Purchasing Management Handbook

edited by
DAVID FARMER

A Gower Handbook

Published by
Gower Publishing Company Limited,
Gower House,
Croft Road,
Aldershot,
Hants GU11 3HR,
England

Gower Publishing Company,
Old Post Road,
Brookfield,
Vermont 05036,
U.S.A.

British Library Cataloguing in Publication Data

Purchasing management handbook.
   1. Purchasing – Management
   I. Farmer, David
   658.7'2   HF5437

Library of Congress Cataloging in Publication Data

Main entry under title:
Purchasing management handbook.

   Bibliography: p.
   Includes index.
   1. Purchasing–Management. I. Farmer, David H.
HF5437.P798   1985   658.7'2   84-18659

ISBN 0-566-02471-3

Typeset in Great Britain by
Graphic Studios (Southern) Ltd, Godalming, Surrey.
Printed in Great Britain by
Redwood Burn Limited, Trowbridge, Wiltshire

Contents

Contents

Editor's preface

It has been a rewarding task to bring together the contributions of thirty people into the collective whole which is this text. In each case the insights and specialist knowledge of the individual authors have contributed to my own understanding of the topic in question as, I am sure, they will for the reader. Clearly, the extent to which any text contributes to a reader's knowledge and understanding depends upon his or her starting point. Thus some readers will gain more than others from each chapter and from the text as a whole. However, in my view even the most experienced and well-read specialist manager will benefit to some degree from 'using' this book. That benefit may come from consideration of broad issues such as policy and strategy; it may arise from analysis of one or more of the fundamental elements of the purchasing mix; or from the insights provided by the writers in the specialist section; but it will emerge.

In this short preface I should like to highlight the verb 'use' in the context of the previous paragraph. Too many managers, in my experience, do not make the time to read. If they purchase a text it tends to be consigned to their bookshelf to gather dust. They are put off using what are often valuable points of reference, by attempting to read a text like a novel. It would be a pity if this book suffered that fate. *Use* it, please! Dip into the chapters which relate to problems with which you are currently grappling. The chapters may not provide you with 'the answer', but you can be sure that the various key issues which relate to the topic will be discussed and, thus, should facilitate your own decision making. Certainly you have nothing to lose and everything to gain from taking this approach.

Finally, I should like to thank every one of the contributors for providing such useful material for our consideration. It has been a pleasure working with you, gentlemen. My thanks, too, to Malcolm Stern of Gower Publishing for his cheerful professionalism and to the many people, known and unknown by me, who have worked to make this book a reality.

At the time of writing Billy Graham is undertaking his crusade to England. My personal crusade with respect to the purchasing function, which has been in progress for twenty years, continues. I consider it to be an accolade to have been labelled the 'Billy Graham of Purchasing'. I wish Dr Graham as much success as we wish ourselves.

David Farmer
Twyford

Illustrations

Illustrations

Notes on contributors

Peter Baily *(Purchasing systems, Purchasing commodities)* worked for several years in the manufacturing sector before moving into management education. He was the pioneer of full-time European lecturers who specialised in purchasing and has a long list of publications to his name. He has considerable experience as a lecturer in many countries and has been a board member of the Business Education Council and has served on several IPS committees.

Richard A. Beardon *(Purchasing from abroad)* was, at the time of writing, Operations Director for T.I. Raleigh Ltd, Nottingham. Prior to joining Raleigh he held senior posts with T.I. Domestic Appliances, the Ford Motor Company and Crane Ltd. His first purchasing experience was gained with Perkins Engines at Peterborough. He has had widely-based experience of international purchasing, and is now Operations Director for Gooding Group.

Richard C.J. Brasher *(Purchasing for the petrochemical industry)* was Head of Procurement for Badger Engineers and Constructors in London from 1975 to 1983 when he transferred to Sterling Greengate Cable Company – another Raytheon company. He was Chairman of the EIC Contractor Vendor Working Party from 1981 to 1983 and of the IPS Oil Gas and Petrochemical Industries

Subcommittee from 1982 to 1984. He is now a consultant with Mervyn Hughes, a leading firm of management recruitment and executive search consultants and a member of the IPS Courses Committee.

Clive Butler *(Purchasing for the pharmaceutical industry)* is Pharmaceutical Purchasing Manager for The Boots Company PLC where he leads a team responsible for purchasing raw and packaging materials used in the manufacture of health care products. He has had over 25 years' purchasing experience mainly with public companies and joined The Boots Company in 1974. He is interested in education and serves as a member of a Nottingham College PTA, and the local branch of the Institute of Purchasing and Supply. Until recently he also acted as Controller of the Institute's Specialist Section for the Pharmaceutical and Cosmetic Industries.

Colin A. Carnall *(Purchasing and manufacturing systems design)* is Director of the Masters Programme at Henley/Brunel University. He has extensive experience in consultancy and research in job and manufacturing systems design. Prior to entering management education Dr Carnall worked with Herbert Morris Ltd.

Barry Castling *(Purchasing forgings)* had extensive industrial experience with David Brown Gear Industries, Pioneer Weston and Eaton Ltd before becoming a specialist consultant. He is the author of several papers relating to his special subject.

Owen Davies *(Purchasing policies, Strategic purchasing, Measuring purchasing performance)* is managing principal of his Australian-based consultancy and was formerly Director of Purchasing for CIBA-Geigy, Managing Director of the Airwick Company and held a board appointment with S & K Holdings. His consultancy experience includes major assignments with international companies in several countries as well as for government authorities throughout Australia and Southeast Asia.

Reginald Dickinson *(Purchasing for the food industry)* is Purchasing Director for HP Foods Ltd, and Golden Wonder Ltd. He has had twenty-five years' experience in the food industry and is an acknowledged expert in the procurement of agriculture-based food commodities.

David Farmer *(Introduction, Competitive analysis, Organising for purchasing, Purchasing and materials management, Purchasing and source selection, Ethical issues in purchasing)* is Director of Henley Management Development and Advisory Service. He was the first European to obtain a doctorate in a topic specifically relating to purchasing. In October 1979 he became the first European to have a professorship conferred on him as a result of his work in the purchasing field. He is widely known for his pioneering work with respect to purchasing management; has lectured, consulted or run seminars in more than thirty countries; is author or co-author of seven texts and over two hundred papers. His industrial experience included management appointments in the aluminium, heavy engineering, timber and refractory industries.

David Ford *(Purchase price management)* is senior Lecturer in Marketing and Director of Postgraduate Research at the University of Bath. An engineer by initial training his industrial experience includes service with American Standard Inc. and British Railways. He has lectured on industrial marketing and purchasing in several European countries and the United States.

Richard J.C. Ford *(Purchasing for retail organisations)* is Merchandise Director with Currys Ltd, prior to which he held senior posts with The Boots Company, Guinness Retail Holdings and R. Gordon Drummond. His wide experience embraces both purchasing and marketing in competitive retail fields.

Ken L. Fox *(Purchasing in local government)* is Director of Supplies for the Greater London Council, a post he has held since 1977. He has had considerable purchasing experience, including periods with the Rowntree Group, the Ford Motor Company and the British Gas Corporation. For seven years he worked as a consultant with Coopers & Lybrand Associates and other management consultants.

Aubrey Grant *(Purchasing castings)* was originally a purchasing trainee with Crompton Parkinson. Subsequently he held management appointments with Smiths Industries, G.E.C.-Elliot Control

Valves and British Twin Disc. Currently a consultant, he is the author of the IPS publication *Guide to Buying Castings*.

Andrew Green *(Purchasing schedule management)* graduated from University College Cardiff in 1976 and joined the purchasing department of a major British company within the automotive industry. After initial experience as a buyer he was, in due course, promoted to become a chief buyer of machine tools, responsible for a budget of £10 million per annum. Further advancement to the position of purchasing agent with a budget of £50 million procuring steel products, led to the appointment of his current position of purchase planning and control manager. With a staff of over fifty people he is responsible for timing, research and administration and reports directly to the purchasing director.

Bernard Hammond *(Purchasing for the paint industry)* is Regional Purchasing Executive for the UK and Ireland region of Berger, Jenson and Nicholson. He is also Purchasing Manager and member of the Executive of Berger Decorative Paints. Prior to joining his present company he was Group Purchasing Manager UK with CIBA-Geigy and was also responsible for logistics, long-term planning and purchasing for CIBA-Geigy Saudi Arabia. He is based at Berger's regional headquarters at Hengrove, Bristol.

Peter Harris *(Purchasing for the construction industry)* is Purchasing Manager for Shephard, Hill & Co. Ltd and has worked in the construction industry for more than thirty years. A member of the Institute of Purchasing and Supply he is currently Chairman of its Construction Committee.

A.E. Hart *(Purchasing print)* worked as a typographic designer, monotype operator and litho estimator, following the completion of a full compositor apprenticeship. His experience with the Greater London Council has included appointments as Manager of the IBM composing unit, senior print buyer and operations Manager of the Council's central reprographic services. He has a C & G Full Tech. Cert. in Printing and is a Licentiate in Printing Administration.

Peter J.A. Herbert *(Financial aspects of purchasing)* worked for several years as a consultant with Coopers & Lybrand Associates before moving into management education. Originally an accountant with a leading international practice, his experience since then has included European and South American assignments. He is a senior member of the staff at Henley, The Management College.

David Jessop *(Foreign exchange and currency management)* is Principal Lecturer and Head of the Business Operations Division at The Polytechnic of Wales. He is the author of several papers, articles and contributing author to a number of management texts.

Brian Kenny *(Purchasing for the defence industry)* is a Principal Lecturer in the Department of Economic and Marketing Studies at Huddersfield Polytechnic. His industrial experience includes working as a Senior Sales Engineer with Ferranti. He has developed his specialist knowledge relating to defence industry structure from that base.

P.T. Kirby *(Purchasing print)* has considerable experience in local government administration in particular in conjunction with purchasing and reprographic services. He is the Head of Central Reprographic Services for the Greater London Council, has an HNC in business studies and the Diploma of the IPS.

Geoffrey Lancaster *(Managing purchasing people)* is a Principal Lecturer in the Department of Economics and Marketing Studies at Huddersfield Polytechnic. His industrial experience includes service with Thorn Electrical Industries and with Whessoe.

James McConville *(Purchasing for the airline industry)* read Economics at St Catharine's College, Cambridge. He then joined Unilever as a management trainee and subsequently worked in the UK and overseas with appointments in finance, purchasing and management consultancy. After joining British Airways in 1977 he held treasury responsibilities for cash management and foreign exchange before taking up his present appointment as General Manager Purchasing Control.

Geoffrey E. Partridge *(Purchasing capital equipment)* is UK

Director of Purchasing for Philips Electronics. A graduate of LSE, he has had extensive experience in purchasing and international trading. He is a Fellow of the Institute of Purchasing and Supply and has served on its management board.

Stephen Parkinson *(Effective negotiation)* is Senior Lecturer in Marketing at the University of Strathclyde. He is the author or co-author of several books and many papers and articles. He has been a consultant to a wide range of companies and has run many 'in-house' programmes for practising managers.

C. Anthony Skidmore *(Purchasing for the motor industry)* is Ford's Manager, Material Procurement Power Train Operations. During his twenty-five years with that company he has held senior management posts in Germany and the UK and has been concerned with reciprocal trade and supply base studies in the Middle East, Eastern Europe and Japan. He is a Fellow of the IPS and BIM and is currently Chairman of the Automotive Committee of the IPS.

Martin Steer *(Purchasing for the aerospace industry)* is Procurement Director for Panavia Aircraft GmbH, Munich. Prior to taking up his present post he was responsible for all supply activities at the Warton Division of British Aerospace. Among other projects, during his career he has worked on the 'Concorde' and 'Tornado' programmes. He is a Fellow of the IPS.

John Stevens *(The make or buy decision, Purchasing for maintenance, repair and operating)* is course leader in Materials Management at Lanchester Polytechnic. He has had considerable consultancy experience in many industries and is the author of more than fifty articles and of the texts *Measuring Purchasing Performance, The Purchasing-Marketing Interface* and *Case Studies in Purchasing and Supply*. He is a Fellow of the IPS and has served on its local and national committees.

Michael M. Taylor *(Legal aspects of purchasing)* has had varied industrial experience including board-level appointments concerned with purchasing with the Thorn, Metal Industries, and Lancashire Dynamo Groups. Later he acted as a consultant to Thorn Electrical

Industries and to Cutler-Hammer Inc. On leaving industry he became President and Director General of the International Federation of Purchasing and Materials Management. In 1977 both the Institute of Purchasing and Supply and the IFPMM awarded him their highest accolades when he became the recipient of the Swinbank Medal and the Garner-Themoin Medal.

Alan Turner *(Purchasing for the aerospace industry)* is Group Computing Manager with specific responsibility for co-ordinating the development of a materials management system throughout British Aerospace Aircraft Group. His former posts included a period in supplies management.

Robin W. Wagstaff *(Purchase quality management)* initially qualified as a metallurgist and worked in quality and process control in the engineering industry. In 1970 he moved into production management with GKN and subsequently became Principal Lecturer at the Polytechnic of North London.

Introduction

David Farmer

Whenever there are business transactions there are those who buy and those who sell. Those who sell may offer a product or a service and those who buy have to decide if the potential supplier is the most reliable, economical and trustworthy of those in the market-place. The problems associated with those decisions are as old as commerce and as new as tomorrow's business. Yet, whilst the basic aspects of the economic transaction which involves buying and selling are the same, the setting of today's business environment make them more complex and more difficult to manage than was the case. They have additional parameters; they require broader vision; they demand a greater understanding of the business system in which buyer and seller operate; and they necessitate an international perspective. Competition, threat and opportunity will appear in all countries in which the trading partners do business.

During the nineteen-fifties and sixties the professional buyer was assured of a broad-based indigenous supply market for most of his needs. Usually that market contained several alternative sources for the buyer's key requirements. Then, if he was obliged to buy from overseas sources, he could be assured of the stability of his home-based currency relative to those of other countries with whom he traded. Whilst the pace of technological development was increasing, the fifties and sixties represented ordered, steady, reasonably predictable progress.

Things have changed. The buyer of today finds himself having to

1

cope with fluctuating comparative currency levels, fewer, sometimes no domestic sources of supply, increasing pressure on profit margins and a pace of change in technological development in some fields which would render an old-time buyer professionally impotent.

The variables then which have to be taken into consideration in making purchase decisions in the eighties are both more numerous and more complex than in the past, and this necessitates more effective decision making and better analysis of data of improved quality. It requires, too, a greater awareness among top management and professional purchasing management of the quality of staff which are needed to undertake the task. Without such understanding, without the corresponding skills, attitudes and knowledge, purchase decisions are unlikely to provide the buying company with competitive advantage in its marketplaces. Indeed, the converse will be true.

During the last decade, the impact of the supply market on manufacturing firms, in particular, has been highlighted by several factors. The oil crisis of 1973/4 emphasised the crucial role which the supply market plays in business economics. The arguments, so prevalent in the purchasing literature, were underlined and, for a short while at least, more attention was paid by management to the supply side of business. Some businesses, indeed, were influenced to the degree that the strategic focus of their management thrust was amended to accommodate supply side considerations. And in the interim, where that was managed effectively, the buying companies have benefited.

An even bigger impact on world markets which has emphasised the need for effective purchasing and materials management, was made by Japanese mass-assembly companies. Most world markets have been affected by the success of Japanese concerns. For example, as Tony Skidmore points out in Chapter 32 Japanese companies which in 1953 produced only 1 per cent of world vehicle production, had by 1982 increased that thirtyfold. The hordes of businessmen, academics and consultants who descended upon Japan to discover the reasons for such success all reported on reliability of quality and assurance of delivery as key issues. The methods by which the assembling companies achieved such standards were analysed and re-analysed. Amid the plethora of conclusions drawn was the commonly held view that the Japanese managed the supply side of their business effectively.

In 1976 Professor Keith MacMillan and I undertook a research project into buyer/supplier relationships.[1] The hypotheses behind the work were based upon the fundamental tenet that buyers and sellers should seek to develop mutually beneficial relationships. That collaboration was infinitely superior to confrontation; that forging continuing, healthy relationships between a buyer and a particular seller would benefit both; that 'shopping around', to use a political slogan of the time, could be ineffective in total acquisition cost terms. The research results confirmed the hypotheses and the workshops which were run subsequently to help establish a better understanding of the concepts were well received. However, the prevailing typical market environment was one of ingrained competition between buyer and seller. In many cases in the intervening years both suffered; both lost market share; and yet more analysis was undertaken.

Today, as we read in many sections of this handbook, the received wisdom has it that, for mass-assembly companies at least, dedicated sources are *de rigueur*. For example, Volvo, Volkswagen and Austin-Morris, among other major European car assemblers, have made great strides towards a single source philosophy and there are few major consultants who do not currently claim skills in developing materials flow systems. Not surprisingly, although supply management had been largely ignored by these same advisers in the past, wherever input costs are a significant element in output revenue, effective purchase systems are now stated to be fundamental to business success.

The point to note here is not that Professor MacMillan and myself were right in 1976 (indeed it is not always appropriate to confine purchases to a single source) rather that the relative ineffectiveness of many businesses over the last two decades has stemmed, in part, from inadequate attention being paid to purchasing management. Nor is that message new. Alfred Chandler, in his classic book *Strategy and Structure*,[2] includes many examples of successful businesses evolving in the US which were built or thrived on balanced strategies which included purchasing as a fundamental aspect. Indeed, in most of the cases which he quotes, the impact of effective purchasing on the success of the business in question and the balance of its system, is evident. Another visionary, Shaw, writing in 1915,[3] argued that:

> The relations between the activities of demand, creation and physical supply . . . illustrate the existence of the two principles of *interdependence* and *balance*. Failure to co-ordinate any of these activities . . . or to place undue emphasis or outlay upon any one of these activities, is certain to upset the equilibrium of forces.

It is sufficient to emphasise at this point that the idea that a system needs to be 'in balance' in order to ensure that it is effective, is irrefutable. And this balance presupposes that the interdependent elements of the system are managed to ensure a mutuality of benefit; that the sum of the whole is greater than the sum of the parts. Clearly, when some of those 'parts', e.g. suppliers, have different owners, objectives and philosophies from the buying company, then ensuring effective liaison to achieve such objectives will necessitate a level of management attention commensurate with the complexities of that task. This text is designed to assist management in performing that exacting role. It seeks to provide a point of reference regarding the key issues which relate to the management of input to the business; to co-ordination with the many outside systems which impinge upon that business; and to integration with the other elements of the company system which purchasing represents. Its purpose is not to emphasise that role in isolation, but to stress the part which the function must play as an influential member of the company team.

The authors of the thirty-seven chapters that follow all contribute to that objective, each presenting his own view. Taken individually the chapters will provide an informed opinion regarding the topic in hand, collectively they represent the most comprehensive text dedicated to purchasing which has been published in Europe to the present date.

THE STRUCTURE OF THE BOOK

Part One of the book addresses the broad issues concerned with purchasing policy, strategy and organisation. In Chapter 1 Owen Davies discusses the importance of thought-through policies as a tool for effective purchasing. Among other things the chapter incorporates examples of written policies. Where formal policies have yet to be developed, these should be invaluable to the practitioner as a starting point for his own consideration. The next chapter examines the important topic of competitive analysis, an area which for too long has been given little attention by management. Clearly, buying companies have competitors in their supply markets as well as in their end markets. Recognition of a company's relative power position vis-à-vis those competitors can be a stimulant to redressing the balance in its favour. Once again the chapter includes an example of an approach to managing such analysis as a model for the practising manager to adapt to his own circumstances.

In the chapter on strategic purchasing which follows, Owen Davies emphasises the importance of not concentrating on shorter-term/operational issues to the detriment of the longer-term. Many supply markets are what they are today as a result of buyers not recognising the dangers of such strategic myopia. And, as Davies argues, much of the fault for such thinking must be laid at the door of top management who, in the past, have over-emphasised price measurement and short-term 'bottom line' results.

The last two chapters in Part One are concerned with organisation. They are grouped with those concerned with strategy for, as Chandler's[2] excellent book stresses, strategy and organisation/structure need to be carefully related if a business is to succeed. Chapter 4 is concerned with the broad issues of organisation and includes examples of different types of structure. The basic argument inherent in the discussion is that each organisation structure needs to be 'tailored' to fit the company concerned. Two broad topics are discussed: How should the purchasing function be organised? and How should it fit into the remainder of the organisation of the business itself? As stated in the conclusion to the chapter, organisation structures and their related systems provide the means by which people may communicate and operate effectively to achieve corporate goals. In themselves they cannot ensure success, for *people* have to make organisations work.

The chapter concerned with materials management puts that particular 'systems approach' into the context of this book. Drawing upon the wide-ranging discussion which materials management has evoked, it stresses the importance of purchasing providing the necessary level of commercial input to the materials system. Otherwise too often, it is argued, materials systems become dominated by 'systems' men who tend to under-emphasise the commercial role of the materials function.

Part Two is concerned with the various elements of the 'purchasing mix'. For those new to this description, it represents the amalgam of the elements of the purchasing transaction. Those elements are included in the traditionally stated objective of the purchasing function, sometimes referred to as 'the five rights'. That is to purchase the right *quality* materials in the right *quantity* from the right *source* at the right *time* and at the right *price*. Each purchase decision, it is argued, implies a trade-off among these elements and the task of the purchasing man is to select the optimum mix as judged against the variables involved in the task in hand. Whilst each topic is discussed individually, the various authors have each considered their topics in the context of the 'total' purchasing decision.

In addressing the complex topic of purchase price management, David Ford has provided an overview of the issues which the buyer faces in this critical area. He also discusses the issues which marketeers face in developing their pricing approaches and illustrates the implications for buyers of some of the different strategies which are adopted. Ford argues that the buyer should take an active role in the price-setting process. In conclusion he describes a number of analytical techniques which may be used for effective purchase price management.

Bob Wagstaff's chapter on managing quality addresses the many aspects of this complex topic. He shows how reliability is an extension of quality which, he argues, has two distinct attributes: quality of design and quality of conformance. Wagstaff discusses the costs associated with quality and the controls which are necessary to ensure conformance.

In Chapter 8 Andrew Green considers some of the problems associated with schedule management. He outlines the basic requirements of a schedule and then demonstrates the application of such an approach in two different production environments. The first of these is a mass-production assembly-line situation and the second is concerned with manufacturing a purpose-built machine tool. Green has firm views on the Japanese 'miracle' and incorporates these in his discussion.

The topic of source selection is addressed in the next chapter. It is argued that selecting, appraising and managing key sources of supply is the most important task of the purchasing function. Sound sourcing decisions repay the effort involved in making them on a continuing basis. Conversely, poor decisions result in additional work, disruption and sub-optimum business performance.

Among the topics considered in this chapter are: one or more suppliers; the monopoly buyer; agent or manufacturer; local or distant sources; reciprocity; purchasing within groups; and the process of selection. A questionnaire relating to supplier service is included so that readers can use the approach in developing supplier profiles which meet their own specific need.

As an extension to the discussion on sourcing, John Stevens, in Chapter 10, considers the fundamental source decision – make or buy? He emphasises the importance of developing effective policies and procedures in order that the best decision might be arrived at. And, in so doing, argues for the purchasing function to be the initiator of such systems and guidelines.

In the final chapter in this Part, Richard Beardon deals with another aspect of sourcing – purchasing from abroad. He underscores the importance of recognising that, for many businesses, purchasing from overseas is a strategic issue with tactical implications. Beardon's discussion includes consideration of market differences; reasons for purchasing from abroad; some of the difficulties which may be faced in such trading, and the priorities which are necessary for success in such source decision making.

Part Three focuses upon systems and functions (including finance). In Chapter 12 Peter Baily traces the course of a typical purchase transaction, referring at each stage to the forms and records which are used. The chapter ends with a brief look at new developments in information technology and their possible impact on purchasing systems.

Colin Carnall's chapter on purchasing and manufacturing systems design illustrates the sometimes radical changes which are being made in this sector. He discusses the pressures and opportunities which these changes imply and emphasises the pro-active role which is necessary for purchasing to undertake. Included in Carnall's discussion is consideration of MRP and 'Kanban' approaches which Andrew Green touches on in Chapter 8.

In Chapter 14 Peter Herbert addresses the important topic of purchasing and financial management. Since purchasing typically disposes of the bulk of a manufacturing company's income, its influence on the finances of the business can be marked. Consequently an understanding of the many issues involved is a key requirement of purchasing management. Among the many aspects discussed, Herbert examines cash management, credit, corporate funding, managing growth, coping with inflation and assessing suppliers financially.

Owen Davies argues that the lack of purchasing performance reports is a sure indicator of poor purchasing management. His chapter on measuring purchasing performance emphasises this view and outlines problems and opportunities which abound in this much discussed area.

In the following chapter David Jessop discusses the topic of foreign exchange and currency management which was touched on by Richard Beardon in Chapter 11. Jessop highlights the risks associated with exchange rate variation which buyers who source overseas need to take into consideration. He provides a description of the backcloth to currency management and suggests a number of techniques which might be helpful in dealing with risk and uncertainty in currency decision making.

Peter Baily's chapter on commodities considers the factors which cause commodity prices to fluctuate both in the short and longer term; he discusses some attempts to reduce or minimise fluctuations and illustrates how future contracts may be used as a means of 'hedging' to reduce risk. Some background information is provided about the organised commodity markets and various approaches which are used to buy price-sensitive commodities.

Each time a buyer arranges a purchase with a supplier he is entering into a contractual arrangement. Thus it is important that, in a book of this nature, an informed discussion is provided which considers the legal aspects of the task. Michael Taylor's chapter is such a contribution. In it he discusses the conflict of laws – which will impinge upon international purchasing; the different concepts of the fundamental law of contract; the difficulties which arise from different legal concepts and then examines internationally acceptable conditions of contract.

In Chapter 19 Geoffrey Partridge discusses the purchase of high-value capital equipment. He argues that such purchases should be managed by a project team which should devise and work closely to a plan which covers every aspect of the transaction from initial investigations through to post-contract management. Partridge lays particular emphasis on detailed specification setting and on the importance of the internal and external negotiations which precede the commitment of all parties to the specification. Throughout, he emphasises the key role which purchasing should play in such management.

Geoffrey Lancaster's contribution, the first chapter in Part Four, is concerned with managing purchasing people. In it he examines the more important aspects of this task in the context of a changing and, seemingly, ever-broadening role for the function in a modern company. He discusses selection, training, leading and motivating and emphasises the importance of the purchasing manager having an understanding of the several issues involved as he faces up to the task of managing his human resources.

In Chapter 21 the topic of negotiation is discussed by Stephen Parkinson. He proposes a set of basic analytical tools which may be used in assessing the negotiator's position vis-à-vis the other party, and suggests guidelines for managing the process of negotiation. Since the ability to negotiate effectively is a key attribute for the purchasing professional, this chapter provides an essential contribution to this handbook.

Probably the most discussed topic among purchasing professionals provides the subject for Chapter 22. Rarely a month passes without one or other of the world's professional journals including letters from readers on ethical issues. Clearly, since the purchasing manager is frequently responsible for spending the largest portion of his company's income, it is extremely important that he behaves in an ethical manner. As illustrated in the discussion, both the UK Institute of Purchasing and Supply (IPS) and the International Federation of Purchasing and Materials Management (IFPMM) have produced ethical codes for their membership, which suggests a genuine concern for acceptable standards.

The purpose of this chapter is to provide information and

guidelines which will enable a manager to formulate effective ethical policies. Whilst a particular position is taken in the discussion (that sound ethical behaviour makes for good business) it must be the prerogative of the reader to tailor guidelines to his own situation and in line with his own beliefs. Nonetheless, it would be a foolish manager who failed to consider the codes and guidelines which wide experience around the world has indicated to be fundamentally important.

Part Five, the final section of the book, is devoted to purchasing in particular fields. Each chapter is by a purchasing professional whose everyday task is to be an effective manager in the environment concerned. As such it should provide practical guidelines for anyone concerned with undertaking or relating to the function in that field. As with the remainder of this book, no claim is made that each contribution is *the* finite guideline. Rather, the professionals concerned have, in each case, sought to indicate what *they* see as the key issues involved. Others may disagree with those views. However, the discussion provided should help the reader to arrive at an informed position with regard to undertaking the task in the environment concerned.

Ken Fox, Director of Supplies for the Greater London Council, has contributed the chapter on local government. Richard Ford, currently with Currys and who has had considerable senior management experience with other major retailers, writes on retailing. Alan Turner and Martin Steer, both of whom hold senior posts with British Aerospace, contribute the chapter on the aerospace industry, an important aspect of which is the use of an on-line computer system in undertaking the task. The construction industry is discussed by Peter Harris, Purchasing Manager with Shepherd, Hill and Co. Ltd. Two authors, P. T. Kirby and A. E. Hart, Head and Deputy Head of the GLC's Central Reprographic Services provide a detailed, helpful contribution on purchasing print. This chapter should prove to be particularly useful to the non-specialist buyer faced with making effective decisions in this complex field. Aubrey Grant is the author of another excellent specialist chapter on purchasing castings. Again, the intricacies of performing the function effectively in this area are examined in detail. Specialist and non-specialist will gain much from this discussion. Barry Castling's contribution on purchasing forgings is of similar value. The guidelines which are included in this chapter will be invaluable for anyone faced with the problems and opportunities of purchasing in this field. The chapter on purchasing for the food industry is by Reginald Dickinson who is Purchasing Director of HP Foods and Golden Wonder. He is particularly concerned here with the commodity-based raw materials which are fundamental to effective management in this industry.

Clive Butler, who has extensive experience in the industry, provides the chapter on the pharmaceutical industry, which includes a profile of this industry and helpful guidelines relating to supply markets, quality and possible future developments. The chapter on purchasing for the motor industry is by Tony Skidmore who has worked for twenty-five years in senior positions with Ford in the UK and Europe. His discussion focuses on the major shifts which have taken place during the last thirty years in automotive production and emphasises the continuing key role of purchasing management.

James McConville is the author of the chapter on the airline industry and illustrates the many challenges inherent in this task. Chapter 34 – on defence – is by Brian Kenny who has made a special study of this complex field. In 'Purchasing for the Paint Industry' Bernard Hammond of Berger Paints covers raw materials, packaging and the important issues concerned with liaison with manufacturing and marketing which is a key to success in this industry.

Chapter 36 is concerned with the petrochemical industry. The author is Richard Brasher who has had extensive experience in senior positions in this industry. The final chapter, by John Stevens, also author of Chapter 10, is on purchasing for maintenance, repair and operating. It stresses the need for a professional approach to what are frequently regarded as tasks of no particular significance.

The final two items are intended as reference material. The Appendix lists the member institutes of the International Federation of Purchasing and Materials Management. As will be seen, there are professional purchasing bodies in most parts of the world, and they could prove to be an invaluable source of information for the buyer wishing to do business in a particular country.

The second item is a list of books on purchasing. These, taken together with the works mentioned in individual chapters, constitute a comprehensive reference for the professional purchasing manager.

No single book can cover every topic of concern to those wishing to be better informed about a particular aspect of management. Nonetheless, it is not unreasonable to claim that what follows is a wide-ranging discussion of many important issues with which purchasing management is concerned. More than thirty people, each a specialist in his field, have contributed. Together they represent hundreds of man-years of experience. No attempt has been made at a uniform style of writing. Apart from some minor editing, each chapter reflects the particular author's approach and presents his own informed view of the subject in question.

REFERENCES

(1) D. Farmer and K. MacMillan, 'Effectiveness and Efficiency between Firms' in *Scandinavian Journal of Materials Administration,* vol. 1, no. 2, November 1976.
(2) A. Chandler, *Strategy and Structure,* MIT, 1962.
(3) A. W. Shaw, *Some Problems in Market Distribution,* HUP, 1915.

PART I
POLICY, STRATEGY AND ORGANISATION

1

Purchasing policies

Owen Davies

Relatively few organisations have published purchasing policies, yet the role which the function performs, probably more than any other, suggests a clear need for such written statements.

Well-constructed purchasing policy statements identify the direction to be followed by purchasing personnel giving them clear, unambiguous objectives, thus ensuring a smooth and orderly progress towards goal achievement in keeping with an expected standard of corporate behaviour. Since they are the source of authority they assist in the process of delegation and are, therefore, to be welcomed in clarifying the job role for purchasing. Equally, of course, purchasing policies assist top management in ensuring a consistent application of the purchasing standards which they wish to apply.

Misunderstandings occur over the difference between policies and objectives. Whereas objectives are a statement of intent, that is the desired result that is to be achieved, policies should clearly and unequivocally specify the process that must be followed to achieve an end result. Policies thereby indicate a performance criterion which is unalterable. Objectives identify the end result to be achieved without delineating the process by which such objectives have to be brought about.

For example, at the front of the purchasing manual of the McDonald's fast food organisation, the following statement is made: 'It is the responsibility of the McDonald's Purchasing

Department and the Regional Purchasing Personnel to purchase – or make available for purchase – quality goods or services at fair prices, from reputable firms, for profitable use by McDonald's operators.'

DEFINITION

Policies have been defined as statements or decisions usually made and communicated by the top management of an organisation which apply universally to a set of circumstances met by personnel and which can be applied repetitively. They represent procedural guidelines which can be followed consistently in decision making throughout an organisation. As such they should be consistent, incapable of misinterpretation and repetitive in application. Finally, they should be capable of implementation without further reference to higher management.

Purchasing policies, therefore, serve as ready guidelines to repetitive questions of significance to the organisation and, by the policy statements, eliminate misunderstandings and uncertainty. Universally applied, they reduce, if not eliminate, concern as to discrimination in the minds of suppliers, including tenderers. They present a prescribed method to be followed by purchasing personnel and, since such policies should be unambiguous, they should not allow for variations or differences in approach.

Purchasing policies, therefore, can be defined as standing (in the sense of performance) decisions made by top management which can be applied consistently to significant recurring purchasing issues without the necessity to refer back to higher management.

DELEGATION

It is clear that purchasing policies represent a clear delegation of responsibility and authority to the purchasing function. They establish the purchasing accountability in an organisation in that the application of the stated policies must be carried out in the manner prescribed. They tend to be long-lived, for while policies can be changed, such changes should not need to occur frequently. Proof of the worth of a policy is its ability to stand the test of time.

Purchasing policies apply to repetitive situations and those issues which are addressed will usually be of significance. It has also to be recognised that, although being repetitive, circumstances can vary to some degree and the purchasing policies will need to be sufficiently flexible to cover these differences.

Purchasing policies are, in fact, sub-policies of those which have been established for the company as a whole. In the same way that objectives are integrated in a hierarchy, all organisation policies should also stem from the basic corporate policy. Purchasing policies should be interpretations of company policy as it applies to the purchasing function. This retains the consistency of overall company approach and ensures proper co-ordination. Purchasing policies, since they are derived from top management decisions, should bear the written approval of management even if individual policies are published by the most senior purchasing executive in the organisation. Indeed it would be prudent to have the chief executive countersign the statement. This will provide unequivocal authority for the purchasing policies.

FRAMEWORK FOR PURCHASING POLICIES

Appendix A to this chapter gives an outline framework for a purchasing policy manual. In formulating such a framework it must be acknowledged that there is no single approach which will provide a universal standard for all organisations. The example of a framework provided here is purely to demonstrate one approach which could be taken to formulate sound purchasing policies. The reader will wish to adapt it to his or her own circumstances.

Nevertheless some guidelines can be given for the development of purchasing policies and the following checklist indicates some of the steps in the process of compiling written policy statements.

1 *User developed* – Since it is the purchasing department which will apply the policies, it would be sensible to invite the users to develop their own policy statements as discussion documents. This can be achieved by establishing sub-committees or project teams and allocating policy areas to each for draft proposals.

These draft policies should be reviewed by the senior management of the purchasing function before final submission to top management.

2 *Policies not procedures* – It is important to emphasise the difference between policies and procedures. Whereas policies specify standing decisions, procedures demonstrate how purchasing tasks should be undertaken in a routine manner. Policies which address the questions 'what, when and where' are those which should be applied in the purchasing area. Procedures question 'how' purchasing work should be performed.

3 *Use experts* – To ensure that purchasing policies are tenable and have a degree of permanence with a reasonable time frame, it would be appropriate to use expert advice in their formulation. This expertise may stem from, for example, the legal department and could readily cover such issues as reciprocity, ethical standards, commitments etc. Financial advice would be sought in respect of policies on credit periods for suppliers, buying of currency, limitations on signing of purchase orders etc. Technical input could come from manufacturing, quality control, design engineering etc.

4 *Take time* – Hastily constructed purchasing policies are counter-productive and it would be sensible to draft and re-draft proposals, allowing other relevant functional areas to comment on the draft policies. Clearly there is a limit to the process of amendment and re-drafting but it would be preferable to err on the side of over-drafting. Consequently allow plenty of time; it is not uncommon for three or four drafts to be developed prior to the production of sound key purchasing policies. It should be clearly demonstrated to top management that care has been taken to integrate the purchasing policies into the overall corporate policies, that they are wholly compatible with other functional areas and that proper advice has been obtained from relevant specialists. Supporting comments from other functions will also demonstrate to top management that proper consensus has been taken and that the purchasing policies have been drafted with full regard for co-operation and co-ordination.

5 *Keep it simple* – The precepts of good written communication

must apply – clear, concise and simple. Since the essence of a well constructed policy is to provide an unambiguous statement, it is vital that the written policy cannot be misinterpreted. Consequently allow for a number of people to read through the drafts and have them write out their interpretation in their own words. If the policies have been written well, the interpretation given by the readers will be consistent. To achieve a lack of ambiguity, the simple direct statement will succeed. Sir Ernest Gowers' *Plain Words* is to be recommended as the standard text in the construction of simple draft statements of policy. The simpler the policies are to understand, the more creditable and authoritative they will be to the purchasing staff that use them. Complicated language and/or jargon should be avoided; in any event, they generally lead to ambiguities. We have all read legalistic policy statements which are incapable of being understood and policy statements of this nature are wholly counter-productive.

6 *Allow for revisions, changes and amendments* – Although it is advisable to develop policy statements which will stand the test of time, circumstances can alter, economic issues can change, as can government regulations. Therefore it is advisable to allow for such amendments to be made as and whenever necessary. Policy statements should be sufficiently flexible to take account of as many variations and contingencies as possible. It will be unlikely that every contingency will be covered. However, policies by definition, seek to cover issues of significance and as such will not aim to provide a total panacea for every purchasing problem that may arise. In any event, a total policy response to every contingency will reduce initiative to a minimum which would remove job authority and reduce delegation to absurd levels.

Foreword to a purchasing policy manual

The foreword to the purchasing policy manual is vitally important in that it should outline the philosophy of the purchasing function. It should, therefore, be signed by the chief executive of the organisation. It should state the support to be given by top management to the purchasing function and delineate the delegated authority to the organisation's purchasing executives. It should state unequivocally that the purchasing department is responsible for all buying within the organisation for which it has corporate authority. Exceptions might include:

- insurance
- property
- certain capital items
- advertising

(though it is important to note that some organisations do not preclude one or all of these).

Whilst the foreword should be brief, it should refer to overall purchasing objectives and invite the co-operation of all parts of the organisation in the achievement of such goals.

Purchasing policy considerations

In determining the various policies outlined in the framework shown in Appendix A, consideration should be given to the following issues in drafting purchasing policy statements.

1 *Definitions* – Whilst not classified as a basic policy, the understanding of the purchasing policies is improved by a statement of definition of purchasing terms used in policy statements.

2 *Policy revisions* – It has been recognised that changed circumstances can require amendment or revision of a purchasing policy. Consequently it would be sensible to make a statement to the effect that whilst deviations or variations to purchasing policies are not permitted, recommendations for amendment and change can be made to the proper purchasing authority. One of the problems in maintaining written policies is to keep them up to date and the purchasing function itself should undertake periodic review. This will ensure a systematic coverage of purchasing policies and demonstrate their continued effectiveness. With the use of word processors in organisations, many companies have placed their policies on computer file so that any amendments can be readily made.

Interrogation of computer terminals can also facilitate the availability of policy statements either through screen copy or hard copy.

3 *Organisation policies* – Policies covering issues of purchasing organisation include decisions regarding centralisation. The policy, importantly, should not deal with reasons for selecting either mode of organisational operation. It is simply a statement of fact that a type of purchasing organisation has been adopted. The delegation of purchasing responsibility, authority and accountability will be clearly defined with specification of limits of purchasing authority stated. The purchasing delegation and limits of authority will cover all management levels within the organisation. In general it will establish that purchasing is the only authority recognised to commit the organisation for the procurement of goods and services, with the exceptions defined. Where financial limits are imposed, the policy will need to specify approved requirements. Whilst the foreword will have provided a broad outline of the objectives of purchasing, it is necessary to define the responsibilities, and thereby more specific objectives, of the purchasing function and its officers. Organisation trees backed by outline job descriptions would be appropriate without detailing the manner (procedures) by which the job is to be carried out. In establishing the reporting line of the purchasing function, it would be appropriate to indicate the reports to be rendered, the timing of such reports, the distribution list applicable and a brief statement of the report content and purpose.

4 *Supplier selection policies* – A series of policies which will deal with aspects of:

- competitive bidding
- negotiation versus tendering
- evaluation of quotations
- supplier visits
- supplier relations
- ethical standards
- contract documentation
- legal aspects

    – reciprocity and preferences

    – pre-award; post award; contract administration.

Since these aspects are dealt with at length elsewhere in this handbook, comments here will be restricted to emphasizing that policy statements in respect of these issues are not a vehicle for instituting discussion. Purchasing policies relating to all these issues must represent clear guidelines for action.

Examples

'It is the policy of this company to use competitive bidding for all purchases. It is the policy of this company that the highest ethical standards will be maintained in the bidding process to ensure equal opportunity for all qualified bidders in competing for our business and to ensure fair dealing with all bidders.'

'It is the policy of this company not to disclose any information relating to competitive bids to any bidder.'

    A further reference is made to the use of external policy 'welcome booklets' in supplier relations later in this chapter.

5 *Pricing and payment* – Purchasing policies in this area cover aspects of unpriced or priced orders, discount and credit arrangements, escalation formulae, rebates etc. Importantly such policies will be derived in full consultation with the finance department.

6 *Relations with other departments* – In the determination of purchasing policies, there is some danger that policies derived will be seen as entirely restrictive by other parts of the organisation. It would be prudent therefore to devote one policy to spelling out clearly that the purpose of purchasing is to provide a cost effective service to user departments. This would also be the appropriate section to define purchasing input to issues such as corporate planning.

7 *Personal purchases* – Since personal purchases represent a potential source of friction, a decision identifying a purchasing policy to undertake or not to engage in personal purchases through the purchasing function should be spelled out. There are no hard and fast rules; some companies see it as an opportunity to improve employee relations, other organisations take an opposite view that it becomes a ready source of

friction and unfair practice. Whatever the decision, a purchasing policy statement on the subject is important.

SUPPLIER RELATIONSHIPS

Since policy statements tend to be used largely for internal communications, suppliers could be at a disadvantage. As a result it is not uncommon for suppliers to complain that they are not informed, are misinformed or are confused about the purchasing policies which are being applied. This leads in the end not only to frustration on the part of suppliers but to the existence of poor relationships between them and the purchaser.

To overcome this communication barrier, many purchasing departments, both private and public sector, have issued what have become known as 'welcome booklets'. These are, in essence, policy booklets which outline any of the company's purchasing policies which affect its relationship with suppliers. In the public sector, booklets are now published for potential suppliers on 'How to do business with the government'. (Some examples of welcome booklets are included in Appendix B.)

There is no doubt that such booklets can significantly improve relationships with suppliers by creating a full understanding of the purchasing policies that apply in the sourcing and selection of suppliers.

Subjects covered in the welcome booklets include:

- an opening statement of 'welcome' by the chief executive and the chief purchasing executive
- a statement of the overall purchasing philosophy
- purchasing policies relating to sourcing and selection
- the purchasing company's obligations to suppliers
- suppliers' obligations to the purchasing company
- purchasing organisation facilities, procedure for supplier visits etc.

The following foreword in the government booklet on 'How to do business with the government' signed by the responsible minister exemplifies the policy approach to vendor relationships:

The government spends a considerable sum of public money

23

each year on the procurement of goods and services for use by its various departments and authorities.

It has been the policy of successive governments that procurement should, to the extent practicable, be conducted on the basis of fair and open competition, with a view to ensuring that the highest standards of probity are maintained, that there is equal opportunity to make offers to supply government needs and that funds provided by taxpayers are spent effectively and economically.

The purpose of this booklet is to explain the policies, procedures and practices followed in (government) purchasing. I hope that the information in the booklet will assist potential suppliers to understand the system and encourage their active participation in the process of supplying (government) requirements.

Importantly, a major derivative of policy related to supplier relationships lies in encouraging them to propose alternatives in the supply of goods and services. For example:

> *Good ideas mean more business for you*
> We need good ideas to help us increase the value of our products by either reducing the cost while maintaining quality, or holding cost while providing additional functions. If you have a better idea with a better product at a better price, it is bound to mean more McCulloch business going your way.
>
> (McCulloch Corporation welcome booklet)

> *Cost reductions*
> Motorola welcomes and encourages your input towards our value analysis/cost reduction programme. We ask for your ideas on component standardisation, substitution and simplification.
>
> (Motorola 'Suppliers guide to opportunity'
> welcome booklet)

CONCLUSION

Purchasing policies are directives issued by top management for guidance and direction where uniformity of action is required. Thus a policy is a command from top management to the purchasing function and directs every member of the purchasing operation to act in a prescribed manner in handling specified purchasing questions. As such, it provides the purchasing function with points of reference and guidelines to be followed without the necessity for reference back to higher authority.

Policies help to eliminate misunderstandings since they are capable of only one universal interpretation and serve to concentrate purchasing efforts towards the achievement of agreed functional goals.

Properly developed and authorised, purchasing policies enable company top managements to make balanced and considered decisions in respect of basic questions of continuing importance that confront the purchasing function.

The opportunity to weigh and consider beforehand eliminates the need for hasty, spur-of-the-moment decisions which, in themselves, might set unfortunate precedents. In addition it makes it possible to bring to bear on important purchasing issues the accumulated knowledge and experience of the purchasing function as a whole. In so doing a consistency of approach will be evident to all who deal with the purchasing function.

Sound policies allow the purchasing function to concentrate on exceptional issues. When he is supported by sound policies, a purchasing executive can think beyond the dimensions of his or her own job and can be more creative in other aspects of work performance. Purchasing policies also provide the means by which responsibility and authority are delegated, thus identifying accountability for the decisions arrived at.

In addition the effective use of sound purchasing policies helps to improve the overall quality of decision making in the purchasing process since it applies to issues generally beyond the scope of a single purchasing individual, who does not require to revert constantly to management for decisions beyond the normal scope of purchasing work.

Since the critical purchasing issues which have to be addressed have already been carefully evaluated and decisions made, there is less opportunity for friction and dispute, or for a wrong decision to be made in the heat of an emergency situation. All of which helps the members of the purchasing team to work together towards a common goal.

Soundly constructed purchasing policies should never cause any reduction in purchasing efficiency through inflexibility. In fact, the reverse should be true, since by clarifying the purchasing executive's role, duplication and overlap are eliminated.

Yet despite all these benefits, a recent survey undertaken in the US across a broad spectrum of private industry and the public sector, identified that 77 per cent of organisations did not have stated purchasing policies. And it is reasonable to assume that similar results would emerge if the survey was undertaken in other developed economies. Among the reasons for this result could be the resources which need to be utilised to develop effective policies. For example, there is no doubt that drafting and issuing written purchasing policies is a time-consuming task; most estimates allow for twelve months to two years to write and implement policies within a framework such as that shown in Appendix A. However, where the task has been undertaken, the establishment of purchasing policies in an organisation enhances the function of the purchasing and results in improved performance. Importantly, purchasing policies will provide the base structure from which a purchasing function can build, demonstrating its clear contribution to the corporate goals.

Finally, the use of purchasing policies demonstrates the support given by top management to the purchasing function in their organisation. It causes top management to think through the attitude they need to adopt in respect of their purchasing operation. The establishment of purchasing policies also allows purchasing management to gain top management acceptance of the importance of the purchasing role to the overall organisation. Effective policies always necessitate considered discussion which will allow the purchasing professional to establish his case.

APPENDIX A – A FRAMEWORK FOR PURCHASING POLICIES

Foreword by the chief executive

Definitions

Organisation policies
1 Major responsibilities and objectives of purchasing.
2 Placement of purchasing in the organisation hierarchy (organisation chart). Central versus decentral.
3 Delegation and authority. Commitment limits to purchase.
4 Job outlines (position descriptions).

Purchasing policies
1 Single and multiple sourcing.
2 Reciprocity.
3 Consideration of small businesses; local supplier preferences.
4 Negotiation versus tendering.
5 Intercompany purchases.
6 Personal purchases.
7 Pricing and payment.
8 Commodity/forward purchasing.
9 Purchasing of currency.
10 International/overseas purchasing.
11 Terms and conditions of contract.

Supplier policies
1 Competitive bidding.
2 Disclosure of information.
3 Evaluation of quotations.
4 Communication with suppliers.
5 Supplier visits.
6 Ethical standards.
7 Contract documentation.
8 Backdoor selling.
9 Complaints and rejections.
10 Quality control.
11 Carriers.
12 Supplier alternatives.

Relations with other departments
1 User specifications; determining the need.
2 Co-operation with user departments.
3 Delegated authority; commitment to purchase.
4 Emergency orders.
5 Value analysis; make-or-buy studies.

APPENDIX B – EXAMPLES OF COMPANY WELCOME BOOKLETS

Welcome

John D. Ong
Chairman of the Board,
President & Chief
Executive Officer

BFGoodrich is engaged in the production and marketing of its chemical, tire, and engineered products throughout the world. To participate competitively, BFG has re-organized its procurement activities so as to improve its communications and efficiency. Our intent is to provide a coordinated approach to purchasing which includes overall economic considerations as well as local, national, and international effects and implications.

We believe this expanded and coordinated purchasing activity can further benefit both BFGoodrich and its suppliers. It should ensure a thorough and consistent review of sourcing considerations. We welcome your participation with BFG in the attainment of product excellence and reliability within the competitive marketplace.

J. D. Ong

John D. Ong

To Our Suppliers

Robert J. Manser
Vice President-Purchasing

Purchasing Philosophy

This booklet is offered as an aid to companies that have had no prior experience or contact with the BFGoodrich Purchasing organization and to those many current suppliers who wish to expand their business contacts with BFG.

Included in this booklet are explanations of BFG's purchasing philosophy, the procedures and responsibilities of each of the partners (BFG and the supplier), a description of the various product groups, and a listing of our purchasing locations.

For more detailed information than this booklet provides, or if there are any questions, complaints, or suggested improvements relative to supplier contacts or purchasing procedures, we hope you will not hesitate to contact this office. We hope you will take advantage of the card enclosed in the fly-leaf to forward to us your comments/suggestions.

Robert J. Manser

The BFGoodrich Purchasing philosophy is to obtain, for our customers, goods and services with the maximum total value. The elements of total value include more than price, quality and delivery. Technical innovation, assured supply, cost reduction assistance, and engineering or process assistance are some of the supplier contributions that BFG considers in determining total value.

We view the relationships with our suppliers as a business partnership in which both parties coordinate and combine their talents and actions to produce mutually profitable and superior results.

As an integral part of this purchasing philosophy, BFG is committed to establishing business partnerships with firms owned and operated by minority citizens. Although we will not relax our strict standards of performance to achieve this goal, we are dedicated to assuring that such enterprises have the opportunity to compete for our business.

Purchasing Procedures/ Responsibilities

As discussed in our Purchasing Philosophy, BFGoodrich views the relationships with its suppliers as a business partnership. As in any partnership, this arrangement imposes obligations on both partners. Outlined below are what we believe are the obligations imposed by the partnership on BFG and its suppliers.

BFG's Responsibilities

1. **Ethics** — High ethical standards, objectivity, integrity, fairness, and total honesty are mandatory, full-time principles that we apply on each and every occasion.

2. **Value** — Each purchase decision we make will reward the suppliers who will supply BFG the best total value.

3. **Competitive Price** — We expect to pay a competitive price for the total value we receive.

4. **Commitments/Access** — We will fulfill our commitments to our suppliers and provide them with access to BFG personnel. We will provide the suppliers with knowledge of our purchasing system, accounts payable system, and other policies and procedures necessary to be an effective business partner.

5. **Professionalism** — We are dedicated to professionalism within the purchasing function at BFGoodrich. Our purchasing people have the responsibility and authority to manage every aspect of our supplier relationships. Only Purchasing has the final authority to commit BFG to a purchase.

Supplier's Responsibilities

1. **Ethics** — Suppliers must pursue all their relations with BFG with the highest standards of ethical conduct. There is no room in our partnership for attempts to compromise either partner's high ethical standards.

2. **Product Value** — Be ready and willing to show that your product or service contributes value; its cost is proportionate to its usefulness; it needs all of its features to do the job and there's nothing better for performing the function; no other supplier can provide the same product at lower cost; and you are not supplying it to others for less than you are offering it to BFG.

3. **Involvement of Support Functions** — Suppliers are expected to involve more than just their sales people in supplying BFG. We expect marketing, engineering, manufacturing, and technical assistance in order to provide our customers with a high-quality product at a competitive price.

4. **Commitments** — Suppliers should not let us lead them into making commitments that cannot be kept, but once made, we expect commitments to be met.

5. **Long-Term Partner** — We expect our relationships with our business partners to endure for a long period of time. As such, we require a supplier's commitment to satisfy our longer range material, volume, quality, cost, service, and technology needs.

We encourage you to become one of our business partners and to come forward with suggestions that will improve our partnership.

Purchasing
at Mead

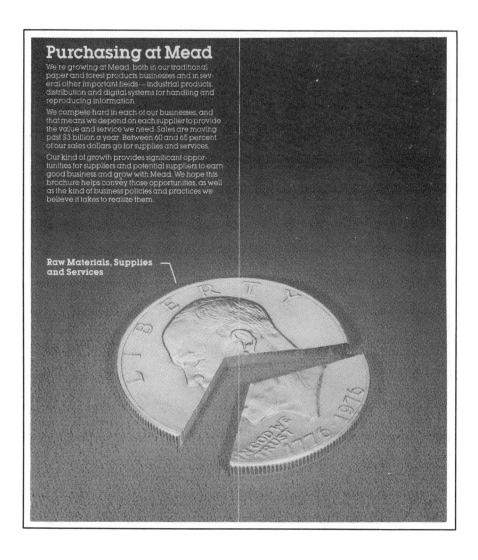

Purchasing at Mead

We're growing at Mead, both in our traditional paper and forest products businesses and in several other important fields — industrial products, distribution and digital systems for handling and reproducing information.

We compete hard in each of our businesses, and that means we depend on each supplier to provide the value and service we need. Sales are moving past $3 billion a year. Between 60 and 65 percent of our sales dollars go for supplies and services.

Our kind of growth provides significant opportunities for suppliers and potential suppliers to earn good business and grow with Mead. We hope this brochure helps convey those opportunities, as well as the kind of business policies and practices we believe it takes to realize them.

Raw Materials, Supplies and Services

Mead

Objectives

Assure supply—Our prime objective in purchasing is to have sufficient supplies of all required items available at the time they are needed.

Best possible value is another key objective. By encouraging all forms of competition, we aggressively seek the best total value in a combination of supply, price, required quality, service and research help.

Pertinent information on values obtainable through our purchasing contacts is often vital at several Mead locations. We try to share it promptly with the appropriate manufacturing and/or research people, keeping management advised on current and projected availability and price information. Suppliers and potential suppliers are encouraged to present new ideas and materials that can help us make better products, reduce costs or otherwise improve our operations.

Ethical and legal conduct—Mead insists its employees observe the letter and spirit of the law and practice the highest standards of business conduct.

Purchasing Organization

Most purchases are made at Mead's individual operating locations.

Major raw materials, MRO (maintenance, repair and operating) supplies and services used at multiple Mead locations are normally purchased or contracted for by the purchasing staff at Mead's headquarters in Dayton, Ohio. Operating plants release directly against these supply agreements.

Procurement and leasing contracts for automobiles and material handling equipment are also handled through the Corporate Purchasing department through the competitive inquiry process.

New construction and related projects are handled through the purchasing section of Mead's Corporate Engineering department in Dayton.

How to Earn Mead's Business

Competitive Inquiries or requests for bids, along with appropriate negotiation, provide equal opportunities for potential and current suppliers to EARN Mead's business.

Long-term value considerations include reliability, price, required quality and service. These form the basis of our purchasing decisions.

Competition: Mead strives to develop all forms of competition; i.e., between sources, materials, different grades of the same materials and processes.

Innovation: Vendors are encouraged to bring Mead new or improved materials, equipment and services.

Profit: We believe our suppliers are entitled to a fair opportunity to make a profit under healthy, competitive conditions. However, they are not automatically entitled to a profit.

Competitive Inquiries to suppliers and potential suppliers regarding our requirements imply that business is or may be available and that it will be placed with those sources offering Mead the best total value.

Unsolicited proposals may be submitted to Purchasing at any time. The potential supplier will be informed if we have made previous commitments.

Communications with vendors normally should be handled through Purchasing. In many situations, technical, engineering or related considerations make direct involvement desirable. Purchasing may make the initial arrangements and should be kept abreast of developments to assure that the supplier receives proper consideration in establishing supply contracts and purchase orders.

Commitments to purchase or changes in existing commitments will be made by authorized Purchasing personnel only.

Confidentiality is of great importance. Suppliers must maintain the confidentiality of competitively sensitive information which is obtained from Purchasing or other Mead personnel.

Mead's Obligations to Suppliers

Non-disclosure: Prices and related information, whether accepted or not, will not be disclosed.

Competitively sensitive information is handled in a completely confidential manner.

Security: Although supplier representatives are to be treated courteously, we avoid revealing competitively sensitive price, usage, and related information. To help avoid breaching security, information is provided only on a "need to know" basis.

Claims can generally be avoided through good specifications and contract terms. If, however, a claim does result, it will be settled promptly and fairly, based on the facts.

Employee purchases: Mead employees are not permitted to receive or purchase goods or services for personal use from suppliers or potential suppliers at price concessions not available to the general public.

Gifts and Entertainment

Business-connected social contacts, on a limited basis, can be in the best interest of the company when properly conducted. Entertainment in any form that would likely result in a feeling or expectation of personal obligation should not be extended or accepted.

Inappropriate entertainment, hospitality, or gifts from companies doing or seeking to do business with Mead are strongly discouraged, and any other than those of nominal advertising value will not be accepted.

Visits to suppliers: Purchasing personnel are encouraged to make only essential business visits to suppliers of major or critical materials to review the strengths/weaknesses of the manufacturing and related facilities and to become acquainted with key management and service personnel. When visiting suppliers, Mead expects to pay transportation, hotel and related living expenses.

Picking up the tab: When luncheon or dinner meetings are necessary for conducting business, Mead expects to host an appropriate share of such meetings. Repetitive engagements are usually unnecessary and should be avoided.

Legal Guidelines

Mead's policy is strict compliance with the spirit as well as the letter of the law. We work hard to educate all our people on compliance.

Legal guidelines have a direct bearing on our day-to-day relationships with suppliers and potential suppliers.

Knowing the law: Mead employees and employees of the companies with which we do business have a responsibility in this respect. They need to be familiar with and understand the law's requirements and the consequences of non-compliance. This is especially important with regard to antitrust laws (e.g., Reciprocity, Tying Agreements and Price discrimination).

Liabilities: It is important to understand that a corporation may be fined up to $1,000,000 if convicted of a criminal violation of the antitrust laws. Convicted individuals may be fined up to $100,000 or sentenced to up to three years in prison or both!

Working Together

Mead strives to build sound, professional business relationships with suppliers. As customers we demand a good deal of value, service and reliability. At the same time we recognize our own obligation to help suppliers and potential suppliers know the company well—its needs, its standards, its philosophy of doing business. We try to keep that obligation in mind as we manage our purchasing programs.

This booklet is a reaffirmation of our commitment to sound judgment and integrity in all our dealings. We hope it will prove informative and facilitate doing business with Mead.

Provisions for open, effective communications are an integral part of the integrity and health of our business relationships. In this regard your constructive comments and recommendations are welcomed.

Burnell R. Roberts

Burnell R. Roberts
President
Mead Corporation
Dayton, Ohio 45463

Hyster Company Purchasing Policies

Hyster Company Purchasing Policies

STANDARDS

Hyster Company subscribes to the following standards of purchasing practice which are similar to those advocated by the National Association of Purchasing Management:

1. To consider, first, the interests of the company in all transactions and to carry out and believe in its established policies.

2. To be receptive to competent counsel from colleagues, and to be guided by such counsel without impairing the dignity and responsibility of the office.

3. To buy without prejudice, seeking to obtain the maximum ultimate values for each dollar of expenditure.

4. To strive consistently for knowledge of the materials and process of manufacture, and to establish practical methods for purchasing conduct.

5. To subscribe to and work for honesty and truth in buying and selling, and to denounce all forms and manifestations of commercial bribery.

6. To accord a prompt and courteous reception so far as conditions will permit, to all who call on a legitimate business mission.

7. To respect the Company obligations and to require that obligations to the Company be respected, consistent with good business practice.

8. To counsel and assist fellow purchasing agents in the performance of their duties, when occasion permits.

9. To cooperate with all organizations and individuals engaged in activities designated to enhance the purchasing profession.

William J. Fronk
President

OBJECTIVES

The purpose of this statement is to outline the Company policies upon which our worldwide purchasing policies and procedures are based. It is to be used as a guide by all purchasing departments and personnel from the initial contact of any supplier to the completion of a purchase order.

It is the responsibility and objective of all purchasing personnel to procure authorized material and services of required quantity and quality at the lowest ultimate cost, on schedule, from sources selected according to approved policies.

Hyster buyers are expected to give proper consideration to costs, realizing that our suppliers cannot continue in business if their prices do not meet their costs plus a reasonable profit.

COMMITMENTS

All Hyster personnel, with the exception of Advertising and Training, work through our purchasing departments for the award of procurement contracts. Advertising and Training make their own commitments, but do subscribe to this policy.

OUTSIDE OF THIS EXCEPTION, PURCHASING ALONE IS AUTHORIZED TO MAKE PURCHASING COMMITMENTS ON BEHALF OF THE COMPANY.

HYSTER COMPANY
Corporate Headquarters
P.O. Box 2902
Portland, Oregon 97208

Worldwide Manufacturing Locations

U.S. Industrial Truck Division
- Berea, Kentucky
- Danville, Illinois
- Portland, Oregon
- Sulligent, Alabama

Warehouse Equipment Division
- Crawfordsville, Indiana

Construction Equipment Division
- Kewanee, Illinois

Fabtek, Inc.
- Healdsburg, California

Non-U.S. Operations
- Craigavon, Northern Ireland
- Irvine, Scotland
- Johannesburg, Republic of South Africa
- Mississauga, Ontario, Canada
- Nijmegen, The Netherlands
- Sao Paulo, Brazil
- Sydney, Australia
- Tessenderlo, Belgium

SUPPLIER RELATIONSHIPS

Hyster Company is aware that we cannot attain our prime objective of satisfying our customers and making an acceptable profit without the continual cooperation and support of those who help supply our needs.

Suppliers will be requested to offer quotations only when the buyer conscientiously expects to consider them as suppliers in the final determination.

Worldwide suppliers, both potential and existing, will be evaluated and monitored on the basis of their capabilities, technical competence, quality, reliability and prices as well as performance.

We encourage small/minority business concerns to participate, and due consideration will be given such concerns in the selection of suppliers.

U.S.A. suppliers will be required to certify their compliance with all applicable Federal and State laws, ordinances and rules, regulations and orders of governmental agencies including, but not limited to, the provisions of Executive Order 11246, as amended.

Multiple sources will be established wherever practical throughout the world to ensure our meeting production schedules and to sustain the competitive aspect of our business.

CONTRACT BUYING

It is our established practice whenever possible to enter into an Annual Procurement Agreement (APA) or Annual Contract (AC) for items which are used in volume or lend themselves to this type of contract. These agreements, usually for a term of one year, commit Hyster Company to procure its annual requirements from a selected supplier. When properly administered by both parties, they should result in additional profit dollars for both our suppliers and Hyster Company.

DECENTRALIZATION

Hyster Company's purchasing activity is operated on a decentralized basis. Each of our domestic and foreign plants has a purchasing operation responsible for fulfilling its own particular needs. However, in a number of cases, annual or corporate-type contracts and coordinated procurements are developed jointly by the Corporate Purchasing Director and the individual Divisional or plant purchasing managers for commodities and services having Companywide usage.

PURCHASING RESEARCH

For new product and development work, purchases are made through the Purchasing Research section of Corporate Purchasing in Portland, Oregon. Contacts with engineers for any new project are to be made through this group.

The Construction Equipment Division in Kewanee, Illinois and Fabtek in Healdsburg, California are responsible for their own development work.

PARTS AND SERVICE

Our goal is the very best available after-market service to Hyster customers. You, as a supplier, can render valuable assistance for the program by prompt, complete reporting of any changes to the product which you supply. Further, our suppliers should understand it is Hyster's policy that our part numbers, drawings, and other business matters are to be considered proprietary information between buyer and seller.

VALUE ANALYSIS

We solicit the suggestions of our suppliers to help reduce costs and yet fulfill the requirements of our products.

Any suggested value-engineered changes recommended by a supplier will be held in confidence and considered proprietary in nature.

TRAFFIC

Each operation has a Traffic Department that operates under this policy.

For those suppliers who furnish Hyster's requirements worldwide, we have established an Import-Export Department at Danville, Illinois for consolidation and containerization of overseas shipments. This department will be your contact in the event that there are any questions or problems. To avoid costly delays, please ensure that this department's instructions are understood and followed.

INTERVIEWING HOURS

Every effort will be made to promptly and courteously receive each caller. To facilitate this and to best utilize the time available, interviewing hours have been established at all Hyster plants.

We suggest that infrequent visitors, and those who must travel long distances, should advise purchasing personnel in advance of the date and time of a proposed visit.

GIFTS AND GRATUITIES

It is Hyster Company policy that no employees or their families are to accept gifts, entertainment or favors from any current or potential suppliers. To avoid any misunderstanding, please ensure that your people are aware of this policy.

APPENDIX C – AN EXAMPLE DRAFT POLICY: LIMITS OF PURCHASING AUTHORITY

1 Delegation of purchasing authorities

1.1 Definitions

Purchasing authorisation – Applies strictly to those nominated to approve purchase requisitions and thereby commit the cost-centre budget over which they exercise control within the limits of authority specified.

Purchasing authority – Denotes the commitment of the company's funds usually through the contractual signature of a purchase document (purchase order or contract).

1.2 Purchasing commitment

The only department permitted to commit the company for expenditure with external suppliers is the purchasing department, subject to the areas of exception listed below:

(*a*)   advertising
(*b*)   real estate
(*c*)   insurance
(*d*)   services (electricity and water)
(*e*)   telephone, telex, telecommunications.

1.3 Associated purchasing commitment

The purchasing department remains the commitment authority for both non-capital and capital purchases of items, goods, equipment, materials and services. In respect of capital purchases, the extent to which the purchasing department is involved is:

(*a*)   preparation of bidlists
(*b*)   issuing requests for quotations
(*c*)   receiving quotations
(*d*)   preparing bid summaries and making recommendations for an award
(*e*)   advising successful and unsuccessful bidders
(*f*)   placing the purchase order.

2 Authorisation to purchase (requisitions)

The purchasing department does not of itself determine the need for, or the specification of, the items to be purchased. The authorisation for the purchasing department to proceed with purchasing action is based on the receipt of completed and properly authorised purchase requisitions. The purchase requisition is the document used by departments to request purchasing action. It may be initiated by any department within the company, but must be signed by individuals having both budgeting and delegated authority to approve a transaction of the type and size in question. The purchasing department will work closely with, and in support of, all user requisitioning departments to ensure, on behalf of the company, that proposed commitments are based on maximum value to the company having regard to price, quality, service and delivery.

2.1 Delegation of authorisation

Authorisation of purchase requisitions will be in accordance with the authority limits specified in the addendum to this policy document. The purchasing department has the responsibility to verify authorisation signatures and personal money authority limitations on all purchase requisitions. The purchasing department should not change the essential facts of a purchase requisition without the agreement of the requisitioner. Minor changes in quantity to develop possible savings through optimising ordering quantities and in descriptions to enhance clarity or conformance are permitted. Whilst it is not the responsibility of the requisitioner to specify source of supply, the requisitioner may recommend known supplier sources without commitment.

3 Authority to purchase (purchase orders)

The purchasing department has the sole responsibility for issuing purchase orders. Signature of purchase orders is delegated in accordance with the addendum to this policy document. A purchase order is a legal document committing the company to a purchase transaction as specified therein. The purchase order form incorporates appropriate terms and conditions governing the transaction. Prior to issue to a supplier, all purchase orders shall be signed only by the person(s) who have been specifically granted purchase order signatory authority. All purchase orders will be in response to documented purchase requisitions signed by authorised management individuals. The purchasing department is responsible for the selection of the supply source, with certain exceptions within the purchase of capital equipment requirements, and will normally place the purchase order with the low bidder in accordance with purchasing procedures. Allowance for technical or commercial justification for single or sole source are included within the purchasing procedures. Where a purchase is in excess of a purchasing executive's authority limit, he/she should send the purchase order and all supporting documentation with appropriate recommendations for selection to the individual who has the appropriate purchase authority level (as per the addendum to this policy document) for review and countersignature.

3.1 Capital expenditure

Capital projects and construction projects of a significant size (above £ x) are the subject of special review and should follow the procedure laid down for 'capital investment appraisal'.

Authority Limits

Authorised signature \ Transaction	Requisitions Non-capital items	Requisitions Capital items	Requisitions Services	Purchase orders non-capital	Purchase orders capital	Purchase orders services	Contracts non-capital up to 1 yr	Contracts capital up to 1 yr	Contracts non-capital 1-3 yrs	Contracts capital 1-3 yrs
	3	3 (1)	3	3	3	3	3	3 (5)	3 (5)	3 (5)
Chief general manager	1M	3M	1M	–	–	–	5M	10M	10M	50M
General managers	0.5M	1M	0.5M	–	–	–	3M	5M	5M	10M
Chief managers and supts.	0.25M	0.5M	0.25M	–	3M (4)	–	–	–	–	–
Group managers	0.1M	0.25M	0.1M	–	–	–	–	–	–	–
Division managers	50K	0.1M	50K	–	–	–	–	–	–	–
Dept heads	10K	50K	10K	–	–	–	–	–	–	–
Materials manager	10K (2)	50K (2)	10K (2)	1M	1M (1)	1M	2M (6)	2M (6)	2M (6)	2M (6)
Purchasing manager	5K (2)	10K (2)	5K (2)	0.5M	0.5M (1)	0.5M	1M (6)	1M (6)	1M (6)	1M (6)
Senior buyer	–	–	–	0.1M	0.1M (1)	0.1M	0.5M (6)	0.5M (6)	0.5M (6)	0.5M (6)
Buyer	–	–	–	50K	50K (1)	50K	0.1M (6)	0.1M (6)	0.1M (6)	0.1M (6)

NOTES: (1) Requires counter-signature of chief engineer
(2) Purchasing department only
(3) Above limits – to board
(4) Chief engineer only
(5) Requires legal vetting
(6) Counter-signature required

2

Competitive analysis

David Farmer*

A key requirement when analysing market situations is to identify the advantages and disadvantages which the various businesses in that market have, one against the others. The marketing and planning literature includes considerable discussion as to the necessity for such analysis and the methods by which it might be undertaken. However, there is little emphasis in that discussion which relates to purchasing. Indeed, even in the purchasing literature, scanty attention has been paid to such issues.

It appears from this that there is, at least, the implication in theory and practice that:

1 Purchasing organisations do not have competitors in their supply markets.
2 They do not seek to develop competitive advantage in those markets.
3 They have not perceived that they could benefit from such advantage.

Yet even cursory analysis of business activity over the years shows that the more perceptive businesses have obtained sustainable competitive advantage because they have been aware of opportunities. In the UK, for example, the dominant food retailers in the high

---

* A version of this chapter first appeared as a paper in the June 1984 edition of *Long Range Planning* (vol. 17, no. 3) and is published here by permission of the Editor.

streets have established themselves, at least partly, as a result of their competitive supply strategies. The British Shoe Corporation, the dominant retailer in the footwear market, was established on the back of a vertically integrated competitive strategy. This was both upstream and downstream-related. In the US at the turn of the century, Durant's success with the embryo General Motors business stemmed largely from a, then, novel supply strategy. Then in the late nineteen-seventies, Savin Business Machines took a major share of the low/medium volume copying market in the US from the Xerox Corporation.[1] They did so by finding competitive advantage both in their supply and sales markets.

In all these cases, it should be noted, a successful competitive strategy at the supply end of the business allowed the company concerned to compete more effectively in its end market. Since many businesses (e.g manufacturing and retailing) convert and/or add value to inputs to meet their own end-market needs, the potential for such action is appealing. Certainly, a business which seeks competitive advantage solely in its end market(s) is ignoring considerable potential. This is particularly true where input costs are a significant element in output revenue, or where a key material/component is essential for end-product configuration. In the latter circumstance, even insignificant items in cost terms can be seen to be significant strategically.

The purpose of this chapter is to emphasise the importance of this deceptively obvious insight. It is to discuss the need for evolving and managing competitive strategies in supply markets which complement those being applied in other areas of the business system. It is to suggest that those strategies can be an effective weapon in the armoury of the corporate strategist and to outline one approach to competitive analysis and strategic action in supply markets. Throughout, the implication is inherent in the discussion that the competitive advantages sought in those markets have as their purpose the enhancement of such advantage in end-product markets; no one is in business purely to buy.

THE CONCEPT OF COMPETITION

Competition is a fact of life. For example, biological systems exist as competitive entities and, as Henderson[2] writes:

> The total competitive environment . . . consists of a . . . web of interfacing competitors. . . . The competition within the web is for resources. These can be of many kinds, but the basic starting point for all of these are the natural resources of energy and materials. Such resources are converted to more complex and specialized use by successive trophic levels. In nature there are rarely as many as six trophic levels. In business there can be more.

In this statement Henderson is underlining the complexity of nature's supply chain, where one creature becomes the food or material by which others live. He is also stressing the fact that business environments can be even more complex than nature's. There is, too, the implication of the impact upon balance and the need to view the supply chain as a whole. For example, the supply chain(s) relating to industrial raw materials, semi-processed materials, components and sub-assemblies, is one such case. And competitive activity may take place at and between each of the levels in the supply chain. Consequently, if only in terms of ensuring supply, awareness as to how crucial each of these levels is, is a key element in the development of an effective strategy. Clearly competition can and does affect behaviour in supply markets just as it does in those concerned with end products.

Figure 2.1, which is a simplified model of the supply chain relating to wood products, is an example. The growth in development of furniture made from chipboard to the detriment of products made from solid timber within this chain is a case in point. That development affected the balance of supply activity at several points within the chain. However, in this case the developments within the supply chain could best be categorised as having been evolutionary rather than revolutionary. Initially they were stimulated by furniture manufacturers seeking a cheaper alternative to solid timber. Subsequently the additionally attractive features of the chipboard product to the furniture manufacturer (stability, uniformity, immediate use) resulted in far larger volumes being consumed. There was, too, the appeal to those who predicted a shortage in the supply of quality timbers. In addition the chipboard product could utilise relatively inferior grades of timber which, in turn, widened the potential scope of supply.

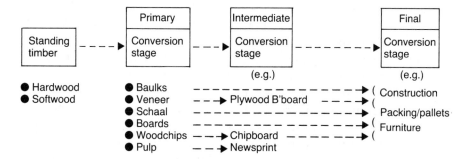

Figure 2.1 A simple model of a wood products supply chain

Consideration of this example will suggest some of the aspects of competition in the supply market and will add credence to Schumpeter's[3] statement that:

> The kind of competition that is decisive is that which comes from the new commodity, the new source of supply and the new type of organisation.

A new product, in this case chipboard, utilised by a manufacturer in his own product allowed him to develop new markets. It also promoted other developments such as 'knocked-down' furniture, where the customer was provided with self-assembly 'kits'. In its turn this allowed initiatives in storage and distribution of flat packs and of retailing modes.

In its way chipboard represented new technology. However the most dramatic effects of this stimulant in modern markets must surely have been beyond the comprehension even of Schumpeter (writing in 1941). For example, the pace of developments in semi-conductor manufacture have been startling. And since much end-product development has been promoted by the sophistication of these intricate components, their impact on the business system has been marked. Clearly those manufacturers who have had the ability to locate, develop and promote competitive advantage for themselves in this supply market have been advantageously placed in their end markets. An example is IBM's courtship of Intel in the

US which allowed it considerable advantage with respect to its own range of personal computers. Despite the fact that IBM produces its own chips, it recognised that the availability of Intel's 16-bit microchip to its competitors could represent a major threat. Whilst IBM do not purchase all Intel's output, their purchases are significant enough to have an impact on availability. In addition, the computer giant's action in purchasing a 12 per cent stake in Intel late in 1972 cemented a relationship which is concerned with the next generation of microchips. Intel is still an independent concern, yet the relationship produces the benefits for both parties which stem from quasi-vertical integration. For IBM it is part of the supply strategy, for Intel it is an element of the marketing strategy. The fact that the result is mutually beneficial should assist in sustaining competitive advantage.[4] At least by inference, the literature suggests that the initiative for such an approach should come from the seller. However, it is obvious that perceptive purchasers can be as creative and dynamic with respect to their input markets as they can to their end markets. Yet there is evidence[5] to suggest that managements in many industries are myopic as far as supply market opportunities are concerned.

ROLES IN SUPPLY MARKET PLANNING

The basic functions of the strategist in respect to supply markets are the same as those with which he would be involved vis-à-vis end markets. It is necessary to analyse, predict, weigh probabilities, define strategies and plan their enactment. In broad terms the task with a supply market perspective necessitates:

1   Analysing the company's supply chains in order to perceive the key points at which competitive advantage may be sought or where competitive threats may arise.
2   Understanding the potential impact of particular strategic interventions upon the complex entity which is the supply market(s). Also, to be able to conceive of the likely rearrangements which may occur and how competitors within the system may react.
3   Having weighed the potential consequences of particular

interventions, selecting those which are likely to be most beneficial to the business.

4 Predicting, with reasonable accuracy, the outcome of such interventions so as to be able to justify the allocation of resources to the project.

5 Convincing colleagues within the business of the benefits of such interventions and of the need to link supply-end strategies with end-market strategies, plans and actions to ensure that advantages are optimised.

Given that there are no unchanging 'rules' within markets, these abilities are demanding of the best executive. Consequently, it might be that one of the reasons for the apparent myopia with respect to supply markets is that end markets in themselves present enough of a challenge. Nonetheless, most management issues concern the effective allocation of resources. And where the company's business system is heavily reliant upon supply market factors, then it is a foolish organisation which does not consider them when allocating its resources.

STRATEGIC INTERVENTIONS

As has been shown elsewhere,[6] strategic action among purchasers tends to be the exception rather than the rule. In most businesses it would appear that the function of purchasing is undertaken, at best, in a tactical fashion. As in any market situation given time, competition will evolve as the 'actors' employ operational or tactical moves. In contrast, effective strategic intervention can result in change in a relatively short time which will provide the strategist with competitive advantage. Given that purchasers tend to be reactive, there is considerable incentive for the strategist with insight into supply market possibilities to take advantage of such myopia. And since the concept of competition presupposes that there will be winners and losers the importance of seeking such advantage is clear.

Presumably the strategist should be seeking to locate the segment in a particular market where his company will be able to influence competitive forces in its favour. This implies both defensive and offensive actions and a broad-based knowledge of the sources, and potential sources of competitive pressure. In supply markets this will involve consideration of, e.g.:

- the behaviour of other existing buyers (direct and indirect competitors)
- the behaviour and strategies of existing sellers
- the effect of new entrants on existing behaviour (buyers and sellers)
- the impact and potential of by-products on existing markets.

None of these is, of course, mutually exclusive which adds to the complexity of the supply market environment made up, as described earlier, of a series of sub-markets. And there will be different competitors at each level.

One approach

Awareness and knowledge of the key competitive forces which impinge or are likely to impinge upon the buying company is the basis for strategic action. Conventional analysis of strengths, weaknesses, opportunities and threats will indicate the 'most likely' sectors for strategic intervention. The priorities for action should then be identified. In many respects the analysis is concerned with identifying comparative power positions – actual and potential. The following section describes one approach to competitive analysis in supply markets as a precursor to enacting selected strategic interventions. The approach is not intended to have universal application, nonetheless it should suggest a framework which can be tailored to most situations.

Stage 1 *Internal appraisal*
Involves consideration of the skills and resources necessary to manage the strategic programme which is envisaged. Included in this is the need for a planning framework which facilitates strategic decision making and which will be beneficial to the integrated business. Clearly this appraisal involves realigning/strengthening the resources available as appropriate.

Stage 2 *External appraisal (general)*
Involves analysis of market(s) and sub-markets as implied

above. Apart from those mentioned so far, other factors involve consideration of, e.g.:
– the general economic environment
– government legislation
– mergers/takeovers
– international market effects
– comparative currency relationships.

Stage 3   *External appraisal (specific market sectors)*
This work is undertaken against the backcloth of the general appraisal. Specific analysis is undertaken along the lines of earlier discussion relating to specific market sectors.

Stage 4   *Alternative approaches considered*
From the specific market analysis strategic alternatives are proposed and considered. Particular interventions are selected from among those generated based upon determined priorities.

Stage 5   *Interventions enacted*
In this phase specific plans are constructed, enacted and monitored.

At Stage 1, a typical problem for the organisation which has not conceived of supply factors being strategic is a shortage of data and skills with which to work. There is often the problem, too, that the attitudes, perceptions and traits of the people involved in supply work fail to match the role which has to be performed. In addition there is the tendency for those who are operating at a strategic level to make false assumptions about supply factors. A powerful method which can help to change attitudes involves bringing a cross-functional team together (*a*) to analyse a problem which has been caused by such myopia; (*b*) to apply the lessons learned from such analysis to some potential new product discussion; and (*c*) to identify key materials/components in particular products which could be the subject of such analysis. Not surprisingly, the extent of the work involved can be considerable, particularly in attitude and skill development and in building an effective information system. For this reason it is important to specify priorities for analysis which have the greatest profit potential.

The work at Stage 2 is a virtual mirror image of end-market analysis. The differences involve tailoring the general data towards supply market issues. Thus, for example, government legislation with regard to UK development areas could indicate potential sources of low-cost products. Mergers and takeovers in the supply market could realign power relationships and indicate detailed analysis at the next stage. Then the difficult question of comparative currency relationships has considerable potential impact upon those businesses which source, or are considering sourcing products, components and materials from abroad.

Stage 3

Assuming that little has been done previously, some method of selecting priority cases for consideration at this stage is necessary. At the outset it is probably best to:

- (*a*) isolate critical materials/components from current listing; then
- (*b*) isolate new materials/components from development plans, and
- (*c*) produce a shortlist, say three or four, of these items for detailed analysis.

It is useful to have a checklist of what is considered critical as a starting point. One such listing might be:

- – If the total expenditure is substantial (particularly on products which are in the 'star' or early 'cash cow' categories)
- – If it is essential for the company's business
- – If there is no other known acceptable supplier
- – If it is a key item which is a company 'policy' sole source
- – If general environmental analysis suggests future turbulence in the market(s) concerned.

Having selected the items for consideration the detailed analysis of the supply market in question is undertaken. Among the factors included in this analysis are:

- – Who else is buying (significantly) in our markets? What are their end products? Have they any alternative?
- – What is the supply industry profile? Does it have a large dominant market captain? Does it have many suppliers?

- Is it regionalised? Is it dominated by multinationals? Is it ripe for rationalisation? How dependent are suppliers upon overseas sources of materials/components/technology/financing?
- What are the comparative power positions of the parties in the market (buyers and sellers)?
- What key factors influence competition in the market (e.g. importance of energy costs, limited sources of key raw materials)?
- What potential substitutes are available? Do they have potential improvement curve benefits? Might they benefit from greater economies of scale?
- Is the product concerned 'generic' or differentiated?
- What new factors may influence supply and demand balance? (For example, as Porter[7] illustrated, high energy costs in the late nineteen-seventies stimulated the recognition of the potential impact of better insulation. Initially fibreglass enjoyed a great demand, subsequently a plethora of substitutes emerged.)
- Which supply businesses are low profit earners but are being sustained through being members of a group?
- Which of the other purchasers of the item are under considerable profit pressure? Will that pressure stimulate action vis-à-vis the material in question? What options are open to them in this respect?
- How difficult is it for new suppliers to enter the market? (e.g.) – economies of scale
  – extent of capital necessary
  – control of distribution channels.
- What is the key to the dominant position of the major suppliers (e.g. raw material source, distribution channel)?

In answering all these and other questions a major purpose is to discover competitive advantages to which other companies in the market are blind. Another is to isolate potential or emerging threats which may be forestalled.

Stage 4

The approaches selected at this stage will, of course, vary with the circumstances. Among those which might be considered are:

- Vertical integration (Ford Motor Company is among the many to have followed this route).
- Realigning expenditure so as to have greater influence over particular suppliers (an approach being adopted currently by several European motor manufacturers).
- Purchasing segments of production capability (security of supply).
- Moving to standard/generic materials/components in formulation so as to increase scope of potential supply.
- Encouraging key overseas suppliers to set up plant in own country.
- Lobbying government to support particular initiatives.
- Stimulating technological development in the supply market on a 'first use' basis (note technological developments could include resource technology, e.g. new ways of obtaining the material; production technology, e.g. electronic components where improvement curve developments have been remarkable; fabrication technology, e.g. in the aerospace industries with regard to combining different heat resistant metals in one fabrication. Clearly factors such as weight, material costs and fabrication costs are all germane to these enquiries.
- Establishing mutually beneficial long-term relationships with key suppliers (Marks & Spencer are among the foremost promoters of this approach).
- Assisting new entrants to the marketplace through, for example, providing base loads for their plants, indicating different distribution methodology which would provide a means of entering the market. (Air Products were assisted in this respect when seeking advantage over the entrenched major competitor, British Oxygen. Instead of developing major centralised plants they worked with major buyers to establish on-site plants. In turn, smaller buyers stimulated a milk-round 'top-up' approach to distribution which favoured both buyer and seller.)

- Making all or a proportion of the items concerned.
- Buying sub-assemblies in lieu of components.
- Buying certain finished products on an own-label basis.

Having decided on the approach, the next stage is the enactment of the plan and the monitoring of progress. As in all competitive situations, surprise can be an extremely important element in success. That that surprise can emanate from supply markets is evident. However, it is important to stress again the importance of considering that source not in itself, but rather as part of an integrated planning framework. The approach can be effective in relatively simple as well as in complex markets. For example, the success of the Dr Pepper soft-drink product in the US was based partly upon lower cost raw materials in the recipe. It can extend across the chain of business activity. In that respect, Savin's early success against Xerox was based upon a liquid technology – as against a powder; on standard parts as against Xerox designed; on an assembly approach to manufacture as against integrated production; on distribution through dealers instead of direct and on sale as against leasing.

In all cases a company's perception of its strengths or weaknesses reflect that of its relative power position vis-à-vis the other parties in the system. Recognition of power or weakness can be a stimulant to redressing the balance in the company's favour. This chapter has sought to emphasise the potential for such action in supply markets. They are sources of considerable potential, worthy of careful attention from corporate strategists.

REFERENCES

(1) David H. Farmer, 'Input Management' in *Journal of General Management,* vol. 6, no. 4, Summer 1981.
(2) B.D. Henderson, 'The Anatomy of Competition' in *Journal of Marketing,* vol. 47, Spring 1983.
(3) J.A. Schumpeter, *Capitalism, Socialism and Democracy,* George Allen & Unwin, 1949.
(4) D.H. Farmer and K. MacMillan, 'Redefining the Boundaries of the Firm' in *Journal of Industrial Economics,* vol. XXVII, no. 3, March 1979.

(5) Robert E. Spekman and Ronald P. Hill, 'Strategy for Effective Procurement in the 1980s' in *Journal of Purchasing and Materials Management*, vol. 16, no. 4, Winter 1980.

(6) David H. Farmer, 'Developing Purchasing Strategies' in *Journal of Purchasing and Materials Management*, vol. 14, no. 3, Autumn 1978.

(7) Michael E. Porter, 'How Competitive Forces Shape Strategy' in *Harvard Business Review*, March-April 1979.

3

Strategic purchasing

Owen Davies

The main failure of the purchasing function is its concentration on negotiation and market price, and in emphasising short-term opportunistic decision making. Such an emphasis ignores a strategic holistic approach to purchasing and falls well short of any long-range planning horizons.

This short-range process derives in large measure from a short-sighted management attitude which measures purchasing perform-ance primarily on price relationships. Yet the same management will respond to a sales strategy that requires the need to buy into a market to derive market share with, for example, differential pricing policies relating to strategic marketing plans.

The objective, therefore, in this chapter is to evaluate the benefits to be derived from the use of strategic purchasing actions, recognising that such a process requires closer relationships through supplier development and problem-solving approaches rather than head-on positional bargaining postures.

The short-term approach in purchasing leads to an imbalance in the investment cycle, with production capacities swinging between buyers' and sellers' markets, with resultant over- and under-utilisation of manufacturing plant. Strategic purchasing seeks to derive a more balanced approach to capacity planning – those of the buying company as well as those of its suppliers.

The market research planning information which suppliers use is dependent on interpretation of customer data. Such data could be significantly enhanced by more accurate dialogue between purchasing and its suppliers. As a body, purchasing tends to be highly secretive in its information attitude, perhaps to its own detriment strategically. Yet such approaches as baseload contracts, longer-term supplier relationships, joint development and supplier utilisation lead to a concept of mutual benefit through adoption of strategic purchasing principles. Such an attitude will strongly influence inventory policies of both buyer and seller – a joint problem-solving approach to minimising the expensive capital tied up in inventory by both parties by maximising the utilisation of facilities, of both parties, and improving the flow of working capital. Strategic purchasing seeks a joint approach between buyer and seller to determine an effective solution to resource management. Such objectives will include zero inventory and zero defects in the mutual enhancement of a longer-term strategic relationship. In broad terms the move of strategic purchasing is away from 'fire-fighting' towards 'fire prevention'. However this will not be achieved without the co-operative understanding of top management of the benefits to be derived from the use of strategic purchasing approaches.

DEFINITION

Strategic purchasing is not an offshoot of the corporate planning function. Strategic purchasing may be defined as the process of taking a longer-term view of a purchasing decision, a cost-benefit relationship between an opportunistic short-term benefit approach and a balanced longer-range analysis of ultimate purchasing rewards. It concerns the review of a total cost approach to purchasing, encompassing all facets of the materials flow from sourcing derivation through distribution inwards, warehouse receipt and inventory control to eventual conversion (or value added) to distribution outwards.

Whilst the approaches used have parallels in corporate planning, strategic purchasing retains a closer involvement in the procurement activity. It is carried out by purchasing people and is not seen as a totally separate functional organisation. It provides both an input to and interface with corporate planning and, importantly, provides an essential, and generally missing, link in the corporate planning chain.

FACTORS INFLUENCING THE PURCHASING DECISION

In recognising that the flow of materials in an organisation is horizontal, the strategic factors that will influence the purchasing decision will be internal as well as external (see Figure 3.1). Many of these factors will provide limitations and constraints on the role of the purchasing function within the organisation, and part of the task of strategic purchasing is to convert such problems to opportunities to build on strengths whilst overcoming weaknesses.

Internal factors

Production and engineering

Traditionally, the manufacturing and engineering functions have been accorded the distinction that they have the ultimate responsibility and authority for what should be purchased, through the determination of the specification criteria. They have also significantly influenced the quantity to be purchased and, in less direct ways, even the source of supply. The role of strategic purchasing is to influence such decision making so as to ensure that effective decisions are taken which balance commercial and technical issues. Unilateral decisions made by production and engineering are as potentially lacking in cost consciousness as unilateral purchasing decisions are potentially dangerous without technical consultation.

Strategic purchasing forms the bridge between the technical functions in the organisation and the operational purchasing arm, setting up the dialogue by which the parties may balance the technical needs alongside the commercial opportunities, particularly with the longer term in view.

This role necessitates strategic purchasing staff having sufficient technical competence and knowledge to ensure the recognition of the strategic purchasing function by production and engineering; to have credibility with their technical colleagues. Among other things this should result in involvement in the capital expenditure

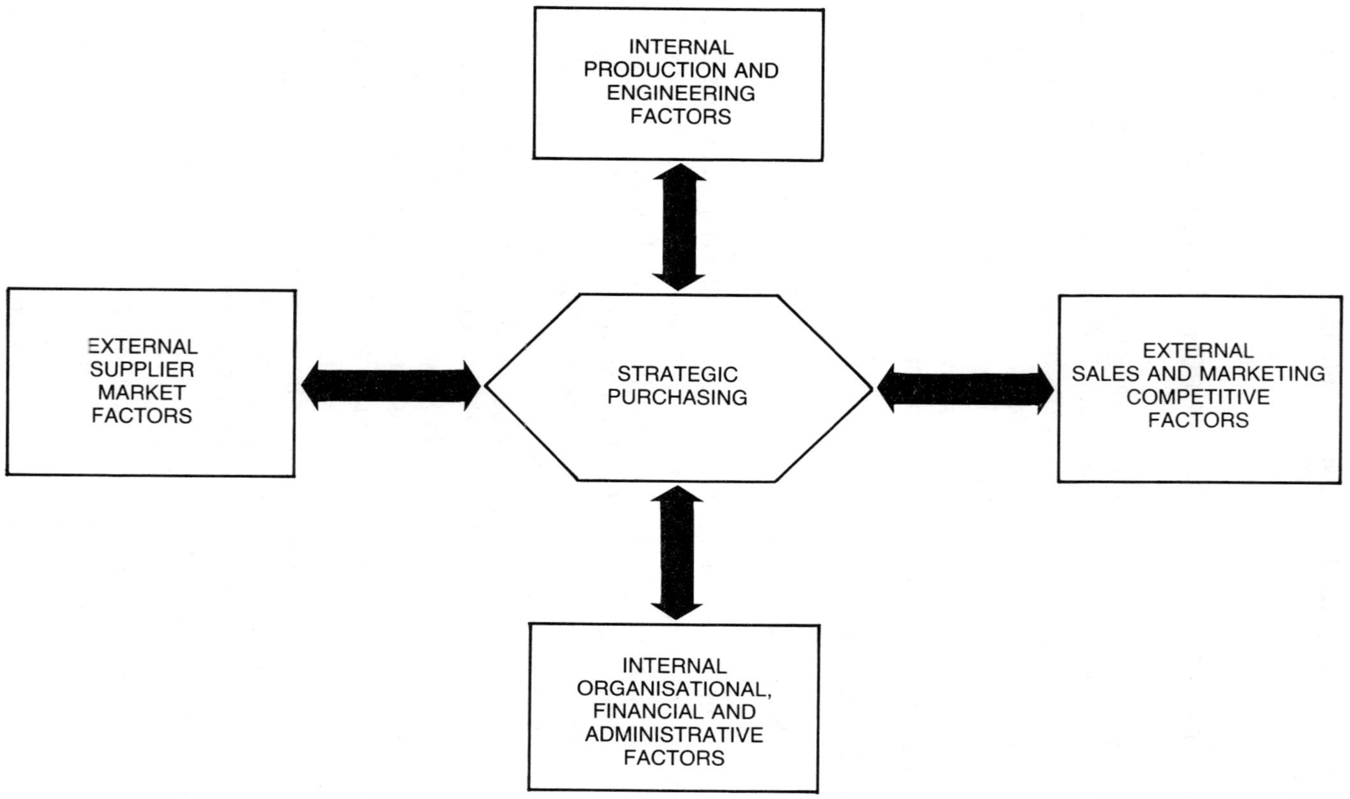

Figure 3.1 Strategic purchasing factors

programme and capital investment appraisals in concert with, for example, engineering and finance.

In addition there is the necessity for strategic purchasing to influence specifications. For example, specifications, if unchallenged, can result in a number of constraints and limitations:

1 The specification can be written in such a way as to preclude open competition in sourcing if it is written around a specific item or equipment.
2 The specification looks for custom-built items when standard items are readily available and at a considerable price/cost benefit to the buying company.
3 The specification is over-engineered, with requirements in excess of the functions which the specification seeks to perform.

There is a case, therefore, for the final writing of specifications not to be undertaken solely by the user departments and to be considered as a 'central service' carried out by specialist specification writers.

Another incentive to balanced specifications is to include the critical importance of life-cycle costing (see Figure 3.2). Using life-cycle costing, the costs of maintaining and operating an equipment or service are taken into account as well as replacement costs and residual values. In making purchasing decisions, the availability and costs of maintenance spares are often ignored and decisions are made on the criterion of the initial capital cost of the equipment alone. This has led to a number of well-documented financial blunders by government as well as private purchasing organisations throughout the world. There is little point in deciding in favour of equipment X if spares support is not readily available, or if the costs of operation are significantly higher than other equipments. Under the life-cycle costing technique, all future costs are estimated using discounted cash flow to determine net present value and equivalent annual values.

However, it should be noted that the use of life-cycle costing techniques in strategic purchasing decisions suffers from a serious limitation. Future costs are estimates, often based on sales brochures, which, understandably, may contain some 'exaggerations'. There is a need, therefore, to develop an information bank

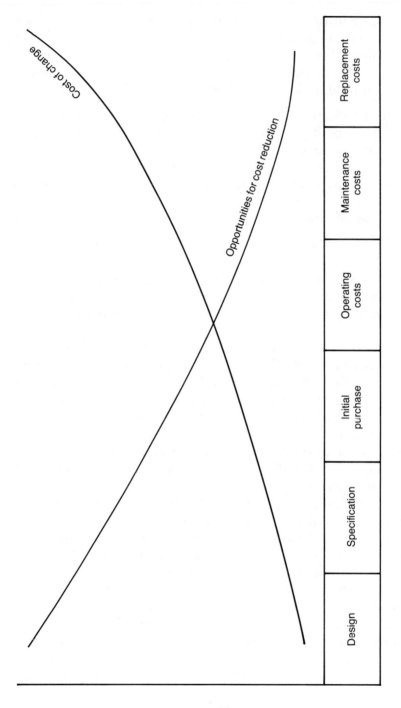

Figure 3.2 Life-cycle costing

within the organisation on performance – maintenance and operating – data for specified equipments. Presumably one means of using believable sales information would be to obtain performance guarantees with consequent contract penalties for non-performance.

Another important aspect of the application of life-cycle costing is the recognition that the best opportunity for cost reductions combined with the lowest cost of change is, understandably, at the design phase. At this time we are dealing with concepts, ideas, design features, prototypes etc. in the pre-specification stage. Yet purchasing is generally not involved in this phase and becomes active only when the initial purchase decision has been taken. Such concepts require the close involvement of purchasing right at the conceptual phase, and take full account of the total life and replacement of the equipment and service.

For example, the decision to utilise a certain computer hardware configuration has long-term strategic purchasing implications. Once installed, the cost of changing to an entirely different hardware infrastructure, no matter how apparently competitive, involves considerable expenditure beyond the actual cost of the competitive hardware. To change over from one major earthmoving equipment to another involves careful cost considerations of spares inventory held, different operating procedures, cost of retraining, high initial technical support etc.

Strategic purchasing, then, has much to offer the production and engineering functions and it is this recognition of the complementary role to be played by strategic purchasing in the affairs of both production and engineering that is essential to a balanced techno-commercial purchasing decision.

Organisational, financial and administrative

It cannot be ignored that, from an organisational standpoint, very few companies have adopted any kind of strategic purchasing concept. Some of the biggest automotive companies in the world such as General Motors are close to strategic purchasing but such organisations represent the exception rather than the rule. Lack of understanding of how dramatically strategic purchasing can contribute to the overall profitability and long-term development of the company has caused managements to ignore the opportunity afforded them. However, there are definite signs in the 1980s that management is no longer sidetracking the impact of strategic purchasing and there is no doubt that we shall see some significant changes through the introduction of strategic purchasing concepts during the present decade. Until that recognition occurs, however, organisational strictures will militate against the successful application of a strategic purchasing approach.

Successful development of a strategic purchasing concept requires the full support of management in terms of allocated resources – time, money and manpower.

Financial and administrative factors are less pervasive within strategic purchasing concepts but nevertheless provide some constraints to successful applications of strategic purchasing techniques. The most critical is lack of funding to introduce computerisation. Strategic purchasing depends to a high degree on detailed, wide-ranging information which can only be derived from an effective purchasing data base. Whilst accounts payable and inventory software packages are being increasingly adopted, a sound purchasing data base is not yet part of the integrated MIS. Nor have too many computer companies marketed, as yet, a worthwhile purchasing data base software package; some claim the presence of an integrated purchasing system but few actually achieve a complete data base information package for strategic purchasing decision making.

Administrative factors, alongside organisation issues, relate to manning levels as well as personnel standards. To staff a strategic purchasing function properly requires high calibre personnel with skill needs above the normal buyer criteria. Analytical, logical, numerative, business acumen, tertiary education preferably to MBA level, do not represent the average skills specification of a purchasing job. Combined with a preferred technical background, the overall man-specification for the strategic purchasing post is demanding. Nevertheless, the rewards to the organisation which recognises the benefits accruing from the use of strategic purchasing concepts are undeniable.

External factors

Supplier market

The build-up of the purchasing data base relates to detailed knowledge of the supplier market place in which strategic purchasing decisions will be made. In order that such decisions are based on sound information, it will be necessary to maintain both supplier profiles and product information files.

Supplier profile

Information on the financial standing of suppliers alone is insufficient to determine the advisability of engaging in longer-term supply relationships. A thorough investigation of the management style of the supplier organisation, manufacturing and R & D capability and, importantly, the industrial relations record of the company, all need to be undertaken. It would also be appropriate to check out the capability of the purchasing department on the basis that, in manufacturing industries, approximately 50 per cent of costs relate to purchased materials. The search procedure will be a combination of questionnaire and on-site visits for key suppliers conducted by a techno-commercial team headed by strategic purchasing. The supplier profile will need to be continuously updated and all major potential suppliers, including new entrants to the marketplace, will require to be investigated in this way.

It is sometimes difficult to obtain profiles of overseas suppliers, nevertheless it is even more important that such profiles are developed, since the security of supply becomes more significant. At the same time the re-supply pipeline between the overseas country and the consignee country should be carefully evaluated to assess the points at which disruption can occur, e.g. at the various ports of despatch, transhipment and entry.

The stability of the overseas currency involved is also a factor to be monitored for it will influence price and costs. In this respect the discussion in Chapter 16 will be found to be invaluable. The co-operation of suppliers in the assembly of their respective profiles should be sought and usually such co-operation is readily obtained. After all, it is in the interest of the suppliers that their profile should be wholly representative of their company situation.

Details of major changes in a supplier's financial or organisational structure – takeover, mergers etc. – must be analysed carefully and evaluated to determine their effect on the present relationship between buyer and seller. In particular, supplier profiles should be analysed to present known or potential areas of supply vulnerability – ownership by our own competitors etc.

Product information files

Product information analysis provides not only data relating to sourcing of supply but identifies price and cost analyses through:

- formulations
- component breakdown
- drawings, specifications
- manufacturing processes

in order to derive as accurate a cost structure as possible.

Monitoring of key ingredients, materials, services (e.g. electricity) which provide the major cost factors in the key products and materials purchased is an essential feature of the product information files. This enables cost increases to be forecast for strategic decisions on forward buying, and price increases submitted by suppliers can be evaluated more effectively.

Alternative and substitute materials will be investigated as part of the strategic purchasing action, together with assessments of new technologies, new and improved manufacturing process of suppliers products, new distribution and packaging methods etc.

Our own sales and marketing factors

The accuracy of a company's own sales forecast and sensitivity to the changed demands of its customers has a considerable effect on its purchasing effort. In less strategically minded companies, purchasing sees itself as starting from a breakdown of production schedules. With a strategic purchasing approach, however, materials planning is closely integrated with the sales forecast and change amendments. It will also concern itself with the accuracy of that forecasting and it is regrettable that the forecasting techniques applied in the sales areas of many companies are woefully substandard when the impact that such forecasts have upon production and purchasing are taken into account.

The close communication between the strategic purchasing function and marketing can improve the sales position markedly by, for example, providing information on:

1 Critical supply issues which will affect the availability of certain finished products. Sales demand always goes up as customers chase supply and salesmen are continually surprised that it is market forces that have caused the demand rather than their assumed salesmanship and sales push.
2 Significant price changes in key bought-in materials which will affect the pricing policies of a company's finished products, up or down.

In turn, the strategic purchasing function will look for early warnings from marketing of changes in their marketplace which will affect purchasing demand.

Internal audit

It will be seen from the foregoing that it is important for the strategic purchasing function to ensure that it has a high level of credibility within the organisation. It is the lack of such internal visibility and poor communications with user departments which adversely affects most purchasing departments and is a fundamental cause of poor performance. A lack of understanding of the needs of users or of their changed requirements leads to friction and dissatisfaction being established between purchasing and internal departments.

One feature of the strategic purchasing approach would be the undertaking of an internal 'audit' of user departments (purchasing's internal customers) to assess the service which purchasing is providing and to determine the means by which that service should be improved on a long-term basis.

FACTORS INFLUENCING CORPORATE PLANNING

Although strategic purchasing is not an offshoot of corporate planning, it should contribute important input to the system. Corporate planning should be concerned with the longer-term aspects of a company and its environment. Whilst this task is undertaken with varying degrees of success few organisations include supply end factors in their thinking.

Yet a company is vulnerable not only in the marketplace in which it is selling but also in the supplier marketplace in which the purchasing function operates. It has threats and opportunities in both markets and should seek to take advantage of the latter while avoiding the former where and whenever possible. There is little point in marketing making a sales thrust to secure a larger share of a market if a competitor manages a takeover of a key supplier of strategic materials or components. There is no gain in mounting a new product launch unless the continued availability of the required raw materials or components is secure and at a bought-in price which allows the new product to generate profitable gross margins. Equally there is no benefit in investing in new or expanded plant capacity if the availability of raw material input is only short term or is to be replaced by alternative, more available and cheaper materials. The role of strategic purchasing in these and similar issues is vital to the success of corporate planning.

Corporate planning as a function has been criticised for stifling creativity and idea generation whilst placing too much emphasis on 'number crunching'. Current management thinking is to de-emphasise formalised central planning to bring it closer to where the action actually occurs. Part of the changed view has stemmed from the apparent unpredictability of external events, particularly in supply markets, e.g. sudden OPEC oil price increases. Clearly input from the purchasing in this and similar regards is extremely important.

In such a corporate scenario, the role of strategic purchasing is important in the provision of information as to what is happening, strategically, in the supplier marketplace. By paying more attention to what the suppliers are thinking and doing, corporate planners believe that they will be in a better position to perceive the corporate future and to reduce the unpredictability of external supply factors.

What are the strategic purchasing activities that will directly input into corporate planning thinking in the future? Certainly an assessment of the vulnerability of the company in terms of the security of supply of strategic materials is critical to the future prosperity of an organisation. This assessment, by the strategic purchasing function, will require firm recommendations for, for example, backward integration including acquisition evaluations. It will require evaluated proposals for possible joint-venture deals so as to ensure that the vulnerability risk is reduced to the minimum.

In addition all corporate investment proposals should necessitate strategic purchasing input as to the viability of the proposal from a supply aspect, e.g. availability of source materials, competitive alternatives and long-term price trends.

Above all, strategic purchasing must maintain a constant dialogue with corporate planners to inform them of critical issues as they occur and as trends emerge in the supplier market place. Such issues are not only of an adverse nature; opportunities to exploit surplus situations and overcapacities leading to potential volume price reductions are as important as short supply and significant price rises.

The critical influence of purchasing on corporate planning has not yet been fully understood by the latter function. It is the writer's opinion that much of the adverse criticism in the 1980s of the lack of results from corporate planning may well be alleviated by greater concentration on strategic purchasing. To date corporate planning has concentrated too much on looking forward and it is a sound military practice to 'secure your rear'.

ORGANISATION

Organisationally and functionally, strategic purchasing has a parallel with the marketing function. Both strategic purchasing and marketing are concerned with:

1 Longer-range planning views of the external marketplace (supplier and customer respectively).

2 Research analysis of what is happening in the external market place as a basis for decision-making advice to the operational buying/selling functions.
3 Continuous investigation of external and internal factors (suppliers/competitors and production issues).
4 Evaluation of new products, new technology, new distribution and packaging methods (see Figure 3.3).

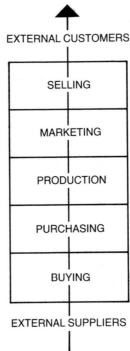

EXTERNAL CUSTOMERS

SELLING

MARKETING

PRODUCTION

PURCHASING

BUYING

EXTERNAL SUPPLIERS

Figure 3.3 Materials flow

Strategic purchasing should therefore have the organisational capability for:

- interpretive research
- project leadership
- systems development
- long-range forecasting
- numerative analysis
- business logic.

It is important that the strategic purchasing role should be undertaken as a part of the overall purchasing function and, ideally, integrated into an overall materials management (MM) concept. Organisation structures for materials management are dealt with elsewhere in this book. However, strategic purchasing gives an added dimension to the organisational spectrum of MM. Materials management is generally defined as unifying the synergies presented within an organisation in the flow and control of materials and services from sourcing to distribution in order to obtain the lowest total cost and most effective service.

The traditional concept of MM lacks the strategic perspective. Whilst MM harnesses the business synergies within an organisation, they are operational, day-to-day events and, as such, represent only the optimisation of the fire-fighting roles. A traditional view of MM ignores the opportunities afforded by strategic applications.

The injection of a strategic purchasing function into MM changes its dimension into one of resource management – capital and materials. Materials represent capital tied up in working assets and add cost without adding value. The philosophy of resource management measures the release of capital to achieve a return on the capital employed, rather than the inventory philosophy which represents not only a stagnation of capital but requires a high percentage gearing to service the capital tied up in goods.

The overview afforded by strategic purchasing concepts converts MM into the next evolutionary stage of business resource management and forms a co-ordination 'bridge' with the finance function. Thus strategic purchasing is a key element in the interconnecting membranes of all the key functions in the spinal column of the overall organisation (see Figure 3.4).

In medical terms we could liken strategic purchasing to the component parts of a spinal cord. The flexible pads (strategic purchasing interface) between the bodies of the vertebrae (organisation functions) are the intervertebral discs which contain the spinal nerves as part of a network of the body nervous system (company strategic communications network). This arrangement allows movement without loss of strength and the discs act as effective shock absorbers.

As part of its organisational structure, the strategic purchasing function will exert a leadership role in initiating value analysis

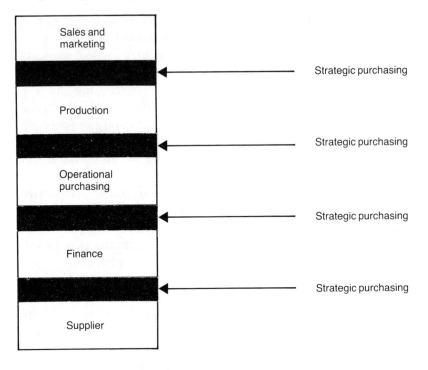

Figure 3.4 The vertebrae of strategic purchasing

projects, and/or quality control circles, as well as make-or-buy studies. VA has been around a long time and yet has still to achieve its potential for achieving significant cost benefits. VA has expanded through the input of statistical analysis techniques and the tutelage of Dr Edwards Deming into the Japanese-inspired Quality Control Circles. QCC has spread in the kind of way that VA did not and is receiving wide acclaim throughout the world. The basis of QCC is nevertheless akin to value analysis and, no matter what the organisational title, it is the remit of strategic purchasing to identify, initiate and lead multi-disciplinary project teams into purchasing-related investigations of:

– materials
– services
– equipment
– distribution systems

  – packaging methods
  – procedures

so as to ensure that functional performance is achieved at the lowest optimum cost on a continuing basis.

Make-or-buy studies represent a continuous programme of investigative research, again on a multi-discipline project team approach (purchasing, production, engineering, finance), to determine the feasibility of manufacturing in-house rather than purchasing or vice-versa. Such studies can sensibly be expanded to include rent, and lease or buy evaluations.

THE UPSTREAM ACTIVITY

Whilst there is a theoretical requirement that operational purchasing staff should allocate a percentage of their time, usually 20-30 per cent, to engaging in purchasing research activities, in practice the pressure demands of the operational, fire-fighting role prohibit this effort towards strategic purchasing.

The end result of course is that an increased pressure of fire fighting demands an ever-decreasing time availability for fire prevention. Strategic purchasing concerns itself with the upstream activity so that the operational purchasing function is not swamped by unpredicted events. The upstream activity also ensures that operational decision making is not spontaneous off-the-cuff type decisions but rational logical decisions which consider not only the short-term but the longer-term issues. Such considered purchasing decisions are thereby capable of withstanding management challenge as reasoned events and, importantly, provide the means for measuring the purchasing performance.

The broad aspects of the upstream activities of strategic purchasing have already been detailed (see Figure 3.5). Some examples of actual strategic considerations would include:

  – supplier development
  – offshore purchasing
  – offsets policies
  – systems development.

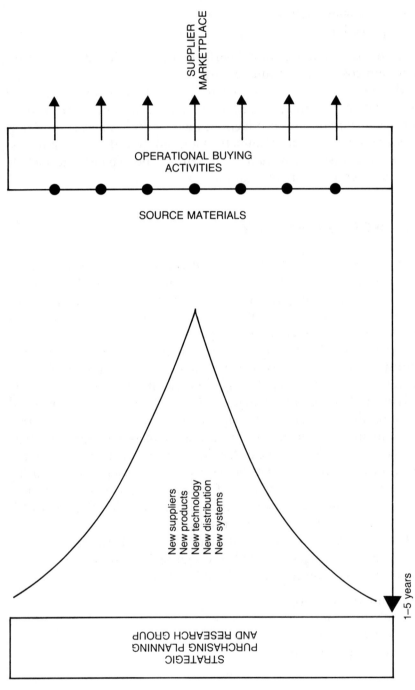

SUPPLIER MARKETPLACE

OPERATIONAL BUYING ACTIVITIES

SOURCE MATERIALS

New suppliers
New products
New technology
New distribution
New systems

STRATEGIC PURCHASING PLANNING AND RESEARCH GROUP

1–5 years

Figure 3.5 The upstream activity

The following examples are based on factual company activities undertaken within the authors knowledge (and guidance) as strategic purchasing stratagems.

Supplier development

The trend in the 1980s is towards establishing relationships with fewer, more trusted suppliers. The selection of the right suppliers with whom to develop long-term supply strategies, given the adoption of such a philosophy, is therefore crucial.

Marks & Spencer in the UK pioneered supplier development by 'tying' suppliers to them on long-term contract arrangements, providing technical assistance and instituting stringent quality control criteria. Toyota have developed the 'Kanban' inventory system, known as the 'just-in-time' concept which enables the Japanese car maker to operate on near-zero inventory. The Kanban system is highly dependent on having dedicated suppliers who will deliver on schedule, often two or three times a day, to a zero-defects programme. These suppliers are often owned in part or in whole by Toyota and operate within a 90 km radius of the main Toyota factory.

Adoption, and adaptation, of the Kanban-type inventory systems alongside a strategy of planned supplier development has enabled other large car manufacturers such as General Motors, Ford and Volvo to reduce their inventory holdings by 50-65 per cent.

Through the process of supplier development giving long-term tenure, subject to performance, to vendors, an international white-goods manufacturer has eliminated its material warehouse with direct deliveries to the production line with guaranteed quality (zero defects) so that the QC department was also dismantled.

Supplier participation in packaging VA teams enabled a US photographic manufacturer to achieve substantial savings through vendor recommendations; a similar relationship with suppliers by an Australian food processor resulted in revised packaging specifications using standard materials and, again, substantial cost savings.

The use of long-term baseload contracts enables suppliers to engage in investment proposals and plant expansion. By such supplier development strategy, an international chemicals group was able to stabilise its pricing, operate more competitively, gain priority of supply in critical supply times and reduce its inventory by increased dependency on its long-term suppliers.

Supplier development strategies thus present wide-ranging benefits to companies which are prepared to engage in this aspect of strategic purchasing.

Offshore purchasing

The strategy of offshore purchasing is not widely used. It involves selecting the area in the world which presents the most competitive positioning for purchasing and then establishing an 'office' in that location to engage in purchasing the materials, items or equipments which are required.

There may be a number of offshore purchasing points established throughout the world dependent on the material needs. Singapore or Hong Kong may be the most suitable for a wide range of electronic or consumer goods; Rotterdam for oil products; Switzerland for packaging machinery etc. Important criteria in the selection process, besides product competitiveness and availability, are the stability of currency, the relationship of that currency with the normal national currency of the buyer and readily available freight movement.

The strategy is especially useful where companies operate within areas where free competition is not readily available or where initial and re-supply problems of spares can occur.

Alongside offshore purchasing, offshore expediting has been well used for some time; this includes the establishment of contract(or) liaison officers who engage in factory visits of suppliers and contractors to ensure the timely delivery of component, material and equipment requirements.

Offshore expediting takes the same strategy one stage further. Reliance on overseas suppliers can be a precarious purchasing strategy; adoption means increased safety stock and close monitoring of re-supply items. To reduce the supply risk factor, offshore expeditors are located in the key supplier overseas areas with the responsibility for 'trouble-shooting', ensuring expediting of requirements not only at the supplier manufacturing plant but also through the distribution shipping network.

Use of offshore expeditors in this way has resulted in significant improvements in pipeline re-supply and consequent reduction in production downtime due to non-availability or late delivery of needed materials. Hard information from a company's own expeditors 'on the ground' can significantly enhance materials planning of overseas supplies.

Offsets policy

Offsets policy is another strategic purchasing variation which is gaining support, particularly in government circles since it assists a country's balance of payments. The strategy can best be described by taking an actual example.

The government purchasing agency in country X decides that a multi-million dollar contract for computer hardware/software based on tender submissions should go to a major US computer manufacturer, say IBM. The government in country X is now faced with an adverse effect on its balance of payments; on the one hand IBM is the most competitive tenderer and on the other hand, payment has to be effected in hard US dollar currency. To mitigate the adverse balance of payments effect and at the same time capitalise on the lowest competitive tender, the government purchasing agency approaches IBM to determine the extent to which the company could offset the balance of payments problem by:

(a) Purchasing component items inside country X;
(b) establishing a manufacturing capability or permitting manufacture under licence in country X;
(c) using local personnel and services in the installation of the IBM hardware/software;
(d) purchasing other components to be exported from country X.

This strategy has the dual effect of not only reducing the balance of payments problem but of creating possible employment and/or export opportunities.

Systems development

The need for a user analyst within the purchasing function has become quite common over the past few years. The rapid escalation of available purchasing and inventory computer software packages demands that a proper evaluation of available packages, or in-house development, be made against user needs. The writing of a user specification for the computerisation of the purchasing function and the systems interface to the overall materials management programme requires specialist knowledge of systems analysis. It is now seen as preferable, and probably less expensive in terms of cost-benefit relationship, to train a suitable purchasing individual in systems design rather than vice-versa. The results from the user writing his own specification, establishing systems flow-charts and liaising directly with the computer programmer has proved to be significantly more beneficial to the user department.

Purchasing has generally lagged behind other functional areas in computerisation, even though inventory systems have been introduced. The requirement for assembling a purchasing information data base has already been stated, and is seen as critical to the successful introduction of a strategic purchasing function. The means of assembling this data base is seen as part of the user specification alongside the selection of a cataloguing and codification system.

The systems development strategy would also embrace the upgrading of the manual purchasing systems to appropriate levels for computerisation. It is important that manual procedures are not simply translated to computer systems without an upgrading process; poor procedural functions are exaggerated under computerisation and the cost of change, once installed, is high.

The longer-term systems development for purchasing is clearly towards a paperless system. The achievement of this objective requires significant co-operation from internal audit to derive an audit trail. In addition the creative utilisation of telecommunications both internally (with departments such as goods inwards, quality control, accounts payable) as well as potential external hook-ups with selected suppliers is essential.

Systems development, then, will increasingly feature as an important work assignment for the strategic purchasing function. Purchasing generally suffers from an overload of paperwork and sound systems development can sharply reduce this burden.

THE PUBLIC SECTOR

The use of strategic purchasing in the public sector has been amply demonstrated over recent years with the introduction of systems such as:

- performance budgeting
- planned, programmed budgeting
- zero-based budgeting.

The most recent systems introduction into the public sector probably emphasises to the highest degree the use to be made of strategic purchasing – programme performance budgeting (PPB). The system is not new in that it evolves from a number of the features of the earlier systems mentioned above which were introduced into the US public sector in the 1970s as well as being developed in Canada, New Zealand, Australia and the UK (particularly the Greater London Council).

In strategic purchasing terms, PPB requires the identification of purchasing objectives related to the long term policy goals of government. PPB for purchasing is defined as a purchasing plan which measures the input resources required (materials, services, equipment) against the expected output results to be achieved (the service provided). In other words PPB as applied to purchasing describes the methodology to relate purchase costs to the benefits to be derived from a particular service or programme. By this cost-benefit analysis it enables governments to allocate resources between programmes to achieve the most desirable outcome having regard to the public priorities. This means that public funds will be expended to optimise the maximum benefits which can be derived from that purchase expenditure.

Purchasing in the public sector has been plagued by the traditional budgeting process whereby user authorities submitted annual budget proposals for materials, goods, equipments, services etc. Such budget expenditures once approved became a target expenditure with a user determination to use the funds allocated to ensure the availability of funds needed in the following annual estimate. The PPB philosophy seeks to change this fundamental attitude to annual purchasing expenditures, by defining required resources to specific programmes unrelated to previous annual expenditure allocations. The philosophy is also definitive as to the time the programme is expected to take, not just annual.

To determine the purchasing expenditure required under the PPB procedures, the expected results of a particular programme are assessed. Based on the outcome, an evaluation of the resources needed to achieve those results is then computed. Finally, the resources are converted to purchasing expenditure to determine the cost-benefit relationship.

A further important facet of the PPB approach is directed towards the actual cost of the supply (purchasing) support service, defined within the PPB system as an inter-agency support service (a service provided by one agency to support the work of other agencies). The costs associated with the purchasing support service could appear twice in the overall programme expenditure definitions – once within the programme structure of the purchasing department as the agency providing the support service and also in the agency programme receiving the supply service. However, it is the intention of the PPB concept that the supply support service will be paid for only by the agency receiving the purchasing service. In such circumstances the supply (purchasing) support service will be clearly measurable and thereby capable of challenge by receiving agencies as to the cost-benefit relationships. Such a concept presents an interesting measurement feature and one that could reasonably be applied to the private enterprise.

Elsewhere within the public sector similar strategic purchasing applications to those described above are used and a number of the purchasing computer applications have been developed in advance of some of the private industry systems, particularly in the area of user friendly codification and cataloguing.

CONCLUSION: BUSINESS RESOURCE MANAGEMENT

Strategic purchasing:

(a)   is not another form of corporate planning;
(b)   should not be isolated within an 'ivory tower';
(c)   is not a central co-ordinating body.

Strategic purchasing:

(*a*) should apply practical long-term planning techniques and approaches;

(*b*) should be undertaken by skilled purchasing practitioners who have conceptual ability;

(*c*) should be a disciplined approach to optimising capital investment;

(*d*) is a problem-solving approach which converts purchasing problems into opportunities.

Any organisation comprises four basic resources: materials (inventory), machinery (plant and equipment), men (personnel), methodology (systems and information). All are convertible to the fifth *M* – money, and all are potentially obsolescent (see Figure 3.6).

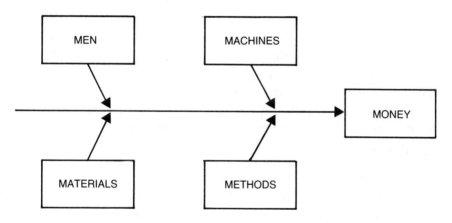

Figure 3.6 The five Ms

Strategic purchasing is concerned with the correct replacement of the asset resources (materials and machinery) and with ensuring that a proper return on such investment secures the continued profitability of the company. In this sense strategic purchasing represents the final link in a complete business philosophy of resource management.

4

Organising for purchasing

David Farmer

It is inevitable that a handbook concerned with purchasing management should include a chapter on organisation. Apart from anything else, the search for more effective organisation structures has continually exercised the minds of managers since the first management thinkers surveyed their field. And it is a truism that no businessman will have progressed through his career without being involved in several reorganisations. Consequently from time to time any thinking purchasing manager will, in the face of circumstances which currently prevail, be aware of the need to re-evaluate his present structure. The question he needs to ask most frequently is not 'Could it be improved?', but rather 'How could it be improved?'

His concerns need to relate to two main issues: 'How should the purchasing function be organised?' and 'How should it "fit" into the remainder of the organisation of the business itself?' A key point in considering both issues is the fact that even if the current organisation was perfect to meet the business needs of x years ago, it is probably not suitable today. People, systems, technologies and the business environment will have changed. It is also necessary to emphasise that even the elusive perfect structure will not, of itself, result in effective performance. People have to make organisation structures work, and unless they are capable, well directed and motivated, even the best of structures will prove inadequate. Finally, the structure which works well for company A may be quite ineffective for company *B*, even if both concerns operate in the same market environment.

In this respect the analogy that an organisation structure is like a suit of clothes is apt. Not only does it suggest the necessary individuality of 'fit', it also indicates something of the inevitability of change over time. As with a suit, where wear and tear and fashion are relevant indicators of the need of change, so it is with organisations. To those who might query the need to draw this analogy, it is worth pointing out that many organisational problems arise simply because the comparisons are ignored. Just as there are no suits which will fit everybody, so are there no organisation structures which can be applied universally. In the same way as the suit bought ten years ago would not meet the buyer's needs today, yesterday's organisation structure is unlikely to meet today's needs.

WHAT IS AN ORGANISATION?

Organisations may be described as being concerned with ways of establishing responsibilities, authorities and controls within a company in such a way that it may achieve its objectives and basic purpose. In so doing the functional and other relationships within the company are determined, together with the communication systems which will be used to manage the concern. An organisation also sets up the decision-making structure within the company.

Purchasing organisations, first as part of the wider organisation and then of themselves, need to be developed with the many implications of this definition in mind. The first question should always be 'What do we want to do?' It is this fundamental question which often clouds the issues as far as the purchasing function is concerned, for in some companies it has diminished responsibilities and authorities not in keeping with the strategic and operational needs of the undertaking in question. In such cases the function is poorly placed in terms of decision making and communication and neither it, nor any of the other functions concerned with materials supply, are in a position to actually control. At least part of this type of problem arises from the diminished view of the function held by the firm's top management. This often results in a quality of staff unsuitable for a broader role, with the result that the ensuing organisational problems are perpetuated.

The argument here is not that purchasing should always be represented 'on the board'. The basic 'What do we want to do?' question has to be asked in the light of the company's strategy for profitable survival. However, increasingly, sometimes through reorganisations, takeovers or mergers, the function is being seen as having a key part to play at strategic level. The organisational problems which the senior purchasing man faces in such circumstances are often quite common.

PURCHASING AND MATERIALS MANAGEMENT IN THE BUSINESS STRUCTURE

As has been suggested, there are those who would argue that the purchasing function needs to be represented at board level. However, the relevance of that argument needs to be carefully examined in the light of the importance of the function to the business. There are, too, those who press for an integrative approach, such as materials management, in which purchasing is structured as part of the materials function. Before addressing the topic of the place in the organisation of purchasing itself, it would be helpful to consider the materials management approach. Among other things this will illustrate the many interrelationships which need to be considered in placing purchasing within a company's organisation structure.

Integration

The concept of materials management is by its very nature integrative. It requires the various functions within the system, which is the business, to collaborate so as to ensure that the whole may be greater than the sum of the parts. It necessitates a business-wide focus rather than a departmental emphasis. And it requires managers to promote effective collaboration with colleagues in other functions and with supplier organisations. The benefits of such systemwide collaboration are readily accepted by most commentators. Yet even in organisations which have wholeheartedly embraced materials management, the quality and effectiveness of integration between departments, let alone buyers and sellers, leaves much to be desired. Some of the reasons for this less than effective application of the concept are mentioned in Chapter 5. However it would be useful at this point to indicate other of the most common factors which have hindered the successful application of materials management in manufacturing businesses.

Some problems

Consideration of the scope of typical materials management objectives suggests many sources of difficulty. Among those most often quoted are:

(a) to ensure that an adequate volume of materials (to the correct specification) is delivered in keeping with the needs of production schedules and marketing activity;

(b) to locate suitable suppliers which are reliable and cost effective;

(c) to minimise the level of capital which is tied up in inventory, and

(d) to minimise the total cost of acquiring, handling, moving and storing materials.

It will be clear to any practising manager that these objectives contain elements of potential conflict. For example, if objective (d) is to be achieved, the price paid to the supplier should not be so low as to result in quality failure or schedule interruption. If inventory is to be kept to the minimum it should not result in additional transportation, delivery and handling costs which would outweigh any advantage gained. Nor should it result in an unacceptable level of 'stockouts' or in interruptions to manufacturing schedules. Obviously the optimal decision should be arrived at having considered the best *balance* between the elements in the particular equation. In marketing, the concept of the marketing mix illustrates a similar requirement at the output end of a manufacturing system. Here the balance is sought between the level of *price* to be charged for the product, the level of *quality* of that product, the level of *promotional* effort and expense, and the particular segment of the market in which the product is placed. Thus the price of, say, a Rolls Royce will reflect its high quality specification and the limited group of potential purchases who may wish to own such a vehicle. On the other hand the Austin City Mini is a fairly basic vehicle at a low price which is within the scope of a vast number of potential owners. With respect to the 'input' end of the manufacturing system the idea of a 'mix' may also be seen to apply. This time, however, it may be thought of as a 'materials mix'. The selected specification should, in value analysis terms, provide the best functional value given adequate consideration of the market segment which has to be satisfied. Yet many designs add unnecessarily to cost in a variety of ways. For example a European company lost a NATO defence contract on the grounds that its price was almost double that of the favoured supplier. Subsequent analysis illustrated that the material costs alone of the unsuccessful bidder were as great as the total selling price of the selected supplier. The successful specification reflected the greater commercial awareness of the particular company's designers. It ensured that the material mix was correctly balanced for the purpose in hand and the contract was won.

This case illustrates one of the component problems in ensuring effective balance in the materials mix. The designers in the unsuccessful company were concerned with design excellence rather than commercial quality. Once the designers' decisions had been taken the purchasing function could only purchase that specification at lowest cost. Discussion with the designers showed that:

(a) they were used to working in a high specification environment;

(b) their job satisfaction came in large part from producing a new design to high standards;

(c) their view of the role of the purchasing and materials functions were that they were there to obtain and provide what had been specified, and

(d) they had little notion of the impact of design decisions on cost and selling price.

For their part the purchasing staff assumed their role to be that in (c) above and obtained their job satisfaction from reducing quoted selling prices and delivery dates. From the various suppliers' viewpoints they were happy to quote against the customer-drawn designs on the basis of special contracts. Yet, in several cases, standard items in the suppliers' range at much lower cost could have been utilised with benefits to both parties, including a considerable reduction in lead time.

The common problem illustrated in this case is the insularity of the various parties within the system. Each took his decisions based upon his own view of the system and his own objectives. Furthermore, leaving aside the suppliers, within the buying company the various parties involved were motivated to behave in the way they did by:

(a)   the source of their job satisfaction;
(b)   the role which they had traditionally played in material decision making, and
(c)   the 'reward and punishment' system which was being applied.

The latter aspect it should be noted, is a particularly powerful motivator. Many managers have emphasised, for example, that the budget systems which are applied within their businesses frequently emphasise functional efficiency rather than system effectiveness. The net result, they argue, is that they may be ensuring a negative departmental result in seeking to make a decision which will benefit the wider system.

While the materials management concept seeks to obviate such problems, in practice 'old habits die hard'. Functional or departmental 'ownership' of decision-making authority, and role specifications which have been the norm for many years are difficult to change. The manager given the task of doing so has to have a broad understanding of the attitudes, values and cognitions of the various managers within the business. And he has to find ways of getting the various specialists to think and act in terms of optimal decision making.

ORGANISATIONAL STRUCTURE

As the above discussion suggests, one of the fundamental reasons in favour of applying the materials management concept is that traditional functional organisations are most often counterproductive. Departmental optimisation frequently results in system suboptimisation, and traditional organisations often nurture such behaviour. The materials management approach necessitates an organisation structure in which a single manager is responsible and has authority for all aspects of materials flow. In so doing the manager will be seeking effective co-ordination and communication between the various functions under his control. The logic of the materials management approach flows from that objective.

The way in which the role of the materials manager is defined in practice will depend upon a variety of factors, for organisation structures, roles and responsibilities vary from company to company. However, in most cases where the materials management concept has been applied, the purchasing and inventory control functions are included among its responsibilities. In one multiplant organisation a basic job description has been devised which is then tailored to meet the needs of the specific location. It should be noted, however, that this very useful basis was itself developed with a particular company environment in mind.

In general it may be stated that all companies which have embraced the materials management approach have defined the role as including some or all of the following elements:

- purchasing
- expediting
- inwards goods control
- stores management
- inventory control, including work-in-progress
- materials control
- production scheduling
- in-plant transportation
- finished product transportation and shipping, including packaging.

Three organisational diagrams from different manufacturing concerns will serve to illustrate the variety of approaches which are in current use (see Figures 4.1, 4.2 and 4.3). Each of the following relates to companies which work in similar sectors of industry, all being largely assembly-based businesses of similar size. The differences which are evident presumably reflect the variety of factors which affect most organisational decisions. These include:

(*a*)   the knowledge and skills of the managers concerned;
(*b*)   their status and reputation within the business;

(c) the historical power base of the various parties within the system;

(d) the size of the company, and hence the complexity of effective communication;

(e) the level of awareness of top management as to the importance and influence of the materials activity;

(f) the economic pressures under which the business is operating, e.g. level of competition and the state of the economy within which the business operates, and

(g) the level and quality of resources which are available to undertake the tasks involved and the quality of their interrelationships.

In Figures 4.1–4.3 the differences in titles in themselves may not be significant. In companies A and C the directors responsible for the materials function have similar titles. In company C however, the production planning and production control functions are clearly separated, whereas in A both are within the aegis of the materials manager. Company B is the only one of the three with a board-level appointment related to materials; the company concerned adopted the materials management approach several years before the other two. It is interesting to note, too, that it is the only company of the three which includes inwards and outwards transportation under the materials umbrella. Without wishing to draw any conclusions from the fact, comparing the same two financial years results of the three companies, B happens to be the most profitable.

BUYER-SELLER INTEGRATION: PURCHASING

All applications of materials management involve the purchasing function. Purchasing has the task of locating and selecting sources of supply and of managing the interface between them and the company's own production systems. At least those are the tasks which are generally located with purchasing in organisations where tasks are formally defined. However, as Robinson, Faris and Wind[1] have shown, and as the case of over-specification discussed earlier indicates, others in the buying company system may be the real decision makers.

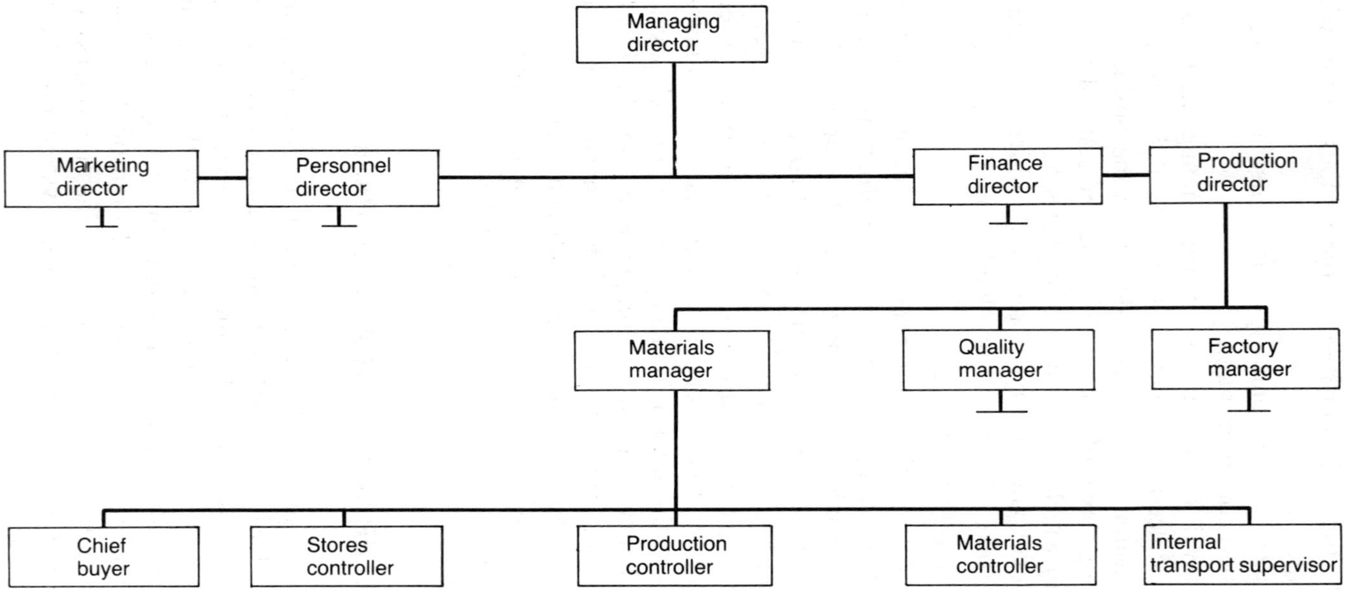

Figure 4.1 Materials management approach: company A

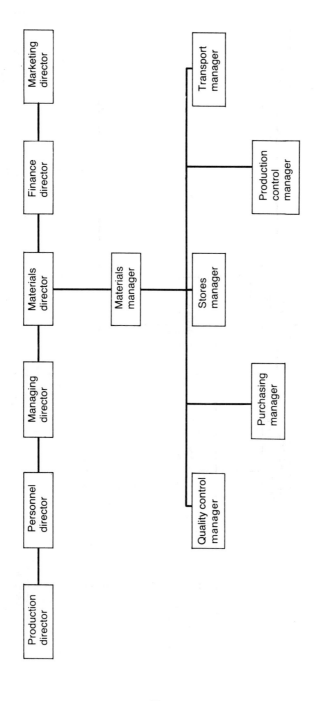

Figure 4.2 Materials management approach: company B

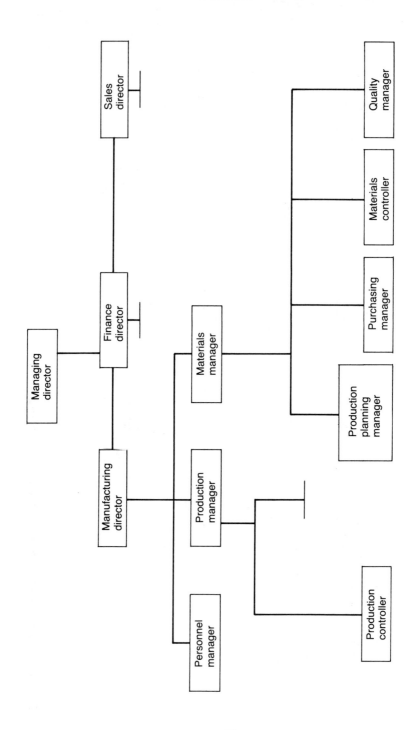

Figure 4.3 Materials management approach: company C

The complications which arise from this situation may have a considerable impact upon the materials system as a whole. Thus a part of this chapter has been devoted to that aspect of integration. However, before addressing that topic in particular it would be beneficial to consider the wider implications of buyer-seller integration.

In the average manufacturing concern in developed countries, more than half the company's income is spent on providing materials and services with which to produce finished goods. Thus in financial terms the materials sector is in most cases the largest single cost centre. This statistic is significant in its own right. However, in addition, when the physical aspects of materials management are considered the impact of materials flow on the business may be seen to be potentially enormous. For example, the effective balancing of production scheduling, materials scheduling and inventory levels can be of critical importance to the effectiveness of the firm. In financial terms this balancing may affect cash flow and capital lock-up. In physical terms it will affect effective resource utilisation in space, equipment and labour terms. The level of success of the buying company's management in balancing this can be of considerable importance.

The difficulties associated with such balancing may be formidable enough within the business itself. They are exacerbated where the buying company's system has to 'mate' with a series of supplier systems. Figure 4.4 illustrates the mutuality of these relationships as regards the efficiency and effectiveness of buyer and seller systems.

It is an important factor that the buying company is required to motivate the supplying company to work with them. In practical terms this will involve ensuring that the supplier delivers products to specification on time at a competitive price. In attempting to meet this requirement the selling company will be seeking to do so profitably. Between these two basic objectives, system effectiveness may be impaired by company (buying or selling) oriented action. For example, if the buying company continually make alterations to their requirement schedules, the supplier's system will be adversely affected, e.g. in production and transportation terms. If the buying company takes extended credit this will obviously adversely affect the supplier's cash flow. As Farmer and MacMillan[2] have shown, it is frequently a feature of successful businesses that considerable

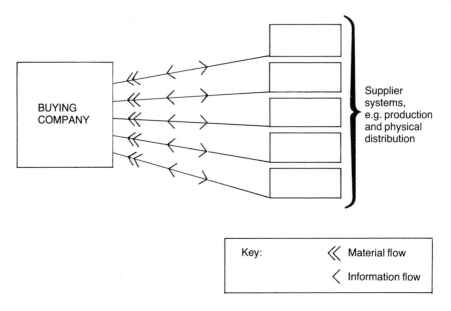

NB: This is, of course, a simplification of the real situation facing many businesses. Each box on the right may represent anything from 20 to 100 suppliers.

Figure 4.4 The company supply system

effort is applied to ensuring that relationships and communications between them and their suppliers are of the highest order. This is not to imply 'cosy' relationships, but those which, recognising the complexity of the situation, aim to develop mutual trust, professional respect and inter-system commercial effectiveness.

Purchasing

It is because of these complexities, and of a concern that the absorption of the function into a materials management structure can be detrimental, that some argue that purchasing should remain a separate function outside any materials grouping. The function is, it is argued, the commercial wing of the company business as far as the supply market is concerned. Too many materials management organisations, the argument continues, are managed by 'number crunchers' often with a production control background. And when that occurs, the commercial aspect of the role is de-emphasised.

Whatever the rights and wrongs of these arguments, they have resulted in some organisation structures retaining purchasing as a separate entity. Sometimes the result is a board-level appointment, in others the function is located under a board member. Figures 4.5 and 4.6 each illustrate a different approach.

Discussion on the structure of the function itself will add factors for the reader's consideration as he examines his own situation. However, before addressing that topic it is interesting to consider another potential complication – that of a purchasing organisation in a group of companies.

PURCHASING IN A GROUP

Figure 4.7 illustrates how a group of companies developed over a period of about 25 years. It relates to a UK-based group which, like all others, has its own characteristics. However, the growth and organisational pattern illustrated is not untypical of the development of many such groups. Among other things the case emphasises that it is rarely possible to design an organisational structure without the problems of history affecting decision making. As suggested by the notes, the figure is a simplification of the real situation. For example, acquisitions were made throughout the period; however important takeovers took place on three occasions.

An interesting aspect of this particular case history is that purchasing arrangements tended to 'follow' the general organisation decisions until phase D. The present senior procurement executive argues that until phase D purchasing was barely considered when such decisions were made. Then, as he put it, 'Despite the efforts of the then senior purchasing staff, the function had to work within a system which did not allow it to use its purchasing power effectively'. At the beginning of phase D a firm of consultants was called in, and an early recommendation was to align the two former groups into a divisional structure. It was when the basic reasons for this suggestion were examined that the group realised it was in no position to develop an effective overall strategy. Unusually, considerable emphasis was placed on an early presentation to top

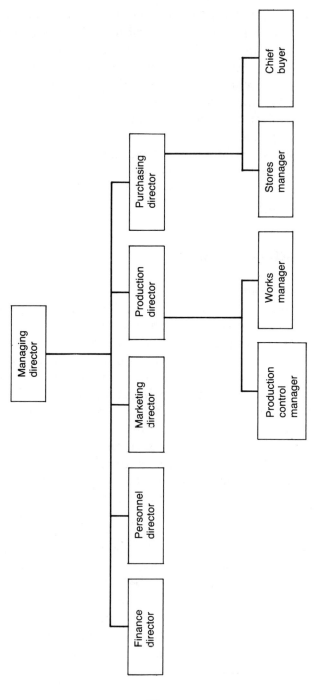

Figure 4.5 Purchasing approach: company X

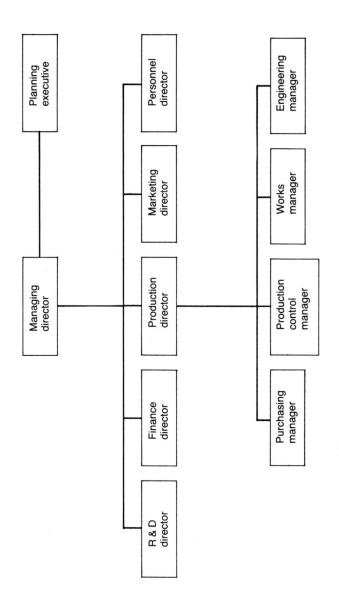

Figure 4.6 Purchasing approach: company Y

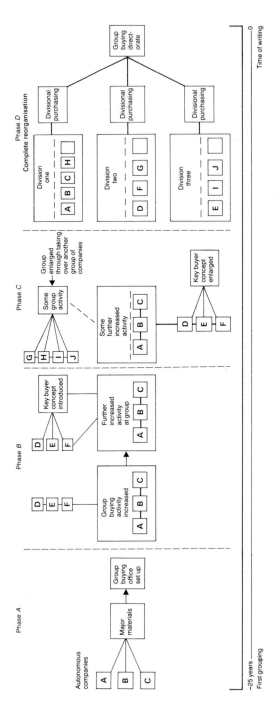

Notes:

(1) The boxes A, B, C etc. do not necessarily represent single companies. The actual number is not included so as to simplify the diagram and help preserve anonymity.

(2) The grouping in phase A was of companies which operated largely in the same industries both as buyers and sellers.

(3) In phase C the group of companies which was taken over was disparate. Group procurement effort was relatively small but there was some attempt to co-ordinate.

(4) In phase D the two former groups were merged through a divisional structure. This meant that it was possible to work on a more rational basis. The group staff was established as a director and two assistants.

(5) The 'Key buyer' concept was retained within the three divisions.

(6) The phases are not to time scale in the diagram.

Figure 4.7 The alpha group – growth and organisation over time

management on procurement. As a result the directors made an immediate decision to appoint a group purchasing director. It says something for the situation that a commercial director from one of the larger companies in the group was given the job on a short-term basis. The appointment involved two important tasks: first to work closely with the consultants and the senior management team involved with the reorganisation; second to find a successor who would take over the job within eighteen months. The suggestion was that the successor should be a purchasing professional of the calibre to do the job as it was conceived.

In the event it took some fourteen months for the new man to be appointed and arrive. Meanwhile the first director had undertaken a great deal of the initial work. When the new man arrived the pair then had a further twelve months working in tandem. There were a number of problems which had to be faced in those initial years. Among them were:

-   a considerable disparity in the quality of purchasing staff across the group;
-   differences in the location and scope of the function within organisations;
-   differences of the perceived importance of the role of the function between organisations;
-   differences of the preparedness of procurement staff and/or their companies to collaborate on a divisional let alone a group basis;
-   considerable differences in systems, procedures, and available information (including a lack of the most basic control information in some cases).

Generally speaking the differences highlighted the individuality of the companies concerned and the approach of their directing managers, and thus some of the points made at the beginning of this chapter. However, some of the differences were affecting the efficiency of the concern, and by 'differences' the director concerned usually meant that some were not up to the standard required. Effective collaboration can only be based upon sound information and control systems.

His early action programme included the appointment of a number of key staff who were of higher calibre than those whom they replaced. Generally speaking these appointments were made to more senior posts than had previously existed. In turn, partly through the 'selling' efforts of these new men, there was a wider recognition of the role that the function was to play within divisions, and the divisional structure allowed this role to be perceived more easily by all concerned. Another key element in the action plan was the use of the computer systems (which were progressively installed across the group) as 'influencers'. As a result, systems and procedures were made more uniform and, together with an in-company training programme, this helped to generate a divisional and thence a group ethos.

Even now, some years after the beginning of phase D, all is not perfect. The present director emphasised this when he said, 'Things are much better than they were even three years ago. The recession helped a lot to break down some of the barriers we had not been able to get around. But most of all I believe that it has been the better calibre people in the function which has made the difference. Nevertheless, we still have a long way to go. The man at the head of division 1 has done far more than his colleagues in the other divisions. Then we are really only learning to get our other key managers, as well as those in the procurement area, to think about strategies in their supply markets.'

He went on to emphasise that the organisation structures within each division and in the companies within those divisions, would never be uniform. 'What we are attempting to do is to work against certain basic principles towards a type of centralised/decentralisation. Then as far as special approaches to solving the organisational problem are concerned we are trying to ensure that we apply them when they suit. For example, as things are evolving, I believe that we will see a form of materials management in division 3, for we believe that it will increase our efficiency in that setting. But I do not see it being effective in other divisions at the present time.'

ORGANISING THE FUNCTION

To conclude this chapter, the task of organising the purchasing function itself is considered. In doing so, of course, many of the points raised in the discussion on materials management need to be considered. These include the importance of effective relationships with peer departments, with the supply market – current and would-be suppliers – and professional competence in managing the myriad of relationships involved.

Lee and Dobler[3] suggest that there are five classifications of work found in a purchasing operation: administration, buying, expediting, special staff work and clerical. Whilst some would argue with the emphasis suggested in this list, the five headings could be interpreted as covering all purchasing activities.

Figure 4.8 illustrates how one purchasing organisation has been structured to take account of these tasks. Purchasing is arranged on a product group basis. Chief buyer 2 and his subordinates are responsible for a particular group of production materials. Their task is to develop special knowledge and relationship about those materials inside and outside the firm. Chief buyers 1 and 3 operate in a similar way. This type of structure often has the concept extended within the unit. Thus, for example, if chief buyer 2 and his group were responsible for electrical and electronic supplies, buyer A would be allocated a specific subsegment of this grouping, as would B and C.

The role of the systems manager has become increasingly important as computer applications have developed. Among other things, this role is extremely important in questions of interfaces with the remainder of the company system.

The purchasing research and planning manager has the tasks of (a) integrating the purchasing function into the corporate strategic planning activity; (b) developing effective purchasing strategies, and ensuring that (c) tactical and operational approaches are in line with agreed strategies.

In this particular case, in addition to their formal role as the obverse of marketing 'product managers', the three chief buyers each have a secondary responsibility. One is the liaison man for new product development, a second has responsibility for value analysis and cost reduction exercises, and the third is concerned with management development and training. All buyers are encouraged to maintain close liaison with user departments and, for example, with production control and stores areas which both, in the company concerned, report to the production director.

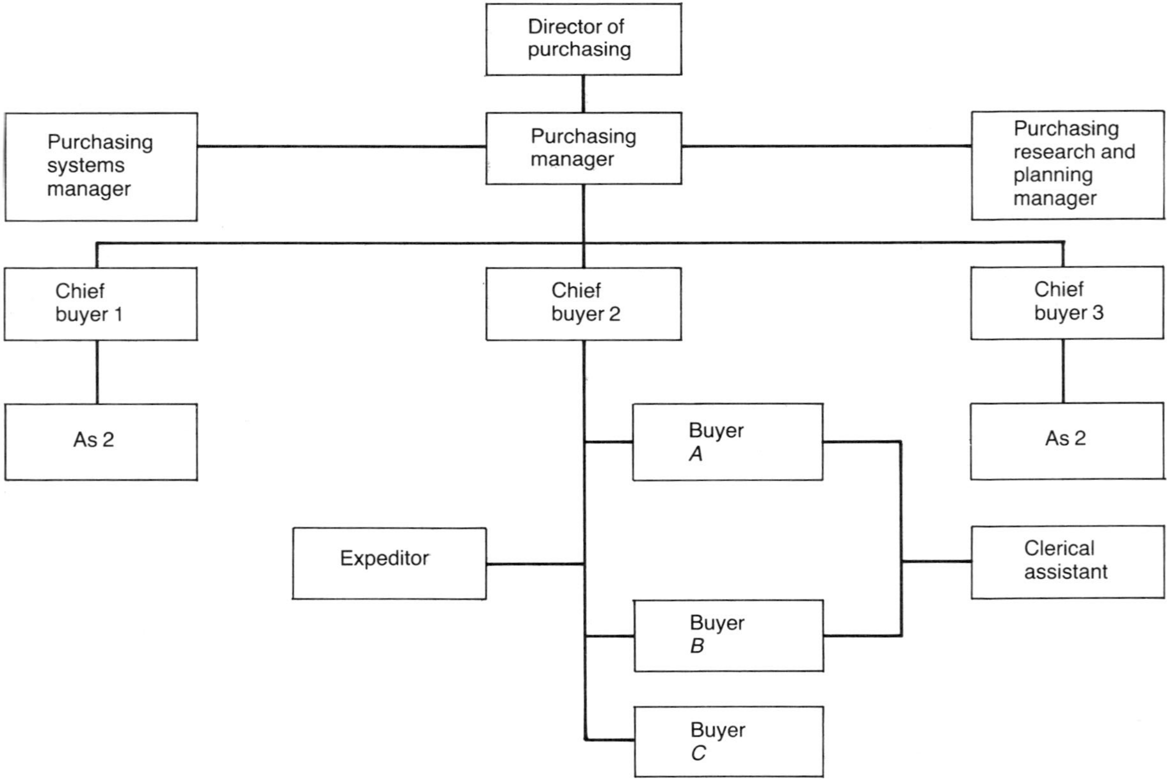

Figure 4.8 Medium-sized purchasing organisation

Other types of organisation

The above company has an organisation structure which, at present, satisfies its needs but, as has been emphasised already, it is not intended to be a model for any situation. Apart from size, which has a considerable effect on any type of organisation, the type of business and the special needs which it has will have a considerable bearing on the structure adopted. For example, construction companies frequently have a project-based organisation. Here particular staff are allocated to a project which may be worth several million pounds and take a year or more to construct. In effect these people tend to act as though they were buyers for an independent business. Usually the structure in these cases has a series of 'service' departments which co-ordinate data, contracts and systems so as to ensure that the organisation is using its purchasing power effectively and that resources are being used to the best effect.

Most purchasing organisations comprise two or three people and in these circumstances the staff are obliged to fulfil many roles. Usually the chief buyer, or whatever title the senior man has, takes responsibility for the most important purchases. His assistants then undertake all other purchases and perform the progressing role. Administration and clerical work is then shared under the direction of the senior man. Policy, systems development and longer-term issues tend to be the responsibility of the chief buyer himself, although wise managers will also seek to delegate some of this work.

In multi-site situations there is, usually, some kind of mechanism for co-ordinating common purchases. Some companies favour centralising this activity in a group buying department, others have a very small staff at group HQ, say two or three people, and use the lead-buyer approach. With this approach the buyer of the largest volume of a product or commodity might negotiate on behalf of the group as a whole. The people at the centre, then, have responsibility for such tasks as co-ordination, systems design support, policy development and management development.

CONCLUSION

Organisation structures and systems provide the means by which people may communicate and operate effectively in order to achieve corporate goals. In themselves they cannot ensure success, for people have to make organisations work. Each structure should be tailored to meet the specific needs of its environment and managers should not assume that someone else's organisational arrangements will meet their own needs. Further, organisations need to develop over time to meet the needs of changing circumstances; thus they should be reappraised from time to time.

REFERENCES

(1) Robinson, Faris and Wind, *Industrial Buying and Creative Marketing,* Allyn and Bacon, Boston 1967.
(2) D.H. Farmer and K. MacMillan, 'Effectiveness and Efficiency between firms' in *Scandinavian Journal of Materials Administration,* November 1976.
(3) Lee and Dobler, *Purchasing and Materials Management,* 3rd ed., McGraw-Hill, 1977.

FURTHER READING

Baily and Farmer, *Purchasing Principles and Management,* 4th ed., Pitman, 1981, Chapter 2.
Leenders, Fearon and England, *Purchasing and Materials Management,* 7th ed., Irwin, 1980, Chapter 2.
E. Raymond Corey, *Procurement Management,* CBI, 1978, Chapters 4 and 5.

5

Purchasing and materials management

David Farmer

Whilst this book is concerned with purchasing management, it is, of course, impossible to separate that role from the wider materials task. For example, inventory levels, quality and delivery scheduling all affect and are affected by purchasing decisions. Then computer-based concepts like MRP and more conceptual systems such as Kanban are forcing companies to reappraise their systems and organisation structures. Thus the purchasing specialist must consider such developments and his potential role with regard to them.

There are those purchasing specialists who perceive of the function as being outside materials management as it is applied in their business. They argue that in many systems there is too great an emphasis on straightforward schedule management and upon production control. Then that, as a consequence, the important commercial aspects of the materials task are under-emphasised both at operational and strategic levels.

However, as this discussion illustrates, the application of the materials management concept has resulted in a wide range of structures and systems. A key issue is always the vision and calibre of the people involved in the materials systems. A purpose of this chapter is to ensure that the purchasing specialist is better able to influence system developments in his own business so that the dangers inherent in de-emphasising the commercial issues involved are obviated.

THE CONCEPT OF MATERIALS MANAGEMENT

In reviewing the advancement of materials management in 1973, Fearon[1] concluded that the real scope and direction of the concept was unclear. His conclusion was based upon a careful analysis in which he showed that:

(*a*) the concept was being applied in many different ways, and

(*b*) the approach taken was based upon the experiences and perceptions of the individuals involved.

Since materials management, like all organisational concepts, needs to be tailored to the specific setting in which it is to be applied, Fearon's conclusions should not have been surprising. Yet in some respects they indicate one of the difficulties which has been a factor in reducing the pace of acceptance of the ideas involved. An aspect of this is that managers frequently approach such concepts as if they were 'packaged panacea' for their operational ills. One result of this is that ideas are misapplied resulting in outcomes which do not meet the expectations of those involved.

All those who have been involved with the successful development of materials management will have realised that it is a concept and not a group of techniques, and that the idea is capable of application in a wide variety of organisational forms. They will have been made aware of the important impact of the calibre, status and personality of the individual managers involved in the application of the concept, including the vital role of the purchasing functionary.

Nevertheless, it is clear that materials management has been adopted as a concept by a growing number of companies despite these and other difficulties. For example, Miller and Gilmour[2] were able to report that nearly half the manufacturers responding to their survey 'now have materials managers . . . compared with a scant 3 per cent in a 1967 survey'. A parallel UK survey showed that 30 per cent of the responding companies had a manager with that title at that time (1979), whereas, as Baily[3] showed from a UK survey ten years before, less than 3 per cent of the firms in his sample had materials managers then. There is also evidence (see Ericsson[4]) that the growth of the materials concept has been similar in several other developed countries.

The reasons for that growing acceptance are as varied as the organisational forms which have been adopted. However, there are key advantages which are seen to be common in most cases and this chapter will examine them along with some of the problems involved. Our objective is to provide the reader with clearer guidelines to assist in the implementation and development of the materials management concept. While Fearon's conclusions are as pertinent today as they were a decade ago, as regards clarity of direction, the advantages and problems involved are now better understood. That understanding starts with the precept that no two materials management organisations are alike. Even if the organisational diagram includes the same boxes and titles; even if the companies concerned are competing or collaborating in the same industrial sector; the personalities which give the organisation life will interpret their roles and undertake their duties in different ways.

THE EMERGENCE OF THE MATERIALS MANAGER

In 1832 Charles Babbage used a term to describe a role in a mining company which included many of the features of a materials management task. In describing the work of the ten key 'officers' who ran a mining business, he included a materials man (who) selects, purchases, receives and delivers all articles required (to run the mine).[5] The US railroads generally adopted a similar approach later in the same century.[6] In this industry it was common to have the functionaries concerned with purchasing, stock control, inwards good receipt, storage and issuing items to users, all to report to the same manager. Fearon quotes Goubeau[7] as claiming that materials management began to emerge in the US in the nineteen-twenties. Then Lewis and Livesey,[8] reporting on a 1944 survey, claimed that the co-ordination of materials was critical to the management of the airframe industry.

It was the benefits of such co-ordination which were emphasised by academic writers starting in the nineteen-sixties. Ammer[9] was the first to use the title for a book, although Lee and Dobler[10] also used it in conjunction with 'Purchasing' for the first edition of their book in 1965. By the late 'seventies several other texts[11] were also incorporating materials management in some form in their titles.

Presumably this adoption of the name in titles reflected the growing market for the materials management concept as much as its theoretical development.

BENEFITS OF MATERIALS MANAGEMENT

The majority of writers concerned with materials management emphasise the core benefits of the concept as effective integration and co-ordination of the various elements involved in the materials system. They illustrate the problems which arise through attempting to optimise at a departmental level and argue that many problems occur between departments as a result of conflicting sub-objectives and poor liaison.

Effective materials management is said to:

– reduce conflicts between departments;
– reduce inventory levels, both in respect of component and raw material stocks and work-in-progress;
– give greater assurance of the availability of necessary materials/components;
– improve liaison with suppliers;
– reduce overall material costs;
– increase inventory turnover rates;
– reduce handling and transportation costs;
– improve liaison with the output end of the business system with a resulting improvement in customer service levels.

The potential extent of these benefits will, of course, vary from company to company. Nonetheless, some of the examples which have been quoted in the literature are indicative of the scope of that potential. Schultz[12] for example, questioned managers on their experiences with improvements in inventory management resulting from materials management. Among the respondents one manager claimed: 'Without materials management good in-process inventory would be $150,000 higher, stores $200,000 higher. Inventory turnover has gone from 2.5 to 4.0 . . . daily shortages have nose dived from 180 to 8. Spare parts order delinquency has dropped from 60 per cent to 13 per cent.'

Another Schultz respondent claimed that about 50 per cent of the (materials) savings occur as a direct result of the materials management structure.

Zenz[13] in a doctoral survey in 1968 found that 38 per cent of his respondents claimed improvement in inventory from applying materials management, 29 per cent indicated dollar savings and 24 per cent improvements in production efficiency. Despite the rather small population, which is not surprising given the timing of the research vis-à-vis acceptance of the concept, these benefits are similar to those quoted earlier.

Writing in 1975,[14] the same author pointed out some of the problems of evaluation of performance in the application of the concept. Nonetheless broad evidence from the literature would appear to confirm the range of benefits which can stem from effectively applying the concept. And, without doubt, the simple logic of the approach has much to commend it.

STIMULUS FOR ADOPTION

The survey carried out by Farmer and MacMillan[15] in 1976 showed that 'Arab oil embargo' and 'raw material shortages' had been the most significant factors in promoting better relationships between buyers and sellers. It is probable that the same factors were responsible for greater resources being applied to seeking solutions to those problems at that same time. Consequently, it is reasonable to argue that the pace of development of the materials management concept in practice was stimulated by those factors and by academic/theoretical and journalistic interest which resulted from the activity. Perhaps the most significant stimulus though was the wider recognition of a key factor which had long been projected in the purchasing literature. That is, that in the developed countries, at least, more than 50 per cent of sales revenue is, on average, spent by manufacturing firms in purchasing goods and services. As such, this sector represents the most significant element of the company's costs and is also the area with the largest potential return for the investment of management resources seeking profit improvement. Yet traditionally supply management has gained limited attention in the literature and in the business schools. And in business it was, and is, often graded poorly in comparison with other functions.

However, developments over the last decade appear to indicate that the significance of materials on total costs will become even greater. As a consequence, in the future it is probable that the management of materials will be recognised as being more important as an element in total mix. Among these developments are:

(a) automation, which by definition reduces the labour element of factory costs;
(b) transportation/logistical developments;
(c) potential material and capacity shortages;
(d) computer developments which facilitate information sharing within the business system as a whole;
(e) the increasing multinational developments in the manufacture of goods of many kinds;
(f) increasing international competition in many markets which will tend to force companies to control the most significant elements in their costs more effectively.

A brief comment on each of these trends will serve to emphasise the argument.

International competition

Without doubt, the most effective competitors in many world markets over the last decade have been the Japanese. Their products have made great inroads into a wide variety of markets in which they have had no traditional presence. Motor cars, motor cycles, televisions, radio and watches are among the most obvious of these. Concerned competitors have attempted to analyse the reasons for Japanese success and after generalisations about cultural differences and 'Japan Limited', the way in which they manage materials is frequently an important feature. In the motor industry, for example, a table credited by Hohn[16] to the Industrial Bank of Japan, showed the differences between Japanese, German and US firms in respect of purchased items expressed as a percentage of gross profits. Over the four years Toyota's figure was in excess of 80 per cent while Volkswagen stood around 55 per cent and General Motors 45 per cent. Hohn[17] also showed a comparison of inventory supplies (stocks × 360) ÷ (gross profits) between the same firms over the years 1972-79. During this period Toyota's ratio was of the order of 5 days, whereas both that of Volkswagen and General Motors had fluctuated from a peak of high seventies to low eighties (days) in 1974 to an average of mid-forty days in 1979.

The implications of these figures in terms of competitiveness in the end market are clear to see, and represent a stimulus to Toyota competitors to match the levels of the Japanese company's efficiency. The implications for more effective materials management are clear in any attempt to meet this objective.

Multinational developments

As multinational companies have developed their manufacturing bases in various countries, the pressures on them regarding materials have usually increased. Among those pressures have been a widespread demand from host countries to increase the local content of their production.[18] In the case of the Japanese they have found that many local supply markets do not measure up in terms of quality and service to the standards which they require. One result is that they have been forced to develop suppliers in those local markets to the standards which they require.[19] Skinner[20] illustrated the same problem relating to US multinationals.

Computer developments

Given the pace of development of both computer hardware and software, the facilities for fast information management now available are formidable. Inventory management systems involving negligible response time have enabled operating costs due to direct labour to be reduced dramatically. What is more, the shared information available through materials requirements planning (MRP) systems has served to emphasise the systemwide impact of poor materials management. The pressures on businesses to reduce inventory costs while improving service response time to customers will probably continue to stimulate these developments. It is reasonable to forecast a far greater emphasis on systemwide issues as a result, incorporating a focus upon materials management.

Potential material and capacity shortages

The idea of material and capacity shortages may appear strange in conditions of (general) world economic downturn. However, those conditions are precisely the potential cause of such shortage in the future. For example, given depressed markets, mine owners are postponing developments which, they argue, current free market prices will not allow them to finance. In the short term, too, existing facilities are frequently more than sufficient for current demands. However, when there is an upturn in certain cases it will be necessary for new mines to be developed. Since there is often a long lead time involved in the development of a mine, this could result in material shortages and inflated prices, at least until new facilities are on stream. A similar argument may be used, albeit with shorter lead times, in manufacturing situations. The materials management response in these circumstances has strategic potential. The assurance of necessary supplies in the longer term on mutually competitive terms is often most effectively arranged in depressed markets. Clearly, such strategic considerations provide for the purchasing specialist in the materials team (see Chapter 3).

Transport/logistical developments

The Arab oil embargo was a further stimulant relating to materials. Most goods in the developed world are moved by transport (land, sea or air) which is oil powered. With the startling increases in oil prices, the transportation element of materials costs was brought into sharper focus. Better, more cost-effective ways of moving products were sought, usually involving better payloads for the vehicles concerned. Coupled with the shortages which were apparent in 1974 this resulted in actions which tended to inflate inventories. The task of materials management then was to consider the business as a whole and aim to optimise across the system rather than in transport costs in isolation. Many companies in the process began to work with their supply system more effectively, seeking benefits from relocating distribution depots and intermediate stocking points.

Despite short-term effects, it is probable that oil prices will continue to rise through the nineteen-eighties. In the face of that development, managements will need to continue to find ways to improve their effectiveness with regard to material flow.

Automation

The latest extension of the English language relating to automation has resulted in the word 'robotics'. Car plants, in particular, have developed systems involving robot assemblers of components and robot painters. At the same time, in the face of increasingly expensive and scarce skilled manual labour, relatively conventional machines such as lathes have been converted into computer-controlled units. Handling, shaping, lifting, moving and assembling tasks of many kinds once performed by human beings are increasingly being automatically performed by machines. One effect of these developments has been to reduce the proportion of manufacturing costs which relate to labour. Another, and in respect of materials management a more important issue, is that in such circumstances the supply of necessary materials to feed the machines becomes even more crucial. Clearly, expensive sophisticated modern machines necessitate effective utilisation if they are to be viable.

A DEFINITION

Ammer's comment[21] that '. . . every study that has been made indicated that there is no agreement as to precisely what activities should be undertaken by the materials manager' is still pertinent today. The type of organisation, size and stage of its development, being among the factors which influence the structural pattern involved. Fearon[22] in his synthesis included several examples to reinforce the point, before developing a broadly-based general definition. One problem in seeking a generally acceptable definition is that different writers, and managers, perceive the scope of concept in a variety of ways. Some, for example, use the term 'materials management' where others use 'logistics management'. Not surprisingly, in such circumstances sensible discussion becomes difficult because the parties involved are basing their comments upon different perceptions. In order to provide a clear understanding of the scope of the concept it is important to attempt to give a definition. That definition, however, should not be considered as a 'straight jacket', but rather as a basis.

It is useful to illustrate the scope of materials management in diagrammatic form, as shown in Figure 5.1. This diagram is a development of that used by Farmer[23] and is a reflection of widely held views of the scope of the various concepts included.

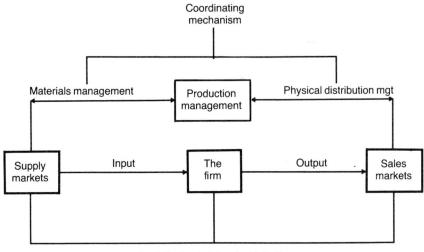

Figure 5.1 The scope of materials management

Within this view, materials management may be seen as being concerned with the management of materials and components from the supply markets into the company. The approach may be more precisely defined as: the concept concerned with the management of the flow of materials into an organisation to the point where those materials are converted into the firm's end product(s).

Within this definition, responsibilities include:

(a) collaboration with designers on material component specifications;

(b) purchasing, which includes the search for and location of suitable sources of supply and monitoring delivery performance at both an operational and strategic level;

(c) incoming traffic;

(d) receiving, inspecting and checking incoming goods;

(e) supplier quality control;

(f) inventory control – raw materials, components and, possibly, work-in-progress;

(g) material control and issuing to production and, in some cases,

(h) internal materials handling.

As with all the systems approaches which are included in the diagram, the main thrust of materials management is to avoid sub-optimisation and seek systemwide effectiveness. In other words, it is to seek to achieve systemwide objectives rather than those which apply to elements within the system (which may result in conflicts which are detrimental to the whole).

Possible conflicts

Ammer[24] provided a useful summary of some of these possible conflicts in an early paper (see Figure 5.2). Ammer's thesis at that time was that effective co-ordination through the adoption of the materials management approach would eliminate many of the problems associated with these conflicts. Several other writers have taken this position and the examples of successful application quoted earlier have stemmed from such co-ordination. In general, all have emphasised the important advantage of seeking to ensure that the whole is greater than the sum of the parts.

Deceptive simplicity

In conclusion it is worth emphasising that the deceptive simplicity of the concept has been something of a trap for some adopters. Ericsson,[25] for example, suggests that suitable management expertise should exist within the company to enable it to be adopted successfully. He also emphasises the important point that costs connected with the materials system should be capable of being analysed and accounted for with a reasonable degree of accuracy. Then he stresses the importance of appropriate communication

	Primary objective	Interrelated objectives that are adversely affected
1	Minimum prices for materials	High inventory turnover, continuity of supply, consistency of quality, low payroll costs, favourable relations with supply sources
2	High inventory turnover	Minimum prices, low cost of acquisition and possession, continuity of supply, low payroll costs
3	Low cost of acquisition and possession	High inventory turnover (sometimes), good records, continuity of supply, consistency of quality
4	Continuity of supply	Minimum prices for materials, high inventory turnover, favourable relations with suppliers, consistency of quality
5	Consistency of quality	Minimum prices for materials, high inventory turnover, continuity of supply, favourable relations with suppliers, low payroll costs, low costs of acquisition and possession
6	Low payroll costs	Maximum achievement of this objective is possible only by sacrificing all other objectives
7	Good supplier relations	Low payroll costs, minimum prices, high inventory turnover
8	Development of personnel	Low payroll costs (other objectives might also be affected)
9	Good records	Low payroll costs (other objectives might also be affected)

Source: Ammer.

Figure 5.2 Possible conflicts between departmental materials objectives

information processing systems, and the need for top management to be wedded to the concept.

The various stimuli suggested earlier may well have a significant effect on top management's acceptance of the concept. And, with such support, several of the other problems may be obviated. The two most common traps which we have observed, however, relate to the kind of misconceptions mentioned earlier in the chapter. For example, in one large multinational concern reorganisation along materials management lines resulted in what could be most kindly described as 'partial success'. A key factor which emerged was that the functionary who was given the materials manager title at the various plants most often came from a system or production control background. This resulted in an over-emphasis on systems and production matters in the approach taken by the manager concerned. The effect was a production orientation in which the problems associated with that idea at the sales market end of the business were mirrored. In short, the functionary lacked commercial skills. For this reason, it is clear that many purchasing specialists need to develop a greater understanding of their materials systems so as to be in a position to challenge for the top materials jobs of the future.

The budget and accounting implications of the problem were also present in this company. Broadly stated, the accounting/measurement systems remained as they were under the previous departmental structure. One result of this was that managers who performed the various subfunctions in the materials system were being measured against norms which encouraged them to suboptimise. In effect there were penalties for the individual in seeking to achieve systemwide effectiveness, while he was rewarded for the narrow results of his own function. The end result, of course, was contrary to the objectives of the materials management concept.

REFERENCES

(1) H. E. Fearon, 'Materials Management: A Synthesis and Current Review' in *Journal of Purchasing*, vol. 9, no. 1, February 1973.
(2) J. G. Miller and P. Gilmour, 'Materials Managers: Who needs Them?' in *Harvard Business Review,* July-August 1979.

(3) P. J. H. Baily, *Media Research Bureau for Modern Purchasing*, 1970.

(4) D. Ericsson, 'MA's Utveckling' in *Scandinavian Journal of Materials Administration*, vol. 4, no. 1, 1978.

(5) C. Babbage, *On the Economy of Machinery and Manufactures*, Chas Knight, 2nd ed., 1982.

(6) 'Purchasing and Care of Supplies' in *The Railroad Gazette* vol. 12, 1890.

(7) V. de P. Goubeau, 'Materials Management – A Realistic Appraisal', AMA Report 35, 1959.

(8) H. T. Lewis and C. A. Livesey, 'Materials Management – A Problem for the Airframe Industry', Harvard University Bus. Research Study 31, 1944.

(9) Dean S. Ammer, *Materials Management,* Irwin, 1962.

(10) L. Lee and D. W. Dobler, *Purchasing and Materials Management,* McGraw-Hill, 1965.

(11) W. B. England and M. R. Leenders, *Purchasing and Materials Management,* Irwin, 6th ed., 1975.

(12) G. V. Schultz, 'The Real Low-Down on Materials Management' in *Factory*, December 1967.

(13) G. J. Zenz, 'The Economics of Materials Management', unpublished PhD dissertation, University of Wisconsin, 1968.

(14) G. J. Zenz, 'Evaluating Materials Management' in *Journal of Purchasing and Materials Management,* vol. II, no. 3, Autumn 1975.

(15) D. H. Farmer and K. MacMillan, 'Voluntary Collaboration vs "Disloyalty" ' in *Journal of Purchasing and Materials Management,* vol. 12, no. 4, Winter 1976.

(16) S. Hohn, 'Material Management as an Integral Part of Corporate Strategy', a paper given at the Schmatenbach Conference, Frankfurt, 1981.

(17) Ibid.

(18) D. H. Farmer, 'Source Decision-Making in the Multi-National Company Environment' in *Journal of Purchasing,* vol. 8, no. 1, February 1972.

(19) D. H. Farmer, 'Input Management' in *Journal of General Management,* 1980.

(20) W. Skinner, *American Industry in Developing Economies,* Wiley, 1968.

(21) Dean S. Ammer, *Materials Management,* Irwin, rev. ed., 1968.

(22) H. E. Fearon, op. cit.

(23) D. H. Farmer, 'Why Materials Management' in *International Journal of Physical Distribution of Materials Management,* October 1977.

(24) Dean S. Ammer, 'There are No "Right" Answers in Materials Management' in *Purchasing,* vol. 46, February 1959.

(25) D. Ericsson, 'Materials Administration' in *Scandinavian Journal of Materials Administration,* November 1975.

PART II
THE PURCHASING MIX

6

Purchase price management

David Ford

The acquisition of goods and services at an appropriate price is an important function of the buyer. Frequently, judgements made by management about the buyer's success in achieving appropriate prices are an important factor in assessments of his or her performance. Further, savings made in the purchased price of inputs into industrial companies can have a profound effect on company profitability. The profit contribution of even small purchase price reductions can often be greater than the effects of considerable increases in sales volume (see Figure 6.1). Additionally, knowledge about prevailing market prices, variations between different potential suppliers and negotiation skills are central aspects of the buyer's stock-in-trade. The buyer may not be able to match the appreciation of technical factors in buying decisions made by R & D colleagues, or knowledge of the interrelationships between different purchased items which are important considerations for his company's engineers. Nevertheless, the buyer's understanding of purchase price and his role in price analysis and negotiation are one of his major contributions to the purchase decision process.

Despite the importance of price to the performance evaluation of buyers, to the purchasing process and to company profitability, understanding of pricing issues is often unclear and confused. For example, the difficulty in assessing the buyer's success in purchase price reduction contributes to the problem of introducing a sound

		£
	Initial sales	100,000
	Profit on sales	10%
	Net profit	10,000
(a)	Cost of purchased items	50,000
	Cost reduction through saving of 5%	2,500
	Increase in net profit	25%
(b)	To achieve a 25% increase in net profit, sales must increase by	£25,000 (£2,500 ÷ 10%)

∴ In this case a 5% reduction in purchase costs produces the same profit increase as a 25% increase in sales

Figure 6.1 Comparison of the effects on profitability of purchase cost savings and sales increases

performance-based reward system for buyers. This difficulty con-trasts with the ease with which the performance of salespeople can be assessed in terms of sales volume achievement and marketing people can be measured through profitability performance. In this way, the problem of measuring price performance by the buyer also contributes to the often relatively lowly status of the buyer within the organisation, when compared to marketing or other colleagues.

It would be difficult to provide a complete analysis in a short chapter of all the pricing issues which a buyer must face. This chapter attempts to provide some guidance for the buyer by examining firstly the pricing strategies adopted by marketing companies and then looks at the current practice of purchase price management in companies. Some of the issues in purchase price analysis are briefly explored in order to draw conclusions for the development of a buyer's strategy for purchase price management.

PRICE AND THE INDUSTRIAL MARKETER

First it is worth emphasising that the industrial marketer is probably no more confident in the correctness of his pricing policy than the buyer is in asserting that he has achieved the best possible prices for his purchases. Pricing is an area of complexity for the marketer and he faces a number of problems, appreciation of which can assist the buyer in strategy and negotiation.

Price and the marketing mix

The industrial marketer, like his consumer colleague, is unwilling to 'sell on price'. Much of marketing strategy is involved with product differentiation. Through this the marketer seeks to cultivate real or imagined added-value for his product and hence avoid the situation of selling a 'commodity' product at a commodity price. It has been argued that it is possible to differentiate any product. Often this differentiation can only occur in other areas of the marketing mix – terms of sale, delivery, pre- and after-sales service, quality and reliability and of course the intangible of reputation or 'image'. Differentiation is not limited to giving the customer what he expects, it may also involve 'augmenting' the product with things the buyer never thought about. Thus on one side of the transaction the marketer is seeking to offer an assembly of product features, including price. It is the buyer's task to 'disassemble' this package as far as possible so that each aspect is individually assessed, rather than being part of some global judgement. It is the buyer's job to buy from a clear understanding of requirements in terms of, for example, delivery scheduling, seller service provision or surface finish so that the unnecessary features can be removed from consideration.

Price and costs

The seller faces problems in relating the price he wishes to charge to the costs he has in producing a product. For example, the sales and marketing manager of a major UK engineering manufacturer recently reported to the author that he had little idea of the 'real' costs of his products now, and even less idea of their costs for the time in the future for which he was quoting. This inadequacy in cost information, and the fact that even small discounts on price can mean large decreases in profit are important factors in industrial marketers' conservatism over prices.

The greatest problem for the marketer is that of cost allocation. Frequently, decisions about this are avoided by adopting fully-absorbed cost-plus pricing. Here product cost is arrived at by adding allocated overheads to the variable production costs of the product. These overheads are usually allocated as a multiple of the labour hours in making any product or of the direct material used. An alternative is to use a combination of both, or any other variable which is common to most of the firm's products, such as machine hours or floor space used. Absorption costing has the advantage of simplicity. For example, the total number of budgeted labour hours is divided into the total fixed costs of the firm and these are subsequently allocated to each hour of labour. There is then no problem of 'under-recovery' of overheads. This 'safety' appeals to many manufacturers, typically job-shops of all kinds.

Absorption costing suffers from three main problems: firstly, the allocation may not be 'fair'. Thus, some products may use large amounts of the facilities which generate fixed costs such as machinery etc., or indeed the machinery may only exist for use on a certain product, while others may not use these facilities. This means that the costs attributed to some products may bear little relationship to the incurred costs of producing them. Additionally, prices arrived at by full absorption costing bear no relationship to market demand. Thus, overhead allocation calculated at one level of demand, say 100,000 units per annum, can lead to under- or over-recovery of overheads if demand reduces or increases. Perhaps, even more importantly, reduced demand over time can lead to ever higher levels of overheads being allocated to each of the fewer units produced, leading to higher prices and hence even further reduced sales, the so-called 'doom-loop'. This leads to the third basic problem for both buyer and seller in absorption pricing: the price arrived at by this method bears no necessary relationship to what the market is prepared to pay.

An alternative to absorption cost pricing is contribution pricing. The initial cost ingredient in price formation is the variable costs actually incurred in producing the product, or in producing additional units of the product. The difference between this and the achieved price is then regarded as a contribution towards the company's fixed costs. The advantage of this method is that it produces greater flexibility for the marketer. In some senses, it transfers control over pricing decisions from the accountant to the marketer. The contribution towards fixed costs becomes an item of discretion or judgement. This is of particular importance to the marketer when considering incremental business, or perhaps business in a new market. Thus the marketer can take the view that the additional business is not 'attracting' further overheads, which are already being covered by existing production. Consequently, additional sales can be considered at any price greater than the actual variable costs incurred. Contribution pricing is often a short-term tactic for the marketer. In the long run he must avoid the danger of under-recovery of overheads.

For the buyer, it is important that his price discussion takes place on the basis of a realisation of the overhead allocation practices of suppliers, e.g. by labour or machine hour, and the reality of these for the products he is buying. It also means that the buyer must be aware of his position as possibly an additional source of volume, which does not in itself attract additional overheads.

Also the buyer must be aware of whether fixed and semi-variable costs make up a large proportion of the suppliers' total costs. If this is the case, then achieving high capacity utilisation, and hence covering these fixed costs, is vital to the manufacturer and his pricing is likely to show flexibility in order to achieve this. If, on the other hand, variable costs are a high proportion of total costs then the manufacturer is likely to price so as to achieve maximum unit prices, even at the expense of some additional volume.

Price and time

Changes in a product's price over time due to 'unavoidable cost increases' are all too familiar. Nevertheless, the relationship between price and time is an important aspect of the marketer's strategy and hence it is a crucial part of the buyer's task of interpreting that strategy. There are a number of elements in the marketer's considerations which will be dealt with in turn.

Setting the introductory price for a product is particularly difficult for the marketer. If the product is relatively innovative, he will have little basis for comparison with the prices of existing products. He can, however, attempt to use the 'economic value' of the product to his customers as an ingredient in his pricing. This involves calculation of the financial benefits to the customer of buying the product. For example, the value of electric forklift trucks can be calculated in terms of elimination of fuel costs. This saving can be discounted to its net present value and expressed as a return on the possibly higher capital investment required when compared to diesel trucks. The marketer must take care in this calculation. Firstly, he must distinguish between the perceived value of the product to his customers as opposed to its potential value. Customers may be aware of risks involved in a changeover, for example, the possibility of union opposition to increased mechanisation, or they may simply be sceptical of the marketer's claims. Secondly, product value may be considered differently by different market segments; for example enhanced acid resistance in an alloy may be of more value to the petrochemical industry than to a manufacture of elements for electric cookers. Thirdly, the value a customer places on a product will depend on the options open to him; for example one manufacturer may be able to choose between plastic and metal for a component, whilst for another only metal will suffice. Thus the marketer can only successfully build customer value into his pricing after segmenting his market and analysing the alternatives available to different customer groups. Also it is vital for the marketer to make this value analysis before engaging in extensive product development. This is one aspect of the mutual interest of buyer and seller shown through buyer co-operation in this analysis.

The seller frequently has a range of discretion in setting the price of a new product. This range is between his perception of the value of the product to his market, or his view of what the market will bear, and the cost of making the product. Marketers often make the distinction between extremes of this discretion – skimming and penetration pricing.

Skimming pricing involves the marketer selecting a price at the upper limit of his discretion. This may be well above the price floor determined by his cost structure and close to his estimate of the value of his product to the market, or what he believes is the maximum price the market will bear. Skimming has a number of advantages to the marketer: it maximises the contribution he receives per unit and hence works towards the recovery of his investment in product development. It means that the product is first employed in the less price sensitive segments of his markets where it has its clearest application, leaving more price sensitive segments for later exploitation. Perhaps more importantly, it establishes the initial price for the product at a high level. Thus the product's value is often seen by the market to be high and subsequent price reductions by the seller are from a high margin position. Of course the establishment of a high market price for the product through skimming is likely to attract competitive entry. Because of this, skimming is most likely to be employed where the initiator has a technological or other advantage which will delay competitive entry. The initiator can then respond to this entry by advertised price reduction of a high priced and, by implication, high quality product, which is then taken into other more price sensitive segments.

Penetration pricing involves price setting near the lower limit of the marketer's discretion. This is often employed where the marketer does not have a technological edge or other barrier to entry. The low price may not only develop the market rapidly, but may also discourage competitive entry because of the low margins and hence high breakeven point of competitors.

The manufacturer's deliberations in initial price setting have a number of important implications for the buyer. Firstly, examination of the seller's price in skimming or penetration terms may affect his decision as to when he will adopt a new product. Secondly, the buyer's management and control of purchase price increases, which will be discussed shortly, can only make sense if his analysis of the seller's cost and price movements are made from a sound basis. This reinforces the value of understanding seller's cost structure through purchase price analysis at the *start* of a continuing purchase.

The product life cycle

Sophisticated marketers are increasingly aware of the life cycles of their products and hence plan variations in mix through the life cycle. From the buyer's perspective there are at least two aspects of this which are important. The first is the movement in costs which the seller can expect through the life cycle and hence the changes in price he can expect or negotiate. These cost changes are often described in terms of the 'learning curve'. There have been a number of studies which have tried to calculate the cost reductions which can be expected through the life of a product. The Boston

Consulting Group suggests that there is roughly a 25 per cent reduction in unit costs of production for each doubling of production output. Cost movements through the learning curve increase the manufacturer's discretion in pricing, particularly if he has adopted an initial skimming strategy. In this way he is able to plan his price reductions either following, or even in advance of, his learning curve in order to forestall competition.

The second implication for pricing of the product life cycle is that the place of price in the manufacturer's strategy will change through the life cycle, due in part to the effects of differences in competition. Thus the growth stage of the life cycle is a time of relatively soft competition, when the rapidly increasing demand for the product means that manufacturers can command comfortable margins without significant price competition. At the same time, the product is entering what has been described as the cost reduction phase. The importance of cost reduction becomes apparent during the maturity stage of the life cycle. Here the slower rate of growth leads to over capacity and consequent price competition. Also the technology on which the product is based becomes more widely known. Product similarities increase and the product tends to assume the characteristics of a commodity. To avoid this, and hence command a higher price, many manufacturers concentrate on tailoring their product to the particular requirements of one or more market segments. In this way, they hope to command a greater price for their differentiated product. However, the combined impact of market saturation and new technology means inevitably that an existing product eventually enters the decline phase. Here the manufacturer's task is that of managing this decline. The critical decision facing him is when to withdraw the product. Nevertheless, competitive withdrawal may mean the seller may have a small but remaining market committed to the product. In this case he is likely to attempt to 'milk' it. Thus, by price increased and minimal investment, he seeks to maximise his return from declining sales.

All of this means that the buyer must be aware of life-cycle considerations and the associated cost and competitive movements in his price negotiations.

Price and competition

We have already noted the changes in competitive influences through a product's life cycle. Competition has a much more pervasive influence on manufacturer pricing than this. The price of near or exactly substitutable competition is an important guide to the pricing of products. In many cases these competitive prices are strongly influenced by those of the price leader. Price leaders tend to be most common in oligopolistic markets, where a small number of companies have a large market share. The leader generally has a large (or the largest) market share, is a low-cost producer, has a strong position in the market through his distribution and sales force, and is often in a position of technical leadership. Such a company has sufficient financial and market strength to make a stand on price in the market. It is also likely that the leader will act to preserve stability in the market and in the interests of the market as a whole. These motivations are related to the stake which the leader has in the current market. The leader holds his position by having initiated price moves which are accepted by customers and followed by competition: false moves tend to destroy the leader's credibility. Finally, because price leaders are often technical leaders their strategy often concerns the price relationship between new and existing products. In this way new products having superior performance are priced at a premium over existing ones and act to preserve price levels and margins on existing products and give less incentive to competitors to indulge in price competition. This preserves the margins necessary to fund further new product development.

Prices and customer decision making

The skilled marketer will relate his pricing strategy to the decision processes of his customers. At least two aspects of this are important. Firstly, the price sensitivity of a buying company will vary depending upon the importance of other factors, such as reliability of delivery or the need for a product to meet a high performance requirement with extended reliability. It is particularly likely to be the case where an engineer has an important role in the purchase decision process. Similarly, the marketer will be aware of the unwillingness of a buyer to take the risks involved in changing suppliers unless the price advantage is significant. This applies both to an already 'in-supplier' or an 'out-supplier' prepared to offer this price difference in the short term at least in order to gain business.

This reinforces the importance of the role of the buyer in the purchase decision process. It is he who is providing information on comparative pricing and hence makes explicit the costs of the respective advantages of different product features. Only through this can objective, as opposed to more judgemental, criteria form the basis of the purchase decision.

PRICE IN PRACTICE

The difficulties that manufacturers face in setting prices have been noted earlier. It will now be useful to examine the methods which they use in practice. The only large-scale study of pricing in British industry is that published by Atkin and Skinner in 1975,[1] which indicates that the main method of pricing appears to be adding a percentage to cost. Further, it seems that the basis for this cost-plus pricing is most often that of absorption costing. The study did show that prices may be modified by non-cost related considerations and that profit margins varied between a company's different product lines and here the influence of competition seemed important.

Perhaps more significantly for the buyer, the study found that acceptability of prices was only formally investigated in even the broadest sense by one-third of the companies. This applied even where price was considered vital to the overall marketing strategy. Company sales forces were almost invariably the means of 'investigating' price acceptability and there was no recourse to outside market research respondents. The implications for the buyer are obvious: industrial marketers frequently have little firm knowledge of the appropriateness of their prices. Their information is gathered by sales forces who are certainly not dispassionate researchers and are often susceptible to influence by buyers.

The majority of respondents in the study believed that the effective price range for their industry is 20 per cent or less, while over one-third thought this range was 10 per cent or less. This can be combined with the finding that nearly 90 per cent of the respondents thought that their own prices were either about average or higher. Only 7 per cent thought their prices were lower than average. Many marketers believe that price competition is of relatively little importance to them when compared to competition on the basis of quality or performance. Further, it seems that many manufacturers may have a somewhat unrealistic view of their market, believing that their prices are above average and that they compete on their superior quality. It emphasises the important role of the buyer in bringing reality into the market, because it is he who has, or should have, a clear idea of competitive prices and comparative quality.

Lack of responsiveness to the market by manufacturers was also indicated by Atkin and Skinner's findings on price changes. It seems that changes in prices are more likely to occur in response to a cost increase than for any other reason. Companies are also likely to follow upward movement in overall market price or to increase in order to achieve greater profit. In contrast, they are less likely to respond to a fall in costs or market price. Price changes are infrequently used as part of a positive attempt to gain market share. Finally, the method most commonly used to assess the effects of price changes is a comparison of sales results over comparable periods. Formal market investigation is rarely carried out and there is little evidence that manufacturers fully assess price change effects on important buyer-seller relationships or long-term competitiveness.

All of this emphasises the importance of the buyer's positive role in price determination. His information on competitive price movements and industry cost changes must be used in negotiation, on the basis that price determination is a joint activity between him and the supplier. Further, it is important that the buyer's involvement in pricing occurs on the basis of a clear assessment of the importance of price and non-price factors to his company.

PURCHASE PRICE MANAGEMENT IN PRACTICE

Farrington's study[2] provides comprehensive information on current practice in purchase price management. Predictably the study found that the majority of buyers believed that management in most companies judge buyers on their ability to buy at the right price.

However, less than two-thirds of the respondents in Farrington's study said that buyers in their company were given specific price objectives. Additionally, many of the buyers who do have such objectives have them set 'passively'. This means that they are set on the basis of historical data – standard costs, previous prices paid or comparison with an index of supplying industry. Only just over 20 per cent had objectives set on the basis of purchase price analysis and only 19.4 per cent set by some cost-reduction objective.

Overall, only just over half the respondents had cost reduction objectives which again indicates a somewhat passive role for many buyers in purchase price management. Long-term contracts were listed by the most buyers as factors in cost-reduction programmes, followed by price negotiation. Changes in specification, standardisation and make-or-buy studies were less frequently used. Perhaps significantly, resourcing studies were mentioned least frequently of all, although here it appears that buyers who do use them use them very often.

A somewhat less passive view of the buyer's role is provided by questioning about buyer's response to a supplier request for a price increase. Less than 2 per cent of Farrington's respondents would accept such a request without further action. The most common action by buyers is to ask for supportive data from the supplier and/or to invite other sellers to quote. However, it is not clear whether these additional quotes are mainly to serve as a check or whether they represent a serious attempt to resource. Farrington notes the importance placed by both buyers and management on delaying price rises. Also approximately one-third of respondents used industry and own-company cost data and indices. However other analytical techniques such as value analysis and consultation with other buyers were relatively infrequently used. Buyer's requests for detailed cost breakdowns are most likely to be stimulated by a price increase request. This was the case with over 70 per cent of respondents, whereas only a little over half of the respondents would seek cost breakdowns when buying an item for the first time.

Another study, conducted by R. M. Hardwick at the University of Bath, investigated differences between the prices paid by 64 buyers within a single UK engineering group. A price scatter of between 30 and 35 per cent was repeatedly found with no real correlation between size of purchase and reducing price. This was for such basic commodities as resistors, fasteners and mild steel tube and sections etc. This wide price variation was also found to exist where attractive 'group agreement' prices had been negotiated and widely circulated. Here the question was almost purely one of communication in that buyers frequently did not use the group terms to negotiate improved deals locally.

The problem is compounded when manufacturer's discount structures are taken into account. These make it increasingly difficult for the buyer to monitor continuously the price he is paying, especially for such differing items as electronic components and bearings etc. Thus the prices of many products largely reflect the degree of commercial attention paid to the product by the buyer, rather than the size of his expenditure. However with standard purchases of wide variety, low cost, low repeatability and high volume, the amount of time a buyer can devote or the expertise he can develop is limited. As products become more expensive or more critical, the buyer's level of attention will be correspondingly greater. Nevertheless, in the standard products area the market prices are often those which reflect the unadjusted pricing policies of suppliers.

This and other studies together provide a picture of a somewhat 'reactive' buyer. Buyers frequently do not have clear pricing objectives, they are often inadequately provided with analytical and information resources to carry out purchase price management. In many cases they do not use the resources available to them. Further, their costs breakdown requests are more likely to occur in response to manufacturer pressure for price increases, rather than as part of the initial price-setting process. This picture, when combined with the findings noted earlier about the ways in which manufacturers set prices, indicates the need for change in many buyers' approach and particularly the strategy and resource allocation process of purchasing management and perhaps more importantly of resource allocation by general management. However, before dealing with conclusions in this direction it is important to examine some of the available techniques of purchase price analysis in more detail.

ANALYTICAL APPROACHES

The importance of information to the buyer in his task of purchase price management has been emphasised earlier. A major source of this information is from within his own company. However, many (or most) buyers must operate without the backup of purchase price analysts. Obviously the value of carrying out expensive analysis is justified only in the case of significant purchases. Nevertheless it is more often the case that buyers lack the essential information on which to base their negotiation. Centralised analysts, working on their own company's cost information and on industrywide cost movements, can provide alternative cost estimates to those supplied by a seller. For a detailed discussion of this, see Farrington.[2] Additionally, analysts should provide information on the 'true costs' of purchases, i.e. the purchase price plus the incremental costs of acquisition or those through the life of the product. An example of this is shown in Figure 6.2. This approach is of particular value with dual or triple-sourced products where the information is vital in sourcing decisions and price negotiation.

	Supplier		
Cost of defect prevention	*A*	*B*	*C*
Qualifying visits	250	250	250
Laboratory tests	200	200	200
Specification revision	300	–	–
Cost of defect detection			
Incoming inspection	600	600	600
Processing inspection reports	1,200	1,200	1,200
Cost of defect correction			
Manufacturing losses	1,590	150	200
Handling and packing rejects	1,500	280	600
Cost of complaints and lost sales	13,200	–	2,043
Total	*18,840*	*2,680*	*5,093*
Total value of purchases	*63,820*	*67,947*	*84,896*
Quality cost ratio (%)	29.5	3.9	5.9

Figure 6.2 Quality cost analysis

The buyer must use both the informational and purchasing resources of his whole company. This means the purchase of products under umbrella or group contracts and the cross-checking of purchase price paid between different buyers and the same supplier or for the same product. The use of centralised computing now makes this exchange of information possible.

The buyer must also establish the analytical basis for subsequent price movements at the start of purchasing from a supplier. Therefore cost breakdowns are required *before* a purchase takes place. It is only then that a sound basis of comparison can exist for the assessment of price increase requests. A second aspect is the use of contract price adjustment (CPA) by the buyer where a formula is derived for price changes on the basis of future cost movements. Such a formula needs to be individually designed for each contracted product. However, it is again important that the buyer is proactive in deriving this formula at the start of negotiations so that not only is future negotiation on a sound basis, but the formula is more likely to be established on his terms. An example of such a formula is illustrated in Figure 6.3.

Conclusions on buyers' purchase price management

This chapter has examined some of the approaches of both sellers

---

$$P_1 = \frac{P_o}{100} \left(a + \frac{bM_1}{M_o} + \frac{cS_1}{S_o} \right)$$

P_1 is the final invoiced price for the item which will vary from the original price at the date of quotation due to movement in the cost of the relevant materials and wages.
P_o is the initial price at the date of quotation.
M_1 is the mean of the price for the materials concerned over the last 3/5ths of the period of the contract.
M_o is the initial price for the same materials at the date of quotation.
S_1 is the mean of the wages of shopfloor personnel over the last 3/5ths of the period of the contract.
S_o is the initial wages for the same staff at the start of the contract.
abc are the contractually agreed proportions of the initial price at the following percentages:
    a – fixed proportions at 15 per cent
    b – materials at 44 per cent
    c – wages and social charges at 91 per cent

Source: Farrington[2]

Figure 6.3 Contract price adjustment for a capital purchase

and buyers to industrial pricing and several conclusions can be drawn about purchase price management.

The buyer has a major responsibility for purchase price management which has a number of elements. It is he who is the source of the company's information on competitive prices and hence the initiator of purchase price comparison on a 'cost per feature basis'. It is the buyer who should seek and feed into decision making information on the relative 'true costs' of purchases. Similarly it is the buyer who must co-ordinate the use of purchase price analysis.

The important profit potential of purchase price management reinforces the requirement for analytical resources for the buyer, both in terms of quantitative cost analysis and the wider aspects of purchasing research.

The buyer must approach price issues on the basis of a realisation of his position in the market, the strategies and tactics open to the marketer, and the life cycle, and costing structure of the product being bought.

The buyer must consider the subsequent purchases of a product at the stage of initial purchase. Price control on these later purchases can only be carried out effectively on the basis of realistic price and cost information for the initial purchases.

Finally this chapter has emphasised the importance of the buyer taking a proactive role in pricing activity. This is based partially on a realisation of the inadequacy of the manufacturers' pricing procedures. However it means that the buyer must be provided with the prerequisites to carry this proactive role. Firstly, he must have a clear brief as to the relative importance of price of service factors in the purchase and secondly, he must have the resources in terms of time to devote to his purchases as well as the necessary information from within the company. This means that companies will have to look afresh at price comparisons between departments and divisions and the establishment of more sophisticated information systems dealing with prices paid both elsewhere and in the past. Also they must re-examine purchases in terms of the likely savings overall, rather than concentrating only on more visible purchases. This structured approach is an essential back-up to the skills of the buyer in his negotiations with individual sellers and his dealings in the market at large.

CHECKLIST ON PURCHASE PRICE MANAGEMENT

To what extent do buyers in your company have specific price objectives? If so, are they set on the most appropriate basis – previous data, purchase price analysis or industry indexes?

Do buyers in your company have the necessary resources to carry out purchase price management?

Do they have access to comparative information from other departments or divisions within the company?

Do they have the back-up of purchase price analysts?

Do buyers regularly seek cost breakdowns for the initial purchase of a particular product?

Do buyers have or develop information on the 'true cost' of purchases from particular suppliers? Is this information fed into subsequent purchase decision making?

Do buyers develop and use contract price adjustment formulae, or accept those of suppliers?

Do buyers insist on and have the information to evaluate suppliers' cost breakdowns for re-pricing requests?

Do buyers operate a system of seeking additional quotes when faced with re-pricing requests? Are these quotes used only for checks, or do they form part of a full purchase re-evaluation?

Do buyers enter price negotiations on the basis of analysis of the seller's perspective, the approach he is likely to take and the factors affecting his pricing policy as well as a sound understanding of the supply market and the extent of his own power in it?

REFERENCES

(1) B. Atkin and R. Skinner, *How British Industry Prices,* Industrial Market Research Ltd, London, 1976.
(2) B. Farrington, *Industrial Purchase Price Management,* Gower, 1980.

FURTHER READING

J. Stevens, *Measuring Purchasing Performance,* Business Books, 1978.

How British Industry Buys, Financial Times Market Research Department, 1984.

IMP Group, H. Hakansson (ed.), *International Marketing and Purchasing of Industrial Goods: An Interaction Approach,* John Wiley, 1982.

F. Livesey, *Pricing,* Macmillan, 1976.

7

Purchase quality management

R. W. Wagstaff

The word 'quality' is commonly considered as implying high quality. A dictionary definition includes statements such as 'degree of excellence; possessing high degree of excellence; concerned with maintenance of high quality (quality control)'. Such implications can be misleading when applied to industrial situations. Excellence is expensive: the quality of bought-in items or manufactured products must therefore be controlled to ensure that they meet the user's requirements, and continue to do so for a given period of time, while avoiding excessive costs due to unnecessarily high quality.

The British Standards Institution defines quality more precisely as:

> The totality of features and characteristics of a product or service that bear on its ability to satisfy a given need.[1]

Reliability is an extension of quality, i.e. the ability of an item to perform a required function under stated conditions for a stated period of time. Reliability can be expressed as the probability that a product will operate satisfactorily for the stated period of time.

In the case of both quality and reliability the first need is to specify precisely the characteristics required, then to ensure that the materials and manufacturing processes used result in products which conform to the specification. Thus two distinct attributes of quality are evident:

1 Quality of design: the quality defined by the specification and a measure of the extent to which this meets the needs of the user.
2 Quality of conformance (quality of manufacture): the extent to which a manufactured product conforms to the stated specifications.

Quality assurance, i.e. all the activities concerned with the attainment of the required quality, thus encompasses all of the following:

1 A satisfactory design of product, thoroughly proven by testing to establish its reliability under service conditions.
2 Specification of requirements, which must be understood by everyone concerned with manufacturing the product.
3 Confirmation that outside suppliers and in-company manufacturing processes are capable of meeting the specified requirements.
4 Motivation of all those concerned with manufacture of the product, inside and outside the company, to achieve the standards set by the specification.
5 Verification that products conform to specification.
6 Accurate and reliable means of inspecting or testing.
7 Feedback of inspection results and user experience to prove that all the above stages are effective.

THE COSTS OF QUALITY

The objective of any quality control system must be to achieve the required level of quality at the lowest overall cost. The quality level desired should be chosen in the light of customer quality demands (and hence selling prices) and the costs associated with producing to various levels of quality (see Figure 7.1).

Only when the quality policy of a company has been defined can appropriate systems of quality assurance be adopted. Although difficult to quantify, it is evident that inadequate control of quality will lead to defective items which may be scrapped, reworked at additional cost, sold at lower prices as 'seconds', or sold (knowingly or unknowingly) as good items, which may lead to loss of customer goodwill. Other costs associated with inadequate *control* of quality

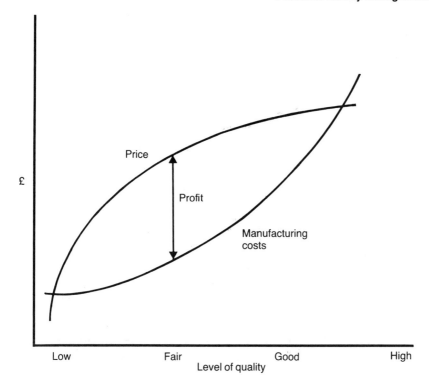

Figure 7.1 Effect of different levels of quality on manufacturing costs and selling prices

are additional inspection, selective assembly, possibly the use of manual manufacturing methods instead of intended automated manufacture, disruption of manufacturing schedules due to required materials or components being rejected, and servicing of customer complaints. The lower the level of quality control in manufacturing, the greater is the likelihood of such additional costs (see Figure 7.2).

On the other hand, quality control activities are themselves expensive. As manufacturing tolerances are tightened, production processes and equipment must be improved to allow greater precision to be achieved. Production rates are usually slower, and additional inspection using more sophisticated techniques may be necessary. The proportion of items rejected because they do not conform to specifications may also increase. In the case of bought-in materials and components, insistence on higher quality usually

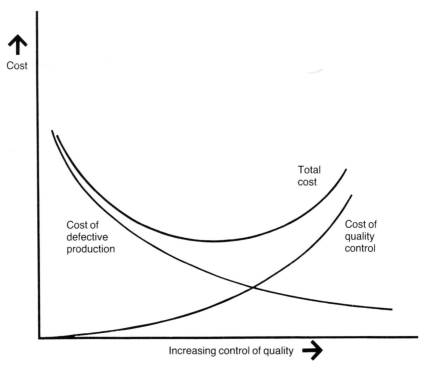

Figure 7.2 Relationship between cost of quality control and cost of defective production

increases purchase costs and may reduce the number of potential suppliers able to meet requirements.

Figure 7.2 indicates the relationship between the costs of quality control and the costs of inadequate control. A company must select the level of quality control which allows it to achieve its quality objectives at the lowest total cost.

It is estimated that the total costs of quality in industry arising from prevention, appraisal (which includes inspection and testing services) and failure (which includes scrap, rework, replacement and repair under warranty, and handling customers' complaints) lie in the range of 4 per cent – 15 per cent of turnover, with an average of around 10 per cent. Based on the 1976 Census of Production figure of sales by UK manufacturers, quality costs in the UK could be of the order of £10,000 million per year.[2]

SPECIFICATIONS

A specification is a detailed description of the requirements to which products must conform. These requirements may include the chemical composition of the material to be used, its physical properties (strength, ductility, porosity, particle size, viscosity, electrical or thermal conductivity), dimensions of the product, its weight, colour, surface finish etc. In each case it is necessary to specify the tolerance on each desired characteristic, i.e. the range of values over which a property may vary without causing the product to become unacceptable.

It is at this stage that the design, quality engineering, procurement and production staff can realise significant cost savings. Too wide tolerances can lead to problems in subsequent manufacture or use, as when a number of components must be assembled together. Typical examples of such problems include furniture manufacture where out-of-square components give poor joints and an unsatisfactory appearance; clothing manufacture where excessive cutting tolerances can lead to badly sewn seams which may pull apart in use, or to garments which vary too much from the stated size. In mechanical engineering inadequate clearance between moving parts can lead to seizure, but excessive clearances may prevent effective operation or allow loss of lubricants and hence premature failure.

On the other hand, excessively stringent tolerances lead to other increased costs. For most items previous experience will indicate the appropriate quality level to adopt but in the case of new designs and materials, testing of a product under actual or simulated service conditions may be necessary in order to establish suitable specifications.

Most of the desired properties of an item can be expressed in figures, e.g.

length 295 – 299 mm
weight 113.40g ± 2.83g

These are termed *variables.* (Note that the method used to illustrate length involves specifying only the upper and lower limits. This format is preferred because it avoids the arithmetic needed to add and subtract tolerances from a nominal figure, which could lead to mistakes.)

Attributes are properties which are not defined in figures, such as:

'all bar ends to be painted green'
'all edges to be free from burrs'
'all items to be stamped with part number'

In all such cases an item can only be classed as acceptable or unacceptable. Attributes are generally less satisfactory as standards because they can be more difficult to interpret. A statement that 'timber is to be straight and free from cracks' does not define precisely acceptable limits. However there are inevitably situations where certain desired properties cannot readily be reduced to figures, such as taste or smell in the food and toiletries industries. Colours are often checked by an experienced person comparing items with a previously agreed standard sample, or with two samples showing light and dark limits.

A standard commodity specification for tomato paste (see Figure 7.3), a widely used constituent of many foodstuffs, illustrates the use of both quantitative and qualitative requirements, and statements of the ways in which certain of these properties are to be measured.

When widely recognised standards exist for a product they should be adopted if at all possible. The starting point when establishing a specification for a product not previously bought or manufactured should be a review of current international, national or industry standards. The ISO Catalogue, *British Standards Yearbook* or appropriate industry associations should be consulted. A company standard should be developed only if no appropriate, more widely used standard exists.

QUALITY CONTROL OF INCOMING RAW MATERIALS AND COMPONENTS

It is a basic principle of quality control that non-conforming items are identified as early as possible. Any work carried out on materials which are unacceptable is simply wasted money; it is not normally possible to recover from suppliers the costs of any work done on such materials.

Most companies operate some system of goods-inward inspection, although reliance on such a system alone is unwise. Incoming

STANDARD COMMODITY SPECIFICATION	No. 0114

TITLE:
 	
      TOMATO PASTE (HOT BREAK)
 	
COMMODITY CODE: 0114
	Date Issued
	      1.4.85
	
	replaces —

DETAILS

1 GENERAL REQUIREMENTS

Tomato paste shall be the product resulting from the concentration of the liquid obtained from clean, sound, well ripened tomatoes of red varieties. Free from skin, seed particles, black specks, foreign material, added salt or colourings and harmful contaminants.

2 ORGANOLEPTIC REQUIREMENTS

2.1 *Flavour and Aroma*
Free from scorched, bitter, green tomato flavours or other objectionable flavours or objectionable odours of any kind.

2.2 *Colour*
Gardner Colour difference meter targets at 12½% total solids by refractometer: L 25 ± 1, a 25 +, b + less than ½a.

3 ANALYTICAL REQUIREMENTS (on sample(s) as designated by an approved random sampling method)

3.1 *Consistency*
Consistency below 10.0 cms measured by Bostwick consistometer at 12½% total solids by refractometer 25°C for 10 secs.

3.2 *Copper (as Cu)*
Not more than 50 p.p.m. calculated on dry residue.

3.3 *Lead (as Pb)*
Not more than 5 p.p.m. on the concentrate.

4 MICROBIOLOGICAL REQUIREMENTS

4.1 *Mould Count*
Not exceeding 50% positive fields as determined by the Howard Mould Count Method.

4.2 *Insect fragments*
Free from insect eggs, hairs or fragments.

5 MANUFACTURING AND PACKAGING REQUIREMENTS

5.1 *Screen Size*
The tomato paste shall be processed using 0.60 m.m. finishing screens.

5.2 *Cans*
In accordance with can specification attached.

5.3 *Filled weights*
5.1 kg Gross for Net.

5.4 *Cases*
In accordance with case specification attached.

Figure 7.3 Commodity specification for tomato paste

goods must be held in quarantine until all inspection has been carried out. Even for relatively simple chemical analysis this may take two or three days from receipt of the material to reporting of the results to production control and the user department. In the case of more specialised tests such as wear tests on textiles, creep or corrosion tests on metals, considerably longer quarantine periods may be necessary. This extends the real lead time for the material, and increases the buying company's stock levels. Holding material in separate quarantine or inspection areas may also involve double handling, but failure to do so allows the risk of material which has not yet passed inspection being used by mistake. Any material rejected after delivery increases transport costs unnecessarily. For these and other reasons many manufacturing companies are placing greater reliance on supplier quality assurance (q.v.). Inspection of incoming goods from approved suppliers can then be reduced to a minimum, which may be little more than a check on documentation and quantities, and possibly a visual check for damage in transit.

Incoming goods inspection will still be necessary for supplies which are bought from non-approved suppliers, at home or abroad, where the cost of a supplier quality assurance approval survey may not be justified. Where incoming goods inspection is necessary it must at least ensure the following:

1 Identification of inspected material to distinguish it from that awaiting inspection.
2 The use of suitable sampling and test procedures.
3 Control of inspection, measuring and test equipment.
4 Segregation of non-conforming material.
5 Maintenance of inspection records which can be related to other documentation (purchase orders, works orders/batch cards, customers' orders).

CONTROL OF QUALITY IN MANUFACTURING

Every manufacturing process suffers from variability. The task of quality control in manufacturing is to ensure that the variations in the properties of a manufactured product are contained within the specified tolerances. The success, or otherwise, of this control determines the conformance quality of the items produced. The emphasis will vary depending on the type of production, but in most cases the following elements will be involved:

1 Specification of requirements: accurate, adequate and up-to-date.
2 Control of incoming raw material, as outlined above.
3 Control of tooling.
4 Control of manufacturing processes.
5 Calibration of instrumentation and measuring equipment.
6 Inspection.

Jobbing production

Production runs are short, work is usually only to customer's order, and often customer's specification. It is difficult to establish standard inspection programmes in such work, and common practice is for skilled operators to be responsible for setting equipment, making or assembling the product, and inspecting it, possibly with additional patrol inspection or technical support facilities. In such circumstances the quality assurance programme would emphasise:

1 Drawing and change control: work instructions to operators must refer to current drawings and manufacturing instructions. Obsolete versions must be withdrawn.
2 Observance of manufacturing and inspection instructions.
3 Maintenance of records of manufacturing and inspection data for each job.
4 Checking that measuring and inspection equipment is calibrated. While this is essential in any type of manufacturing, it can more easily be overlooked if each operator retains instruments such as micrometers or gauges for his own use.

Batch production

Three main forms of inspection are available:

1 Inspection of all items produced in a batch (i.e. 100 per cent inspection).
2 Inspection of a sample of items from a completed batch.

3 First-off inspection at the start of a batch, followed by periodic sampling during manufacture.

One hundred per cent inspection is time consuming and is normally used only for small batches. Sample inspection after manufacture would be used where an entire batch is processed together but where it is unnecessary or impractical to inspect every item, e.g. heat treatment of metal items, firing of pottery.

Most batch production involves setting a machine, then processing a quantity of items individually before re-setting for a subsequent batch of different products. In such cases it is normal to carry out first-off inspection to verify that tooling, setting, operating methods and material are in accordance with specification. Where a machine is set by a skilled setter, but subsequently operated by another person, the first-off samples should be those produced by the production operator, to ensure that the operator is using the correct method. Typical problems which might arise are failure to coat a pattern or die with a mould release agent, or failure to apply lubricant correctly in presswork operations.

Once initial samples have been approved, further samples should be taken throughout production of the batch. The frequency of sampling should take account of production rate, the quality levels required, the variability of the production process, and the need for periodic re-setting. Control charting (q.v.) could be an appropriate aid for periodic inspection.

Process production

In continuous process production the emphasis lies on process control, with inspection at intermediate and final stages to verify that controls are operating satisfactorily. Continuous in-process measuring of sizes, temperatures etc. can be linked to process controls. A typical example would be the rolling of continuous steel strip or rod, where measurements of gauge and temperature at one stage can be used to adjust automatically the settings of rolls (roll gap, speed) at earlier stages (feed-back control) or subsequent stages (feed-forward control) to compensate for variations in the product.

STATISTICAL QUALITY CONTROL: CONTROL CHARTS

All manufacturing processes suffer from variability, and all products will exhibit variations in their measured properties. Even two items with apparently identical dimensions will be found to differ if measured with sufficient accuracy. The use of statistical techniques to recognise and hence control such variability is an essential element of every quality assurance programme, two common applications being control charts and acceptance sampling. A thorough grounding in statistical theory is not generally necessary. Both techniques can be adopted by reference to standard procedures.

The theory underlying the use of the control chart originated by Dr W. A. Shewhart is that the variations in the quality of manufactured products can be divided into two categories: random variations and variations due to assignable causes. Random variations are those resulting from a large number of chance variations, each too small to isolate, but which together lead to the expected variability in final quality. If this expected pattern changes, it is inferred that some additional, or assignable, factor has caused this change.

The method relies on inspecting small samples, typically four or five, measuring the property under investigation, and using the results obtained from this small sample to deduce the properties of the parent population from which the sample was drawn. The charts are constructed to give three signals which can be considered as a set of traffic lights:

green = safe to proceed
amber = warning, re-check process
red = action, stop process.

Let us consider the production of an engineering component having a specified diameter of 9.78 to 10.00mm. Suppose the manufacturing process is set to produce pieces with a diameter of 9.90mm, and that the inevitable random variations lead to the items having a standard deviation of 0.03mm as shown in Figure 7.4.

If a single item was inspected it might be found to have a diameter of 10.00mm, i.e. at the upper limit of tolerance, and one might therefore deduce that the process needed adjustment. There is,

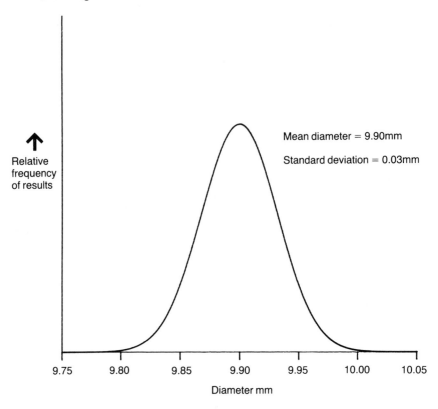

Figure 7.4 Distribution of diameters

however, a chance of about 1 in 2,000 of the process producing this size even when it is correctly set at 9.90mm.

Other problems which may arise when using single items as the basis for control are that the distribution of the parent population may neither be normal nor may it follow any standard distribution; it is difficult to detect changes in the process average from individual measurements unless the change is large; and there is no indication whether a change is in the mean or the standard deviation, or both.

If, on the other hand, a sample of four is taken, it is extremely unlikely that all four pieces will lie towards one extremity of the distribution as long as the process is operating normally.

The use of a small sample instead of individual results overcomes other problems.

1 It is immaterial whether the parent population is normally distributed or not, since the sampling distribution of the means will be sufficiently close to normal for all practical purposes.

2 The number of sample means which fall more than a specified distance away from the overall mean will indicate the degree of control in the process.

3 The ability to detect changes in the process average is greatly increased.

4 Samples allow detection of changes in process variability as well as process average.

Suppose four such pieces have diameters of 10.00mm, 9.88mm, 9.95mm, 9.89mm, giving an average of 9.93mm (although the machine may still be correctly set at 9.90mm). There is no apparent need to adjust the process, but we must decide how far the average diameter of our sample can be allowed to vary before adjustment becomes necessary.

Knowledge of the properties of the normal distribution shows that the standard deviation of the sampling distribution of the mean σ_m is related to the standard deviation of the parent population σ as

$$\sigma_m = \sigma/\sqrt{n}$$

where n = sample size. With samples of four, the distribution of the means will have a mean of 9.90mm with a standard deviation of 0.015mm as long as the process continues unchanged. Detection of changes from this pattern provides the basis for the control chart.

Figure 7.5 shows the principle of the control chart. The chance of the mean diameter of a sample of four items falling above 9.945mm (or below 9.855mm) is only about 1 in 1,000. When it does happen, it is most likely that the process has changed, and that individual items may therefore be larger than 9.99mm (or smaller than 9.81mm). The process should therefore be stopped, the reason for the change investigated, and corrective action taken.

The chance of the sample mean lying above 9.93mm (or below 9.87mm) is about 1 in 40, i.e. it would be expected to occur once in every 40 samples. When it does happen, however, there are grounds for suspicion and the usual procedure is to take another sample immediately before deciding whether adjustment is necessary.

The sample means can be plotted on the chart using time or

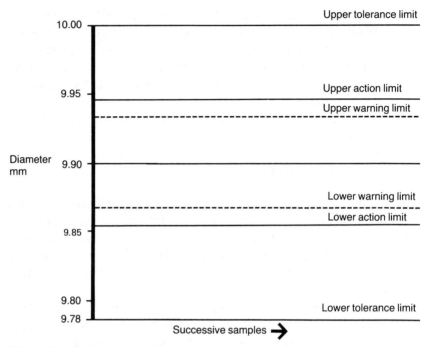

Figure 7.5 Control chart for averages

number produced on the horizontal axis, which will highlight any drift in the manufacturing process, as often occurs due to tool wear. As illustrated in this example, the control chart limits do not need to be set symmetrically within the tolerance. They may be moved towards one extremity (in this case towards a nominal diameter of 10mm), but this of course reduces the effective tolerance available to the producer.

This example also illustrates the importance of the relationship between process variability and the specified tolerance. If the production equipment is set to give a mean product diameter of 9.90mm, the variability quoted ($\sigma = 0.03$mm) would result in five items in 10,000 having a diameter greater than the upper tolerance of 10.00mm. If the mean diameter shifts to 9.95mm, as illustrated in Figure 7.6, we would expect 4.85 per cent of the output to exceed the upper tolerance, i.e. nearly 5 per cent of the items would be defective.

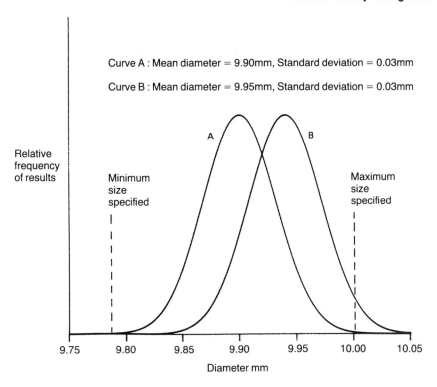

Curve A : Mean diameter = 9.90mm, Standard deviation = 0.03mm

Curve B : Mean diameter = 9.95mm, Standard deviation = 0.03mm

Figure 7.6 Shift in the distribution of diameters

A production process with less variability is illustrated in Figure 7.7, where the standard deviation on diameter is 0.02mm. In this case when the process is set to give a mean diameter of 9.90mm we would not expect any items to be produced outside the tolerance limits (if they are, we should immediately look for an assignable cause). Furthermore, even if the process drifts so that the average diameter increases to 9.95mm, we would still only expect about six items in 1,000 to fall outside the upper specification limit.

This simple example illustrates the importance of determining process variability, and comparing it with the required product tolerances. From a buyer's point of view the converse should be considered: given the specification for an item, what normal degree of process variability must a supplier achieve if he is to be regarded as being capable of producing consistently acceptable output?

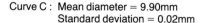

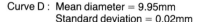

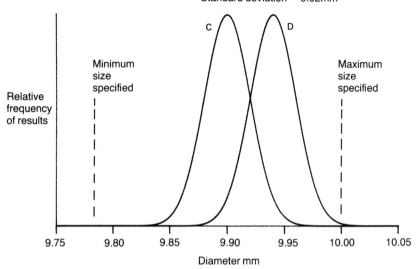

Figure 7.7 Distribution of diameters with less variability

DETECTION OF CHANGES IN VARIABILITY

It is possible for the process mean to remain the same (i.e. 9.90mm) but for the variability to increase. The sample means would lie outside the warning and action limits more often, and action could be taken to adjust the process (both up and down) more frequently, but the process would still not be under control.

Another form of chart, the range chart, is necessary to control this aspect. To construct a range chart, the normal range between the largest and smallest measurement in each small sample (four in the above case) is found for about 20 samples taken when the process is operating normally. Range limits are set by multiplying the average range from the initial 20 samples by a factor which depends on sample size. For the case illustrated, warning and action limits could be set as shown in Figure 7.8.

Control charts can be constructed for attributes, where the decision to accept or reject a batch depends on either the number of

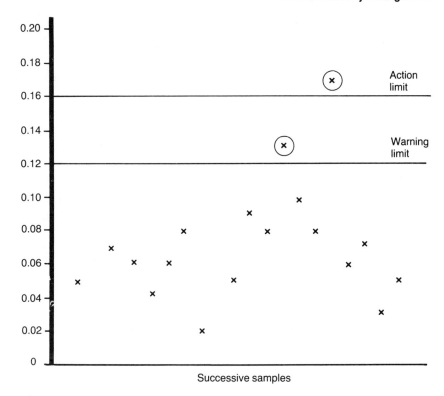

Figure 7.8 Range chart for samples of four items

defective items in a sample, or on the total number of defects in an article. The basic principles of construction are similar to charts for quantitative data, but the method is less sensitive.

ACCEPTANCE SAMPLING

Inspection is an expensive activity. Products where defects are not critical need not be subject to 100 per cent inspection. To allow a few defective items to get through is not a serious matter. In a box of 100 cheap ball-point pens it is not critical if two or three do not write properly, but the proportion which are defective should not be allowed to rise significantly.

In industries where the product is a vital one, where lives may depend upon its quality, or where the costs of failure would be abnormally high, every effort must be made to ensure that every item is satisfactory. There is no substitute for 100 per cent inspection, in fact it may be necessary at various stages of manufacture, and at final assembly.

Even 100 per cent inspection is not necessarily absolutely reliable. An interesting paper by Peter Cavanagh and Alec Rodger reports results of 100 per cent visual inspection of glass jars. Jars, from three different suppliers, were divided into three grades based on initial inspection results. Each jar was then inspected by each of four inspectors on 30 separate occasions, making 120 inspections for every jar. The research showed significant variations in the results of the inspections. The authors add:

> You may be interested to learn, in passing, that not a single one of the 648 survived without at least one rejection. For a time it looked as if one jar would escape condemnation. After going through 60 of its 120 inspections its reputation was still intact, even if the jar itself was not unblemished. When the investigators got out this apparently perfect jar to have a good look at it, they found a surface flaw an inch long on its side. Reference to the log book in which marked particularities of jars had been noted confirmed that it had been there from the outset.[3]

Some experiments have indicated that if inspectors are faced with batches for 100 per cent inspection, then the inspection tends to be less reliable than if sample methods are used.

Other obvious applications of sample inspections are when inspection is costly or time consuming, or when destructive testing must be used.

If it is recognised that some proportion of a batch of products is likely to be below the specified quality, but a certain proportion of such defective items in a batch can be tolerated, it is possible to apply sampling plans which give reasonably reliable results at minimum cost.

All too frequently sampling inspection is used without adequate consideration of the appropriate sample size. Instructions such as 'inspect 10 per cent' are given, but testing one sample from a batch of ten tells one nothing about the other nine. Testing 10 per cent of a batch of 50,000 would be quite unnecessary; a reasonable sample from which sufficiently reliable results could be obtained would be 500 items, i.e. 1 per cent of the batch.

Statistical sampling plans must be tailored to each particular inspection situation. Once a sampling plan has been chosen, it gives an inspector a simple set of instructions for inspecting each batch of items. In essence the sampling inspection tables say:

> For a batch of size N take a random sample of size n.
>
> Inspect all items in the sample.
>
> If the number of defective items is less than or equal to the acceptance number c, accept the entire batch.
>
> If the number of defective items is more than c, reject the entire batch.

For any given set of conditions a small, *known* risk is taken of making a wrong decision on the evidence from the sample.

The sampling plan depends on four factors:

1 *The batch size* A batch is a definite quantity of items which have been produced under conditions which are presumed to be uniform. If one type of item has been produced on two alternate machines, it would be normal for the manufacturer to keep separate the output from each machine, and to draw a sample from each batch. In this way the output of each machine is checked, and should quality decline the cause may be attributed more easily. When using sampling inspection for incoming goods, each consignment from a supplier would normally be regarded as a separate batch. The assumption is made that items sent in one consignment are more likely to be alike than are items in different consignments.

2 *The acceptable quality level (AQL)* The AQL is the level of quality, i.e. the percentage of defects, which is only just acceptable as a process average. For example, if an AQL of 1 per cent is set, we should be prepared to accept up to this percentage of defective items without question. The fact that an AQL is stated should not be construed as meaning that a manufacturer has the right knowingly to supply defective products. It is always better to have no defective items than any specified proportion.

3 *Inspection level* The inspection level defines the relationship

between batch size and sample size. Normal inspection is used unless otherwise specified. This seeks to balance inspection effort and reliability. If greater reliability is required, e.g. if there is reason to suspect that the process average has deteriorated, tighter inspection may be called for and larger samples would then be taken. Conversely, if the inspection effort can be lessened, reduced inspection and hence smaller samples may be appropriate. Special sampling plans are available for situations where very small samples must be used, e.g. when inspection is extremely expensive or where destructive testing must be used, and where low reliability of sampling inspection can or must be tolerated.

4 *Whether single, double or multiple sampling is to be used* Single sampling plans, which are the simplest to operate, accept or condemn a batch on the evidence of a single sample taken from the batch. The inspection effort may be reduced without loss of reliability by adopting double or multiple sampling. A smaller initial sample is taken, followed by a second if, and only if, the result of the first is inconclusive. For example:

Take a sample of 32 items. If there are no defectives accept the batch. If there are two or more defectives reject it. If there is one defective only, take a further sample of 32 items. If the second sample contains no defectives or only one defective, accept the batch. If it contains two or more, reject the batch.

Using this plan, the decision would in most cases, be made on the evidence from a sample of 32 items; only occasionally would two samples be taken. If single sampling were used under the same conditions a sample of 50 items would be taken from every batch.

The risks involved in acceptance sampling

While the use of acceptance sampling is straightforward, the selection of an appropriate sampling plan for any given situation requires an understanding of the risks which are being taken. Suppose that we are concerned with inspecting large batches of items, which can be classified as good or bad. A simple example might be checking electric light bulbs to ensure that they work. A manufacturer, major user or distributor of such items may wish to verify that quality control in production was effective and that there had not been excessive damage in transit. It would be unrealistic to insist that every bulb works; an acceptable quality level of 2.5 per cent might be agreed between supplier and purchaser. We would thus be prepared to accept batches with one or less defective bulbs in 40. A simple inspection plan might therefore seem to be to take a sample of $n = 40$ and inspect them, i.e. test to see if they light. If one or no bulbs are defective, accept the batch; if two or more, reject the batch. The maximum number of defective items permitted in the sample is called the acceptance number c; in this $c = 1$.

However, it is of course not certain that a random sample of 40 bulbs out of a large batch would contain two or more defectives even if the batch itself contained significantly more than 2.5 per cent. The probability that any given number of defectives will occur in a sample from a large batch may be calculated from the binomial distribution. If a batch contained no defective items (and assuming that inspection itself is faultless) clearly our sample of 40 would be accepted correctly. We can say that the probability of no defectives (P_0) is 1.0000.

Another batch may in fact contain 5 per cent of defective bulbs, although we do not know this. The probability of taking a sample of 40 which contains no defectives may be calculated as $p_0 = 0.95^{40}$, i.e. 0.1285.

Similarly, the chance of a sample of 40 containing only one defective may be calculated as

$$p_1 = 40. \ (0.95)^{39} \ (0.05)^1, \text{ i.e. } 0.2706.$$

The chance of our sample containing either no defectives or one defective is therefore $0.1285 + 0.2706 = 0.3991$. We can see that the sampling plan proposed ($n=40$, $c=1$) will give a result which leads to the batch being accepted on about 40 per cent of the occasions even when the actual percentage of defective bulbs is 5 per cent, i.e. twice the acceptable quality level.

The calculation may be repeated for various values of the percentage defective in the batch as shown below:

% defective in batch	Chance of sample of 40 containing 0 or 1 defectives
0	1.0000
0.5	0.9828
1.0	0.9393
1.5	0.8874
2.0	0.8095
2.5	0.7358
3.0	0.6615
5.0	0.3991
7.5	0.1877
10.0	0.0665
15.0	0.0121

Plotting these results gives what is known as the operating characteristic, or OC curve, of the specified sampling plan as shown in Figure 7.9. Note that the OC gives the probability of accepting a batch with any given percentage of defective items on the evidence of a sample of 40 and an acceptance number of 1 (or less) defectives.

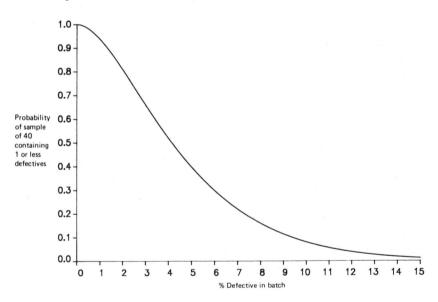

Figure 7.9 Operating characteristic (OC), curve for the sampling plan $n = 40, c = 1$

Now the risks involved in operating this particular sampling plan can be appreciated. Although we have agreed that up to 2.5 per cent of defective bulbs is acceptable, there are 4 chances in 10 that a batch containing 5 per cent of defective bulbs will be accepted, nearly 2 chances in 10 ($p = 0.1877$) of accepting a batch with 7.5 per cent of defectives, and even a slight chance ($p = 0.0121$) of accepting an exceptionally bad batch containing 15 per cent of defective bulbs.

On the other hand there are about 2 chances in 10 ($p = 1-0.8095 = 0.1905$) of rejecting a batch containing only 2 per cent of defective bulbs, i.e. a level of defectives which is less than the maximum we have agreed to accept. We may therefore decide that the risks of making an incorrect decision on the evidence from this sampling plan ($n=40$, $c=1$) are too great. Compare this scheme with two others: $n = 80$, $c = 2$; and $n = 200$, $c = 5$ as shown in Figure 7.10.

Comparing these three OC curves we see that the larger the sample, the more discriminating is the sampling scheme, but even a large sample ($n=200$) involves risks of making incorrect decisions. A more discriminating scheme is not inherently a 'better' one. It is

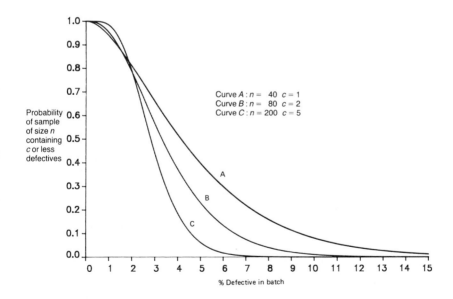

Figure 7.10 Three OC curves for different parameters

more reliable, but involves inspecting larger samples and hence is more expensive. It is, therefore, more appropriate in some circumstances and less appropriate in others.

In deriving these illustrative OC curves it has been assumed that the probability of defective items being present in the sample remained unchanged throughout, i.e. remained as the proportion defective in the batch. Where finite batches are involved there are, of course, only a limited number of defective items in the batch and the probability of drawing a defective item varies from trial to trial. For example, if one has a very large number of packs of cards, the chance of drawing an ace is 1 in 13. Even if one has already drawn three cards at random, and all were aces, the probability of drawing another is still 1 in 13. However, if one draws three aces from a single pack of cards, the probability of drawing a fourth has changed considerably; there is only one ace left in the remaining 49 cards, and the probability is therefore 1 in 49.

The OC curves derived for sampling from finite batches therefore take account of this aspect, but the principles for selecting a sampling plan remain the same. Both producer (supplier) and consumer (purchaser) carry some risk. The producer's risk is the chance that the manufacturing section or supplier wrongly rejects a batch of material which contains less than the maximum acceptable percentage of defects. In most cases the producer would submit such a batch to 100 per cent inspection to sort good items from bad. At the end of this exercise he would find that the percentage of defects was in fact less than the maximum allowed, and he would thus have incurred unnecessary inspection costs. This risk is therefore termed the 'producer's risk'.

On the other hand a user or purchaser carries a risk of wrongly accepting a batch which contains more than a maximum permitted percentage of defectives. This is termed the consumer's risk, and is often set as 10 per cent. This does not mean that 10 per cent of all batches accepted should have been rejected. It means that the plan gives the wrong answer on 10 per cent of the occasions when the percentage of defects exceeds the permitted maximum level. Suppose that over a period a supplier sends 100 batches of bulbs, 80 batches being good and 20 batches containing more than the permitted maximum percentage of defects. We would expect to accept wrongly 10 per cent of these 'bad' batches:

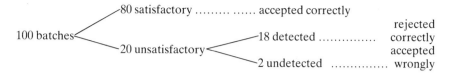

100 batches
— 80 satisfactory .... accepted correctly
— 20 unsatisfactory
— 18 detected .... rejected correctly
— 2 undetected .... accepted wrongly

Sampling schemes may therefore be tailored to give a high level of protection to either the producer or the consumer. In the former case the maximum allowable percentage of defectives is called the acceptable quality level (AQL). In the latter case the maximum percentage of defects is referred to as the 'lot tolerance percent defective' (LTPD); the consumer therefore seeks a high degree of protection against accepting batches containing more than this figure.

Once the degree of protection required is known, standard sampling plans may be drawn from standard tables such as those given in BS6001:1972. A guide to the use of these tables is also available (BS6000:1972). Where the particular property being checked can be measured, rather than simply classified as good or bad, and where the variability in that property follows the normal distribution, inspection can be based on the measured property in much the same way as for control charts. The sample sizes are usually much smaller than those for sampling plans based on attributes. For details see BS6002:1979.

SUPPLIER QUALITY ASSURANCE

Maintaining the necessary levels of quality of bought-in raw materials, components or finished products is a key part of any quality assurance programme, and the inspection of incoming supplies is frequently necessary. But inspection at this stage cannot change quality levels: it can only sort bad items from good. Increasingly, buying organisations are seeking to ensure that their suppliers operate adequate quality assurance systems, so that the buyer can rely on incoming goods being of acceptable quality. Among the many factors contributing to this shift of emphasis are the following.

1 In high volume manufacturing industry (e.g. assembly of cars,

electrical appliances etc.), rejections of incoming items could lead to costly stoppages in production.

2   With many complex products, the required level of quality can be assured only by adequate quality control throughout all stages of manufacture. It is not adequate, nor practicable, to rely only on inspection of incoming products to detect faults. The buyer has no option but to rely on the supplier operating a sound quality assurance system, and may therefore seek reassurance that the supplier's QA system is adequate. In many cases this reliance on the supplier extends to his design capabilities also.

3   The growth of legislation placing greater demands on manufacturers to ensure the quality of finished products means that they, in turn, are demanding better quality assurance from suppliers. Industries particularly subject to such legislation include aircraft and automotive engineering, nuclear power plant manufacturing, and food processing. The growth of product liability legislation is likely to give a further boost to the vetting of suppliers' quality systems.

Large organisations generally carry out their own assessment of major suppliers. Alternatively such assessment might be carried out by a third party: the Kitemark scheme operated by the British Standards Institution is a widely known example of such a scheme, giving purchasers an assurance that items so marked comply with a British Standard. It involves not only the testing of the product, but also inspection of the manufacturer's works. More recently, BSI has established a system for the registration of firms of assessed capability,[4] which involves assessment of firms which are applying against specified quality system requirements including scrutiny of the firm's quality control manual and periodic site visits. Firms which meet the appropriate quality standards are then included in the register.

The initial widespread use of formal schemes to assess the quality capabilities of suppliers, as opposed to inspection of finished products, was in the field of military procurement. The NATO Allied Quality Assurance Publications were adopted in slightly modified form as a series of Ministry of Defence standards (05/21 to 05/29). The requirements laid down in these provided the basis for a series of guides (BS5179:1972) on the assessment of manufacturers' quality assurance systems. The recommendations given in BS5179 were subsequently incorporated in BS5750:1979 as requirements. A series of guides to BS5750 parts 1, 2 and 3 have subsequently been issued as BS5750, parts 4, 5 and 6 respectively, and have replaced BS5179.

The appraisal of the manufacturer's QA system needs to reflect the type of work which he is to undertake. Many systems for vetting suppliers' quality capabilities classify work into three categories, reflecting the extent to which one relies on the manufacturer.

QUALITY SYSTEMS

For final inspection and test

At the simplest level it may be possible to assess the quality of a product by final inspection. If one is to rely on the supplier for such final inspection, it would obviously be wise to check that the supplier does, in fact, use appropriate inspection facilities, that instruments and test equipment are properly calibrated, that sampling inspection methods are sufficiently reliable, etc. One would also seek reassurance on other factors such as the ways in which the manufacturer checks incoming materials and segregates any rejected materials or items.

For manufacture

For many manufactured products, conformance with requirements can only be ensured by proper control throughout production, including inspection at a number of intermediate stages. Work of this nature inevitably requires that the manufacturer has a more extensive system of quality control if a customer is to rely upon it. In addition to those aspects involved in quality systems for final inspection and test, the manufacturer must use a reliable system of giving work instructions to production operatives, and therefore needs a reliable system to ensure corrective action if faults arise during manufacture.

For design and manufacture

In both the above categories, the supplier is responsible for manufacture but is not responsible for design. Where a supplier is to be responsible not only for manufacturing a product, but also for its design, a buyer would seek further reassurances that design activities and any related product testing were also sufficiently rigorous.

These three levels of quality requirements provide a rational basis for assessing potential suppliers. The *minimum* criteria to be satisfied if a buying organisation is to rely on a supplier's quality system are suggested in Figure 7.11.

QUALITY AUDITS

Any management system should be subject to periodic reviews to check its effectiveness. The quality audit is to the quality system what the accounting audit is to the financial system. The accounting audit seeks not only to verify the accuracy of a company's accounting and financial records, but also to review the effectiveness of the control system itself. Similarly, the quality audit seeks not only to check on the quality of a finished product and the performance of the inspectors, but also to review the adequacy of the entire quality assurance system. Most aspects of the quality audit are the same as the aspects investigated under a supplier quality assurance survey. Specific aspects would include:

1 Checking that measuring and testing equipment is correctly calibrated, that calibration has been carried out regularly and that records support this.
2 Checking that operators and inspectors have, and follow, up-to-date drawings, work instructions and inspection methods, and that practice conforms to the quality control manual.
3 Review of inspection records and analysis of rejections.
4 Review of customer complaints.
5 Rechecking work passed by inspectors. A typical example from the motor industry illustrates the extent of such rechecking.

Requirements	Level of approval		
	Final inspection	Manufacture	Design and manufacture
Appropriate quality system	✓	✓	✓
Appropriate organisation and defined responsibilities	✓	✓	✓
Periodic review of the quality system. Records of such reviews to be available to purchaser's representative		✓	✓
QA planning system			✓
Control of design activities, including design reviews			✓
Documentation and change control to ensure up-to-date production and inspection procedures are followed		✓	✓
Work instructions to ensure adequate standards of workmanship		✓	✓
Manufacturing operations carried out under suitable conditions		✓	✓
In process inspection at appropriate stages		✓	✓
Inspection and testing of completed items	✓	✓	✓
Control and calibration of inspection measuring and test equipment	✓	✓	✓
Use of specified sampling procedures	✓	✓	✓
Adequate records of inspection etc. to substantiate conformance to specified requirements	✓	✓	✓
Quality control of purchased materials, components and services		✓	✓
Control of purchaser-supplied material		✓	✓
Effective systems to distinguish between inspected and non-inspected materials and products	✓	✓	✓
Identification, control and disposition of non-conforming material	✓	✓	✓
Suitable packaging, handling, storage and delivery to maintain product quality	✓	✓	✓
Appropriate staff training schemes	✓	✓	✓

Figure 7.11 Requirements to be satisfied by suppliers for each level of approval

Complete vehicles are taken periodically from final assembly, together with the production inspectors' records. The vehicle is then completely disassembled by a quality audit team, who recheck the quality of items used (dimensions, surface finish etc.) and the quality of manufacture. The latter includes checking the torque applied to fasteners used in assembly, the quantities of lubricants and coolants used, the fit and alignment of sub-assemblies such as lights and steering, and numerous similar checks.

QUALITY POLICY AND MANAGEMENT

Figures 7.1 and 7.2 indicated the need to select the target levels of quality and quality control. Increasingly the activities of customers and other bodies, particularly governmental, are influencing the quality policies and practices of manufacturing companies. A manufacturing company which wishes to sell, directly or indirectly, to organisations which operate supplier quality assurance systems, will have to operate a quality assurance programme adequate for the desired class of approval.

Industries such as automotive, aerospace and electrical equipment manufacture, where finished products are subject to legislative control on standards of safety, already have extensive quality assurance schemes. Manufacturers in other industries can expect to have to follow suit, if this is not yet the case. Other, more general, legislation will also lead to manufacturers extending their QA systems to meet customer demands.

Organising for quality

Quality is everybody's business. The achievement of the desired level of quality requires effective contributions from every function. It should be appreciated that:

1 Responsibility for defining customers' quality requirements rests primarily with the marketing function.
2 Responsibility for the design and specification of a product rests primarily with design and production engineering.

3 Responsibility for producing goods to specification rests primarily with manufacturing.

What, then, is the role of a quality assurance department? Rather than try to usurp the quality responsibilities of other functions, the quality department should advise and assist on all quality tasks, and co-ordinate and monitor them throughout the whole organisation. Activities which are likely to be the direct responsibility of an independent quality function are:

1 Developing the quality assurance programme and quality manual.
2 Operation of the quality control programme.
3 Exercising control of incoming and defective materials.
4 Metrology and calibration of test equipment.
5 Analysis of quality records, particularly defect/failure analysis.
6 Measurement and reporting of quality cost.
7 Ensuring that training in quality matters is effective throughout the company.

It should perhaps be emphasised that the responsibility of the quality department for operation of the quality control system (2 above) must give adequate authority to quality control staff to reject defective items and, if necessary, to halt production. Many organisations assessing the quality assurance system of a supplier place particular emphasis on the organisational aspects:

> Effective management for quality assurance should be clearly prescribed, and delegated personnel should be given both the responsibility and authority to identify and evaluate quality problems and to initiate, recommend or provide solutions.
> The supplier shall appoint a management representative, preferably independent of other functions, who shall have the necessary authority and the responsibility for ensuring that the requirements of this standard are implemented and maintained.[5]

QUALITY CIRCLES

The belief that quality is everybody's business underlies the concept of quality circles which are helping to improve quality in a number of companies. Examples include Rolls Royce's Aero Division in Derby, where cost savings of over £500,000 were achieved in 2½ years. Machining problems on turbine blades leading to scrap rate of 4 per cent were investigated. As a result of improvements identified by the operatives concerned, rejections were cut to 0.5 per cent, saving £26,000 per year. Defective welds on turbine blades were reduced from 24 per cent to 1.8 per cent. Investigations showed the need to amend welding techniques, and led to annual savings of about £77,000.[6]

Quality circles originated in Japan and are now used on a wide scale, over 10 million workers being circle members. About 250 companies in the US have adopted the concept, and at least 40 companies in Britain, including BL, Ford, Marks and Spencer (and a number of its suppliers), Mullard and Wedgwood.

The concept is simple, although the practice requires a change from traditional management attitudes. A small group of operatives selects and investigates quality problems in its own area of work under the guidance of a suitably trained leader. In order to work effectively, the group members should be provided with appropriate training in carrying out systematic investigations, problem solving and the presentation of their proposals.

The quality circle is entirely voluntary, selects its own problems for investigation, and puts forward its own proposals. The involvement and commitment generated by this process encourages those directly involved, who are likely to know most about the causes of quality problems, to contribute their experience, knowledge and skill to the solution of these problems.

REFERENCES

(1) British Standards Institution BS 4778: 1971. Glossary of General Terms used in Quality Assurance.
(2) *A National Strategy for Quality: a Consultative Document*, Department of Prices and Consumer Protection, 1978.
(3) P. Cavanagh and A. Rodger, 'Some Hidden Determinants of Inspectors' Judgements' in *British Journal of Occupational Psychology*, July 1964.
(4) British Standards Institution System for the Registration of

Firms of Assessed Capability BSI 1977.

(5) British Standards Institution BS 5750: Part 6: 1981, p. 1.

(6) D. Hutchins, 'How quality goes round in circles' in *Management Today*, January 1981.

8

Purchasing schedule management

Andrew Green

A schedule is a request made by a company for material requirements compatible with the production process. A schedule is placed between the company and its suppliers or within different manufacturing units of the same organisation.

This chapter outlines the basic requirements and mechanics of a schedule and demonstrates the application of this system in two different industrial production environments. The first example is a mass-production assembly line producing washing machines, and the second, the building of a special purpose machine tool.

The application of material schedules to each example is discussed in detail, but then, concentrating on the mass-production assembly line, several different approaches to effective schedule and materials management are discussed.

Schedule management is about risk. With correct forward planning and by taking real account of shopfloor problems a materials manager can reduce the risk to production to an acceptable level and at the same time maintain low stock levels and inventory costs.

However, in the future whilst the stock levels may be low at the receiving or assembly factory, the stock levels within the supplier matrix may be higher than in recent times in order to give increased flexibility to build.

The skill of the scheduling manager is to persuade the board of directors that effective control of supplied material cannot always be carried out by obeying the rigid rules of low inventory equals low cost. In addition, the myth of the Toyota system of Kanban which is not properly understood by the majority of senior managers within British industry, needs to be replaced by a materials movement system which will work into the 1990s.

THE SCHEDULE

A schedule is a document of instruction to procure material, produce and supply goods which passes from a company to a supplier, or from unit to unit. In most cases the document cannot be prepared and issued prior to the negotiation and establishment of a contract or order between the two companies.

The order must define the price and supply guidelines, i.e. minimum order quantity, but the schedule which is then prepared based on the foundation of the order must transmit more detailed information of current and future requirements. The order can be of two types: type 1 is closed and the total commitment is defined, i.e. '17,000 parts to be delivered in batches of 1,000 between 1 January and 31 March'; type 2 is an open order, i.e. 'Delivery to be in accordance to schedule requirements'. In type 1 the schedule produced simply calls in the parts in line with the production build programme and in type 2 the schedule must define current and future requirements with an ongoing plan.

The raising or creation of a schedule, therefore, requires a wide variety of data from departments outside material and schedule control. The range of data required for type 2 is outlined in Figure 8.1.

Before the schedule can be issued, a material requirement plan (MRP) has to be agreed between production control and the scheduling department. It is important that this accounts for historical reject levels and the damage of goods within the factory.

The schedule is then prepared. At all times it must carry the following information:

Date
PT no. or ref code
Contract or order number and date of issue

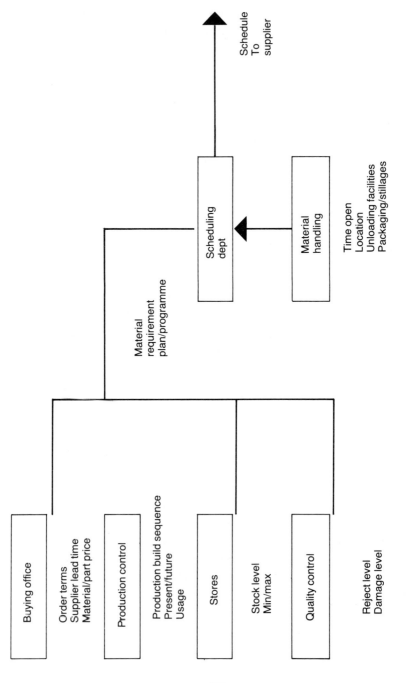

Figure 8.1 Range of data for type 2 order

Date goods required
Number required
Packaging or stillage requirements

A description of the goods should not be required, provided the part number or reference code is understood by both parties. Preparing a schedule is simple and its application to two examples demonstrate the different types:

Mass production

The supply of material to a moving assembly line presents a variety of problems to the materials manager, above all production must not stop because of the shortage of components. In most cases the components supplied are divided into separate groups, this method or Pareto analysis easily defines the critical components.

In this example of a washing-machine assembly track the components are divided into three groups based on the following factors:

Cost
Inventory/stock cost
Supply/supplier lead time
Production immobility/rework potential
Size/storage space
Material handling characteristics

Group *A* parts, which are high on cost and vulnerability, have a lead time in excess of 10 weeks, account for only 15 per cent of the parts but contribute 55-60 per cent of the cost. Group *B* parts are medium cost, have a lead time below 10 weeks, but are specially designed and procured for the product; they account for 35 per cent of the parts and 20-25 per cent of the cost. Group *C* parts, approximately 50 per cent of the total, are low cost and are mainly standard parts which are readily available from the market, e.g. fasteners and castor wheels.

All the parts need to be available to build the finished product, but each will have a different vulnerability rating or factor as far as production is concerned dependent on their location within the washing machine. In general groups *A* and *B* have higher vulnerability, but the shortage of some group *C* parts may stop production and the ability to fit parts off-track which have become a shortage needs to be considered.

The method of scheduling of each type of component is different.

Group A

In general the high cost goods are the key to production and a special and stable relationship has to exist between the assembler and supplier. The effective scheduling and material control of these parts to limit stockholding and commitment, without jeopardising production, is the key role of schedule management.

The schedule must provide a long-term future commitment to material and parts, variations must be kept to a minimum to allow the supplier to support the schedule. A balance has to be reached between the need for a high stock to protect production and a low one to reduce costs.

The schedule issued is generally an 8/16 type, this has a five-week commitment to a precise number of components, i.e. this week and four weeks forward; a further three-week commitment to parts with a plus or minus variance of 15 per cent, and then a further eight-week commitment to raw material. The schedule also shows a cumulative figure of parts delivered since the start of the year, or period.

A schedule of this type can only be adjusted within 15 per cent six weeks forward and within 100 per cent, i.e. to nil within eight weeks for parts. Therefore it is important, when changing the production build sequence, to include in the review and decision-making process the forward or committed costs. The 8/16 schedule is protective to the assembler and the supplier. It demands precise forward planning and is cumbersome and inflexible.

Group B

The schedule is similar to group *A* except the forward commitment to parts is only four weeks and material eight-ten weeks dependent upon the components. However, unlike group *A* parts which are delivered every week, group *B* parts can be delivered every two or three weeks, decreasing delivery complexity.

Group C

These parts can be treated in an entirely different manner, the components in this group are standard and available from several sources. Often the number required compared to the total number produced by suppliers each period is low and therefore the assembler is just one of many customers.

It is in the interests of the assembler not to complicate the supply of these parts by using running schedules at all, but rather to issue, say, one document every three months calling in 25 per cent of year's requirements.

This method allows the buying office to establish better prices, requires the schedule department to issue one document and then monitor closely the bulk delivery to that schedule. The inventory or stock costs are not dramatically increased by this method, but the production line is better protected from shortage. The schedule department can then concentrate on the weekly deliveries of group *A* and *B* items and maintain the schedules for these parts; group *C* items can be subdivided into three groups and each group ordered and delivered every quarter.

Machine tool

The development and planning of schedules in a machine tool company is entirely different from a mass production environment. A machine tool is a capital investment and usually the builder only commences action after an order or contract is received.

The schedule department becomes a timing function and, again, the components required can be divided into sub groups.

Group A

Bought-out casting or fabrications which require final machining with the building factory.

Group B

Bought-out parts which require sub-assembly within the builder's factory prior to assembly onto finished machine.

Group C

Bought-out standard part – valves, fasteners etc. – which require sub-assembly and final assembly to the finished machine tool.

Timing plan

In order to plan the procurement and supply of components a basic timing plan is developed. It is in the best interests of the builder that this action is taken at the quotation stage. For illustration purposes five components are shown in Figure 8.2.

In each case the procurement activity starts at a different time and, therefore, the scheduling department provides to purchasing a procurement or activity programme.

The timing chart is developed so that each sub-component arrives exactly as required; this is the most cost-effective method of building, but also has the highest risk, unless additional planning is undertaken. Again the components are subdivided into three groups, but not on the basis of lead time or cost, but on build vulnerability (see Figure 8.3)

Each layer will contain components of at least two of the timing groups. Therefore, a group B component with a short lead time and no in-factory machining may be required to be available at the start of final assembly. This does not relate to the time period of assembly; it is necessary because of its sequential requirement to other components. Therefore, having developed the basic timing plan based on lead-time analysis, the triangle of sequential build needs to be drawn for each major assembly and then be considered in conjunction with the basic timing plan.

The final stage is to take an overview on risk and costs, in the event that the components arrive three weeks, three days, or three hours before, or after, they are required. Again vulnerability to the achievement of the finished machine on time needs to be considered, as does consideration of the performance of suppliers. The timing chart is then completed and the order sequence established. Regular monitoring and updating is then required to ensure achievement of the plan.

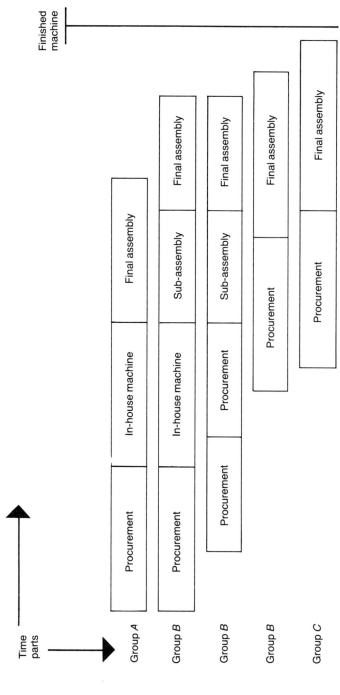

Figure 8.2 Machine tool timing plan

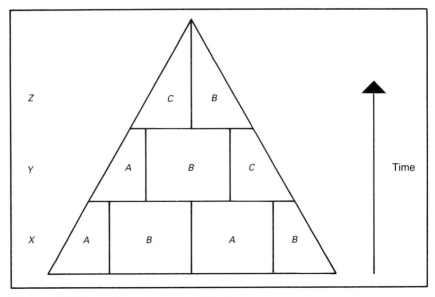

Figure 8.3 Triangle of sequential build

SCHEDULING AND THE BUYER

The method of scheduling adopted in most high-volume production environments delegates the responsibility for obtaining components away from the buyer to materials managers. This situation is not the rule in industry, and in most small industrial companies the material flowing inward only does so against an individual or discrete order.

The adoption of the scheduling method takes away from buyers the day-to-day progressing of orders and allows them to concentrate on other aspects, particularly the search for new suppliers.

The scheduling method changes the role of the buyer and its adoption can only be recommended where buying staff are of sufficient calibre and are motivated to adapt quickly to their new role. Too often, the buyer who is no longer required to progress delivery of material finds it difficult to take advantage of the time available, and quickly becomes a second-line part progresser.

In all companies which adopt schedule management techniques the buyer must become involved if the chosen supplier does not deliver to the requirements of the schedule. However, in too many cases the threshold at which the buyer is contacted is too low, and the buying staff, experienced in dealing with such problems, immediately respond and become involved.

The introduction of schedules also affects the buyer regarding price increases. Again, in the past, the price of components was established prior to the order and price movements over a twelve-month period took place in a series of small steps. With the forward security of an 8/16 schedule the buyer can resist increases until an annual agreement pattern is established. The contained impact of the series of small increases all coming at once can often produce something of a surprise for the buyer. However, this offers the opportunity for the buying staff to negotiate effectively. Opportunities open to them include re-sourcing, using other quotations to improve the competitiveness of an offer; or working with the existing supplier to reduce his costs. Nonetheless in many cases the same problem remains – buying staff not trained, educated, or prepared for twelve-month negotiations and agreements, often fail to take advantage of the opportunity offered.

Individual orders to scheduling

Before a company makes the transition from individual orders to scheduling the following basic questions must be asked:

1 Are the suppliers able to respond?
2 Are the buyers able to respond?

Too often such questions are not asked and the resulting confusion acts against the original intention.

Until the mid-seventies the inward flow of material needed active progressing and in many cases the buyer was able to use the 'power' of the next order to persuade suppliers to make and deliver components in preference to other orders. The situation has now changed. Inwards progressing is often more toward stopping deliveries over-schedule than chasing delinquent suppliers.

If the role of materials management is properly carried out the buyer can be free to make a powerful impact on profitability by reducing component costs, fully searching available markets and firmly limiting supplier price increases to justifiable levels.

SCHEDULING AND PRODUCTION CONTROL

The use of schedules for obtaining components for delivery direct to lineside from suppliers can reduce inventory and stock levels and, thereby, manufacturing costs. However, one penalty which results is a reduction in build flexibility. This occurs because the production line can only build to the established plan which was used to develop the MRP and against which parts are then delivered. Because the stock levels are reduced, production flexibility decreases and this may highlight other, so far, hidden problems in the production process.

This scheduling method demands that suppliers deliver according to programme. In addition it forces the assembler to predict build sequence up to five weeks forward. This disciplined build pattern is only possible with a steadily increasing and stable market for the final product. The requirement to be more flexible, to build more to short-term market demands and trends can send shock waves throughout the supplier matrix. Schedules which have been stable for many years can be decreased or increased with no apparent warning, and the stable relationships established between suppliers and assembler is adversely affected.

The resulting stress which impinges upon a stable scheduling relationship is detrimental to effective materials management and in the extreme can result in the collapse of the scheduling system. As markets have become more competitive this threat of failure is often used by companies who do not use the method as the reason why they do not wish to adopt it.

SCHEDULING AND FLEXIBILITY

The rules and discipline necessary for controlled supply of materials against a schedule would seem at first to limit the flexibility of build sequence or product variability. If this is so, how can the scheduling methods which have been discussed thus far be modified to cater for the greater flexibility required to allow the assembly industry to meet changing market demands?

The first obvious solution is to increase line stockholding. If six weeks' stock of components is held then any combination of product can be built. At first this seems to be against the other principles of low inventory and storage cost, but the assumption that this stock is held lineside or even that it is the property of the assembler would be wrong.

Many of the assembly industries are established in factory sites built before the recent advances in material handling technology, particularly before the advent of 34-ton trailers detachable from the delivery tractor unit. While new factories can be built on green field sites, which offer specially designed unloading facilities, the majority of industry cannot shut down existing facilities. Apart from anything else, the limited funds available for investment must be put to develop new products.

Kanban

Many materials managers have learnt of the Japanese system 'Kanban' – indeed this over-used word is often cited as the solution to all problems. Kanban is a system used by Toyota, and the word actually means card. The basic principle is to limit stockholding to a minimum and deliver goods to trackside 'just in time'. It is incorrect to assume this system is used throughout Japanese industry; it is only introduced where the receiving factory can unload its daily requirements of components direct to lineside and where the build sequence is defined and does not change.

Toyota uses a repeating assembly cycle for each day for as long as a month. This is called 'Tacto' time and it sets the monthly production rates for all parts and assemblies. Toyota is the largest producer of vehicles in Japan and, to date, its monthly cycle of production has always been achieved to the programme. The company has a unique relationship with its suppliers. Acting as 'overlord', it supports and cultivates supplier relationships and investment, but also has a reputation for demanding the lowest priced components.

The Kanban system which works for Toyota cannot be applied without modification to British industry for one other fundamental reason. The employment structure of a Japanese supplier allows the workforce to complete its daily production of components precisely to the next day's requirements of Toyota. Therefore if Toyota builds 500 Corolla models with alloy wheels per day, the supplier must produce 2,500 wheels (remember the spare) the day or period before, and must do so before the workforce or shift leave the factory.

With correct production rates the Japanese supplier works a shift pattern, which, contrary to the popular view, keeps the worker at the factory for eight or nine hours a day. The fundamental difference is that if the production process fails through a machine breakdown then the workforce remains at the factory until the quota of parts is achieved. This allows in-line stockholding between supplier and assembler to be kept to a minimum because supply security is virtually assured.

Surprisingly, the Kanban system also relies on flexibility. The material control method is a card system maintained by a large number of clerical staff, often young people or women. If a supplier over-delivers by 10 per cent this is accepted and the record card manually adjusted. In addition, the forward daily schedule is changed to reflect a reduction sometime forward to cover the over-supply and return to the agreed schedule. Minor over-deliveries are tolerated and, despite the publicity generated by Japanese manufacturing industry which presents the view of no overstocking and of deliveries exactly matching the production cycle, minor under-delivery does not stop build. The system allows up to 10 per cent over- and 7 per cent under-delivery without jeopardising the build, and this situation is immediately corrected by manual alteration of the card system.

A system similar to Kanban operated in the British motor industry in the late nineteen-fifties and early -sixties. Because the supply industry operated a piecework pay system, a supplier always produced, for instance, 2,500 wheels per day and because the vehicle market was growing, the assembly industry produced in line with the build programme and offered suppliers the required security. It will be seen, then, that the Kanban system can work in Europe as well as in Japan. Indeed, it is applicable in any situation where there is stability of demand throughout the manufacturing and supply matrix.

Because of the perceived success of the Kanban method, many material managers advised its adoption in British industry without fully appreciating the differences in work practices or the requirement for a more flexible approach. Kanban was introduced at the same time as material control staff monitoring card records were replaced by computers programmed with rigid rules. It was introduced in factories designed to accept one lorry unloading at one time and which were incapable of accepting multi-deliveries. The position was often further exacerbated as a result of suppliers utilising, for cost reasons, larger vehicles capable of carrying more than one day's stock. Inevitably the system failed; Kanban is not the answer to all problems and the material control functions suffered because the panacea of 'just in time' did not work.

Consequently, it is necessary to develop a new approach which takes into consideration the mistakes of failed 'just in time' systems. A new method is proposed: this is termed 'just in time, but somewhere else'.

Just in time but somewhere else

It has always been assumed that in order to allow multiple daily delivery to an assembly factory that the material or fabric of the building must be modified to cater for all the supplier vehicles which are likely to arrive on any single day. However, many factory sites are not suitable for modification and, even where there might be limited space available for expansion, could be better used for manufacturing purposes than for a super unloading bay. The following proposal seeks to accommodate such factors.

Stage 1 At this stage it is necessary to categorise the components supplied into separate groups; the key components – group *A* and some in group *B* are used for the new approach.

The suppliers are contacted and a separate site acquired away from the assembly factory, the site must contain adequate unloading facilities and storage space. The suppliers then deliver to the site in loads compatible with their current transport method. The goods are repacked into containers compatible with the lineside storage facilities and transported from the warehouse to the track on a continuous basis.

At first sight this seems expensive since the space required for decanting and repacking is larger than that necessary for dumping a load of components trackside. However, this method does not require expensive alterations to the assembly factory. In addition, the benefits are mutual to assembler and suppliers; the transport vehicle can be unloaded immediately and the traditional employment rules applying at the factory need not apply at the warehouse. The responsibility for unloading can be given to the supplier, and the warehouse does not have to be heated to the same level as the factory.

The parts stored at the warehouse need not become the property of the assembler until taken to the track, although this arrangement with the suppliers needs to be carefully negotiated. In any event, the stock cost should not exceed the previous method's frustration costs.

With the introduction of Stage 1 to the major suppliers, build flexibility is re-established, since more inventory is available at no greater cost and the impact on the factory is to reduce the flow and number of incoming delivery vehicles.

This method also helps to obviate the problem of supply interruption. Among other things it allows the supplier to accept short delays in production without jeopardising supply and without holding excess finished stock at his premises. Whilst providing added security to the receiving company, the supplier's production and material plans can be more cost effective, while machine utilisation can be planned to produce components at a lower cost. The idea of raising stock levels is never popular because on first analysis the cost is high. However, because of the avoidance of frustration costs and the benefits in manufacturing cost the total financial picture is not as adverse as it might appear at first.

The effect of this method on schedules is dramatic. Since the required short-term flexibility does not immediately affect the supplier, the schedule returns to stability, the short-term waves are smoothed by the stock buffer, and with the increasing confidence and required forward commitments – previously 8/16 weeks – can be reduced to a 4/8 ratio.

A disadvantage of this proposal is the potential production of obsolete or unusable stock, say as a result of a model line finish. Although this problem is often quoted, very few industrial markets collapse completely overnight and provided the sales department liaise closely with production and material control, such commitment can be kept to a minimum.

Stage 2 of this method can only be introduced after Stage 1 is successfully in operation. The objective here is to extend the method so that the assembler utilises one transport fleet to collect the components from the suppliers. A benefit of this is that unloading and repacking is obviated since the components are collected in the required sequence.

It is attractive to propose moving to Stage 2 immediately, but the complexity of collecting the components exactly in the correct sequence for unloading, could only be approached following experience with Stage 1.

In summary, it is the writer's opinion that the Kanban system will not work in the traditional assembly industries, while the standard scheduling systems are not capable of responding to the flexibility requirements of the next decade. To overcome these two problems, materials managers must introduce a different approach and one solution recommended here, which at first sight is against the recent trends of nil stock, low-cost inventory, is to set up storage facilities or buffer stocks. The introduction of this proposal is possible because of the strong tactical position of the 'buyer' in a supply market which is suffering from over-capacity, but the benefit is long-term security to the supplier and increased flexibility to the assembler.

SCHEDULING AND THE FUTURE

This chapter has demonstrated the basic methods of scheduling in two industrial applications. Concentrating on a high-volume production environment, the application of certain scheduling techniques has been recommended in order to allow the major advantage of freeing the buying department to achieve other, more creative, objectives than progressing parts supply. However, this transition has failed too often because of lack of preparation or recognition of the major impact this change can make.

It is suggested that scheduling techniques should be developed to increase build flexibility through planned stockholding at a separate site funded jointly by suppliers and the assembler.

9

Purchasing and source selection

David Farmer

The importance of choosing the right supplier cannot be emphasised too strongly. The supplying company which delivers the material or service required to the right quality and at the right time is potentially contributing in considerable degree to the profitability of its customer. Consequently there is great merit in spending a commensurate amount of time, effort and resource in thoroughly evaluating key would-be suppliers and in appraising and managing existing suppliers on a continuing basis. And this evaluation and management should take into consideration medium and longer-term issues as well as those concerned with day-to-day operations.

Because this is so, where purchases are significant organisations with sophisticated purchasing procedures are prepared to devote relevant resources to both source selection and source management. Clearly there is not the need to devote the same level of key resources to, say, the selection of suppliers for office consumables as would be utilised in seeking a major production materials supplier. As in every aspect of business, the manager has to exercise judgement in deploying his resources. However, recognising the contribution which suppliers can make to the effective management of the business system, major suppliers at least should be subject to careful management.

Generally speaking, one of the major factors affecting the extent of a supplier investigation will be the scale of requirements from that source. These may be measured in financial terms, and even the one-man department can effectively isolate what might be called his 'top ten' for such evaluation. In all probability he will spend 80 per cent of the money he utilises with approximately 20 per cent of the companies with whom he deals and as a rider to that, probably on about 20 per cent of the range of materials he purchases. Time utilised in such investigations is most likely to show the most productive return, since management effort is being concentrated where the potential is greatest. This is not to say, of course, that other items should be ignored.

Another factor which affects the necessity for thorough supplier investigation is the state of competition in the market. For example, it may also be necessary to evaluate thoroughly a source for a one-off piece of equipment or service. For instance, a one-off machining job involving extremely close tolerances could well justify such an investigation. Certain companies will have the reputation for working to extremely fine limits. Because of their specialisation in precision machining, their investment in machine tools will be extensive. In addition, the specialist craftsmen employed will tend to be of higher calibre than their counterparts in the jobbing machine shop. In view of these and other factors the price of work done will tend to be high, but the real cost in terms of drawing queries, spoiled work and delivery delays will often be low.

In one such case, where a source investigation was merely cursory, a casting in a particularly fine grade of iron was spoiled by a machining subcontractor. The lead time on the replacement casting was sixteen weeks and, despite urgent action, a valuable export order was lost to the buying company. The fact that the machinists had to pay for the replacement casting was of little consolation. A thorough investigation at the time the order was placed would have shown up deficiencies in machine tools at the chosen supplier in addition to the fact that the labour there was not used to working to such fine limits.

The main factors involved in supplier selection are time, quality, quantity and price; but there are other important considerations. For example, the financial stability of an organisation can affect each of the factors mentioned. If, for instance, a supplier's cash flow is badly managed, then he may well be dilatory in paying his accounts and may find difficulty on occasions in obtaining materials. This may affect delivery time and/or quality. A financially unsound supplier can be as great an embarrassment to a company as could a customer similarly placed. It is extraordinary how little attention is paid to the financial position of suppliers by some organisations. Yet the same companies maintain a close check on all new customers. The latter is important, but in certain cases no more so than with respect to a key supplier. The implications of the Lockheed decision to source the engines (RB 211) with Rolls Royce are illustrative of the possible effects at the extreme.

Another important factor is the extent of service provided by the supplying organisation in terms of, for example, research and development, information/liaison facilities, technical assistance and value analysis. While such service is difficult to quantify, it can make a valuable contribution to the reduction of real purchase costs.

The management expertise and technical competence of the supplier is a further area for consideration. Efficient management will be striving to improve methods and reduce costs; to initiate development where possible and to ensure the continuing training of personnel. These things affect labour relations and morale. The old naval saying 'an efficient ship is a happy ship' may well be applied to a factory. Sound management and high morale are likely attributes of a successful source of supply. In considering management, we should also take into account higher management and the possibility of amalgamations or mergers. It is not unknown for an industrial giant to buy out a successful smaller competitor and then close it down. Alternatively the larger company may well install its own management which, particularly in the short run, might affect morale in the supplying organisation and/or the service provided by it.

One or more suppliers

In considering the question of the right supplier, one problem which needs to be examined is the number of suppliers which are used for any material or service. Should a company ensure that all its eggs are not in one basket, or should it go for the advantages of a single source? Within these basic alternatives, should it use three or four on an equal basis? Or should it give the bulk of business to one and keep a second 'in reserve', producing small quantities?

In some cases there is no alternative available to the buyer because he is purchasing from a monopolistic source by virtue of patents, special processes, nationalised utilities, or simply because of reasons of available capacity. In other circumstances he is limited to a single source because of high tooling costs or of technological 'know how'. He may also be obliged to use a single source for spares for existing equipment or supplies for office equipment by virtue of the terms of a rental contract.

Given these alternatives it is necessary to consider the arguments for and against using one source of supply as against more than one.

Where a single supplier is used and considerable quantities are involved, the supplier may be motivated to a great degree to meet the requirements of his customer. Because of the volume of guaranteed business, continuity, and the effects of the learning curve he should be able to quote the keenest prices. Against this it may be said that if more than one source is used, if there is a fire, a strike or a machinery breakdown at one, then supplies may be obtained from the others. In addition, where more than one source is used, the effects of competition will help keep prices keen and may encourage design improvements and better service.

At the time of writing the received wisdom among major assemblers such as Ford, Austin Rover and Volvo, is to operate a single-source policy. The arguments for doing so are appealing, particularly with regard to system efficiency and reliability. Nonetheless it is clear that there is no stock answer as to which is the better system. Each situation must be reviewed in relation to the circumstances which apply. It is evident that even if Jack Bloggs placed all his business with ICI it would mean very little in terms of turnover to the supplier. Whereas Ford could have considerable influence on a component manufacturer if it was their single source for a particular item.

SINGLE OR MULTIPLE SOURCING: A COMPARISON

Some advantages of single sourcing

1 The supplier ought to be able to offer price advantages because of economies of scale.
2 Personal relationships can be more easily established, thus

making communications more effective.

3 Administrative work in the buyer's office is reduced.
4 Closer relationships and a reasonable tenure can result in mutual cost-reduction effort.
5 Buyer-tied research can be undertaken.
6 Tool and pattern or fixture costs are reduced and long-run tools may be used.
7 Transportation costs can be lower and, where pallets are used, common pools can be established.
8 Quality control is made easier since there is only one location.
9 Scheduling is made easier.

Many of these arguments lose weight if the business involved represents a small proportion of the supplier's total sales.

Some advantages of multiple sourcing

1 With several sources there is insurance against failure at one plant as a result of fire, strikes, quality, delivery problems etc.
2 A competitive situation can be developed; no one supplier can afford to become complacent.
3 In cases of standard items, no tooling cost is involved and there are often no advantages for added volume.
4 The buyer is protecting himself against a monopoly and may have the advantage of two sources of new ideas or new materials.
5 There is no moral commitment to a supplier as when the total quantity would be a considerable proportion of the supplier's total sales.
6 Giving orders to a number of suppliers increases flexibility in case of large additional call-off or decreased needs.
7 Part business can be used as a base-load in conjunction with which a smaller supplier may be developed.
8 With two suppliers holding stock, the buying company can reduce inventory levels.

THE MONOPOLISTIC BUYER

Is it good policy to take all or almost all a supplier's capacity? Both ethical and commercial considerations affect this question. Stories of big buyers taking the whole of the output of a small supplier and then gradually 'squeezing' their prices are not uncommon. Most thinking buyers would agree that, quite apart from the doubtful ethics of such action, it is bad buying practice. Good suppliers are a potentially valuable asset. If they are to survive then they should be allowed a reasonable profit. Clearly, this does not mean that they should achieve such a profit when they are inefficient. The buyer has a duty to his own business to ensure that he is purchasing supplies and services at the most advantageous cost. However, suppliers should be given every reasonable opportunity to conduct their business in an efficient and effective manner. In the process, the fact that they make reasonable profits which allow their businesses to thrive should be in the interests of the buying company. When this interchange is managed effectively it is certainly not philanthropy on the part of the buyer. It should be motivation to the supplier to improve his product, service, pricing and, thus, retain the business.

There are other dangers inherent in a supplier being tied to a buyer. Not the least of these dangers being that when things are slack with the big buyer, they may be even slacker with the small supplier. A small supplier without the financial reserves of his customer will then find himself in financial difficulties. At the worst this could lead to bankruptcy and at the least to difficulties with raw material supplies, replacement of machinery and, inevitably, a cutback in research and development.

While it is possible for the medium-sized organisation to be a monopoly buyer with, say, a one-man concern, it is most often the larger organisations which are in such a position. It is significant, therefore, that many companies actively discourage their suppliers from concentrating too much business with them. And, of course, the better suppliers will be unlikely to allow themselves to be placed in such a vulnerable position.

AGENT OR MANUFACTURER

Another problem in the selection of a source of supply, is whether to buy direct from a manufacturer, through an agent, a stockist, or through a wholesaler. Once again the benefits and disadvantages of each alternative need to be considered carefully. Some years ago the National Industrial Distributors Association in America listed 'eight essential major marketing functions which are consolidated in the local industrial distributor'. These included advantages in storage and distribution, risk-bearing, selling and product service. They claimed that their service 'added value' in the marketing process by 'performing functions as economically or more economically to free the buyer to pursue other responsibilities, therefore effecting greater efficiency in his entire operation. These economies realised by the buyer are the values added by the industrial distributor.' While these arguments were put forward by an organisation with a vested interest in pressing the case, this does not invalidate them. For example, a buyer could consolidate a wide range of C items from his range. He could then require the stockist to provide a level of service and price which would be more attractive than if he were to buy and stock each item himself. Apart from any other benefit, administrative costs per unit would be dramatically reduced.

One of the major arguments often used by stockists is their proximity to the buying company. As a result, they argue, they are able to provide faster service. However, objective evaluation of the many factors involved will show that what really matters is the efficiency and economy of the function performed by the stockist rather than his location. This, of course, is why the more efficient national stockists expand their field of operations often to the detriment of the 'local' man.

Stockists are often used with advantage in maintaining stocks of small tools, spares and other articles in common use in perhaps a number of companies in their area. They guarantee to keep stocks to meet the various buyers' requirements and thus allow them to dispense with stocking these items themselves. The items may be called forward from the stockist as and when required, often under some monthly order arrangement which also saves paperwork. An extension of this idea used in some places is for the stockist to maintain a rack in the buyer's own stores, which he keeps replenished with an agreed range of materials or parts. The prices of these parts are agreed in advance and those used are paid for each month against an agreed stock check. This idea, sometimes called consignment stocking, is being used, too, by manufacturers as an extension of their service. With the high cost of money, this approach has gained considerable favour in recent years.

In the final analysis, the decision to buy direct or from a stockist must be based upon a comparison of real costs and benefits of the alternative services. The right choice is, then, that which is found to be most economical and reliable, though like every source decision it should be reviewed from time to time.

LOCAL OR DISTANT SUPPLIERS

'Everything else being equal, buy from the local man' is the axiom by which many buyers live. While everything else is rarely equal, it is true to say that the local supplier has many advantages over a distant competitor. Nevertheless, direct comparisons sometimes reveal advantage to the buyer in placing his business with firms which are not local, but which are more efficient in operation and thus able to offer a more economical service in the given circumstances despite the disadvantages of distance. Sometimes, what may be called 'political' considerations have to be taken into account and the business placed with local sources even when they are not the most competitive. For example, this may be a policy decision from the company's top management regarding certain aspects of its trading. The buyer's task here is to ensure that top management is aware of the real cost of applying the policy.

The local source is sometimes used because it facilitates liaison regarding urgent requirements, or because close contact will assist in resolving possible disputes. In other cases, the local source is used because there is a feeling of responsibility to the local community, particularly perhaps in the development areas. Personal and social relationships add further reason too, for even allowing for the highest standards of objective decision making by the buyer, the local supplier will generally be extremely keen to hold the business. The implications of losing local business to a distant supplier could well have an unhappy effect on his overall business.

If a distant supplier is in effective competition with a local source, it may be because he is operating on a national scale or specialising in a narrow area of materials or services. As a result of economies of scale operating in his favour, he is able to offer a better service or quality or both at a lower price than the local source. Some national organisations have tried to provide a service which allows the best of both worlds to the buyer, by establishing depots or local branches. Small tools, bearings and motor spares are three areas where such chains are well established. In the construction world, more and more of the larger organisations have set up regional units to operate in this way. Wimpey, by virtue of their extensive advertising on the theme 'the local contractor with the national organisation', are probably best known outside the industry for such an operation, but while being the largest are only one of the companies operating in this way.

With the increase in takeovers and amalgamations in every industry, such arrangements are becoming more common. One big advantage to the buyer comes when he is part of a similar organisation himself. Centrally negotiated terms may then become available to his own local organisations in various parts of the country from 'local' branches of the supplier. As a result, the decision maker should consider carefully the various implications of the decision. In the final analysis it is his judgement which must be exercised.

RECIPROCITY

Another thorny question which the majority of buyers have to face some time in their careers is reciprocity. This is probably more in evidence in times of national economic recession. One of the effects of recession is, often, to reduce the volume of business which is available to manufacturing companies. As a result sales organisations, anxious to maintain as large a share as possible, are urged to greater efforts. One question which is frequently asked at this time is: 'Which are the companies from which we make substantial purchases who could utilise some of our products, but are currently buying elsewhere?' This is followed by: 'Can we bring pressure to bear on these organisations to buy from us on the basis that we are good customers of theirs?' Or the sales department may simply ask for the help of the purchase department in applying pressure to a possible customer who is a supplier.

The buyer is charged with making the best purchase possible for his company. When a selling organisation solicits his business on reciprocal grounds, he should consider why the approach has to be made on such a basis. Does it really amount to: 'Even though we aren't really the best source, buy from us because we're good customers of yours'? If so, the buyer can hardly claim to be making the best possible purchase if he accedes to the request. But he should also consider how the decision will affect the organisation as a whole; that is, whether his company's own sales could be seriously affected. The danger in deciding reciprocal trading questions on narrow departmental grounds is of sub-optimising; that is, finding an optimum solution from the viewpoint of one department or section of the organisation which is not the optimum for the organisation as a whole. Gaining sales at the expense of costly and unsatisfactory purchases could be sub-optimising from the sales angle; making the best possible purchase at a ruinous cost in lost sales could be sub-optimising from the purchasing angle.

The task of the purchasing man is to ensure that, in discussion with his colleagues and general management, all issues are carefully weighed. Short, medium and long-term issues are relevant.

What happens, for instance, if one party wants to cut back on its purchases from the other? Has a reciprocal cutback to be negotiated? What does the buyer do if he succeeds in finding a new, greatly superior source? Normally he would be free to switch his purchases; but when the previous sourcing decision has been taken on reciprocal grounds, presumably he will have to raise the whole question once more with general management. Is a supplier who has won the business on reciprocal grounds going to keep up a high standard of service, or will complacency and a take-it-or-leave-it attitude develop? What does reciprocal trading do to purchase department morale, to its zeal in systematically comparing and evaluating sources and materials, to its opportunities to achieve cost reductions? The better the purchase department is at its job, the better placed it is to insist that full weight is given to these somewhat intangible considerations in deciding reciprocity questions.

Three-way reciprocity deals also occur: for example, when *A* requests his supplier *B* to purchase certain items required by *B* from a third party *C* on the grounds that *A* supplies *C* with raw materials for those parts. The same principles apply to this more complicated situation. The most efficient purchase departments are fully aware of the importance of their own suppliers having efficient purchase departments in their turn. Far from attempting to impose reciprocal limitations on their suppliers' purchasing, they will look for efficiency in the purchasing activities of those suppliers, for such efficiency will have considerable effect on the price they will have to pay for their supplies from that source; at least in the long run.

MUTUAL BUYING WITHIN GROUPS

Similar problems to those above can present difficulties in the application of purchasing policy on buying from other companies in a group. In the course of consultancy assignments over the last two decades the writer has noted a variety of approaches to the establishment of policy in this area. There are those groups which insist that group suppliers are given the same opportunity as 'outside' suppliers and that they are treated in the same way. Another approach requests group companies to buy from sister organisations 'when and wherever possible'. There is a third type which, whilst stating that group suppliers should be given the opportunity to quote, add something like: 'Where a group company submits a quotation which is less advantageous than a competitor, it is to be given the opportunity to meet this competitor on equal terms.'

What must be remembered in striving to make the best decision in this type of circumstance is that inefficiency in purchasing, even if a group company benefits instead of an outside supplier, is still inefficiency. In the final analysis, a group would seem to gain far more by a policy of outward-looking efficiency than by some form of communal philanthropy. If the companies in a group are efficient and economic, their service, price, and quality will be competitive and thus attractive to their fellow group members. In certain circumstances of course group members are afforded special discount rates by virtue of their membership of the group concerned. This again embraces group and company policy at top management level. While the price advantage in such circumstances may tend to make the group company's offer more attractive, the other factors in source selection need to be examined carefully. There is often the danger that the supplying organisation tends to take group orders for granted, giving priority to other customers.

After all, there is often more direct profit to the supplying unit in an outside order than in an in-group order. The incentive is thus with the former.

Source selection involving group companies and policy making in this area needs, as much as any other factor in source selection, careful consideration. A large discount and thus a lower price does not always compensate for poor service and may result in a high real cost.

THE PROCESS OF SELECTING SUPPLIERS

This chapter has examined some of the factors involved in source selection. The final section examines the process of selection itself.

Whilst the approaches which are used in selecting suppliers tend to differ from extremely detailed supplier appraisal schemes to relatively simple procedures, there are common elements in all procedures. These may be summarised as:

- define the need
- search market for potential sources
- match sources to need
- obtain proposal from selected supplier(s) to meet the need
- evaluate alternative proposals and suppliers
- select most suitable/economic
- place business/control
- assess performance: re-evaluate source decision
- continue trading or seek alternative(s).

As has been suggested, the detail or sophistication associated with each of these elements will differ according to the circumstance/company/market. For example, the most sophisticated companies tend to have elaborate supplier assessment schemes. These frequently include quality audits, facility audits and careful financial appraisals along with a management audit, and are undertaken by a technical/commercial team. Smaller businesses, without the same level of resource, may use a simple checklist approach which reminds the buyer concerned of the information about the potential supplier which he should obtain.

Among the other issues which need to be considered in evaluating a would-be supplier are:

1 His product/service range.
2 The volume of business which he is capable of handling.
3 The 'technical' back-up which is available to support the buyer.
4 'Track record' with regard to meeting delivery schedules (reliability).
5 Similarly the quality record. (If the source is new to the buying company it is sensible to take up 'references'.)
6 The people with whom the buying company will interface. (People who can work well together can make a considerable difference to the efficiency and effectiveness of any system.)
7 To whom are key services subcontracted? (For example, many firms use transport contractors to deliver goods. The quality of their service could be crucial to the buyer's satisfaction.)
8 The quality of after-sales service, e.g. with capital equipment, spares service and, where relevant, credit arrangements.

One useful tool for supplier selection and evaluation is the questionnaire shown in Figure 9.1. The responses can be used to develop a supplier profile for both assessment of current performance and decisions on future sourcing.

DEFINITION OF NEED

Frequently the user is involved at this stage. His requirement may appear in a number of ways:

(*a*) a purchase requisition;
(*b*) a bill of material or parts list (hard copy or via a computer system), and
(*c*) a permanent order card, for stock items.

In other cases the need may evolve from a statement of, say, the function to be performed. The specific definition may emerge in internal discussions and talks with potential supplier(s).

		Please circle as appropriate			
Frequency of delivery	1	2	3	4	5
Time from order to delivery	1	2	3	4	5
Reliability of delivery	1	2	3	4	5
Continuity of supply	1	2	3	4	5
Orders filled completely	1	2	3	4	5
Advice on non-availability	1	2	3	4	5
Ease of order placing	1	2	3	4	5
Accuracy of invoices	1	2	3	4	5
Quality of sales representation	1	2	3	4	5
Regular calls representatives	1	2	3	4	5
Credit terms offered	1	2	3	4	5
Reliability of quality	1	2	3	4	5
Effective materials-handling methods	1	2	3	4	5
Quality of consultation on new product development (ours)	1	2	3	4	5
Quality of co-ordination with production	1	2	3	4	5
Competitive prices	1	2	3	4	5
Quality of engineering support	1	2	3	4	5
Quality of market information (short and long term)	1	2	3	4	5
Early information on new product development (theirs)	1	2	3	4	5
Quality/effectiveness of packaging	1	2	3	4	5

Figure 9.1   Supplier service questionnaire

OBTAINING PROPOSAL

Where specific requests for quotation are sent to potential suppliers, it is important to ensure that the buyer will be able to consider offers which are based upon the same need. Variations from the standard make true comparison more difficult. Whilst it is not impossible to accommodate such consideration, the variations need to be highlighted and costed clearly.

One other important guideline is to ensure that, as far as possible, functional specifications are provided for supplier consideration. There can be considerable benefits in avoiding the branded product or the differentiated one as regards monopoly source problems.

EVALUATING PROPOSALS

By following the foregoing guidelines this stage will be simplified. However it is important to ensure that any assumptions about any of the potential quotations should be validified *before* decisions are made. As discussed in Chapter 22, the degree to which and the method by which quotations are subject to subsequent negotiation is a matter of individual policy. Nonetheless, all key sourcing decisions will involve subsequent discussion with the selected supplier. There is little doubt that effective time spent at that stage will prove to be extremely beneficial in the longer run.

It is reasonable to argue that selecting, appraising and managing key sources of supply is the most important task of the purchasing function. Sound decisions repay the effort involved on a continuing basis, while, conversely, poor decisions result in additional work and disruption. The costs associated with effective selection are usually higher than poor decision making. However, the benefits associated with the former far outweigh the costs involved, whilst allowing the purchasing manager to concentrate upon the important rather than the urgent.

10

The make or buy decision

John Stevens

The make or buy decision arises through three routes. There is the problem of the new product, assembly or part – should this be made in or bought out? There is the existing product, assembly or part which is already being made in which might be more economical to buy out. There is the problem in reverse, something being bought out might better serve the interests of the organisation making it in. Who should make a contribution to these decisions? Should manufacturing, say, dictate the choice?

In many organisations purchasing has emerged as a distinct activity as a result of the buying job being delegated by the production director. As a result, it may then continue to report to the production director, in which case it may be highly likely that make or buy decisions will be made with some bias – favouring viewpoints which coincide with arguments to maintain the level of in-plant manufacturing, possibly regardless of cost and economic considerations. This, of course, is just one reason amongst many for arguing against such a reporting situation.

Whether a company makes or buys is a very important decision, which has far-reaching effects and will determine the profitability of the enterprise as a whole. Clearly in a new product situation the decision can relate to the complete end product itself. At a lower level it might be applied to major assemblies or major inputs, and at the lowest level to components and other less important inputs (see Figure 10.1).

Long-term strategic decisions	1	Do we buy new product and factor it?
	2	Do we make new product?
Strategic tactical decisions	3	If 2, do we buy major assemblies/items?
	4	If 2, do we make major assemblies/items?
Tactical operational decisions	5	If 4, do we buy components/minor items?
	6	If 4, do we make components/minor items?

Figure 10.1   The various levels of the make or buy decision

The figure suggests that the decisions are of differing significance. The answers to questions 1 to 4 would require board deliberation. Because purchasing should know more about the supply market and what it might do in the future than any other function, it should hopefully be represented at board level and put some input into make or buy decisions at the strategic and tactical levels. At the tactical/operational level the decision might be made as a straight purchasing/production interface, with purchasing not being dominated by production through an inappropriate reporting posture.

Once production starts this should not be the end of the affair. The situation should be reviewed and the review period should be shorter or longer according to whether the decision is strategic, tactical or operational. It may not be possible to make an early change to a strategic decision once made, but the constraints for altering an operational decision to, say, make a minor item in-house rather than buy it at present, may not be great.

The suggestion being made is that a policy should exist with regard to make or buy decisions. Furthermore, any policy should require such decisions to be made in a formalised way with a balanced view being arrived at, based upon the contributions from at least manufacturing and purchasing, and at the strategic levels from other functional heads. A checklist of questions would also require to be asked in order to make correct initial make or buy decisions, and also to reconsider those decisions when the situation came up for review. The following topics, if reviewed, might serve to enhance the decision-making process when considering the make or buy question.

POLICY IMPLICATIONS

There are a number of fundamental situations which may point the decision-making group in a particular direction before other factors are considered.

The first is where the product is an extension of an existing type of production, or a replacement unit for an obsolete model. Very serious efforts must be made to manufacture, even if new expert knowledge has to be brought into the company from outside. You cannot afford not to embark on such an exercise under these circumstances, and it is highly dangerous to place yourself at the mercy of rare or inadequately developed raw material.

The second case is a product where it is a major extension of an existing type of production. Here again the choice must be the same. Clearly, the total capacity of plant and the manpower situation have to be considered, and the capacity of your raw material sources, but at least the decision must be to keep the final assembly, the test, the control of quality of the end product under your own wing. If other capacity factors are deficient, then you could well start looking outside for machined parts, fabricated parts etc. You are paying a profit margin to that supplier and, unless the parts are very specialised indeed, it is probable that the operation could be conducted more economically within the company.

The third case is where there is a completely new type of product which is broadly within the industry which your company currently serves. By examining the existing companies or manufacturers who are already in the field in that particular line of product, it is possible that your company can get alongside somebody, and tie up with them, and go in on a joint-exercise basis. This has happened in the nuclear energy field in recent years, where some of the major electrical companies have linked up with heavy engineering companies to provide a nuclear engineering service.

Where the product is unknown and constitutes the invention of a complete new industry, the obvious step is to merge with or buy up an existing unit which has sound technical personnel and adequate production facilities. Whilst your company is in the broadest sense buying the product, it is really doing more than that, it is buying the facility to make the product. If there is the likelihood of making, then consider whether the projected product is within the orbit of experience of members of the board who are called senior executive management. Questions must be asked about the marketing and sales skill within your organisation. Are they suitable for the project which you are planning? Look at the company's sales coverage, sales skills, sales knowledge, in order to assess the line which the company should follow.

SUPPLY SECURITY

Examine the change from made-in to bought-out from a supply security point of view: aspects will include service; also the price you have fixed is one which is going to hold good for the peak business; and there is some long-term future in the economics which has prompted you to make a change. Union increases in wages and materials affect this issue, and if you are making parts in you have to bear the full brunt of these increases yourself. Whereas a purchaser, in the majority of cases, is able to make a settlement with the component supplier which does not necessarily mean that he can pass on the whole of these charges.

Supply security would also involve being confident of getting the deliveries when you want them, and comparative flexibility of supplies as between your own manufacture and that of the supplier, when you have a joint production. There is also the question of engineering changes. If any parts or components are subject to frequent engineering changes, it would be a factor in favour of keeping such parts under your own control.

However, the reverse may be the case. Where the supplier may have special skill and experience which would have to be developed within your own company if you decide to make it in, and it may be that to divert work into your plant requiring this special knowledge may not be the best or most profitable use of your executive's time. This latter point can be the important issue where a company concentrates its efforts on that work and manufacture of which it has special knowledge and skill, and so avoid dissipating the efforts of management, engineering and technicians over a much broader field. It is a question of utilising the best judgement on the merits of specialisation.

CAPITAL AND CAPACITY

Let us suppose a new and substantial requirement arises which is being considered as a made-in unit, but where capacity does not exist. To get the answer as to whether it is more profitable to the company to make or buy, and considering cost factors along the broadest terms, the next stage would be to find the amount of capital that would have to be invested in the new capacity facilities, which could involve buildings and plant, and then to estimate as accurately as possible the overheads that would be created in the setting up of a new section. These two basic requirements would then enable us to see how the future made-in cost would compare with the bought-in cost.

Generally, on this base the made-in cost would be less expensive, but a problem remains to find out how much would be saved by making in over buying out, in order to determine whether the amount of money invested on the new capacity gets a sufficient and reasonable return from the savings to be made over buying these parts. Most companies look at this and ask the question as to how many years it will take to get back the money which they have invested; three to five years would be a satisfactory pay off. These same arguments, which all represent a question of good business, apply in the same way to the question of parts which you may be at present buying out, and which could be made in cheaper, although they would involve the creation of additional capacity.

It might be as well at this time to refer to the question of cost figures, because in comparing costs and make or buy, we are trying to find out the effect of the total cost to the company. For the purpose of cost-accounting systems, many firms operate different kinds of accounting principles. Some companies, for example, talk about standard costs or flat costs where they include only the bare cost of the material and the direct wages concerned. In the case of direct wages in some cases this may be again the bare wages without any bonuses paid, or it may include incentives.

You must have some sort of an answer on these questions of costing materials before you get involved in the analysis of capital investment. Under normal conditions it is possible to get a fairly accurate assessment of the investment required to cover the cost of the plant, buildings and land. There are, at the present time, two complications in the UK. The first is the policy of successive governments which relates to the location of industry. Whilst one cannot disagree with the needs of certain regions as regards employment and the efforts at relocation, policies directing industry geographically must be operated intelligently. The second complication is that the very regions which have been given incentives are often in the more remote areas which incur high initial expense and high training and operating costs.

We must all have experienced the case where during boom times capacity is fully employed, and yet still more output is required. Production then look round and say: 'Well, if we can off-load this, that and the other, it would give us capacity for further tight-spot parts which would enable us to put the output up a certain amount.' Subcontracting or bought-out action then takes place. However, as soon as the boom falls off and production become short of work, there is pressure to get back in the parts which were subcontracted or bought out. In some cases labour relations and the retention of the labour force can be just as powerful a factor as price considerations.

SUPPORTING SERVICES

The existence of supporting services is fairly straightforward. If in some existing organisation there are already perimeter roads, heating, power supply, a tool room maintenance service etc., it is most likely that the company will build a more economic project than if it has to put up a completely new factory out in a remote area, where the business will have to start all the ancillary services from scratch. Existing in-house supporting services favours making in.

LABOUR

There could also be labour problems. By changing from made in to bought out you may be faced with redundancy or there might be some reason that a job should be made in because it helps to maintain the organisation in a certain balanced form.

It might also help to know whether the labour rates are likely to be comparable as between your own and that of the prospective supplier due to geographical position, or the fact that the supplier is able to use female labour on jobs which is not the practice in your own company. There may be trade union considerations in your shop which prevent the organisation of labour on as economical a basis as the supplier might be able to do.

The potential for the subcontractor or for the in-house workforce to show improved results through the learning curve must also be considered, because in the long term this can have dramatic effects on relative costs.

RAW MATERIAL

Another element in the analysis is raw material availability. Take care not to ignore the changing patterns in the development of material at the present time. It obviously makes sense to locate a manufacturing unit as closely as possible to its source of raw material. Where these sources of supply will be, according to whether you make or buy, can be quite dramatically different. The question of free-issuing material must also be examined carefully because this may produce improvements in price, quality, delivery and service performance if entertained.

FLEXIBILITY

Another factor which might be considered is the fluctuation of trade on a seasonal basis. Over the years the supplier has learnt to live with varying schedules and short-notice adjustments. The supplier may be able to balance his plant better to these conditions than would be the case in your own shops where it would in any case be lying idle to the extent of the capacity reduction.

PRICE COMPARISONS

Purchasing prices are not always what they seem. It could be the bare purchase price, or the purchase price plus delivery plus receiving, handling, inspection and overheads of the purchase department, material control cost etc., so that it is extremely important to know you are talking about the right cost and, when making comparisons, you are comparing like with like. When considering making a change, consider also the time factor and not only what the circumstances are at that moment, but what they might be in two or three years time.

These are just some of the questions that need to be answered before a logical make or buy decision is arrived at. The writer does not claim this to be a comprehensive list nor has he claimed to approach the solving of the problem from a cost/quantitative approach such as Levy and Sarnat.[1] The argument here is that there should be a formalised approach to make or buy decision making.

Does this cool, objective, quantified, structured approach to a very important decision, commonly faced, get adopted in British industry? A survey conducted in the Midlands elicited the following facts. Readers are invited to compare what occurs in their own organisations with this piece of empirical evidence. The original questionnaire is shown in Figure 10.2 with the results of the survey shown mostly in percentage scores.

CONCLUSIONS DRAWN FROM THE QUESTIONNAIRE

The size of company contacted ranged from small engineering firms to large car manufacturers. It is clear that practices vary widely, but consistent statements showed that the following conclusions could be drawn:

1 Make or buy decisions occur fairly often.
2 Some formalised procedure for reviewing does exist.
3 Production and purchasing most commonly initiate investigations.
4 Production and purchasing most commonly process the investigation.
5 Purchasing is often an active participant in decision making.
6 Decisions are finally made at director level.
7 Ultimately the question of price or comparative unit costs are overriding reasons for deciding whether to make or buy.

8 Design secrecy is the least important factor in deciding the make or buy issue.

9 Reviews of existing situations are probably not reconsidered often enough, given the changing circumstances over the last few years.

---

1 Number of employees on site ....
  Number of purchasing department employees on site ....

2 Does the company utilise make or buy criteria in its decision-making process?   Yes 85.7%   No 14.3%

3 How frequentyly has a make or buy decision arisen in the past twelve months?
  Not at all nil   Once only 7.1%   Several times 35%   Frequently 57.1%

4 Is there an established make or buy procedure operating within the company?   Yes 75%   No 25%

5 Which department(s) initiate make or buy investigations?

Research and development or equivalent	42.9%
Production	78.6%
Purchasing	85.7%
Finance	28.6%
Marketing/sales	21.40%
Other	7.1%

6 Which department(s) actively participate in the make or buy investigation, e.g. have a representative on a committee?

Research and development or equivalent	50.0%
Production	85.7%
Purchasing	92.9%
Finance	57.1%
Marketing/sales	28.6%
Other	28.6%

7 How would the purchasing department's role best be described from the following in a make or buy investigation?

(a) Overall control.	14.3%
(b) Active participant (i.e. specifically researches item under investigation).	57.1%
(c) Passive participant (i.e. formulates views on other department's research).	7.1%
(d) Used as an information source.	NIL

8 At which managerial level is the final decision taken?

Managing director or board level	21.4%
Director	35.7%
Executive	21.4%
Committee	14.3%
Manager	7.1%
Other	7.1%

9 Which of the following factors are considered most important when deciding make or buy policy? (Number in descending order of importance.)

Security of supply	(3)
Design secrecy	(6)
Price advantages	(1)
Quality aspects	(4)=
Capital outlay necessary to make in-house	(2)
Excess/shortage of in-house capacity	(4)=

10 How often is a make or buy situation reviewed?
  Annually 21.4%   Every 3 years 14.3%   Every 5 years 21%   Never 7.1%

11 How are the cost factors in make or buy investigations evaluated?

Payback	42.9%
Discounted cash flow	35.7%
Return on investment	35.7%
Yield	12.0%
Other formula	NIL

12 Brief details of recent make or buy investigations ....
  .... (3 case histories received) ....

Figure 10.2 'Make or buy' questionnaire

A few companies made brief replies to question 12, concerning recent make or buy investigations. A commentary on these replies is given below.

One company was having difficulty producing cheques to the required quality. Because of this quality problem, plus internal moves to modernise the in-house processes, the cheques are at present sourced externally. It is hoped that when new general-purpose equipment is installed, a make or buy study will be undertaken.

A second company stated that items similar to those already made in are automatically costed on a 'make' basis, and capacity available checked. New, and different from normal, 'make' items are subjected to 'buy' routines.

The engine and car production and assembly companies emphasise their introduction of new models each year, which causes them to carry out make or buy reviews on a continuous basis.

This survey was carried out in the Midlands and may not reflect the national situation. Even here, 25 per cent of respondents indicated that there was no formalised procedure for dealing with the make or buy decision. Purchasing appears to have a strong voice, but the influence of the motor industry environment should be mentioned. However, this sample in a particular geographical region suggests there is a realistic interface between purchasing and production and that Midlands-based purchasing men hold their own with their production colleagues in deciding what is to be sub-contracted.

Evidence from another source[2] emphasises the fact that purchasers see their role as contributors to the make or buy decision, and indeed measure their own performance, in part, by their improving input to this important policy area. A short extract from the book referred to above clearly indicates this:

> Who measures purchasing performance on the basis of its level of contribution to the make or buy decision?

Responses from 105 organisations

1 By reporting position:

		n	No.	%
(a)	purchasing reports to non-board member	30	11	36.7
(b)	purchasing reports to board not managing director	42	16	38.1
(c)	purchasing reports to managing director	33	17	51.5*
(d)	all respondents	105	44	41.9

*Note the reply of the highest reporting group.

2 By spend on revenue items per annum:

(a)	– £500,000	12	5	41.7
(b)	£500,000 – £1,000,000	16	5	31.3
(c)	£1,000,000 – £2,000,000	15	6	40.0
(d)	£2,000,000 – £5,000,000	12	6	50.0
(e)	£5,000,000 – £10,000,000	20	6	30.0
(f)	£10,000,000 – £20,000,000	8	3	37.5
(g)	+£20,000,000	22	13	59.1*

*Note the role of purchasing managers as perceived by those in the larger companies in the sample.

Considerable expertise has been developed by purchasing departments to ensure that outside supply prospects are viable from the points of view of quality, production capability, direction of personnel and financial stability. All of this comes within the general heading of 'supplier assurance' – a pre-sourcing checkout. Coupled with this is the development of monitoring systems once the prospect is a supplier; these 'vendor rating schemes' are often computer supported and buyers have a great deal of information on both potential and existing sources of supply outside the company. It is but a small step to make similar objective judgements of the buyer's own in-house facility – purchasing should have the wherewithal and the expertise to do it.

REFERENCES

(1) H. Levy and M. Sarnat, 'The Make or Buy Decision' in *Journal of General Management*, vol. 4, no. 1, 1976.

(2)   John Stevens, *Measuring Purchasing Performance*, Business Books, 1978.

FURTHER READING

S. A. Bergen, 'The Make or Buy Decisions' in *R & D Management*, vol. 8, no. 1, 1977.

J. W. Culliton, *Make or Buy*, Harvard University Graduate School of Business Administration, 1942, 4th reprint, Boston, 1956.

N. Davies, 'Discussion on Japanese Production Methods', *Institution of Mechanical Engineers*, 24 September 1981.

D. H. Farmer, 'Developing Purchasing Strategies' in *Journal of Purchasing and Materials Management*, vol. 6, no. 11, Autumn 1978.

Harry Gross, *Make or Buy*, Prentice-Hall, Englewood Cliffs, New Jersey, 1966.

H. Gross, 'Make or Buy Decisions in Growing Firms' in *The Accounting Review*, vol. 14, no. 4, 1966.

H. Gross, 'Purchasing Procedures for Make or Buy Decisions' in *Journal of Purchasing*, vol. 2, no. 4, 1966.

R. W. Haas and T. R. Wotruba, 'Marketing Strategy in a Make or Buy Situation' in *Industrial Marketing Management*, vol. 5, no. 2, 1976.

C. C. Higgins, 'Make or Buy Re-Examined' in *Harvard Business Review*, March-April 1955.

M. J. Hubler, 'The Make or Buy Decision' in *Management Services*, vol. 3, no. 6, 1966.

L. R. Jaunch and H. K. Wilson, 'A Strategic Perspective for Make or Buy Decisions' in *Long Range Planning*, vol. 12, no. 6, 1979.

J. Morley, 'Buy or Make: Its Not Just a Matter of Cost Comparison' in *Business*, vol. 96, no. 7, 1966.

National Association of Accountants MAP Committee, 'Criteria for Make or Buy Decisions' in *Management Accounting*, vol. 55, no. 3, 1973.

D. A. Raunick and A. G. Fisher, 'A Probabilistic Make-Buy Model' in *Journal of Purchasing*, vol. 8, no. 1, 1972.

K. Uyar and H. M. Schonfeld, 'Integrating Production Scheduling, Capacity Acquisition, and/or Abandonment and Make or Buy

Decisions' in *Management International Review*, vol. 13, 1973.

F. C. Weston, 'The Multiple Product Make or Buy Decision' in *Journal of Purchasing and Materials Management*, Winter 1981.

P. Wulff, 'Make or Buy Decisions Shift Like Quicksand' in *Purchasing*, vol. 73, no. 6, 1972.

11

Purchasing from abroad

Richard Beardon

In the context of most industrial and commercial enterprises the question of purchasing from abroad is a strategic issue which can be viewed without regard to the influences of politics and the interests of the national economy. Such influences are the subject of continuous debate elsewhere. It is sufficient for this chapter to focus on the strategic and tactical aspects of purchasing abroad.

MARKET DIFFERENCES

There are a number of factors which differentiate purchasing abroad from local sourcing. The relative importance of each will also differ from market to market and between commodities. However, the presence of any or all of these factors adds complication and risk to the purchasing process. A few of the most significant factors are mentioned here in order to give the reader insight into the complexity of purchasing abroad. Understanding these factors can help towards achieving success in purchasing abroad.

Language is perhaps the most obvious difference likely to be involved. No general rules apply here. It is unsafe to assume that all business can be successfully conducted in the native language of the purchaser. In the case of English this will frequently be possible, but there are many situations in which the purchaser can perform better if he has the ability to trade in the language of his supplier. Each case should be looked at on its merits and if language presents an opportunity to win, decisions should be taken accordingly.

Currency is possibly the most complicated factor. Exchange rates are dynamic indicators reflecting the ever changing relationships between competing economies. They represent an area of significant risk and constant uncertainty. Frequently the decision to purchase abroad can be taken regardless of the currency exchange factor. However, there are many instances where the exchange rate is the prime motivator in the decision to purchase abroad. The buyer, in these cases, must quantify the risk and take appropriate action to safeguard his position. Such circumstances require specialist knowledge and skill.

Legal requirements pertaining to business differ greatly between countries. This is another area of risk completely beyond the control of a buyer. Not only are laws developing all the time within countries but there are now many parts of the world where trade is conducted under collective laws. Examples are found in EEC and OPEC and it is reasonable to expect an extension of these influences as similar organisations develop among the developing countries.

Politics may be ignored by an enterprise, but to ignore the politics of overseas countries when considering purchasing abroad is perilous. This is another factor which can frequently add significant risk to the purchasing decision and underlines the frequent difficulty in justifying purchasing from abroad.

Economic performance of overseas countries is another key factor which differentiates purchasing abroad from local sourcing. It is hard enough to understand and forecast performance trends of the buyer's own economy; to attempt such an understanding of one or several overseas economies adds a significant dimension to the tasks of a purchasing department.

Cultural differences, though frequently overlooked, play an important part in determining the success or failure of purchasing abroad. The prospective purchaser should be aware of the differences between his own business and sociological culture and that of his prospective trading partners. He must evaluate and take account of the effects of such differences.

Ethical standards differ widely throughout the world and trade is frequently conducted to the standards of the supplier rather than the buyer. Here again, the buyer should understand the differences and act accordingly in his own company's best interest and within the laws which pertain.

Financial practice is another variable factor. The capital structure and credit financing arrangements available to buyers varies considerably from one country to another. Ignorance of the custom and practice in potential supply markets will involve the buyer in lost opportunity.

Lead times when purchasing abroad are usually different from local sources – not always greater!

REASONS FOR PURCHASING ABROAD

The world is becoming a smaller place, or so we are frequently informed by the air travel industry. Undoubtedly the volume of international trade has increased significantly, but also there is an ever increasing range of products which are available from many parts of the world. This situation will always be changing in line with the industrial and economic development of individual nations.

Perhaps this is the most important reason why purchasing operations should always be open to the idea of purchasing abroad. Each year there will be numerous changes to the industrial base of scores of countries, and each change presents new opportunities to buyers.

Apart from this generally opportunistic reason for considering overseas sourcing, there are several particular factors which, frequently, provide compelling reasons for purchasing abroad.

Quality

Quality is more often than not involved in the decision to look abroad for sourcing. But quality in this context can mean several things. For instance, the buyers of raw materials for process industries may find what is apparently the same commodity available from several countries, but the quality available from each can vary greatly (e.g. the inherent purity of the raw material in question). To other buyers the quality factor in purchasing abroad can be associated with the reliability or consistency of manufactured goods produced under different conditions and methods in each source. An awareness of such differences places the buyer in an advantageous position in negotiation with both local and foreign sources.

Price

Price is most frequently quoted as the major reason for purchasing abroad. The explanation for this is peculiar to each situation but can usually be explained by identifying one or more of the following:

- lower raw material cost perhaps associated with proximity to source
- lower wage and social cost
- economies of large-scale production
- government subsidy
- higher productivity
- lower transportation costs.

However, price comparisons are misleading if taken at face value. A more appropriate criterion for decision making in purchasing abroad is the total through cost of the sourcing decision. This is one of the main difficulties associated with overseas purchasing and is dealt with in a later section in this chapter.

Availability

Availability and delivery performance are also relevant to many overseas sourcing decisions. In the same way that certain grades or levels of quality may be available from specific markets, so, also, may some types of manufacturing process or manufactured goods have their availability restricted to overseas markets. Furthermore, it is common to find overseas sources offering their products or service with more competitive availability than local sources. This is, usually, the result of an overseas source electing to compete more on availability than any other aspect of his total service. Sometimes the buyer needs such advantageous delivery service even at the expense of higher prices or lower credit terms.

Customer preference

In many consumer product markets the matter of customer preference plays a key part in the sourcing decision. For example, a merchandising operation dealing with fashion goods, will not survive unless it provides its customers with a 'fashionable' product. This might originate abroad and is likely to change at frequent intervals. The buyer must understand the advantages offered by different markets in relation to such fashion demand. Customer preference may also be based upon perceived quality or value, or on the reliability of foreign goods in comparison to those of local origin. This preference may only be based upon general impressions of overseas supply markets as in the situations referred to above.

Brand

On the other hand, customer preference influences the purchasing decision most clearly when product brand is involved. In situations where a particular brand is desired by customers or specified by product designers, the buyer has few options other than to purchase abroad if that is where the particular brand originates. However, if other aspects of the purchase decision are particularly unfavourable, the buyer may decide to seek a local source which can supply the foreign brand under licence or other arrangement.

Technical

Technical reasons for sourcing abroad are frequently cited by organisations importing manufactured goods and foodstuffs. Technological development is taking place simultaneously all over the world but at differing rates. Consequently there may be advantage to the buyer from sourcing with the technically most advanced suppliers who may be abroad. Such technological advantages may be in the products themselves or reflected in the product price or quantity already mentioned. In the case of foodstuffs the buyer should take account of overseas market achievements in growing, breeding, rearing or cultivation, all of which are affected by the rapid technological developments of recent years.

Product features

Special product features offered by overseas suppliers can often attract a buyer. These may be separate from the technical or product brand characteristics referred to above. For instance, a particular overseas supplier might offer products with longer service intervals, or smaller overall size, or lower weight. Such features of a product design can be sufficient to justify purchasing abroad despite having to manage the difficulties referred to later.

Whilst each of the issues discussed here may be of critical importance, in most situations where purchases are made abroad the reasons are complex, being based upon a number of the factors described.

Reciprocal trading

Eastern bloc nations and many countries in the underdeveloped and developing regions use reciprocal trading practices to help balance their foreign currency transactions. These situations usually arise where domestic exporting companies are trying to sell into one of these soft currency countries. The customer country then tries to sell some of its own products as a condition of purchasing from the domestic exporter. In these situations the domestic company buyer is usually involved in finding something to buy from the country in which his organisation seeks a sale. The buyer may have a possibility to buy something he needs but may have to sacrifice some quality, cost, or availability in order to secure the two-way arrangement. In many cases the buyer cannot find anything he wants for his normal business. In that situation the buyer can consider joining forces with an import-export house which specialises in handling goods arising from reciprocal deals, or he can effectively purchase and attempt to resell the necessary product himself. In either case the buyer should attempt to evaluate the risks and opportunities of the reciprocal trade before committing his company to it in conjunction with his sales operation.

Export markets

Companies which are involved in home market and export markets may find that the requirements of their export markets dictate some foreign product content. Nationalistic prejudice or preference is sometimes a significant factor which may preclude offering home market specification to export customers. The buyer who is involved in such circumstances will need to understand clearly the value which is attached to the item he is required to purchase abroad. Failure to do so may involve him in unsuccessful protracted price or specification negotiations.

The inclusion of export market requirements and reciprocal trading as reasons for purchasing abroad is not intended to imply that either is undesirable in business. These can be difficult matters for purchasing staff, but they can also be profitable opportunities and provide a stimulus to competition. In addition to the reasons already described which are associated with marketing strategy, there are several reasons for purchasing abroad which may be linked to a purchasing or manufacturing strategy.

Capital expenditure projects

This is an area in which buyers become involved in purchasing abroad. The selection of capital plant and equipment is usually motivated by technical staff within the buyer's organisation. In these cases the buyer's role is to ensure that the many peculiarities of the overseas supply source will not put his company's investment plans at risk. Further, there is likely to be considerable negotiation involved around the commercial aspects of capital expenditure abroad.

Supply security

The frequently debated subject of supply security is a strategic issue to most organisations. It is possible that a firm wishes to increase supply security and consider that this may be best achieved by developing additional sources abroad. A contrasting strategy might consider that supply security is best achieved by single sourcing a key material into a stable overseas market. These apparently contradictory approaches are each worthy of consideration in relation to the needs of the buyer's business.

Capacity

A manufacturing strategic reason concerns capacity. This may be a need for more capacity than is available in the domestic supply market. On the other hand it might involve a decision to encourage the expansion of capacity in an overseas market which has intrinsic advantages to the buyer; perhaps lower wage or material cost.

Alternatively the buyer may require capacity which is more flexible than domestic sources. This might enhance the service given to the buyer's customers in terms of delivery time or response to seasonal demand fluctuations.

Stimulus to competition

Purchasing abroad can be a strong stimulus to competition. The desire for more competition in a supply market may be good reason for a buyer to source part of his requirements abroad. This may result in some improvement in service or trade terms offered by domestic sources if the buyer's custom is desired by those domestic suppliers. On the other hand this reasoning has a serious risk that sourcing abroad will actually weaken the position of the domestic sources resulting in even less good performance from them.

DIFFICULTIES

Careful consideration of the factors which differentiate markets and give reason for a purchasing abroad decision will suggest to the reader the presence of many difficulties which are not present in domestic sourcing arrangements. The most difficult aspect is the cost comparison. This has several elements which put it into the area of considerable risk and uncertainty.

In the first instance the buyer should seek to compare domestic and foreign sources at the ex-works price level. This will show, in most cases, whether there is a real difference in selling price. To the extent of this difference, calculated at the exchange rate ruling during the comparison, the buyer can begin to assess the competitiveness of the foreign source. This in turn must be analysed or judged whether the difference seen is caused by true cost factors, or commercial policy.

At this point it is worth returning to the question of culture. This plays a big part in determining the behaviour pattern of foreign sellers. The buyer should be aware of who will negotiate his price, who will expect a dutch auction, and who will substantiate his price with cost information. Such information is of paramount importance to the buyer in determining the real price for comparison purposes.

Detailed analysis of quotations and prices from abroad should be the buyer's rule otherwise the opportunity presented by the foreign bidder may be misunderstood. For example, the foreign source may operate a different accounting convention regarding depreciation of plant and amortisation of special tooling. This may cause a price quoted to look uncompetitive at first sight, but when analysed may in fact offer some distinct advantages to the buyer.

The cost comparison is relatively simple when based upon ex-works prices at current exchange rates. But many sourcing decisions involve commitments for considerable time periods. In these cases the buyer will need to assess the current competitiveness of the foreign source and make a forecast of how that might change over time. Two complicated factors, both beyond the control of buyer and seller, and different for each country, are involved: currency exchange rates and cost inflation rates. The buyer is well advised to adopt one or a combination of the following ideas in an attempt to minimise the risk of purchasing abroad:

- consult several of the leading professional economic forecasts, for example NIESR or Henley Centre for Forecasting
- seek the view of the seller
- specifically negotiate price variation clause to protect competitive position
- agree base price to be subject to movement in line with domestic economy
- agree to renegotiate price after initial fixed period in order to preserve competitive position established at the outset.

Although this chapter is not intended to be the buyer's guide to international trade, it is important to note that the terms of trade between two countries as reflected in their currency exchange rates are to a great extent determined by the relative performance of those economies and, in particular, their rate of inflation. Thus, a buyer making purchase agreements with a strong currency may find his costs affected adversely by exchange rate movements; on the other hand, had the buyer opted to remain locally sourced, his costs could be affected adversely by higher domestic inflation.

A further difficulty concerning currency exchange rate uncertainty affects an organisation which both buys and sells in the same overseas markets. If such trade can be balanced the exchange risks to both sides of the business can be protected.

Freight

Freight is another element in the total cost of purchased goods, particularly from abroad, and is frequently ignored as a major profit opportunity. A buyer who is considering purchasing abroad must give serious thought to this element. Above all the golden rule is to ensure that transport is carried out by professional organisations who obtain the business on the basis of free competition. But the haulage contractor or shipping line or railway is not the only potential weak link in the chain. The selection of contractor and negotiation of freight cost can be carried out by the seller or the buyer or by an agent acting on behalf of either seller or buyer. For full control on the cost and the operation itself the buyer is well advised to carry this responsibility himself. In circumstances which preclude that approach, the use of a freight forwarding company is usually appropriate, but the buyer should discuss arrangements with several agents before placing this type of business.

Administration

The administration associated with purchasing abroad is another essential ingredient to the menu of difficulties. It is comprised of work associated with the cost comparison tasks mentioned above and with the procedural intricacies of importing goods. The importation procedures required by HM Customs are not difficult and do not constitute a barrier to entry of goods to the UK. This subject is frequently detailed in textbooks but the writer suggests it is better handled by the buyer making enquiries direct to HM Customs and Excise and to reputable freight forwarders.

Lead times

By comparison with administrative procedures the implications of lead times for purchases abroad is more difficult. The lead time will normally be greater when purchasing abroad than local procurement. This may impact on several aspects of the buyer's business. For instance, a longer supply lead time may adversely impact on a company's ability to react quickly to changes in its customer demand volume or mix. This inflexibility could cause a consumer goods manufacturer to miss a sudden seasonal upsurge. The buyer will probably not be required to exercise sole judgement on such difficulties. The issue about supply lead time could be strategically important and might result in a company deliberately turning away from some other attractive aspects of purchasing abroad. In some cases the importance of this problem could result in a company seeking to develop local suppliers in order to achieve the advantages offered abroad and yet retain the benefits of shorter local source lead times.

Extended purchase commitment and stock obsolescence

If lead times are longer than local sources it implies a greater financial commitment associated with the longer pipeline. This is an important matter for the buyer to deal with in his negotiations with overseas suppliers. They are asking the buying company to accept greater financial liability if they purchase abroad. The buyer might be able to use this as a lever to obtain some compensating advantage from the contract, such as extended credit. Stock obsolescence is an inevitable risk if a company decides to purchase long lead-time goods, or if it decides to hold higher levels of inventory on account of the longer lead time. A corollary of obsolete stock is the increased time involved in the implementation of specification changes where items are purchased abroad on long lead times. This is a definite disadvantage to companies involved in highly dynamic product development and change; and is particularly true for manufactured consumer goods.

Misunderstandings

Purchasing abroad is prone to difficulties of communication resulting in misunderstandings. The best known example of this is found
in trading relationships with Japan. In this example the Japanese
character finds it very difficult to say no. Thus, a Japanese seller will
normally say yes or nod his head and smile to every question. A
buyer who is unfamiliar with the social customs of Japan can easily
misunderstand his position. Language difficulties are also likely to
result in serious misunderstandings from time to time. When
business is conducted in English the buyer must be cautious that the
seller is not misunderstanding the spoken or written word. English
grammar, and in particular, sentence construction, is so different
from many other languages that a foreigner may understand
individual words but misconstrue their meaning when phrased in a
certain way.

Rejections

Rejections of faulty goods purchased abroad are more costly and
difficult to handle than from local sources. During early negotiations
sellers, naturally, play down the risk of rejections, yet experience in
several industries suggest that the buyer must exercise caution on
such promises. Goods may be rejected for several reasons many of
which cannot easily be anticipated. At the time a rejection occurs
the buyer must decide whether to seek immediate replacement or to
use the faulty material under a specification concession, or after
rework and repair. Such decision making is usually constrained by
some of the other difficulty factors described above. For instance,
the lead time may preclude replacement unless rapid premium-cost
freight is available.

Supplier appraisal

Supplier appraisal is more difficult abroad. The activity of assessing
potential sources prior to contract placement is accepted in the UK,
but in many parts of the world sophisticated buying techniques are
not well received or understood. Furthermore, the cost of performing such assessments on faraway sources may not be justifiable.

PRIORITIES FOR SUCCESS

Supply strategy

A consistent supply strategy which forms part of an overall corporate strategy is the first priority for successful purchasing abroad. There is no advantage to be derived from adopting a casual or haphazard approach to overseas sourcing. Such an approach is likely to place the buyer and his company into a perilous position resulting from a failure to manage the difficulties mentioned above.

People

The second priority is people. The buyer who purchases abroad must be intellectually capable of analysing market differences. Further, the buyer has to manage the difficulties and understand thoroughly the reasons for purchasing abroad. These requirements demand high calibre staff who will need training in specific skills such as freight and importation procedures. Further, it is often appropriate to give staff who purchase abroad the facility to study appropriate foreign cultures and languages.

Market research and intelligence

Market research and intelligence is a key factor for success. The scope for this work is unlimited if the buyer treats the whole world as his market. However, it is usually a simple matter to research foreign markets to identify their strong industries and to pursue research in those directions.

Travel and communication

This is another high priority. The buyer who trades abroad must at all times ensure that communication is prompt and clear. This will be facilitated by travel to the intended sources. There is no substitute for face-to-face contact of supplier capability.

Having paid attention to the above priorities which are pre-requisite for success, the buyer is ready to do business abroad. The remaining success factors are common to local sourcing and include professional negotiation, clear specification, secure freight arrangement, and concise and agreed contractual terms.

The following is a summary checklist for managers considering how well they are placed to cope with the task of purchasing from abroad.

Checklist

Do I know why I should buy abroad?
Is the reason for buying abroad consistent with corporate objectives?
Are the buying staff capable or trained to purchase abroad?
Can I manage the freight aspects internally?
Do I understand the risks and opportunities of buying abroad?
Can I manage the difficulties listed above, and in particular, will the currency exchange problems be manageable?
Are there any cultural or ethical problems involved?
Have I completed a thorough cost comparison before deciding to purchase abroad?
Are the communication channels effective?
Is the supply secure and quality assured?

PART III
PURCHASING SYSTEMS AND FUNCTIONS

12

Purchasing systems*

Peter Baily

A purchase department which makes many thousands of purchases every year, and trades with hundreds of suppliers, and works with many other departments in the organisation it serves, has to perform quite a complex set of administrative tasks. Its work can be considerably facilitated if the systems it uses are efficient. Good systems and records do not of themselves produce an effective, efficient or successful purchasing operation. But poor purchasing systems and records make it hard even for able purchasing people to function effectively.

Because organisations differ considerably in the tasks they take on, the problems they face and the solutions they adopt, it is not feasible to put forward a standard system suitable for all requirements. However, it is possible to analyse a typical purchase transaction into its successive stages and to consider some of the forms and procedures which are in common use at each stage, and this should be useful to anyone who is designing or redesigning a purchasing system.

The four successive stages in a typical purchase transaction are:

Stage 1 – origination
Stage 2 – selection

---

* This chapter is based on *Purchasing Systems and Records* by Peter Baily, 2nd edition, Gower 1983.

Stage 3 – ordering

Stage 4 – completion.

These will be considered in turn.

ORIGINATION

Purchases normally originate outside the purchase department. Exceptionally, buyers may be responsible for determining requirements in addition to procuring them: for instance, the buyer/first sales in a department store, or a specialist raw material buyer in certain types of manufacturing. Purchasing may also be a section or subdivision of a materials department which also includes stock control or production planning and control; but the purchases which originate with these other sections or subdivisions need to be notified to the purchasing section just as if they originated in a different department.

The normal situation is that purchasing acts when it receives a purchase requisition. This document serves three purposes:

1 It requests that a purchase be made.
2 It authorises the expenditure.
3 It serves as record, for audit and other purposes, of what was done.

Three versions are in common use: the general-purpose requisition, the travelling requisition, and the blanket requisition.

An example of a general-purpose requisition is given in Figure 12.1. This would be date-stamped on receipt in the department and passed to the appropriate buyer for action. The buyer checks that the bottom righthand box, 'authorised by', has been signed or initialled by an authorised signatory. These general-purpose requisitions are used to indent for anything from a box of chalks to capital equipment. Capital expenditure is usually approved by an authorised committee responsible to the board of directors. A box of chalks could obviously be approved at a much lower level. A list of authorised signatories, with their cash limits where appropriate, is kept in the purchase department.

The buyer also checks that the description of the goods given on

PURCHASE REQUISITION	Department _____		
	Date _____		
To purchase department: Please obtain the undermentioned	Number _____		
Suggested supplier	Quantity and description	Price	Required for
	Requisitioned by	Authorised by	

Figure 12.1 General purpose requisition

the requisition is adequate commercially. Requisitioners do not always express their needs in terms suitable for communications with suppliers; some editing may be required after checking buying records and specification files.

Order number, and a note of any preliminary investigations such as requests for quotations, are entered in the bottom lefthand box before the requisition is filed. Two years is normally long enough to keep old requisitions on file.

Travelling requisitions save time and effort in repeat ordering or regular purchases. Unlike the general-purpose requisition, printed on flimsy paper for once-only use, the travelling requisition is printed on card for repeated use. It is used for maintenance, repair and operating supplies (MRO). It was also widely used for stock replenishment and production components and material until computer systems offered better ways of doing it.

A travelling requisition is a permanent order card kept by the originating department on which is entered permanent data such as description of the goods and requisitioning department. Space is provided to enter variable data such as date, quantity required etc. There is usually a column in which the authorised signatory can write his initials (see Figure 12.2).

									Date received purchasing department	Purchase order number				

PURCHASE REQUISITION CARD   Card number

Classification _____

Code number _____   Description _____

Approved suppliers

Minimum stock _____

Average monthly consumption _____

Contract

Inquiries issued

Date	Present stock	Quantity required	Unit	Delivery wanted	Required for	Approvals	Date received purchasing department	Purchase order number	Supplier	Price	Carriage	Settlement terms

Figure 12.2 Travelling requisition

The travelling requisition is sent to purchasing whenever another purchase is required. Order details are entered on the card by purchasing and the card is returned to the originator, who files it until he needs to re-order. Usage rates, ordering frequency, and other useful data can be deduced from the data recorded on the form. There is no problem as to correct description of articles, since both the shorthand description used in company jargon and the normal commercial description used in the trade can be shown on the form.

Finally, there is the 'blanket' requisition which is used when a large number of requirements arise at the same time. No special form is in common use for these schedules of requirements. Indeed, they may not be printed out in hard copy format, with some computer systems.

Many stock-control systems are based on periodic review of sections of the stock range. This review may be done by physical check or stock count, or by examination of records kept manually or by computer. Each review of a section of the stock range results in a blanket requisition for stock items which need to be replenished. Obviously it would be wasteful to prepare individual general-purpose requisitions for each item required.

Many production planning and control systems, such as materials requirements planning (MRP), and period batch control, also produce periodically a schedule of requirements or blanket requisition, which it is pointless to convert into a host of individual requisitions.

A typical MRP system is implemented on a computer connected to a number of workstations or visual display units (VDUs). Starting with a master production schedule, or list of finished products to be completed each week, the system explodes this into time-phased schedules of sub-assemblies, parts and materials requirements, allows for stock on hand and orders due in, and produces a schedule of net requirements per period. This can be printed out to serve as a blanket requisition for purchasing. But if the system includes a purchase order module, there would be no need for hard copy. The net requirements can be shown on the VDU screen as required, and gradually converted as work is done on them into proposed orders, firm orders and order releases.

SELECTION

After notification of requirement, the next stage is to decide where to buy it. Sometimes two stages are involved: detailed specification or brand selection, and source evaluation or supplier selection. These two stages often interact: you decide to replace your brand X car with another brand X car, but when you look at net cost of replacement after taking account of trade-in allowance, brand Y looks very attractive; then you shop around the distributors to establish the variety of discounts and other inducements which are on offer.

Three buy-classes or types of buying situation may be distinguished: the straight rebuy, the modified rebuy, and the new task. New task purchases tend to involve more people, in more departments, in the search for suppliers and the selection of ordering policy and preferred source.

For major subcontracts and for complex, unique, high-cost requirements of this type, it is normal practice to start with a request for information (RFI) document. This is sent to a large number of possible suppliers and in effect asks them if they would be interested in quoting for the supply of the goods or services, of which brief particulars are given. It may be that existing commitments, future plans or some other reason rule this out, in which case the supplier can simply state that he is unable to submit a bid. Suppliers who are interested in the business give particulars of the information which the purchaser needs to know before proceeding to the next stage, which is to decide on a short list of suitable suppliers and to send them a request for quotation (RFQ), or as the form is often called, an enquiry, together with full details of the requirement.

At the other extreme, the 'straight rebuy' normally involves very little in the way of supplier selection since there is a strong preference for continuing to deal with existing suppliers who have proved their capability to satisfy the needs of the purchaser. In fact for such items the ordering policy may be to place annual contracts, possibly covering the requirements of several different branches or divisions of the organisation, so that the buyer's first action after checking the details of the requisition would be to refer to a contract file, and if there is a group or period contract in existence an order would be placed immediately, mentioning the contract reference number. If no contract exists, reference to the purchase record will show where orders have been placed in the past and whether supplier performance has been satisfactory in respect of price, delivery, service and quality. A repeat order on the same supplier will normally be placed if all is well; otherwise the 'buy-class' becomes similar to a 'modified re-buy'. However 'normally' should not be interpreted as meaning 'indefinitely'; sooner or later the offering even of a satisfactory supplier should be compared with the offerings of other potential suppliers.

It is hard to say when this should happen – when a buyer should go to the market and invite quotations from new sources of supply even though an existing source is felt to be reasonably satisfactory. Energetic marketing by a new source, or an unexpected request for a price increase from the old source, are often the reason. In the absence of trigger events of this kind, it may be confidently said that three months is too short a time, and twenty years is too long a time, before the buyer should check on what alternative suppliers are prepared to offer. Experience and knowledge of the market are the buyer's best guide in this connection.

In the 'modified re-buy' situation then, whether the modification is due to some change in the nature of the requirement, or to some change in the market itself, or to some change in the relationship between buyer and seller such as a requested price increase, or failure to meet quality or delivery or other requirements on the part of the seller, the first step the buyer takes is to make a shortlist of feasible sources. This would also be his first step in the case of 'new task' purchases which were less demanding in terms of the supplier's capacity and resources than those mentioned previously. Requests for quotation are then sent to the names on the shortlist.

In compiling a shortlist of potential suppliers, buyers may make use of trade directories, their own knowledge and experience and that of colleagues, or various computerised directories. A large organisation might even maintain a centralised computer facility giving details of possible suppliers and subcontractors by trade and geographical location, plus details of existing suppliers with statistics on business placed with them by various branches or divisions and 'vendor rating' information. There may be a technical library, maintained by purchasing services unit or drawing office services. Computerised supplier directories have been set up by polytechnics and other organisations to cover particular areas and national directory and enquiry services are becoming available, which can be consulted on line or by telephone.

The request for quotation or enquiry form, which has been mentioned several times, is shown in Figure 12.3.

It should *not* be modelled on the purchase order form, as this will inevitably result in careless recipients sending the goods instead of a quotation. A better model is the company letterhead, with some form of words such as 'please quote your price, terms and delivery period for the supply of the under-mentioned'. The example shown in Figure 12.3 is a neat form designed by a printer as a multipart carbon-interleaved set. The three boxes at the upper lefthand side allow for three names and addresses; if more than three suppliers need to be contacted, additional forms would be used.

When quotations are received, they will of course be compared on a basis of price, terms and delivery period; but many other things may be taken into account. The Department of Industry booklet, *Delivering the Goods: A code of good practice for purchase and supply*, published in 1983, points out that:

243

INQUIRY FOR QUOTATION

BRITISH SUGAR CORPORATION LTD.
CENTRAL PURCHASING DEPARTMENT
P.O. BOX 26, OUNDLE ROAD
PETERBOROUGH PE2 9QU
TELEX: 32149 & 32273
TELEPHONE: PETERBOROUGH 63171
TELEGRAMS: SUGARCROP, PETERBOROUGH

Please quote this Reference in any correspondence or Telephone call

Reference	Date	Contact
— — — — —		

Please quote us, delivered carriage paid on the conditions specified overleaf, your lowest fixed price for goods enumerated below. A Cash Discount of 2½% M/A will be deducted from Invoice (unless otherwise stated in your Quotation).

Your Quotation should reach this office by:

For and on behalf of **BRITISH SUGAR CORPORATION LTD.**

Specification:

Delivery date of goods _____

Delivery of goods to be made to

Figure 12.3 Request for quotation

Value for money should not be judged solely on the basis of lowest initial cost; life-time costs and other relevant factors should also be taken into account. Factors such as:

- reliability of delivery
- design
- performance, durability and maintenance costs
- productivity improvements and improvements in user efficiency

will affect the total cost over the life of the product and can justify a higher initial cost. Actions to promote the competitiveness of suppliers can also justify an additional initial cost or greater technological risk if over the longer term the purchaser expects to gain improved value for money.

Where the purchase is not of standard merchandise, or goods which can be seen and inspected before purchase, but is for the manufacture of goods or the supply of services in accordance with the purchaser's specification, it will also usually be necessary to make a check on the supplier's quality control system, and in some instances on the supplier's total quality capability, as considered in Chapter 7.

Analysis of quotations received is often followed by negotiation with the preferred suppliers. It is not considered good practice simply to try to beat down the quoted prices, but there is often plenty of scope for constructive negotiation to improve the terms and conditions of contract or to arrive at a more cost-effective way to order. The request for quotations may itself be structured in such a way as to provide a basis for these negotiations, and if a supplier has a reasonable chance of obtaining a large slice of business he may well be willing to make several alternative offers, on the basis for instance of annual contracts or separate orders, of quantity discounts or annual rebates etc.

It should be borne in mind that the buyer's objective is not to get the lowest possible price on a series of isolated, independent transactions. It is to construct a comprehensive sourcing system which includes major and minor sources, innovators and cash cows, and to develop sound long-term working relationships with satisfactory suppliers. Also of course the buyer is, and ought to be, subject to audit. When the highest of three independent quotations is the one selected, the audit trail must include reasons and documentation for the choice.

One approach to this is supplier rating, a system of evaluating suppliers ('vendors') by measuring their scores on delivery performance, service, quality conformance, and other factors including perhaps price. The most controversial aspect of supplier rating is the attempt to attach weightings to these scores so that they can be combined into a single overall figure of merit – and thus justify perhaps the award of the contract to the highest bidder; or maybe the lowest bidder, but in any case the best buy. This aspect is dealt with in greater depth in Chapter 15.

THE ORDERING STAGE

This is the crucial stage at which buyer and seller formalise their agreement, on the one hand to supply goods and services at the price and on the terms which have been negotiated, and on the other to accept and pay for them. This would be the stage at which a contract is signed if each transaction could be considered in isolation; but in reality where thousands of transactions occur continually it is necessary to make a clear distinction between an order and a contract, and also to give consideration to the options available in the choice of ordering policy.

A contract could be defined in this connection as a business agreement for the supply of goods or services in return for a price. It is subject to the law of the land; for example, in the UK the Sale of Goods Act and a number of other statutes and parts of the common law are pertinent. It can be the subject of legal action for breach of contract, and in addition to the terms and conditions which are written into the contract by the law of the land, a large number of special terms and conditions may be devised and agreed by the parties to the contract.

An order, on the other hand, is an instruction to a manufacturer or trader to supply something. Confusion can arise because in the typical purchase department for the majority of purchases a single document, the purchase order form, serves as order and as evidence of the contract. This applies both to minor occasional purchases and to major isolated purchases, for instance large capital expenditures.

But for an important group of repeat purchases separate documents are often used for the contractual agreement and for the orders or 'call-offs' which are subsequently made against contract.

The four sorts of document to be considered are general-purpose purchase order forms, period contracts and blanket orders, contract releases or call-offs, and simplified order forms.

General-purpose purchase order form

A typical general-purpose purchase order form is of similar format to Figure 12.4. Normal practice is to make a firm rule that every purchase must be made by means of the official purchase order form, or one of the approved variants. This is not for legal reasons, since no law requires an organisation to use an official order form; it is for practical reasons, to establish clearly what the organisation is committed to accept and pay for and to prevent unauthorised purchases being charged to the firm. In emergencies it may be desirable to instruct firms to supply goods or carry out work immediately, without waiting for the formal procedure, but the position should be rectified as soon as possible by issuing an official order marked 'Confirmation: This order confirms the arrangements made on . . . by . . .'.

The form normally comprises:

1 The words 'Purchase order' in bold type at the top.
2 The name and address of the purchasing organisation, with phone number and telex code where appropriate.
3 A space to enter the name and address of the supplier.
4 The instruction 'please supply –'.
5 A space to enter the quantity, description and price of what is to be supplied.
6 A space to enter date and order number, unless this is preprinted.

Other information given on the form may include delivery address if this is different from that printed on the heading; delivery date or period; payment terms; special inspection arrangements etc. The order is usually signed by an authorised buyer in a space provided.

Three to six copies of the order are usually produced. The top

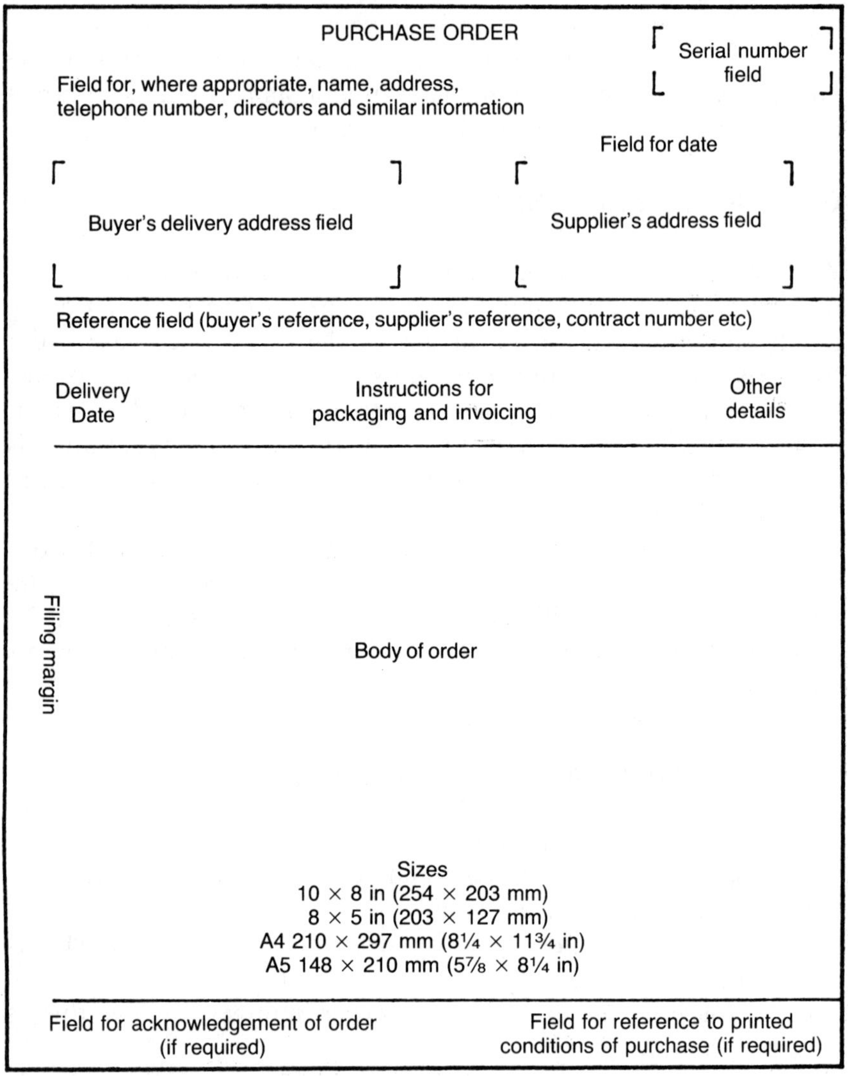

PURCHASE ORDER

⌐ Serial number
L field ⌐

Field for, where appropriate, name, address,
telephone number, directors and similar information

Field for date

⌐ ⌐

Buyer's delivery address field   Supplier's address field

L ⌐ L ⌐

Reference field (buyer's reference, supplier's reference, contract number etc)

Delivery Date	Instructions for packaging and invoicing	Other details

Filing margin

Body of order

Sizes
10 × 8 in (254 × 203 mm)
8 × 5 in (203 × 127 mm)
A4 210 × 297 mm (8¼ × 11¾ in)
A5 148 × 210 mm (5⅞ × 8¼ in)

Field for acknowledgement of order   Field for reference to printed
(if required)   conditions of purchase (if required)

Figure 12.4 Purchase order format

copy goes to the supplier, and sometimes a second copy called the acknowledgement copy is sent as well. In this case the supplier is required to sign and return this as evidence that he has received the order and accepts it on the terms stated. Unfortunately many suppliers will not comply with this requirement without a lot of follow-up and administrative pressure, and a 70 per cent return rate is not good enough to serve the purpose. Consequently many purchasing managers do not use acknowledgement copies. Another copy is filed in an outstanding order file, or open order file, until the transaction is completed, when it is transferred to a closed order file. Closed orders are commonly kept for seven years and then destroyed. Of the remaining copies one goes to goods receiving, another copy is used for invoice certification, and there may also be a follow-up copy, as considered later.

Period contracts and blanket orders

These are all ways of aggregating a variety of requirements into a single contract in order to obtain better terms. For instance corporate headquarters or head office may place contracts on behalf of the whole organisation against which local branches and divisions may be able to place orders on more advantageous terms than would be available if they were to order their individual requirements separately. The period for which the contract runs is usually one year, although both longer and shorter periods are also used, and it is good practice to stagger renewal dates so that each month a number of contracts are reconsidered and renewed, rather than have them all expiring in December for example.

Another version of the period contract is used when a manufacturing establishment knows that for the whole of the year it will require a certain component or material to make one of its products, but the quantity required is not exactly known because it depends on sales. A contract is then made for, say, 50 per cent of the estimated annual requirement, and the actual requirements as they arise are ordered against this contract. This arrangement is mutually advantageous. The advantage to the supplier is that he is assured of a substantial workload and can plan capacity and commitments accordingly. The advantage to the purchaser is firstly a lower price for a larger contract, and secondly better delivery times because of advance booking of capacity.

Blanket orders are another kind of period contract. The term literally means an order which covers a number of different items, but it has come to be used for a contract, usually with a local stockholder, for the supply of a large number of maintenance, repair and operating (MRO) items. A great variety of these is required by any large establishment, and individual requirements are usually for retail quantities. By consolidating the requirements into a single blanket agreement and arranging for a single monthly invoice for goods called off against the agreement, considerable savings in paperwork can be made for both buyer and seller.

Period contracts and blanket orders are not usually instructions to deliver goods, rather they are agreements as to the total quantities, descriptions, prices and terms on which goods are to be supplied. They are used in conjunction with another document, called contract release, call-off, or simply order. Of course the general-purpose purchase order form can be used for this purpose, and this is normal practice when branches or divisions are ordering goods against a period contract placed by head office. Alternatively a special simplified order form may be used, as considered later, and this seems to be normal practice with the so-called 'blanket orders'.

Naturally in both cases reference would be made to the date and number of the main contract against which goods are being ordered.

Contract release form

When the normal purchase order form is used for the period contract, against which a series of delivery instructions later need to be issued, it is felt that confusion could be caused if the same purchase order form is used for the delivery instructions. A special contract release form, such as the example shown in Figure 12.5, is then adopted.

More complicated forms are often found, in which the supplier is instructed to deliver the next period's requirements, and is also authorised to manufacture but not deliver requirements for the following period, in case he finds this advantageous. In addition he may be authorised to purchase materials but not to carry out work on them for a further period. The aim is to enable the supplier to make the most economical manufacturing arrangements open to

DELIVERY INSTRUCTION

Division _____

If you cannot comply with this instruction or
disagree with any figure shown please notify us
immediately

If no such notification is received it will be recorded
that the quantities and conditions are acceptable to
you

Contact _____

Date _____

Authorised _____

Please note conditions overleaf

Part number	Description	Order number	Details of last delivery	Total quantity received	Arrears from periods	A Delivery required		B Manufacture only authorised – not delivery		C Raw material only authorised – not manufacture	For internal use only
						Period	weeks ending	Period	weeks ending	Periods	

Figure 12.5 Contract release

him within the quantity bracket which the purchaser is committed to accept and pay for. In addition, it enables him to place orders for materials with long lead times if this is necessary in order to meet future manufacturing requirements, while at the same time limiting the purchaser's commitment to pay both for work done and for materials bought. In conjunction with an efficient, tightly controlled materials requirement planning system, approaches of this kind can work very well.

Simplified order forms

These are often used for the large number of small orders for routine requirements, especially MRO requirements, which occur in most organisations. According to the well-known 80-20 law, 80 per cent of the transactions account for only 20 per cent of the expenditure, and vice versa. Eighty per cent of the administrative effort and purchasing man-hours will naturally tend to be taken up with these numerous but relatively insignificant transactions, unless a deliberate attempt is made to concentrate on the more important work and to streamline procedures for the less important items.

Blanket orders have already been mentioned as a form of period contract for MRO requirements. They are often used in conjunction with a simplified two-part order form, very similar to a purchase requisition except that it is addressed to a supplier instead of to the purchase department. It often carries a legend to the effect that it is not valid for amounts exceeding £25, or other appropriate small amount, and it can then be signed by the person who is the authorised signatory for requisitions without going through the purchase department at all.

A 'laundry list' type of order is also used with period contracts of this type: the user fills in his weekly requirements on a preprinted order form, which the supplier collects each week, delivering the requirements on his next visit a week later.

A combined requisition/order/cheque form for small orders was devised by an American firm some time ago, and has been adopted by several other organisations including at least one local authority. The document which the user prepares as a requisition is made to serve as an order, and goes to the supplier with a blank cheque attached. This cuts out a good deal of paperwork on both sides of the counter, and an additional attraction for the supplier is that he gets prompt payment.

Standing orders, cash purchases using an imprest account, and a specialist small order buyer who gives immediate service, exemplify the various approaches which are adopted with a view to giving a good service to users for the small orders which often seem so urgent and important to users, but which do not add up to a lot of money in annual terms.

ORDER FOLLOW-UP AND PROGRESSING

Between the ordering stage and the completion stage a period of time elapses which is sometimes regrettably longer than expected. Some firms, whether unscrupulous or desperate, quote delivery times they cannot achieve in order to get the order. Others quote delivery dates in good faith, but when circumstances change and the dates are rescheduled they fail to tell the customer. Others, perhaps the majority of firms who fail to deliver on time, just are not very good at production planning and control.

Nor is the fault all on the side of the seller. Too often purchasers who suffer from late deliveries have only themselves to blame. When suppliers know and are fully aware that the delivery schedule they have received is firm and accurate, and that whenever they fail to deliver on schedule they will have to explain it to their customer, then experience shows that 99 per cent on-time deliveries are by no means unusual.

Nevertheless, order follow-up and progressing is something which needs to be done, not indeed for all orders, but for an important minority of them. In this section we will look briefly, not at the whole process of ensuring delivery on time, but just at the reminder systems which are used to indicate which orders may need to be progressed on any particular day.

The first step is obviously to decide, at the time the order is placed, whether it may need to be progressed, and if so when? Over-kill systems in which every order is followed up a month before it is due by means of postcards and letters saying in effect 'this order is due a month from now; do you expect to deliver at this date?' are quite ineffective, since most of the postcards and letters go straight into the suppliers' wastebaskets. It is necessary to be selective.

Although it is only a minority of orders which need to be progressed in most organisations, it is also true that some orders need to be progressed at more than one stage: for instance towards the completion of design work, at about the time prototypes should be ready for inspection etc.

Having decided that a particular order should be followed up, and having decided also at what date this should be done, the next step is to enter the date into some sort of reminder system. This should all of course be done within one day after placing the order, preferably the following morning.

If a high proportion of orders needs to be followed up, a simple reminder system can be based on producing a special follow-up copy of the order as shown in Figure 12.6. One system requires that each morning the previous day's follow-up copies are sorted by follow-up date and put into suspension files numbered from 1 to 31 (for days of the current month), from January to December (for the next twelve months), plus two or three files for later years. Also, each day the copy orders from the file for that day are taken out and those which have been received or are in transit are destroyed. Those which are

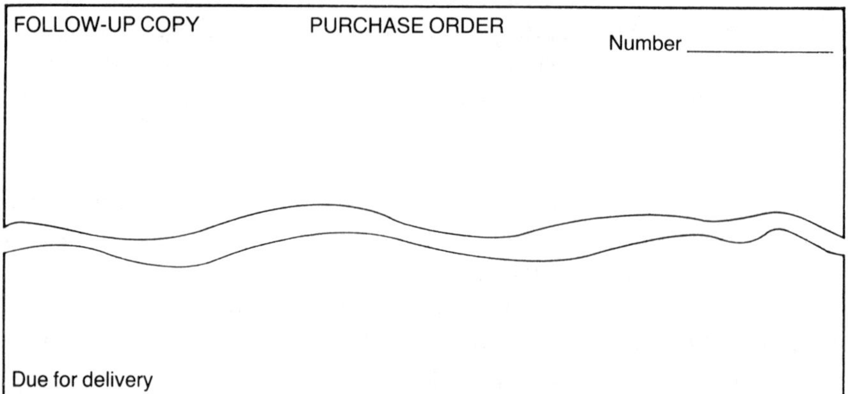

Figure 12.6 Follow-up copy

left are those which may need to be followed up. Each month end the contents of the new month's file are sorted into day order and transferred to the 1 to 31 files.

Other systems are based on progress cards, strip index, coloured tags attached to the top edge of the copy order in the open order file etc. If the number of orders which need to be progressed is not too large, a desk diary can be used. Each day the orders placed the previous day are noted under the date at which progress action will be considered. And a system which is similar in principle, though obviously different in practice, is used in the increasing number of purchase offices whose open order files are maintained on computer storage.

It is simple to devise a program which on request will scan the open order file and produce a list of orders due to be progressed today. Systems have been used in which the computer proceeds directly to the next stage of printing out progress letters which are sent to the suppliers, but in most cases human intervention is desirable before this is done. It is counter-productive to progress orders which are not in fact needed yet; it damages the credibility of the purchase department in the eyes of suppliers to expedite orders which are already in transit, when written notice has been given that they have been dispatched; generally speaking the responsible buyer should consider and approve the proposed list of orders for progressing before progress action is actually taken.

THE COMPLETION STAGE

The final or completion stage of an order or contract occurs when work is completed or goods are delivered and accepted and payment is duly made. Just as the purchasing section does not normally initiate a purchase, so it does not normally carry the main responsibility for the completion stage, although it must be notified of receipts and inspection results and will normally deal with suppliers in connection with discrepancies in quantity or price, rejections and other problems.

The purchasing section also needs to take note of supplier performance for future use in the case of straight re-buys and modified re-buys, as mentioned earlier under the heading of 'selection'. What is required is hard evidence rather than subjective impressions as to whether supplier performance has been satisfactory in respect of price, delivery, service and quality. This should be entered into the supplier record or the purchase record, where these are kept; otherwise it should be filed so as to be accessible the next time a purchase decision needs to be made.

The paperwork associated with the completion stage usually starts with an advice note received by post, which advises that goods have been dispatched (and consequently is sometimes called a dispatch note). These may be routed through the purchasing progress section, so that note may be made on progress documents that goods are in transit, but must be delivered to the goods receiving section the same morning. Each morning the goods receiving section will also look through their collection of advice notes (and dispatch notes) to see if any are overdue, so that action may be taken.

When goods are delivered, they are identified with the aid of the packing notes or advice notes included with them, the advice notes or dispatch notes previously posted, and the copy orders provided for the purpose. Occasionally goods arrive which are not covered by an official order, and the normal procedure is to refuse to accept them. Before the goods have to be taken away again, however, the goods receiving section should contact purchasing in case some emergency arrangement has been made which has not yet been ratified in the paperwork.

Goods delivered may be subject to anything from a quick visual check to a thorough technical inspection before they are accepted. The usual procedure is to prepare a goods received note after acceptance. This is a multipart form with copies to purchasing, accounting, and perhaps the relevant user department. Rejection notes and inspection reports may also be produced. Small organisations sometimes use a goods received book or sheet instead, while a special goods received copy of the purchase order form can save time when most orders are completed by a single delivery.

The next document received by post from the supplier is the invoice, which will eventually be the basis for payment. Before the accounts department makes payment, checks need to be made to ensure that the goods were properly ordered in accordance with authorisation procedures, have been duly received and not rejected on inspection, and that the price and terms shown on the invoice are correct. These checks are clerical procedures almost entirely consisting of the comparison and reconciliation of documents, and can be carried out by a section within the purchasing department (with perhaps some economy in documentation), although it is more usual for them to be carried out by a section within the accounts department. An outline of the whole sequence is shown in Figure 12.7.

ELECTRONIC SYSTEMS

Reference has been made in the course of this chapter to computer systems, but the purchasing systems described have mostly been those which nearly all firms use in the early 1980s, and these are not computer-based. However it seems very likely that this situation will change dramatically in the near future.

The cost of electronic data storage on floppy discs or Winchesters is coming down, and the convenience of access is going up, so rapidly that we may shortly expect to see the purchase department using electronic systems as the norm. The technology is exploding rather than expanding and the pace of development is extremely fast. Already it is practicable, and quite possibly cost effective, for the buyer to have on his desk a keyboard and a visual display unit, comprising his executive workstation. On this he can call up his supplier records showing for each supplier not only name, address and telephone number, but names of contacts, dates of visits, transaction history and performance record; his purchase records showing for each regular purchase the sources used, the prices paid and other information; alternative sources and alternative materials if they exist. Blanket requisitions and schedules of requirements can be shown on the screen, suppliers can be contacted, orders can be drafted, amended, and eventually released for print out. Open order files can be maintained, scanned for progressing purposes and updated etc.

A drawback at the time of writing is that the buyer needs to be able to type. Familiarity with the qwerty keyboard has for some time been regarded as a low-level skill, best left to those who did not expect to rise from the ranks into executive positions. This is not

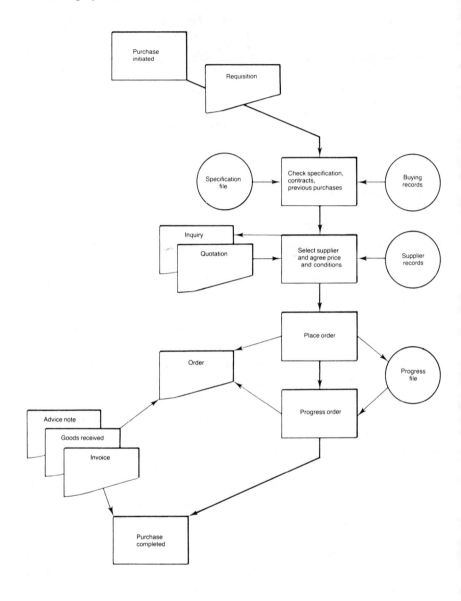

Figure 12.7 Typical purchase transaction

true at present, when access to computer files and instructions for computer action cannot be achieved without typing some message, however brief, into the keyboard. However this situation is likely to change in the near future; voice recognition programs are already in use for some applications, spelling correction programs are available as additions to many word processing systems, and the voice-operated typewriter cannot be far into the future.

Information technology is developing so quickly that this chapter must in some respects become obsolete within a few years. However it will still be true that a typical purchase transaction may be thought of as comprising four stages. The administrative systems and the appearance of the paperwork may change, but there can be little doubt that in ten years' time people will still be doing deals, organisations will still be making difficult decisions as to which suppliers to choose and how many suppliers to use, and price will still for many transactions be settled by person-to-person negotiation rather than emerging from computer routines.

13

Purchasing and manufacturing systems design

Colin Carnall

In many companies the design of manufacturing systems is currently going through a process of radical review. A number of pressures and opportunities seem to be providing the impetus for change and development. The rate of introduction of new technology has accelerated in recent years; robots, computer-numerical control machines, computer-aided design and micro-technology for process control are but a few of the developments under continuous review by those interested in manufacturing. Moreover, the impact of recession, greater international competitiveness and increased uncertainty in product and currency markets form much of the context and are the source of pressure for change. More importantly, many managers are beginning to recognise and exploit opportunities created by some of these developments.

The use of computers in manufacturing provides one example. Computer-aided manufacture (CAM) is well established, comprising the use of computer-based information to plan and control manufacturing plants, inspection and test equipment. The use of computers in design (CAD) is growing rapidly, including applications in design analysis, component design and the preparation of manufacturing instructions and numerical control. From these two basic approaches there is now emerging the concept of the 'linked business system' in which CAD/CAM systems are coupled to marketing, purchasing, production, planning and control, and financial systems. Such a system would include data bases of customer requirements, product design information, manufacturing plant, availability and capacity. Linking all of the information requirements is the definition of parts, sub-assemblies and assemblies. These definitions provide a 'picture' of the customer's requirements, provide purchasing with essential information of specification and purchasing requirements, manufacturing specifications and the information needed to plan and control manufacture.

Another development is the flexible manufacturing system. Here multi-function machine units are combined with an integrated, computerised materials-handling system. Many now refer to a logic of development which emphasises a trend towards increasingly integrated and automated processes, leading ultimately to the 'automatic factory'. In the view of the writer it is all too easy to become obsessed with the 'automatic factory'. Whether or not this can be seen as the culmination of our technical ingenuity, it seems clear that effectiveness and achievement are not related to technology in any simple way. For example Takamiya[1] has found that British plants may be more automated than 'equivalent' Japanese plants and the efficiency of Japanese plants may rest on the meticulousness and dedication to detail of various employees, particularly with respect to quality and reliability.

This leads to a crucial point regarding the developments which have been discussed thus far. It is now generally agreed that a new philosophy of manufacturing is required to take advantage of each of them. Traditional thinking about manufacturing has been too readily dominated by the technological issues. Much of it has been based on the experience of expanding homogeneous mass markets and either stable or growing demand for specialised products over time. The present environment is characterised by more differentiated and shifting market patterns which demands flexibility and adaptability in manufacturing.

In summary, a philosophy of manufacturing is required which provides flexibility, adaptability, low costs and the application of new technology and methods. Moreover, it is necessary to deal with the problems of integrating these elements. The conventional way of achieving greater output and flexibility was to hold inventory, but competitive and financial pressures have changed this situation. Thus the advent of group technology (GT) in batch manufacturing was an attempt to introduce flow principles and was aimed, partly, at reducing inventory levels. More importantly, manufacturing management needs to recognise the increasing importance of relationships and integration, both between departments within a company and between a manufacturing company and its suppliers. Modern technology increasingly demands higher quality standards of the materials and components which are supplied to the production process. In addition the demands of flexibility and low acquisition cost imply the need for more effective co-ordination between suppliers and manufacturer. The role of purchasing in spanning the boundary between the company and suppliers is crucial to this end and the developments on CAD/CAM discussed earlier provide an opportunity which can be of considerable assistance. The concept of the 'linked business system', recognising the 'part' as the basic unit of analysis, can provide a sound data base giving purchasing better access to control information.

An integrated view of manufacturing demands that the importance of managing boundaries is understood, while the need for timely and accurate information as an input to that process is a key to success. Effective integration is not directly a question of automation, although new technology can provide considerable impetus in improving performance. In this chapter the role of purchasing in manufacturing organisations is considered and two developments in the area of scheduling, namely materials requirements planning (MRP) and 'Kanban' are reviewed.

MATERIALS REQUIREMENTS PLANNING (MRP)

MRP is a system designed to control the flow of raw materials, components and sub-assemblies to the final stages of manufacture. This has become increasingly popular in volume production situations. MRP takes the forecast for each item and calculates the requirement for materials and components to match that forecast. A master schedule, detailing output requirements of the company, is converted by means of a parts explosion, into a definition of the requirement for all inputs. For a company with a diversified product range, MRP is feasible only with some form of data processing. MRP provides an information system which produces data relevant to the co-ordination of finished items, raw material/component/sub-assemblies, inventory levels and scheduling throughout the system. In practice MRP systems can either be changed completely at the beginning of each planning period or changed incrementally. Hill[2] reports that the use of MRP will help reduce some of the problems of the fixed re-order point system, including high inventory costs and obsolescence. Moreover, he includes in his discussion details of a survey of 326 companies who use MRP indicating improvements in increased inventory turnover, improved delivery, reduced split-batching due to shortages, reduced numbers of 'progress chasers' required, and reduced lead times. Disadvantages of MRP include the fact that it is oriented toward assembly situations and that the accuracy of data is crucial to the whole process.

The main problem in most discussions regarding MRP (or other 'systems' for that matter) is the idea that the system provides control. It does not do so! It provides the information necessary for control to be established; it does not control anything. People provide control! This may seem a minor distinction but it is crucial. The idea that systems provide control is as fallacious as the idea that 'automation' is the answer to manufacturing problems. Later in this chapter it will be argued that much of our failure to understand the success of Japan lies in our unwillingness to accept this fundamental point. Suffice it, for the moment, to say that the purchasing manager plays an important role in the control of materials and components quality and supply by, firstly, assessing the relationship of each supplier to the company, and secondly, by developing an appropriate strategy to deal with that relationship.

What MRP can provide is the information needed for control to be achieved. Moreover it is a system which focuses upon future loads and on requisitioning replenishment when shortfalls are predicted. Thus it provides a means by which manufacturing, material movement and financial planning data can be generated. Computer based, it can provide data on various manufacturing options enabling the manager to assess the impact of changes to schedules. This is perhaps the main difference between MRP and 'Kanban' which is essentially a static system, ordering replenishment only when material is depleted. Thus 'Kanban' is suitable to stable, high-volume production situations.

THE KANBAN SYSTEM

Toyota's Kanban philosophy has attracted considerable attention, in particular the just-in-time concept which is central to the practice of Kanban. With Kanban two ideas are fundamental: the first is to visualise production as a series of small factory units delivering components to one another in successive stages of the production flow until final assembly. Secondly each factory unit, and therefore each employee, works to a lead time of one day. Thus each unit delivers to the next unit the quantity which that unit needs for one day's production each day. To achieve this Toyota sets monthly production schedules for each product and hence establishes a uniform daily demand throughout the whole system. In practice quantities delivered may vary from the day's requirement but within fairly tight limits, subsequent deliveries being adjusted to allow for this variation.

The main features of this system include a focus on reducing work-in-progress to an absolute minimum, to eliminate bottlenecks, to reduce machine down-time, to reduce set-up and changeover times and to have more frequent deliveries of small numbers of parts. Clearly the operation of such a system requires stability of demand at every stage, good and close relationships with suppliers and a material movement system which can handle the deliveries. In practice many Japanese companies are unable to work to lot sizes of one unit, rather working to minimum and standard lot sizes. The important point to note is the attempt to maximise labour and equipment utilisation by achieving stable plant loads and flow principles. In the process both parties gain benefit. Group technology aims at very similar objectives. Thus, in system terms, there is little that is novel here. The achievement has more to do with working practices, attitudes and relationships than with 'systems'.

Before these latter aspects of Kanban are considered it is necessary to discuss systems-related problems which are often put forward as reasons why Kanban cannot be applied easily in the UK. To do this it is necessary to draw the reader's attention to Chapter 8 by Andrew Green. First, Kanban demands very close relationships with suppliers. Green suggests that Toyota has a unique relationship with its suppliers, acting as 'overlord'. It supports and cultivates supplier relationships and investment. More importantly, the

Japanese worker is prepared to remain at work until a quota of parts is finished. Green argues that a system similar to Kanban was operated in the UK motor industry in the 1950s and 1960s. He argues that this depended upon the operation of a piecework system and a growing vehicle market. Moreover he states that:

> Kanban was introduced at the same time as material control staff monitoring card records were replaced by computers programmed with rigid rules. It was introduced in factories designed to accept one lorry unloading at one time and which were incapable of accepting multi-deliveries. The position was, often, further exacerbated as a result of suppliers utilising larger vehicles capable of carrying more than one day's stock. Inevitably the system failed; 'Kanban' is not the answer to all problems . . .

Clearly there are difficulties here which should not be overlooked. Just as clearly some of them derive from mistakes in other areas; thus computers 'programmed with rigid rules' are increasingly becoming outmoded, or at least there is every reason to work for this end. Most importantly the 'system failed'. But this is the least important part of any philosophy of organisation. Kanban as a philosophy is an ideal which assumed that people will work toward certain ends, that employees will be committed to performance and quality and that purchasing will be concerned to establish effective working relationships with suppliers. Kanban is clearly not the answer to all problems. The belief that it might be is the real problem of management that must be faced. No system can ever solve problems, only people can, by attacking difficulties positively and with energy and commitment.

Green also identifies various operational problems associated with Kanban. He is, of course, quite correct. Some factory layouts make the principles of Kanban problematic. However, it is reasonable to argue that this will not apply to every factory in the United Kingdom and it certainly does not apply to many new factories. In any event, it is worth asking whether or not the reduced work-in-progress, which is potentially possible through Kanban, might not provide the necessary additional space for access. Green's suggestion of 'just-in-time-but-somewhere-else' seems sound enough, particularly where these problems predominate. It is worth noting, however, that in essence the idea is to establish a buffer store of parts, the costs of which are to be incurred, at least partly, by the supplier. This seems sound and probably reflects current practice, even within Kanban. There appears to be some advantage in establishing such stocks by negotiation, for example where costs are the joint responsibility of supplier and user. But only if this leads to effort to review and minimise those costs through improved co-operation and effort on a continuing basis.

Nonetheless, it is the writer's view that to argue that Kanban will not work in Britain is to miss the point; what is essential is the necessity to overcome the tendency to accept problems as being determined and unavoidable and that existing attitudes and behaviour are fixed, for all time. Whether or not the typical UK assembly plant can be run on Kanban lines is not really at issue. As Green notes, most of Japanese industry is not run in this way and, in any event, Kanban is an ideal even with Toyota; its practice allows for flexibility. The real issue turns upon whether or not it is possible to work toward the advantages claimed for Kanban.

Getting quality right and reducing inventories are desirable ends to work for even if they can be only ideals in the ultimate. Reducing set-up times and utilising flow principles in batch manufacturing are also desirable ends, and ends which have attracted wide attention and commitment in Britain since the 1960s. For example, group technology, a philosophy of manufacture which aims to gain for batch manufacturers the advantages of flow processes, has been mentioned earlier. This is achieved by grouping 'families' of like parts together (whether on operations required, shape, size or other criteria must be decided in each particular case) and manufacturing them on one or more group layouts, each comprising a range of processes. Such systems can lead to various advantages (see NEDC 1976[3]) including reduced lead times, reduced work-in-progress, reduced setting-up costs and simplified control. Moreover there seems to be some evidence to suggest that job satisfaction can be enhanced through group technology work organisation. Hill notes that there is one significant limitation to the application of these ideas. A group technology layout effectively dedicates a number of processes to the manufacture of a family of products or parts. Therefore a company needs a stable product mix in order to ensure that the volumes are sufficient to sustain this position over time. In any event, numerically controlled machining (NC) or computer numerically controlled machining (CNC) can provide the advantages achieved by group technology in lower and less stable production volume situations. The main point here is to emphasise, again, the importance of establishing an appropriate manufacturing philosophy in the business as a whole.

PURCHASING AS 'BOUNDARY MANAGEMENT'

Earlier it was emphasised that the crucial role which purchasing plays is in managing the 'boundary' between suppliers and the company. In essence this demands the development of effective links with suppliers, passing information on schedules, quality specifications and delivery and other operational requirements. It demands that effective relationships be formed and maintained at personal and corporate levels. The aim must be to minimise disruption to flows inside the firm by seeking to help suppliers to work to compatible schedules and to appropriate levels of quality. All of this cannot be achieved through systems. Systems can provide the information needed and may comprise the objectives to which the company aspires. Only people can manage these 'boundaries'. This point, that integration, co-ordination and co-operation are based upon the efforts of people, has been central to much that has been written about organisations. To understand the problems of boundary management it is necessary to analyse the nature of the relationships involved in terms of relative power and the implications of that for supplier-buyer relationships.

Kraljic[4] emphasises the importance of this problem area when he argues that:

> In many companies, purchasing, perhaps more than any other business function, is wedded to routine. Ignoring or accepting countless economic and political disruptions to their supply of materials, companies continue to negotiate annually with their established networks of suppliers or sources. But many purchasing managers' skills and outlooks were formed 20 years ago in an era of relative stability and they haven't (sic) changed. Now, however, no company can allow purchasing to

lag behind other departments in acknowledging and adjusting to worldwide environmental and economic changes.

Thus purchasing cannot be seen in isolation from other elements of a company. There is a great need for improved integration and stronger cross-functional relations and co-operation in order that the information on which purchasing staff base contracts with suppliers is both timely and accurate. Kraljic emphasises the systems support essential for all of this to be developed, as follows:

(a) improved operational flexibility through rolling demand forecast systems, coupled with systematic evaluation of supply market data;

(b) integration of purchasing systems with other departmental systems, Kanban being one such system;

(c) effort to improve efficiency, reduce through-put times.

All of this is sensible and is necessary for effective purchasing and supply management in a complex and changing environment. But it is not sufficient of itself. Managing on the 'boundary' of an organisation demands good information and the deployment of special skills. Clearly, improved information can help suppliers and purchasing management to develop unambiguous schedules and specifications of supply. To the extent that it is necessary to reduce lead times and in-process inventory it is essential to examine ways and means of achieving greater integration of supplier and user.

To understand how to achieve this latter objective it is necessary to define the skills which can be deployed. Regrettably, most discussions of management in general, and purchasing or supply management in particular, stress the systematic tasks and activities: e.g. making sure that specifications are clear; that items are not omitted; that costs, performance and schedules are monitored. It is easy to be deceived about the work of a purchasing manager, particularly since computerised systems now play such a crucial role in many companies. Ultimately the development and maintenance of effective relationships with suppliers depends upon reciprocal benefit. Both parties must benefit from the arrangement. This is not all, however. The relation is one of exchange and dependence. The user depends upon the supplier for the delivery of a schedule of items at a specified quality. The supplier may depend upon the user as a source of continuing business. A supplier who has maintained deliveries over a long period of time, providing materials and items which the user company cannot obtain easily elsewhere and whose business is only minimally dependent upon the user company, provides an entirely different case from the new supplier whose business is entirely dependent upon the user company.

Realistically, in the former case it makes sense to seek alternative sources of supply and in the latter case to negotiate low prices and improved quality. More importantly the purchaser will use a variety of strategies to cope with suppliers, the balance being a reflection of the relative dependence of supplier or user on the relationship and on the need to ensure reciprocal benefit, a sense of fair and reasonable treatment. In many cases the experience of supply in practice has been a constant round of late deliveries, non-availability, interruptions, changes of specification and quality problems. Purchasing can influence key people in supplier companies urging them to continue to 'fight against time' and to maintain effort and impetus to 'solve' these problems. Moreover the purchasing manager spends a great deal of time bargaining. In part this is in response to continuing streams of unanticipated problems or opportunities. New problems, design changes, short cuts, inaccurate estimating of cost, time or quality and errors of quantities, all demand solutions. But rational criteria do not always exist, and different people will have different views on how to proceed. Rational solutions not being available, flexible give-and-take can become the order of the day!

The importance of the role of purchasing in developing, establishing and managing relationships with suppliers to ensure system success cannot be overstated. Personal intervention, attention to relevant detail, as well as the enactment of effective strategies are all essential elements for success. Purchasing should work closely with suppliers to help them solve their own problems as well as with production to facilitate such action. There is little doubt that effective information systems will be of considerable assistance in managing this exacting task. However, judgements about people at the supplying company, uncertainties in economic, technological and other areas, provide for an exacting purchasing role. Formal systems become, as it were, an 'agenda'. Control becomes future-oriented with the drive to reduce uncertainty through shortening the instruction/demand time.

CONCLUSION

So far this chapter has discussed some recent innovations in manufacturing systems. An argument for the adoption of an integrated approach has been presented, and the crucial role of purchasing, managing the input to the manufacturing system has been identified. It has been suggested that there is a real need for manufacturing systems to become more integrated, and that there is a key role for purchasing in managing the interface between user, designer and supplier. Further, that the mutuality of the interests of buyer and supplier needs to be better understood if input systems are to be effective. Clearly, purchasing has a principal role in managing such relationships.

Throughout the chapter it has been emphasised that 'systems' such as MRP and Kanban can provide only some of the conditions for improved performance. Only the actions of people, albeit using the ideas involved, can effect improvements, and purchasing people have considerable responsibility in managing the vital interface with suppliers. In order to better understand some of the issues which underlay such relationships, it is worth examining, briefly, some of the ideas of academics working in the social science field concerned with problems of applying academic findings to improve practice in organisations.

These problems are often conceived of as being based upon the divide between theory and practice, between academic and practitioner. It can be said that values, modes of expression and interests differ. The academic is concerned with theory, with questioning and with change, whilst the practitioner is concerned with 'answers', with action, with 'getting things done'. Without wishing to be disassociated from this view, the author believes the argument to be dangerously oversimplified. Managers often tend to be suspicious of theory and frameworks. Similarly they tend to be suspicious of techniques, whether they have their origins in the behavioural sciences or elsewhere. It is all too easy to say that this is because of 'values', or because people tend to be innately 'conservative' and will resist change. Such a view must be based on the notion that a researcher develops understanding and theory which managers could use if only their value systems would allow them to question current methods. However this does not tell the whole story.

The limits of systematic or scientific methods for predicting and providing for the control of human behaviour are well recognised. Particularly striking is the example of the development of PERT (program evaluation and review techniques, otherwise known as network planning or critical path method (CPM)) for the US Navy to control the development of the Polaris Missile. Subsequently, the Polaris Missile was deemed to be an example of a successful development programme and PERT was taken as having made a major contribution to that success. Yet, Sapolski[5] found that:

> In interviews with contractor executives reviewing their experience with the original PERT system, *not one of them* said that he had used the data generated by that system. . . . Instead, many thought it was the technical officers and engineers that actually had used the PERT system data. The technical officers and engineers, in turn, denied ever using PERT data . . .; they thought it was the program evaluators. . . . Plans and Programs, however . . . never used the system; rather, they thought, it was . . . the plant representatives who worked with the PERT reports. The plant representatives were similar in their response: 'No, it must have been elsewhere'.

If PERT was deemed to be a 'success story' and not used for planning or control purposes, then for what was it used? Sapolski suggests that it was used as a means of justifying and defending budgets; to generate 'facts', demonstrating progress and performance, to articulate a view of management's confidence in the project using an approach apparently neutral and scientific in form and content. Whether or not this conclusion is accepted, it allows the point to be made which is central to the present argument. Clearly, 'getting things done' and 'making change' in organisations is a 'political' process. Change requires that resources be mobilised, that support be generated, and then the efforts of people be organised. Sapolski's retrospective explanation for the 'success' of PERT refers to the political value of the data which can be generated by such a system. Increasingly, the literature on change refers to influences such as the 'politics of implementation'. If this is accepted, it follows that any change proposed for an organisation has to be conceived, practically, and in terms of the assumptions and data on which it is based, and also in terms of its impact on the organisation, including the impact of actually introducing it into the organisation. This is also true with systems such as MRP and Kanban.

All of which points to the important conclusion that the problem of developing an integrated approach in manufacturing is inherently attitudinal. It is a problem of philosophy and of change and not of 'system' as such. Green's appealing argument necessitating a two-stage approach to the adoption of Kanban is supportive of this.

It is clear that the problems 'inside' an organisation in breaking down 'compartments' are formidable. When other parties, e.g. suppliers, are involved, those problems are exacerbated. Apart from anything else there are many different corporate cultures which have to be 'mated' with that of the buying company and, geographically at least, they may be far removed from the purchaser.

Progress towards more effective system management must, of necessity, be a gradual process, more gradual in some cases than in others. Indeed, it might be argued that rapid change, even if it were possible, could be counterproductive. Close relationships and mutual trust with and between suppliers and buyers need to be nurtured over time. The key issue is to understand the importance of those relationships and work towards mutual, constructive 'marriages'. As the Japanese lucidly put it, to becoming 'co-workers'.

Systems such as MRP and Kanban may well provide an effective framework within which this exacting task is undertaken. However, only the deployment of appropriate skills and the development of effective policies, strategies, tactics and operations, particularly by purchasing, will bring them to fruition. In the turbulent, rapidly changing environment of the nineteen-eighties it seems likely that the successful enterprise will be adaptive, resilient and responsive to the needs of its customers. To achieve this, companies need to develop flexibility and a more integrated approach. Purchasing should play a major role in these developments.

REFERENCES

(1) M. Takamiya, *Japanese Multinationals in Europe: Internal Operations and their policy implications,* International Institute of Management, Berlin 1979.

(2) T. Hill, *Production/Operations Management,* Prentice-Hall, 1983.

(3) NEDC, *Why Group Technology?* London 1976.

(4) P. Kraljic, 'Purchasing must become supply management' in *Harvard Business Review,* vol. 83, no. 5, pp. 109-17.

(5) H. M. Sapolski, *The Polaris System Development,* Harvard University Press, 1972.

14

Financial aspects of purchasing

Peter Herbert

Credit taken from suppliers of goods and services constitutes the single largest source of short-term funds to UK companies. This pattern is frequently encountered abroad. It should scarcely be surprising then, that corporate treasurers and finance directors will display keen interest in those policies pursued by their purchasing colleagues, so far as they affect the crucial task of corporate funding. And yet purchasing executives could be forgiven for concluding that the glamour and technical sophistication of stock market share issues and the like, cause credit management to be artificially relegated in the minds of their financial colleagues until a parlous cash position provokes crash stock reduction programmes and the clarion call 'Stretch the creditors for all you can get!'

In this chapter the origin of the several sources of relationship between purchasing and financial management will be examined. The purpose will be to identify the nature of the many competing interests which can arise and the means by which they may be resolved efficiently in the pursuit of mutually accepted corporate objectives. Although it is true that constructive, and sometimes destructive, tension will often characterise the resolution of these dilemmas, there is much territory where coincidence of purpose and responsibility can be found. The latter is nowhere better illustrated than in the joint pursuit of raw material and other costs designed to maximise profitability. Nevertheless, conflicting pressures do arise when, for example, attractive input costs can only be 'bought' at the expense of early settlement or abnormally rapid delivery dates.

This chapter is divided into four sections, reflecting the principal areas in which the responsibilities of purchasing and financial management interact. It begins with an exploration of the roles of price and credit terms in the negotiating armoury of the buyer so far as these affect the profitability and liquidity positions of the business. In the second section, evaluating the cost of trade credit as a source of capital is examined, paying particular attention to the implications of abnormally short or long credit terms. The third section examines the management of credit as a key component of financial policy; problems of growth and inflation receive special attention. The final section is devoted to the financial evaluation of suppliers.

MOTIVES IN PURCHASING AND FINANCE

If asked to provide three policy guidelines to his purchasing colleague, the finance manager or accountant might typically respond: 'Get the lowest prices you can and the longest credit terms possible, but make sure the supplier, not us, holds the stocks'. Of course there is an assumption here that trade credit and its management is either costless or at least cheaper than some alternative source of finance, e.g. a bank overdraft. As will be seen later, this point often merits greater attention than is generally assumed necessary.

Why should a treasurer respond in the manner suggested? What are his motives? Do they make sense and if so, for how long and under what conditions? These are some of the key questions which purchasing managers need to understand when pursuing policies which are both rational to themselves and sensible from a general management point of view.

Simple economic intuition might be sufficient to explain the financial motives behind the advice given to our purchasing executive. Unfortunately, this will not provide a set of tangible, operational guidelines sufficient to recognise not only the complex interrelationships which may exist, but also the very real limits for manoeuvre which the likes of commonsense, prudence and custom and practice will dictate. Analysis of the so-called 'operating cycle'

275

does, however, provide a useful means for disentangling the impact of several key variables which affect profitability and the funds needed to generate it.

The operating cycle is a generalised picture of the time interval which elapses between the initial investment in materials and services required to produce a product and the eventual receipt of cash for the sale of that product. For the typical multiproduct-process company the length of the cycle is in the nature of some hypothetical 'average' of all the individual patterns of buying, stockholding and production, together with the supplier and customer credit lines associated with each product or product group in the company's portfolio. The start and finish of the operating cycle cannot, of course, be identified as discrete points in time. However, for most businesses, it is possible to calculate the approximate length of the cycle. In the case of a manufacturing business, reference must be made to the average duration of the activities shown in Figure 14.1.

The data required should be readily accessible from the firm's accounting or finance department, although it must be stressed that a number of simplifying assumptions will often prove necessary, even if these do 'stick in the gullet' of the more pedantic breed of

Activity sequence	Duration calculation
Credit taken from suppliers	$\dfrac{\text{Average level of trade creditors}}{\text{Period supply of raw material}}$
Holding raw material inventories	$\dfrac{\text{Average investment in raw material}}{\text{Period consumption of raw material}}$
Production/conversion process	$\dfrac{\text{Average investment in work-in-progress}}{\text{Period value of production output}}$
Holding finished goods inventories	$\dfrac{\text{Average investment in finished goods}}{\text{Period cost of sales}}$
Credit given to customers	$\dfrac{\text{Average level of trade debtors}}{\text{Period value of sales turnover}}$

Figure 14.1 Duration of operating cycle elements

accountant! It is also worth mentioning in advance of the more detailed examination of the financial health of supplier companies which will be undertaken later, that a crude version of the operating cycle can be gleaned from published annual reports and accounts. The cycle length can be calculated in terms of days, if the necessary information is of sufficient quality. However, typically it is adequate to work in units of one week.

The length of the operating cycle can now be determined and, for best effect, portrayed graphically (see Figure 14.2). It can be seen that the overall length of the operating cycle is twenty weeks, made up from each of the five key components.

Whilst the absolute length of the operating cycle can provide startling news for the uninitiated and, usually, inefficient business, it has little intrinsic value except for highlighting the relative significance of each of the corporate functions involved. Its real potential derives from two sources. First, informative comparisons can be made between different products produced by the same organisation and between similar products produced by different organisations. Analysis of this type can serve to highlight product priorities in the first case and comparative efficiency in the second. The second potential benefit lies in the opportunity to contemplate variations both to the length of the operating cycle as a whole and to each of its constituent parts. However, in order to appreciate the full range of influences which the purchasing function may exert on

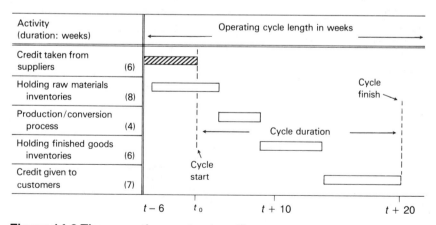

Figure 14.2 The operating cycle : length

corporate efficiency, the financial consequences of the extant cycle need to be recognised. In Figure 14.3 the cash flow consequences of each of the operating activities are shown in the form of a cumulative profile.

It can be seen that the operating cycle constitutes an ever-increasing hole in the corporate purse, until such time as the product's customer actually delivers his cash. There are two key messages here. First, both the length and the depth of the operating cycle will have vital impact upon the cash flow and liquidity positions of the business, not only at the level of the individual product or product group but also for the business in total. Second, the firm's profitability will be directly influenced by the level of holding costs, including financing charges, incurred as a product of the length and depth of the cycle. If the length of the cycle can be curtailed, then both cash flow and profits will improve; if the depth of the cycle can be reduced then profits and cash flow will also improve; and if both can be achieved simultaneously then the effects will be multiplicative.

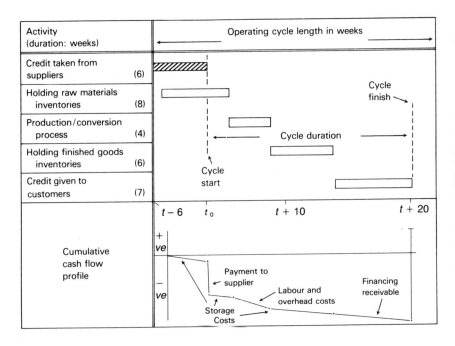

Figure 14.3 The operating cycle : cash flow profile

Where, precisely, can purchasing management influence the shape and duration of the operating cycle? Plainly, there are several sources:

1 Extend the period of credit taken from the suppliers of raw materials and thereby reduce the period during which the cash deficit is at its most sizeable.
2 Organise delivery of supplies so as to reduce inventory levels and thereby the 'tie-up' of one's own capital, at the expense of the supplier.
3 Negotiate input prices not only of raw materials but also other goods and services consumed in production, distribution and the like so as to minimise product costs and therefore maximise profitability.

Although the analysis so far does not capture the contribution which purchasing management may make through decisions covering, for example, capital expenditure and 'make or buy', it should be clear already that there is ample scope for enhancing corporate prosperity.

Naturally, the objective of efficient purchasing must be to achieve a sensible mix of priorities when negotiating supplier contracts. The purchasing levers which have been mentioned cannot, usually, be operated entirely independently of each other, nor will their travel be unencumbered by the objectives and instincts of the suppliers themselves. Moreover, the skill of the purchasing manager lies in the ability to accommodate important financial motives whilst recognising the more subtle qualitative attributes of the supplier/buyer relationship.

SUPPLIER CREDIT AND CORPORATE FUNDING

The importance of trade creditors or accounts payable as a source of corporate finance has been stressed already, at least in general terms. A specific example will better illustrate the point. The following table summarises the manner in which ICI funded its multinational operations at its financial year-end 31 December 1983:

Short term	£m	£m
Trade creditors	669	
Other creditors	880	
Short-term borrowings	538	2,087
Long term		
Grants and deferred liabilities	792	
Loans	1,400	
Capital and reserves	3,342	5,534
		7,621

If we assume that this position is typical of the company's funding policy over time, then it can be seen that trade creditors accounted for some 9 per cent of total funds – equivalent to 12 per cent of the long-term capital invested in the business. Plainly this item will feature strongly in the mind of that company's finance director as he seeks to organise an efficient portfolio of liabilities. In principle, the volume of credit taken from suppliers will reflect the commercial conditions prevailing in those sectors in which ICI operates, the current liquidity position of the business, and several other factors – including the cost of this particular source of finance. For like any other source of capital, supplier credit attracts a cost even though it may be less conspicuous than that of dividends on share capital or interest on bank and other borrowings.

Leaving aside the example of ICI, corporate treasurers will be concerned to optimise the use of cash discounts for early settlement, to manage cost effectively the administration of supplier accounts, to evaluate late or stage payment opportunities and to optimise the mix of short-term sources of finance which may include payables, bank overdrafts, acceptance credits and trade bills.

THE COST OF TRADE CREDIT

The cost of supplier credit normally has two components. These are the administrative cost of managing supplier accounts, e.g. computers and account clerks, and the opportunity cost entailed in forgoing options to take cash discounts. Both of these costs will normally fall within the responsibility of the finance and accounting department, even though cash discounts may be a potent ingredient in supplier/buyer negotiations. It is important in these circumstances for the buyer to appreciate the true benefit of discount opportunities as well as the cost of disturbing established methods and systems of supplier payment. In other words, though we are concerned with what amounts to a financing decision primarily, the purchasing function should recognise the financial dimension of its work and be prepared simultaneously to exert and accede to pressures on the finance function.

In general, credit terms will offer two alternative means of settlement, i.e. payment within a specified period following the transaction date, or settlement within a prescribed shorter period in exchange for deduction of a specified discount. The difference between the two options constitutes an opportunity to borrow for the duration of the difference between the two settlement dates at the cost of the cash discount to be forgone. The annualised cost of this source of funds is illustrated in the following example.

Computing the cost of cash discounts

Assume that normal settlement terms call for payment of the entire debt within 30 days of the invoice date. A cash discount of 2.5 per cent is available if settlement is made within 7 days of the invoice date.

$$\text{Annualised discount cost} = \frac{2.5}{(100-2.5)} \times \frac{365}{(30-7)} \times 100$$
$$= \frac{2.5}{97.5} \times \frac{365}{23} \times 100$$
$$= \underline{40.7\%}$$

It is plain that the cost of credit terms such as these is not trivial! Where annualised costs are of this order of magnitude, then serious consideration must be given to the use of alternative cheaper sources of finance such as bank overdrafts. In fact, where overdraft finance is judged to be the realistic alternative, then comparative interest costs must be expressed in compound rather than simple terms. If, in the example, interest was to be compounded at 23-day intervals, then the effective annualised cost would rise to approximately 48 per cent. Whichever method of calculation is used, there is a clear incentive for the buying function to recognise credit costs when negotiating suppliers' prices and to convey the significance of these to the treasurer's department. Two problems arise here. First, costs expressed in percentage terms are not readily identifiable in their 'bottom-line' effect. Second, the circumstances envisaged in the example are incomplete in the sense that an extra administrative charge may need to be incurred in order to give special treatment to an account which would normally be settled by standard accounting and computing systems. The following example illustrates how credit costs may be expressed more informatively:

Invoice value : £10,000
Supplier's normal credit terms : 30 days following invoice date
Early payment (2.5 per cent discount) : 7 days following invoice date
Marginal administration cost : £20
Bank overdraft cost : 15 per cent p.a.

$$\text{Value of normal credit period} = \frac{30 \times 15\% \times £10,000}{365}$$

$$= \underline{£123}$$

$$\text{Value of early payment credit period} =$$

$$\left(\frac{7}{365} \times 15\% + 2.5\%\right) \times £10,000 - £20$$

$$= \underline{£259}$$

Net cost saved by taking cash discount $= \underline{£136}$

Practical difficulties can be encountered in estimating the true incremental cost of special administrative arrangements to handle early payment opportunities. However, once these are known the profitability consequences of early or normal settlement can readily be seen – in the example, £136 of additional profit arises by adopting early payment. But one word of warning! The temptation often arises to ascribe excessive potency to arithmetic calculations and conclusions such as illustrated. It is vital to stand back in order to judge whether or not other, perhaps unquantifiable, factors should be taken into account. For instance, adoption of early settlement terms may serve to reduce flexibility in negotiations or the risk may arise that the supplier will become excessively dependent upon the buyer's liquidity position, to the detriment of his own financial standing. Other points to watch out for include difficulties in recovering overpayment where insufficient time exists to check the quantity and quality of supplies before early payment is due, reduced leverage on suppliers when contractual disputes or litigation arise, and the risk of being locked into early payment when financial exigency may make it essential to delay payment as long as possible.

Developing creditor payment policies

In addition to recognising cash discounts in terms of their annualised percentage cost or absolute value, it is also essential to appreciate their effects in relation to the volume of credit settlement transactions. Broadly, the higher the proportion of 'credit input costs' to the total costs of the organisation, the greater will be the significance of discounts policy for profitability and cash flow planning. Figure 14.4 illustrates this point, where a company's projected revenue, cost and profit plans are divided as shown.

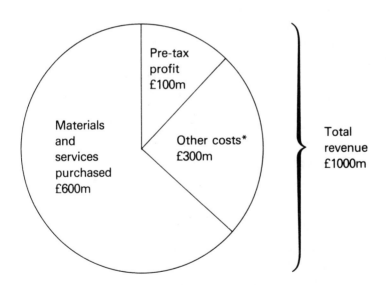

* Assumed to be cash costs (e.g. wages) and depreciation.

Figure 14.4 Breakdown of company costs and revenues

Assume that this company planned on obtaining an average 2.5 per cent cash discount on all materials and services to be purchased during the forthcoming year. Pre-discount purchases would be:

$$£600m \times \frac{100}{97.5} = £615m$$

That is, a cost saving of £15m (£615m−£600m) would have been anticipated in the process of earning pre-tax profits of £100m.

If, for whatever reason, cash discounts were assumed to be unobtainable then, other things being equal, pre-tax profits of only £85m would be expected. Taking cash discounts at an average level of 2.5 per cent will generate pre-tax profits some 17 per cent ($\frac{£15m}{£85m} \times$ 100) greater than otherwise possible. The scale of this profit impact is of course the direct consequence of creditor costs constituting two-thirds of total costs. A simple calculation will show that when the relationship between creditor and cash costs respectively is inverted, then the leverage effect of discount policy on profits is correspondingly reduced. It can be seen then that the profitability consequences of a specified early settlement policy are a direct function of both the rate of cash discounts and the volume of transactions to which they apply.

Cash discounts apart, frequently settlement policy will involve opportunities to take extended credit, even perhaps where these involve late payment penalties. In general, these opportunities should be evaluated on lines similar to those for early settlement. For the large organisation which has ready access to a greater variety of cheaper sources of finance than its smaller counterpart, the cost of extended credit is likely to be uncompetitive. Nevertheless, these opportunities should not be discounted altogether where, for example, the supplier refuses to negotiate on price or is employing credit as a marketing device and will not reflect the credit benefit in an alternative, cash price. Complex financial subsidy packages can also be encountered and, again, it is important to stress that other commercial considerations may be sufficient to sway the balance of the decision.

In any event, the development of coherent policy must be based upon a realistic judgement of the costs and benefits of routine payment and allied processes which should apply in the majority of cases, together with the special costs or benefits of early and late settlement opportunities. Moreover, it is vital that whatever policy is ultimately agreed on, it should not be allowed to become sterile or, worse still, a straitjacket which inhibits entrepreneurial skill and refuses to accommodate fundamental changes in the financial and commercial circumstances of the organisation and its environment. It is to two particular types of change – actual and apparent growth – that attention is now turned.

MANAGING GROWTH

Paradoxically, the task of financial management becomes the more exacting when growth, rather than contraction is the order of the day. The economic recession of recent years has served to cause many companies to accumulate large quantities of cash, as surplus assets have been sold or run down to levels consistent with reduced activity. In sharp contrast, the most prevalent cause of corporate collapse, other than that caused by sustained loss making, is the mismanagement of growth and the financial strain which it frequently imposes. In short, this discussion is concerned with the problems of cash flow management and the impact which purchasing management may have on them.

Before proceeding it is necessary to distinguish between two types of growth which may occur independently or simultaneously. Real growth, as the term suggests, implies progressive expansion to the physical attributes of the firm, be these the number of personnel employed, the physical volume of output generated, the number of customers or the size of market share. None of them need be measured by means of money – other measures will suffice to capture genuine rates of change. Once the yardstick of money is used, its inherent instability can serve to distort or disguise the underlying real position. Inflation will make growth apparent rather than real: deflation the opposite. Whilst this problem besets the interpretation of financial statements as shown later, the present concern is for the real demands for cash which derive from unreal changes to the substance of the business. Nowhere is this phenomenon better illustrated than in the increasing need for cash to finance the inflating prices of supplies whose physical levels do not change. The financial consequences of real growth are examined first.

Real growth

Real growth may be achieved either organically or by acquisition. Which route is chosen will depend on a number of factors including the degree of hunger for growth as well as diversification objectives. Whilst these two routes may be pursued simultaneously, the choice of appropriate strategy will need to reflect, for example, preferences as between horizontal and vertical integration. The former may arise from a desire to obtain a suitable measure of market dominance, whereas the latter is frequently motivated by the need to secure a guaranteed supply of critical downstream resources, such as pulp supply in papermaking.

The problems of financing rapid growth, particularly of the organic variety, lie in the freedom or lack of it with which the particular firm may exercise choice between different alternative sources of finance. Notwithstanding the existence of a highly developed capital market, UK companies typically fund 60-70 per cent of their capital requirements by means of profits retention. This dependence is often exaggerated for the small firm, which does not have access to stock market share issues or long-term institutional lendings. Heavy reliance will often be made on bank borrowings, retained profits and, of course, trade credit. The next example illustrates some of the issues involved.

Visualise a company, perhaps one of your own suppliers, which seeks to expand operations (see Figure 14.5). It aims to achieve this result by offering new extended credit terms to its existing and potential customer base. What cash flow consequences would be encountered by this change of policy?

Whereas in the small, steady-state condition to the left of the diagram, the rate of cash remittances per week or month would have been virtually identical to the rate at which sales were being achieved, the effects of the new promotion would be first to generate additional sales turnover, but then to experience a delay in the rate at which cash receipts would accelerate until the new credit terms began to 'bite'. Eventually, it is reasonable to expect a new steady-state condition reflecting the increased size of the business where the rates of sales turnover and cash receipts once again coincided at the new, higher level shown on the right in Figure 14.6. The key question for the treasurer of this company concerns his

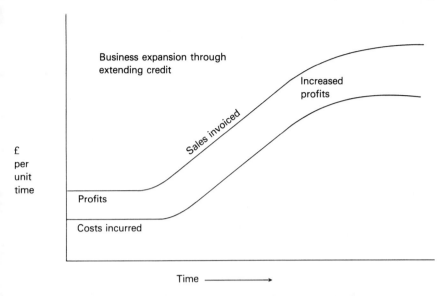

Figure 14.5 Business expansion through extended credit

ability to tolerate the delay in cash receipts, given that he must fund the purchase and production of the additional output in advance of its sale; moreover, he must be prepared also to finance a larger permanent investment in customer debts. What are the options open to him and will they be sufficient to meet the full requirement?

An important contribution to solving this funding problem could be made by the purchasing function of the company. As Figure 14.7 shows, it may be feasible to mitigate the scale of the expected cash flow deficit by obtaining extended credit terms on the additional inputs required by the intended expansion.

It can be seen that the size and duration of the cash flow deficiency (hatched) are both substantially smaller than would have been the case had the 'cash paid' line continued to coincide with the 'costs incurred' line, perhaps to the critical extent that the expansion exercise could not be sustained. In this sense, it is worth stressing the financial and other strains which a customer company, intent on growing itself, may impose upon suppliers who are exhorted to participate in such growth. Such interdependency of fortunes has, of course, prompted the very intimate relationships which can be

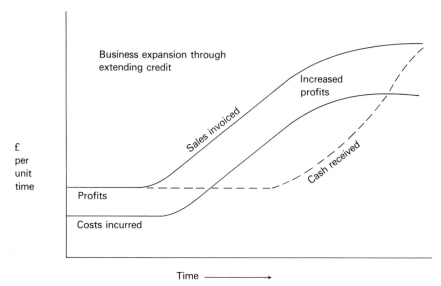

Figure 14.6 Delay in cash receipts

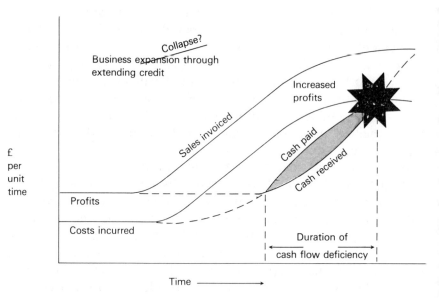

Figure 14.7 Effect of extended credit

encountered between High Street retailers of clothing and furniture and their manufacturing suppliers, particularly where the latter's output is heavily or even exclusively devoted to one major customer.

Two important conclusions emerge for purchasing managers. First, as a party to the real growth of their own businesses they can influence materially both the scale and the nature of the funding tasks required of their financial colleagues. Growth is not easy to manage, and it should be apparent that procurement plans can assume crucial significance in exacerbating and/or solving its attainment. Second, informed susceptibility by purchasing managers to the problems they may pose when stimulating rapid growth in supplier companies can pre-empt unpleasant surprises and even demises.

Coping with inflation

Inflation holds two threats to corporate prosperity and survival. The first danger manifests itself in declining real margins. This problem can be particularly acute for the business which depends upon fine margins and high volume, i.e. characterised by high break-even points, in highly competitive markets. If retained profits hold the dominant place that they do in corporate financing, then the importance of maintaining profit margins is self evident. However, the ability to maintain margins is governed typically by several variables, many of which are within the purchasing sphere of responsibility. These variables are dealt with elsewhere in this and other chapters, but one in particular is worth emphasising here. As much as anything else, speed of response to changing price levels is the key to maintaining profitability and this requires quick and efficient management accounting systems. These systems will need to anticipate and convey the consequences of price increases which purchasing management can neither directly nor indirectly avoid, to those other functions which will become affected. Surprising though it may seem, many management accountants responsible for such systems are frequently amenable to constructive ideas from their non-financial colleagues! Purchasing managers are in a unique position to influence the design of information systems which will

289

alert the organisation to the threat of inflationary input costs and it is vital that they take this initiative.

The second major risk attending inflation derives from the fact that it consumes real cash for no productive purpose. Not only is this effect felt in the escalating cost of replacing obsolete or worn-out fixed assets, e.g. plant and machinery (magnified frequently by deteriorating exchange rates on imported equipment), but it can have an insidious impact on the various components of working capital which themselves affect the solvency position of the firm. The latter phenomenon can be readily observed in the following illustration. Imagine two companies, A and B, which are identical in all respects except for the different requirements for working capital which each experiences to achieve the same sales turnover and pre-tax profits. The results for both companies in year 1 are shown in Figure 14.8. It can be seen that the consequence of B requiring

	Company A	Company B
Trading account	£	£
Sales	1,200,000	1,200,000
Depreciation	30,000	30,000
Surplus on trading (7½%)	90,000	90,000
Bank interest (see below)	(16,000)	(32,000)
Profit before tax	74,000	58,000
Tax at 50%	37,000	29,000
Profit after tax	37,000	29,000
Working capital		
Debtors (A = 2 months of sales)	200,000	
(B = 3 months of sales)		300,000
Stocks (A = 1½ months of sales)	150,000	
(B = 2½ months of sales)		250,000
Creditors (A = equivalent to stocks)	(150,000)	
(B = same as A)		(150,000)
Working capital	200,000	400,000
Bank interest at 12% on facilities being equivalent to two-thirds of working capital	16,000	32,000
Cash flow		
Profit after tax	37,000	29,000
Depreciation	30,000	30,000
Capital expenditure	(30,000)	(30,000)
Positive cash flow	37,000	29,000
Difference between A and B cash flows		£8000

Figure 14.8 Comparison of requirements for working capital

twice the level of working capital of A, whether the reasons be valid or not, is that B incurs higher bank interest charges and thereby achieves lower post-tax profits than A. This difference of fortunes is also realised at the level of net cash inflows for each company.

Figure 14.9 sets out the results for both companies on the assumption that each experiences 15 per cent inflation in the following year's trading. The results of the two companies can be summarised as follows:

- Both achieve identical levels of sales turnover and trading profit, albeit that margins have suffered during the inflationary period.
- Whereas the working capital requirement of A has risen by £30,000 to £230,000, B has experienced an increase of £60,000 even though the credit and stock cover periods of each have not altered between the two years.
- The bank interest charges, arising from the overdrafts required to fund two-thirds of the working capital in both companies, have risen as a product of the higher interest rates required to discount debasement of the currency.
- Higher bank interest charges, especially for B, have dented the pre- and post-tax profits of both companies.
- The cash flow positions of the two companies are entirely different. Whereas A has achieved a modest cash surplus even after consuming £30,000 in inflated stocks and debtors, B experiences a major cash deficiency all and more of which can be attributed to its adverse working capital position.

The essential point to grasp is that the different profit and cash flow conditions of the two companies arise as the exclusive product of inflation – not real growth.

The role of purchasing in maintaining margins has already been discussed, but there are other forms of assistance which can mitigate the effects of inflation. In so far as trade credit is a cost-competitive source of finance, then it should be used to counterbalance inflationary pressures on stocks and debtors particularly. Of course, the degree to which this is feasible will depend upon the circumstances of the individual company, its suppliers and the several interacting considerations which have already been discussed. Excessive investment in stocks is a further source of vulnerability in

No growth in sales volume or surplus on trading	After 15 per cent inflation	
	Company A	Company B
Trading account	£	£
Sales	1,380,000	1,380,000
Depreciation	30,000	30,000
Surplus on trading (6½%)	90,000	90,000
Bank interest (see below)	(21,500)	(43,000)
Profit before tax	68,500	47,000
Tax at 50%	34,250	23,500
Profit after tax	34,250	23,500
Working capital		
Debtors (A = 2 months of sales)	230,000	
(B = 3 months of sales)		345,000
Stocks (A = 1½ months of sales)	172,500	
(B = 2½ months of sales)		287,500
Creditors (A = equivalent to stocks)	(172,500)	
(B = same as A)		(172,500)
Working capital	230,000	460,000
Bank interest at 15% on facilities being equivalent to two-thirds of working capital	21,500	43,000
Cash flow		
Profit after tax	34,250	23,500
Depreciation	30,000	30,000
Capital expenditure	(30,000)	(30,000)
Increase in working capital	(30,000)	(60,000)
Positive/(negative) cash flow	4,250	(36,500)
Difference between A and B cash flows	£40,750	

Note: Bank interest at 15 per cent (up from 12 per cent in year 1) has been applied to the *average* working capital for year 2.

Figure 14.9 Comparison of results

inflationary conditions. If the debilitating effects of savage stock reduction programmes on supplier relations are to be avoided, then purchasing management must look for opportunities to curtail stock build-up. These may include resisting the temptation of bulk purchases, rescheduling supplier deliveries onto a more continuous pattern thereby reducing buffer stocks and, sometimes, reducing the speculative purchase of goods expected to rise in price. The latter point may seem perverse, yet it precisely epitomises the need to shift emphasis away from profitability and towards cash flow in severely inflationary times – better profits tomorrow than insolvency today!

This section has dealt with the financial problems involved in securing growth (be it real or illusory). When these two forms of growth occur simultaneously it is to be expected that the task of funding, and purchasing management's contribution to it, will be magnified. But the task of integrating the aspirations and motives of purchasing, financial and other functions lies not only with the buyer's own organisation, it also faces suppliers. The success or failure which they achieve can have direct and often substantial influence upon the buying company's destiny. It is incumbent, then, to assess the strengths and weaknesses of supplier companies and it is the financial aspects of that task that will now be discussed.

ASSESSING SUPPLIERS

The following quotations come from an interview which the author held recently with the purchasing manager of a major photographic company:

> I like to review the financial viability of a concern I am dealing with. . . . It would be bad news to get three months into a project, to find that a company failed. There may not be any direct cash lost but the failure may indirectly affect our concern by slowing or cancelling a project.
>
> I look to make sure that my purchases do not exceed a certain proportion of a company's sales. . . . Not so bad with an extraneous purchase, but on a regular basis it could become morally difficult to drop a company, i.e. that company may fail when your business is taken away.
>
> I review suppliers' accounts regularly to make sure they are consistent, e.g. I would be concerned if R and D was suddenly arrested, or . . .
>
> When discussing/negotiating with suppliers I look for signs of financial pressure, i.e. specific pressure to pay bills earlier.
>
> . . . during negotiation I try to obtain breakdowns of costs from suppliers. It may be possible to get a percentage split of their product. . . . This will help in following years to

substantiate changes/increases. I always keep notes of discussions with suppliers.

These observations serve to highlight many of the strategic and tactical responsibilities of purchasing management when developing relationships with suppliers.

At the strategic level, a key preoccupation will be to decide on the merits of single or multiple sourcing and the risks of buyer/supplier dependency which may arise. This problem is illustrated in Figure 14.10, where the concern is with the strategic stance of company $B(1)$ in each of two different scenarios.

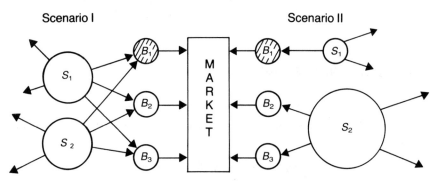

NOTE: Disc sizes to give approximate effect to corporate size/strength

Figure 14.10 Alternative consumer/supplier relationships

In scenario I the market is supplied equally by three competitors, $B(1)$, $B(2)$ and $B(3)$. Each of these companies buys inputs from two similar suppliers, $S(1)$ and $S(2)$. By contrast, scenario II assumes the same competitors as in scenario I but that $B(1)$ is supplied exclusively by $S(1)$, and $B(2)$ and $B(3)$ are supplied jointly by $S(2)$.

In scenario I, $B(1)$ has no obvious strategic strengths or weaknesses when compared with its competitors. Suppliers $S(1)$ and $S(2)$ are both of sufficient size and stability that the demise of either is unlikely. If either should fail then $B(1)$ loses little or no strategic strength vis-à-vis its competitors. In scenario II, however, $B(1)$ is supplied exclusively by $S(1)$ which is comparatively smaller and weaker than its competitor $S(2)$.

Plainly there are different policy implications for $B(1)$ in each of the two scenarios. In the first case, the company will need to develop competitive strategies so as not to suffer to the advantage of competitors $B(2)$ and $B(3)$. In the absence of any serious concern about the financial viability of its two large suppliers, $B(1)$ may find it sufficient to ensure that it is not taking substantially more or less than one-third of the output of each of its two suppliers.

In scenario II, $B(1)$ may need to shift the emphasis of its intelligence gathering. Whilst the incentives for a solus relationship with $S(1)$ may be substantial, $B(1)$ will need to guard itself against two key sources of risk. First, it will need to monitor the extent to which $S(1)$'s survival and prosperity may become dependent on $B(1)$, by virtue of its own growth or the retreat of $S(1)$'s other customers. Second, it will need to appraise, regularly, the financial stability of $S(1)$ so that, in advance of the possible failure of that firm, either supply links can be established with $S(2)$, or $S(1)$ can be acquired to ensure continuity. Of course, this implies a need for $B(1)$ to monitor the position of $S(2)$ even though no commercial relationship exists at present.

An abstraction perhaps, but the illustration serves to highlight the need for purchasing management to gather important commercial and financial intelligence about existing and potential key suppliers, as a matter of routine. This will serve to develop not only intelligent strategy over the choice of suppliers, it will also provide powerful levers when negotiating supply contracts. But what specific types of financial intelligence are actually useful?

FINANCIAL INTELLIGENCE

Experience shows that information is a seductive creature! The more we can get, the more assured we feel – even if much of it is of the 'nice to know' rather than 'need to know' variety. Analysing a set of published accounts is no exception. It is a very time-consuming process even for the skilled analyst who knows his needs precisely. However, the exercise can be made relatively straightforward by asking three simple questions at the outset:

- What do we need to know?
- Where can we find the answers and how reliable are they?
- How much reliance can we place on supplier survival?

Each of these questions will typically spawn subsidiary lines of enquiry which reflect the particular circumstances of the buyer/ supplier relationship. Consequently, generalisations about the types of question and answer which may be relevant are of limited value. Nevertheless it is useful to speculate on one or two of the more important ones, bearing in mind that access to suitable information will typically extend beyond the scope of published annual reports and accounts. Indeed, one of the key objectives of financial appraisal should be to use its results either to stimulate questions whose answers can and should be found elsewhere, or to confirm qualitative intelligence gleaned from the marketplace, trade and financial press, business contacts and other sources.

Defining necessary information

At the outset it is necessary to be clear about just which existing or potential suppliers should merit close scrutiny. Often the 80:20 rule will apply: that is, 20 per cent by number of suppliers will account for 80 per cent of purchasing activity. Whilst modest intelligence may be sufficient for the bulk of suppliers, the weight of investigative effort should be devoted only to those of substance, or those which are new but which could become important.

Central to the understanding of annual reports and similar data is the body of knowledge which all users will need to have whatever their standpoint. The following types of question will usually be relevant:

- What do I already know about the company?
- What sort and mix of products does the company make?
- What principal industry(s) is the company in?
- Does the company operate at home and overseas?
- Do the company's products have a worthwhile reputation for being advanced and reliable?
- What do other people think about the company?
- Is the company in the news?
- Who are the leaders of the company and are they in the news?

- How do you expect the current economic situation to affect the company?
- What are the market trends for the company's products?

By beginning with a checklist such as this it quickly becomes apparent that a company's report and accounts serve to complement or supplement the knowledge which is already possessed from financial or other sources.

With this 'broad brush' picture in mind, the next task should be to formulate specific questions about the existing or potential supplier. The precise nature of these questions will vary according to the perspective of the enquirer, but for the purchasing executive the following will probably be uppermost in importance:

- Is this supplier progressing, stagnating or withering?
- Do we/will we feature significantly in the interests and future of this supplier?
- Can this supplier survive, given the financial and other risks to which it is exposed?

Of course there may be other questions which can acquire special significance in non-routine situations. These can include: 'Is this supplier worthy of acquisition?' or 'Are there signs that this supplier might be taken over by a competitor in its own field or in ours?' or 'Would this supplier collapse if we were to cease trading with it?' Questions such as these are very broad in their scope and the financial acumen required to answer them will typically lie with specialists elsewhere in the organisation. Nevertheless the purchasing executive can be expected to discover for himself, largely if not exclusively, the solutions to the three basic questions.

Finding the answers

An early exercise in any task of intelligence gathering is to familiarise oneself with the form of the information available. This applies not only to annual accounts but also to other sources of financial information to which we shall refer shortly.

Whilst it is true that annual reports are subject to legal and other requirements, it is also true that companies have a fair measure of discretion over the way in which information is compiled and displayed. Regrettably it is commonplace for particular information located in one section of one company's report to be found in an entirely different section of another company's report. Be prepared to keep your eyes wide open!

The content of an annual report can be broken down into a number of separate sections. All reports will contain the following:

- the annual accounts and notes relating to them
- the auditor's report
- the directors' report.

Most company reports will also contain the following:

- the chairman's statement
- a review of the company's activities
- a short summary of the company's results
- a statement summarising the company's principal results for the past five or ten years.

Once familiarity has been obtained with the layout of an annual report, a crucial first step is to examine the auditor's report. This will not indicate whether the company is in good financial shape, but it will show whether the accounts have been prepared correctly or not. Beware particularly of reports which contain such phraseology as 'The financial statements have been drawn up on a going concern basis which assumes that additional borrowing facilities will be obtained. We have been unable to satisfy ourselves . . .' If, nevertheless, you have a real interest in such a company, it is worthwhile seeking professional advice either within or outside your own organisation.

Assuming that the supplier company has a 'clean bill of health' from the auditors, the next important stage is to review the statement of accounting policies. Here it is important to look for any major changes in accounting policies which may affect your interpretation of the results of the company, year on year. A quick check should also be made to discover whether the accounting policies which are used differ from those normally adopted by similar companies. Again professional advice may be worthwhile.

Protected by the two 'early warning' tests which have been suggested, the recent progress of the target supplier can be investigated. The best source for a quick overall view of the company's performance is the five or ten-year statistical summary. The purpose here is to look for trends over a number of years without attempting to undertake any complex calculations. These summaries typically include financial and non-financial information which can be used to trace such variables as sales turnover, number of employees, capital expenditure, number of sales or production units and earnings per share. Graphical presentation of these figures will often serve to dramatise the progress, or lack of it, which the company has achieved. Frequently this stage of the analysis provides the best opportunity to gauge the scale and impact of your own dealings with the company in question. Growth trends of your business and that of the supplier can be correlated to discover significant patterns or discontinuities. But a word of warning! There are two key limitations of annual accounts to be aware of. First, although it is true that the UK accounting profession has been wrestling with the problem of inflation for many years, heavy reliance is still placed on so-called 'historic cost' figures. Although this is but one of a series of technical principles or conventions underpinning accounting statements, the fact is that historic cost data can easily distort the true progress implied by time-series comparisons. The more enlightened of publicly listed companies will provide inflation-adjusted figures to aid your interpretation. For other companies it can suffice to recalculate published figures by reference to a suitable price index, e.g. RPI.

The second problem concerns the fact that annual accounts need make no mention of the plans which companies have in mind. In special situations such as share issues or takeover bids, forecast information may be publicised in prospectuses or offer documents. More fruitful sources can include stockbroker's reports, press cuttings and trade publications.

Although the emphasis so far has been on published financial information, several other sources of data are available and can be used to build up a picture of the target company – including its history, its present status and at least some indication of its future. The appendix to this chapter shows a selection of sources of information in the United Kingdom. They are all readily accessible and have been listed under two headings:

1 Possibly within your own organisation or the commercial

section of a public/central library.

2 Commercial organisations.

ASSESSING CORPORATE SURVIVAL

Predicting corporate failure is itself a hazardous business. Many attempts have been made to construct predictive models which, by means of combining a series of more or less conventional financial ratios, aim to anticipate incipient failure. Some of these approaches are more successful than others. However, their common disability is that they impute a degree of inexorability about decline which self-aware and intelligent management teams should find intolerable. Nevertheless, the following are key financial ratios for which declining trends should be a source of concern, if not panic!

1 Current ratio = current assets: current liabilities.
2 Quick ratio (or acid test) = liquid assets: current liabilities.
3 Gearing ratio = $\dfrac{\text{Interest-bearing capital}}{\text{Ordinary shareholders' equity.}}$
4 Interest cover = $\dfrac{\text{Operating profit before interest}}{\text{Interest on borrowing.}}$

Current ratio

This ratio can be constructed by reference to the current assets and current liabilities listed in the company's balance sheet. It is a crude measure of liquidity but useful as a first indicator of a company's ability to pay its creditors. It is difficult to specify what the current ratio for a particular company ought to be, but as a 'rule of thumb' there should be at least £1 of current assets for every £1 of current liabilities; for complete safety, some analysts prefer to see certain types of company exhibiting a substantial excess of current assets, that is with a current ratio approaching 2:1.

Liquid ratio or acid test

A more incisive measure of liquidity, this ratio excludes those items in current assets which may not be immediately available as cash to meet short-term liabilities. Normally this means excluding stocks from the calculation, although in food retailing, for example, this may be thought an artificial restriction. A rule of thumb relationship of 1:1 is often suggested for this quick ratio but, again, circumspection is required in the application of such yardsticks – like most averages they seldom apply to any one individual!

Both the current ratio and acid test are absolute measures of solvency and like all 'snapshot' ratios their value really lies in comparison over time or across similar businesses. The supplier which displays steadily deteriorating solvency ratios may be heading for disaster, but it is almost certain that it will wish to exert pressure on its customers to settle their accounts rapidly. If, as a buyer, you are sure that failure is not imminent then, of course, such weakness can be capitalised on in price negotiations.

Gearing

Sometimes known as leverage, this ratio expresses the relationship between interest-bearing capital (debt + preference shares) and equity capital (including reserves). A company with a large proportion of debt to equity is said to be highly geared and vice versa. High gearing may be interpreted as a source of vulnerability in the sense that the company concerned may be subjected to distracting pressure from its lenders. Moreover, in the event of receivership the providers of secured borrowings will naturally hold preferential rights over the assets of the company – usually sufficient to ensure that any residue for unsecured creditors will be small or zero! Again caution must be exercised in the interpretation of gearing ratios, for they vary greatly between business sectors according to the mortgageable nature of the fixed assets involved, e.g. land and buildings for property companies.

Interest cover

This measure illustrates the extent to which profits are pre-empted by the need to make interest payments. If interest cover begins to decline, perhaps to the point where profits are scarcely sufficient to meet them, pressure can be anticipated from the providers of loan capital. In fact, inspection of trust deeds attaching to borrowings, which can be undertaken at Companies House or via a company search service, will often reveal very precise stipulations for interest cover which can be tested against the annual accounts.

Whilst none of these ratios is capable individually of anticipating collapse, they can be used in combination to good effect. But beware of slavish adherence to arithmetic; it is its origins which matter. In this respect it is worthwhile mentioning the availability of credit ratings from such organisations as Dunn & Bradstreet in the UK, and Moodies in the USA. These ratings are obtained as an amalgam of several ratios of the type discussed and can give useful indication of the creditworthiness of supplier and other companies. Whilst UK ratings have yet to acquire the status of their US counterparts, the latter provide ample evidence of the degree to which financial manoeuvrability may be restricted or enhanced by the level of the rating. Changes to these ratings are often publicised and can give useful indication of the financial community's shifting mood.

APPENDIX – SOURCES OF FINANCIAL INFORMATION*

Possibly within your own organisation or commercial section of the public/central library

Financial Times
Daily newspaper, excellent coverage of business, commercial management, United Kingdom company news, international companies and finance, etc.
Financial Times Ltd,
Bracken House,
10 Cannon Street,
London EC4P 4BY
(Tel 01-236 1340/1).
(Library open to general public 10.30-12.00 and 14.00-15.30 daily.)
A useful publication to consult would be *A Guide to Financial Times Statistics,* edited by D. Bell and A. Greenhorn, published by Financial Times Business Information Ltd 1984.

The Economist
Weekly review of the latest facts and figures on the world economies and on commodity and financial markets.
The Economist Newspaper Ltd,
25 St James's Street,
London SW1A 1HG
(Tel 01-839 7000).

Investors Chronicle
Weekly guide to investment, city and financial news, reviews of companies and industries.
Financial Times Business Publishing Ltd,
Greystoke Place,
Fetter Lane,
London EC4A 1ND
(Tel 01-405 6969).

British Business
Weekly news from the Department of Industry and Trade.

---

*Reproduced from 'Accounting for Managers', a Henley Open Management Education Programme, by kind permission of Henley Distance Learning Ltd.

Economic Trends
Monthly – brings together all the main economic indicators. The tables and charts illustrate trends in the United Kingdom economy. Prepared by the Central Statistical Office in collaboration with the statistics divisions of government departments and the Bank of England.

Monthly Digest of Statistics
Prepared by the Central Office of Information in collaboration with the statistics divisions of government departments. Areas covered United Kingdom of Great Britain and Northern Ireland.

Bankers' Almanac and Year Book – organised in three sections
(*a*) British banks – information on all those companies that have been granted recognition as banks under the 1979 Act and are registered in the United Kingdom and on the list issued by the Bank of England.
(*b*) details of companies which have been granted a licence as a licensed deposit taker.
(*c*) the international banks.

Britain's Top 1,000 Foreign Owned Companies
Annual. Provides a detailed analysis of companies registered in Great Britain with more than 50 per cent of their voting share capital in the hands of corporations registered overseas.

Britain's Top Private Companies: the First and Second Thousand
Britain's Top Private Companies: the Third and Fourth Thousand
Provide a detailed analysis of the financial performance of selected lists of private companies.

Directory of Directors
Annual. Lists the directors of the main public and private companies in the United Kingdom, and gives the names of the concerns with which they are associated.

Europe's 10,000 Largest Companies
Annual. Financial and statistical information on industrial and trading companies. There are also sector lists for the banking, transport, insurance, advertising and hotel/restaurant industries.

Kompass (2 volumes)
Annual. Volume 1 – a detailed listing of companies by products.

Volume 2 – company information contains over 33,000 company entries and business data. Each main company entry gives information on company structure, directors, senior executives, number of employees and nature of business.

Major Companies of Europe (2 volumes)
Volume 1 – companies in the EEC.
Volume 2 – companies in Western Europe outside the EEC.

The Stock Exchange Official Yearbook
Annual. Details of securities quoted on the London and Federated Stock Exchanges are given. Also information on the company, registrars, directors, capital, accounts, dividends and transfers.

The Times 1000
Annual. Lists *The Times* top 1,000 companies, giving details of chairman, turnover, capital employed, net profit before interest and tax, number of employees and equity market capitalisation.

Who Owns Whom, UK & Republic of Ireland (2 volumes)
Annual. A directory of parent, associate and subsidiary companies. Volume 1 lists parent companies with their subsidiaries. Volume 2 lists United Kingdom subsidiary and associate companies showing parent company.
There is also a –
Who Owns Whom, Continental Europe, Australasia and Far East and North America

Guide to Key British Enterprises (2 volumes)
Annual. A-Z listing of leading public and private United Kingdom companies. Gives information of headquarters' address, factory location, line of business, trade names, sales turnover, number of employees, directors, telephone, telegram and telex numbers.

Kelly's Manufacturers & Merchants Directory
Annual. Manufacturers, merchants, wholesalers and firms listed within their trade descriptions, addresses, telephone and telex numbers and telegraphic addresses. There is also a list of exporters and importers.

London Gazette
Four times weekly. Official notices relating to companies, bankruptcies and partnership dissolution.

Register of Defunct and Other Companies
Annual. This information now appears as a section in the Stock Exchange Official Yearbook.

NB: Don't forget telephone directories (particularly London Business), local directories, trades and professional directories.

Commercial organisations

Information is provided on a commercial basis in the majority of cases.

Companies Registration Office
Companies' House,
Crown Way,
Maindy,
Cardiff CF4 3UZ
(Tel 0222-388 588 X 2223).
London Search Room,
Companies' House,
55-71 City Road,
London EC1Y 1BB
(Tel 01-253 9393, Mon-Fri 9.45-400 pm).
The office where companies are registered, their annual returns and accounts are deposited. The public are allowed access. The London Search Room has facilities for the examination of documents held in Cardiff.

CBD Research Limited
154 High Street,
Beckenham,
Kent BR3 1EA
(Tel 01-650 7745).
Provide guides to organisations, directories and other sources of information on business enterprises, management associations and to sources of statistics.

Datastream International Ltd
Monmouth House,
58-64 City Road,
London EC1Y 2AL
(Tel 01-250 3000).

A comprehensive databank of company, industry and economic statistics. The service can be provided either on *Time sharing* with direct terminal access to the central computer by telephone, or on *Fact-finder* for users without terminals.

Extel Statistical Services Limited
37-45 Paul Street,
London EC2A 4PB
(Tel 01-253 3400).
Financial and background information provided on any of the limited companies registered in the United Kingdom, either one-off or continuously updated as information becomes available, either in Extel Card format or as photocopies of companies' filed accounts. In addition to updated services, Extel Cards and Searches are available on a one-off basis. There is also an overseas companies' service.

Financial Times Business Information Service
Bracken House,
10 Cannon Street,
London EC4P 4BY
(Tel 01-248 8000).
On-line facilities for searching every article from the *Financial Times* (London and Frankfurt editions) which mentions a company name.

McCarthy Company Information Services
Manor House,
Ash Walk,
Warminster,
Wilts BA12 8PY
(Tel 0985 215151).
Daily press cutting service on quoted and unquoted United Kingdom registered companies on the London and regional stock exchanges. Also overseas information available.

Prestel
London Prestel Centre,
Post Office Telecommunications,
10th Level International House,
Canterbury Crescent,
London SW9 7QT
(Tel) 01-583 9811
On-line facilities which can be provided in your own home. Covers amongst other information, company accounts, income and funds, news search services, and company services.

Textline
Produced by Finsbury Data Services Ltd,
68-74 Carter Lane,
London EC4V 5EA
(Tel 01-248 9828).
On-line information on companies from leading daily financial and general newspapers, journals, annual reports and press releases.

Warwick Statistics Service
Business Information and Statistics for Industry,
University of Warwick Library,
Coventry CV4 7AL
(Tel 0203 418938).
A commercial information service giving access to the full resources of the university library.

Other useful sources of information can be obtained from the following publication:–

Dare, G. A. and Bakewell, K. G. B., *The manager's guide to getting the answers,* 2nd edition, Library Association, 1983.

15

Measuring purchasing performance

Owen Davies

If you were to stand on the scales and announce to your colleagues that your weight was 196 lbs, such a statement might evoke mild interest. However, if you were to advise that, as a result of a specially prepared diet programme, your announced weight represented a reduction of 5 lbs over your weight two weeks ago and that you still have another 15 lbs to shed, this would cause significantly more interest – the point being that the statements included measurement against stated objectives and a measurable programme.

If you wished you could also introduce comparisons of your weight relative to World Health Organisation standards for a man/woman of your age, height and body frame and even introduce aspects of eating habits related to your country of residence. Further, you might introduce other comparative measurements illustrating how you have progressed during the diet programme, comparative weights over past years and the likely weight standards you intend maintaining in future months and years. Finally, you might comment on other influences which have had a bearing on your weight comparison to other standards, which may take into account economic and behavioural issues etc.

Already, therefore, in this simple introductory analogy on measurements, it will be seen that effective performance measurement includes:

- an information data base
- objectives
- trends (analysis, interpretation, forecasting)
- variations
- exceptions
- indices.

It would also be important to differentiate between measurement of performance and information or workload statistics.

To return to the analogy – suppose you were to decide that you could gauge your weight based on intuition and past experience and did not require the use of the scales. It is likely that you would adjudge yourself to be somewhat lighter than you were, whereas your colleagues would estimate you to be somewhat heavier than you really were. Equally, if you claimed to have lost an excessive amount of weight in a short period without providing evidence to back the claim, your colleagues would be likely to find your estimate somewhat lacking in credibility.

All of which suggest other measurement aspects to be considered. These include:

- a willingness to be measured
- credibility of 'savings' claimed
- acceptability of the measurements
- accuracy of the measurements
- accuracy of the measurement 'instruments'.

Of course, some of your colleagues might also be on the same or a similar diet programme and you would be made aware of their progress relative to your own. This introduces yet another element of performance criteria:

- competitor's performance
- comparative standards
- interfirm comparisons.

The dietary programme might require special foods which are often more expensive than your normal food intake; it might even be necessary to undertake a special course at a clinic or health farm and/or obtain some special fitness equipment. This introduces a further dimension into a measurement programme. In the work situation this could involve:

- department costs
- cost/benefit relationships
- systems costs
- budgets.

From all this it will be seen that measurement of performance is, on the one hand, relatively simple in its systems approach and relatively complex in its analytical determinants. Finally, 'you' can be represented as an individual or a functional group, but both require performance measurement. The sum of the departmental performance should be greater than the sum of the individual performance, although that is not necessarily the case.

OTHER FUNCTIONAL MEASUREMENTS

It has been said that the purchasing function avoids performance measurement criteria because the function cannot be properly measured. Yet elsewhere in any organisation adequate measurements are identified and used as a means of determining performance.

Sales and marketing

Sales and marketing measure their performance against wholly accepted criteria, e.g.:

- gross margins
- market share
- market penetration
- selling expenses
- distribution costs
- marketing ratios
- movement off shelf
- product recall
- customer attitude/acceptance.

Production

The manufacturing operation details performance to estabished and wholly measurable criteria:

- production throughput
- production downtime
- standard costing
- manhours
- technical production data
- manufacturers' data
- rejection rates
- rework costs
- overtime
- over-runs.

Finance

The whole basis of financial measurement determines the profitability, or otherwise, of the organisation and the results of such measurements are evidenced in the profit and loss account and the balance sheet.

It is important that the acceptability of these performance measurements hinges on the fact that finance acts as the third party 'auditor' to specify, agree and monitor the functional performance areas. It is through the finance function and the establishment of an effective management information system (MIS) that the senior management of an organisation can assess the performance of its various functions and the organisation as a whole. At this point it would be helpful to review the applicability of performance measurement criteria to the purchasing functional area.

PURCHASING INFORMATION SYSTEM

With the increased use of computerisation in the purchasing area, the assembly of a complete data base is possible. This will provide for an effective systems approach to purchasing and enable purchasing to interface with the organisation MIS through a purchasing information system.

The purchasing information system will collate and present data covering the following functional aspects, including:

- pricing information and trends
- vendor performance
- stockturn relating to inventory movement and velocity
- supplier selection criteria
- critical supply issues including shortfalls in supply.

PURCHASING WORKLOAD STATISTICS

It is essential that differentiation be made between workload statistics and performance indicators.

Workload statistics are defined as those pieces of information, historically derived, which identify the amount of work input/output but do not of themselves provide measurements of efficiency and effectiveness. Examples of purchasing workload statistics would be:

- number of purchasing employees
- number of purchase orders raised
  - local
  - overseas
  - standing orders
- number of requisitions received
  - travelling
  - standard
- number of releases against requisitions
- department costs
- number of inventory line items.

The clear danger of using workload statistics as evidence of performance was well exemplified by a purchasing manager who took the following statistics to derive efficiency indicators:

- number of purchase orders raised
- value of purchase orders raised
- number of purchasing personnel
- department costs
- value of purchases per purchasing personnel
- $ cost per $100 expenditure.

The faults in this system are obvious. Statistics are being manipulated to derive spurious indicators of purchasing performance. As a result the whole basis of measurement of purchasing performance is called into question.

PURCHASING STANDARDS AND OBJECTIVES

Purchasing objectives must be determined in consultation with senior management so as to ensure that such objectives are properly integrated with those of the company as a whole. The use of management by objectives (MBO) remains a most useful medium for creating both individual and departmental purchasing objectives (see Figure 15.1).

Purchasing standards determine when an objective has been met and importantly are established at the time the objectives are set and before action is initiated to achieve the objective. This means that purchasing standards can then be established as criteria of purchasing performance since they are measurable, limited by time, and allocated to specific purchasing personnel for achievement. Evaluation of these purchasing standards allows management to assess critically the contribution made by the purchasing performance in respect of the overall profitability of the enterprise.

Within an MBO system, purchasing objectives and standards can be modified but only by agreement with top management. By virtue of the fact that identified purchasing objectives and standards are agreed and accepted by management, they represent commonly agreed objective measurements rather than subjective assessments – an important criterion.

STANDARD ACQUISITION PRICES

Where a standard costing system exists within an organisation, the input of estimated pricing for the purchase of goods, materials and services will be undertaken by the purchasing function. Since standard acquisition prices represent a forecast of what purchasing expects to pay for goods and services acquired over a given forecast period (month/quarter, six months, annual), it is important to the

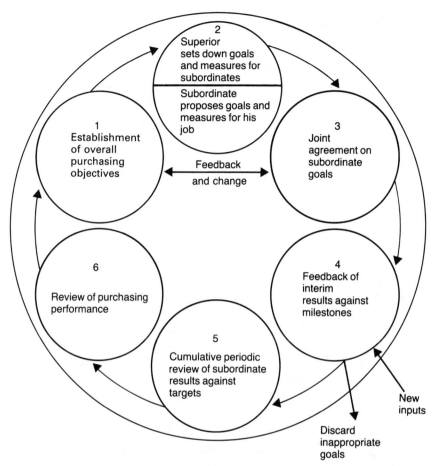

Figure 15.1 The cycle of management by objectives

acceptance of such standard prices that the assumptions on which the estimates were made are stated, clearly and unequivocally. The assumptions will cover the area of:

- fiscal, e.g. currency
- economic, e.g. inflation
- political, e.g. tariffs, government regulations
- supplier market trends
- product availabilities, under-/over-supply

together with specific assumptions for key materials, goods and services.

SAVINGS

A primary cause of concern in the measurement of purchasing performance relates to the claims for 'savings' made by purchasing. The credibility of the function will be called into doubt when purchasing lays claim to 'savings' against standards which are themselves estimates forecast by purchasing. Excessive 'savings' will be assumed to have been achieved by insurance 'buffers' included within the standards set.

It is imperative that where purchasing is measured, the performance measurements are accepted as being wholly credible by other people within the organisation. Further, that savings claimed are acknowledged, where appropriate, to be the result of joint departmental effort; purchasing should never lay unilateral claim to savings where other functions have contributed to the effort (engineering, manufacturing, quality control etc.).

Savings, then, are defined as those planned, predetermined actions undertaken by purchasing, or by purchasing and other departments, which result in measurable cost/price reductions, value improvements (through VA projects, quality control circles etc.) or avoidance of a higher cost. In other words, a general 'across-the-board' price reduction by a supplier would not qualify. Nor would 'savings' achieved by purchasing which cause increased costs elsewhere; the obvious example being volume discounts taken by purchasing which increases stockholding costs. A total acquisition cost approach is essential to the measurement of savings.

Whilst savings should be categorised into recurring and non-recurring, they should be reported only once, based upon the first year of applicability.

Alternative management synonyms to the use of the word 'savings' might be:

– cost minimisation programmes
– profit contribution programmes
– cost reduction programmes.

The use of the word 'savings' could be considered provocative and it may be prudent to help ensure management credibility by erring on the side of parsimony in reporting such 'savings'.

VARIATIONS AND EXCEPTIONS

One danger in reporting savings against standard is that many purchasing managers ignore the fact that standard acquisition prices are forward estimates of the expected average price to be paid over the forecast period. It is clear, therefore, that in the first half of the forecast period, the actual prices paid will be below the standard, to be compensated in the second half by prices higher than standard (see Figure 15.2). If the standard acquisition price is wholly accurate, then of course the pluses and minuses will cancel out. If the standard is inaccurately forecast, the variations will not be in balance. However, savings are not in any event applicable since all that the imbalance of pluses over minuses proves is that the standard was inaccurately set; though the difficulty of establishing accurate standards should not be underestimated.

Purchasing variances are deviations, plus or minus, that fall within established tolerance limits. Clearly, since standards are forward estimates based on stated assumptions, a degree of error is to be expected. The further out in time a standard is projected, the wider will be the degree of error (see Figure 15.3). It would be prudent at the time of setting standards, to identify tolerance limits (plus/minus degrees of error) so that variances occurring within such

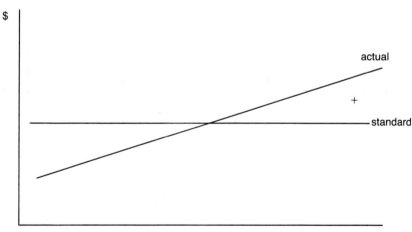

Figure 15.2 Use of standard pricing

tolerances are accepted, though reported, but are not used in any way as 'savings'.

The theory and practice of control by exception is important for purchasing, since it is a management control system which can establish clearly purchasing delegation and authority. Exceptions to purchasing standards occur outside the set limits of tolerance and thereby require the attention of the senior purchasing management (see Figure 15.4). This control process clearly identifies where work is not progressing according to purchasing standards and is, therefore, a clear performance indicator.

USE OF INDICES TO PROVIDE TRENDS

In the process of measurement of purchasing performance there is the need to evaluate an organisation's performance against a norm.

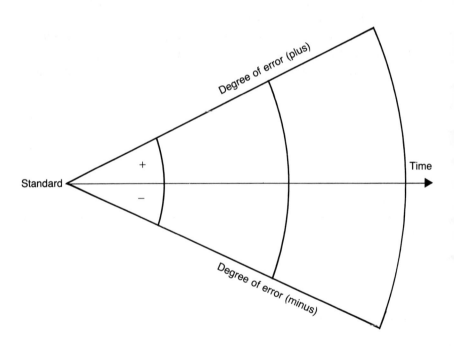

Figure 15.3 Forecasting error

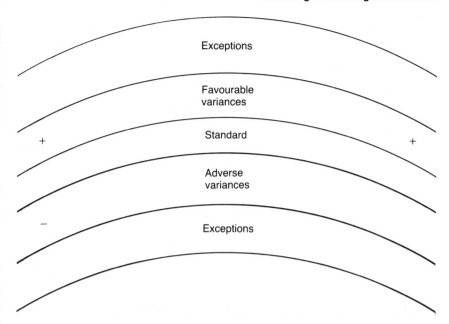

Figure 15.4 Variances and exceptions

One useful method is to convert actual purchasing performance to an index and measure its trend against a published or universally accepted index.

If, for example, a company purchased materials whose major ingredient was steel, it could convert actual price history to an index and plot its relationship to the published steel price for the same period. If the bought-in price index followed the line taken by A in Figure 15.5, then this could be taken as adjudged indicating that since the gap was narrowing, the price line indicated a poor performance. Conversely, if the trend line reflected B, then it might be interpreted as a favourable performance. The index lines can be also converted to a points scale which gives percentage variations from which to measure the purchasing performance. There are published indices for just about every commodity, either obtainable from government statistics or from published technical journals and information media, e.g. *LME Bulletin* which could be used in this way.

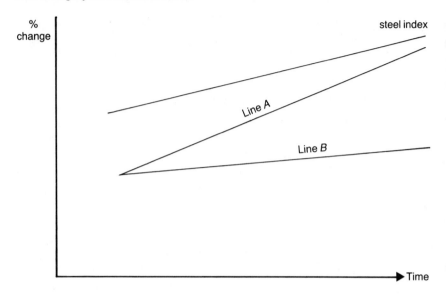

Figure 15.5 Gap analysis in purchasing performance

It could also be possible to introduce purchasing performance measurement through averaging out a 'shopping basket' of key materials/services, giving a weight/volume allowance and converting the result to an index which is plotted against, for example, the published inflation rate or consumer/wholesale price index.

A final use of indices is to determine the materials content of key product groups sold by the company and demonstrate the percentage change that occurs in the materials content, either in percentage or index terms. This will give a guideline to the impact of materials cost content on the gross margin of the key selling product groups and give some measurement of cost improvements which occur in the materials content.

It is important to understand that comparison of purchasing price indices against published statistics gives only a guideline for performance measurement purposes and should not be taken as a critical performance indicator. Extrapolation of the trends demonstrated by the indices should also be carefully interpreted and provided as forecast trends to management.

PURCHASING EFFICIENCY INDICATORS

A number of organisations have endeavoured to provide meaning-ful indicators of purchasing efficiency and effectiveness. One example is shown in Figure 15.6 which is taken from the United States Air Force, and another is shown in Figure 15.7 which is from a major international food manufacturer (the sales figures etc. have been changed).

USE OF PURCHASING RATIOS

The use of ratios as a means of measurement is well established and accepted by management. The following purchasing ratios not only provide a control check but also enable management to see the trend of purchasing performance in various areas and to take corrective action where necessary.

Purchasing operating ratios which appear to be most applicable are:

> sales: purchases
> working assets: purchased inventory
> debtors: creditors
> cost of purchases: inventory.

The buying rating formula is based on seven variable factors:

$$\text{Standard output} = \left[\frac{x_1 + 2(x_2 + 10x_3)}{x_4} \right] \times \left[1 - \frac{x_5}{2} + \frac{x_6}{x_2 + x_3} - \frac{x_7}{x_1} \right]$$

where:
x_1 = line items (number of items purchased per month, regardless of quantity per item)
x_2 = actions under \$2,500 (this includes the vast majority)
x_3 = actions over \$2,500 (these estimated to take 10 times longer to handle)
x_4 = number of manhours worked in a month
x_5 = delinquency rate (per cent of orders shipped late)
x_6 = major and minor errors (one point for major errors, 0.25 for minor errors)
x_7 = cost savings (one point for saving under \$100, two points for over \$100).
A *minor error* is defined as the failure to act on requisitions within 30 days or the failure to mention a delivery date on the order.
A *major error* would include the failure to include required legal clauses and the failure to obtain competitive bids.

Figure 15.6 USAF purchasing rating formula

	1981 (Actual)	1982 (Actual)	1983 (Actual)
Group sales value	$51.3m	$57 m	$63.8m
Total purchases	$18.9	$20 m	$22.2m
1 Purchasing ratio	36.8%	35.1%	34.8%
suppliers	127	152	160
agents	7	5	4
staff (purchasing)	9	8.5	9.5
staff (company)	612	618	642
Packaging staff %	1.47%	1.38%	1.48%
Inventory level/month	$723 K	$696 K	$690 K
2 Inventory %	3.8%	3.5%	3.1%
3 Purchasing commitment	7.62	5.0	5.0
4 Purchasing efficiency index	.188	.587	.779
		i.e. 3.12 times 1981	i.e. 4.14 times 1981

1 PR = GSV ÷ TP
2 I% = IL per month ÷ TP × 100
3 PC = Total $ on forward contracts × avge. # Months contracted ÷ TP
4 PEI = TP × # Supp ÷ # A ÷ # Pur. staff ÷ IL ÷ PC ÷ PR

Figure 15.7 Food manufacturer's purchasing formula

Sales to purchases

The average percentage of purchases to sales in manufacturing companies is between 52 and 56 per cent. By maintaining a ratio comparison over the years, some analysis of the trend for purchasing can be determined.

Working assets to purchased inventory

Working assets primarily consist of inventory, both finished and raw materials etc. It is important to determine the relationship between the purchased inventory, work-in-process and finished products.

Debtors to creditors

This ratio should essentially be in balance, i.e. equal to one. However, an improvement in the ratio could be sought by, for example, obtaining increased credit facilities from suppliers.

Cost of purchases to inventory

This ratio represents inventory turnover and is an important indicator of productivity in this area.

INTERFIRM COMPARISON

One key objective for the purchasing function is to place its company in a preferred position with respect to its competitors in the marketplace. It would therefore be a sound measurement of the purchasing performance if it was possible to compare acquisition prices paid by your organisation against those paid by competitors. Whilst interfirm comparisons are undertaken on the sales end (A. C. Nielsen, for example), they are not generally available on the purchasing operation.

Companies should, nevertheless, give serious consideration to undertaking interfirm comparisons within their own organisation and even on an interdivisional basis. Clearly, care must be taken, in such circumstances, to ensure that the comparisons are equable otherwise the end results will be counter-productive.

SUPPLIER RATING SYSTEMS

With the use of computers supplier rating systems are becoming more sophisticated and can provide a useful guide to the measurement of purchasing performance. It has been said that there are no poor supplier performances only poor purchasing selection performances. Suppliers are rated on the basis of price, quality and service with sub-categories dependent on the industry and manufacturing process. Whilst there are a number of formulae to derive a supplier rating the following measurement process provides a sound base for most systems.

Price index

Take the total price quoted, or accepted, for each supplier related to the product or service to be measured. The price index for a supplier is then the ratio of his price to the lowest price.

Example:

Suppliers	A	B	C
Unit price	155	165	135
Price index	$\dfrac{155}{135}$	$\dfrac{165}{135}$	$\dfrac{135}{135}$
(Integer) =	87.1	81.8	100.0

Quality index

Whilst this is basically the ratio of accepted, or rejected, parts to the total parts received, allowance has to be made for the number of shipments made between suppliers. In other words, a weighting factor has to be included to differentiate between one supplier with a single shipment and another with multiple shipments of the same product. A weighting factor commonly used is:

$$\sqrt{\frac{ST}{ST + 1}} \quad \text{where } ST = \text{the number of total shipments}$$

The total formula derived would be:

$$\frac{PA}{PT} \times \frac{SA}{ST} \times \sqrt{\frac{ST}{ST + 1}} \times 100$$

where PA = parts accepted
PT = total parts received
SA = no. of shipments accepted
ST = total no. of shipments received.

Example:
Supplier A 1 shipment
100 parts total
96 parts accepted

$$\text{Quality index} = \frac{96}{100} \times \frac{1}{1} \times \sqrt{\frac{1}{2}} \times 100$$
$$= 96.0$$

Supplier B   4 shipments
3 shipments accepted
600 parts total
580 parts accepted

$$\text{Quality index} = \frac{580}{600} \times \frac{3}{4} \times \sqrt{\frac{4}{5}} \times 100$$

$$= 65.0$$

Supplier C   2 shipments
2 shipments accepted
200 parts total
180 parts accepted

$$\text{Quality index} = \frac{180}{200} \times \frac{2}{2} \times \sqrt{\frac{2}{3}} \times 100$$

$$= 73.48$$

Delivery index

The delivery index is computed on the basis of the number of times the supplier meets his delivery promise. Allowance has to be made for determining the degree of lateness related to the production downtime; the later the delivery the more serious is the effect on manufacturing. The degree of lateness is therefore exponential and the weightings have to be determined, probably in conjunction with production planning; e.g.

Days late	Weighting
1 – 5	1
6 – 10	2
11 – 21	3
21 +	4

The delivery formula would be:

$$100 - \frac{(AD \times F) + (AD \times F) +}{TD}$$

where AD = no. of days late
F = weighting
TD = total no. of deliveries.

Example:
Supplier A = 4 deliveries
          1st – 4 days late
          2nd – 0 days late
          3rd – 12 days late
          4th – 5 days late

$$\text{Delivery index} = 100 - \frac{(4 \times 1) + (0 \times 1) + (12 \times 3) + (5 \times 1)}{4}$$

$$= 88.75$$

Supplier B = 2 deliveries
          1st – 5 days late
          2nd – 2 days late

$$\text{Delivery index} = 100 - \frac{(5 \times 1) + (2 \times 1)}{2}$$

$$= 96.5$$

Supplier C = 1 delivery
          6 days late

$$\text{Delivery index} = 100 - \frac{(6 \times 2)}{1}$$

$$= 88.0$$

Overall index

These price, quality and delivery indices are sometimes combined to give an overall supplier performance measurement with an additional weighting to allow for the rating of price over quality over delivery. If we were to adjudge that price represented a factor of 50, quality 30 and delivery 20, we could use these weighting factors to arrive at an overall performance indicator for the vendors *A*, *B* and *C* as follows:

Suppliers	A	B	C
Price index	$50 \times 87.1 = 43.55$	$\times\ 81.8 = 40.90$	$\times\ 100.00 = 50.0$
Quality index	$30 \times 96.0 = 28.80$	$\times\ 65.0 = 19.50$	$\times\ 73.48 = 22.04$
Delivery index	$20 \times 88.75 = 17.75$	$\times\ 96.5 = 19.30$	$\times\ 88.0 = 17.60$
Overall index	90.1	79.7	89.64
	(preferred supplier)		

The above represent basic decision rules for measurement of supplier performance and can be varied to suit organisation needs.

INTERNAL DEPARTMENTAL PERFORMANCE

It would be appropriate to conduct interdepartmental performance comparisons between divisional purchasing departments where the organisation is of a size to have more than one purchasing department. The purpose is not to provide some kind of competitive league, though the motivational aspects of this should not be wholly ignored, but to identify where management intervention may be necessary.

One system which is being researched is the use of the 'add-on costs' system to measure purchasing performance. Let us take the example that no purchasing department exists in an organisation. Thus users go directly to suppliers to obtain quotations. Suppose that a price of 100 units is offered in such circumstances for a product. The intervention of the purchasing department into this procedure is clearly to derive an improved positioning for the user department in relation to the supplier through the use of its professional expertise.

In the example, by negotiation, the purchasing department obtains an improved price of 85 units for the product. The measurement of performance, therefore, of purchasing is 15 per cent favourable. However, this is the gross margin of performance and from which should be deducted the cost of purchasing intervention. If this latter departmental on-cost was 10 per cent, then the net effect of purchasing performance is only a 5 per cent improvement over the original user-to-supplier direct commercial link.

This is the basis of the added-cost measurement, and analysis of various purchasing departments has revealed some on-cost examples as follows:

- In a number of government purchasing departments evaluated, the added-cost factor, taken as a total cost basis, from sourcing through inventory to internal issue to users, varied from 9 to 18 per cent.
- In a number of private enterprise companies evaluated, the added-cost factor, again on a total cost basis, varied between 6 to 15 per cent.

Thus the variation between the public and private sectors was not significant and the evaluation suggests that the more efficient purchasing operations reflect an added-cost of around 6 to 8 per cent. At the higher end of the study, it may be appropriate to ask whether user departments may not obtain a better service by going direct to suppliers than 'paying' an internal on-cost of between 15 to 18 per cent for what clearly is an inefficient purchasing operation.

AUDITS OF PURCHASING PERFORMANCE

A neglected area of measuring purchasing performance is the conduct of audits:

- internal 'customers'
- external supplier view
- consultant led.

Internal customer

Since the whole purpose of the purchasing task is geared to provide an optimum service to user departments, purchasing should engage in an audit to determine the effectiveness of its service level and inventory holding (see Figure 15.8). It is clear that there are issues other than stockouts and production downtime which measure the overall effectiveness of the purchasing function including:

- speed of response
- efficiency of communication
- flow of information on requisitions
- courtesy.

Once purchasing understands the attitude necessary to service its internal 'customers' and that the very presence of the purchasing function is to provide an efficient and effective service at optimum cost, then the internal relationships with user departments, can be improved considerably.

A simple questionnaire will provide an excellent audit document to measure purchasing service to internal customers.

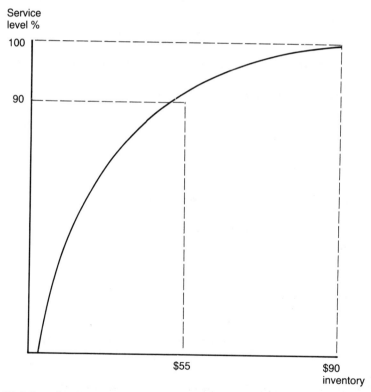

Figure 15.8 Service level

SALES PERSON'S OPINION SURVEY
MOTOROLA PORTABLE PRODUCTS DIVISION
FORT LAUDERDALE, FLORIDA 33322

1. How long have you been calling on Motorola? _____

2. How often do you visit us? _____

3. Which section of the Purchasing Department do you normally visit?

ELECTRICAL	MECHANICAL	MRO
____ IC's/Semi's/Crystals	____ Plastics	____ Test Equipment
____ Coils/Transformers	____ Metal Parts/Hdwe	____ Tools
____ Capacitors	____ Castings/PC Boards	____ Furniture
____ Resistors	____ Chemicals	____ Construction
____ Switches/Pots	____ Packaging/Wire/Cable	____ Janitorial
____ Speakers/Connectors	____ Rubber/Leather	____ Office Supplies
____ Other	____ Other	____ Other

4. Are you now a supplier to Motorola? _____ Yes _____ No

5. Are you aware of our policy on gifts, gratuities, and entertainment? ____ Yes ____ No

6. Do you usually call ahead for an appointment? _____ Yes _____ No

7. Is the buyer you ask to see usually able to grant you an interview with reasonable promptness? _____ Yes _____ No

8. What do you think is a reasonable time to wait to see the buyer? _____

9. Please check the line that indicates your rating of the Motorola Buyer(s) whom you visited.

	VERY GOOD	GOOD	FAIR	POOR
Attitude	____	____	____	____
Product Knowledge	____	____	____	____
Decisiveness	____	____	____	____
Negotiator	____	____	____	____
Open Mindedness	____	____	____	____
Professionalism	____	____	____	____

10. Are you requested to submit ways to reduce the cost of materials we buy?
_____ Often _____ Sometimes _____ Never

Figure 15.9 Sample questionnaire of supplier's view

11. What is your overall opinion of Motorola's Purchasing Department, its policies and people, compared to that of other companies on whom you call?
_____ Superior _____ Above Average_____ Average _____ Below Average _____Inferior

12. What do you consider to be the major strength of our Purchasing Department and also indicate that area that you feel offers opportunity for improvement?

_____

_____

_____

_____

_____

_____

_____

THANK YOU FOR COMPLETING THIS OPINION SURVEY.

(FOLD THIS FLAP, Staple with Return Address Out, and Mail)

AN INVITATION TO SALES PERSONS WHO VISIT MOTOROLA:

The Purchasing Department has the objective of cultivating and maintaining good relations with our suppliers. You can help us evaluate our progress by stating your opinion on the opposite side of this self-mailing form.

We value your opinions, and we hope you will see fit to participate in this survey. To do so, merely check your responses to the questions and write in whatever comments you care to make. YOU ARE NOT ASKED TO SIGN, but merely to re-fold the questionnaire with the return address outside, staple and drop in any mailbox. In doing so, you will be performing a service for us by monitoring our efforts to be effective toward our responsibilities and responsive to your time spent with us.

Thank you
Manager of Purchasing

Figure 15.9 *concluded*

External supplier view

Another attitudinal perspective which will provide guidelines to the efficiency of the purchasing function could be derived from seeking a supplier's view of the purchasing department. Again, a questionnaire could be a useful tool to derive such measurement information. A sample questionnaire used by Motorola is shown in Figure 15.9; this example should provide a very useful basis for any company considering such an approach.

Consultant

A consultant audit should provide an objective analytical assessment of the purchasing function and provide a total evaluation of purchasing performance. If it is conducted as a diagnostic process it will return to management a 'balance sheet' of strengths and weaknesses of the purchasing operation. The objectives of a consultant-led audit may be seen as:

- Identifying the criteria by which purchasing performance can be measured.
- Applying such performance indicators to determine the extent to which purchasing performance meets or fails to meet those criteria.
- Reporting to management on the objective assessments of the purchasing function based on the evidence of purchasing performance.

INDIVIDUAL BUYER PERFORMANCE

The best form of individual purchasing appraisal is self-appraisal which requires the individual buyer to evaluate his or her own performance. To do so requires the availability of some form of appraisal document which relates specifically to purchasing performance. This will enable the buyer to think through his/her own performance in purchasing in terms of the standards by which he/she will be measured.

However, self-appraisal alone is an insufficient measurement and must be backed by an organisation appraisal document. Reference has already been made earlier to the MBO system which provides a sound basis for appraising the individual buyer through reviewing individual action programmes. Since these action plans clearly identify purchasing performance standards which are agreed by the individual buyer and his/her manager, they form a base for both self-appraisal and manager appraisal.

The Kodak Corporation has instituted an individual purchasing appraisal scheme which is known as the 'best accomplishment programme' and whose purpose is to give recognition to outstanding individual purchasing performance. The stated objectives of the programme are to:

1 Motivate individuals to higher levels of achievement.
2 Inform management of outstanding purchasing contributions.
3 Provide awareness of techniques and ideas to increase purchasing effectiveness.

On a monthly basis individual buying accomplishments are rated on a ballot basis with the votes cast evaluating the individual accomplishments against three criteria – effort, innovation and savings. The top five accomplishments are recognised by publishing the results of the balloting with the top buyer having his/her name inscribed on the 'best accomplishment programme' plaque outside the purchasing director's office. The aim is to stimulate individual creativity and advancement towards individual and department goals.

The definitions given to the individual criteria for assessment are:

Effort is the special attention given to a project over a considerable period of time or a concerted attack on a problem in a short time or repeated entries into a problem over a medium time.

Innovation is the art of introducing something new to an effort or making a novel change which contributes to a purchasing accomplishment in a non-routine way and demonstrates some professionalism or imagination on the part of the buyer.

Savings is the result of avoiding unnecessary waste or expense and may be divided into direct and indirect savings. An example of direct savings would be the negotiation of a lower price with a new or current supplier whilst an example of indirect savings would be the elimination or reduction of related costs, such as service calls and replacement within the warranty period.

REPORTING PURCHASING PERFORMANCE

Purchasing reports generally are poorly executed and do little to further the professional approach that the purchasing function seeks to demonstrate. Reports to top management which announce 'the department typewriter needs replacement' or 'the purchasing department lost the services of Mr X on his resignation' surely announce to top management the inadequacy of their purchasing department (these are actual report items seen by the author).

Reports need first to be categorised between content, format and readership – who wants to know what, when and how often? Figure 15.10 gives a breakdown table of a suggested report frequency and reporting lines.

Whilst the actual content of purchasing reports obviously depends upon the type of industry and the type of organisation involved, the following examples indicate the kind of item that might be included.

Market and economic conditions and price performance

1 Price trends and changes for major materials and commodities purchased. Comparison with standard costs where such accounting methods are used.
2 Change in demand-supply conditions for the major items purchased. Effects of labour strikes or threatened strikes including shipping (home country and overseas).
3 Lead time expectations for major items.

Inventory investment changes

1 Dollar investment in inventories classified by major commodity and materials groups.
2 Days' or months' supply and on order for major commodity and materials groups.

Readership	Performance area	Frequency	Function	Department head	Individual
Top management		A	1 Plan	Selected ratios/ statistics (M)	MBO performance reports (M)
		Q	2 Forward look		
		Q	3 Key product review		
		Q	4 Critical shortages		
		Q	5 Key price changes		
Dept. heads	Sales and marketing	M	6 Opportunity areas		
		M	7 Shortages		
		M	8 Price variances		
	Finance	M	8 (as above)	Forward orders	
		M	9 Forward currencies		
	Production	M	7 (as above)	Lead times	
	Others			Service level	Training needs
Immediate superior		M	8 (as above)	Ratios/stats.	Appraisal (A)
		M	10 Indices		

A = Annual   Q = Quarterly   M = Monthly

Figure 15.10 Purchasing reporting

3 Ratio of inventory dollar investment to sales order volume.
4 Rates of inventory turnover for major items.

Purchasing operations and effectiveness

1 Cost reductions resulting from purchase research and VA studies.
2 Quality rejection rates for major items.
3 Number of out-of-stock situations which caused interruption of scheduled production.
4 Number of requisitions received and processed.
5 Number of purchase orders issued.
6 Employee workload and productivity.
7 Transportation costs analysis.

Operations affecting administrative and finance activities

1 Comparison of actual department operating costs to budget.
2 Cash discounts/credit period – analysis and changes.
3 Commitments to purchase classified by expected delivery dates.

Special reports

Initiated by purchasing research.

CONCLUSION: PRICE IS NOT THE SOLE CRITERION

Measuring purchasing performance is a complex task which many purchasing managers approach in too simple a way. Yet the correct reporting of purchasing performance represents a clear opportunity for informing top management of the effective contribution which purchasing makes to the profitability of the enterprise. As such, it is an opportunity which demands the careful attention of the professional purchasing manager. To ignore such an opportunity or to present a poorly constructed report will itself be a measure of the quality of purchasing function in the eyes of senior management.

Performance reports to top managements should serve to provide important purchasing information upon which top management can base decisions in respect of company operations. Secondly, and in that order of priority, the reports enable management to measure, in credible terms, the overall performance of the purchasing function as a key role in the business.

In the absence of a measurement system for purchasing, judgements of purchasing performance will still be made, albeit in a highly subjective manner. Such judgements will have little regard for what is happening in the supplier marketplace, or the inflation effects on price movements, or shifts in the availability of key materials. Thus the lack of an effective measurement procedure for purchasing performance, with proper reporting methods conducted in a timely manner, robs the purchasing function of the opportunity to present itself in a professionally competent and credible light.

It is important that the purchasing performance measurement criteria which are used should reflect areas of significance to the organisation and should, therefore, eschew trivia, concentrating on key issues which have important effects on the company's business. In assembling the criteria for performance measurement, the purchasing manager should review the criteria used by other functions and the method of presentation by those departments of their performance measurements. If it is meeting its objectives, by careful presentation of purchasing performance measurements using both narrative and numerative methods, purchasing can clearly demonstrate its effectiveness within the overall performance of the company's business.

The purchasing function, in many organisations, continues to be disregarded in its proper light and there is no doubt that this results at least in part from a lack of properly presented, meaningful information on purchasing performance. It is not suggested that purchasing should 'blow its own trumpet' simply for the sake of so doing, but it is important that colleagues in other functions are aware of the contribution which purchasing is making and can make.

16

Foreign exchange and currency management

David Jessop

Foreign exchange, the act of converting the currency of one country into the currency of another, is not a modern development, it has existed for as long as there have been different countries. However, foreign exchange as currently practised has only existed since the end of the First World War. Prior to this time the values of currencies were generally determined by the amount of gold or silver that they would purchase and many currencies were convertible into these precious metals.

Convertibility into gold or silver is no longer a practicable proposition. After 1918 most countries abandoned the full gold standard because there simply was not enough gold in existence to back the large numbers of notes made necessary by inflation in the war-damaged economies.

In 1925 Great Britain did attempt to reintroduce a modified version of the gold standard, but this lasted only until 1931. During the period between the wars there were a number of devaluations by various countries who were attempting to stimulate their domestic economies during this difficult period, and the whole area of foreign exchange was somewhat chaotic.

In 1945 the western countries met at Bretton Woods in an attempt to organise and rationalise the international monetary system. This conference replaced the pure gold standard with a dollar-gold standard and established the International Monetary Fund (IMF) to administer the system.

This agreement was a great success. Following a revision of the value of the pound from US $ 4 to US $ 2.80 in 1948 the external values of the world's leading trading currencies remained remarkably stable against one another until 1967, but between 1967 and 1971 the agreement began to break down; one by one the major subscribers to the agreement broke away, being no longer able, or perhaps willing, to control the values of their currencies within the bounds of the Bretton Woods agreement. The final stroke came in 1971 when the US Treasury decided to break the link between the dollar and gold; there was no longer a fixed rate of exchange between the two.

In view of the remarkable success of the Bretton Woods agreement it is not surprising that an attempt was made to replace it. Towards the end of 1971 the major trading nations met at the Smithsonian Institution in Washington and made a new agreement which revised currency values in terms of the dollar which was itself devalued. Unfortunately the Smithsonian agreement was not successful and the major international currencies, the US dollar, the pound and the yen began to 'float' freely on the world's money markets. The oil crisis of 1974 further destabilised money markets, and led to the present era in which there are massive and largely unpredictable changes in the relative values of currencies. There have been, and continue to be, attempts to limit the extent of these relative changes, the 'snake' set up by the European Economic Community (EEC) being a case in point. However, it does seem that large fluctuations in the world foreign exchange market will only be avoided in the long term by co-ordinating the management of the various national economies, a prospect which appears to be remote.

Accordingly, the organisational buyer who acquires some of his needs from overseas countries needs to be alert to the probability of exchange rate fluctuation and, more importantly, needs to be able to minimise the financial risk associated with such fluctuation.

WHY EXCHANGE RATES FLUCTUATE

A currency, just like any other commodity, will vary in price according to the interaction of supply and demand. The price of a currency may be thought of as its value in exchange for another currency. If the supply of a particular currency at a certain time exceeds the demand for that currency, then its exchange value will automatically fall because a seller of the currency will have to offer more of it in exchange for a fixed amount of another currency in order to induce purchasers to act. The converse is also, of course, true. If demand exceeds supply then would-be buyers of a currency will have to offer higher prices in order to induce sellers to part with their holdings. It is easy to see that the 'rate of exchange' which is simply the 'price' of a currency will fluctuate continuously as the supply of, and the demand for, the currency changes.

According to economic theory purchasing power parity will limit the extent of fluctuations and will tend to bring currencies into a reasonably stable relationship with each other. Purchasing power parity theory suggests that the rate of exchange between two countries will reflect their relative purchasing powers. For example, if a certain quantity of goods costs £10,000 in Britain and DM 40,000 in West Germany, then the rate of exchange ought to be DM 4 = £1. If the rate of exchange alters to, say, DM 3 = £1, then British goods will become cheaper in Germany, because the German buyer will need to pay fewer marks for the same number of pounds. On the other hand, German goods will be more expensive in Britain. The result of this, so the theory suggests, is that the demand for British goods, and hence pounds, will rise in Germany, and the demand for marks will fall in Britain, and the two currencies will resume their former parity. Whilst there must obviously be some truth in this theory, there are a good many factors other than commercial transactions which influence exchange rates, and the situation is much more complicated than the simple interrelationships between currencies that the theory assumes.

Inflation is one of the factors which has a great bearing upon exchange rates. If all countries were to suffer inflation to the same degree then the relative values of their currencies would not alter; exchange rates would remain the same. However, what happens in reality is that the inflation level is different from one country to another, and those countries where the level exceeds the prevailing level will need to take some appropriate action. This might take the form of monetary or fiscal measures or of a reduction in the value of the national currencies. Inflation, deflation and reflation are factors relating to the domestic economy of a nation, having an indirect affect on the value of its currency.

A primary indication of the strength or weakness of a nation's economy (and its currency) will be given by the country's balance of payments, since this balance has an immediate effect on the country's gold and foreign currency holdings. Any surpluses or deficits which show up in the figures will indicate the direction of the overall flow of money into or out of the country, and the volume of that flow. However, distinction must be made between short-and long-term flows, for example short-term outflows are not of great significance if they are investment outflows, since they are likely to affect the balance positively in the not too distant future.

The visible balance of trade is probably the most important component of the balance of payments. The nations whose economic viability depends upon international trade are, naturally, judged on their trade performance rather than by other factors. A country with a sound balance of payments including a positive visible balance of trade is likely to possess a strong currency.

Other factors influencing the value of a particular currency include the fiscal policy of a nation. Changes in taxation, on the extent to which duties and other levies will be charged and other factors which influence spending power will be analysed and will have their effect on exchange rates.

The increasing tendency for governments to use the supply of money as an instrument of policy means that frequently exchange rates move rapidly in response to policy decision. An increase in the money supply in a particular country will usually cause the value of the currency to fall; an increase will have the opposite effect.

Domestic interest rates constitute a very important factor in determining the value of a currency. The immense strength of the US dollar at the time of writing is attributable to the fact that relatively high interest rates available in the United States have caused holders of other currencies to discard them in favour of the dollar, the dollar rising and other currencies falling as a result.

There are numerous other factors which might be said to have a bearing upon exchange rates, but it would be a mistake to assume that a careful study of all of these factors would lead to an 'understanding' of the market and an ability to predict movements accurately and consistently. There are too many random and unpredictable factors for this to be the case, an added complication being that in addition to attempting to forecast the direction of movement the analyst has to assess the extent of that movement. Little wonder that the movement of currency values is regarded by some as following a 'random walk'.

RISK AND UNCERTAINTY IN CURRENCY MARKETS

By far the greatest risk for most importers is that of currency fluctuation. Fortunately there are several ways in which the buyer can reduce the risk of loss or, and this is sometimes preferable, remove the uncertainty. It is important to distinguish between risk and uncertainty in this context, since in everyday usage the words are often interchangeable. This may be done by way of example.

A farmer who wants to be certain as to his income next season could agree to sell his forthcoming crop of wheat at a fixed price per bushel, irrespective of market conditions. The buyer might be a pasta manufacturer who wants to be certain of adequate supplies of wheat to keep production running smoothly. Both farmer and manufacturer have removed uncertainty as to the price of wheat for the next season. But the risk is still there. If the open market price is high next season, the farmer will have lost and the manufacturer gained by contracting in advance at a fixed price. Equally, of course, the reverse could be true.

The most obvious way for the UK buyer to achieve certainty as to import cost is to arrange that the price is stated in sterling. This is not always possible, nor does it eliminate the risk, since either the buyer or the seller might benefit most. 'The market' is made up of countless informed opinions. If the market thinks the pound is due for a fall, holders will try to sell and the price will in fact fall. The price of sterling at any time is basically the equilibrium price, which means that in view of the market the price is just as likely to rise as to fall. It follows then that the buyer who agrees to pay a fixed amount of sterling at a future date is as likely to lose by his action as to gain. For the same reasons, this would be equally true if the seller's currency were agreed upon as the medium of exchange.

Agreement to pay in either of the currencies of the contracting parties is, in a sense, sharing the risk, though any movement in the relative values of the two currencies will result in one party bearing all the loss, and the other making a commensurate gain. For this reason it is sometimes found appropriate that some unit of account other than the currency of one or other of the parties to the contract is used, particularly when the currencies of the two parties are fluctuating markedly in their relationships with each other. In the days when the values of most currencies were pegged to that of gold, fluctuating exchange rates were not a problem, but it should be remembered that there is no reason why buyers and sellers cannot work out their own 'gold standard'. A third uncertainty is introduced here, in that the price of gold itself now fluctuates, but it might be thought that this is a preferable uncertainty in that it spreads the risk and ensures that the price paid is not tied to the value of one particular currency.

TECHNIQUES FOR DEALING WITH RISK

Gold is, of course, not the only possible medium through which exchange rates can be pegged. A mutually acceptable third currency could be used, or possibly some notional unit of account based on a formula agreed upon by the two parties. The European Unit of Account might be found to be suitable, as it is a very accurate accounting currency based on a 'basket' of European currencies. Although the relative values of European currencies change frequently, a weakening of one currency implies a strengthening of another, and the value of the unit will remain more stable than that of any single currency.

There is, however, a lot to be said for a straightforward agreement between buyer and seller about what to do in the event of a currency fluctuation. The use of a third medium does not ensure that the risk is equitably shared, only that it is to some extent shared. It is entirely practicable to include a clause in a contract design to ensure that the risk is exactly halved, or indeed that any other apportionment of risk as the parties see fit be applied. A simple clause, designed to cater for a 50-50 sharing of risk might be worded as follows:

The exchange rate on which the contract is based is to be £1 =

x. In the event of there being a different rate of exchange prevailing when payment is made, calculation of the amount due will be made according to the formula £1 = $\dfrac{\$x + \$y}{2}$, $\$y$ being the value of £1 at the date of payment.

The purchasing techniques used when buying an item or commodity which has a fluctuating price are occasionally suitable where it is the exchange rate, rather than the price, which is fluctuating. After all, the end result, reflected in costs, is the same. One such technique is the well known 'pound cost averaging' technique. This is based on a very simple principle and is often used by investors when buying shares. The buyer merely allocates a set amount of money per fixed period for whatever it is that is to be bought. For example, a processor of copper might choose to enter into a direct contract with a producer in, say, Zambia, rather than buy through the LME. The output in Zambia will be priced in Kwachas, which are 'pegged' to the US dollar, so the processor might ask for £100,000 worth of wirebars to be shipped each month. If the price of copper, in terms of sterling, falls as a result of a change in the rate of exchange between the pound and the dollar, or indeed for any other reason, then £100,000 will buy more of the material. If the reverse happens, then less of the expensive copper will be added to the stockpile.

'Volume timing' of purchases is another technique which could possibly be employed to cope with varying exchange rates. If the buyer is in a position to select a rate of exchange which he can adopt as a realistic rate at which to buy from a particular source, and if there is scope for him to vary the quantity of goods purchased at a given time, then it will be possible to vary the quantity bought according to whether the prevailing rate is above or below his 'datum' rate. If the prevailing rate is more favourable than the 'datum' rate, then the buyer can buy in quantities larger than are necessary to cover his immediate needs. He will take advantage of his fortunate circumstances to 'stock up'. When the current rate of exchange is worse than the 'datum' rate, then the buyer must engage in 'hand to mouth' buying, that is to say that he should buy only if absolutely necessary and only that amount which will fulfil his immediate needs. This unfortunate state of affairs could, of course, exist for a considerable period of time, and when this is the case the buyer will have to employ his judgement to determine whether an alternative source of supply has become preferable.

Sharing the uncertainty involved in buying from a source involving foreign currency is not the only way open to a buyer. The banks play a major role as risk takers for the world of commerce, and a proportion of their profit comes from the premiums charged for so doing. There are over 200 authorised dealers in foreign exchange in London, most of these being banks, with just a small number of foreign exchange brokers. Currencies are the most homogenous of commodities, one pound, franc or dollar is absolutely identical with another, so the currency markets can approach very closely the perfect market. There is a very effective system of communication on the foreign exchange market, so it is most unlikely that the buyer will be able to obtain competing quotations for a foreign currency in the same way as he might be able to do for many other purchases unless he is spending very large sums. It is, however, a simple matter for an importer to be sure of the exact amount he will have to pay in sterling to meet a future indebtedness of a known amount of foreign currency.

An obvious and straightforward way of doing this would be simply to buy the foreign currency 'spot' and hold it until payment is due. The disadvantage of this is that the buyer is deprived of working capital for a longer period than if money did not have to be found until payment was due. A solution often found convenient is to buy 'futures' in the currency. The principle is exactly the same as that involved in buying futures in commodities such as zinc or coffee, the important advantage being that payment is not made until the foreign currency is transferred to the supplier.

It is also possible to buy foreign currency and invest in an interest bearing account in that currency.

'Hedging' is a very valuable technique for coping with exchange rate fluctuation, and has become a much more viable proposition since the opening of the London International Financial Futures Exchange (LIFFE).

The London International Financial Futures Exchange (LIFFE)

This exchange, which opened on 30 September 1982, is situated in the Royal Exchange in London. It provides a regulated market for financial futures, trading contracts of four kinds:

1 Short sterling interest rate contracts.
2 Long gilt interest rate contracts.
3 Short eurodollar interest rate contracts.
4 Currencies – against $ US
                 – sterling
                 – deutschmark
                 – yen
                 – Swiss franc.

It is the provision for foreign currency contracts which is of the greatest interest to the organisational buyer, allowing him to provide for known commitments to protect his exposure to future price movements by 'hedging' these commitments.

Contracts are standardised, and trading in them is by open outcry, so all prices are therefore publicised. The buyer can be sure that he is dealing at the 'going rate' for his particular currency, but against this advantage must be placed the disadvantage that, because they are standardised, contracts are inflexible compared with the forward currency market.

As in any other commodity market, hedgers minimise the risk to themselves of unfavourable movements in interest or currency rates of exchange. They are usually seeking to protect a genuine commercial transaction for the purchase or sale of goods or services. A future exchange rate can be 'locked in' by taking a position in future contracts which is equal and opposite to an existing position.

Illustration of the principle of a hedge

Suppose that on 10 March a buyer contracts with a supplier in the USA for machinery at a cost of US $ 150,000, payable 10 June. The US supplier agrees to accept payment in sterling, but only at an agreed exchange rate of $1.5 = £1, the rate current on 10 March. The buyer could, if he wished, buy dollars at this time and thereby 'lock in' to the current exchange rate, though this would depend upon the availability of cash and would require that the money was tied up for the contract period.

He might decide that a better alternative would be to protect himself by entering into a hedging transaction on the futures market. He could do this, on 10 March, by selling a contract to mature on 10 June for $150,000. Naturally he would not have to make delivery of the dollars until this time.

His protected state of affairs would not involve any immediate outlay on his part, and might be summarised as follows:

Current currency market	The hedge
10 March – (£1 = $1.5)	10 March – (£1 = $1.5)
Buyer agrees to pay US supplier £100,000 (equivalent to $150,000)	Buyer sells contract for US $ 150,000 (valued at £100,000 at current exchange rate)
10 June – (£1 = $1.6)	10 June – (£1 = $1.6)
Buyer pays US supplier £100,000 (equivalent to $160,000)	Buyer buys US $ 150,000 for £93,750 in order to meet contract maturing today.
A 'loss' of $10.000 (or £6,250 at current exchange rate)	A 'gain' of £6,250 (or $10,000 at current rate of exchange)

This is a somewhat simplified illustration of a 'hedge', with the two sides exactly counterbalancing each other. There are technical reasons why a perfect hedge of this kind is unlikely in practice, though the fundamental principles as illustrated will apply, and a very large measure of protection can be achieved. It is perhaps worth pointing out that had the opposite type of currency fluctuation occurred, with the pound weakening against the dollar, then there would have been windfall gain on the main transaction, but a compensating loss would have arisen from the hedge.

FORWARD EXCHANGE CONTRACTS

A forward exchange contract is a legally binding agreement between the bank and its customer whereby each party agrees to deliver at a specified future time a certain amount in one currency in exchange for a certain amount in another currency at an agreed rate of exchange. Cash is not normally exchanged at the time the contract is taken out, but both parties enter into a commitment to transact on the maturity date at the originally agreed rate.

By entering into a forward exchange contract with a bank a UK importer is able to:

1 Fix at the time of the contract a price for the purchase or sale of a fixed amount of foreign currency at a specified future time.
2 Eliminate the risk of future foreign exchange rate fluctuations.
3 Calculate the exact sterling value of an international commercial contract, although payment is to be made in the future in a foreign currency.

Hence covering forward is not speculative but rather a form of insurance that is taken out by prudent traders who wish to be relieved from the constant anxiety concerning fluctuations in rates of exchange, which are influenced by forces outside their control.

The date for delivery of the foreign currency is specified in the forward contract either on a particular business day (fixed forward contract) or a day to be chosen by the customer between two previously specified future dates (an option forward contract). This is not an option to deal, but merely an option with regard to the timing of the delivery when one currency can be exchanged for another.

If a customer has a forward exchange option contract, he does not have to make or take delivery of all the currency at one time. He may, if he so wishes, arrange for several separate deliveries.

In the event of a customer being unable to complete his forward foreign exchange contract on maturity, it must be closed out by means of a compensating spot deal that involves the purchase or sale of the foreign currency at the spot rate ruling at the time. This rate may differ considerably from the original forward rate and therefore, the customer will be faced with a loss or a profit.

On the other hand, if the reason for the customer failing to complete the contract is due to a delay in receipt of funds, a new forward contract may be entered into based upon the spot rate used to close out the original forward contract. This is known as an 'extension', which will tend to neutralise the profit/loss situation brought about by the initial closing out.

Forward exchange market rates can and do fluctuate hourly, in either direction, as a result of the factors mentioned elsewhere in this chapter.

When calculating rates the rule to remember is that a bank would always 'sell low' and 'buy high'.

Banks will offer two types of contract for commercial clients who wish to purchase foreign currency.

Spot deals

These are current deals for which the dealer will quote two rates – buying and selling, with the small difference between them, i.e. the spread, representing a profit margin on dealings. For example, if the dealer quotes US$ 1.4930/1.4940 this means that he is selling 1.4930 US dollars for every pound sterling and buying 1.4940 US dollars for every pound sterling.

Forward deals

Forward rates are not quoted as such, but rather as the difference expressed in decimal points between spot and forward prices, i.e. premiums (where the currency is dearer relative to sterling) and discounts (where the currency is cheaper relative to sterling).

In order to calculate the rate of exchange to be employed at the future date, the spot rate has to be adjusted by the amount of the appropriate margin. The rule is that the premium is deducted from the spot rate and the discount added to the spot rate.

ARRANGING PAYMENT

When a buyer imports goods from overseas it is not necessarily the case that currency will move from one country to another. What will most probably happen is that an arrangement for settlement will be made through the banking system, whereby one debt is offset against another. The banks of the trading nations have accounts in each other's countries in the domestic currency, and as credits are transferred the financial relationship between the banks will vary. Adjustments will be made when necessary by the banks buying or selling currencies.

Depending upon the foreign supplier's ability or willingness to offer credit terms the buyer has a variety of methods available to him through which he can make payment. Advance payment, or cash with order is one such method, but this is fairly uncommon because, apart from extending credit to his supplier the buyer is also running the risk that he will not be sent the goods as agreed. However, where contracts for capital goods are concerned it is sometimes the case that 'deposits' or partial advance payments are made, typically between 10 and 20 per cent of the contract price. 'Stage' or 'progress' payments may also be made. It is possible to request that a supplier should arrange with his bank that a guarantee be issued as security for any advance payment you may make.

The least difficult arrangement whereby a customer might pay for imported goods is through an open account. There are several ways in which payment can be sent to a supplier on this basis, although these have in common the fact that the paperwork is relatively simple, and payment is normally not made until after the goods have been received. Examples of ways in which money can be sent under open account are as follows.

Telegraphic transfer is an instruction from the importer's bank to the exporter's bank to transfer some of the balance of its account to the person named in the transfer. The buyer will pay his own bank in his own currency, and the bank will convert to the exporter's currency and will make charges for the transfer which will either be paid by the buyer or deducted from the currency paid to the exporter. These transfers are very rapid, it takes only a few minutes to process urgent payments and even the routine ones take only two hours or so.

Mail transfers are, naturally, less immediate than telegraphic transfers, but are generally similar in that they take the form of an instruction from a UK bank to an overseas bank to pay a stated sum of money to the suppllier. Airmail is generally used, but even so the process might easily take a couple of weeks. It is slightly less expensive than telegraphic transfer.

Cheque payments are very slow indeed to be completed as the cheque has to be processed through the international clearing system before the supplier receives credit. This might take as long as a month, and it is not surprising that suppliers are, generally speaking, not keen on this method of payment. Another disadvantage is that the supplier is likely to have to pay a fee to his own bank which arranges clearance of the cheque.

Banker's draft payments can be arranged whereby your bank issues a draft drawn on an overseas bank. This is sent to the supplier who can usually pay it straight into his account. A banker's draft can be in any currency.

International money orders are convenient for payments of small amounts. Readily available in US dollars or sterling they are simply posted to the overseas exporter who receives immediate credit from his bank.

Aside from the 'open account' methods already mentioned, there are two very popular ways of arranging payment offering benefits to both buyer and seller: a documentary bill of exchange and a documentary letter of credit.

A *documentary bill of exchange* which is legally defined as 'an unconditional order in writing addressed by one person (the drawer) to another (the drawee) signed by the person giving it (the drawer) requiring the person to whom it is addressed (the drawee, who when he signs becomes the acceptor) to pay on demand, or at a fixed or determined future time a sum certain in money to, or to the order of, a specified person or to bearer (the payee)'.

In effect a bill of exchange is a demand for payment from your supplier. His bank will forward it to a bank in the UK for 'collection', along with the documents relating to the transaction. The bank will release the documents to you provided that you either pay the amount in full on presentation or, in the case of a bill drawn payable in the future you 'accept' the bill by signing across it your agreement to pay on the due date.

A *documentary letter of credit* is in effect a promise given by your bank to your supplier, usually via a bank in his own country, that you will pay for the goods providing that he follows exactly the conditions laid down in the credit. This method ensures that the supplier will receive payment for goods and protects the importer by guaranteeing that no payment will be handed over until the stipulated requirements have been met. Letters of credit are normally irrevocable, measuring that they cannot be altered or cancelled without the agreement of both parties to the transaction. Occasionally, however, a revokable credit is encountered, whereby the importer can alter or cancel the credit at any time before the supplier presents his documents for payment.

An important point for the buyer to note is that an offer to pay by means of a documentary letter of credit can be a useful negotiating point, as you are reducing the risk 'to' your supplier.

When selecting the method by which payment is to be made do not forget that a bill of exchange can provide a useful method of arranging for credit. If the supplier consents, then a bill of exchange payable in, say, 90 days might be advantageous to the buyer. The seller will not necessarily wait 90 days for his money, he may arrange with his bank for them to advance him the money.

FURTHER READING

R. G. F. Coninx, *Foreign Exchange Today,* Woodhead Faulkner, 1980.

G. Dufey and I. H. Giddy, *The International Money Market,* Prentice Hall, 1978.

H. E. Evitt and R. F. Pither, *A Manual of Foreign Exchange,* Pitman, 1973.

L. C. Jacque, *Management of Foreign Exchange Risk,* Lexington Books, 1978.

T. W. McRae and D. P. Walker, *Foreign Exchange Management,* Prentice Hall, 1980.

D. P. Whiting, *Finance of Foreign Trade,* M. and E., 1977.

D. P. Whiting, *Finance of International Trade, M and E.; Foreign Exchange Yearbook,* Woodhead Faulkner; *Support for World Trade* (booklets), Barclays International; *Notes on Foreign Exchange,* Lloyds Bank, 1981.

17

Purchasing commodities*

Peter Baily

The primary commodities are natural products rather than manufactured products, although they normally enter into trade in partly manufactured or processed form rather than simply as harvested or mined. Cocoa, coffee and tea, for example, are dried and processed before being put on the market. Many primary commodities are traded locally but do not enter into world trade. This chapter deals only with those which are traded in such volume that there is a world trade in them, and organised commodity markets to serve that trade.

The main problem in buying such commodities is the very large fluctuations in price which occur, sometimes in quite a short period of time. This price variability is a real challenge to the purchaser if he needs large quantities of price-variable commodities to feed factories making products whose prices cannot be varied in the same way. Adverse price changes can also have serious effects on the manufacturing costs of producers who use secondary products incorporating price-variable primary commodities.

Cable manufacturers use copper; chocolate manufacturers use cocoa; wool carpet manufacturers use wool; tyre manufacturers use rubber; battery manufacturers use lead; food container manufacturers may use tin. Copper, cocoa, wool, rubber, lead and tin are all

---

*This chapter is reproduced with permission from *Purchasing Principles and Management*, Pitman Publishing Ltd, 4th edition, 1981.

commodities traded on organised commodity markets which offer facilities for hedging by the use of futures contracts.

This useful method for reducing risk is considered later. First, a brief look at the factors which cause commodity prices to fluctuate.

WHY DO PRICES FLUCTUATE?

Anyone who buys food for a household or a restaurant is familiar with the way prices change for farm products. In England, the first new potatoes, Jersey Royals perhaps, appear in spring at very high prices. Potato prices fall as the months pass and the bulk supplies, first of earlies, and then of main crop potatoes, reach the market; until by autumn old potatoes are selling for less than one-tenth of the price of the first new potatoes in spring. The first asparagus reaches the market at astronomical prices; there is not a lot to sell, but at those prices there are not many who are willing to buy. Supply and demand are brought into equilibrium by means of these price changes. Price also changes from year to year; in some years potato prices stay high all year because the weather or some other reason has resulted in a major shortfall in supply.

Exactly the same considerations affect the prices at which the 'soft' commodities are traded on commodity exchanges, but there are also additional considerations. As well as producers and consumers, participants in these markets include speculators, dealers and jobbers. Prices react continually to expectations – of present and future supply, of present and future demand, of stock situations etc.

Consequently, even though prices for some commodities stay much the same for long periods of time, the typical commodity price changes are much larger in amount, and occur in much shorter periods of time, than changes in the prices of manufactured goods. Also, commodity prices have in the past been almost as likely to move downwards as upwards, which has not been the case for manufactured goods. The high amplitude and short period of the price changes which can occur can be illustrated from the commodity price boom which occurred in 1973/4. Cocoa, for instance, sold at £187 a ton at the beginning of 1973, yet it was selling for as much as £1010 a ton in 1974. Copper sold on the London Metal Exchange for £450 a ton in January 1973; by April 1974 its price reached an unprecedented peak of £1400 a ton, yet only five months later it was back down to £600.

Price fluctuations of such amplitude are unwelcome both to consumers and to producers. A major British consumer of cocoa announced halfway through the period in question that certain purchasing staff had made 'transactions in the company's name on the cocoa terminal market which were not disclosed to the Board and which will involve the company in substantial costs'. These costs were later shown to amount to trading losses of £32.5m. Managements of manufacturing firms prefer not to be exposed to the risk of losses of such magnitude. A major producer of copper is the developing country of Zambia in Africa, whose main export revenue is derived from the sale of copper. The government of such a country faces an impossible task in planning capital investment programmes such as the construction of hospitals, schools, highways and ports, which will take years to complete, when the export revenue required to finance them can increase by over 300 per cent in a year, only to be cut in half in a few months. It is generally agreed that consumers and producers alike would prefer a more stable level of prices, although they might take different views as to what level is appropriate.

Price stability, however desirable, has not in practice proved easy to achieve. Commodity price changes reflect changes in the supply of commodities and in the demand for them.

Flood, drought, plant disease and crop failure can produce a shortfall of agricultural produce, while exceptionally good harvests can produce a glut on the market, and the natural results are high prices and low prices respectively. Wars, strikes, revolutions and changes in government policy have also had serious repercussions on the supply of commodities. Changes in economic activity in the industrialised countries, which are the main customers, have immediate effects on demand, and changes in taste or technology or the availability of substitutes have long-term effects on demand.

In the case of many commodities, the effect on price of any changes which occur in supply or demand is increased by the length of time it takes for any attempt to adjust supply to demand to take effect. Newly-planted coffee, rubber and cocoa trees take years to come into full production. Small changes in metal output can be made with existing facilities, but a large increase in output might require a lengthy process of re-opening old mines, or digging new mines and providing housing, transport and shipping facilities to exploit them. A large reduction in output is equally difficult to achieve because of the serious effects on employment and export revenue which would result.

PRICE STABILISATION SCHEMES

It might at first appear easy for producer and consumer to agree on a stable price if this is what both parties want. There is considerable use by large manufacturers of direct contracts with the producer, the producer's agent or the shipper. Although the commodity markets provide a medium for hedging and speculation, a means for buying and selling commodities, and a consensus of trading views on market conditions, reflected in market price, the fact is that a large part of world trade does not pass through these markets. If both buyer and seller prefer a stable price, surely they are free to negotiate a fixed-price contract.

But, in practice, if such a price gets much out of line with world prices it becomes almost impossible to resist the pressure to re-negotiate it. Prices payable under direct contracts between producer and consumer are usually referred to the basis price set by the commodity markets for this reason. Prices for major individual contracts can be stabilised in general only if the world market price can also be stabilised.

A number of schemes have been successful in damping down short-term price fluctuations on commodity markets, although long-term changes are a different matter. Short-term fluctuations tend to occur about a mean, until a change in the supply/demand ratio triggers off an upwards or downwards trend.

A typical scheme would be administered by a governing body, perhaps a producer cartel, or possibly a council with representatives appointed by consumers as well as producers. This governing body would appoint and finance a buffer stock manager and fix the floor and ceiling prices between which he is to operate. The buffer stock manager buys for stock when price tends to fall, and sells from stock when price tends to rise; and if operating on sufficient scale the result is to stabilise market price. Such market operations have worked well for appreciable periods of time; but they break down once a long-term trend develops. They cease to work in the case of rising price when the warehouses are empty and the buffer stock manager has no more to sell, and in the case of falling price when the financial reserves are exhausted and he has no money to buy.

For long-term price stabilisation to be successful, the governing body needs also to monitor world demand and to make appropriate changes in output in order to keep the tonnage which reaches the market in line with market requirements. This is much more difficult to achieve than short-term buffer stock operations, because output is affected by unplanned events, planned changes cannot in many cases be implemented quickly, and governments of some producer countries may feel that a change which is agreed to be in the general interest does not advance their own particular interest.

HEDGING WITH FUTURES CONTRACTS

Both consumers and suppliers of commodities thus find themselves exposed to serious risk of loss, as well as of windfall profit, because of unpredictable changes in price. It is the sort of risk which might be insured against, in the same way as insurance is taken out against the risk of loss through fire, theft or flood, if this were feasible. Unfortunately it is not feasible. Insurance is based on the fact that only a small, statistically predictable minority of those at risk will actually suffer loss in a given period. Consequently, compensation can be paid to them from a fund which is provided by premiums collected from all those insured and calculated according to the degree of risk. Fire insurance is feasible because only a few of the buildings insured actually catch fire in a given period. But market changes affect all those trading in the market, not just a small minority.

Although normal insurance is not available, a different form of risk reduction technique is possible because, while price changes affect all traders, they affect some adversely and others favourably. Some stand to lose and others to gain if the price rises, for instance; and those who stand to gain if it rises are also at risk of loss if price falls. In either case the risk can be reduced by hedging, which in this context means balancing a trading position by making compensating transactions in futures contracts.

Futures contracts should not be confused with, for instance, a construction contract to be completed in two years' time, or an order for castings to be delivered two months in the future. They are a special kind of commodity contract, which originated in the nineteenth century as world trade expanded and the markets developed arrangements whereby traders could agree on the sale or purchase of standard quantities of goods to standard descriptions for completion at a stated future date and at a fixed price. These contracts were made alongside the physical transactions in which actual goods were sold by sample and description for immediate delivery and constituted a facility whereby traders were able to reduce the risk of trading loss. Modern futures markets trade in titles or rights to commodities rather than actual goods, known as actuals, physicals, spot or cash. Futures contracts do not normally lead to actual deliveries of goods, although this is technically possible on some markets; they are closed out before completion by means of a reverse transaction.

How this works may best be seen by example. Suppose a copper producer ships 100 tons of copper to a British cable manufacturer. The goods will take three months to reach Liverpool and will be priced at the London Metal Exchange (LME) settlement price which applies on the day of arrival. On the day the goods are shipped from the country of origin, the producer hedges his position by selling 100 tons of copper futures at the ruling price, say £800 a ton, the spot price being £750 at that date. Three months later prices have declined by £100. On arrival at Liverpool, the copper consignment realises only £650 a ton. But on the same day the shipper 'buys back his futures' for £700 a ton, thus closing out his hedging operation. The 'loss' due to the decline of £100 a ton between shipment and arrivals is exactly compensated (in this simplified example) by the profit of £100 a ton on the futures transaction, and the net realisation is £750 a ton. If price had moved the other way and increased by £100 a ton, the consignment would have realised £850 a ton on arrival at Liverpool, but this would be reduced by a loss of £100 a ton on the futures transaction so that the net realisation would again be £750 a ton. The producer is removing the uncertainty from his transaction, the risk of making either more or less than expected.

Meanwhile, let us suppose that the cable manufacturer sold to a European customer a quantity of cable requiring 100 tons of copper to complete. The price is based on the spot price of £750 a ton ruling at the date the contract is signed. Between this date and delivery of the cable three months later, the manufacturer is at risk; so he hedges his position by buying 100 tons of copper futures at £800 a ton. If price increases by £100 a ton, the manufacturer 'loses' £10,000 on the physical transaction, but makes a compensating gain by selling his futures for a £100 a ton profit. If price falls by £100 a ton, the loss on the futures transaction is compensated by an equal gain on the physical transaction. Again, the uncertainty has been removed.

Gain or loss on physical transactions is compensated exactly by hedging transactions with futures contracts only if prices in both markets move in the same direction by the same amount, giving a perfect hedge. An imperfect hedge may, however, be better than none. Selective hedging is also common; but spot price and futures price do often move in step.

SOME BUYING TECHNIQUES

One cautious policy which is sometimes adopted is known as 'back-to-back' or averaging. Ideally, no stocks are held, and the exact quantity required is purchased at the time of requirement. This ensures that the cost of commodities consumed is the same as the market price. No expert knowledge is required and no risks are taken. However, it does not work so well when stocks have to be carried.

An ingenious formula approach, sometimes called budget buying, can ensure that the cost of commodities consumed is *less* than market price, provided that average market price can be predicted successfully and that actual prices fluctuate in random fashion about this average. The idea is to spend a standard sum based on the average price at regular intervals of time. This 'budget' amount buys a larger amount when actual price is below average and a smaller amount when price is above average. This can best be illustrated by taking simple, exaggerated figures. Let us suppose that one ton a week is required of a commodity of which the average market price is £100 a ton, and that in three successive weeks, actual market price is £150, £50 and £100. With the back-to-back or averaging policy, one ton would have been bought each week; but with the budget-buying policy, £100 would be spent each week, the budget amount to obtain one ton at the average market price. In the first week, £100 would buy two-thirds of a ton at £150 a ton. In the second week, it would buy 2 tons at £50. In the third week, it would buy 1 ton. Over the three-week period, budgeted buying would have resulted in 3⅔ tons being bought for £300, at an average cost below the average market price. The averaging policy would have resulted in three tons being bought for £300, at cost equal to the average market price.

A more sophisticated approach has been developed by operations research workers and is known as dynamic programming. To illustrate this technique, let us suppose that 100 tons a week are required of a commodity the price of which fluctuates randomly between £200 and £300 a ton, and that the buyer is authorised to purchase up to ten weeks' supply (1,000 tons). We will also assume that futures contracts are not available. Having found a method of determining each week how much to buy, we will then reconsider these simplifying assumptions.

In order to establish a yardstick, by which we can measure how well the dynamic programming technique works, let us first see how well we could buy if we knew in advance what the market price would be each week. Over a fifty-week period, let us assume that prices each week are going to be as follows:

Actual market prices

Weeks	*Weekly prices in £/ton*				
1–5	277	265	220	209	280
6–10	234	246	202	205	204
11–15	215	240	206	287	288
16–20	217	218	277	266	214
21–25	268	227	285	211	217
26–30	226	295	268	297	273
31–35	275	264	227	245	201

36–40	287	220	202	219	236
41–45	245	242	296	272	298
46–50	278	281	252	231	288

Assuming we start with no stock, we must buy 100 tons in the first week to meet the first week's requirements, but as price is falling we buy only one week's supply. The same applies in weeks 2 and 3, but in week 4 the price of £209 is the lowest until week 8, so we buy 400 tons to last until week 8. In week 8 the price of £202 is the lowest which is going to apply for a considerable time, so we buy ten weeks' supply, the maximum authorised. Each week we look ten weeks ahead and buy as little as necessary to meet requirements until we can stock up at a low price. With the advantage of advance knowledge of price we would be able to supply the fifty-week requirement at an average price of just below £210 a ton, as follows:

Week number	Opening stock	Price paid	Amount bought	Total expense
1	NIL	277	100	27,000
2	NIL	265	100	26,500
3	NIL	220	100	22,000
4	NIL	209	400	83,600
8	NIL	202	1000	202,000
10	800	204	200	40,800
13	700	206	300	61,800
20	300	214	100	21,400
24	NIL	211	1000	211,000
25	900	217	100	21,700
35	NIL	201	1000	201,000
38	700	202	300	60,600
39	900	219	100	21,900
49	NIL	231	200	46,200
Totals			5000 tons	£1,048,200

Average price paid = £209.64/ton

If, on the other hand, we took no chances and had no advance knowledge, and simply bought 100 tons a week at the going price, the average cost would be £248 a ton.

THE PRICE OF INDIFFERENCE

In order to decide a buying rule for the practical situation in which advance knowledge of market prices is not available, the procedure is to determine a *price of indifference* at which it does not matter if an order is placed or not. If market price is above the price of indifference, no order will be placed, and if it is below the price of indifference we make a further calculation to decide how much to buy. Clearly the price of indifference is affected by the amount of stock in hand; with nil stock we cannot afford to be indifferent but must buy whatever the price. We will denote the prices of indifference by P_0, P_1, P_2 ... P_{10}, where the suffix denotes the number of weeks' stock in hand. These prices can easily be calculated on the simple assumptions we have made, that:

(*a*) demand is 100 tons a week;
(*b*) orders are for multiples of 100 tons;
(*c*) maximum stock is 1000 tons;
(*d*) price varies randomly and evenly from £200 to £300 a ton.

With nil stock we must buy whatever the price; but price will not exceed £300, so P_0 is £300.

With one week's stock, the price of indifference is determined by the fact that we must buy next week if we do not buy this week. Next week's price we do not know, but on the average will tend to be halfway between £200 and £300, so we should buy this week if the actual price is below £250; and this gives the value of P_1 as £250.

With two weeks' stock, the situation is more complicated. If we do not buy this week, next week we will be down to one week's stock and P_1 = £250. The chances are even that next week's price will be below £250, and if it is on the average it will be £225. Consequently,

$$P_2 = \text{(probability of price being below } P_1) \times \text{(expected price if it is)} + \text{(probability of price being above } P_1) \times P_1$$
$$= 0.5 \times 225 + 0.5 \times 250$$
$$= £237.5$$

With three weeks' stock, a similar calculation can be made:

$$P_3 = \text{(probability of price being below } P_2) \times \text{(expected price)} + \text{(probability of price being above } P_2) \times P_2$$

Since prices are assumed to be evenly distributed, if the price is below P_2 it will on the average be halfway between £237.5 and £200, so:

$$P_3 = 0.375 \times 218.75 + 0.625 \times 237.5$$
$$= £230.5$$

Proceeding in this way we obtain the following prices of indifference:

$$P_0 = £300$$
$$P_1 = £250$$
$$P_2 = £237.5$$
$$P_3 = £230.5$$
$$P_4 = £225.8$$
$$P_5 = £222.5$$
$$P_6 = £220.0$$
$$P_7 = £218.0$$
$$P_8 = £216.4$$
$$P_9 = £215.0$$
$$P_{10} = £214.0$$

These are shown in graphical form in Figure 17.1.

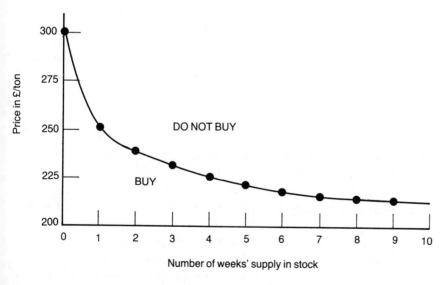

Figure 17.1 Indifference prices

Now we can work through the 50 weeks' prices previously given once more. In week 1, with nil stocks, P_1 applies and we must buy. The quantity to buy is also derived from the above list; if market price was £218, equivalent to P_7, we should buy enough to supply 7 weeks' requirements. But in week 1, market price is £277.5, higher than P_2, so we buy just one week's supply. In week 2 we again buy just 100 tons. But in week 3, price is £220, corresponding to P_6, so we buy six weeks' supply, in addition to our requirement for the current week. Proceeding in this way, by the end of the year our buying record is as follows:

Week number	Opening stock	Price paid	Amount bought	Total expense
1	NIL	277	100	27,700
2	NIL	265	100	26,500
3	NIL	220	700	154,000
4	600	209	400	83,600
8	600	202	400	80,800
9	900	205	100	20,500
10	900	204	100	20,400
13	700	206	300	61,800
16	700	217	100	21,700
20	400	214	500	107,000
24	500	211	500	105,500
33	100	227	300	68,100
35	200	201	800	160,800
38	700	202	300	60,600
48	NIL	252	100	25,200
49	NIL	231	200	46,200
			5000 tons	£1,070,400

It can be seen that the 5,000 ton requirement would have been bought for an average price of £214 a ton. This is much better than the average market price of £248, which is the best which could have been achieved by the risk-reducing policy of averaging, or in this case buying 100 tons a week. While it is not quite as good as the average price of £210, which is the best possible obtainable with complete advance knowledge, it really is pretty close to it.

It may be objected that anyone can set up a simplified illustration and devise a winning strategy; how applicable is this to the real world? Well, the simplifying assumptions that demand was a fixed 100 tons a week, and that prices varied once a week, and that buy decisions were made in multiples of 100 tons are made only for ease of explanation and can be relaxed without affecting practice. The assumption that a maximum of ten weeks' supply could be bought reflects the fact that in reality some limit must always be set to the buyer's discretion and that he must seek special authority from higher management if, in his judgement, commitments can with advantage be made beyond that limit. Finally, it was assumed that price distribution was rectangular, or flat between the two limits stated. In practice a price forecast with its likely error distribution could be used instead. B. G. Kingsman[1] has given a fuller account of this technique, which he says can also allow for futures contracts as a less expensive alternative to holding stock.

A brief glossary of commodity market terminology follows.

GLOSSARY

Arbitrage Buying in one market, e.g. London, and selling in another, e.g. New York, in order to profit from price anomalies. This in fact smooths out the anomalies.

Backwardation When the cash price is higher than the futures price.

Basis Difference between cash price and futures price.

Bear One who speculates for a fall in price; *bear market,* one in which price is falling.

Broker One who buys or sells for others in return for a commission.

Bull One who speculates for a rise in price; *bull or bullish market,* one in which price is rising.

Commission Charge made by broker for buying or selling contracts; rates of commission are fixed by market authorities and brokers are not allowed to depart from them.

Contango When the cash price is lower than the futures price.

Long Owning physical commodities or futures contracts which are not fully hedged.

Short Selling physical commodities or futures in excess of what is owned.

REFERENCE

(1) B. G. Kingsman in D. H. Farmer and B. Taylor (eds) *Corporate Planning and Procurement,* Heinemann, London, 1975.

FURTHER READING

T. Watling and J. Morley, *Successful Commodity Futures Trading,* Business Books, 2nd ed., London, 1978.

18

Legal aspects of purchasing

Michael Taylor

A well-informed manager is expected to acquaint himself with many subjects under the law. Among them are employers' liability, agency, trade descriptions and restrictive trade practices, patents, trade marks and copyright, negotiable instruments and the carriage of goods. Beside all this he must, if he is a purchasing director or manager, have special knowledge of the law of contract and the sale of goods. That is the subject of this chapter. It will deal with the acquisition of goods and services, not with the control of them. The term purchasing manager will be used, not to exclude the materials manager, but for brevity. The materials manager too must understand the law of contract and the sale of goods since purchasing is an integral part of his responsibility.

The domestic law of contract and the sale of goods is well charted territory. The excellent short courses organised by the British Institute of Purchasing and Supply and the authoritative articles currently appearing in *Purchasing and Supply Management* provide the most up-to-date information on recent case law and legislation. The principles are well established in the textbooks. Together these sources supply the practitioner with all he needs to know about the domestic legal problems of his profession.

What is not so readily available is digestible guidance on the complexities of the law relating to international trade. The basic problems will be stated and some of the solutions available will be outlined under the headings overleaf.

1 The conflict of laws.
2 Different concepts of the law of contract.
3 Difficulties arising from different legal concepts.
4 The doctrine of the proper law of the contract.
5 Conventions for harmonising the law of contract.
6 Internationally acceptable conditions of contract.
7 Domestic conditions of contract suitable for international trading.

THE CONFLICT OF LAWS

Sovereign states, about 170 in number, have assumed an inalienable right to govern their affairs by:

(*a*) making certain acts illegal and punishing offenders (criminal law);
(*b*) setting up machinery for enforcing settlement of disputes (civil law).

In many countries this single jurisdiction runs throughout the land but, in some, departments within the sovereignty apply the rules of law in different ways. There are, as is well known, differences for historical reasons between the laws of England and Scotland. In this chapter the law of England will be cited but where there are no differences, e.g. in recent legislation on contractual matters, the term UK law will be used.

In Switzerland there are *droits cantonneaux* within the confederation. In Canada provincial law in Quebec differs from law in other provinces. In the USA legal regulation exercised by the states varies between one state and another. The differences include the law of contractual obligation. It is therefore not enough for the purchaser from the USA to be acquainted with federal law. He must enquire into the relevant state law.

Although variations between laws are formidable it is possible to distinguish in the world four legal systems or, better, families of systems which have concepts different from one another.

DIFFERENT CONCEPTS OF THE LAW OF CONTRACT

Common law

In England the law of contract developed under the system known as common law, the basis of which is to use judicial decisions rather than legislation to settle disputes. At first it was little more than a means of keeping the King's peace by preventing disputants from resorting to arms. Later, persons aggrieved by decisions in local assemblies could appeal to the King to settle their grievance. This was done by the use of principles established in one trial as binding authority in subsequent causes. Thus the law of contract in common law countries is not the work of legal scholars but of trial judges in action using the experience of their predecessors.

To them we owe the distinguishing features of contract law in England: unequivocal offer and acceptance, consideration, agreement on essential terms, willingness to be bound at law and limited capacity to act. These concepts have been adapted in many countries which formerly had political links with England: the USA, Canada, Australia, New Zealand and some of the countries in the Middle East, in South-East Asia and in Africa. In some of these common law has been accepted only in part, for example in Muslim states and in India where it has stood alongside traditions of other civilisations.

Romano Germanic law

The basis of Romano Germanic law is Roman law adapted in the twelfth century to prevailing conditions in the relics of the Roman Empire. It was developed mainly by legal scholars who formulated a series of rules based on the sixth century Code of Justinian. In this system the task of the judges was not to adduce principles of law, but to settle disputes by applying the rules laid down in the code.

The Roman law of obligations is the key to the law of contract. It is a very different concept from the sanctity and freedom of contract under common law. The difference finds clear expression in the treatment of breach of contract. In Romano Germanic law it was not considered improper for defaulting parties to pay a penalty for failing in their legal obligations. In common law a penalty could not be written into a contract because it could be exacted oppressively by a powerful against a weak contracting party.

In France the Romano Germanic law was coded under Napoleon. In Germany it was coded in 1900, thirty years after the unification of Germany under Prussia. In the Nordic countries a code has developed from judicial rules drafted in the sixteenth century. As in common law, Romano Germanic law has extended its influence to former colonial empires of European origin, to Latin America, to countries in Africa and the Middle East and in part to South-East Asia and Japan.

Socialist law

The USSR and other European socialist states have preserved some of the characteristics of Romano Germanic law to which they adhered before they became socialist. The rule of law is still conceived in the form of a general code of conduct and the divisions of law and terminology remain as they were constructed in the universities of Europe in the Middle Ages.

This is the shadow. The substance is very different. The purpose of socialist law is not to preserve basic concepts of justice. It is to create conditions for a social order in which the state and the law are synonymous. The law of contract, as it is understood in the West, has been extinguished. It is subordinate to economic and political purposes and is little more than an aspect of state policy. In the West failure to execute undertakings carries redress. In socialist states it causes penal sanctions. The raison d'être of contracts is not to avoid dispute but to be a tool for economic development and eventual world domination.

Law based on philosophy or religion

The various legal systems in this category are independent of one another but they do have some common characteristics. Almost all emphasise the duties of a just man but the idea of the right of individuals to equal treatment under the law is unknown. They are not legal systems in the same sense as the two bourgeois systems of the West. They are called legal because the body of rules which they propound are intended, in the minds of their adherents, to fulfil the role which in the West has devolved upon the law.

Of these systems Muslim law is the most important. It is not the law of Islamic states. It is the law to which in certain matters the faithful are supposed to adhere. Muslim law has few binding provisions. It leaves wide scope for initiative and personal freedom. According to one Hadith (an authoritative saying of the prophet) there is no harm in drawing up private agreements (i.e. contracts) except in matters forbidden by the law of Islam. It is therefore easy to assume contractual intent even though it may be no more than a legal fiction which cannot be enforced in the courts.

Similarly Jewish law is not the law of the state of Israel. Hindu law is not the law of India. They are both precepts which govern the conduct of the faithful and subsist behind the veneer of legal systems imposed by the state. So also the customary laws of Africa continue to exist in some countries but do not have the sophistication of Hindu, Jewish and Muslim law. They are elemental, tribal rules behind the façade of systems which recognise the rights of the individual. This concept is foreign to customary law in the African countries; it was imposed by colonial powers in the nineteenth century. With their departure the concepts of the common law and Romano Germanic law are ebbing away from the governance of many countries.

DIFFICULTIES ARISING FROM DIFFERENT LEGAL CONCEPTS

In this diversity of legal concepts there are some daunting conclusions to be drawn. Even in the system most like common law there are differences of which no purchasing manager could reasonably be expected to know. In so simple a matter as offer and acceptance a contract which is valid under common law may be invalid under Romano Germanic law. At common law acceptance by post is complete when the letter of acceptance is posted. Under Romano Germanic law acceptance is not complete until the offeror receives it.

Much greater is the diversity between socialist law and the bourgeois systems of the West. Negotiation *ab initio* and complete specifications on all financial, technical, production and commercial matters are essential because under socialist law there is no redress. On this *Czarnikow v Rolimpex* is a cautionary case for purchasers. Rolimpex is a Polish state trading company with exclusive rights to export and import sugar. After a bad sugar harvest world prices rose above the contract price to be paid by Czarnikow and the Polish government decided that the contract should not be honoured. The Western purchasers lost £40m in meeting contractual obligations to their customers and sued Rolimpex. Rolimpex claimed that the government ban amounted to *force majeure* and relieved them of their duty to supply the sugar under the terms of the Refined Sugar Association agreement.

With awe inspiring unanimity the arbitrators, the Court of Appeal and the House of Lords, ruled that even though Rolimpex was a state organisation it was not so closely connected with the government as to preclude it from relying on the government ban as *force majeure*. The House of Lords further decided that Rolimpex, having fulfilled its warranty under the contract to obtain an export licence, had no obligation to maintain the licence in force until the sugar had cleared Polish customs. It is a worrying judgement for all who trade with the USSR and her satellites. State trading companies are clearly instruments of state policy yet acts of government may be claimed to relieve a state company of its legal obligations.

In countries with a philosophical or religious background to the law the problems are somewhat different. They are more subtle than the draconian attitudes of socialist states and they are less calculable. A particularly difficult concept is the idea that a ruler's word is law. If it is, it is a waste of time to negotiate contracts. Examples abound of the difficulties of doing business with Saudi Arabia and the Arab Emirates. Lawyers practising in these countries deny that the written word of contractual obligation can be over-set by the absolute power of the ruler. They claim that this power itself helps to defend and enforce rights under contract. This is a dubious claim but at least there are some legal rules and procedures which are respected by governments and the courts.

A basic rule is that from the start only an Arabic version of an agreement will be supported in the courts. A translation of contract documents into Arabic is essential. It must be not only grammatically correct but must clearly reflect the spirit of the contract and the intention of the parties. Even if it is agreed that a Western law is to be the law of the contract Arab courts will interpret it in the light of their own legal tradition. It is therefore dangerous to contract in general terms in the hope that what is reasonable or good business practice in the West will govern any dispute. Western purchasers must spell out as clearly and concretely as possible what is intended by the contract. Litigation is to be avoided and a Western party to a contract should not appeal to Arab courts unless there is so strong a case that it cannot be refuted.

The basic Islamic law of the Koran has been overlaid by nineteenth-century legislation of the Ottoman Empire under French influence. Both Romano Germanic and common law have been adopted in part and recently there has been a spate of legislation on the conduct of business with foreigners. There is also in the Emirates federal legislation but not every federal law is accepted in all of them. The judges can choose between one law and another to reach their decisions in a manner unknown to the West. Judgements depend very much on the background and training of the trial judge. In this labyrinth of legal pitfalls Western purchasers need the guidance of a sponsor and his knowledge is of prime importance in framing a suitable form of contract as well as in enforcing it. It is not prudent to extend to a sponsor the powers of an agent to act in the name and on the account of the purchaser. Sponsorship is a defensive device and it can be valuable in any country where the law is based on philosophical or religious concepts foreign to the legal systems of the West. But it must be laid down clearly in writing exactly what the sponsor has and has not authority to do.

THE DOCTRINE OF THE PROPER LAW OF CONTRACT

To overcome these difficulties there has emerged the doctrine of the proper law of contract. The proper law is the law to be applied in determining rights and obligations under a contract. In Romano Germanic law the proper law is that of the country in which the contract was made. This rule is not applied in common law courts. There the principle is to establish what was the intent of the parties. This may depend upon their relative strength in negotiation and the existence of a buyers' or a sellers' market. If there is no clear intent preference is given to the law of the country with which the contract has the most real connection. This could be the country of manufacture. It could be the country where erection takes place. It could be the country where purchases or sales are to be made.

Albeko Schumaschinen v the Kambovian Shoe Machinery Co. illustrates the point. Kambovian, an English company making and marketing shoe machinery, wrote to Albeko, a Swiss company, offering them an agency in Switzerland. Under the proposed agency commission would be payable on sales in Switzerland. When Albeko claimed commission Kambovian said Albeko's acceptance of Kambovian's offer had not been received. Albeko said they had posted their acceptance and this was sufficient to complete the contract under English law. Albeko then sought remedy in the English courts.

At the trial the court held that the issue must be judged not under English law but Romano Germanic. The contract was to be performed in Switzerland even though the machinery was made in England. Romano Germanic law was therefore the proper law of the contract. The offeror had not received the offeree's acceptance so there was no contract under that law. Under English law there would have been a contract because acceptance had been posted even though the offeror had not received it.

Another hazard is the effect that attitude or opinion in one country can have on international purchases and sales in other countries. These can virtually overturn the execution of the proper law of contract. The best known example is the imposition of sanctions on the USSR by the USA after the declaration of martial law in Poland. The effect in international trade was to interfere with contracts by European countries to supply equipment for the gas pipeline from Siberia to Western Europe. There is growing concern about the damage which can, in this way, be inflicted by one country upon the trading interests of another by legal sanctions.

The USA also claims that companies with more than 25 per cent US stockholders are subject to US law, even though they neither buy nor sell in the USA. Also such agencies as the US Securities and Exchange Control Commission and the Commodities Futures Trading Commission seek to impose disclosure requirements which may not be in the interest of traders in other countries. So too in the EEC the commission seeks to enforce disclosure regulations on companies outside the Community which have subsidiaries within it.

The seventh company law directive seeks to make multinational companies controlled outside the EEC publish consolidated accounts for their EEC activities, irrespective of the company's legal structure within the EEC. The issue of jurisdiction over companies whose operations are located in one and controlled in another country is a disturbing influence on contractual obligation. The doctrine that rights can be enforced under the proper law of the contract is not always available to contracting parties. An international arbiter such as the International Court of Justice in the Hague may be the proper forum for deciding whose law rules. For purchasers, the problem is not so much whose law rules but whose law overrules the proper law of the contract.

CONVENTIONS FOR HARMONISING THE LAW OF CONTRACT

From all that has gone before it is clear that the law of contract needs to be harmonised so that international trade is not damaged by different concepts and different uses. A proper instrument is required for international agreement. It is called a convention. The process to produce a convention can be initiated by an international agency or a sovereign state. An invitation is sent to other countries inviting them to meet to discuss a particular problem. Generally a politician is sent, accompanied by technical experts. The politician does the talking; the technical experts do the work. A draft convention is prepared which purposes to solve the problem. It is signed by the representatives present, with or without reservation. This does not commit the countries represented to the terms of the convention. This can only be done by a specific act of government: ratification. The draft convention is then open to governments for ratification. Sometimes the text specifies how many states must ratify to make the convention effective. Generally a time limit is set for ratification, together with a procedure for subsequent ratification by countries which wish to adhere to the convention at a later date. There are four conventions relating to the law of contract at various stages of negotiation.

UN convention on international contracts for the sale of goods

The history of this convention goes back to long before the advent of the United Nations. In 1930 the International Institute for the Unification of Private Law (UNIDROIT) began to prepare two draft conventions but they were not ratified before the Second World War. In 1951 the Netherlands government called a conference to resume work and two uniform laws were produced, one for the formation of international contracts, the other for harmonising practice between parties to an international contract. Only eight countries ratified the conventions when they were opened in 1964. Among them was the UK and the Hague Conventions were accepted into UK law by the Uniform Laws on International Sales Act 1967, but it was not until 1972 that an order was published on the application of the Act. The order made an express reservation that the uniform laws were not to apply to a contract unless the contracting parties specifically agreed that they should.

In 1968 the UN questioned all member states on their attitude to the uniform laws. States with different legal, economic and social systems put forward difficulties and the conventions were redrafted to accommodate them. In 1978 the two uniform laws were combined and designated as the draft convention on international contracts for the sale of goods. The convention was published by the UN and opened for ratification in 1980. To September 1983 only six countries had ratified. They were Argentina, Egypt, France, Hungary, Lesotho and Syria. The convention does not come into force until the deposit of the tenth instrument of ratification, so it remains a dead letter. Why have so few countries, including the UK, not adhered to the convention?

A major difficulty is that the convention is intended to be obligatory unless the contracting parties expressly contract out of it. In the UK this is considered burdensome, especially on small traders who cannot reasonably be expected to know how the convention works and possibly not to know of it at all. The Institute of Purchasing and Supply has made a number of reservations to the Department of Trade about the convention as it stands and has suggested amendments. To the writer's view differences from UK law are not necessarily objectionable. But there are difficulties in the convention on the passing of title, product liability and offer and acceptance procedure.

For the convention it can be said that it defines clearly the obligations of the buyer and the seller, the obligations common to both, the passing of risk and remedies for breach of obligation. It would overcome some conflict of law problems and provide a single, up-to-date and comprehensive code which would particularly benefit those who do not wish to concern themselves with legal matters in detail on each contract. It is time that the adherence of the UK to the convention is considered again.

EEC convention on the law applicable to contractual obligations

This convention was signed by seven members of EEC in 1980 and the remaining two, one of which was the UK, in 1981. It is therefore in operation and available to contracting parties who expressly agree to use it. When there is no such agreement the contract is to be governed by the law of the country with which it is most clearly connected. Despite this, consumer contracts are not to have the effect of depriving a consumer of protection afforded to him by mandatory rules of law in the country where he resides. Professional purchasers cannot rely on this: they do not have the same protection under the law.

The law applicable to a contract in particular governs questions of interpretation, performance, the consequences of breach, the ways of extinguishing obligations and the consequences of nullity of the contract. It also provides that where a member state comprises several territorial units, each of which has its own rules of law in respect of contractual obligations, each territorial unit is to be considered as a separate country for the purpose of identifying the law applicable under the convention. Even in the EEC there still remains this fragmentation which makes the international law of contractual obligation such a complex subject.

Council of Europe draft convention on reservation of title

This draft convention of 1982 deals with a problem that is very much in the minds of purchasing managers in the UK since the Romalpa case. In *Aluminium Industrie Vaassan BV v Romalpa Aluminium* the Court of Appeal held that when title had been reserved a seller could trace goods into the hands of third parties to secure payment of money owed to him by the purchaser. This concept was new to

UK law. It is well established in Romano Germanic law but there are many variants of application in the Romano Germanic law countries.

The Council of Europe limited itself to simple reservation of title because of the complexity of the subject. The draft convention deals only with contracts for the sale of goods under which the parties have agreed that ownership will not pass to the buyer until he has paid in full for the goods. This enables the seller to recover from third parties goods for which the buyer has not paid.

The draft convention is back in the hands of the Committee of Experts to deal with objections made by Council members. The UK has not accepted the convention because the priority given to sellers to recover goods when attachment of bankruptcy proceedings have begun may not accord with changes in the UK law of bankruptcy now being considered.

International Chamber of Commerce conventions (INCOTERMS)

These conventions on the interpretation of trade terms and uniform customs and practice for documentary credits were first published in 1936. They have been revised twice. The definitions contained in them are now so standard that fob, for, c & f and cif are used even when contracts are not drawn in English. The rules, which are optional, are based on the greatest common measure of practice current in international trade in order to obtain the widest possible use of them.

There is in Incoterms an attitude of realism not always present in conventions on international trade. They do not seek to incorporate improvements in commercial practice. They are intended to codify what practical business men have evolved over the years as convenient. This is considered by the International Chamber of Commerce to be better than theoretical improvements which do not get implemented. Three problems are dealt with in particular, the applicable law, the consequences of inadequate information and difficulties of interpretation. On the whole Incoterms lean towards minimum liability on the part of the seller. It is for the purchaser to ensure that sellers' liabilities not in the rules are imported into the contract if he so desires.

INTERNATIONALLY ACCEPTABLE CONDITIONS OF CONTRACT

United Nations Economic Commission for Europe (UNECE)

In 1951 a modest first step was taken towards harmony in international contracts for the purchase and sale of engineering products. By 1953 the ECE delegates had completed a set of conditions for supply without erection. All the essential terms of contract were included except terms of payment. These vary so much in the international market that standard terms of payment would not have been useful. This first convention was signed by nine countries from Western Europe and Yugoslavia.

When a second set of conditions to include erection was being worked out, the Soviet Union and other East European countries decided to co-operate. Two versions were produced, one for the West, the other for the Soviet Union and her satellites. They are identical except that in the latter there is no mention of the circumstances which would give rise to relief in the event of industrial dispute and there is no procedure for arbitration. There are now nineteen signatories to the ECE conditions which include, beside the machinery conditions, conditions of contract for engineering stock articles and for soft commodities such as timber and cereals.

The ECE conditions are not binding on participating governments. They are model general conditions for optional use by contracting parties. These conditions, with slight modifications to suit local custom and practice, have become standard conditions for engineering contracts between all the Scandinavian countries. In other European countries their use is wide and is spreading outside Europe to countries whose law and practice are geared to the Romano Germanic and common law patterns.

The particular advantage of ECE conditions is that they make no attempt to change the law of the states concerned with them. The task of the draughtsmen was to provide a framework which remains consistent whatever legal system is applied. This is a considerable achievement. It has the effect of reducing to a minimum the time and expense spent on legal and commercial argument when an international contract is being drawn up. The ECE conditions

379

should be compulsory reading for anyone who has to battle with the legal complexities of international trade.

Organisme de liaison des Industries Metalliques Européenes (ORGALIME)

These conditions deal with four important areas in metal industries contracts:

(*a*) import and export of semi-processed goods and components for incorporation in other goods;
(*b*) provision of technical personnel abroad;
(*c*) exclusive agreement with a foreign distributor, and
(*d*) exclusive agency with a foreign distributor.

Fédération Internationale des Ingénieurs-Conseils (FIDIC)

More than 80 national associations of consulting engineers belong to FIDIC. Their broad interest as consultants in international trade has engendered two very comprehensive conditions of contract:

(*a*) for works of civil engineering construction, and
(*b*) for electrical and mechanical works, including erection.

There are also special sets of conditions for agreement between the client (purchaser) and the consultant. These conditions are very strong on the problems of plant erected on site and on turnkey contracts. There are indications that their use is rapidly growing. This is because of the increasing size of projects and the length of time required for completion of work. These factors of size and time encourage the use of consultants as project managers. The FIDIC conditions confer on consultants wide power and independence of the purchaser but they reflect current practice for large-scale contracts and should be better known.

DOMESTIC CONDITIONS OF CONTRACT SUITABLE FOR INTERNATIONAL TRADE

Many learned institutions have published conditions of contract which are not, in general, unfavourable to the interests of their members. Some of them are used by non-members. Possibly the most widely used are those published jointly by the Institution of Electrical Engineers and the Institution of Mechanical Engineers (IEE/IMechE conditions). There are variants for home and export contracts, for supply only and for delivery with or without erection as well as fob, cif and for. Conditions of contract are also published by the Royal Institute of British Architects, the Institution of Civil Engineers (some jointly with IMechE), the Institution of Chemical Engineers and the Institute of Purchasing and Supply.

The IPS conditions are of particular interest because of the wide field which they cover: supply/erection; services; agreement for contract staff; secrecy undertaking; dismantling/demolition, and repair/modification. There is a valuable summary of points to consider in international trade, for which the IPS conditions can be adapted. They include the applicable law, arbitration, formation of contract, terms of payment, passing of property and risk, shipping, bills of lading and customs formalities.

Many trade associations also publish conditions of contract. Probably the best known are those of the British Electrical and Allied Manufacturers' Association because of their exemplary price adjustment clause and formula. There are also the conditions of the British Mechanical Engineers' Federation, the Association of Consulting Engineers, the National Association of Scaffolding Contractors, the Chemical Plant Manufacturers' Association, the Mechanical Handling Engineers' Association and many more.

Standard conditions are supposed to save time and expense. There are now so many sets of conditions applicable to different industries that it is not possible for a purchasing manager to be familiar with them all. But at least the well informed manager will know where to look. There can be no quick guide to deal with every situation which may arise in the international law of contract and the sale of goods. There is almost always complexity and often uncertainty. As every good purchasing manager knows, he who acts as his own counsel in these matters has a fool for his client.

19

Purchasing capital equipment

Geoffrey E. Partridge

The purchase of capital equipment can cover a wide range of values – from relatively inexpensive items of production equipment or instrumentation to multi-million pound turnkey projects. This chapter will cover high value equipment purchases but will not deal with building and construction contracts, which are beyond the scope of the handbook.

Capital purchasing differs significantly from the purchase of components, raw materials and indirect materials because many or all of the following will apply:

- The cost is high.
- It may be a one-off transaction, for a plant of which nobody in the purchasing company has any considerable experience.
- The budget process has been prolonged and time pressures are considerable.
- Timely operation of the equipment may be vital, especially if installation has been preceded by dismantling of a facility which is being replaced.
- The choice of supplier may be critical if performance is to be assured, and that may limit competition.
- The cost of finance is high during the manufacturing, assembly and commissioning stages, and if the equipment fails to perform this cost is on-going.
- Negotiations may prove difficult, especially where the supplier has all the experience.

- A new and wider range of problems arises on the writing of the contract, which calls for a high level of competence and considerable experience.

A major factor which can give rise to difficulties is that the purchasing company's engineers or production staff may have been contemplating such an investment for years. Their technical investigations, study of publications and general enquiries in the supply industry or the various fields of application may have led them to tentative or even firm conclusions well before the professional buyer became involved.

On major projects the potential risks are high and it is the responsibility of the purchasing manager to ensure that they are minimised. This requires the devotion of time and resource over a long period, well in advance of signing the purchase contract, the co-operation of everyone concerned with the project and the full support of management.

THE PROJECT PLAN

For any major project it is essential to nominate a project team who should prepare a plan, secure agreement regarding individual responsibilities and obtain the commitment of everyone concerned to the individual stages and the timing of them. Normally the team should be nominated and the plan drafted at the earliest stage, before initial enquiries are made and budget proposals prepared. The project plan would usually cover the following aspects:

Preparatory stage:
- drafting of preliminary specification of purchasing company's requirements;
- investigating the supply market and identifying potential suppliers, at home and overseas;
- establishing factual information on potential suppliers – their facilities and capacity, management competence and financial viability and their experience in the relevant field;
- where possible visiting users who have already installed similar equipment;

- establishing tentative lead times, prices, operating and maintenance costs and production rates;
- consideration of the above and agreement upon a list of suppliers to be asked to quote.

The initial enquiry:
- issue by the purchasing department of a formal request for quotations against a detailed specification and against detailed terms and conditions of contract;
- evaluation of quotations received, followed by discussions with those suppliers to ensure that there is full understanding of the purchasing company's requirements and how they will be met.

The budget proposal:
- submission of an investment proposal, with supporting documentation in terms such that wherever possible there remains full scope for competition between a number of suppliers.

Negotiation with suppliers and conclusion of the final specification and contract with the selected supplier:
- the detailed process resulting in a firm commitment by the supplier and all parties in the purchasing company as to what is to be provided, how, when and on what terms and setting out precisely the responsibilities of all concerned.

Post contract management:
- progress monitoring;
- delivery and installation;
- negotiation and agreement of variations;
- acceptance and operation;
- payment;
- problems, documentation and claims.

At this stage two aspects of the project plan should be emphasised. The first is time-scale and the second is commitment. The project team must include members with experience of the time necessary to handle the plan effectively and of the high costs and potential failure that may follow skimping or rushing any stage. They must also have the ability to convince management of the validity of their views. Those concerned must be satisfied that the plan allows adequate time to complete each stage and the individuals responsible must be committed to satisfactory completion in that time. The successful completion of the internal negotiations in the purchasing company, leading to agreement on and publishing of the project plan, provide the essential foundation for a successful purchase contract.

THE ROLE OF THE PURCHASING MANAGER AND HIS STAFF

Whilst there should be strong purchasing representation on the project team, it would rarely be appropriate for purchasing to provide the team leader at the project plan stage. However the purchasing delegates are the logical ones to obtain the necessary information from and about potential suppliers and they must perform that task. In so doing, purchasing will be able to familiarise themselves with the requirements to be met by the equipment, satisfy themselves that specifiers and users have stipulated precisely what is required and ensure that the wording is clear and unambiguous from a legal viewpoint as well as being sound commercially. Purchasing thereby becomes fully committed to the investment proposal, which strengthens their position in subsequent negotiations with suppliers. Moreover their presence at this stage demonstrates to suppliers that they will have negotiating responsibility at the contract stage and at the same time allows them to take the necessary steps to safeguard the company's negotiating position.

This is the critical period when sellers will do everything possible to bypass purchasing and by one means or another so influence the specification or persuade the end-users, that single-source supply appears the only possibility. If purchasing fails to play its proper role at this time, or has inadequate resources to do so, or if management permits other departments to take over its role, the costs resulting can be considerable, even disastrous.

Purchasing must play a strong supporting role in the early stages, namely the preparatory stage, the initial enquiry and the budget proposal, but thereafter it must take the lead, assuming responsibility for negotiations, supplier selection and the final specification and contract terms. However this stage of the process should be a continuation of the team approach and by no means a stand-alone purchasing operation. All the members of the project team, this time under the leadership of the purchasing manager or his nominee, will need to be satisfied of the validity of the proposed deal overall and if that is to be achieved they must, in some degree, be party to the negotiations.

At the outset the negotiation team must settle their strategy and tactics, agree upon the role that each member will play and decide how to ensure that a competitive situation is maintained as far as possible throughout the process. The negotiation process leading to final contract can be subdivided into the following different segments:

- supplier selection;
- specification
  of the equipment itself or the process it is to perform
  and its relationship to the company environment;
- contract terms
  general terms and conditions,
  specific conditions relating to delivery installation, performance testing, acceptance and final operation,
  provisions concerning maintenance, spares and subsequent back-up service,
  purchase price and payment conditions.

In practice they tend to merge one into the other because of the interrelationship between them, but each individual segment has an impact on final cost. It is this overall negotiation for which purchasing is responsible and must clearly provide the team leader.

A full study of each of the segments of the negotiation would fill a complete volume but certain aspects can be highlighted here.

SUPPLIER SELECTION

This is critical. If you select the wrong supplier who is incapable of providing what is required, you may have the best price and an ideally worded contract, but all you will have at the end of the day is a pile of scrap, a law suit on your hands and all the costs of failure in your own environment, such as high production costs, loss of market share or even damages for breach of sales contracts. Equally a supplier who could have performed but went into liquidation halfway along the road can prove to be just as damaging.

The problem is one of risk evaluation. The market leader may be so well established and so sure of his dominance that he will hold out for a high price and reject any contract terms which impose damages for poor performance. The next in line may, or may not, have the same competence to complete to the agreed standard and on time, but may be in no position to reject terms which put pressure on his performance. One supplier may successfully have installed many similar plants; another evidently has the competence but not the specific experience and another, a 'break-away outfit', has pioneering management, experience in the industry and may be willing to buy its way into the business.

Each member of the project team will measure the risks differently. At one end of the scale the extreme possibility would be the technically perfect item at ruinous cost and at the other the 'bargain' that never works. Between the extremes lies a band of acceptable solutions or sometimes, just a choice of one.

The author recalls a major project many years ago undertaken by the company for which he was then working. There were two technical solutions to a problem and several suppliers for each. The company had a strong preference for one of the solutions and one supplier stood out above his competitors. The problem was that despite all his claims the buying company still had doubts as to credibility of performance. A competitor had purchased similar equipment from the same people and after payment of the contract price had had to incur further costs, nearly equal to the purchase price, to make it function properly. Based on this knowledge the buying firm drew up a contract that they thought to be watertight. All the supplier's assurances were written into contract terms. The buying company considered that the supplier's viability was assured and that it would be unaffected by a heavy loss on the contract in question. They also assumed that their management would not tolerate two failures in succession. They were right – the supplier signed the contract and finally completed to specification, although later than scheduled. He 'lost his shirt' in the process and not a penny of extra cost was passed on to the buying company. A fairly high risk decision, but it was judged as the least risk alternative.

To be able to operate effectively in this process, purchasing must have done all its 'homework'. Technical staff who may feel that their careers are at risk in the event of a failure will expect convincing reasons why they should not favour the high price low risk alternative. Purchasing must establish those reasons, otherwise a low price is just a low price and nothing more.

THE SPECIFICATION

In some instances the right approach is to purchase a standard product and ensure that the supplier is committed to the related specification. Custom-built equipment presents more problems. It is possible to make a contract with a very short specification which is sufficiently clear to buyer and seller so that equipment, newly designed from scratch, performs exactly as was intended. One of the author's first experiences of capital purchasing fell into that category. When delivery was due the supplier tested the machine he had built whilst it was still in his own works, and it failed miserably. He wrote apologetically, explaining that he had scrapped the machine and was starting to redesign and rebuild. Six months later – not a disaster as it happened – he delivered a perfect machine that went into full production within days. He sent an invoice for the contract price but explained that future machines would cost three times as much!

As has been said, it is possible – but don't count on it. The author has never met another supplier like that in the thirty intervening years. The specification is the key to a successful purchase contract and every hour or day spent on it will be amply repaid in the end.

In general, custom-built capital equipment is purchased from specialist suppliers with perceived competence to apply expertise and knowledge to the solution of specific problems. To provide the best and most economic solution the supplier will need to adduce his know-how, existing designs and resources and he can do this only if the buyer stipulates a functional requirement rather than a solution. If the buyer states the results that he requires, the nature of the input materials, the quantity per unit of time and the operating conditions, it is for the supplier to choose from possible solutions available and make his proposal accordingly.

Consequently whenever economically possible a functional specification should be the buyer's objective. Many advantages follow from this approach:

1 Demands on the buyer's own engineering and design resources are minimised.
2 New technology may be applied, of which the buyer was unaware.
3 Responsibility and risk remain with the supplier.
4 The buyer purchases equipment with guarantees of performance rather than equipment which matches the prescribed description but may not perform.

To reinforce the argument it is worth mentioning a major raw material supplier who some years ago promised supplies of a high grade product derived from a new process. When the time came for deliveries the buying company knew the process plant was 'in-and-running' but the new material was still not available. There was some reluctance to discuss the question, but it finally transpired that the equipment had been purchased by description. Liquidated damages for late delivery had been written into the contract and the supplier had successfully negotiated a bonus clause for early delivery. Delivery was made early and the bonus claimed. Full payment was made – and a very substantial sum was involved – and the plant never operated successfully. Shortly afterwards the raw material supplier was taken over by another company!

An important aspect of the equipment specification is its relationship to the environment in which it is intended to operate. This is a very broad subject and unless great care is taken it is very easy to fail to cover some vital aspect. Major headings for consideration include:

- safety requirements, including guards, fail safe etc.;
- noise and vibration limits;
- pollution and radiation stipulations;
- building/enclosure requirements such as fireproof, dustfree, inert gas flooded, humidity limits;
- foundation requirements and fixing details;
- weights, operating forces and space requirements/limitations;
- power requirements, water pressures, heat dissipation rates, coupling and interface operations.

There are however many other points which need to be considered. With adequate study and discussion, costs to the buyer can be minimised and potential problems for both parties can often be circumvented. A checklist process has proved to be invaluable at this stage.

Figure 19.1 includes four checklists covering such questions. It need hardly be stated that no checklist, however comprehensive, can ever cover all aspects of a particular project. There is no substitute for thought!

Site facilities	Off loading and storage
1 Define site facilities available.	1 Who unloads items and at whose risk and liability?
2 Define any special site facilities required by the supplier.	2 Who provides unloading/lifting equipment and at whose cost?
3 Any site facilities used by the supplier, used at supplier's risk and responsibility (e.g. workshops tools etc.).	3 When items will be unloaded/stored – what are the labour requirements?
4 Procedure for use of any special site facilities.	4 Who moves the items to required positions – risk and liability?
5 Services/temporary services:	5 Define storage requirements – size, special conditions, access etc.
(a) what services are required (electrical points, water etc.)?	6 Who is responsible/risk for storage.
(b) the quality of services to be provided;	7 Insurance for items stored.
(c) timescale/quantity of services required;	8 Liability for costs involved.
(d) responsibility for connection;	
(e) position of services;	
(f) liability for cost incurred.	

Installation and commissioning	Risk and liability
1 Who prepares site/environment?	1 When and under what conditions does risk in items pass to buyer – i.e. final acceptance, provisional acceptance, delivery, passing of title etc.?
2 Who is liable for ensuring site/environment suitable for installation?	2 Which party carries risk and liability for injury or damage to persons or property while work is carried out by supplier on site i.e. the buyer, the supplier, both parties in prescribed circumstances?
3 Who unloads items and moves to required position?	
4 Who provides unloading/moving equipment and labour and at whose risk?	3 Who arranges delivery, off-loading etc. and at whose risk and liability?
5 Timescales involved.	
6 What services are required, who provides them and is responsible for connecting to items?	4 What obligations and what incentives can be placed on supplier to replace items damaged or lost during shipment, or work on site?
7 Responsibility for ensuring installation suitable before commissioning commences.	5 Who arranges, protects and carries liability for storage of items on the buyer's site?
8 Procedures if delay caused by buyer (other equipment not ready) or supplier.	
9 Procedure when installation or commissioning is complete.	

Figure 19.1 Checklists for capital equipment contracts

GENERAL TERMS AND CONDITIONS OF THE PURCHASE CONTRACT

It has already been stated that the initial enquiry to potential suppliers should require quotations to be submitted against detailed terms and conditions of contract. At this stage, however, many aspects of the proposed contract may well be tentative. The terms themselves may be changed in the light of revisions to the initial specification and in the course of subsequent negotiation.

It is always possible, although very time consuming, to write tailor-made contracts for every capital purchase. In earlier years, the author and his colleagues did so. Later they developed a comprehensive set of general terms and conditions of supply for the purchase of high-value capital equipment. These span ten pages and the aspects covered are:

- definitions
- scope of the work
- warranty and guarantee
- liability
- price
- terms of payment
- testing and provisional acceptance
- final acceptance
- right to withhold provisional or final acceptance
- delay in testing and acceptance
- completion and delivery dates
- progress, progress reports and site meetings
- liquidated damages
- cancellation
- maintenance
- availability of spares
- training
- drawings, design and operational manuals
- health and safety at work
- indemnity
- temporary services
- site preparation and civil work
- removal of rubbish

- confidentiality
- title
- insurance
- supplier to inform himself
- assignment
- arbitration and law
- waivers
- contract amendments and notices.

In addition they have, as part of the general terms and conditions, standard forms for provisional and final acceptance.

Over and above the foregoing there are many other aspects of a contract that should be considered and where appropriate written in. Examples of these are performance bonds and *force majeure*.

Many large companies draw up their own general terms for purchase contracts. Trade associations and professional bodies in engineering and similar spheres of activity often publish model forms of contract and some suppliers propose that such documents should be used as the basis for business with them. Other suppliers have their own standard sales terms on which they prefer to make contracts.

In the UK the Institute of Purchasing and Supply has published documents providing model forms of contract and notes for guidance explaining the intention and advising on the application of the terms.[1,2]

Whilst it is preferable, from the buyer's viewpoint, to base negotiations on standard terms that are well known to him and generally acceptable, this may not always be an available option. It depends on the relative strengths of buyer and seller and the importance of the contract to each of them. However, whatever the terms under discussion it is vital that every word is considered and agreed in advance of signature. Where modifications to standard wordings are so agreed, they should all be fully recorded as a part of the contract documents. In practice the most effective way of dealing with the problem is to provide a schedule of variations in which deletions, additions, insertions and amendments are listed in full.

The preliminary investigation and discussion process within the buyer's organisation is facilitated by the checklist approach, which is also recommended for use during actual negotiations with suppliers. It is desirable to have a checklist for every aspect of capital purchase contracts and some examples of such lists are shown in Figure 19.2.

SPECIFIC CONDITIONS

The general terms and conditions will normally cover the general principles on which the contract is based. For a standard machine tool of which the buyer may already have several in operation it may be desirable to purchase simply 'delivered buyers works' with a guarantee that performance will match existing machines. For more expensive and complex installations that approach would be quite inappropriate. Having agreed the intended performance of the new equipment, in terms of the function it is to perform, and established

Item warranty	Performance bonds
1 Against materials and workmanship – period and from what date.	1 Value of bond as percentage of total contract price
2 Against design defects – generally no time limit.	2 Provisions of bond, i.e. as surety for supplier's compliance with all terms and conditions of contract.
3 Related to performance e.g. produce stated quantity of components/operate stated period of time.	3 Form of bond.
4 Conditions for warranty to apply, e.g. buyer maintains to agreed procedures.	4 Bank or insurance co. acceptable.
5 Software warranties, support and period.	5 Agreed date and/or conditions for bond to expire.

Title	Training and documentation
	1 Where training takes place.
6 Supplier's reponse and period to effect repair/replacement under warranty claims.	2 Duration of training programme.
7 Additional warranties from sellers to supplier to apply.	3 Content of training programme.
	4 Number of participants.
1 When and under what conditions title passes.	5 Educational level of participants.
2. Does risk, acceptance, or liability pass with title?	6 Cost/price breakdown of training programme – included in contract price.
3 Can and under what conditions does title revert to supplier?	7 What documentation will be provided and what areas will it cover (e.g. operations, maintenance)?
4 Is title to the whole or part of the work or items required as security for payments?	8 Number of copies.
5 If title to items passes in supplier's premises, how are items segregated or marked to signify buyer's ownership?	9 In the English language.
6 Buyers right to inspect the goods at the supplier's works.	10 Cost of documentation/cost of extra copies.

Figure 19.2 Further checklists for capital equipment contracts

which party will deliver, assemble, install and test run, it is necessary to agree upon a series of tests sufficient to demonstrate adequate measured performance. The agreed tests and procedures should be spelled out in detail in the contract which should also stipulate the number of hours of sustained performance that will satisfy the test criteria. Provisional acceptance will normally follow successful completion of the acceptance procedures.

Final acceptance will follow some considerable time thereafter on the basis that 'the proof of the pudding is in the eating'. Here again, the longer-term criteria that must be satisfied should be clearly recorded in a schedule to the contract.

At each stage it is wise to write in clear procedures that will be followed in case the equipment fails the acceptance tests. Firstly these should envisage one or more re-tests and also establish the consequences of delayed acceptance, such as delayed payment. Secondly they should usually spell out the consequences of repeated failure to pass the tests. At one extreme the buyer may wish to reject the equipment outright and recover all moneys paid, whilst at the other he may gladly accept an established reduction in price to offset substandard performance.

Finally the contract might envisage supplier supervision or simply occasional visits by supplier representatives to oversee the initial weeks or months of operation under production conditions.

MAINTENANCE, SPARES AND BACK-UP SERVICE

This is an aspect that calls for careful study. It is quite common for suppliers to list 'recommended spares' or include a spares package as part of their initial proposal to supply the equipment itself. Acceptance of such a proposition involves significant cost to the buyer and rarely solves the problems that arise following installation of major equipment.

Some so-called spares are in reality consumable items which require replacement on a more or less regular basis. The buyer needs assurance of minimum life, minimum wear or whatever is appropriate coupled with the supplier's commitment to replace free of charge or at a reduced price should the items not perform to specification. He will normally look to the supplier to hold stocks of these at agreed prices fixed for a period ahead or alternatively provide the information necessary to enable the buyer to obtain them direct from the sub-supplier, or indeed other potential suppliers direct. Suppliers may even agree to hold stocks on the buyer's premises and only charge for them after they have been drawn from stock.

Other spares may rarely be required in the future, but in the event of breakdown must be promptly available. It may be necessary to purchase a stock of these, but it is often practicable to arrange for the buyer's own stock to be backed by supplier commitment to deliver from stock in his own warehouse throughout the useful life of the plant.

Where 'specials' are concerned it is normally essential for the purchase contract to require the seller to provide the buyer with a full set of specifications and drawings to enable him to acquire his own spares. These can be provided at the time of delivery and installation, but if the supplier is unwilling to do so then the documents must be deposited with a third party, such as a bank, who must have clear written instructions as to the circumstances (such as supplier bankruptcy) under which they must be made available to the buyer free of charge.

In some cases maintenance or back-up service may be provided by the supplier. Settling the terms for this after the purchase contract has been signed can prove to be a costly affair. Far better, where possible, to agree in advance in detail the actual services that are required, how they will be provided and monitored, and the cost to the buyer over a long period. At this stage it is usually going to be easier to persuade the supplier to agree a fixed annual charge, regardless of the number of calls made and spares replaced!

PURCHASE PRICE AND PAYMENT CONDITIONS

Establishing the price appropriate to the specification for the equipment and ensuring commitment to performance of the contract by the supplier in return for payment are critical aspects of the contract. This is not the place to dwell on the art of negotiation, or the process and techniques involved nor with the buyer's aspirations to achieve the best possible price. However there is one aspect that must be underlined: the initial purchase price is only part of the total sum associated with capital investment. The cost of ownership and operation must be added, and where appropriate the end-of-use resale value deducted, to establish the total cost or life-cycle cost as it is generally known. The cost of labour to operate the equipment and the power consumption must be set alongside the expected cost of maintenance and repair. The anticipated downtime, or more positively uptime, can have an overwhelming impact on costs and price – assuming, that is, that the equipment can profitably be operated at a high rate. All of these aspects need careful consideration when evaluating the purchase price and comparing one proposal against another. When significant sums are involved, discounted cash flow calculations are the only valid approach.

If the supplier is overseas, currency considerations arise and have to be fully understood, whether the seller agrees to a selling price in sterling or in some other currency. In addition a judgement must be made as to the credibility of the overseas supplier's maintenance and spares service and its possible impact on uptime and life-cycle cost.

The buyer will normally wish to discuss a fixed price but if this is not achievable he will need to establish precisely how the quoted price will be varied and in what circumstances. A thorough understanding of price adjustment formulae is essential before agreeing to their application, since failure to think the problem through may result in a final price that really cannot be justified by the underlying facts.

There is one point which must be emphasised: there is no necessary correlation between cost and price in the capital equipment business. Large sectors of the capital supply industry are vulnerable to wide variations in demand, reflecting the general level of business. This implies that, where there is real competition, suppliers will if necessary during times of recession, agree to sell at low prices. This can result in low profit margins, no profit at all or even a willingness to sell at prices well below total cost. A buyer who fails to recognise this fact may happily agree to a price that has no validity in the marketplace. Conversely, when demand is strong and effective competition is diminished by the scarcity of available capacity amongst credible suppliers, the buyer must live with a situation where profit margins are high.

When it comes to terms of payment, sellers and buyers may have entirely opposed views. Sellers frequently ask for substantial payments at the time of ordering followed by large progress payments as manufacture proceeds, culminating in final payment on, or just before, delivery. The buyer on the other hand should normally look to pay nothing until the equipment has been delivered, assembled and has been shown to be operational. The major payments should, from the buyer's viewpoint, be due only when the equipment has been first provisionally and then finally accepted.

The background to this potential battleground is that very often production lead times are long, the amount of money involved is large and the cost of finance is high. Either the selling or the buying company may go into liquidation before the contract has been completed; the equipment may not function on delivery and installation or the buyer may fail to meet his obligations to make payment when due. Predictably each party will try to protect his own interest and negotiate accordingly.

Standing back from that situation it is necessary to consider the size of the contract, the size of the buying and selling companies in relation to each other and to the size of the contract, and the availability of finance to the parties involved. If Goliath buys from David he will not normally expect David to be able to finance major projects from internal funds. However if David has a good track record, Goliath might reasonably expect David's bank to fill the gap, or a large part of it.

On a major project the cost of finance can be one of the largest elements in total costs. It can be argued that it is in the interest of both parties to ensure that the cost is minimised by utilising the cheapest source of finance available to both parties. It is considerations such as these that may lead the buyer to modify his stance that payment must only follow delivery, performance and acceptance.

The buyer should expect finance to be provided by the seller and generally should refuse advance payments, as a matter of principle. When for any reason it is necessary or desirable to concede some part payment in advance, then the buyer must protect his position against the possibility of liquidation of the supplying company, failure of the supplier to deliver in a stipulated time, or failure of the equipment to meet the specification. An advance payment guarantee provides that essential protection. This would normally be provided by a bank. It must be irrevocable, relate specifically to the contract and have a validity commencing on receipt by the supplier of the first advance payment. The guarantee should expire, say, six weeks after satisfactory delivery and final acceptance of the equipment in accordance with the contract terms, or on some other date, say, one year after the delivery date agreed in the contract, whichever shall be earlier. In the document the bank must guarantee to repay the buyer on his first written demand, the total sums advanced in return for the buyer's written declaration that the supplier has refused or failed to perform the contract in question.

The cost of obtaining an advance payment guarantee depends upon the creditworthiness of the supplier and normally ranges from 0.5 to 2 per cent per annum. The buyer would not usually envisage any increase in the contract price to cover that cost, although if he is obliged to do so the added cost may well be worthwhile: indeed the higher the cost, the more worthwhile it may be! If a supplier is unable to obtain a bank guarantee because his bank judges the risk to be excessive it may be wiser to find another supplier.

The contract should include a provision that all invoices shall be accompanied by an advance payment guarantee for not less than the agreed value of the claim. The wording of the guarantee must be in the agreed form, which should be an appendix to the contract, and be signed by a bank approved by the buyer.

Returning to the more normal situation the contract should be carefully worded to ensure that payments may be claimed only on provisional acceptance. It should stipulate that the invoice(s) must be accompanied by a photocopy of the acceptance certificate duly signed by the buying company's authorised representative. There should be no doubt that should the seller fail to achieve acceptance he is not entitled to payment. That need not preclude subsequent negotiations to modify the situation, but in such circumstances the pressure remains on the seller to perform.

Leasing must be mentioned here as a means of finance which is frequently used to acquire capital equipment. Although it is always essential to discuss proposed payment terms with potential leasing companies, in principle it does not affect any of the points made above – the lease document merely provides for transfer of title to the lessor who in turn provides finance and then leases the equipment back to the buying company, which becomes the lessee. There are many types of lease appropriate to different circumstances and the buyer should study the matter in depth and acquire the necessary expertise, or rely heavily on skilled advice available from colleagues elsewhere in the company or from financial advisers.

POST-CONTRACT MANAGEMENT

Once the task of negotiating and finally agreeing the terms has been completed, the first step must be to ensure that both parties have copies of identical documents, all signed and initialled by authorised signatories from both parties.

At this stage the purchasing manager would normally hand over leadership of the project team to a colleague who has overall responsibility for monitoring progress on the installation. The extent to which it is necessary or desirable to check progress in the supplier's factory or with his subcontractors depends very much on the nature of the project and the same is true when it comes to overseeing the work done by the contractor's staff on site. A well-written contract will include or call for a workplan which lists the major activities and the dates at which completion of each stage is to be achieved. Critical path analysis (PERT charts) may be desirable to demonstrate the validity of the supplier's delivery promise and regular updates of the PERT charts provide an invaluable tool for project control. The leader of the project team will need to verify that all is proceeding to plan and involve his purchasing colleagues when necessary to persuade the supplier to meet his obligations. This process must continue through to provisional and final acceptance, operation and final payment.

The reader may consider the above so obvious that it is not worth stating, but experience suggests otherwise. It may be, for example, that despite all the efforts made earlier to elaborate a valid specification, it is in some respects found to be wanting. The parties must agree some change and at the same time establish who suffers extra costs arising or benefits from any savings. At the same time any impact on the agreed delivery and operational dates must be established, although the buyer may well wish to insist that no changes are made to those dates, nor to the wording of the liquidated damages clause tied to delayed performance.

Regular site meetings, with published minutes highlighting problems, attributing cause and blame and recording agreed actions are essential on large projects. A purchasing representative should be present at all formal meetings and be responsible for agreeing the wording of the minutes. Failing that, it is very easy for the buying company's technical staff to become so involved in the process of assisting the supplier to meet the buying company's needs that the buyer's rights under the contract are blurred; blame for failures can to some extent be passed over to the buyer's engineers and in extreme cases the supplier can avoid all responsibility. It is natural for the supplier's engineers and their counterparts in the buying company to work closely together, and in the interest of both parties that they should. However when serious problems are likely to arise there must be commercially-oriented management control of the process to ensure that the buyer's legal position is protected.

A well drawn specification and carefully worded contract usually prevent or minimise later disputes, but we are all fallible. Most disputes are settled on a friendly basis, and formal claims are fortunately limited. Very few indeed give rise to legal action. However there can be no doubt that friendly, or unfriendly, settlements are facilitated by the keeping of proper records of problems as they arise. The task of the purchasing manager and his staff has not been completed until the equipment is fully operational and paid for and the project team formally disbanded.

CONCLUSION

The author has endeavoured to describe the best practice in relation to capital equipment purchasing. He believes some companies follow many of the principles most of the time. Possibly some may apply all of them, all of the time. On the other hand it is evident that many organisations have no understanding of the process, nor intention of putting it into practice. Baily and Farmer[3] quote two remarks from a 1975 survey by Cunningham and White:

A works manager: The buyer always gets four quotes, that's his job, but I only look at the one I want to buy.

Another respondent: We are required by the finance function to buy the cheapest. I therefore obtain a quotation for the machine I want and two quotations from more expensive suppliers.

The economic environment has changed in the intervening years and it is harder now for industrial companies to make a profit, or even to survive. One wonders whether the two respondents, and their companies, are still active today. Be that as it may there seems little doubt that increasing attention will be paid in the future to this vital business activity.

REFERENCES

(1) R. W. Oliver and A. D. Allwright, *Terms and Conditions of Contract,* Institute of Purchasing and Supply, 1978.

(2) *IPS Model Form of Conditions of Contract for the Supply and Installation (Purchase) of Computers,* Institute of Purchasing and Supply.

(3) P. Baily and D. Farmer, *Purchasing Principles and Techniques,* Pitman/Institute of Purchasing and Supply, 1977, Chap. 14.

FURTHER READING

M. R. Leenders, H. E. Fearon and W. B. England, *Purchasing and Materials Management,* Richard D. Urwin Inc., 1980, Chap. 9.

PART IV
PEOPLE AND PURCHASING

20

Managing purchasing people

Geoffrey Lancaster

The success of any organisation is closely linked to the effectiveness of the individuals it employs. Sophisticated management techniques, the application of electronic data processing, automation of tasks and functions, and many other approaches to improving productivity and profitability, in the final analysis, all depend on the effective management of people. This is as true in purchasing as in any other functional area of business.

The objectives of purchasing which can be found, duly expanded, in most purchasing textbooks are as follows:

> To purchase requirements of the correct quality, in the correct quantity, at the right time, at the right price, from the right source, to be delivered as and when necessary.

The rather prosaic activities which such definitions suggest, belie the fact that the relative effectiveness of the purchasing function can play a key role in the degree of success which an organisation enjoys. For example in many manufacturing organisations direct materials can often account for up to 60 per cent of prime cost, and as the labour element is constantly being taken out of prime cost through automation, the direct material element is increased proportionately. Improving the effectiveness of the purchasing function, therefore, is increasingly recognised as a route to improved profitability. Thus in many organisations we have seen the purchasing function elevated from the position of being a relatively unimportant subfunction in the organisation acting merely as a requisitioning service, to that of a major function with activities that span buying, expediting, materials control and storage, and purchasing research. In addition, and concurrent with this changing status, we have witnessed the development and application of increasingly sophisticated techniques, many of them mathematically and/or computer based, as aids to improved purchasing effectiveness.

It is interesting to note that a similar process of an increased recognition of importance followed by a change in status occurred in the United Kingdom in another management function during the 1960s and 1970s, namely the marketing function. Increasingly companies have been exhorted, cajoled, and required to pay more attention to marketing, with the result that many more companies now have a marketing function, represented at board level supported by an array of specialist marketing techniques. Does this mean that all those companies which have adopted this so called 'market oriented' stance have invariably been successful? The answer to this question is, of course, no. There are a number of reasons for this not the least of which is the fact that in business there are no certain recipes for success. Nevertheless, it is interesting and informative to note just how many of the 'failures' of companies in this area can be traced to poor organisation, and in particular to the ineffective management of people. The lesson is simple – no amount of commitment to new techniques and ideas will generate success without the application of sound principles of organisation and people management. To be effective, purchasing must be planned, co-ordinated and controlled in its organisational setting. Similarly many of the 'standard' textbooks on purchasing neglect the fact that, in the main, things get done through people. The modern purchasing manager ignores at his peril the behavioural issues raised by the need for effective management of his staff.

THE ORGANISATIONAL AND BEHAVIOURAL SKILLS REQUIRED

We have seen that the effective operation of the purchasing function requires certain organisational and behavioural skills on the part of the purchasing executive. We must recognise, however, that once we stray into those areas of purchasing management we leave behind the relatively closed and ordered world of make or buy decisions, economic order quantities, and the like. There are no instant solutions to the issues raised by the need to organise the purchasing function and the individuals within it. Having said this we do, however, have a body of knowledge from which to draw. This body of concepts and knowledge, variously defined as, for example, management theory, organisational theory or, more broadly, administration, does at least point to some of the key issues in the organisation and management of functions and individuals. For example, Williamson[1] suggests that the soundness of an organisation may be judged against a number of criteria, including the extent to which the organisation enables work to be performed efficiently, whilst at the same time making full use of its human assets on a flexible but controlled basis. Similarly the so called 'principles of management' stem from the essential managerial activities of planning, organising, co-ordinating and controlling. Clearly management theory represents an area of study in its own right.

In this chapter we cannot hope to cover in depth all the aspects of organisation theory applicable to purchasing. In any event, one might argue, many of the skills required for the effective utilisation of the human resource are the prerogative of the personnel function. The intention here is to explore some of the more important issues which the effective management of the human resource in purchasing gives rise to. Specifically we shall be concerned with the selection, training and development, leading and motivating, aspects of managing purchasing people.

SELECTION, TRAINING AND DEVELOPMENT: JOB ANALYSIS AND JOB DESCRIPTION

As we saw earlier these aspects of managing human resources are, in many organisations, the responsibility of the personnel department. Nevertheless the purchasing executive will often be required to play a key role in these activities. After all the fact that a manager gets things done through other people means that he would be well advised to be involved in choosing, training and developing his 'raw material'.

The process of recruitment and selection begins with job analysis which in turn forms the basis for the job description. In essence, the job description is simply a document which sets out the objectives, duties and responsibilities of the job incumbent. In turn, the job description may then be used in the selection, training and development of purchasing staff. The preparation of the job description is preceded by a job analysis, the objective of such an analysis being to investigate and clarify the exact work to be done, the nature of the work, the most effective way of doing this work and, in turn, to determine the experience, skills and characteristics required to perform this work. It is worth noting that although we tend to think of a job description in terms of recruiting and selecting new applicants, its preparation and in particular the process of job analysis which precedes it has a wider value to a company. Job analysis, for example, requires that we think carefully about the tasks which we require our purchasing personnel to perform and in addition what constitutes effective performance. The process of job analysis, therefore, is of value even when we are not thinking simply in terms of recruitment, and is a procedure which should be carried out not on a once-and-for-all basis but on a recurrent basis. This is particularly important in an environment where the traditional activities of a function are changing or are required to change by force of circumstance. From time to time an organisation needs to re-assess whether or not the nature of the work, performed by a function, and therefore the criteria for effective performance of this work, are still relevant. Such an environment of change is in fact one in which the purchasing function now finds itself.

As mentioned earier the status of the purchasing function is changing from that of a relatively unimportant sub-function in the organisation to that of a major function. This has been accompanied by a broadening of the activities encompassed by purchasing, which has, in turn, resulted in a change in the activities and therefore skills required of purchasing personnel. It is not the purpose of this chapter to describe what should comprise a list of detailed activities of the modern procurement function, indeed the function of job analysis is to determine what specific activities are required for each particular organisation.

An indication of the scope of possible activities is provided by the work of Moncza[2] in his research on the buyer performance measures used in a range of organisations. Some of the measures he discovered are reproduced below.

1 Price/cost of items purchased.
2 Quality of items purchased.
3 Timeliness of buyer work:

    (*a*)   completion of proposed cycle;
    (*b*)   award of subcontracts;
    (*c*)   subcontractor progress through design and development;
    (*d*)   delivery of prototypes;
    (*e*)   completion of qualification;
    (*f*)   defining product changes;
    (*g*)   rejection disposition;
    (*h*)   tracer processing;
    (*i*)   placement of purchase orders;
    (*j*)   delivery, and;
    (*k*)   scheduling.

4 Supplier availability and workload.
5 Telephone expense.
6 Lost discount expense.
7 Participation in technical interface meetings.
8 Communication with other functional departments.
9 Actual expense versus budgeted expense.
10 Communication with management.
11 Number and unit value of long-term pricing agreements.
12 Supplier development.
13 Document processing accuracy.
14 Substantiation and documentation of purchases.

Regular job analyses, then, ensure that the activities of a function are consistent with what is required. In addition to ensuring that job descriptions are up to date and accurate, job analysis also forms the basis for the assessment of performance, training and development programmes.

SELECTION: CHARACTERISTICS OF EFFECTIVE PURCHASING PERSONNEL

The selection of the right raw material is essential for effective performance. The validity of the selection procedure, therefore, may be judged by the extent to which the individuals selected are capable of performing effectively; actual performance, of course, being a function of both ability and motivation. Ideally we would wish to have a selection procedure for our purchasing staff which ensures that the right selection is always made. In practice selection remains a risky business with inevitable errors of judgement. As discussed earlier, the role of the job description in selection is to reduce such errors to a minimum by indicating the experience, skills and characteristics required of the potential job incumbent. These may then be incorporated in a clear specification of what is required and against which candidates may be assessed. Aspects which such a specification might cover include, for example: personal data – age, physique, health, marital status etc.; educational, technical qualifications and training; work and general experience, and personality and motivation. In addition the specification may distinguish those skills, qualifications etc. which are essential and those which are desirable. Finally the specification will indicate the most appropriate choice of selection devices including interviews, intelligence and aptitude tests, personality tests and physical examinations. This is not the place to discuss in detail the relative merits of the various selection devices available to a company, suffice to say that of all the selection devices, the interview is the most widely used, and careful attention should be paid to its organisation and conduct.

Clearly, it would help the process of selection if we knew the characteristics and skills which distinguish between effective and ineffective purchasers. Understandably, however, there is little consistent evidence on this aspect. In addition, what little is available is of a very general nature, and we should be careful of incorporating this evidence in our selection procedures. Nevertheless this is an area which is attracting increased attention with some interesting results. Reck[3], for example, in an American study completed in 1977 discovered that more effective purchasers perceived themselves as having a superior ability to use their interpersonal skills, evidenced by the fact that they tended to rate themselves higher on personal skills, departmental co-ordination, negotiation and interfirm co-ordination than less effective purchasers. Effective purchasers were more self-confident, more in control, more tolerant of uncertainty, more progressive and expressed a higher level of satisfaction with their overall work situation. He concluded by saying that the more effective purchasers tended to be more interested in developing themselves professionally, evidenced by the fact that their formal education was higher than their less effective counterparts and they tended to participate in more professional development activities. Although this was an American study, there is no reason to suppose that the same situation should not apply in the United Kingdom.

In addition, the nature of the purchasing task points to enable us to make some observations about the general characteristics and skills required in purchasing staff. For example the nature of the purchasing task often means that there are certain temptations for less scrupulous individuals to take advantage of a position of trust; honesty to the employer and fairness in dealing with suppliers are two ideal attributes. If the commodity being purchased is technical in nature, then the ability to assimilate readily technical knowledge would be an advantage. However, this trait should not be over-emphasised to the exclusion of only employing technically qualified personnel in the purchasing function. It is probably more important that the person has perception which will enable him to assess trends in prices and play a meaningful part in such matters as price and contract negotiations, and be able to assess what is value for money. In fact there is a positive danger in insisting on the technical qualification aspect, because such personnel, by virtue of their training tend to be production oriented. One of the tasks of purchasing is to ensure that specifiers do not over-specify – which is an easy thing to do, in that the specifier likes to operate within safe margins or tolerances to protect himself. Over-specification costs money, and one of the tasks of purchasing should be to query suspected over-specification and not purchase blindly from a requisition.

TRAINING AND DEVELOPING PURCHASING PERSONNEL

Having discussed how a company might attempt to ensure that it selects the best available staff for its purchasing function, it must then make every effort to ensure that each individual's potential contribution is fully utilised. The new entrant to a company may have potential, but often this must be developed and refined. In the same way it may be found that the skills and abilities which at one time served the existing staff well in their jobs have become outmoded. The nature of the purchasing function is changing, which in turn requires a developing set of skills on the part of purchasing people.

Training and development of staff then, is crucial to effective performance, a fact which has increasingly been recognised by companies. Indeed as Campbell et al.[4] point out, in many companies training costs have increased to the point where they now represent one of the major costs. The term 'training' covers a wide spectrum of activities including induction training, training in the application of new techniques and computing skills, leadership training etc. Regardless of the specific nature of the programme, however, all training is aimed at changing behaviour. Consequently the process is successful if, after undergoing training, an individual behaves differently, whether through the acquisition of new knowledge, new skills, new attitudes, or some combination of these.

The organisation and design of training and development programmes is a skilled task, and in all but the smallest of companies would normally be assigned to a professional training officer. Nevertheless, the importance of adequate training and development requires that each functional manager, including purchasing, has at least a basic understanding of the steps in the development, implementation, and appraisal of training and development. These steps are outlined, briefly, below.

The first step in a training and development programme is the determination of training needs and objectives. For example, a company may have a problem associated with excessive damage to stocks of raw materials, which may be due to a number of reasons. Procedures for goods inwards inspection may be at fault, or the problem may be due to storage and handling procedures. Indeed there may be a great many potential causes of this problem. The important thing is that the cause of the problem must be accurately identified and specific training objectives developed to address it.

Having identified specific objectives, a training programme can be developed. According to the specific training objectives, decisions can be made with respect to the most appropriate programme content. For example, the training objective might be: 'To improve the negotiating skills of purchasing staff with respect to the selection of suppliers'. The general content of the training programme then is aimed at the improvement of negotiating skills. The specific content is aimed at those special skills and techniques applicable to negotiating with suppliers. The training officer is now in a position to select the most appropriate training techniques.

A wide number of techniques are available for training purchasing staff. For example the development of the negotiation skills described earlier may well be suited to a training programme based on role playing techniques. With these techniques the trainer is required to simulate a real-life situation for the trainee through some kind of exercise. The purchasing director may play the role of an aggressive potential supplier and each member of the purchasing team will be required to play out a negotiation procedure with the 'supplier'. The whole process may be recorded on video and later replayed as a basis for suggesting improvements. Again, it should be stressed that the selection of the most appropriate techniques will stem from the previously mentioned training objectives.

The final step in a training and development programme is the assessment of its effectiveness. Once again, this assessment should be based on a comparison of results against objectives, having in mind that effective training changes behaviour. It is important that the assessment of behavioural change be based on change in the trainees' on-the-job behaviour. A frequent criticism of training schemes is that behavioural change is often limited to the training session and is not reproduced in the day-to-day work environment. As Porter et al.[5] have pointed out, a key person in the process of changing job behaviour is the trainee's superior. In particular, they suggest that it is important that the trainee's newly acquired skills and behaviour be encouraged and rewarded by his superior in the work setting.

MOTIVATING PURCHASING PERSONNEL

Having discussed the importance of the selection and training of purchasing staff, it is stressed that these two activities are essential to provide the raw material which has the necessary skills, experience, and so on to perform effectively in their allotted tasks. Abilities, however, represent only one side of what may be termed the performance equation, effective performance is a function of both abilities and a willingness to utilise those abilities. This willingness, or otherwise, to use abilities or to expend effort in the performance of tasks is conventionally referred to as motivation.

Because of its relevance to organisational performance the topic of motivation has attracted considerable attention in the management literature. Theories of motivation abound, the problem being that the various approaches to motivation are often complex and conflicting. Nevertheless, the purchasing manager is faced with the very real issue of how to motivate his purchasing staff; in doing so he must at least be aware of some of the more significant contributions to this important aspect of managing individuals in order that he may assess his own leadership role in the process.

Perhaps one of the most widely held notions as to what motivates individuals at work is that, primarily, individuals are motivated by financial inducements; money is the motivate. Effective performance, then, will be induced if people are sufficiently well paid. This view has increasingly been criticised as representing too simplistic, and in particular, too narrow a view of the nature of individual needs. Among the more notable contributions to this criticism is that of Maslow[6] whose, so-called, hierarchy of needs approach has had a considerable influence on our understanding of motivation. The main features of Maslow's approach are summarised below:

1 Individuals have a wide variety of needs ranging from physiological needs such as hunger and thirst, to needs for autonomy, independence and a feeling of competence.
2 These can be represented in the form of a hierarchy from lower-order to higher-order needs, being arranged as follows:
    (*a*)   existence needs;
    (*b*)   security needs;
    (*c*)   social needs;

(*d*) a need for esteem and reputation;
(*e*) a need for autonomy and independence;
(*f*) a need for competence, achievement and self-actualisation.

3 The lower-order needs are satisfied first, before moving on to the next level in the hierarchy.

4 A satisfied need is no longer a motivator.

What this hierarchy points to is the diversity of human needs and the ensuing complexity of motivation. The insights of Maslow have been instrumental in spawning a whole set of approaches to the issue of motivation which stress the fact that money is only one of a range of factors in the inducement of human effort. Among these approaches, the notion that the nature of the work itself may be a motivating factor and the consequent importance of job design is of particular interest to the manager of the modern purchasing function.

Research has shown that many of the higher-order needs in Maslow's hierarchy can be fulfilled, and therefore provide a source of motivation, if work is designed so as to give the individual a real feeling of responsibility and achievement. The design of work in order to provide this source of motivation has been explored most fully by Herzberg[7] with his proposals for job-enrichment.

Assuming that the broader role to be attributed to purchasing is adopted, there will be more opportunities for job enrichment within the purchasing function. There will also be more possibilities for job rotation between, say, buying and stock control or expediting and stores. This will avoid the danger of personnel becoming 'stale', and it will enable them to enrich their work and learn the wider aspects of the purchasing function. This should be good for morale and could lead to improved supplier relations and more effective purchasing personnel. Hopefully, this broader knowledge will lead purchasing personnel to realise that such luxuries as over-stocking are very costly and considerable savings can be effected through tighter inventory control. All of this should lead to more motivated purchasing personnel, concerned with wider aspects of business rather than being a mere requisitioning function. They will be able to partake in value analysis exercises and make a positive contribution, rather than being there merely to provide data on material costs. It has often been said, unkindly perhaps, that the prime attributes for purchasing are loyalty, perseverance and accuracy and there is little room for imagination or innovativeness. It may be that the broader role suggested for purchasing will allow these latter characteristics to develop.

Reck[8] perhaps best summarises the situation when he recommends that purchasing could be made more effective by redesigning purchasing jobs to include variety with the opportunity to use a number of personally valued skills, autonomy with the chance to feel responsible for one's work, task identity to give the opportunity to perform a whole piece of work and feedback which will provide the opportunity for an individual to find out how he is performing.

LEADERSHIP AND PURCHASING PERSONNEL

It has been stressed throughout that many of the important aspects of managing purchasing people are the prerogative of specialists: training officers, personnel managers and the like. It was also suggested, however, that the purchasing manager too, has an important contribution to make. Nowhere is this contribution more in evidence than in the leadership role which every manager must play.

As with motivation, the concept of leadership, and in particular the factors associated with effective leadership, remain controversial in the management literature. What we do know is that there is no one single style which will ensure that a manager is effective in his leadership role. The styles usually compared are along what Handy[9] refers to as an authoritarian versus democratic dimension. At one end of this dimension, the authoritarian style of leadership is characterised by centralised decision making and power. The leader determines policy, decides what tasks need to be accomplished and in what manner and then instructs his subordinates. At the other extreme the democratic leadership style is characterised by a much greater degree of participation in decision making, subordinates being encouraged to make suggestions and choose their own methods of working etc.

Neither of these approaches works best in every circumstance; rather the evidence suggests that the effective leader must adopt his style according to the nature of the leader, the task and the subordinates. For example, research has indicated that where the task is very easy or very difficult, an authoritarian style of leadership is more effective with the leader concentrating on achieving the task with little or no attention to interpersonal relations. More supportive, democratic styles of leadership are more effective where the task is of intermediate difficulty, i.e. neither purely routine, nor very complex and ambiguous.

In practice the purchasing manager must achieve a balance between providing the motivation to achieve the task whilst encouraging his subordinates in the fulfilment of their personal needs and aspirations. Selection, training, motivation and leadership are important aspects of the purchasing manager's function.

REFERENCES

(1) R. J. Williamson, *Business Organization,* Heinemann, 1981, pp. 1-3.
(2) R. M. Moncza, 'Buyer Performance Evaluation: Major Considerations' in *Journal of Purchasing and Materials Management,* November 1974.
(3) R. R. Reck, 'Purchasing Effectiveness', Michigan State University PhD thesis, 1977, p. 165.
(4) J. P. Campbell, M. D. Dunnette, E. E. Lawler and K. E. Weick, *Managerial Behaviour, Performance and Effectiveness,* McGraw-Hill, 1970.
(5) L. W. Porter, E. E. Lawler and J. R. Hackman, *Behaviour in Organizations,* McGraw-Hill, 1975, pp. 210-2.
(6) A. H. Maslow, 'A Theory of Human Motivation' in *Psychological Review,* vol. 50, 1943, pp. 370-96.
(7) F. Herzberg, B. Mausner and B. Synderman, *The Motivation to Work,* Wiley, 1959.
(8) Reck, op. cit., p. 166.
(9) C. B. Handy, *Understanding Organizations,* Penguin, 1976, pp. 90-1.

FURTHER READING

V. H. Vroom and E. L. Deci (eds) *Management and Motivation,* Penguin, 1970.

P. Drucker, *Effective Managerial Performance,* BIM, 1974.

E. J. Singer and J. Ramsden, *Human Resources,* McGraw-Hill, 1971.

P. E. Drucker, *People and Performance,* Heinemann, 1977.

C. Argyris, *Integrating the Individual and the Organisation,* Wiley, 1964.

W. J. Paul and K. B. Robertson, *Job Enrichment and Employee Motivation,* Gower, 1970.

R. G. Revans, *Developing Effective Managers,* Longman, 1971.

G. A. Thomason, *A Textbook of Personnel Management,* IPM, 1978.

21

Effective negotiation

Stephen Parkinson

Negotiation with suppliers can cover a wide range of subjects, and continue through several transactions. Broadly speaking, negotiation between buyer and seller is most likely to occur when the conditions of purchase or sale cannot be completely controlled by both parties. Control exists for example when a tight specification on the original drawing may compel the purchasing manager to source from a particular supplier. A proprietary item which is heavily promoted to the end-user may also give the purchasing manager similar problems in sourcing widely. Clearly the effective negotiator does not let himself get into such situations if possible but once in such a situation, he will still try to find alternatives – for example, could the item be respecified, or a substitute found? To the successful negotiator nothing is taken as given and everything is negotiable.

AREAS FOR NEGOTIATION

It would be shortsighted to view negotiation as a process which occurs between purchasing manager and the representative of the supplier at the point immediately prior to signing the contract. There are a variety of situations where negotiation is important and each should be viewed as an important part of the overall negotiation responsibilities of the buyer. Figure 21.1 illustrates these situations in terms of a stylised view of the industrial buying decision.

NEGOTIATION TOOLS

The principal negotiation tool is effective preparation which provides the points for focus in negotiation itself. The effective negotiator is well prepared, with a detailed knowledge of the case he

Buying decisions	Negotiation activity	Negotiation partner(s)
Determination of need	Establishing ordering routines, EOQs, fixing budgets, choice between alternative priorities (e.g. capital investment)	Other members of our organisation (production control, finance, marketing, etc.)
Definition of requirements	Establishing right specification in terms of value for money through value analysis/engineering	Engineering, sales marketing, in house
External contact/search	Agreeing extent of search/ supplier evaluation	Engineering, sales marketing, in house
Qualification of suppliers	Supplier rating and supplier development activities	Supplier's representatives and members of our organisation
Tender administration		
Discussion with bidders, commonly seen as the only or principal negotiation arena	Price, fixing, delivery specification and all other associated aspects of the agreement	Supplier's representatives and members of our organisation
Choice		
Part tender discussion	Discussing unsatisfactory performance, e.g. price rises, quality wrong, delivery unsatisfactory	Supplier's representatives and members of our organisation
Performance evaluation seen by many as the second major arena	Discussing unsatisfactory performance, e.g. price rises, quality wrong, delivery unsatisfactory	Supplier's representatives and members of our organisation

Figure 21.1 Negotiation situations in the buying process*

* Obviously all of these stages are not likely to be present in every buying situation and this table should be seen as indicating potential areas where negotiation could take place rather than an illustration of every situation.

is presenting, and a strategy to present his case to achieve his overall objective. Effective preparation depends upon a knowledge of specific techniques which have been discussed in detail in other chapters of this book. In each negotiation situation different types of information will be required.

The principal analytical tools for the purchasing manager at the preparation stage are supplier assessment, price-cost analysis, value engineering and profit-volume analysis (break-even analysis). Each of these can be used to prepare the case for negotiation.

Supplier rating, the evaluation of suppliers on a series of general factors of performance, has been discussed extensively elsewhere. The extent to which supplier rating is used as a tool varies considerably between companies and situations, but is influenced primarily by the size and importance of the purchase and the time available to the buyer. Where time is available, then it can provide a very useful appraisal of the supplier prior to negotiation.

Many of the factors which are considered in a supplier rating exercise are subjective and it is useful for the purchasing manager to attempt to quantify as much information as possible so as to provide an appreciation of the prospective supplier. The use of financial ratios is one way of developing such an appreciation.

Under the Companies Act 1981, British companies have to report a limited amount of potentially useful information in their annual return. The negotiator can glean information for use in negotiation from this source. Figure 21.2 indicates useful financial ratios which can be calculated for some prospective suppliers. Such ratios are of limited use without a point of comparison. Where there is more than one supplier, ratios can sometimes be compared between competing suppliers. For example, suppose supplier A has a higher ratio of value of assets (plant and machinery) to sales turnover than supplier B. What questions does this raise about the quality of A's manufacturing capability? Such comparisons depend on obtaining comparable information which may be difficult. It is also necessary to make several assumptions about the meaning of the ratios. If the ratios in Figure 21.2 can be calculated, they will provide a basis for discussion with the supplier about general performance factors, such as response time, product development activity, purchasing efficiency, labour efficiency, distribution, administration and selling efficiency. Such factors are crucial determinants of the prospective

Ratio	Application
Plant and machinery: sales turnover	Production efficiency
Stocks: sales turnover	Response time
Development costs: sales turnover	Development activity
Cost of materials: sales turnover	Purchasing efficiency
Cost of wages and salaries: sales turnover	Labour efficiency
Distribution costs: sales turnover	Distribution efficiency
Administrative costs: sales turnover	Administration efficiency

Figure 21.2 Useful financial ratios in supplier appraisal

Depending on the schedule which each company has adopted to report its accounts, some or all of these ratios may be available

supplier's position in the negotiation itself, and will inevitably influence the supplier's response to the purchasing manager's proposals.

Where there is only one prospective supplier, the ratio can frequently be compared with those for the industry in which the firm is operating. Ratios are available from sources such as Inter Company Comparisons for several industries. There are problems of comparability of information, but the statistics may provide a starting point for analysis.

The reader may feel uneasy about the extent to which such ratios provide a basis for final decisions about suppliers. This is not the purpose of collecting such information. Such ratios indicate potential areas for discussion and provide a starting point for an analysis of prospective suppliers. This information must necessarily be complemented by information of a more subjective type, for example experience accumulated in previous dealings with the supplier, and/or visits to the supplier and other managers' opinions.

Other broader considerations include the number of competing suppliers and the intensity of competition, the number of other customers in the market, the extent to which the supplier appears to need the business and the amount of time available for discussion. Each of these factors has some influence on the outcome of negotiation, and the effective negotiator will attempt as far as possible to anticipate their effect.

In addition to general supplier characteristics, the purchasing manager must also analyse the actual purchasing situation as carefully as possible. When negotiations are likely to cover the performance of a specific contract, then consideration has to be given to the individual components of the deal. At this stage the buyer must consider carefully what the objectives of negotiations are to be.

These will reflect how the item will be used, and its role in the manufacturing process should indicate the priorities to give to achieving price, delivery or quality requirements. Such priorities must be established together with other members of the organisation, which may in itself involve some negotiations.

Once these priorities have been fixed the purchasing manager is better positioned to develop his case. Price-cost analysis has been discussed elsewhere in the text, and this technique should be applied to an analysis of each cost separately (engineering and tooling, materials labour and subcontracting, overheads and profit).

In a perfect world the purchasing manager might be expected to develop an understanding of the various stages in the manufacturing process, and the role of each item or service to be acquired. However this would be a daunting responsibility and it would be more realistic to expect the purchasing manager to call upon the expertise of others in establishing the basic components of cost involved. These are best seen in terms of the typical breakdown of costs which make up the selling price. Figure 21.3 presents a typical breakdown and identifies the potential opportunities for analysis, prior to negotiation.

In most instances the purchasing manager will only be able to develop an approximation of the likely costs from such an analysis. However, even if the information is imperfect, developing an insight into likely costs and using this in negotiation is extremely useful, since it will provide the purchasing manager with a series of points of leverage to discuss with the potential supplier.

Systematic appraisal of the requirement to be satisfied by buying the item, will also often identify points of leverage. The typical questions of a value engineering/analysis exercise which identify the use of an item and the relative costs and benefits of alternative

Cost component	Activity
Materials	Establishing market price for materials/components where possible
Labour	Estimating labour content assuming 'best practice' techniques equipment, and learning curve effects
Direct expenses	Estimation assuming 'best practice' techniques, and equipment
Indirect expenses	Examination of general sales, administration and distribution overhead against competition through analysis of reported company information
Profit	Comparison with 'going' rate for industry

Figure 21.3 Factors to consider in price cost analysis

solutions to the requirement, provide information which can also be useful.

This type of exercise makes considerable demands on the buyer's technical skills and frequently the buyer may need the assistance of other members of the organisation, to provide the necessary technical information, and to identify potential areas of flexibility. There are a variety of potential reactions to the buyer's indicated intention to become involved or influence the specification of a company's products. The maxim in such situations is that the buyer should not take over the specification of products. This is not his job and it is unlikely that he would possess the range of skills which would make this feasible in any case. Rather the buyer should reserve the right where possible to challenge the specification and attempt to identify key areas of potential cost reduction through discussion with the engineering staff responsible for the original specification. Such discussion may frequently open up new areas for negotiation when the buyer finally meets the supplier's representative.

The technique of break-even analysis is also appropriate to many negotiation situations. When the buyer is faced with requests from the supplier for upward movement of prices due to cost inflation, or is attempting to negotiate prices downwards by ordering in larger quantities, then break-even analysis is very useful.

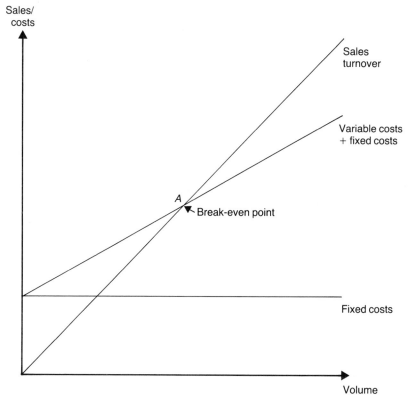

Figure 21.4 General illustration of break-even chart

Broadly speaking the break-even chart in Figure 21.4 illustrates the relationship between fixed and variable costs, sales and profit. Increases in fixed or variable costs, or decreases in the selling price will move the break-even point to the right. The supplier will have to produce more before total costs are covered and profit is made. Decreases in fixed or variable costs or increases in the selling price will move the break-even point to the left with an opposite effect. As the level of fixed cost increases or the unit price increases so changes in volume have an increasing impact on either profit (moving right of the break-even point A in Figure 21.4) or loss (moving left of the break-even point A).

For the negotiator the break-even chart can be a particularly useful tool of analysis provided that he can collect the necessary information to make certain assumptions. It is very difficult to develop a break-even chart for a specific product. Unless the supplier is a single-product company the fixed costs will be shared between the product range. There are also problems of assessing variable costs discussed under price analysis earlier. At best the negotiator can attempt to produce a summary break-even chart from the reported trading accounts of a potential supplier, and use this in negotiation.

The use of each of these tools of analysis depends on the circumstances of the negotiation situation. Where more time is available then the buyer can approach each situation more carefully and prepare the case fully. Where the purchase is an important one, either in absolute cost or in a strategic sense, again the buyer has to examine the case in greater detail using the techniques discussed as far as possible.

MANAGEMENT OF THE NEGOTIATION PROCESS

The best prepared negotiator may be unsuccessful if implementation is weak. No amount of careful collection and presentation of information can compensate for an inappropriate approach to negotiation itself. This aspect of negotiation has increasingly come under scrutiny in recent years and various approaches have been suggested to improve the negotiator's chances of success.

Such approaches have been derived from the observation of negotiation taking place in a wide range of situations and provide a general prescription for negotiation behaviour. In the same way that the techniques of analysis discussed in earlier sections are not necessarily all appropriate to a specific situation, the suggested approaches to negotiation are also not necessarily appropriate in every situation. Figure 21.5 compares two alternative approaches which have been suggested by two authors, who have extensive experience in negotiation training. Winker's[1] approach is considerably more extensive than Kennedy Benson and MacMillan's[2] model, but both cover essentially the same issues.

In each approach the initial stages of preparation include the collection of information and identification of the bargaining position. At this stage the negotiator is concerned with assessing the position and determining the bargaining power of the other party. It

Winkler[1]	Kennedy, Benson and MacMillan[2]
Information gathering	
Diagnosis of situation	
Assessment of bargaining power	
Setting objectives	
Developing strategy	
Structuring their expectations	
Exploration of their needs	
The opening moves	Signalling
Obtaining movement	Proposing
Reviewing objectives	Packaging
Tactical ploys	Bargaining
The settlement area	Closing
Closure	Agreeing
Documenting agreement	

Figure 21.5 Alternative approaches to negotiation: two methods compared

is crucial at this stage to assess the likely goals/objectives of the party with whom negotiations will be conducted.

Another important consideration at this time is that negotiation is not a competition, or rather should not be seen as such. Unfortunately there is a tendency to view negotiation in this way, and to see the outcome in terms of winners and losers. In effective negotiation, at the end of the process both parties ought to feel that they have reached an agreement which is mutually satisfactory, at least at the time that the agreement was reached. Prescriptions for effective negotiation are essentially prescriptions for reasonable behaviour. Therefore the process of setting goals should be based on an assessment of the company's bargaining position, including its purchasing policy, and an assessment of the negotiation partner's position and likely objectives. Kennedy suggests the MIL approach in setting such objectives. There are some objectives the negotiator must achieve if the negotiation is to be deemed successful. There are others which the negotiator would intend to achieve if possible and finally there are some which the negotiator would like to achieve. Objectives should be ranked accordingly to give the negotiator priorities for the negotiation itself. If more than one negotiator is involved, it is also important at this stage to consider the roles of the negotiation team. Each must have a clearly defined part to play in the implementation of the negotiation strategy. Where a team is operating each member must be able to integrate his efforts according to the priorities or objectives of negotiation. Team members must be compatible therefore, and it is advisable to rehearse the negotiation in advance to ensure that each member knows his or her role. Where there is only one negotiator rehearsal is also important, with a member of the negotiator's own company playing the negotiation partner. The use of closed-circuit television, with record and playback facilities, will enhance the effectiveness of the performance of the negotiation. Where such facilities are available the participants can greatly improve their negotiation effectiveness.

At the initial stages of negotiation each party is seeking to establish the other's position. Therefore each is likely to attempt to determine the other party's attitudes, and to explore what dimensions are important for negotiation. If the negotiator has prepared carefully there should be few surprises at this stage. Winkler refers to this stage as 'structuring their expectations'. The negotiator is essentially establishing the ground which the negotiation will cover, and is obviously interested in covering the ground which he or she has prepared.

To progress beyond this stage the negotiator must have indication of the direction in which negotiation should go. Kennedy, Benson and McMillan advise the negotiator to look for 'signals' prefaced by 'if'. For example, 'if' we are prepared to reduce our quoted price would you be prepared to increase the size of your order? Such signals indicate whether or not the partner is willing to move from the initial position, and what would have to be exchanged. Exchanges may last for a considerable time as the negotiators explore different dimensions. The negotiator can also provide such signals in the form of similar conditional statements.

As a result of this initial discussion the negotiator will ultimately be in a position where all alternatives have been examined and the partner's stance on each issue clarified. At this point Winkler suggests evaluating the original objectives against the full information now available on the negotiation partner's position. Where it is clear that the original objectives may not all be achieved then some rethinking may be necessary, possibly to the extent of withdrawing from the negotiation temporarily to re-examine the position. Beyond this stage a solution to the problems under discussion is required, and the parties must find some way of bringing the different aspects of the negotiation together in some way which is acceptable to both (packaging). A suitable combination of offer and counter-offer must be developed to satisfy both parties and here again preplanning is required in order to identify concessions which are possible (bargaining).

If both parties have adopted a professional approach, and if it is a real negotiation situation where both parties lack some element of control over the final outcome, then ultimately it should be possible to find an area where a settlement can be reached which is to the advantage of both parties. Once this happens agreement can be reached and the terms of agreement documented. It is obviously important to document the final agreement as carefully as possible to ensure that subsequent disagreements do not result.

CHOICE OF NEGOTIATOR

The outcome of negotiation is likely to depend crucially upon the personal characteristics of the negotiators involved. These characteristics will include the background, attitudes, formal education and motivation of the individuals involved. Such factors are likely to influence the negotiator's perception of the issues involved, and response to the other party. Negotiation is frequently based on a mixture of clearly identifiable facts and subjective opinion and the effective negotiator must be able to separate the two elements.

From the discussion of the negotiation process above it should be evident that the negotiator must be skilful in asking questions, and be able to guide discussion in the desired direction by introducing relevant issues at the appropriate moment. Personal characteristics such as patience, tact, an ability to think quickly and a sense of humour could be extremely useful. These factors stress the importance of carefully selecting and training negotiation personnel.

The criteria for managing effectively the negotiation process itself have been established by a variety of authors. Their advice is essentially a prescription for reasonable behaviour. Hence negotiators are advised:

(*a*) show empathy – put yourself in the supplier's shoes and try to understand what he or she really wants;

(*b*) never force a showdown – if either party loses face neither gains ultimately;

(*c*) try to satisfy the other parties' needs too;

(*d*) follow a structured and logical approach;

(*e*) be flexible enough to vary this approach depending upon changing circumstances;

(*f*) consider concessions which would benefit the supplier and not harm your position;

(*g*) discuss issues logically on the available information and structure discussion around negotiation objectives.

CONCLUSION

This chapter is a brief overview of the area of negotiation between buyer and seller. It points to the importance of two basic aspects of negotiation, namely preparation and implementation, and provides an introduction to the conduct of each stage. The outcome of negotiation depends not only upon a knowledge of the main elements described here, but also upon the experience of the individual negotiator. This is inevitably acquired through experience and therefore it is appropriate to refer to negotiation, in part at least, as a skill which must be practised to be effective.

REFERENCES

(1)   J. Winkler, *Bargaining for Results,* Heinemann, London, 1981.
(2)   G. Kennedy, J. Benson and J. Macmillan, *Managing Negotiations,* Business Books, 1981.

22

Ethical issues in purchasing

David Farmer

Peter Drucker is credited with having made an appealing statement regarding ethics. He stated that there is no such thing as business ethics, only ethics – and his point is well made. Nonetheless, what could be argued in a philosophical sense is that the raison d'être for a particular code of behaviour in life in general may be different from that associated with business activity. Some, of course, would take the view that, because of their religious or moral standpoint, the two codes are inseparable. However, without wishing to deny that, there is also the argument that sound ethical behaviour is good for business per se:[1] that, for example, when both parties to a transaction behave ethically towards one another, that one outcome is mutual trust, and since trust is a key requirement in effective buyer-supplier relationship that it makes good commercial sense to develop and enhance such an environment.

Clearly, it is the responsibility of the managers in any organisation to establish policies which they perceive as being most beneficial to the business. Since this handbook is concerned with the purchasing function, the reader will wish to ensure that those which are applied with respect to transactions with suppliers are most beneficial to his or her own business. It follows that the purpose of this chapter must be to provide information and guidelines which will enable the manager to make decisions to help ensure such outcomes. Nevertheless, perhaps inevitably, a position is taken in the discussion which should be stated at the outset. That position is that sound ethical behaviour makes for good business: that the author believes that such standards are also rewarding in life in general must be left for another platform.

ETHICS AND BUSINESS

It is an interesting fact that much of the history of commercial transaction has been enacted against the backcloth of a Latin tag – *caveat emptor* – let the buyer beware. Hardly, it would seem, indicative of the trustworthiness of sellers or the ethical behaviour of man in general. Then, from time to time, the media is filled with strident comment on what Edward Heath called the 'unacceptable face of capitalism'. During the last two decades, for example, exposées in the western world have seen public figures including royalty and heads of state associated with bribery charges involved with the influencing of major purchasing decisions. Indeed, virtually all the major cases reported have involved purchase decisions, although it is worth noting that in the majority of those cases, people other than professional buyers have been cited.

Carl Madden,[2] in a thought-provoking discussion on business ethics, provides ammunition for the cynics who might argue that the ethical standards adopted in business are, at best, pragmatic. He includes among the forces which influence ethical behaviour:

- competition
- salesmanship
- 'the bottom line'
- government regulation
- political influences
- group behaviour.

Most of these issues were also cited in an extensive study by Raymond Baumhart[3] who found, for example, that:

> It is easier to be ethical in jobs involving fiduciary relationships such as the accountants' or engineers' than in those jobs involving competitive relationships, such as the salesman's or purchasing agent's.

and that

Though most business men oppose increased governmental involvement in business, many acknowledge that governmental regulation has improved United States business practice.

Overall, then, the business scene might be thought of as being one within which any attempt to establish and enact sound ethical policies would be thwarted. It will also be the position of many that short-term pressures, such as the 'bottom line', are so great that even where certain ethical standards are believed to be laudable, they are impractical. As one businessman put it recently in discussion with the writer: 'Business is a jungle. If I am to survive then I must behave in a way which will protect me from predators.'

Yet the view persists, and it is visible through the policies and actions of organisations which are effective in extremely competitive sectors, that sound ethical purchasing standards are not only desirable in business, they are necessary. (See, for example, the relevant sections of the policy statements included in the appendix to Chapter 1.)

WHAT MAKES GOOD ETHICAL STANDARDS NECESSARY?

The purchasing role, more than any other, involves the management of corporate expenditure. Purchasing people have access to the corporate purse; it is their job to choose between one source and another and to use the organisation's money wisely. In many cases the decision to choose between several potential suppliers is complex. It involves judgement on quality and performance standards and on non-tangible issues such as longer-term viability. Thus it is difficult if not impossible to develop systems which will enable, for example, effective objective post-decision audit on a purely quantitative basis. Consequently, the people who spend the money must be trustworthy, which in the eyes of most thinking organisations means that they should have ethical standards of the highest order. The fact that purchasing people are not the only ones involved in making source decisions complicates the issues. Nevertheless, it is clear that the people who have authority to sign purchase orders are, at least, the final point of control in the source-making chain. It follows that their authority and responsibility includes that of the keeper of the corporate purse. If their ethical standards match those which are thought to be necessary in performing such a task, then there is a greater chance that those standards will be applied.

There are, too, other aspects of the purchasing task which if they are to be undertaken effectively will necessitate the application of proper standards. For example, there are the broader aspects of relationships with particular suppliers; there are those concerned with dealing with competitors, such as disclosure of information; there are those which relate to reasonable opportunity to bid and to supply; and there are those which are concerned with honest information in respect of expected volumes of usage of a component or material. Such issues are relevant where and whenever purchase decisions are made. The standards which are applied in such decision making will, invariably, affect their outcomes. The effective purchasing manager will be seeking to ensure that those which he and his staff apply result in the most favourable outcomes for the organisation by whom he is employed. In the experience of most effective businesses that implies ethical purchasing standards of the highest order. As the old saw has it: 'It takes two to tango'. Even the most corrupt supplier is unable to influence purchase decisions through bribery if no one in the buying organisation is prepared to be so influenced.

FORMS OF BRIBERY

The Christmas season abounds with the dispensing of what are sometimes termed 'goodwill business gifts'. Turkeys, liquor, cigarettes, cigars and gifts of a variety of types are dispensed by sales forces in all markets. It should be noted that they are not only given to buyers; engineers, production men, designers and users are all included in the distribution. Indeed, in many sales organisations the discussion as to which people should be included or excluded from the list has produced many heated arguments. Yet in the majority of cases the gift which is to be given is of relatively low value. Certainly a bottle of whisky or a box of cigars ought not to influence any decision-maker. Yet the fact that a majority of firms involve themselves in distributing such gifts suggests that the managers concerned believe that they do enhance relationships. And attempts to nurture relationships are not confined to Christmas.

The business lunch, visits to Ascot, Twickenham, Wembley, major football and athletic events, theatre performances, trips on the QE II, Concorde and Orient Express and 'seminars' or 'conferences' in holiday resorts are among the many incentives offered on a regular basis by suppliers. Again, presumably, these concerns justify the expenditure involved in the light of the business which it helps generate. There are, too, more overt efforts to persuade people to do business with the firms concerned, such as direct bribery when money changes hands or where money value in products is provided. Whilst this latter group is far less evident than the first, where such cases have been brought to court, the sums involved have been considerable. Indeed, in the cases involving US aircraft sales they have been huge.

The points about all these attempts at bribery (and even the smallest attempt in a business sense must surely be regarded as such) is that they suggest a single question:

> Why is it necessary for the supplier to provide such incentives if his product quality, price and level of service is competitive?

There is, too, the argument that whoever makes a buying decision based at least partly upon the hope of some personal gain, is guilty of a dereliction of duty. Leaving aside any moral issue, the person who accepts a gift of any kind is compromised to a greater or lesser degree with regard to his or her decision making. And this applies both before a source decision is taken and in the management of a supplier's performance subsequently.

Given the extent of the distribution of such incentives, presumably there are many thousands of people who regard these arguments as extreme. Justifications abound, such as:

> I always ask them if the gift is for services rendered or services to be rendered.
> A gift worth £10 will not affect my judgement.
> It's the practice in this industry, everyone does it.

However, when those concerned are asked if they report the receipt of such gifts to senior management, there are very few who do. It seems that most concerns of any size have written or unwritten policies which preclude the acceptance of anything other than a token gift. In turn this suggests that:

1 Most organisations believe it to be important that the agent who is given the responsibility for spending their money is above reproach in terms of his decision making.
2 The people concerned do not report receipt of gifts because such things imply bribery, however modest, and would necessitate explanation to justify acceptance.

It is important that not only should the highest ethical standards be employed in source decision making, they must be seen to be so.

ENSURING THAT CORRECT STANDARDS ARE APPLIED

Because purchase decisions are made by human beings, it is necessary to ensure that the function is staffed by people who apply correct standards as a matter of course. To support them, ethical guidelines should be published as policy statements and these statements should be available throughout the organisation. When new staff are recruited, either in the purchasing function or in those which may be involved in source decision making, they should be made aware of the policies. Further, the practices and behaviour of senior staff should reinforce, on a continuing basis, the standards which have been set. Then the procedures adopted within the organisation and with respect to outside parties should be designed to create an environment which is supportive of the stated policies.

Many leading companies have published ethical policies which are promoted in these and other ways. Presumably this is indicative of their soundness as an aid to effective business. In other words, they are good for business. It would be foolish to deny that a business which is perceived to behave in an ethical fashion will enhance its image and reputation. However, few businesses would be interested in a cosmetic benefit. The costs, and there are always costs involved, associated with such behaviour will need to be recouped through the enhancement of the business which is done.

Space does not permit the publication here of examples of corporate policies relating to purchase decisions. However, the code of conduct which was developed by the Institute of Purchasing and

Supply covers the field at issue in a thorough manner. Consideration of this code should provide the reader with clear guidelines against which more specific organisation-related codes may be developed where none exist. Also it should provide those who have published policies with a model against which those guidelines may be measured.

THE ETHICAL CODE OF THE INSTITUTE OF PURCHASING AND SUPPLY[4]

Introduction

1 In applying to join the Institute, members undertake to abide by the Constitution, Memorandum and Articles of Association, Rules and By-Laws of the Institute'. The Code set out below was approved by the Institute's Council on 26 February, 1977 and is binding on members.

2 The cases of members reported to have breached the Code shall be investigated by a Disciplinary Committee appointed by the Council; where a case is proven, a member may, depending on the circumstances and the gravity of the charge, be admonished, reprimanded, suspended from membership or removed from the list of members. Details of cases in which members are found in breach of the Code will be notified in the publications of the Institute.

Precepts

3 Members shall never use their authority or office for personal gain and shall seek to uphold and enhance the standing of the Purchasing and Supply profession and the Institute by:

(*a*) maintaining an unimpeachable standard of integrity in all their business relationships both inside and outside the organizations in which they are employed;

(*b*) fostering the highest possible standards of professional competence amongst those for whom they are responsible;

(*c*) optimizing the use of resources for which they are

responsible to provide the maximum benefit to their employing organization;
(d) complying both with the letter and the spirit of:
  (i) the law of the country in which they practise;
  (ii) such guidance on professional practice as may be issued by the Institute from time to time;
  (iii) contractual obligations;
(e) rejecting any business practice which might reasonably be deemed improper.

Guidance

4 In applying these precepts, members should follow the guidance set out below;
  (a) *Declaration of interest.* Any personal interest which may impinge or might reasonably be deemed by others to impinge on a member's impartiality in any matter relevant to his or her duties should be declared.
  (b) *Confidentiality and accuracy of information.* The confidentiality of information received in the course of duty should be respected and should never be used for personal gain; information given in the course of duty should be true and fair and never designed to mislead.
  (c) *Competition.* While bearing in mind the advantages to the member's employing organization of maintaining a continuing relationship with a supplier, any arrangement which might, in the long term, prevent the effective operation of fair competition, should be avoided.
  (d) *Business gifts.* Business gifts, other than items of very small intrinsic value such as business diaries or calendars should not be accepted.
  (e) *Hospitality.* Modest hospitality is an accepted courtesy of a business relationship. However, the recipient should not allow him or herself to reach a position whereby he or she might be or might be deemed by others to have been influenced in making a business decision as a consequence of accepting such hospitality; the frequency and scale of hospitality accepted should not be significantly greater than the recipient's employer would be likely to provide

in return;

(f) when it is not easy to decide between what is and is not acceptable in terms of gifts or hospitality, the offer should be declined or advice sought from the member's superior.

5 Advice on any aspect of the precepts and guidance set out above may be obtained on written request to the Institute.

THE ETHICAL CODE OF THE IFPMM[4]

Precepts

1 Members shall not use their authority or office for personal gain and shall seek to uphold and enhance the standing of the Purchasing and Material Management profession and the Federation by:

(a) Maintaining an unimpeachable standard of integrity in all their business relationships both inside and outside the organizations in which they are employed,

(b) Fostering the highest standards of professional competence amongst those for whom they are responsible;

(c) Optimizing the use of resources for which they are responsible so as to provide the maximum benefit to their employers;

(d) Complying with the letter and the spirit of:

(i) The laws of the country in which they practise:

(ii) The Federation's 'Principles and Standards of Purchasing Practice' and any other such guidance on professional practice as may be issued by the Federation from time to time;

(iii) Contractual obligations;

(e) Rejecting and denouncing any business practice that is improper.

Guidance

2 In applying these precepts, members should follow the guidance set out below:

(a) Declaration of interest. Any personal interest which may impinge or might reasonably be deemed by others to impinge on a member's impartiality in any matter relevant to their duties should be declared to their employer.

(*b*) Confidentiality and accuracy of information. The confidentiality of information received in the course of duty must be respected and should not be used for personal gain; information given in the course of duty should be true and fair and not designed to mislead.

(*c*) Competition. While considering the advantages to the member's employer of maintaining a continuing relationship with a supplier, any arrangement which might, in the long term, prevent the effective operation of fair competition, should be avoided.

(*d*) Business gifts. To preserve the image and integrity of both the member and the employer business gifts should be discouraged. Gifts, other than items of very small intrinsic value such as business diaries or calendars, should not be accepted.

(*e*) Hospitality. Moderate hospitality is an accepted courtesy of a business relationship. However, the recipients should not allow themselves to reach a position whereby they might be or might be deemed by others to have been influenced in making a business decision as a consequence of accepting such hospitality. The frequency and scale of hospitality accepted should not be significantly greater than a recipient's employer, through the recipient's expense account, would be likely to provide in return.

(*f*) When in doubt of what is acceptable in terms of gifts or hospitality, the offer should be declined or advice sought from the member's superior.

3 Advice on any aspect of the precepts, guidance or principles and standards may be obtained by contacting the Ethics Committee through the International Office of the Federation in Denmark.

The various statements made in this code are clearly supportive of the basic argument put forward in this chapter so far. Perhaps it is best summed up by the second statement in the code. To paraphrase: 'no member shall misuse his authority for personal gain'. It is a statement which belies compromise of any kind.

HOW ETHICAL ARE BUYERS?

Whilst little UK data exist, the findings of Browning and Zabriskie[5] provide insight into the standards applied by respondents to a US survey. It would be interesting to hypothesise whether similar results would be obtained were the research to be replicated in the UK; some of the findings of this work are worth consideration in this light.

The synopsis of their paper includes the statement that: 'Available evidence indicates that . . . buyers are ethical in dealing with them (suppliers)'. This is followed by the telling comment: 'After all, who wants to do business with someone they do not trust? . . . trust is a basis of ongoing relationships between buyer and seller'. Who indeed?

These authors addressed four key questions:

1　Are buyers as ethical in dealing with salespeople as they are with their own companies?
2　Are buyers' beliefs consistent with their behaviour in specific situations?
3　Do buyers think that other buyers (peers) act and behave more ethically than they do themselves?
4　Can simple demographic variables identify buyers who are more apt to think and act unethically?

In general the researchers found that:

Re 1　Buyers were consistent in their behaviour inside or outside the company.

Re 2　Buyers appeared to behave more ethically in practice than their beliefs seemed to warrant.

Re 3　The respondents believed themselves to be more ethical in beliefs and actions than their peers.

Re 4　(a) The larger the firm and the greater the respondent's age, the more likely it was that the buyer believed that it was acceptable to be entertained, or to receive favours from suppliers who were not currently doing business with the buyer's company.

(b) The higher the educational level and younger the age, the more likely that the respondent would view gifts from the suppliers as bribes and, therefore, unethical.

In general, then, the basic tenet of this chapter is confirmed by the study, though the results have some interesting facets. For example, the response to question 3 suggests that the correspondents had evidence, or perhaps perceived, that many of their peers did not act ethically. And it would be interesting to examine that belief in the light of the broad evidence from the survey. A second interesting feature relates to question 4. It seems that older, less qualified, buyers are more susceptible to influence. Does this finding suggest, too, a less well-rewarded staff group? Unfortunately, responses to the survey were anonymous, thus the researchers could not question respondents further. As a result the reader will need to draw his own conclusions, based upon his own experiences.

OTHER ETHICAL ISSUES

As suggested earlier, there are ethical issues other than bribery in its various forms which relate to the purchasing task. Many of these concern honesty in transactions with a supplier; though it should be emphasised that this should not be taken as implying naïve, uncommercial disclosure. For example, it would be foolish for a buying organisation dealing in a speculative market, to reveal its total requirements for a given period. It could be detrimental to a supplier and to his relationships with the buyer, if the latter gave other competing suppliers information on his processes. In certain circumstances, it would be foolish for a buyer to volunteer information to a supplier which would confirm that he is the sole viable source of a product.

Assuming that these and similar caveats are accepted, the following are among other aspects of purchasing behaviour in conjunction with which ethical standards should be carefully considered.

Fair and equitable treatment of suppliers

One example of this would be giving each bidding firm the same opportunity when competing for a tender. Some companies do not allow variation from a tender specification for this reason. Others argue that if supplier *A* is creative enough to suggest cost-saving ideas then they should benefit, while some firms insist that all suppliers should be allowed to requote against the new specification. The point here is not so much that one of these is the correct approach, but rather that whichever is chosen, all bidders should be aware of the 'rules'.

Other examples of this relate to such things as payment arrangements and access to a company's buyers for representatives.

Disclosure to suppliers and potential suppliers

This has been mentioned in the introduction to this section. It relates to providing third parties with the ideas which have been developed by one supplier and which give him commercial advantage. Presumably because of previous experience, some suppliers build agreements on this question into their contracts. Once again, the 'rules' should be stated and adhered to.

Reliability of information

Clearly, no buyer can foresee exactly how many items he will need in a given year. His task should be to provide a genuine best estimate of his requirements. Yet a frequent complaint of sellers is that, for example, estimates are inflated by buyers so as to achieve a more favourable contract price. The ethical implications of this are quite clear, but there are also straight commercial outcomes. When a supplier has been affected detrimentally by such bogus information, it will inevitably impinge upon his judgement when a contract comes up for renewal.

Genuine supplier errors

This topic, once again, has commercial as well as ethical implications. When a supplier under-invoices or under-estimates his costs in a major contract through error, post-contract repercussions could be considerable. In the extreme the buyer, apart from any ethical issue, could find himself with a bankrupt supplier half way through a contract. Again, opinions will differ as to what should be done in such circumstances. One buying manager when discussing this topic said: 'If it involves a long-term relationship then I would always point out the error. If it was a one-off I'd accept it'.

The bulk of opinion, however, appears to be in favour of disclosure and discussion. As another manager put it when emphasising the close relationship between sound business decisions and good ethics: 'I would always point out the discrepancy. Honest dealing is good business and I cannot afford to put my company at risk through disadvantaging a supplier'.

Payment arrangements

Any first year accountant will be able to show that the buying company can benefit through delaying payment to suppliers. Indeed UK practice in this area is such that many suppliers are obliged to give credit to the extent of three and four months when, for example, the contract states: 'Payment end of month following delivery'.

Strictly speaking such behaviour is contrary to the terms of the contract. Certainly in commercial terms it is detrimental to goodwill and could be extremely dangerous with regard to the cash flow of the supplier.

It could be argued that a strictly ethical company should pay its bills when it has agreed to do so. And, after all, if the buying company intends to take extended credit, should not this be an aspect of the contract negotiation? Cash flow management can only be effective when uncertainty is reduced, and reliability of payment for services rendered is extremely important in that respect.

Soliciting quotations without intending to purchase

This practice is cited by suppliers as being fairly common in industrial purchasing. Some are able to quote examples where alternative quotations are used purely to ensure that the existing supplier remains competitive. Inevitably what tends to happen is that once a potential supplier recognises this practice he ceases to collaborate. Clearly the problem of checking existing prices is a real one for any buyer. The ethical issue is whether he should make potential suppliers aware of his purpose when asking for quotations.

CONCLUSION

The topic of this chapter can cause most heated discussion among purchasing people, for it is one about which everyone seems to have an opinion. Yet whilst the need is fundamental, stated policies on ethical issues are conspicuous by their absence from too many organisations. This chapter has examined some of the many issues involved but there are many more.

It is interesting to quote from an intriguing article which appeared in the *Harvard Business Review*, under the title 'Ethics without the Sermon'.[6] The author reported upon an eighteen-month research into business ethics. She suggests that individuals should ask questions of themselves, such as: 'What will I say when my child asks me why I did that? and 'Would you want your decision to appear on the front page of the (New York) Times?' If the questions implied earlier in this chapter are added then an individual can make a judgement of his own position. From the company viewpoint, the development of effective ethical policies should prove to be rewarding. If nothing else they will provide guidelines on expected behaviour which will be visible to all concerned, internally and externally. A commercial company, as the name implies, employs a variety of people acting on its behalf. If the 'company' is to behave and be seen to behave in a prescribed fashion, this necessitates an agreed uniform set of standards.

More than any other, the purchasing function is open to influence by sellers who are intent on acquiring business. When sellers restrict that influence to proper commercial practice, the function will respond in the prescribed manner. This should be true too when methods are used which involve judgement as to ethical behaviour. However, unless those charged with taking purchasing decisions are clear as to the particular standards which the company wishes to apply, there will be, at least, variations in those adopted. If everything else is discounted, this is a powerful reason for developing and publishing ethical policies. And, as stated earlier, there is a widely held view that sound policies in this area can prove beneficial to a concern in a strictly business sense. If that is so, then the use of 'often scarce' resources to develop and publish ethical policies will be rewarded.

Note

Readers who wish to develop ethical policies for publication will find Laura Nash's article[6] and the detailed chapter in Aljian[7] extremely useful as reference material.

REFERENCES

(1) D. H. Farmer and K. McMillan, 'Redefining the Boundaries of the Firm' in *Journal of Industrial Economics,* vol. XXVII, no. 3, March 1979.

(2) Carl Madden, *Clash of Culture; Management and the Age of Changing Values,* The National Planning Association, 1976.

(3) Raymond Baumhart, *Ethics in Business,* Holt, Reinhard and Winston, 1968.

(4) *Code of Conduct,* Institute of Purchasing and Supply (reproduced with permission); and International Federation of Purchasing & Materials Management (reproduced with permission).

(5) J. Browning and N. B. Zabriskie, 'How Ethical are Industrial Buyers?' in *Industrial Marketing Management,* no. 12, 1983, pp. 219-24.

(6) Laura Nash, 'Ethics without the Sermon', *Harvard Business Review,* November-December 1981.

(7) G. W. Aljian (ed.), *Purchasing Handbook,* 3rd ed., McGraw-Hill Book Company, 1973.

PART V
PURCHASING IN ACTION

23

Purchasing in local government

Ken Fox

In order to understand local authority purchasing and its organisation it is necessary to explain local government itself. English and Welsh local government comprises 6 metropolitan and 47 non-metropolitan county councils, 36 metropolitan and 333 non-metropolitan district councils and 10,153 parish councils. Local government in the administrative area of Greater London is unique in that it comprises the City of London and 32 London boroughs with the Greater London Council (GLC) responsible for major strategic issues in the area and many of the executive responsibilities lying with the boroughs. In contrast local government in Scotland is based on 9 regional authorities and district councils at the lower tiers within the regions.

Within these diverse local authorities the internal management structures vary. Most of the larger councils are organised on a committee system appointed to determine and administer discrete programmes or services. For example, arts and recreation, environmental services, housing etc., are all controlled by individual committees and are usually serviced by departments charged with that particular area of responsibility.

The procurement decisions flowing from this committee/departmental organisation are determined by a wide range of factors including the council's political structure and its election manifesto, central government economic, fiscal and monetary policies, pressures from the local community and the activities of any previous administration, particularly if previous capital investments constitute commitment to future revenue expenditure.

It is against this background that the procurement of goods and services is organised and the 'insularity' of the individual programme/department system can tend to fragment the procurement decision-making process as far as contract negotiation, purchase of goods and services, distribution and similar activities are concerned. Unless a conscious decision is taken to combine the procurement of similar products and to employ professional purchasing staff to co-ordinate purchasing, the activity will be located at departmental level frequently carried out by staff without buying skills or knowledge of the market.

Some indication of the relative importance of local authority purchasing in the public procurement scene in Britain can be gauged from Figure 23.1. Of the total public expenditure by programme provided for in the central government's budget strategy, some 25 per cent or £28,000m is spent by local authorities on a mixture of capital and revenue items. Part of this expenditure is financed by a rate precept on the local population and part by the central exchequer's rate support grant.

The broad 'programme' base of local authority expenditure (see Figure 23.2) is subject to a number of constraints imposed by central government. Controls over capital and 'prescribed expenditure' (defined as expenditure required to be included in capital by the central government) severely constrain local authority expenditure. Other forms of direct control over local authority programmes are frequently imposed without regard to commitments already entered into. These directives can substantially change the nature and volume of procurement.

Given the basis of local authority revenue expenditure of approximately £28,000m in 1982-3, if staff salaries and wage costs are excluded, a very approximate 20-25 per cent of this expenditure, or £5,000m, is spent on goods and bought-in services. Local government tends to be labour intensive and the major proportion of the £28,000 of revenue expenditure is comprised of staff costs including teachers, policemen, social workers etc.

In addition to the employment of specialist contractors on capital projects, a considerable amount of purchasing of goods and services for large capital projects is performed by contractors and

	1981-82 outturn	1982-83 estimated outturn	1983-84 plans
Central government			
Current			
Goods and services	33,151	36,720	39,401
Subsidies and grants	37,308	41,819	42,236
Capital			
Goods and services	2,173	2,685	2,896
Grants	2,097	2,388	2,321
Net lending to nationalised industries and some other public corporations	1,960	1,858	1,582
Other net lending and capital transactions	304	398	173
Total excluding debt interest and other adjustments	76,993	85,867	88,608
Local authorities			
Current			
Goods and services	20,618	22,527	22,247
Subsidies and grants	2,734	3,234	3,969
Unallocated margin			1,024
Capital			
Goods and services	2,537	1,937	2,729
Grants	276	537	687
Net lending and other capital transactions	499	507	558
Total excluding debt interest and other adjustments	26,664	28,742	31,213

Source: 'Central Governments Forecasts of Public Expenditure', HMSO.

Figure 23.1 Total public expenditure by spending authority and economic category (£ million cash)

subcontractors under the direction of local authority project managers.

From Figure 23.2 it is possible to gauge the relative importance of goods and services purchased under current or revenue expenditure and, as expected, a large proportion of the specialist purchasing activity tends to be found in the procurement of materials for activities in education, housing, social services, environment, public health and similar activities.

	1981-82	1982-83	1983-84
Current expenditure in England			
Agriculture, fisheries, food and forestry	80	95	102
Industry, energy, trade and employment	113	134	127
Transport	1,549	1,765	1,462
Housing	508	549	384
Other environmental services	2,130	2,299	2,250
Law, order and protective services	2,613	2,957	3,030
Education and science, arts and libraries	9,912	10,533	10,337
Health and personal social services	1,795	1,998	2,020
Social security	486	866	1,832
Unallocated margin			904
Total current expenditure in England	19,187	21,196	22,449
Total current expenditure in Scotland	2,575	2,853	2,947
Total current expenditure in Wales	1,169	1,258	1,358
Total current expenditure in Great Britain	22,931	25,307	26,754
Capital expenditure in England			
Agriculture, fisheries, food and forestry	102	115	50
Industry, energy, trade and employment	36	47	47
Transport	563	572	766
Housing	789	430	1,096
Other environmental services	445	353	487
Law, order and protective services	76	102	127
Education and science, arts and libraries	380	327	301
Health and personal social services	67	102	108
Total capital expenditure in England	2,459	2,049	2,982
Total capital expenditure in Scotland	626	663	678
Total capital expenditure in Wales	179	215	259
Total capital expenditure in Great Britain	3,264	2,927	3,919

Source: 'Central Governments Forecasts of Public Expenditure', HMSO.

Figure 23.2 Local authority expenditure in Great Britain (£ million cash)

In reviewing purchasing activities within local authorities it should be noted that the responsibilities of each local authority are closely prescribed. For example, the county councils in England and Wales will have exclusive responsibilities for education, social services, police and fire in their area and may not delegate these responsibilities to enable district councils to undertake them on an agency basis. They may, however, consider using district councils as agents for refuse disposal or as a consumer protection agency. The organisation of purchasing can vary according to the prescribed functions of each local authority and any agency arrangements that it has made.

LEGAL AND ADMINISTRATIVE FRAMEWORK OF PURCHASING

Local authority purchasing in England and Wales is controlled by a number of Acts and statutory instruments. The Local Government Act of 1972 established new local government areas and authorities in England and Wales. The Act also laid down certain regulations concerning contracts and tenders and covered the development of councils' contracts and standing orders. One of the requirements of the Act is that all local authorities shall make standing orders which ensure competition is present in the tendering and award of their contracts for both the supply of goods and materials and the execution of works. These standing orders (SOs) cover the level of authority and broad procedures for securing competition and for regulating the manner in which tenders are invited, evaluated and awarded.

The Act does not allow persons entering into a contract with a local authority to enquire whether the SOs have been complied with and, indeed, non-compliance does not invalidate a contract. There would, however, be grounds for a possible challenge from either a ratepayer or at audit if standing orders were not followed without due authority from the relevant committee. To assist local authorities in the development of their SOs, the former Ministry of Housing and Local Government issued model standing orders which all authorities were recommended to use as a basis for their own documents. These model standing orders are now outdated and have been criticised as encouraging authorities to develop archaic and ponderous regulations governing the award of contracts. They are however not mandatory and not widely used in professionally staffed purchasing departments.

The Local Authorities (Goods and Services) Act of 1970 allows authorities to co-operate in joint purchasing action. Under this Act local authorities are empowered to supply goods, materials, administrative, professional and technical services and to carry out works of maintenance on behalf of other authorities, provided these bodies are specifically listed in the attachment to the order. A feature of all the authorities which may co-operate in joint action and use each others' services is that they must be non-profit making public bodies. In addition to the metropolitan, county and district councils a wide range of educational bodies, voluntary aided and independent non-profit making associations can participate in these joint purchasing arrangements. Central government, nationalised industry and other similar bodies cannot participate in these arrangements and have their own purchasing agencies. This Act has enabled a large number of local authorities to develop fully professional purchasing services on a shared cost basis and to enjoy the economies of scale, standardisation of product and other advantages which the large purchasing bodies can secure. Under these arrangements, joint contracts are placed on the basis of combined requirements enabling extremely competitive prices to be secured, to operate quality control, inspection and the many other advantages which joint purchasing action can secure. The organisation and management of inter-authority co-operation is discussed later.

There are, of course, a number of other Acts which apply to local authorities as they do to undertakings in the private sector. For example, the Sale of Goods (Implied Terms) Act and the Competition Acts have particular importance to local authority purchasing. The control of anti-competition practices in the Competition Act of 1980 prevents persons in the course of business pursuing conduct which is likely to have the 'effect of restricting, disturbing or preventing competition in connection with the supply of goods in the United Kingdom'. For the purposes of this, and many other Acts, local authorities are classified as 'businesses'.

The award of contracts may also be influenced by powers under other local government Acts. For example, the relative social costs of placing contracts with companies outside the immediate area of an authority may be considered in the final award of contracts. Local authority members may feel that the difference in costs between the local competitor and one from outside the area may not be sufficient to outweigh the employment opportunities offered by placing the contract locally. Local authority members are perfectly entitled to take that view and there may be, therefore, a division of interest between securing for the ratepayer the best value for money identified by the purchasing agent as a result of competitive contracting and the indirect advantages to the local economy of placing it with a (moderately) higher priced local offer.

All the activities of public buyers and members are subject to surveillance not only by the relevant management committees but by internal auditor and the district auditor; the Audit Commission also inspects and comments on the purchasing activity. Both district auditor and the Audit Commission are external services set up under statute and they may employ the services of management consultants when reviewing specialist functions like purchasing. All these examiners are active not only in preventing or exposing corrupt practices and undue influence in the award of public contracts; they will also investigate 'challenges' by ratepayers and are required to assure themselves that the (purchasing) activities represent value for money.

Of fundamental interest to all local authority purchasing officers are the Prevention of Corruption Acts of 1898 and 1906. These Acts govern the award of penalties where officers and members are found to have accepted remuneration or other gifts from suppliers as a result of their office. There is a presumption of guilt which the officer or member must rebut if it is demonstrated that he has received a gift or other consideration during the course of his duties. Similarly, if a works contractor or supplier has attempted to influence the award of contract by gifts or other forms of consideration, he may be prosecuted.

ORGANISATION OF LOCAL AUTHORITY PURCHASING

The diversity of size and function of local authorities is matched by a similar diversity in the types of purchasing organisations. The functions and authority of the purchasing organisation finally adopted by individual councils varies considerably and is not to be fully explained by the size of buy or authority.

Organisation

Responsibility for purchasing may be organised under one of the following main headings:

- departmental level
- main user as joint buyer
- centralised contract-making unit
- centralised purchasing
- joint or consortia purchasing.

Each of these arrangements may be appropriate for a given type of product or project and a mixture of these methods may occur in the same authority.

Procurement at departmental level essentially means that each department buys its own requirements without reference to similar purchases by other departments in an authority. A variation of this arrangement occurs when the major using department acts as the joint buyer for selected products throughout the authority.

Some authorities have developed a 'centralised' contract-making unit for products and materials in common use with the *individual* departments purchasing goods against the central contract arrangement. A further development in some authorities is to allow a central contract-making *and* purchasing unit to be developed for common products with storage facilities and in some cases distribution systems managed by a central purchasing unit. Joint or consortium purchasing may be organised on the basis of a major local authority offering its services to adjoining authorities or as a joint arrangement between a number of authorities where the management of the consortium may be under the control of a members committee drawn from the participating authorities. Formal contractual agreements between participating authorities may or may not exist and most arrangements are on a purely voluntary basis.

Purchasing in local authorities can contain a mix of these arrangements, each employed according to the value offered, level of service and support obtained by the individual authorities.

Contract and competitive sourcing

The majority, but certainly not all, of local government contracting, particularly for revenue items, is carried out under a competitive sourcing arrangement. Contracts are let under:

(a) an *open tender system* in which all intending suppliers can participate provided they satisfy certain minimum financial and performance criteria;

(b) an *approved list system* in which the suppliers to be invited to tender have previously been checked and as a result not normally subject to any further checking for a prescribed period unless subsequent information suggest such checks would be appropriate;

(c) *call-off arrangements* whereby terms are negotiated for the supply of individual products or a list of items from specific manufacturers, wholesalers, etc.

These three main forms of contracting are used with variations by both technical service departments (works, engineers, architects) and, where established, central purchasing activities in local government. Although the buyers make recommendations as to the suppliers to be invited, the dispatch and evaluation of tenders is controlled by a separate contract section and usually involve a sealed tender box procedure closely defined by a local authorities Tenders and Contracts Codes of Practice. These Codes, in addition to laying down the levels of authority to commit the council and the need or otherwise to seek competitive contracts, cover such items as 'fair wages clauses', i.e. wages established for the trade or industry in the district, equal opportunities, protection of home workers and other conditions designed to ensure that wages paid and working conditions are 'fair' in relation to similar employers in the neighbourhood and unfair discrimination of an ethnic or sexual character does not take place in the company.

Approved list arrangements

In contrast to the open tender list, most local authorities operate approved list procedures from which companies are selected and invited to tender. The objective of the 'approved list', which is usually organised on a commodity or specialist service basis (for example, chemical supplies or coach hire services) includes:

(*a*) avoiding the necessity of repeated checks of suppliers' references, quality of work, financial standing, capacity and quality assurance facilities;

(*b*) providing other departments within an authority with approved firms should they carry out their own local contracting;

(*c*) ensuring common standards covering the requirements laid down in the authority's standing orders (for example, the payment of 'fair wages', non-discriminatory employment policies, health and safety standards etc.).

Once a company is admitted to the approved lists, and subject to reviews usually carried out not more frequently than every two or three years, these firms may be freely invited to tender for work. In many commodities and services these lists tend to be extensive and can reach 200 to 300 firms; it is not usual to refuse applications to these lists.

With certain approved lists, particularly where services to the public are involved, it is necessary to check services and equipment on a more frequent basis. For example, a coach hire company undertaking the transport of school-children must ensure that it operates only roadworthy vehicles using experienced drivers. In addition the competent and regular inspection and repair of its vehicles needs to be checked, usually on an annual basis, so as to ensure that serious accidents or disruption of the education curriculum is avoided.

Other purchasing techniques and systems

The degree of sophistication in purchasing systems varies considerably in local government and again the adoption of up-to-date systems is not necessarily a function of size. Some of the smaller authorites have installed highly professional purchasing procedures using computer-aided monitoring. There are no mandatory or statutory regulations requiring certain purchasing methods to be adopted or prescribed suppliers to be used. The criterion against which the purchasing activity is judged in local government is basically 'value for money', given compliance with standing orders and the contracts and tender procedures of the individual council. The criterion is seldom in the experience of the writer 'lowest price' without reference to life costing, technical support etc.

The purchasing systems currently in use include extensive application of computer systems covering supplier monitoring, contract performance, price and volume analyses. The size of computer systems used in purchasing vary from small stand-alone, to main frame systems with some of the larger authorities, and particularly the consortia, utilising large distributed processing systems based on mainframe installations.

The development of product specification, vendor analyses, make or buy analyses, life costing are widespread in the professionally staffed purchasing units and are of a standard which match the large international corporations. Computer-based interchange of information and requirements with suppliers, exchange of catalogue tapes and other information systems given computer compatibility are also to be found. Both single and multi-sourcing is widely practised and internal manufacturing facilities for such items as exercise books, joinery and furniture are used by some large local authorities.

Purchase research especially into major commodity price trends and product supply markets including oil, paper, building materials, vehicles etc., is also undertaken by the larger units. Where the purchasing activity is combined with warehousing and supply, the computers also control invoice clearance, item picking, distribution and the monitoring of turnover.

If the local authority purchasing activity tends to form part of the general administrative process, and particularly where purchasing is carried out at departmental level, separate budgets and budgetary control covering the purchasing activities are seldom developed; the administrative and other overhead costs are frequently not accounted for as separate items, and the true costs of these activities can be difficult to determine.

With the introduction of a central purchasing unit in the larger authorities and in local authority purchasing consortia, budgetary

461

control is widely established and, because the purchasing activity is a cost centre in its own right, all costs are identified and monitored against budget. It is essential to identify these costs as they are usually recovered from the user of the service by a 'mark-up' or an addition to the basic purchase price. The function of central purchasing particularly within local government is examined in some depth in the publication of the Chartered Institute of Public Finance and Accountancy's Finances Information Service Volume 7, 'Central Purchasing'.

GOVERNMENT AGENCIES IN LOCAL AUTHORITY PURCHASING

All local authorities in the United Kingdom are subject to the EEC directives on public contracts. They are not, unlike central government and other public buying organisations, subject to GATT regulations. For example, the EEC Regulation 77/62 (Public Supply) lays down thresholds above which it is necessary to advertise contracts in the EEC *Journal*. Tender offers received as a result of such adverts must be treated fairly and the grounds for evaluating the tender must be stated in the advert. Failure to advertise contracts falling within the scope of the directives can be the subject of investigation by the EEC Commission.

There are exceptions and exclusions in the directive. Authorities claiming the use of the exception procedure which would otherwise need to be the subject of competitive tenders are required to report annually on the value and type of contract on which the exception clauses have been invoked. The current threshold for the EEC 77/62 is 200,000 ECUs or approximately a sterling equivalent of £110,000 at the present exchange rate.

A further EEC directive 71/305 covers public works. The threshold on this directive is 1m ECUs or the sterling equivalent of £550,000.

Although both directives were designed to improve competition and to open public procurement in the European market to all competent suppliers, the directives have been singularly unsuccessful and very few contracts for local authority goods and services (supply) or building and engineering contracts (works) have been placed with European-based organisations as a result of these directives. Similarly, very few UK companies appear to have gained additional turnover as a result of these directives. There is widespread concern that by one means or another the directives are being evaded. Given general agreement that both directives are in need of substantial revision no attempt has been made to revise them since they were issued.

In July 1980 the UK central government announced a new initiative in public purchasing in which it sought to encourage all public sector purchasing bodies to use their influence in the market to maintain or improve the competitiveness of their suppliers. The government, for example, has been pursuing these policies with its own purchasing agencies, i.e. Crown Suppliers, HMSO, Ministry of Defence etc., in a programme designed to promote British standards, to reduce the proliferation of specially designed products and in an effort to improve industrial efficiency and expand exports. It seeks to encourage local authority purchasing agencies to support this programme.

The particular aspects of this policy which have major interest to local authorities include:

1 The development of 'best purchasing practices' in relation to suppliers. These practices would include a closer user/supplier dialogue, earlier details of future requirements and support for product and process innovation.
2 Specifying products in *performance* terms rather than developing detail design specifications which take no account of either industrial efficiency or the requirements of other markets. This objective also embraces the development and greater use of British standards and some of the working parties of the National Economic Development Office (NEDO) are actively pursuing this objective.
3 Developing regular 'order patterns' to allow efficient forward production planning and more material buying.
4 Debriefing unsuccessful tenderers so that they are aware of any weakness in their products in relation to local government needs, particularly if the successful tenderer is not UK-based.

The initiative seeks to obtain wider acceptance of life costing and Tero technology in determination of purchasing decisions. On more tenuous grounds it seeks to encourage public bodies to purchase 'innovatory' products which might capture overseas markets and encourages local authorities to be seen to be endorsing these products and where possible providing a 'showcase'.

In the publication 'A New General Policy for Public Purchasing', introduced by the central government in 1981, all public buyers were exhorted to apply wider 'value for money' criteria and to take into consideration the advantages of local (UK) supply and life costing when evaluating tenders. Most *professionally* organised purchasing departments in local government recognise in the New General Policy a set of principles long established and widely implemented in their departments. With so many small authorities whose aggregate spend is very significant there clearly are activities where these principles may not be fully applied.

Inter-authority co-operation

With some 10,000 individual authorities in England and Wales, many purchasing goods in quite small volumes, it will be obvious that the employment of specialist commodity buyers may not be possible. The government's White Paper in 1967 recognised the problems of joint action and commented that improvement in unit purchase prices paid and the reduction in administrative, inspection, quality assurance, product proliferation specification, distribution and inventory holding costs which joint action could provide were not being realised. The first steps in joint action as a result of the White Paper were introduced in 1970 when a central source of purchasing information was set up using the services of professional purchasing officers in local government on a voluntary basis. The formation of a Joint Advisory Committee on Local Authority Purchasing (JACLAP) sought to encourage joint action and the sharing of specialised purchasing staff and facilities between local authorities throughout the UK. JACLAP was subsequently merged with the Local Authority Management Services and Computer Committee (LAMSAC) in 1977. Currently the main LAMSAC monitors local authority purchasing at policy level and although it has no executive authority over individual councils it can and does encourage joint action. It is supported and advised by a panel comprising of purchasing officers and local authority staff of other disciplines. The purchasing panel also includes central government assessors and representatives of BSI and other bodies. Within the guidelines agreed with the main committee, LAMSAC seeks:

(*a*) to improve purchasing by the provision of guidance on good purchasing techniques and practices by the exchange of information and systems between similar authorities;

(*b*) to assist local authorities on the organisation of central and co-ordinating purchasing; and

(*c*) the definition and promotion of common product specifications and the development of new specifications suitable for local authority needs in conjunction with British Standards Institution, central government and other bodies.

Forms of joint consortia purchasing arrangements now cover most areas of England and Wales and major areas of Scotland. These consortia may be based on the main county councils and their supplies organisations, for example, Kent, Essex, or Leicestershire; they may be joint undertakings where independent councils agree to consort, for example, the Yorkshire Purchasing Organisation. Others are based on the metropolitan areas and include the Greater London Council (GLC), City of Liverpool and similar metropolitan supplies organisations.

Naturally, the commodities which form the major turnovers of these purchasing consortia consist of items in common use, frequently to a common specification. Joint arrangements and consortia tend to predominate therefore in the purchase and supply of educational materials, supplies for social services, building, clothing, oil, food, general textiles, cleaning materials and similar commodities where the combination of buying skill and market knowledge is allied with common product specifications matched to the requirements of participating authorities. These consortia also undertake quality assurance and testing products and may offer design and installation facilities. Some consortia cover the purchase of a detailed range of the common commodities described above. Still others specialise in a restricted range, for example, petroleum products, furniture etc.

Most, certainly not all, purchasing consortia also provide warehousing and distribution (supply) facilities. Whilst in theory the supply of the range of commodities quoted above could be delivered

465

by private contractors, in practice there is limited competition from the private sector for a number of reasons.

For example, participating authorities frequently wish to keep their user point inventories at a minimum and therefore demand frequent deliveries to small stores of a wide range of products in small quantities without minimum order surcharges. Many of these products are special to local authorities and may be unique to particular local authorities. The inter-authority consortia – and indeed some central purchasing departments within individual authorities – not only meet these requirements for widely dissimilar products in a single delivery at extremely competitive prices: many provide specially tailored ordering documents, computer billing and other systems compatible with the individual local authorities data processing needs. These services provide substantial administrative economies.

The consortia may comprise a joint management committee of members of the participating authorities. Most operate joint consultative councils at officer level in which the educationalists, trade unions, finance and other staffs of the participating authorities can identify product, supply or other administrative problems, suggest new commodities and services for joint action and can deal with any local difficulties raised by the user.

FURTHER READING

Local Government Act, 1972, HMSO.
London Government Act, 1963, HMSO.
Model Standing Orders (Contracts), HMSO.
Local Government (Goods and Services) Act, 1970, HMSO, and Statutory Instruments.
Completion Acts, 1980, HMSO.
The Public Bodies Corrupt Practices Act, 1889.
The Prevention of Corruption Act, 1906.
CIPFA Financial Information Service No. 7, 'Central Purchasing'.
'A new General Policy for Public Purchasing', Report Committee of Accounts, 1981-2, HMSO.
'Public Purchasing and Industrial Efficiency', 1967, HMSO.
Baily and Farmer, *Purchasing Principles and Management,* 4th ed., Pitman, 1982.

24

Purchasing for retail organisations

Richard Ford

The retailer is the last link in the distributive chain before the consumer. The retailer can be on the high street, can sell by mail order or "off-the-page", out-of-town, neighbourhood corner shop, from a market stall, or from a big department store. No one needs reminding that Marks & Spencer started as the Penny Bazaar. The product can be goods or services: services of insurance, estate agency, building society, banking etc; and goods, classically separated as food or non-food.

In the UK over the last ten years, there has been a progressive shift of business towards multiple retailers, not just the big food chains – Sainsburys, Tesco, Waitrose and mixed food/non-food hypermarkets – but also clothing, footwear and other specialist retailers. Many chains of shoe shops are ultimately controlled by one group, and several of the TV rental companies – Radio Rentals, DER, Multibroadcast – are owned by one group, Thorn.

This progressive concentration of ownership and of volume of trade comes as no accident, but is as a result of:

(*a*) well-managed companies finding the correct mixture of ambition and efficiency, and developing

(*b*) the buying power which stems from higher volumes.

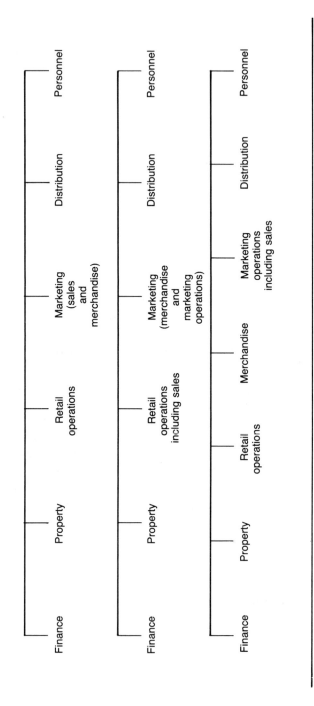

Figure 24.1 Organisation options at board level

PURCHASING ORGANISATION

Organisation and management are covered elsewhere in this book, but just what and who are the retail buyers and how are they organised?

At board level, at the top of an organisation will be director(s) of marketing. Whether the title be marketing, sales or merchandise (buying) will depend much on the company's interpretation of those words. Opinions do differ, but classically the options would be divided as shown in Figure 24.1. Of course, organisations and personalities differ as do opinions. Property, distribution and personnel functions do not always hold board appointments, and on occasion are performed as a main group service to its subsidiaries. In some cases the retail operations – shop management – hold responsibility for sales. Purchasing (or merchandise) invariably holds a board appointment in some guise, and in many cases is responsible also for warehousing and distribution of the goods it has purchased.

The most simple definition of retailing is in two parts:

(*a*) making the most efficient use of sales area and
(*b*) just buying goods and selling them profitably.

However it is stated, the retail organisation must buy its goods efficiently and purchasing must be central to its success.

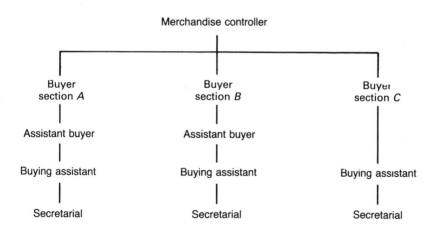

Figure 24.2 Organisation options of buying department

469

Titles vary also down the line and below board level there may be merchandise (buying) departments such as those shown in Figure 24.2.

The progression of an individual from assistant buyer will come from experience, efficiency and ability. Features of the incumbents and most importantly of candidates at recruitment will be:

- numeracy
- literacy
- creativity
- quick wittedness
- commercial acumen
- social skills.

By the time the manager has reached the rank of merchandise controller, sometimes senior buyer, he or she will be a skilled negotiator, able to deal with all manner of people, quick to spot commercial opportunities, to convey them within his own organisation, and with the ability to manage and train others to do likewise.

And one more point for clarification: there are many senior and very able lady buyers in retailing, so where 'he' is used in the discussion, please read 'he/she'.

ACCOUNTABILITY

As in other areas of responsibility, the merchandise management will be bound by and be working within the corporate plan and company policy. It seems trite to emphasise this point, but it is important to any company that its policies are fully understood, then followed. It is equally true that merchandise directors and controllers hold an ideal position to predict changes in product, demand etc., and to contribute to company policy.

What, then, of the accountability of the merchandise controllers? We see them in the three following parts: sourcing, stocking and selling.

Sourcing

To many buyers this is the most interesting part of the job. There can be an intense pleasure for the young buyer in developing an idea, arranging manufacture, and launching the product into the market and it is not unusual that a young person could have achieved just that two years or less after leaving school or university.

There are other disciplines, though, and other constraints. For example, each company will have its own hierarchy of decision making, maybe even selection committees, its rules and precedents, its standards of packaging and the quality standards which it expects to adhere to.

As regards standards and quality, then the buyer will be responsible on the company's behalf for ensuring compliance with all legal standards and special requirements of the product, its packaging, description and probably pricing.

Supplier relationships

This is a delicate and vastly important subject. It is delicate for many reasons. First, and better stated than unstated, because the buyer can be put at risk by a supplier willing to buy his favour. Whilst this may not happen frequently, it is important that every buyer is aware of the hazard and both to be, and be seen to be, entirely honest, for his own sake and for his company's. There is the fine line to draw between the business lunch, the annual diary, the Christmas bottle of Scotch to what comes next?

In addition it is important to remember that the supplier is the source of goods which the buyer and his company want to sell. On occasions the supplier will have the balance of power, stock will be limited. On occasions he will need payment quickly, or the buying company will be watching its own cash flow. There can be a thousand different scenarios.

Successful supplier relationships also necessitate well-tuned negotiation skills and personal relationships. The skill, if that be the word, to be pleasant to someone you really do not like; and the reverse – to be really difficult and to go to the brink with someone with whom you are really friendly. There is the need, too, to have the skill to negotiate at all levels of seniority and the skills to handle these situations and these people in different social circumstances and in different cultures.

The reality of dealings between supplier and buyer embraces five elements. Their 'deals' include:

- the product
- the price
- payment terms
- delivery and distribution
- advertising and promotion.

The product With a new or scarce product which is successful the supplier will have the balance of power. In other cases the buyer may himself have developed the idea, found a manufacturing source and agreed the product specification. Clearly there are many other aspects relating to the product and we will revert to this topic.

The price This is often the key point of negotiation, especially with a commodity product. It is key to the buyer, because one of his principal accountabilities will be gross margin, the percentage profit between his buying and selling prices.

Having located a product and agreed a price the buyer is left with at least three further important questions.

Payment terms Other things being equal, cash must be better in your own bank than the other man's. This simple truth is brought into question when a discount is offered for early settlement, and at a rate of greater benefit than the investment income. It is also under question when either buyer or seller cannot easily part with his cash. Cash flow may be difficult, or there may be a 'false' position for a company's year-end balance sheet.

Delivery and distribution Knowledge of the costs of warehousing and of distribution is becoming better understood by buyers. Company policy may dictate the desirability of delivery to individual shops or to regional/central warehouses or redistribution centres. It is important that the buyer has detailed knowledge of these costs in order that he can calculate whether the mix of buying price, payment terms and delivery terms is the optimum in a particular circumstance.

This topic is also of particular importance in the management of imported merchandise, for here the buyer's knowledge must include costs of shipping – sea, sea-air, road, rail, insurance, UK freight and pertinent duty rates.

Advertising and promotion Retailers have become almost the biggest buyers of media advertising and few have spent their own money in doing so. A small number of concerns, e.g. Marks & Spencer, hardly advertise at all and some others claim not to use anyone else's money. The majority of retailers, however, acquire funds to cover their A & P (advertising and promotion) from their suppliers. Many suppliers have come to expect this, and in all probability try to cost it into the buying price. Others, however, see product, price A & P etc., as having quite separate budgets, and the skilled buyer will seek to obtain maximum revenue from each source. Nevertheless, as with all forms of buying it is necessary to consider the whole mix – product, price, payment etc. Still, the buyer will look for straight media money, merchandising costs, local promotion payments, prizes for staff competitions, annual/quarterly overriding discounts, and many other features which will be beneficial to the buyer.

Despite all these factors the most skilled negotiator will have failed if he does not purchase the right product.

The shrinking world

The commercial world is no longer bound by Chesterfield and Canterbury, and no retail buyer will be able fully to explore his sources without knowledge of international sourcing. This does not only involve foreign travel but also seeing all pertinent foreign sales persons who wish to visit the UK, of making sure that the right ones do, and of making better arrangements than competitors.

Travel of course can be expensive, thus it is important to plan overseas trips carefully. Whilst travel can be exciting, it is important not to buy from that good source in Timbuctoo because the trip is attractive or because they have the most wonderful local cuisine, or wine. And if it can be avoided, do not make source decisions until you are back in the more objective setting of your office. It is good to make quick decisions, and it may be necessary from time to time. Nevertheless they will usually be better decisions, particularly when you have discussed the issues with knowledgeable colleagues, if the decision process takes a little longer.

As the company becomes a bigger importer, it will face the question of whether to establish offices in certain countries, to use agents, or to send buyers abroad regularly. Like it or not, there will be products which are not available in the UK, and the source countries themselves will change as time goes on. It is an expensive business to purchase from overseas but it is an integral part of the sourcing task in the retail world.

Inventory

Stock control is the more dreary part, the grammar of the buying function. After the glamour – for so it can be – of developing a product, employing the designer, finding the factory, negotiating the price, travelling the world and getting the advertising money; after all that, there is the necessity to consider stock control.

In some organisations this function is delegated to other departments of the company, but in the majority the buyer will have the stock control responsibility. He will be accountable for the stock held by the company, be it in the shops, in any central warehouse unit or in transit. This inventory which, of course, is the company's working capital is likely at most times to be the company's biggest investment. It is a heavy responsibility.

It is in controlling inventory that management information is the most vital, and where the more modern computer systems are of greatest value. It is vital to have details of sales and of stocks – shop and warehouse; to have them by volume and by value; and to have them as quickly as possible. EPOS (electronic point of sale) systems are becoming less expensive and more essential in reducing delays in information. The best decisions are made with the highest level of management information.

Distribution of stocks

There are two distinct levels of stock control. One is at individual shop level, ensuring the optimum volume stockholding to maximise sales potential. This is not easy, even with the most sophisticated EPOS aids. The weather can affect shopping patterns, seasonal uptake may vary and fashions may or may not be accepted by the consumer and nothing will sell unless the buying public want it and it is there at that time. Distribution of valid quantities must be in-store and the buyer must ensure effective merchandising support.

At the other level, the buyer will be accountable for the

company's total stockholding and commitment: holding reserves in stock, at factory, or just production capacity, and for maximising sales opportunities. There is also the fact that the most sophisticated analytical systems can never replace what might be called the buyer's gamble. Because there are so many variables he can seldom get it all right. Nevertheless, he has to consider how he can have exactly the right additional stock for what proves to be a winner and how he can select the right time to stop purchasing when a line is in decline. He can never guarantee results, but he must make maximum use of all management information, work within company policies, and must aim to make decisions with the minimum risk having in mind the profit opportunity.

Selling

Retailing is all about selling. This chapter has been concerned with the buyer's position, and he will be accountable for the merchandise range, for the product, its stock level, the profit margin, gross profit, advertising and. sales. Of course, everyone else is also concerned about sales. For example, the shop manager will be targeted to increase his sales and the advertising manager will take credit for his contribution, but when it comes to the level of a product line, or a whole category, then the buyer is accountable.

Nearer the customer

The retail buyer has one great privilege, one advantage in that he sees almost at first hand how the customer is behaving. He will naturally try to 'second guess' his competitors, and to second-guess his suppliers and even customers – by providing early data on the product and the price that his experience indicates. In this his decision making involves risk and it is necessary for him to call upon all his creative skills.

Firsthand knowledge of customer behaviour enables the buyer not just to be creative but to be reactive to the trends which he perceives. The better the quality of the management information and the faster it is in his hands, the more time he will have to react.

Marketing man

Since he has accountability for product sales the buyer has to use all the marketing tools available to him. Organisation structures may differ and show that although the advertising manager, or the promotions manager are on different lines of management, they will still need to be involved. The buyer will need, within company policy, to establish the optimum level of promotion, of PR, of media advertising, the best displays, point-of-sale material and merchandising. It is unlikely that he will be directly responsible for these functions, but he will need sufficient knowledge of marketing 'in-the-round' to invoke the most appropriate support.

Pricing

This is the most fundamental marketing tool of all. As far as the buyer is concerned, in most cases it is probable that he will be responsible for the retail prices of his products. (Clearly he could not be accountable for gross profit margin unless he can control both cost and selling prices.) He will of course be guided by company policies on pricing and competitive posture, but he will face three pressures:

- the buying price/package,
- the company margin requirement, and
- the customer's reaction.

On a commodity, or non-fashion product, most buyers with experience will know the effect of retail price fluctuations. And it is not just a question of price reductions; there will be many occasions when he will wish to raise prices, for instance when there is a shortage of stock and (so long as he does not lose credibility with customers) he can afford to extend his margins.

EVALUATION

A buyer's performance will be measured against the three accountabilities described above, and he will have agreed forecasts and/or targets with management.

The norm will be an annual forecast of which the main elements will be

(*a*)   sales – volume and value;
(*b*)   gross profit – volume and percentage margin;
(*c*)   stockholding – within agreed limits;
(*d*)   other benefits – advertising revenue, settlement terms;
(*e*)   expenses – departmental, travel etc.

This will be the framework, but fundamentally the simple definition of retailing is the use of space, in which to buy and sell. None of the theories will work if the *product* is not what customers want to buy. Consequently the role of the buyer in selecting and sourcing the right merchandise is vital to the success of the retail organisation. In this short chapter it has been possible only to provide the reader with some indication of the key features of that role. Nonetheless it will be seen to be a challenging, exciting, though frustrating task.

25

Purchasing for the aerospace industry

Alan Turner and Martin Steer

The procurement cycle in the aerospace business is typical of many companies. It starts with the centralised capture of purchase requirements for production parts, spares, subcontract manufacture and items required to support the factories. Having confirmed the purchase authority and checked stockholdings, a purchase requisition is placed in the appropriate buyer's work queue. The buyer then selects a supplier, negotiates the price and contractual terms and formally places the order. Deliveries can then be progressed, receipts registered and the parts tracked through inspection and test to the designated store.

The aerospace industry has a number of characteristics which result in rather more complications than usual in specifying the requirement for a system:

1 Extensive delivery schedules result in long-life orders and a high workload maintaining and progressing against both production and contractual schedules.
2 Accounting arrangements have to cater for Ministry of Defence (MOD) contracting requirements as well as various export contracts. Consequently, each purchase order item may relate to several accounting codes and this complicates the calculation of financial commitment to each contract.
3 Pricing arrangements which involve multiple currencies and price escalation.

4 Invoice release arrangements which involve progress payments, limited liabilities, supply of free-issue components and supplier prefunding.
5 Changing programmes and design standards are a feature of high technology products and result in a high rate of order amendments.
6 Parts may be delivered to more than one factory and are also delivered direct to the customer or a collaborative partner's factory.
7 Many items require acceptance testing on delivery; the location of these items needs to be tracked whilst on site, and significant numbers are returned to the supplier for repair or modification.
8 Stocks of the same part may be held in different stores and at times are reserved for particular aircraft or contracts. Nevertheless, it is necessary to determine free stock, transfer stock costs and establish the ownership of stock.

The Warton Division of British Aerospace is a typical aircraft manufacturing unit. It operates on three sites and places some 250,000 orders per year, whilst provisioning for 100,000 stock bins and 100,000 non-stored items. In order to function efficiently, an on-line procurement system is highly desirable, and the following describes the development of such a system during the period 1976 to 1983 by the supplies department at Warton.

BACKGROUND TO THE PROJECT

The development of the project commenced in 1976 when it became obvious that the existing system was not capable of coping with the increased volume or complication of the trinational Tornado programme (see Figure 25.1).

Up to that time, systems had been traditionally designed to handle the peculiarities of a particular aircraft programme. They did not assist or monitor the progress of the buying activity and were geared to progressing the order only after it had been placed. They were batch systems capturing data by means of paper tape or

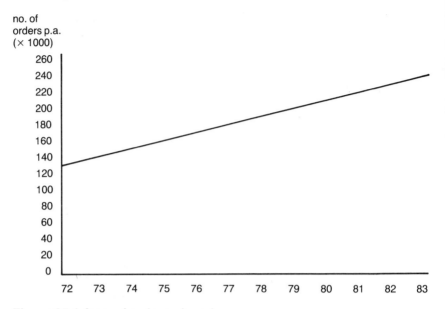

Figure 25.1 Annual orders placed

punched card and therefore involved tedious error correction the following day.

To improve the way in which tasks were handled by the supply department it was decided that a totally new on-line system should be introduced which would span the activities of collecting purchase requirements, buying and stock recording. It was recognised that this would be a large system and expensive both in cost and time. The first step therefore was to see whether an existing software package which covered these major functions was on the market. An American system approximated to the requirement and a feasibility study was completed by early 1977.

The conclusion of the study was that the cost of adapting the package would not be significantly less than that of developing a new system which more exactly matched Warton's requirements. Consequently it was decided to develop a tailor-made system.

THE SYSTEM

The feasibility study was not wasted however, in that it focused attention on fundamental objectives. The data processing specifications which emerged required:

1 A totally on-line system with a file security/recovery facility so that the user would never be required to re-enter data in the event of computer operation problems, i.e. it was not necessary to prepare or retain records of specialist data preparation sheets – indeed data entry could very often be direct from existing factory paperwork.

2 VDU terminals to be installed in each buying section and to be regarded as any other piece of office furniture, operated by both buyer and clerk, i.e. no specialist data preparation section.

3 A system which generates microfiche archives of all key transactions.

4 A test copy of the system was to be used both for testing new software before acceptance for production and as a staff training aid, where the user could practise and overcome any fear of 'corrupting files' whilst learning a new skill.

5 The system design should be flexible enough to accommodate all Warton Division purchase orders including all aircraft projects, commercial items, sub contracts, spares etc.

The user specification included progressive building up of files of information which supported tasks such as:

– maintaining a computerised register of all requirements and progressing outstanding actions against each buyer;
– printing draft copies of orders, if required, and the multi-copy formal orders;
– progressing imminent and overdue orders;
– monitoring total and outstanding financial commitment;
– recording deliveries and acknowledging completion of non-delivered items; printing receipt paperwork;
– reconciling invoices, deliveries and orders and releasing invoices for payment;
– monitoring stockholding usage patterns and ensuring full visibility of stock and on-order assets.

It was decided that the system should be based on a 'mini' computer, which was seen at that time (1977) as the best way of developing business systems. The intention was that a network of distributed processors would be gradually built up within the company. Further, it was decided that rather than use their own limited programming resources on such a major project, the system design and programming would be subcontracted.

A software house was selected and the system was named ORION (ordering, receiving and inventory on-line). A management team was set up which comprised a senior BAe user and a senior programming consultant. Each acted as a central point for clearing problems and generally co-ordinating the project. Within BAe, a team of users met regularly and acted as representatives for the different, and sometimes conflicting, groups and departments. The software house fielded a small team of on-site representatives during the specification stage. The actual coding and program testing was undertaken at the subcontractor's premises. When the programmers were satisfied, each major suite of programs was formally delivered and supply then conducted detailed user trials on the test system.

COMPUTER FACILITIES REQUIRED

The production system was estimated to need two, possibly three, DEC PDP 1170 computers, each of 1½ Mb CPU plus 600 Mb of disk storage and two magnetic tape drives for security back-up. Two 900 line per minute printers would be needed for printing orders and reports. In addition, a teleprocessing network capable of managing up to 150 local VDUs and printers was required. The network had to be capable of not only linking the three divisional sites but also the other BAe divisions and partner companies in Europe.

IMPLEMENTATION PROGRAMME

By the time the selection and feasibility stage had reached a satisfactory conclusion, some two years had elapsed (1978) and it was evident that, taking into account relative priorities of the major tasks and the problems of project management, a phased installation was sensible.

Phase 1

The Tornado programme was now under way and an in-service provisioning system was required to deal with the initial requirement for approximately 30,000 items, none of which was fitted by BAe on the production lines, but were required for ex-supplier delivery to the UK, German and Italian air forces. The requirements for this 'auto spares' sub-system were to be transferred daily on magnetic tape from the IBM mainframe divisional spares department order book system. This phase of the system was put into operation in Spring 1980.

Phase 2

The next priority was to develop a requisition, purchasing and receiving sub-system which would operate on aircraft production line requirements. The plan was to commence with the Tornado aircraft items (implemented Autumn 1980) and progressively expand through all aircraft projects over the course of the next two years. In general, the policy was to raise new orders for selected parts of the business from a given date, but not to transfer the backlog of thousands of existing orders. By the end of 1982, virtually all aircraft orders were on the system and the outstanding balance of the small percentage of long-life orders were then cancelled and reinstated on the new system.

Phase 3

This involved extending the system to include the peculiarities of the subcontract and commercial ordering areas. As with autospares, a magnetic tape link with the mainframe factory work in progress system was to load subcontract purchase requisitions. Work on this commenced early in 1983 and the transfer was expected to be completed during 1984.

Phase 4

As can be seen in phases 1-3, the initial priorities were to develop a multi-project system, up to and including the receiving bay. The progressing and provisioning sections spend considerable time tracking goods through the inspection, test and stores departments on the three factory sites, also at partner companies' factories, and when they are returned to the supplier for repair. This phase of the project was deferred because a mainframe stock system for the production stores already existed. A temporary batch system interface was established which linked ORION to the stock system and produced a combined monthly report of order/stock assets. In the meantime the plan to develop an on-line PDP/ORION bought-out stock system has changed. BAe Aircraft Group has the task of developing a combined bought-out/factory-made stock system to operate at all divisions. In 1983, therefore, a daily transfer of stock data into ORION via magnetic tape was established. ORION, therefore, now effectively meets the objective of displaying require-ments, orders and stock on-line. Figure 25.2 summarises progress.

SCOPE OF SYSTEM

The present scope of the system is best described in Figure 25.3. Requirements are entered via magnetic tape for Tornado break-down spares and subcontracted work. Other requirements are entered by VDU and vetted on-line. The system progresses these requirements through the buyer work queue, ordering, progressing, receiving and into the stock record. Key documents such as purchase orders and goods receipt dockets, and a variety of action, exception and selective retrievals are printed. These are normally printed in the computer room overnight but urgent orders can be printed on-line in the supply office. There are a wide variety of on-line enquiries and the system generates a number of microfiche archives and statistical analyses.

At present there are over 50 VDUs and 15 local printers installed in various offices. The system supports over 150 on-line transactions and over 100 printed reports. The present monthly transaction rate is 150,000.

SOME OF THE PROBLEMS

Especially in the early development days, there was inevitably a
conflict of opinion between user and programmer as to how much of
the existing and varied procedures should be programmed into the
system and how much individual groups should change and conform
to a standardised discipline. Despite strenuous attempts to document requirements in detail, the early user trials discovered quite
large numbers of program 'bugs'. Both supply and the software

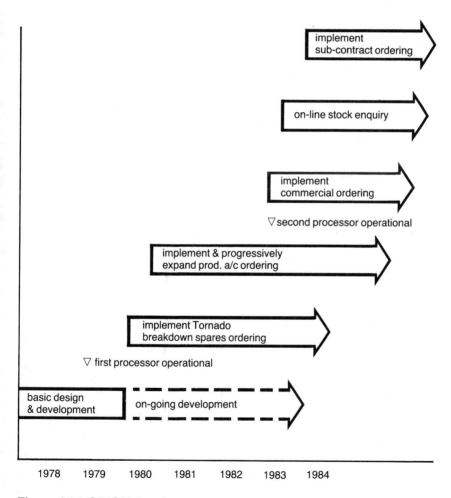

Figure 25.2 ORION development programme

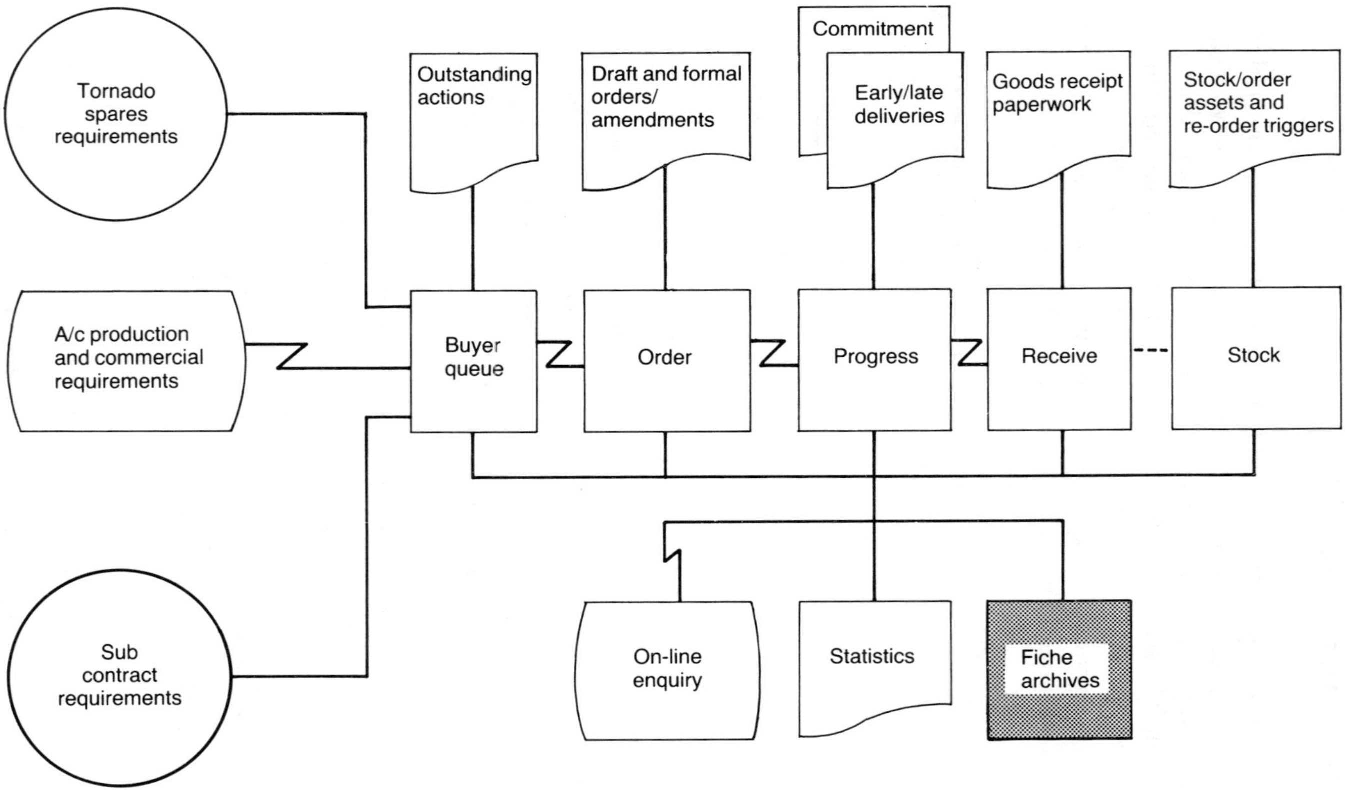

Figure 25.3 Scope of the system

house learned to understand each other's needs and the quality of specifications and programs progressively improved.

Initially the main problem with the production system was system response time. Some of the high transaction volume programs required tuning. Later on, due to a rearrangement of the computer room, there was a delay in installing the second processor, the result being that the first processor was overloaded and consequently response times increased again. The major residual problem with the system is the recovery technique, which irrespective of whether the system is out of commission for operator, software or hardware reasons, takes too long to rebuild the files – the system is very much a part of the day-to-day operation and much frustration builds up if the user cannot gain access to *his* files. It must be remembered however that the user now takes the improvements gained by the new system for granted and, human nature being what it is, soon forgets the problems of the 'old days.'

With regard to staff training, it was decided at an early stage that this should take place as a programme of progressive expansion through the various buying groups. It was felt that extensive user system manuals would not be read or adequately maintained and that the best way was to allow sections to train 'live' on the test system where mistakes did not matter. In addition, for those users who only operate a VDU occasionally, the system is designed to operate via a series of menu screens which guide the user to the correct screen. He can, of course, enter the transaction directly if he wishes. Over a period of time, operating knowledge has built up and succeeding sections have benefited by this process.

The change in style of day-to-day working, the gradual replacement of manual records and paperwork with VDU enquiries, and the building up of confidence all required the passage of time and, of course, some persistence on the part of management. For some two years, the department operated a dual system of new orders being raised via ORION whilst old orders continued to be progressed, amended and delivered on the old system. This had the effect of making change from old to new procedures more difficult and the system could not produce the much needed management summaries, statistics and archives for a whole project or buying section. There is often a dilemma as to whether it is easier and cheaper for a buyer to enter data relatively slowly at a VDU or to annotate paperwork so that a higher speed clerical assistant can enter data on his behalf. The balance of this division of work between buyer and clerk continues to be tuned and varies between groups.

Departmental policy is that the purchase order should be a total single statement of BAe requirements and commercial conditions. As a consequence of this there are occasions when it is tedious to prepare extensive clauses and contractual conditions on the face of the order. There is a similar problem maintaining extensive requirement, contractual and promise schedules and the present technique is overcomplex.

At the outset, it was decided to adopt a style of operation whereby the system generated a preformatted screen layout for a selected transaction and the operator entered data into the appropriate fields. In certain areas, for example where there are a number of simple options, a 'question and answer' style is now being considered.

In summary therefore, such working, as opposed to monitoring, systems are more than an efficient data processing arrangement. They require a change in style, culture and attitude. Provided flexibility is designed into the system and persistent management is applied, people will gradually adjust to find the most convenient and cost effective way of working. The most essential need is to ensure that the system captures all the data as efficiently as possible. The analyses and displays can be developed and modified in the light of experience.

SYSTEM ADVANTAGES

What progress has been made? In a word, the answer is visibility. The number of people requiring information about a given part or order extends across the three sites of the division. Information can now easily be obtained by authorised personnel using VDUs and microfiche distributed around the division. Answers are available to questions such as:

- What orders are outstanding for a given part, when will the next deliveries be and what have we received already?

- Are there any outstanding purchase requisitions in the buyer queue and when are they likely to be ordered?
- What is the current stock, in which store, at what rate is it being consumed, and therefore, taking into account both stock and orders, how many period assets do we have?
- What is the value of the stock?
- What is the total value committed and how much is outstanding for a particular project, supplier, contract or store?

Management makes an endlessly variable series of demands. In the past this required extensive clerical effort. Information is now available, or more easily derivable, in the form of exception reports, summaries and statistics. The policy with new projects has been to insist that 100 per cent of orders are covered by the system and greater demands are now being placed as it is realised that the system is capable of providing a total history.

The introduction of the system has brought some of the traditional procedures into question and has resulted in rationalisation and simplification. The system serves the buyer in that it brings problems to his attention in order of priority, and also serves as his conscience since it relentlessly reminds him of outstanding actions which in the past were lost or forgotten.

Again, the key ingredient, not only with the system but within the working department is flexibility and open mindedness.

THE FUTURE

British Aircraft Group comprises a number of divisions/factories which are engaged in the manufacture of both civil and military aircraft. Collectively, they place in excess of 600,000 orders per year. The formation of British Aerospace in 1977 brought together British Aircraft Corporation and Hawker Siddeley Aviation which in themselves comprised a number of old established aircraft companies. To date therefore, because of the evolution of the company, the different cultures and the different commercial climates in which they operate, various divisions have developed and installed computer systems to support the purchase organisation with differing degrees of success. Each division is aware of the strengths and shortcomings of their systems and naturally future planning included significant further development and enhancement.

In order to consolidate this experience and ensure minimum cost and duplication of effort, the Group has decided that a common materials management system will be developed which can be used by all divisions. The system should take full advantage of rapidly expanding computer-processing capabilities.

The most successful of the last generation systems have brought computer terminals into the daily activities of the purchasing department. Real time processing and rapid enquiry has lead the way to foreground systems where the user interacts directly with the system, rather than background monitoring systems indirectly fed by DP specialists. Computer technology has developed so that systems can become fully interwoven with office and management procedure and practice. The system design for the next decade needs to be able to react to commercial and organisational changes, remain flexible at all levels and yet impose constraints where management feel it appropriate.

Today, the majority of data entered into the on-line updates is via a VDU. By linking materials management systems with production planning and engineering systems, purchase requirements will be automatically transferred into the provisioning function with consequent savings in time and improvement in consistency. Similarly, electronic links with kitting systems will decimate the tremendous volume of stock issue transactions. By printing bar or magnetic codes onto goods receipt paperwork, for example, location tracking and recording inspection results will be reduced to a formality. Optical character readers may be used to capture extensive contractual verbage and word processors will allow this to be edited before being incorporated into the purchase order. In short, by interlinking computer systems and selecting appropriate equipment, the cost of data capture can be substantially reduced and the work pattern of the office will change as a consequence.

This next stage should go further than simply improve data capture however. Data becomes information when it can be manipulated directly by the user. In this context the user may be the material controller, the buyer, the purchasing manager or a director. Only when this stage is reached will a system design be seen to be flexible through the eyes of such users. Computer tools now allow the user to develop on-line enquiries, selective reports and summary statistics without becoming computer programmers. Should the business, the problem or the questions change tomorrow, then the user should be free to amend his enquiries and reports and so return to being fully in control of, and accountable for, his actions. Where appropriate, data can be stripped off mainframe divisional files into departmental or personal computers for local temporary storage, consolidation and possible modelling.

Therefore this next stage will comprise specialist data capture and file maintenance programs where performance, integrity and standardisation remain important. There will be a migration of information processing capability out of the DP department and directly into the hands of the user. The electronic office, interlinked with such systems, will reduce paperwork and filing. Beyond this, electronic linking with suppliers and the development of knowledge-based systems with inbuilt commercial and managerial expertise will result in a purchasing department of the 1990s radically different from that of today.

26

Purchasing for the construction industry

Peter Harris

The successful performance of construction work depends heavily on a large supplies industry. To some manufacturers of building materials and components it offers a sole outlet for their products. To many others a major portion of their turnover is dependant upon new construction work.

This is a widely diversified industry that calls for experienced and professional buyers with special skills. They are required to provide an important service to a host of other specialists and tradesmen who may be working in extremely difficult and trying circumstances.

PROBLEMS WITHIN THE INDUSTRY

The construction industry faces many challenges not least of which is the environment in which the majority of projects are constructed. It should be remembered that nearly every project is different from the last. Basic skills are constant but must be readily adapted. Personnel and materials vary from place to place.

Others areas of particular difference from the normal production facility are:

1 Most sites are 'greenfield' sites.
2 A large proportion of sites are in difficult geographical locations or are difficult because of the close proximity of other buildings and roads.

3 Almost every operation on site is affected by weather which may be good or bad.
4 Sites may spread over large areas.
5 Sites generally exist for a very short time.
6 The main method of winning contracts is for the lowest price to be the most successful.
7 Material management techniques become most important to maintain production with restricted stocks and stocking area.
8 Tenders become contracts in a very short time and require cost effective purchasing immediately.

The value of construction projects can vary from a few hundred to several million pounds. In order to provide legal and contractual security for the client and the contractor they enter into an appropriate form of contract. The type of construction project will determine the terms under which this contract will be formed as there are several different types in use within the industry. Among the principal contracts in general use are:

1 *Standard form of building contract issued by the Joint Contracts Tribunal* – this applies to building contracts with variations to suit particular clients and types of projects.
2 *General conditions of government contracts for building and civil engineering works,* known as CCC/WORKS/1 (Edition 9) – generally used by central or local government and public utilities, such as the National Coal Board, together with some amendments and additions to suit particular types of work.
3 *Institution of Civil Engineers conditions of contract* – used for all works of civil engineering such as water works, sea defence contracts, road and bridge works and sewer reconstruction. Many of the larger construction companies and some public authorities such as the Central Electricity Generating Board produce their own forms of contract or variations on those standard conditions already available.

Most of the contract conditions follow similar patterns, but it is important when dealing with subcontractors to make them aware of the conditions under which they are to submit their offers. When completing the order documentation procedure it will be necessary to ensure that the subcontracts carefully impose upon the subcontractors the same conditions that are contained in the main contract.

The need to make this clear at the tender stage will therefore be apparent.

CONSTRUCTION PURCHASING OFFICERS

Purchasing in construction means the spending of money to procure materials, goods and subcontracts to support production.

Whether this operation is carried out in a centralised or decentralised situation is the subject of considerable debate, but the location does not alter the dimension of the duty.

The purchasing officer in construction companies may have a variety of functions which contribute to the profitability of their respective companies. In smaller companies, for instance, not only will all materials and subcontracts come under the umbrella but also transport, construction plant hire, scaffold purchase and hire, together with procurement of temporary materials, such as piling and steelwork for use in the construction of the project. The last item will require close liaison with the design department to make the best use of available materials and produce the most cost effective solution. Stores and stock control may also be added to the more traditional purchasing functions.

In larger companies many of these operations will be big enough to become solely defined areas of responsibility not necessarily undertaken by purchasing staff. The purchasing officer is then solely responsible for the procurement of materials and subcontracts. This again may be divided into types of material or particular projects.

The skills required for construction purchasing are more than just the requirements of the purchasing profession.

The Institute of Purchasing and Supply diploma will have supplied the commercial expertise, and construction endorsements provide the basic understanding of building construction and services. Many of those currently working in the profession follow several avenues of education before moving into purchasing. Surveying is one such course sometimes followed in the early years, as are building technician courses by The Chartered Institute of Building.

All of these academic requirements will be required of the construction buyer. Above all he must be able to exercise self control and to cope with the extreme frustration that working in the industry produces. To be truly effective he must know and understand the construction process.

THE TRADITIONAL METHOD OF SECURING CONTRACTS

The majority of major construction projects follow the traditional procedure outlined below:

1 The client briefs a professional engineer, architect or surveyor or a team of all three as to his requirements.
2 This team then prepares suitable designs and details and draws up a tender document based on one of a series of documents based on one of a series of conditions of contract previously referred to.
3 The client and/or the team prepares a suitable list of prequalified contractors from which usually between six and ten companies will be invited to tender.
4 Tenders are received by the client and the lowest price is accepted provided nothing has changed to alter the credibility of the contractor.
5 The team then supervise the construction process in accordance with specification and agree the contractor's accounts.

Management contracting is another form of contract which has increased ten-fold over the past five years from about £50 million of work let under the system in 1978 to about £500 million in 1983. By definition management contractors do not build anything. Their role is to control and organise other firms that do. Suitable contractors are invited to put forward their ideas after having received outline details of the project and its problems. They also put forward suggested teams for carrying through the project. Management teams are based around the project manager and his team will include purchasing staff. The whole team are collectively assessed by the architect, or engineering partnership, and possibly the client at an interview. The contractor is awarded the contract on either a fixed or variable percentage fee of the contract value.

Target price or maximum price contracts are also occasionally used. Under this system a contractor negotiates a target price for a project and exposes his accounts to the client. This type of contract poses particular purchasing problems as almost every item used on the contract will need approval from the client before proceeding to order.

Irrespective of the type of contract, it is at the pre-tender stage that purchasing should begin. However, it highlights one of the differences from the other industries. With most construction projects 60-70 per cent of costs are materials and subcontractors. Therefore it follows that, to obtain the contract, every effort must be made to get these prices right. In so doing the element of risk of any project is reduced to an acceptable level.

It is at this stage that the construction buyer starts to follow a pattern not similar to other industries. The difference is that more often than not there will be no contract to complete the purchasing process he is about to commence.

SOURCING SUPPLIES AND SUBCONTRACTORS TO MEET TENDER DEADLINES

In order to be competitive, construction companies must make the best use of their purchasing power. For the buyers to derive the maximum job satisfaction and perform to the best of their ability it is preferable that they are involved at the tender stage.

Project details generally arrive in tenderer's offices complete with drawings, bills of quantities, specification and details of expected completion times. In general this information is incomplete and leaves a lot to the imagination, experience and good sense of the reader. Others will arrive with drawings only or outline specification details only.

The type of project will affect the quality and quantity of the information given. In the case of buildings, the above ground details will generally be considerably better than the foundation details. Civil engineering projects are, by their general nature, more difficult to identify and therefore subject to considerable variation.

Irrespective of the amount of information given, lists giving quantities of materials and types of subcontractors required must be formulated. This is commonly known as the 'take off'. The responsibility for performing this task varies with each company but, should the buyer not carry out the take off, it is important that he/she at least has a close liaison with the estimator so that he is able to apply commercial requirements to the details being given.

The size and complexity of the proposed project will be the prime consideration of the buyer on receipt of the take off.

He must consider particularly:

(*a*)   location of the project;
(*b*)   deadline for return of quotations and tenders;
(*c*)   quantity of the main materials;
(*d*)   numbers and types of subcontractors.

Whether or not the deadline for return of quotations is reasonable will be influenced very much by the location of the project. Above all, the necessity to provide to the estimating department competitive prices on time is paramount, as the date for submission of bids is unlikely to be extended. Having satisfied this criteria, the identification of the key materials and subcontractors is the next phase to receive attention.

In the case of large bulk items the expected rate of deliveries must be ascertained from the estimator or tender programme in order to pursue:

(*a*)   the availability of suitable local materials;
(*b*)   the availability of any other materials which may have to be transported to site by road, rail and sea;
(*c*)   the possibility of winning suitable material within the confines of the site or in an immediately adjacent area.

Any one of these possibilities may require additional analysis and testing to determine its suitability and compliance with specification limits. All will require careful investigation, the results of which may have considerable bearing on the conclusion in the final bid analysis.

Specialist subcontractors will have to be identified to ensure that those best suited to carry out an operation are invited to tender. For instance, all piling contractors do not drive all types of piles, and all plasterers do not lay floor screeds.

The construction industry is full of subcontractors who will carry out various works but many without the necessary skill to produce an entirely satisfactory and acceptable job.

All subcontractors will need to receive full copies of the relevant contract documents and drawings. They will also need detailed programme requirements and may need to visit the proposed site. In particular subcontractor's tasks must be clearly defined.

The remainder of the materials requiring prices should also receive considerable attention for it is here that great care must be exercised. Amongst these items there may be one or two with difficulty in sourcing or lacking in specific detail. The effect of poor attention to any one of these items could be disastrous to the completion of the project when it reaches the contract stage. Under-pricing these items, if they are very expensive, will also have a direct effect on the final tender price.

Provided that the time given to suppliers and subcontractors was adequate and the details given were sufficient to formulate an offer, quotations and tenders should arrive in good time.

The method of collating and analysing these details may well vary with each organisation, but the end result will be the same.

It is likely that many of the offers received for supplies or services will not entirely meet the necessary requirements. In the case of bulk items it is possible that:

(*a*)   there is insufficient quantity available to meet the contract needs from one particular source;

(*b*)   the material offered does not quite fall within the specific limits;

(*c*)   there are planning restrictions on all or part of the materials offered which may require expensive reinstatement to satisfy environmental regulations;

(*d*)   there are limitations on the number and capacity of vehicles using access roads;

(*e*)   rail-born materials may only be loaded on certain days and certain times;

(*f*)   quality control will be more difficult from multi-source suppliers supplying the same material.

In the case of fabricated items there may be size and dimension limitations both for construction and delivery. This may involve special design to allow final construction on site.

Depending on the type, size and nature of the project many other variations will become apparent from the analysis sheets. These may well necessitate inspection of the production facilities and considerable discussion with designers, technicians and managers all, or any of which, will result in further price negotiations. These discussions may well come to the conclusion that the specification is misleading or unnecessarily rigid. It is then that the buyer must put forward all the commercial information and assumptions that have been made. In the event that these assumptions cannot be verified or confirmed a decision may have to be taken to qualify the tender on the known details.

With materials that meet the required needs, the buyer's task follows the normal procedure of satisfying himself that the prices to be put forward for inclusion in the tender are:

(*a*) in accordance with the specified requirements;

(*b*) from a financially reputable company of adequate capacity and resources to meet these requirements;

(*c*) the most competitive available within these limits.

It is at this stage of the tender procedure that the construction buyer is the most frustrated, for, like buyers in all industries, he will have sourced the materials, checked the suppliers and negotiated rates and prices. However, unlike other industries that mainly carry out this operation for positive items, he cannot finalise anything until the contract is secured.

TRANSITION OF TENDER TO ORDER

The time between the submission of tenders and the award of contracts can vary from a few days to a few months. Often there will be meetings between client, engineer or architect to discuss various aspects of the tender. These may involve the buyer, but usually relate to problems in the programme or design and management areas of the contract.

At the time the award of the contract is made, the construction buyer is faced immediately with the problem of time. Most contract conditions in general use contain a clause about starting in a very short time, sometimes only days. This change from possibility to certainty almost overnight is peculiar to the construction industry. It is made more difficult by the necessity to set up operations in difficult locations and open sites which will be vulnerable to the vagaries of the weather.

The necessity of involving buyers at the tender stage is now most apparent. Re-issue of enquiries should be unnecessary provided the work was properly carried out for the tender. It is therefore possible to move directly into the ordering situation and to consolidate all the pre-tender work carried out.

Further investigation of materials may be both necessary and desirable. In spite of adequate precautions when tendering, considerable time may elapse which will bring about a change in the circumstances of the proposed supplier. Changes in the design of the structure may also force enquiries to be made from entirely different suppliers and subcontractors. There is also the attitude of any one supplier not offering the best prices at the tender stage of any project. He prefers to save the most attractive prices for the successful contractor.

It will be important to establish as soon as possible the procedure for agreeing the materials to be used. All major items will almost certainly require approval. Samples suitably labelled with the supplier, source of origin and date of submission should be obtained. Although this may well be in the site management area of responsibility, close co-operation will be needed with the buyer. It is important that materials submitted for approval are those which are intended to be used.

An early decision regarding the supply of concrete to site must be made. If it is decided to batch on site, then the procedure outlined above should be implemented. However, if ready-mixed concrete or mortar is to be used, verification of proposed plants should be carried out. Currently two organisations, British Ready Mixed Concrete Association and British Aggregate Construction Materials Industries Limited, offer plant certification schemes which require their members' plants to meet acceptable standards.

Ideally contracts are let in the spring with the possibility of long working hours and when the weather may be expected to be at its best for some months ahead. The need to take the maximum advantage of this position will require the immediate attention of the buyer for all the various necessary materials. Sourcing prices for the tender will ease the burden at this stage.

MATERIALS AND THEIR MANAGEMENT

The level of material management effectiveness in head office and at site level is very much for each individual construction company to determine. That material procurement and processing represent a major financial commitment and form a major part of any administrative system, has now been widely accepted.

Building materials, components and services are expensive. New materials have been introduced and traditional materials are manufactured and processed into different products. The range of materials available to the construction industry today is greater than ever before. Together with mechanisation, these changes require that effective materials management has a key part to play in the successful completion of a project.

Materials purchased for construction cover almost anything that is available from kitchen and catering equipment, carpets and curtains to computers. To this must be added the 'bricks and mortar' which form the very heart of any project.

Purchasing in almost any other industry has certain defined restrictions. Construction has many of these restrictions, but to this must be added the weather and time. Weather is perhaps the one single factor which affects every other operation. It amends programmed deliveries, produces tremendous variations in stock held, and controlling becomes that much more difficult because of the 'knock-on' effect. Techniques such as economic order quantity calculations, cyclic provisioning and Pareto analysis cannot be used except on very infrequent occasions because such stock-controlling techniques have little benefit for contracts which are short in duration.

Above all the approach to procurement of materials for construction projects must be flexible while sourcing skills and techniques must be 'geographically mobile'.

Good relations with suppliers and subcontractors must be promoted and maintained. Associations formed for one project may well be revitalised in later years when further contracts arise within the same geographical area. In many cases suppliers may be on a national or annual contract basis and supply more than just one project wherever the location.

The overriding requirements, however, must be that ethical and professional standards are applied to procuring materials of the right quantity, right quality and, above all in the time limit.

PURCHASING ATTITUDES TO STOCK CONTROL, STORAGE AND WASTE OF MATERIALS

The construction process on site comes at the end of a complex financial, design, manufacturing and administrative control process. The day of inexpensive materials has gone. Instead, the construction industry is faced with ever rising material cost and shortages which must result in the industry becoming more 'resources conscious'.

In the late nineteen-seventies the Building Research Establishment reported that materials wasted or illegally removed from construction sites amounted to 10-20 per cent of all deliveries to site. Waste therefore is a financial loss to the contractor and operative as well as the client. This direct or indirect loss also represents a deprivation of resources for future generations.

Consequently stock control, storage and prevention of waste of materials on site must take on an even more important role in the future.

It should be remembered that, unlike factory situations, most construction sites are 'greenfield' and storage areas must be created. It is also a fast moving operation which may result in materials having to be placed in areas miles apart. Also craneage for offloading may not be readily available.

Purchasing for construction sites therefore needs understanding of the site situation, positive information regarding quantities and careful study of quantity related offers. The buyer must consider for example whether:

(a) bricks and blocks should be shrink-wrapped and self off-load;

(b) reinforcement is cut and bent, in straight bars cut to length, or stock bars, and if the site can handle large lorries and has adequate stacking areas;

(c) timber, which is affected very much by climatic conditions, should come in large loads, which is the most economic, or be delivered in parcels which will be used up more quickly (this brings about an additional programming problem to avoid holding up the construction process);

(*d*) other materials affected by weather can be adequately protected and stored, such as plasterboard and cement.

Items that are small and highly vulnerable to theft should be delivered when checking procedures can be satisfactorily implemented, and then such items should be securely stored.

Scheduled delivery dates must also be considered in detail. These dates of delivery should be arranged carefully to take maximum advantage of trading terms offered. The buyer must at all times be aware of the effect that large deliveries to site have on company cash-flow forecasts.

THE FUTURE AND USE OF ADVANCED TECHNOLOGY

The construction industry is almost certainly the slowest to accept change in either its operation, management or the materials it uses. It is after all a basic craft industry governed by established professional thinking. Management of the industry has been carried on by architects, engineers, surveyors and financiers within a defined role, for which they each take responsibility. Protection of these roles has been maintained by institutes and federations. Change of any kind has to contend with this background of entrenched attitudes. Purchasing as a separate function, able to contribute to profitability, has only over recent years gained some recognition. During that time the industry workload has declined, resulting in very competitive tendering for projects. In this climate purchasing officers have been better able to demonstrate the contribution that they make. The need to make management even more cost effective may encourage the use of various forms of advance technology now becoming available.

The construction industry has taken up certain aspects of computerisation which have been limited to accounting, estimating, design, bill of quantity preparation and costing.

Writing in *Purchasing and Supply Management*, the monthly journal of the Institute of Purchasing and Supply, Richard Dand, director of purchasing for Bovis Construction, listed (as quoted below) some of the possible areas for which construction buyers are responsible and which lend themselves to automatic data processing (ADP):

- sourcing for subcontractors and suppliers
- raising enquiries for materials and sub-trades and obtaining quotations
- price and cost comparison
- placement of orders for material and subcontract services
- vendor rating
- record of price movement and cost indices
- the projection of price movements
- storage and stock control
- technical library services and reports
- security and vehicle control on site
- materials and scheduling and processing.

Few companies have yet to take advantage of the possible uses for ADP in purchasing departments.

The former president of the Royal Institute of British Architects, Owen Luder, when asked to think about the industry at the end of this century said:

> Construction is about thinking, communicating and then building. Micro computers with the information technology revolution already raging will help the thinking process but humans will still need to do the creative thinking. Physical building and manufacture of components will be helped by computers but not to the extent of robots as in the car industry.

Communication is perhaps the area in which the most changes have already and will continue to happen. Hitherto most construction sites have been equipped with telephones which, together with typewriters, have become very much more sophisticated. On some larger projects computer terminals are to be seen giving instant displays of information that previously took considerable time to reach the site and be implemented. The construction industry of the future is likely to be smaller but more efficient. The technology to provide systems in hardware and software terms are available albeit they have been designed with little understanding of the construction industry.

Although the industry has been slow in accepting change, the pace at which these changes are happening inevitably means construction must fundamentally alter. It is up to professional purchasing people to pursue, diligently, the completion of changes which will both improve their operation and efficiency, and will enhance the image of the industry and the purchasing profession.

27

Purchasing print

P. T. Kirby and A. E. Hart

Little recognition of the range and depth of the technology involved in the buying of print is acknowledged by those not engaged in the activity. Even many of those buying print are themselves not well enough versed to make the best buy. The purpose of this chapter is to set out some of the skills required in a print buyer for the benefit of those who will be employing a buyer, and to provide a guide for action for those organisations not large enough to employ a specialist.

How do you know if you are buying a sufficient volume of print to warrant a specialist? Savings can be achieved of between 15 and 20 per cent if print buying is properly organised, although if an organisation has been adopting an unskilled approach it may find that savings will reach 30 per cent. However, if 15 per cent is taken as a basis and a salary plus overheads of £15,000 is assumed, then simple arithmetic implies that £100,000 is the minimum annual value of print purchases for the employment of a specialist print buyer.

Cost reductions will be derived from two factors:

(*a*) by seeking competitive tenders from a range of good contractors;
(*b*) by the knowledgeable selection of the right firm with the right equipment for the job, preferably a specialist.

EMPLOYMENT OF SPECIALIST PRINT BUYERS

The print buyer

For the successful achievement of continuous cost reduction without sacrifice of product quality it is fundamentally important to appoint the right person. In choosing a buyer, attention needs to be given to the following:

1 He will be expected to be responsible for the complete production of jobs for:
   (*a*) discussing the brief with the client (author, sales manager, editor, computer manager etc.);
   (*b*) advice to client on likely cost of proposals and opportunities for cost reduction;
   (*c*) identifying suitable contractors;
   (*d*) selecting materials;
   (*e*) inviting tenders;
   (*f*) awarding the contract;
   (*g*) progressing proofs etc. through to completion of job.
   If the organisation is large enough it will wish to reinforce internal checks by separating the functions of buying, contracting, and invoice payment.
2 The buyer's experience and personal qualities should include:
   (*a*) a thorough knowledge of print processes;
   (*b*) an in-depth knowledge of the trade and trends;
   (*c*) an appreciation of graphic design; it is difficult to separate entirely printing from an appreciation of graphic design. The ability of the print buyer to design minor items, as well as having a general appreciation of graphic design is a quality which should not be overlooked;
   (*d*) completion of printing apprenticeship;
   (*e*) an appropriate qualification;
   (*f*) good communication skills;
   (*g*) the ability to work under pressure.

Before appointment it would be advisable to require candidates who are interviewed to take a small test to verify, in a simulated real situation, abilities claimed.

The designer

Depending on the type of printing work handled by the organisation, design work may be carried out by an agency or a specialist graphic designer.

If an organisation's printing needs are largely concerned with, for example, illustrated catalogues, it may be appropriate to reverse the emphasis to a graphic designer with a good knowledge of the printing industry who will also do the buying.

An organisation should seek the following qualities:

1 Ability to interpret visually a client's imprecise and often vague concepts.
2 Ability to produce own 'paste-ups'.
3 Ability to work on own initiative.
4 A commitment to meet critical deadlines with acceptable material (a superb design which misses the deadline may abort other elements of a promotion campaign).
5 A thorough knowledge of typography.
6 A working knowledge of print processes.
7 Good communication skills.

As far as experience is concerned the following should be sought:

1 A good basic education.
2 A qualification in graphic design.
3 Work experience as a designer for at least three years.
4 A variety of graphic design experience.
5 Submission of work specimens.

Generally

Additional points important in this context are:

1 Motivation to achieve commitment and good performance. Much unforeseen overtime is demanded by the printing function. In the critical path between the concept and the finished publication, all 'slack time' is frequently used up by the authors and designers. The print buyer and his assistants must, therefore, be sufficiently well motivated to work overtime at short notice.

2 The ability to be up to date with and be aware of the degree of acceptance in different areas of the trade of the new technological developments in printing. In particular:

(*a*) computerised phototypesetting including single key stroking, i.e. the capture of author's key strokes on a word processor and its interface with computerised phototypesetting.

(*b*) the developments in digitising and scanning so far as the reproduction of monochrome and colour illustrations are concerned.

This technology can be highly cost beneficial and is now within reach of most medium-sized organisations.

3 Underlying all must be a good knowledge of the English language; 10,000 copies of a spelling mistake in 24 point detracts from the impact on the reader and unnecessarily damages an organisation's image.

4 Print-buying staff must understand printing processes in order to be able to make valid quality judgements of the final product.

THE METHOD

Background

A print buyer will bring with him a wealth of knowledge about the trade and who does what in it. In fact one of the fundamentals of present day successful print buying is knowing who does what, because firms in the printing trade are increasingly becoming specialised. This is because new technology equipment is not only still relatively expensive but also becoming more and more productive, thus in seeking to fill spare capacity, work is taken on for specific machines and skills. Also as the trade becomes more competitive it is now unacceptable, in terms of the basic cost of the equipment and the expensive floor space it occupies, to have a wide range of equipment (to satisfy all the customers' requirements) which is only used intermittently.

The use of specialist companies is the essence of professional print-buying. However one must qualify the term specialist. In addition to the normally accepted specialist (e.g. a company with rotary presses specialising in computer stationery) many firms may have a very limited range of general purpose equipment, but be a specialist in the sense that they have the ideal plant to produce your particular job. For example, if you have a range of A4 or A5 short-run letterheads to be printed a small jobbing printer with a very limited range of A4 and A3 presses may prove ideal, although in the generally accepted interpretation of the word he would not normally be called a specialist.

Consequently it is necessary to build up and maintain a database of information organised by the types of work likely to be called for. A card index is perfectly adequate and is unlikely to exceed 300 cards. Each card will need to hold the following data:

- name of firm
- address
- telephone number
- representative
- inside contact
- origination and typesetting facilities
- printing machinery
- finishing equipment
- workforce.

These cards will need to be organised alphabetically by firm and also by the type of work of which the firms are capable. The headings which are likely to arise are as follows:

Heading	Comment
Instant print	Useful for short-run urgent, uncomplicated work, normally done on in-house copiers.
Lithographic – small	Letterheads, business stationery, short-run form and short run pamphlet and booklet work.
– medium	As above but longer run.
– large	Very long-run form work, long-run leaflet and booklet work, books, catalogues etc.

Letterpress – small – medium	Short-run stationery, pamphlets and bookwork, with little or no illustrations. Ideal where there are frequent changes to text or cover 'on the run'. Also suitable where cutting and creasing is involved.
Rotary – letterpress	Very little of this still remains. Useful and cheap, working from rubber plates for low quality form and bookwork (paperbacks). Also better quality working from nylon (Dyrcil) plates.
Rotary – gravure	For very high quality colour reproduction and very long-run (normally in excess of ½ million) magazine and catalogue work.
Rotary – offset litho (Web offset)	Continuous stationery (generally computer) and long-run form sets on specialist presses. Also newspapers, broadsheets, booklets and books on uncoated paper, with a run length generally in excess of 10,000 copies, on 'cold set' presses. Booklets, books, catalogues, newspapers on a coated paper with a run-length in excess of 10,000 copies on heatset presses.
Artwork	Preparation of line illustrations, cartographic work, artists work of all kinds for reproduction, page make-up and graphic design.
Binding (casebound books)	Firms specialising in all the operations for making case bound (hard back) books, from the flat printed sheet.
Die stamping	High quality stationery invitation cards etc., expensive but with a unique appeal.

Direct mail	Many direct mail companies can handle the whole operation, from printing, folding and inserting to mailing, sorting and despatching (either through the public delivery service or the company's own). Are they happy to handle your product produced from another printer?
Finishing	Specialist companies equipped to deal with the more simple print finishing operations (as opposed to case binding), i.e. folding, stitching, creasing, numbering, perforating etc.

The buyer will need to be very well appraised of the capabilities of the firms from which he intends to invite tenders. He needs to know:

1 What equipment they have.
2 What types of work they are capable of producing.
3 What type of work is suited to which machines.
4 Have the firm a stable workforce skilled in using the equipment?
5 Is the management and organisation good?
6 What is their record of performance on other jobs?

It is only possible to know all this by visiting the premises where the printing will be done. It is impossible to visit all the firms who seek invitations to tender and it is recommended that only lowest tenderers are visited before the letting of a contract. Thus over a period of time a body of knowlege will be built up in an effective way.

Getting on with the job

1 Clarify the brief. The work may range from simple forms to complex colour work with illustrations and it is important for those staff originating text etc. to discuss with the print buyer at the earliest stage possible what the final product is expected to look like and achieve. The competent buyer will have much to

offer in terms of advice and will wish to identify and clarify issues such as:

(*a*) Is the author's concept compatible with what is achievable within his budget or at reasonable cost?

(*b*) What is the timetable for completion; how urgent is it; is there any slack in the critical path?

(*c*) What will be the proofing arrangements?

(*d*) He will wish to emphasise the disadvantages of late changes in the plan and cost penalties involved when amendments are made at and after proofing.

(*e*) Has any artwork been prepared?

2 The buyer will then wish to analyse the job in terms of:

(*a*) What will be the paper needs?

There are substantial opportunities for cost reduction at this stage:

(i) What size will the product be? Adherence to international sizes will always be a saving as against other sizes. For instance to choose 12½″ × 9″ instead of A4 (11″ × 8¾″) will result in considerable paper wastage, together with machine capacity wastage. Both paper and printing machines are generally designed around the international 'A' sizes and to adopt a dimension slightly in excess of these sizes could result in having to buy the next paper size up, and in using the next machine size up, resulting in both areas of a wastage of up to 80 per cent.

(ii) What weight of paper will be used and how good is the opacity? The buyer must be able to identify the minimum weight in grammes per square metre (gsm) that will fulfil the client's needs and should advise him accordingly. It is, of course, a matter for the client's decision.

(iii) What finish will the paper have? By well informed choice a paper can be used which looks a good deal more expensive to the layman than it really is.

(iv) What method of buying should be adopted? Many people (including some print buyers) will assume that paper is a commodity that the printer will always supply, but this need not be so. A large organisation may well employ a paper buyer, but even when the company's paper purchases are not large enough to justify this, there are advantages in supplying the paper to the printer.

The printer will normally supply the paper for your job charged in accordance with the volume used (i.e. the 'smalls' rate for quantities of up to 200 kilos, the 200 kilo rate for quantities of 200 kilos – 1 tonne, etc.) plus a handling charge to cover storage of around 10 per cent. If your company uses a large volume of one type of paper it will probably be worth entering into a contract with a merchant or mill for a one or two-year supply. If your requirements are diverse but still considerable it may be worth entering into an arrangement where a merchant will supply most or all of your needs at his list price, less a discount or at the 1 tonne rate.

Where a printer is producing a large quantity of small jobs (i.e. departmental letterheads in quantities of 1,000-5,000) it will prove cost beneficial to supply a large quantity of paper for him to hold in stock, and draw against, for each individual job, rather than for the printer to supply and charge at the smalls rate. (The smalls rate can be as much as 50 per cent dearer than the 1 tonne rate.)

In certain instances, such as when the quantity of paper required is less than a ream, or when the printer has certain constraints as to the paper specification (i.e. rotary printer, where the paper must be supplied in reels to a maximum diameter, width and core measurement) it may be better for the printer to supply.

Also when the printer is a specialist and it is known that he buys paper in large quantities, it is worth wording the tender enquiry so that he quotes for the supply of paper separately. In this way the buyer can weigh up the benefits of the printer supplying the paper or a merchant.

In the past there has been some resistance from printers to customers supplying their own paper, but with increasing problems of cash flow, most informed printers now welcome it.

(b) Printing. What is the volume of the run and what bearing will this have on where to place it? What are the break points of the different processes? Which of the printing processes will be the appropriate one and what would be the ideal plant on which to produce this job. Having determined this it immediately identifies which group of contractors should be invited to tender.

(c) Should external or internal typesetting be used?
Each system has its advantages:

   (i)   External – many firms available

                     – urgent work can be done overnight if necessary (though this will be expensive)

                     – competitive situation can keep costs down

                     – very cost beneficial if author's keystrokes on disk can be handled by typesetter.

  (ii) Internal – only large organisations will have their own inplant typesetting facilities the costs and benefits of which need careful weighing against external typesetting; close relationship between authors and typesetters can be advantageous

                     – opportunity of substantial cost saving by processing author's keystrokes if word processing equipment and typesetting equipment are compatible and linkable (up to 50 per cent)

                     – page make-up device can speed up production

                     – substantial paper savings (about one-third) are obtainable if used in conjunction with in-plant printing of certain kinds of work (text).

A beneficial half-way situation can exist if WP floppy disks can be handled by an external typesetter, however, the matching of disk formats can be difficult to achieve and is not as simple as many claim. In the case of both internal and external typesetting if a good 'dialogue' exists between word processing operator and computerised phototypesetting substantial cost savings can be made.

(d) Preparation of artwork. This can vary from pasted-up typesetting to four-colour artist work. Some printers will have facilities for preparing artwork within their organisation. On other occasions it will need to be commissioned separately from a free-lance designer, studio, or agency. The print buyer's involvement may vary enormously but at least may include:
   (i)   selection of agency
   (ii) liaison between author, agency and printer
   (iii) ensuring that made up artwork is suitable for printing reproduction and ready on time to fit in with production timetable.

(e) Finishing arrangements. This consists of all the processes occurring when the work comes off the presses. Care must be taken to ensure that the contractor is clear as to requirements since the correction of errors can be very costly and time consuming. The buyer may have to give instructions to the contractor concerning:
   (i)   guillotining
   (ii)   folding
   (iii) creasing – the pressing of a rule into heavy papers or board to facilitate folding without cracking
   (iv)   gathering and collating. It is important that pages and sections are placed in the correct order before binding
   (v)   perforating – this is done simultaneously with the printing
   (vi)   numbering
   (vii) lamination – the application of transparent plastic film to enhance appearance and increase durability
   (viii) varnishing – the application of oil, spirit, cellulose,

water or synthetic varnish to enhance appearance or increase durability.

(*f*) Binding. This can range from simple wire stitching to the binding of hard cover books in vellum (rare these days). The most common options are:

(i) Wire stitching in which staples are made inserted and clenched by machine from a continuous roll of wire:

Saddle stitch – the centre of the fold is placed across a 'saddle' in the machine so that wire staples can be driven through and clenched on the inside.

Stab or side stitch – staples are punched through from front to back at the binding edge, single or double.

(ii) Thread stitching in which strong thread is used to fasten together the leaves:

Single stitch – single loop drawn through centre and tied.

Double stitch – two loops of a single thread are fastened in the centre of the fold.

Machine stitch – incorporates a lock stitch.

Side stitch – as for wire but using thread.

The binding of books is a complex subject which would need lengthy coverage. It is, therefore, omitted here.

(*g*) Delivery. This may be to a finisher or to the customer's premises and must be detailed in the tender document. There may be special arrangements necessary:

(i) Are all the copies wanted at once? Or will a supply be sufficient on the delivery date specified by the customer, with the balance to follow?

(ii) Any special packing instructions, i.e.

Maximum size of parcel and weight for efficient lifting 20kgs

For large jobs, a particular pallet size to match the needs of a special racking system

Kraft wrapped or shrink wrapped

Bulk wrapped or wrapped in 10's, 100's or 1000's for easy despatch and stocktaking

Contents of parcel marked clearly on the outside,

i.e. order books etc. which may be numbered, and may need to be issued in the correct numerical sequence.

On some heavy case-bound book jobs it may be necessary to commission a specially made carton for each volume to protect it against damage in general handling or through the post.

(iii) The contractor will want to know how many delivery points will be required and the approximate location. If there is a very large quantity of delivery addresses you may wish to have some copies delivered to a mailing house, who may be better equipped to despatch by post or his own door-to-door delivery.

3 With a clear brief and a firm specification the buyer will then be ready to invite tenders. At this stage one is able to take advantage of the increasing specialisation of the printing industry. By identifying and specifying each separate element of the job one is able to invite tenders in respect of each element thus reducing to a minimum the cost of each. The reasons for this are as follows:

(a) The tenderers, knowing the competitive situation, will be putting forward their best price.

(b) By going to, say, half a dozen specialists simultaneously you are more likely to locate one with spare capacity anxious for the work.

(c) Because of their specialisation they will have the ideal equipment for your job and will have lowered unit costs.

The aggregation of the prices thus obtained will be substantially lower than prices tendered by general printers (who may be subcontracting elements anyway).

In view of the urgency of much of the work in the printing environment it is important that the buyers should be able to work in a flexible way. Many of the tender prices will be submitted by phone and confirmed later. The buyer needs not only the freedom of delegated authority below pre-set contract values but also the support and safeguards of a disciplined system of internal check and good audit trail.

Underlying everything is the need to adhere to sound basic principles:

(*a*) competitive tendering (abjuring the temptations of offer back);

(*b*) separation of functions (buying, contract, finance);

(*c*) strict contractual procedures to ensure fair treatment to all tenderers.

4 Also needed is a clear contractual situation. Large organisations will have prepared conditions of contract which cover the generality of their purchasing business but these will not cover the speciality of the printing industry. Here, by way of guidance, are the main features of the Standard Conditions of Contract issued by the British Printing Industries Federation:

(*a*) estimates are at current costs and subject to amendment;

(*b*) copy which is illegible will incur extra costs;

(*c*) additional proofs charged extra;

(*d*) margin for overs and unders are:

Normal work	*Under 50,000*	*Over 50,000*
One colour	5%	4%
Other work	10%	8%

Continuous stationery	*Under 10,000*	*10,000 to 50,000*	*Over 50,000*
Single-part or one process	10%	5%	4%
Multi-part or multi-process	10%	10%	3%

Overs charged, unders deducted.

(*e*) standing material supplied by the customer remains the customer's property – the printer may reject unsuitable materials; materials must cover normal spoilage;

(*f*) the printer may refuse matter which he considers illegal or libellous.

In the event of failure to specify otherwise the above conditions are likely to apply. Full conditions as recommended by BPIF are in the *Printers' Yearbook* which at £35 (1983) is good value for money.

5 Important to the question of timely deliveries is the matter of progressing. In the hurly burly of a busy print-buying office it is easy to overlook the need to enquire after the progress of time constrained jobs. This is particularly the case if the work has been let to a general printer who is expected to cover all the matters in 1 and 2 above.

6 Schedule contracts – if the volume of printing is sufficiently large it is possible to group types of work into a period contract which will set out all aspects of the work against which tenderers can quote prices. The contract can be for one or a number of years and will include a formula for renegotiation of prices, say, annually. Once let, a schedule contract can save a substantial amount of time and staff since it will be unnecessary to invite individual tenders for the types of work covered. However, care must be taken to keep prices under review since it is possible for costs to be rising while at the same time competition is forcing prices down.

THE NON-SPECIALIST PRINT BUYER

It has to be recognised that many organisations will not be large enough to employ a specialist. The options open to such organisations are:

1 To nominate a person who will take responsibility and action in addition to other duties. It is hoped that such a person would use such parts of the preceding information as may be possible and at least invite tenders. Few non-specialist print buyers will have the knowledge, ability, or time to split the job up into elements and even fewer the ability to choose the firm with the right equipment.

2 To invite tenders from general printers who will incorporate most of the elements given above in their price. It must be appreciated that no single printer will be able to produce all your printing requirements at the best price. This is the most common trap into which non-specialist buyers fall.

3 To seek out a 'print farmer' who will be organised in the way set out in 'Getting on with the job' and who recovers his costs

by adding a percentage to the costs incurred. There are not many such agencies and if a good one is found this is the preferred option in this section since you gain a specialist without the overheads of employment.

THE IN-PLANT OPTION

Many large organisations have an in-house print shop. It is very tempting to have work done internally on the marginal cost principle. This temptation must be resisted unless urgency overrides economy. Very few internal printing shops are properly costed and managerial job satisfaction tends to result in the acquisition of equipment with greater capability and sophistication than can be fully utilised or cost justified. The proper function of the typical in-house printing unit is short run and very urgent work, e.g. turn round times of two hours to two days.

In terms of cost the large in plant will be hard put to match the cost effectiveness of the specialist commercial contractor.

Large in plants generally fall down where they attempt to satisfy most or all the printing needs of their parent company. This frequently leads to the purchase of a very wide range of equipment which is underutilised, or alternatively work being put on machines which are inefficient for the needs of that particular job. If a company can identify a specific type of work which is printed in sufficient quantity to justify the purchase of specialised plant and can assure itself that it will be fully utilised, there is a chance that the operation will be cost effective. Additionally, in-plant printing units should adopt the best commercial practices to achieve maximum output and economy, such as double or triple day-shift working, good production management to achieve best utilisation of plant with the minimum of redundant or underutilised plant and premises. The large in plant, like the large commercial printing company, cannot afford amateur management – professionalism and specialisation are the key.

Computerisation

Printing technology is increasingly becoming computerised. The

521

best known aspect is computerised phototypesetting using text created via a VDU, but microprocessors are increasingly being adapted to a wide range of machines. The buyer needs to keep abreast of these developments. Many print buyers will work in large organisations where considerable computerisation of basic processes has taken place, e.g. sales and bought ledgers, stock control, ordering processes, factory processes; however, very little work seems to have been done on computerisation of the print buyer's activity. The authors feel sure that this is to come but are so far unaware of any successful developments.

CONCLUSION

The printing trade is highly diverse and solutions to the problems are also diverse. What will be the best for one organisation will not be the best for another. In determining the way in which to organise print buying it is important to ensure that all costs are taken into account. What is the best for the reader, is for him to decide; this chapter has opened up a few avenues of thought and it is hoped that large, medium and small organisations will benefit from what has been written. However, the practical solutions of day-to-day problems have been only lightly touched upon. Similarly the range of knowledge which underlies the technology of printing, and which is vast, has been hardly referred to; books have been written on subjects dismissed here in a paragraph or not even mentioned.

To summarise:

1 Employ a well-qualified buyer.
2 Exploit the increasing specialisation of the trade using competitive tendering.
3 Keep abreast of new technology and adopt it when it becomes cost beneficial, but remember that computers can damage your wealth.

28

Purchasing castings

Aubrey Grant

For a wide range of engineering products the casting process can be described as the shortest route to the finished component and, for this reason, it is often preferred to forging, stamping, fabrication or machining from the solid. To take advantage of the versatility of the casting process the buyer should be well informed regarding the properties and suitability of metals in the cast form. A knowledge of foundry methods, the factors involved in the choice of pattern equipment, and the quality assurance techniques are also important.

The choice of material will usually be determined by the mechanical, electrical, corrosion or abrasion resisting properties desired, but the possibility of more than one material meeting the requirements should be examined. Within the range of ferrous materials, for example, there is considerable scope for investigating the cost benefits of steel, nodular iron (SG) and malleable iron. In suitable cases, the properties of the casting may be enhanced by heat treatment, a point which is sometimes overlooked. The relationship between wall thickness, mechanical strength, pressure tightness and castability should be carefully examined and consideration given to the limitations of some types or grades of material.

Although technical decisions would normally be taken by the design department, it is important that the castings buyer has an understanding of technical aspects, sufficient at least, where necessary, to act as a catalyst between supplier and those responsible for determining the specification. The range of cast materials is extremely wide and the buyer should develop an interest in the characteristics of the various metals which are featured in the purchasing programme. Space considerations preclude the inclusion of details of all the metals available in the cast form, although an outline of those in common use may be appropriate.

GREY IRON

Grey iron is the most widely used material for cast products. Castability and machinability are good and a range of tensile strengths from $150N/mm^2$ to $400N/mm^2$ (10 to 26 Tons/in^2) is available. Machinability, although remaining good, reduces with increasing tensile strength.

NODULAR IRON

In the nodular (spheroidal graphite) specifications, toughness and ductility are combined in a range of tensile strengths from $370N/mm^2$ to $800N/mm^2$ (24 to 47 Tons/in^2). Although ductility decreases with increasing tensile from 17 per cent to only 2 per cent, those grades with characteristics similar to low carbon steel are easier to machine. A 25 per cent improvement over machining times for carbon steel is fairly typical.

MALLEABLE IRON

The malleable irons represented by three basic grades – whiteheart, blackheart and pearlitic – offer a range of tensiles similar to the nodular irons, but the hardness and elongation characteristics vary according to grade. All grades are hard and brittle in the 'as cast' condition.

Whiteheart after heat treatment which removes most of the carbon, has a structure which consists of a soft, ductile outer layer surrounding a tough, high tensile inner section.

Blackheart is produced by an annealing process which removes very little carbon which, instead, is precipitated as graphite nodules. This gives a dark grey appearance to the fracture which is uniform throughout the section.

Pearlite is produced from the original white cast iron, either by specially controlled heat treatment or by increasing the manganese in the charge prior to casting and using the same heat treatment as for blackheart. In the higher grades, tensile strength is improved at the expense of elongation.

ALLOY IRONS

A range of alloy irons is available for special purposes. Alloys such as nickel, chromium, molybdenum, copper and vanadium are used to increase heat, corrosion, or abrasion resistance, to provide extra strength or special magnetic properties. It would not be helpful to attempt to summarise these irons and those who are interested should refer to published information on the subject.

CAST STEELS

The range of cast steel varies from the general engineering, 28-ton tensile grade to a large number of sophisticated alloys for virtually every purpose. There are grades for high strength, corrosion resistance, impact resistance, high and low temperature applications, wear resistance and combinations of these characteristics. Space considerations make it impossible to provide the reader with a useful outline of all the alloy steels available, but foundries with the appropriate capability, publish comprehensive information on the subject.

COPPER ALLOYS

In the copper alloys there are specifications for sandcastings, diecastings and investment castings covering a range of requirements which include corrosion resistance, pressure tightness, high and low temperature conditions, wear resistance, high electrical and thermal conductivity and other desirable properties.

ALUMINIUM ALLOYS

Aluminium alloys are available for sandcastings, gravity and pressure diecastings covering a wide range of applications from general purpose to specialised grades used principally in the automotive, aircraft and marine industries.

ZINC ALLOYS

The zinc alloys consist of two grades, one of which is used extensively for automotive and consumer products – refrigerators, washing machines etc. The other is used where surface hardness is important – zip fasteners are a good example. Both alloys have useful mechanical properties, combining strength with ductility, but there is deterioration of these properties with age.

PROCESS SELECTION

Selection of the foundry process is, perhaps, the most critical of all the decisions affecting ultimate cost. This is an area where the well informed buyer should be able to make a positive contribution to the technical decision. A balance has to be struck between a number of factors, in particular the standard of quality, accuracy and surface finish required and the economics of machining versus casting costs. The stability of the design and possible constraints on pattern equipment costs must also be considered.

The following is a broad outline of processes in common use. A much closer understanding is desirable and further reading on this subject is strongly recommended.

Sandcasting

This is the oldest, most versatile and most frequently used casting method. Castings can be produced in most metals, in high or low volume, and size tends to be limited only by melting capacity, box sizes and the facilities available at the foundry. There are, however, some difficult materials, notably titanium, monel, pure copper and others for which special techniques have to be adopted. Hand and machine moulding methods can be employed and in recent years, fully automatic machines have been introduced, the most widely known being the Disamatic. As a general rule, foundries employing automatic moulding techniques reserve this type of capacity for very long runs, although some are now prepared to accept relatively low volume work.

Shell moulding

This is a popular method of achieving closer tolerances and better surface finish than is generally available using sandcasting methods. In some circumstances, homogeneity is improved, but this depends on design. Shell moulding should be seen as an important cost-effective foundry method to be used selectively and not regarded as a panacea. Even so, a high degree of complexity of design is possible and, indeed, whenever shell moulding methods are chosen, the designer should seek to take advantage of the additional accuracy of the process to eliminate or reduce machining costs. Shell moulds are produced by 'dumping' resin bonded silica or zircon sand on to a pre-heated pattern plate. The profile of the two halves of the casting in the form of 'biscuits', with the cores in position are glued and clamped together to form the complete mould.

Investment (lost wax) process

This process is especially useful for castings in alloys which are difficult to machine. Exceptionally fine finish, high standards of accuracy, and flexibility of design are outstanding features. Used mainly for very small castings, the process is suitable for low and high volume production. The economics tend to favour high volume, intricate castings but the process is used for critical aircraft components which may be neither high volume nor particularly small. Tooling, although often extremely costly especially if the ultimate in terms of accuracy is desired, compares satisfactorily with similar equipment for other precision processes. The difference will be in the cost of the adjustments necessary to achieve the closer tolerances possible using the lost wax method. Once the metal die has been produced, consistent standards of quality and accuracy may be expected as a matter of routine.

The process involves injecting wax into the die to form a precise impression of the desired component. This wax impression is then assembled on a 'tree' which is then immersed in a fluidised bed of refractory material to form the initial layer of the ceramic mould. This mould is dried and the process repeated until a mould of adequate thickness is built up. The wax is then melted out and recovered for further use and metal is poured into the resulting cavity in the mould.

Diecasting

The main use of this method is for zinc and light alloy castings. Consistently high standards of accuracy can be achieved using either gravity or pressure methods. A good deal of design flexibility is possible, but tooling costs tend to be high and increased complexity involves still greater cost. Set against this, unit costs are low, especially for pressure diecastings where exceptionally high rates of production can be achieved. Porosity is sometimes a problem with pressure diecastings and where pressure tightness is of paramount importance, epoxy resin vacuum impregnation may be necessary.

Permanent moulds

Permanent mould methods are in limited use for the production of castings in iron and materials other than light alloys. Constraints on design inhibit wider use of this method which produces castings of consistent accuracy, metal structure and soundness, at unit costs which tend to be lower than sandcasting or shell mould.

V. process

This is a comparatively recent development, particularly suited to the production of shallow castings. Dimensional accuracy, finish and freedom from gas hole defects are the principal advantages. The moulding material in unbonded silica sand and the specially constructed pattern plate is covered with a pre-heated, flexible plastic sheet to cling to the pattern contours. The two halves of the mould, each consisting of a special moulding box with a vacuum chamber, are assembled and the casting poured with the vacuum on.

CASTING DESIGN

This is possibly the area of greatest neglect. Seldom does the designer seek the advice of the foundry at a sufficiently early stage. The buyer should, therefore, use all possible means to influence technical colleagues to ensure that early and effective consultation takes place. The failure of castings users to observe this simple rule is responsible for much of the misery, high cost, delivery and quality problems which are so much a feature of the foundry customer experience. Foundries are always pleased to offer castings engineering advice when invited to do so, but much more needs to be done to promote a better understanding between casting users and producers. The buyer should take the initiative and secure the benefits of a flow of technical information from foundry to design department. If independent advice is preferred, there are a number of organisations competent to perform this task.

One method, known to have been used by a large company in the early stages of introducing a new product range, is to provide facilities for prospective suppliers to meet together to arrive at a consensus regarding non-functional modifications to preliminary drawings. This obviates the possibility of any one supplier influencing the design to favour his own capability. Whether such a course of action is justified is a matter of judgement for the buyer.

Whatever method is adopted, there are some very simple rules which are often overlooked, and perhaps the most important of these is the tendency to overspecify. Designers in the pursuit of high standards of quality, all too frequently fail to take into consideration the heavy cost penalties attached to unnecessarily tight tolerances, insufficient moulding taper, undercuts, large flat areas and rapid changes of section. Unsuitable material specifications and attempts to reduce weight, in the mistaken belief that cost is based mainly on weight, are factors which can lead to problems. Unbalanced cores, or cores which cannot be properly supported, give rise to high reject rates resulting from core movement as metal enters the mould.

In summary, the designer should:

(*a*)   use rounded surfaces and generous radii where possible;
(*b*)   avoid rapid changes of section;
(*c*)   use strengthening ribs on extensive flat surfaces;
(*d*)   ensure that, wherever possible, bosses are 'D'd to the joint line;
(*e*)   use cored holes to reduce machining costs where feasible;
(*f*)   consider the use of cores to avoid changes of section;
(*g*)   aim to locate cores to provide adequate support;
(*h*)   take into consideration the stresses involved in cooling;
(*i*)   recognise the difficulty of producing homogeneous heavy sections;
(*j*)   avoid feeding heavy sections via thinner sections;
(*k*)   study the minimum thickness of the metal to be cast;
(*l*)   observe the limitations of the process to be used; and
(*m*)   try to strike the best balance between the cost of machining, complexity of the casting, ease of withdrawal of the pattern from the mould etc.

PATTERN EQUIPMENT

The choice of foundry process will, to a large extent, determine the type of pattern equipment (or tooling) required, but the suitability and quality of this equipment will have a profound effect on the useful life and/or repair costs, and the accuracy, consistency and freedom from defects of the castings produced. Many of the better foundries, jealous of their reputation, refuse to use substandard pattern equipment; others, under the pressure of economic circumstances, or to placate the customer, suffer reluctantly the frustration of using equipment which carries a high risk of quality failure, low rates of production, increased fettling and higher unit costs.

As a general rule there are no pattern equipment bargains. Cheap patterns are a poor investment and, whilst the buyer should seek to obtain the best value for money, it is essential that all price comparisons are between equipment made to identical standards. The probability that low cost patterns produce high cost castings should be constantly borne in mind. Quality failures are enormously expensive and can frequently be traced to poor pattern equipment. Delivery failures due to unsatisfactory patterns are not so readily identified, but it is obvious that troublesome work, yielding low profit margins, will always have a low priority.

The decision regarding pattern equipment for sandcastings presents greater difficulty than for other processes and it is important that the buyer has a knowledge of the advantages and disadvantages of the various options. If, for example, there is the need to produce prototypes which may later require modification, this is clearly a time when a cheap wooden pattern may suffice. The possibility of this equipment being used to produce resin patterns should not be overlooked.

Normally, excellent resin patterns can be made from cheap wooden masters, always assuming that dimensional accuracy and general condition are good. Unlike metal patterns, no extra contraction allowance is required for resin. All patterns, of course, have a single contraction allowance to compensate for shrinkage of the metal on cooling. The higher the melting point of the metal the greater the allowance and, if dimensions are critical, it will not be possible to use the same pattern for say, steel and iron.

Prior to the introduction of resin patterns, the choice was between cheap wood double contraction masters suitable for producing metal equipment, and hardwood, usually mahogany. For long life, durability and dimensional stability, hardwood patterns should be of laminated construction, but it is always worth discussing with the foundry the suitability of resin, especially if multiple impressions are required.

The skills for loose moulding have virtually disappeared and, whenever practicable, all patterns should be plated (mounted on a board or metal plate) with the method (runner system) as an integral part of the equipment. For shell moulding, because the process involves heating the pattern plate, all patterns must be metal (usually cast iron). Metal patterns can be produced by machining from the solid or machined from castings. They tend to be extremely costly but are, nevertheless, essential for very high volume production.

Dies for gravity or pressure diecastings are always of metal construction and always very expensive. Machining to close tolerances, arranging moving cores and making adjustments prior to bulk production are all factors in the cost equation. Dies for investment castings are usually of metal and carefully adjusted to extremely high standards of accuracy.

NON-DESTRUCTIVE TESTING

Although it is impossible to deal with the subject in detail, a brief description of the quality control techniques in common use is necessary to complete the background of technical knowledge required by the castings buyer.

Mechanical and chemical properties may be examined using:

(*a*) standard Brinell or Rockwell hardness testing methods;

(*b*) test bars cast from the same molten metal as the casting may be subjected to chemical or spectrographic analysis, and/or machined to permit tensile, Charpy or Izod tests. Spectrographic analysis uses machined test pieces to verify the existence of the desired elements in the correct proportions. Charpy and Izod tests both measure the energy absorbed in fracturing a carefully prepared specimen when it is struck by a pendulum type device.

Internal defects can be detected either by the use of ultrasonics or by radiography. Ultrasonic testing involves the use of a probe to pass high frequency, above audibility, signals through the casting. Defects are identified from reflected signals which are reproduced on an oscilloscope. A skilled operator is able to interpret this information and determine the position of the defect. Radiography (X-ray and gamma ray) is a technique which because of the high cost is used only on high integrity castings. Results are recorded on film and accurate interpretation is a specialist activity.

Crack detection is normally carried out using dye penetrant or magnetic particle testing methods. Both are fairly inexpensive. Dye penetrant involves the application of a fluorescent dye to the area under examination. Faults are easily discerned under ultra violet light. Magnetic particle examination is only possible on ferrous materials. Magnetic powder is applied to a previously painted white magnetised surface. Cracks are revealed by the accumulation of magnetic powder along the line of flux leakage.

Apart from proof machining to reveal faults in suspect areas, and visual examination for obvious faults, one other test is used for castings which are required to be pressure tight. Pressure testing necessitates sealing the casting apertures and filling with water or oil and applying the required test while the casting is examined for leaks.

Obviously, the non-destructive tests described attract an element of extra cost, but the identification of faults at the foundry is often more than adequate compensation. In some circumstances the foundry may, on their own initiative, carry out one or other of these tests. Normally, however, the buyer would specify and agree the extra cost.

SPECIFYING THE REQUIREMENT

The surest way to achieve high cost and a low standard of satisfaction in the procurement of goods or services is to use vague specifications. This is particularly true of castings buying and there is an overwhelming case for rigid adherence to British or international standard specifications wherever possible. Brand names are a device for ensuring customer loyalty, and are based on a claim or inference that the product or material has some feature or ingredient which guarantees superiority over the competition. The castings buyer will do well to examine very carefully all these claims and to ascertain the precise cost benefit and decide if the special properties, assuming they exist, have any relevance to the particular need. The buyer should, therefore, with the co-operation of technical colleagues, ensure that the mechanical properties and, where appropriate, the chemical properties and the performance characteristics are clearly defined and the following checklist will be of assistance in this task.

Casting specification

    Grade of material
    British or international standard specification

Description
Part number and/or drawing number
Batch quantity/annual quantity
Casting weight, if known or estimated
Pattern equipment available – type, pin centres, plate size etc.
Pattern equipment proposed (if enquiry) – ask for details on quotation
Tensile strength, if not covered by standard specification
Special hardness characteristics
Tolerances
Location of part numbers or trade marks
Gauging points
Corrosion resistance
Abrasion resistance
Shock resistance
Finish
Cleanliness
Pressure tightness
Operating temperature
Heat treatment
Inspection and non-destructive tests
Delivery requirements
Point of delivery
Payment terms
Special arrangements regarding rejects

Although an elementary point to make it is, nevertheless, worth underlining the fact that the purchase order is the document which commits both buyer and seller to certain actions. It is a legal document but, perhaps more importantly, it is a document which immediately involves cost. It should, therefore, be sufficiently detailed and unambiguous as not to be the subject of repeated queries. The protests of casting buyers will be heard for miles but the fact remains that too few companies specify their requirements clearly and the order is more a declaration of intent to purchase rather than a clear indication of the requirement. The specification is eventually defined after many telephone calls and/or visits. Increasing urgency leads to error and error adds substantially to cost.

Assuming all the points included in the checklist have been covered, it is advisable before completing the order to make a final check on conditions of sale and, if the requirement involves the manufacture of new pattern equipment, that samples are called for and the responsibility for marking out clearly established. Enclose with the order a certified copy of the drawing cancelling and superceding all previous issues and instruct the supplier to destroy all other copies.

If the pattern equipment is being transferred from one foundry to another, make sure the new foundry is aware of the problems previously encountered. Make a point also of advising the foundry of any special machining methods.

With regard to enquiries, difficulty in calculating casting weights is often the reason for long delays in obtaining quotations. This is not to suggest that foundries estimate price solely on weight. Indeed this method of casting has long been superceded. Nevertheless, weight is an important factor, especially in the more exotic materials. For this reason, the weight if known or estimated should always be disclosed. The practice of withholding this information, presumably in the hope of gaining some advantage, cannot be recommended. In the same way, all the relevant points included in the foregoing checklist should be included on enquiries. Omission of any of the important details is likely to distort the results, leading to incorrect sourcing decisions and costly panic action.

SELECTING THE FOUNDRY

Foundries tend to divide into categories based on the materials cast and the processes used. Further segregation arises from differences in melting methods, the industries served or some other specialisation. There are still some foundries producing a wide range of metals, but increasing pressure on costs has encouraged a trend in the opposite direction. Electric melting has enabled some foundries to offer a wider choice of materials and often this capability is developed to facilitate production of, for example, alloy irons or exotic materials to meet a perceived opportunity to improve profitability per ton of castings produced.

Cast iron and nodular (SG) iron are often produced in the same foundry and, similarly, sand and shell moulding facilities frequently co-exist. Jobbing foundries capable of supplying small quantities or making temporary alterations to patterns to produce special features, are tending to disappear. The shortage of this type of capacity causes many problems for the buyer with only an occasional requirement. Prototype capacity offered by some foundries is normally reserved for customers who have volume business to place. The buyer seeking mechanised sandcasting capacity is in the fortunate position of having an array of options ranging from conventional jolt squeeze machines to high pressure and sophisticated automatic moulding methods. Disamatic, V process, shellmoulding and lost wax methods are also available if the design, quantities or material suggest this type of capacity may be appropriate. Diecasting and centrifugal techniques have clearly defined applications and seldom overlap with other methods.

The first stage in the selection process involves collecting together all the relevant data concerning the requirement – the material specification, approximate weight and any special features which indicate the foundry method to be used. Moulding box size will have a profound effect, not only on the ability of the foundry to produce the casting but also on the cost of the castings. It is essential to optimise the number of impressions on a plate (pattern) and significant variations in quoted prices can often be traced to moulding box size. This may be a decisive factor in the choice of foundry.

Pattern-making facilities available at the foundry may be an important consideration, although it must be said that many foundries having no in-house capability, have extremely satisfactory subcontract arrangements. Indeed, some specialist equipment can only be produced by high class pattern makers whose only activity is the provision of a service to the industry.

Matching the foundry to the requirement cannot be achieved by the random selection of names from a buyer's guide or other advertising material. A more scientific approach is essential. It is suggested that a record of existing and potential supplier capability is compiled, listing such details as materials produced, processes used, weight range, standard box sizes, preferred batch quantities and quality approvals. Other factors which may influence the purchasing decision are pattern-making and/or machining facilities, geography and transport arrangements. Enquiries should only be sent to those foundries having capacity which is obviously suited to the need.

If possible, in advance of any enquiries and certainly before actual orders are placed, new sources of supply should be visited by quality control personnel and a report on their findings made available to the buyer. Satisfactory source selection and economic procurement are only possible with good teamwork within the buying organisation and although the final decision should rest with the buyer, the opinions and advice of technical colleagues must be taken fully into consideration.

PURCHASING POLICY

A soundly based, carefully considered policy is essential to the economic procurement of castings. It is important to regard the foundry as an extension of manufacturing capability, involving long-term relationships and good communications. The objective should be to use the minimum number of suppliers consistent with the different types of castings required and the level of demand. By concentrating demand on fewer suppliers, bargaining power is increased and the buyer is able to exert greater influence over future developments at the foundry, which will, in all probability, have a beneficial effect on costs, quality and service.

Buying castings should be regarded as buying a complete service – technical consultation, production, quality control and delivery monitoring. Costs per unit of output decrease as volume or expenditure increase. The astute buyer will be able to take advantage of this to negotiate lower costs and closer attention to requirements.

Visits to and from suppliers should be encouraged at the technical and commercial level. The buyer should make a point of becoming known to as many as possible of the supplier's personnel. Every effort should be made to ensure a free exchange of information between buyer and supplier on all matters relevant to existing and future business. Close relationships do not weaken bargaining positions. On the contrary, the more is known about the supplier's organisation, methods and future plans, the greater the opportunities for cost reduction.

Policies and actions based on taking short-term advantage of a castings supplier's temporary weakness cannot be recommended. Good suppliers develop a dependence on their traditional customers and are therefore extremely vulnerable. This dependence sometimes leads to an excessive percentage of output becoming devoted to a single customer. This is not in the interests of either buyer or seller and care should be taken to avoid this situation.

Having established a shortlist of suppliers, the buyer is advised to draw up a 'league table' based on expenditure levels and supplier performance. Suppliers should be aware of their actual and potential placings in this league table. Negotiations linking expenditure to performance, and the setting of financial targets can be the means of achieving mutual objectives.

Some attempt should be made to agree with the foundry the probable cost of rejections. Accurate measurement would involve extremely detailed study which the buyer is unlikely to be in a position to undertake. Nevertheless, an assessment can be made and it is suggested that, having regard to the value of wasted machining, the loss of production (which, incidentally, can never be recovered), overtime working, the possible loss of customer goodwill, paperwork and handling, a figure of at least five times the cost of the casting would often be applicable.

The adoption of a formula of this kind underlines the importance of good quality. In some highly structured organisations the link between purchase price, quality and delivery performance is not fully recognised. These various aspects are the responsibility of separate departments and in these circumstances the buyer must take steps to ensure that purchasing decisions are based on considerations of ultimate, rather than initial, cost.

To many it is a source of irritation that foundries refuse to accept a charge for lost machining. The subject is controversial but the case for maintaining the status quo is a good one. Inevitably, prices would reflect and overestimate the risk, and the administration and negotiation of claims on the foundry would be difficult and time consuming.

Far better to persuade the foundry to accept the 'five times' formula when price comparisons are being made. To say the least, attention is focused on the importance of quality and, if the policies and procedures already outlined have been followed, a quick solution will be found to any problems which may arise.

A policy of prompt payment of invoices, i.e. payment in accordance with the terms of the contract, is essential to the negotiation of satisfactory prices and reliable deliveries. The buyer who is responsible for placing the contract must be fully informed regarding payments to suppliers and must be in a position to ensure that the terms and conditions of the contract are observed. It is both dishonourable and costly flagrantly to violate the terms of a freely negotiated contract. Although it may not be possible to assess the cost of extra expediting effort and the lack of enthusiasm on the part of the supplier to provide supporting services, there is a cost which more than cancels out the advantage which it is sought to gain.

It is impossible to overstate the importance of quality and delivery reliability in the cost equation. The buyer who neglects these considerations and makes purchasing decisions based solely on price is behaving irresponsibly. The management which fails to allow the buyer to exercise judgement in these matters has either a misguided view of the purchasing function, or is making the mistake of assuming it is in the nature of castings buying to experience bad quality and late delivery.

Some companies, encouraged by this belief, tend to insulate their production line and maintain output by a massive increase in stocks. This is positively the wrong direction. If the foundry is failing and supplier selection is not in doubt, look first at the pattern equipment and examine production methods and/or production control procedures. Follow this with an investigation into design features which may be causing the problem. If delivery is the only problem, ascertain that orders and schedules are allowing sufficient lead time and that payments are not substantially in arrears. Extra stockholding is enormously expensive. Not only is there a direct cost of holding unnecessary stock, the possibility exists of a quality problem remaining unattended because latest supplies of castings are taken into stock rather than on to the production line where the fault would immediately be revealed. Foundries protect themselves against loss in this regard by inserting a clause in their conditions of sale which limits the period during which credit is available for faulty castings. It is sometimes possible to waive this clause but the buyer is advised to have an agreement with the foundry on this point.

Suppliers should be made aware of purchasing policy and should understand the contribution they are expected to make in keeping the buyer informed of changes within their organisation or any other circumstances which affect the timely supply of castings. This applies particularly to lead times due to capacity changes. The buyer has a right to insist on being informed of impending maintenance to cupolas, or the shortage of raw materials and given the opportunity to increase schedules in advance or obtain supplies from a temporary second source.

Equally, the buyer should discuss with foundry suppliers any changes which might involve new capacity, dual sourcing or even reductions in demand. This exchange of information enables both buyer and seller to optimise their production arrangements and thus reduce cost.

If communications with foundry suppliers are good, the buyer will be well informed with regard to the condition of pattern equipment. In some circumstances, the foundry should be asked to report the condition of patterns at the end of each production run. Alternatively, some other means of regular reporting should be devised. Irrespective of the way in which the information is provided, the buyer should seek to avoid having to renew patterns on an emergency basis. The foundry should be aware that it is their responsibility to give adequate warning of the need for major pattern repairs or renewals. In most organisations the buyer will be required to prepare a budget for pattern expenditure on an annual basis. It is desirable, therefore, to invite foundries to comment on the condition of equipment and estimate the cost of necessary work well in advance of each year end.

Finally, the aim of buyer/supplier relationships should be to achieve cost reduction and mutual prosperity. Suppliers must be made to realise that they have a duty to assist the cost reduction process, but the buyer must be prepared to share the benefit in some way. This may take the form of increased business or it may permit improved profit margins.

In most organisations with a sizeable castings spend there will be considerable scope for cost reduction from minor changes in design. It is a particular failing of foundries, although they very properly preach early consultation on design, once the job is in production it is not until some expensive quality failure takes place that any effort is made to identify improvements which could be made.

QUALITY ASSURANCE

Whatever the type of casting and the machining operations to which it is subjected, quality is a significant factor in determining ultimate cost. Good quality begins with good design and suitable pattern equipment, but it is essential that the foundry has adequate control at all stages of the casting process. This necessitates careful checking of the cupola charge, regulating the moisture content and permeability of the sand, and monitoring pouring temperatures, in addition to inspecting the results after the casting has been fettled.

To achieve all this, the foundry must have laboratory and non-destructive testing facilities. But white coats and sophisticated equipment are not of themselves a guarantee of quality; management attitudes are equally important. Moreover, in the interests of cost, the temptation to source every requirement with the foundry possessing the most impressive range of equipment should be resisted. The emphasis should be on facilities to suit need. For best results, close liaison between the castings buyer and quality control personnel is essential. The relationship should be one of mutual respect and the twin objectives of lowest cost and satisfactory quality fully recognised.

It is important that a record of supplier quality performance is maintained and that, in addition to global statistics, the system provides the means of examining results item by item. This record should be scrutinised on a regular basis and immediate action taken whenever an unusual event occurs.

Sudden quality failures can sometimes be traced to deteriorating pattern equipment. Good quality can seldom be achieved with badly worn equipment and it is a false economy to ignore the advice of the foundry if attention is called to this condition.

Test certificates serve a useful purpose in establishing quality standards for high integrity castings intended for use in hazardous environments or particularly demanding service conditions. Whether or not test certificates are called for, it is always advisable to specify the service conditions if the castings are required for use in corrosive atmospheres, unusually high or low temperatures, or subjected to impact, constant vibration or high pressure.

Common faults in castings are sand inclusions, porosity (gas holes), cracking, excessive flash and distortion. Sand inclusions can be avoided by good moulding methods. Care must be taken not to confuse sand inclusions with porosity. Porosity (gas holes) is due to pockets of gas which cannot escape through the mould. Shrinkage porosity is caused by bad design or insufficient feed metal in the runner system. Suitable foundry techniques can usually overcome these problems.

Cracking is often due to stresses in the material arising from bad design or excessively thin sections, but the possibility of careless handling should not be overlooked. Flash often suggests worn pattern equipment or badly positioned cores. Removal can be very costly although it is wasteful to pay for this operation at the foundry if the offending area is to be machined.

Although in many companies it will be the responsibility of quality control personnel to identify and report faults, directly or indirectly, to the foundry, in order to participate effectively in the ensuing discussions, the buyer should develop an understanding of casting defects, the causes and the remedies.

Quality monitoring is part of the 'package' purchased from the foundry and routine visits from suppliers for this purpose should be positively encouraged. Systems and communications both internally and externally should reflect the importance attached to the maintenance of satisfactory quality standards.

DELIVERY RELIABILITY

Foundries are generally held to be unreliable with regard to delivery. Arguably, the root of the problem is their extreme vulnerability to changes in economic climate and the way in which this affects the attitudes of both management and workforce.

There are, however, certain actions which can be taken by the buyer to alleviate the situation. In all cases of excessive expediting, a complete reappraisal of purchasing policy is indicated. Often it is found that capacity is unsuitable or that priority is being given to more important customers.

Unsatisfactory payments, badly worn pattern equipment and, in particular, insufficient lead time or unrealistic scheduling, all adversely affect the delivery situation. Difficult work or castings which have been incorrectly priced may become impossible to obtain.

If there is substantial business with a supplier, it is probable that capacity can be reserved in terms of the number of boxes per week or per month. Details of the actual castings requirement can be changed at short notice provided that, within reason, the capacity allocated is taken up. This arrangement can benefit both user and producer because optimum use is made of the capacity available instead of being absorbed in building unwanted stocks.

Production control systems employed by foundries tend to be less sophisticated than might be desired and unrealistic demands and requests for special assistance all play a part in disrupting production arrangements. In response to customer pressure, spectacular deliveries are promised with little hope of achievement. The resultant action leaves two disappointed customers – one whose work is displaced and the other whose 'miracle' is not performed.

A statistical method linking price to delivery performance is described in a publication by the Institute of Purchasing and Supply. This system has the effect of focusing foundry management attention on the problem of deliveries and provides the buyer with valuable information when reviewing annual contracts.

Communications with the foundry should stress the importance of adherence to schedules. Visits to discuss schedules and estimated future demands will assist in getting this message across. Effective expediting requires a resolute approach but bullying tactics should be avoided. In the final analysis, there is no substitute for good purchasing policy, intelligent planning and civilised behaviour.

29

Purchasing forgings

Barry Castling

The forging buyer should always challenge the proposals which reach his desk. Paperwork and drawings should be studied carefully and not accepted at face value. The buyer must ascertain the precise details of the requirement and examine the overall capability of the supplier, the resources available and the way in which these are used.

Detailed forging requirements should be specified at the enquiry stage and should cover material specification, heat treatment, tests to be carried out and machining data. Engineering liaison with the supplier should be encouraged at all times with a keen awareness of the cost reduction opportunities.

Caution should be exercised in the comparison of alternative offers to ensure that these are assessed in like terms and with a view to identifying potential hidden costs. The forging drawing is an important element of the supply contract and its relationship to recommended good practice in establishing forging tolerances is discussed.

SUPPLIER ASSESSMENT

The forging buyer should make a critical appraisal of existing and potential sources of supply. The forge should be visited to make sure it exists, and the plant on which the requirement would be produced should be inspected. Conceivably, the facilities could be antiquated and therefore unlikely to give reliable service over long periods. It is also possible that only one item of plant is capable of producing the requisite forgings, thereby introducing the risk of interruption of supplies in the event of plant breakdown or heavy demands from other important customers. Contrasting with this situation, an alternative source may have several suitable machines which would virtually eliminate the risk of delivery failure due to these causes.

Quoted prices must be based on equipment already installed and in use rather than hardware in which the supplier would invest if the order were obtained. The supplier's technical capability should be judged by quality control personnel or other engineer qualified to undertake this task. Reports of their findings should, however, be communicated to the buyer.

The majority of forgings are produced in carbon or low alloy steels. There are, however, specialist forgemasters producing components in aluminium, magnesium, titanium, high nickel alloys and high temperature stainless steels. The raw material which is to be used by the forging supplier should be clearly identified in terms of:

- material specification
- source
- section/size.

The buyer should seek to establish the strength or frailty of the raw material link in the supply chain. It is possible that the supplier might be unable to purchase in sufficient volume or in economic batch quantities. If the material is non-standard, the forgemaster may be a minority buyer with little effective influence over the source of supply.

The following questions should be asked in the process of evaluating the resources of the forging supplier:

- Does the forge have the capability of manufacturing forging dies in their own toolroom?
- Are there in-house facilities for the maintenance of dies?
- Are there heat treatment facilities, if these are needed, and suitable shotblasting or other de-scaling facilities?
- Is the supplier dependent upon the services of a subcontractor

which could involve transport problems, especially if there is a shifted responsibility for the final shipment?

– Are the necessary quality control procedures and equipment adequate to provide ultrasonic testing, crack detection and spectrographic analysis of the material?

In assessing the performance of an existing supplier, the buyer should take into consideration problems experienced with regard to late delivery or poor quality and should try to measure the effect of these factors on the cost of components. The question should be asked: How good are the communications between the forging supplier and other functional levels, i.e. engineering, quality control, production planning, accounts etc? Does the purchasing department bear an unnecessary administrative burden because of supplier attitudes or systems?

The buyer should take all reasonable steps to ensure continuity of supply. Where a large batch or 'flowline' production unit is being served, late delivery can have a disastrous effect on inventory balance and hence the availability of completed units for despatch. It is often necessary to have two or more sources for the same forging. This is particularly important if high volume or critical items are involved.

PRELIMINARY TECHNICAL CONSIDERATIONS

It is the responsibility of the buyer to ensure that all necessary technical information is communicated at the enquiry stage to all potential suppliers. It is normal practice for the customer to furnish a finished machining drawing of the component so that the forgemaster is able initially to supply a marked-up drawing showing the proposed forging and, should he obtain an order, supply a final forging drawing for engineering comment and subsequent customer approval.

The following technical information should be sent to the supplier:

1 Form of supply – whether the forging should be supplied in the machined or unmachined condition.
2 Heat treatment requirements – e.g. normalising, annealing,

tempering etc. and details of the hardness range which these treatments should achieve.

3 If heat treatment by the supplier is called for, it is usual to specify on the purchase order any shotblasting or other treatment required to remove scale (oxide layers caused by the heat treatment).

4 If the forgings are required in the 'as forged' condition, it may be necessary to qualify the location at which this hardness should be measured.

5 The material specification must be clear. Normally, a cast analysis defining the chemical composition will refer to each cast ingot from which the rolled section and subsequent forgings are produced. This analysis should comply with the relevant material specification stated on the customer's drawing and should accompany the material through all the processes prior to forging delivery. The chemical cast analysis is not normally communicated in detail to the customer unless specifically requested, but the reference number should be quoted on all despatch documentation and a record kept by the forging supplier for any subsequent investigation which may be necessary.

6 Details of any testing prior to forging delivery should be laid down at the enquiry stage, so that the prospective vendor can incorporate the effect of these requirements into the cost proposal:

e.g. hardenability (Jominy test)
impact resistance (Izod test)
crack detection (ultrasonic or dye penetrant)
test pieces to accompany bulk production parts.

7 The forging manufacturer may not refer to the production method in the price proposals. If a specific method is required, this should be stated on the enquiry (e.g. upsetting or extrusion forging). There may be an engineering requirement to optimise grain flow to enhance strength, or it may be a prerequisite to suit subsequent manufacturing methods.

8 It is good practice to encourage manufacturing engineering liaison with the forging supplier. The forgemaster should be made aware of intended machining methods. He may then be able to make helpful suggestions which, conceivably, would

avoid costly misunderstandings later on, or which may lead to important cost benefits from reduced forging tolerances on some dimensions. For example, it may be possible to incorporate in the forging process operations such as coining close to form, or the piercing of holes, resulting in significant savings in machining times.

COMMERCIAL CONSIDERATIONS AND PRICE ANALYSIS

Quite apart from the technical aspects of the forging requirement, it is the buyer's responsibility to agree the following salient points of any contract with the prospective forging vendors in an unambiguous manner:

1 *The delivery destination of the subject forgings*
   The price quoted may be 'ex works' or delivered to the customer's works, depending on the buyer's requirements. Care should be taken to make realistic comparisons of offers from alternative bidders bearing these points in mind.
2 *The method of shipment*
   Forgings may be delivered in sacks, stillages, or crates, or may be transported loose in the case of large individual items. Containers are normally supplied and returned on a non-chargeable basis, although some companies may seek a deposit or some financial contribution from the customer.
3 *The proposed method of payment for the goods supplied.*
4 *The manufactured (or delivered) batch sizes*
   This is a critical consideration. As a general guide, economic batch sizes should be:
      suited to the forging equipment used;
      convenient for the machining methods adopted by the customer;
      consistent with customer inventory standards.
   Often there is incompatibility between these factors and the buyer must use his skill to compare the price per unit in relation to the batch size. To illustrate this point let us consider the following example:
      A particular forging is used at the rate of 6,000 per year. The

minimum (buffer) stock level in plant is considered to be 500 pieces.

Prospective suppliers *A* and *B* propose the following prices and delivery arrangements for identical forgings:

A	*B*
Unit price – £10.00	Unit price – £9.80
Produced and delivered batch sizes – 1,000	Produced and delivered batch sizes – 4,000
Average stock 'in house'	Average stock 'in house'
$= \dfrac{500 + 1,500}{2} = 1,000$	$= \dfrac{500 + 4,500}{2} = 2,500$

Difference in actual purchase costs per year
$= (10 - 9.80) \times 6,000 = £1,200$ per year.
Difference in inventory costs, assuming cash tied up could yield a return of, say, 10%
$= (2,500 - 1,000) \times 10\% \times 9.80 = £1,470$ per year.
Therefore, it would be more economical to source with *A*.

5 *The estimated weight of the forging supplied*
This would enable the price per kg. to be calculated for each prospective supplier so that more meaningful comparisons of alternative bids could be made.

Additionally, if the weight of actual forgings supplied were below that upon which the price estimate and quotation were based, the buyer would be well within his rights to insist on renegotiating the unit price.

Knowledge of forging weights is also useful information when the buyer wishes to analyse the effect of raw material cost fluctuations on forging prices.

6 *Cost of tooling to produce and supply forgings*
This could include:
   initial manufacturing cost of forging dies;
   testing or gauging equipment;
   fixtures and jigs for machining.
Some prospective suppliers may itemise these costs separately. Normally, particularly when larger runs are envisaged, tooling costs are amortised into the unit cost of the forging. Once again the buyer must satisfy himself that he is comparing like with like. Considerations of useful die life, repair and replacement costs are normally embodied in the unit price proposals by the forgemaster.

THE FORGING DRAWING

The forging drawing, together with the details given on the purchase order, constitute a contractual arrangement.

This chapter does not deal with the enquiry, quotation, order and acknowledgement procedure for procurement, which are discussed elsewhere in the handbook. However, it is important that the forging buyer understands the responsibilities implied by the forging drawing. Once the respective engineering departments of buyer and vendor have agreed upon a forging drawing, which indicates the appropriate machining allowances, the buyer should obtain signed acceptance from an authorised member of the production engineering department. A signed copy of this drawing should be returned to the supplier as part of the contract and instructions to proceed. A further signed copy should be retained in the purchasing department file. Sample forgings for acceptance, preproduction batches and series production forgings must all conform to this forging drawing.

The forging drawing must specify the material to be used and indicate the location of forgemaster's and customer's reference numbers. The forging buyer should be familiar with and should recognise the importance of British Standard 4114. This should be referred to whenever necessary and the salient points of this specification are included in this chapter. It is pertinent to mention that the forging buyer should be aware of his obligations when engineering changes occur.

First, it is necessary to decide if the change affects the forging drawing and, therefore, the forging supplier. Next, there is the effect on cost and lead time of the introduction of the proposed forging changes. Finally, there is the question of the buyer's liability in terms of raw material commitments and components in production at the forge.

IMPORTANT FEATURES OF BRITISH STANDARD 4114

British Standard 4114 refers to steel forgings – dropforgings, press forgings and upset forgings. The most important elements which concern the buyer are: (a) tolerances for normal requirements, and (b) closer tolerance forgings.

Where forgings are of a specially complicated design, or materials have difficult forging characteristics, standard tolerances can form only a basis for the agreement of appropriate modifications between customer and supplier.

Considerations of other special tolerances are individual and vary widely. They are best discussed at the design stage between purchaser and supplier to ensure optimum use of the forging process whilst at the same time fulfilling the buyer's special requirements at the lowest additional cost. Interpretation of tolerances to BS4114 must be qualified by:

(*a*)   the weight of the forging;
(*b*)   the shape of the die line (flat or symmetrically cranked or assymetrically cranked);
(*c*)   type of steel used (based on carbon and alloying content);
(*d*)   shape complexity factor of the forging (deduced by relating weight of the actual forging to the weight of the overall shape necessary to accommodate the maximum dimensions of the forging).

The categories of tolerances covered by this standard are essentially:
–   diameter tolerances
–   length, width and height tolerances
–   mismatch tolerances (relating to both sides of the die parting line)
–   residual flash tolerances (or trimming flats)
–   pierced hole tolerances
–   thickness tolerances – covering those due to die closure, die wear, and shrinkage relative to dimensions which cross the die parting lines
–   ejector mark tolerances – where these are necessary to facilitate forging production, the position must be indicated to the purchaser before production commences
–   straightness and flatness tolerances – where required, should be indicated on the approved forging drawing
–   tolerances for centre-to-centre dimensions
–   fillet and edge radii tolerances
–   burr tolerances – burr location will be indicated on the forging drawing prior to approval

551

- surface tolerances – relating to pits and depth of surface dressing (on surfaces for subsequent machining, the maximum depth of such characteristics shall not exceed one-half of the machining allowance)
- tolerances on draft angle surfaces – heavy die wear can occur if these tolerances are inadequate (it is important that there is agreement between supplier and purchaser in this regard)
- eccentricity tolerances for deep holes
- tolerances for unforged stock
- tolerances for deformation of sheared ends.

To optimise die and tool design by the forging supplier and facilitate forging inspection procedures, the buyer should supply a finished part drawing detailing dimensions of machining locations and other relevant information on machining operations and component function. The forging drawing produced either by supplier or purchaser, with mutual approval, is the only valid document for inspection of the forged part. Any special features agreed between the purchaser and the supplier must be clearly stated on the forging drawing and all such drawings must be endorsed 'Tolerances to conform with BS4114 unless otherwise indicated'.

Normally, for quotation purposes, the forgemaster will indicate a proposed forging outline superimposed on the finished part drawing. Alternative proposals should be compared carefully in the selection of a suitable supply source. Marked-up drawings should not be used as a basis for the final contract. The buyer should insist on a properly dimensioned forging drawing incorporating all the features ultimately agreed between the two parties.

CHECKLISTS FOR ACTION PLANNING

1 Formulating purchasing policy:
Are all high total value items being constantly researched?
Are there effective communications with suppliers at all important functional levels, e.g. engineering, quality control, production control and accounts?
Is sufficient value analysis taking place between suppliers and our own production engineers?

Is there an excessive burden of costs due to quality problems or delivery failures?

2 Source selection:

Has a sufficiently broad range of supply sources been explored?

Is the source selected the only one capable of meeting the requirement?

What would be the effect of discontinuity of supplies?

Has the supplier invested in sufficient plant to enable production of anticipated requirements without overload?

Does the supplier have adequate stocks of raw material to respond well to requirement changes?

How much investment in component stock is necessary to accommodate economic batch quantities at the supply source?

Would the supplier be in a position to 'steamroller' price increases without submitting their claim to justifiable analysis and negotiation?

Is the method of manufacture efficient in the use of plant, manpower and materials and how does the situation compare with that of other producers of similar components?

30

Purchasing for the food industry

Reg Dickinson

Out of every £1 spent in Britain, 17p is spent on food, adding up to a massive £22 billion a year. The food processing industry is the country's fourth largest manufacturing industry, employing around half a million people and this pattern is similar in all the developed countries in the western world.

Two unusual aspects of the food processing industry have significant implications for purchasing and supply and its role within the individual business. These are the unique industry cost structure, heavily weighted towards prime cost materials, and the growing concentration within the retail grocery market. Grocery buying power is moving into fewer and fewer hands.

Figure 30.1 is a generalised average cost model for the food processing industry which illustrates that prime cost materials and energy account for about 78 per cent of manufacturing costs plus profit before tax.

As the industry is geared to the world soft commodity markets, it is not surprising that the purchased element of cost varies considerably between manufacturers, industry sectors and even within the same business by season.

Figures 30.2 and 30.3 show the growing domination of the major multiple retailers within the UK retail grocery market and the shift in balance of power from the manufacturers to the large retailer. The multiple retailers have increased their share of the food market from 42 per cent in 1970 to 55 per cent in 1980 and are projected to

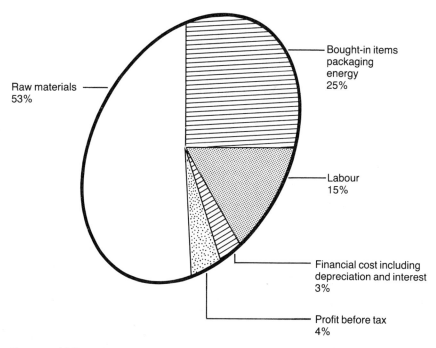

Source: IGD.

Figure 30.1 Financial model: basic food processing industry cost structure

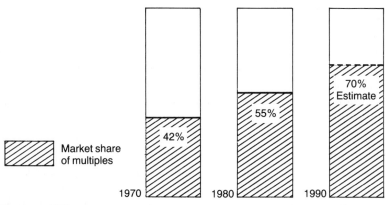

Source: IGD.

Figure 30.2 Multiple grocery retailers: market share

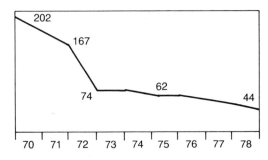

Source: IGD.

Figure 30.3 Multiple grocery sector: buying points

grow to 70 per cent by the end of the decade. The significance of this for the food manufacturer is that the number of retail grocery buying points reduced from 202 in the multiple sector in 1970 to 44 less than ten years later. Five names now account for half the grocery business, with two enjoying 30 per cent between them. Such buying 'clout' inevitably squeezes food processors' profit margins and costs and, in turn, demonstrates the potential impact of effective buying policies and strategies.

Consumer demand for those food products which are generally termed 'fast moving consumer goods' (FMCGs) can be notoriously difficult to predict. The influence of the weather, for example, on the ice cream, soft drinks and snack foods industries is very significannt, and food processors have to gear their production and stockholding policies to accommodate short-term unpredictable and violent fluctuations in demand. Buyers and materials controllers need to take a totally pragmatic and flexible approach to the logistical problems created by the climatic impact on demand, for in such circumstances production forecasts can be hopelessly inaccurate. The problem for the raw materials buyer can be further exacerbated when, as is frequently the case, the raw material or the finished product has a limited shelf life. The introduction of 'best before' date declarations on many manufactured food products as a result of the Food Labelling Regulations of 1980 added an extra dimension to the inventory management problems within the food processing industry. The 'traditional' stockholding costs can pale into insignificance if outdated surplus stocks have to be destroyed.

THE NEED FOR EFFECTIVE PURCHASING

For the individual business, strategy concerns competitive advantage. A competitive advantage exists where (a) a company produces a product or service which customers rate equal to industry standards at a cost lower than that of its competitors, or (b) the company must provide it at the same cost as competitors, but clearly demonstrate some superior attributes that the customers will pay a higher price for.

One clear way for manufacturers to obtain competitive advantage is by ensuring that costs are lower than their competitors. With up to three-quarters of a food processor's costs being in the purchased materials area, corporate strategy must focus on establishing and maintaining a professional and effective purchasing resource.

THE NATURE OF FOOD PURCHASING AND THE RAW MATERIALS BUYER

Agricultural raw materials account for about one-half of the European food processor's costs – sourced internationally, but with a growing tendency towards geographical concentration in Europe. This recent phenomenon has been brought about by the various protection regimes of the EEC's Common Agricultural Policy (CAP) which have led to the UK food industry processing up to 70 per cent of the produce of British farms. Certain sectors such as sugar, dairy, meat processing and milling account for most of this concentration of materials sourcing; the remaining sectors being primarily geared towards the imported tropical or semi-tropical materials not readily produced within Europe.

If one looks for examples of purchase price volatility, the agricultural raw materials, or soft commodities area is a rich prospect, with price fluctuations of up to 100 per cent in any one season being common place, and up to 500 per cent not unheard of. Clearly purchasing's impact on corporate profitability and competitive advantage is significant and calls for a supply strategy which recognises the specialist procurement skills needed to perform effectively in these esoteric markets.

Primary or traded commodity	Principal downstream products and applications
Oil seeds:	
Soyabeans	Animal feedmeal, flours, textured proteins
Rapeseed	edible oils
Palm Kernels	
Groundnuts	
Edible oils/fats:	
Palm	Cooking/frying oil, bakery fats, confectionery fats
Coconut	Ice cream bases, confectionery fats
Olive	Salad dressing, mayonnaise
Soyabean	Cooking/frying oil, bakery fats, margarine
Rape	Cooking/frying oil, bakery fats, margarine
Groundnut	Cooking/frying oil, salad dressings
Lard	Cooking fats
Tallow	Cooking fats, margarine
Marine	Margarine, bakery fats
Meats/fish	Fresh/frozen/dehydrated/canned/chilled
	Powder flavours
	Animal and marine fats/oils
Dairy products:	
Milk	Skimmed and full fat powder, butter, cream, cheese, whey
Butter	Confectionery, baking
Cheese	Flavourings in snacks and biscuits
Cereals:	
Wheat	Flour, starches, semolina, pasta, animal feedmeal
Maize	Breakfast cereals, snack extrusion grits, starches, syrups
Rice	Milled, parboiled and pre-puffed, puffed, breakfast cereals
Sugars:	
Molasses	Animal feed, pickles and sauces
White granulated	Icings, liquid sugars, sweeteners
Cocoa beans	Powder, manufactured chocolate
Coffee beans	Ground, instant, flavourings
Tea	Blended leaf extracts and flavourings
Edible nuts	Whole, chopped
Spices	Whole, ground, oleoresins, extracts, essential oils
Fruit and vegetables:	
Various fresh	Dehydrates, pulps, concentrates, juices, powders, natural flavourings
Dried fruits	Whole, chopped, mascerated
Pulses	Peas, pea beans, lentils

Figure 30.4 Food processing: major raw materials

Figure 30.4 gives some idea of the wide range of raw materials bought by food processors. Primary materials traded on international markets such as wheat and maize will be bought in their original state by large breakfast cereal manufacturers, coffee and cocoa beans by the beverage producers, whilst some manufacturers will buy the semi-processed derivatives as ingredients for their own recipes. In practice most major food manufacturers produce such a diverse range of products that their shopping lists will range from vast tonnages of primary commodities down to a few kilogrammes of semi-processed materials such as seasonings, essential oils and flavourings. Some manufacturers will 'contract grow' their own fresh primary materials, for example, in the manufacture of frozen and canned vegetables and potato crisps. In this situation procurement efforts are directed towards seed buying and production, contract growing negotiation with farmers, and the free market buying of additional supplies during the harvest season. It is not unusual for the purchasing department to be involved in all of these activities as a matter of routine.

The food processor's materials purchasing function must be structured and manned to meet this varied demand for specialist skills. The basic professional skills of negotiation, purchase price management and source development etc. form a very necessary fundamental requirement in any food raw materials buyer. The additional skills of commodity market analysis and buying judgement are simple to define, yet difficult to measure, particularly when in the process of recruiting buyers. Demonstrations of past performance of necessity calls for experience. Experienced buyers with good track records in commodities are a rare and expensive breed; to the extent that most companies prefer to train their own. The training costs are high both in terms of time and on the job judgemental error. Nevertheless the prize, in terms of profit contribution from successful market judgement, creates a real competitive advantage for the buyer's employers through lower costs.

A variety of operational research techniques for soft commodity price forecasting are available to the buyer either as computer software packages for in-house use, or through specialist commodity consultants and brokers. Such complex models attempt to measure such variables as chance and risk, and the strategies of competing buyers and sellers. Thus far these tools can only be used as a decision-making aid. Market psychology and sentiment have little or no quantitative underpinnings and so major market forces will continue to require qualitative evaluation by the buyer. Science and art continue to work together in the commodities buying arena with a growing emphasis on the quantitative aspect.

CAP COMMODITIES

Agriculture and the production and marketing of its products has, since time immemorial, received considerable attention from national governments around the world. The continuing expansion of food production from a country's own resources in an effort to become self sufficient owes its origins to the need for home production during war years, and to the balance of payments benefits of reducing the food import bill.

In the early years of the development of the EEC, it was argued that the food processor would enjoy a greater supply security for his raw materials which are covered by the CAP regime. Self-sufficiency and insulation against wildly fluctuating world market prices are the key objectives in community agricultural policy making. To some extent these objectives have been fulfilled at a crippling cost to the member states. In 1983 66 per cent of the total EEC spending of 25.1 billion European Currency Units (ECUs) went to agriculture with the dairy sector soaking up 19 per cent and creating enormous surpluses of cheese, butter and skimmed milk powder.

The reasons for this apparent market mismanagement revolve around one fundamental problem: *agriculture is the main industry in many remote regions of the community with few alternative sources of employment.* This is a predominant feature in the politics of EEC agriculture and it is not surprising that the laudable economic objectives become overwhelmed by the social problems and measures to resolve them.

The agricultural problem is one of the most perplexing difficulties facing community policy-makers today. The objective of price stability has been achieved through huge surpluses which eventually must be dumped, via export subsidies, on world markets or at the extreme, destroyed. The raw materials buyer, with an ear to the Commission in Brussels, can seek out the occasional opportunities when they occur and profit from procuring surplus commodities at advantageous prices. Indeed, the major buyer can sometimes influence the timing and pricing of such disposals by astute lobbying.

In such a dynamic political environment the buyer has a key role to play in industry and national lobbies to form or modify CAP legislation; particularly as such issues have a direct impact on price and availability.

The commodities in Figure 30.5 show a striking resemblance to the major food processing raw materials in Figure 30.4. Consequently very few EEC manufactured foods will escape totally the effects of CAP. Sugar and cereal products are outstanding examples. Buyers not constrained by CAP can still enjoy the benefits of cheaper world prices in times other than extreme scarcity. Since 1967 the sugar buyer within the EEC has been severely handicapped by internal prices frequently far in excess of world free market levels. Similar situations arise in several other CAP commodity areas. The buyer will find his main route of escape in substitution by acceptable alternatives which are either cheaper or not constrained by EEC policy regimes.

Sugar is perhaps the most ubiquitous of food ingredients and in some sectors of the industry is a very costly raw material. During 1983 the UK government gave food and drugs clearance to a variety of artificial sweeteners, infinitely superior to saccharin, which may now be used as sugar alternatives in soft drinks and manufactured foods. Notwithstanding the dietetic benefits in low calorie food products, the cost benefits can be significant for food processors who are able to incorporate these into their recipes. Similar substitutions can be made in the area of dairy products and cereal-based raw materials such as thickeners which are not only cost effective, but have no detrimental effect on the end product. Some food processors have been pleasantly surprised at the product improvement side effects of some ingredient substitutes. The buyer must often be the prime mover in stimulating such change, as he is invariably the only individual within the organisation so immersed in the problem that he can pinpoint opportunities as they arise.

	Year[a]	World market[b] price	EEC support[c] price	EEC price as % of world market price
Wheat, soft	1979-80	158.23	149.17	94
	1980-81	170.35	155.88	92
	1981-82	179.19	166.23	92
	1982-83	169.50	179.27	107
Barley	1979-80	115.53	149.17	129
	1980-81	141.06	155.88	111
	1981-82	139.78	166.23	118
	1982-83	121.97	179.27	147
Maize	1979-80	101.18	149.17	147
	1980-81	142.79	155.88	109
	1981-82	134.54	166.23	123
	1982-83	146.15	179.27	123
Rice	1979-80	318.78	382.28	120
	1980-81	455.59	408.16	90
	1981-82	380.50	450.50	118
	1982-83	397.34	496.69	125
Butter	1979-80	792.50	2849.70	360
	1980-81	1160.07	2916.00	251
	1981-82	2017.06	3178.04	158
	1982-83	2003.20	3497.00	175
Sugar	1979-80	331.01	410.09	124
	1980-81	539.04	432.07	80
	1981-82	315.08	469.05	149
	1982-83	250.06	514.01	205
Beef	1979-80	882.43	1391.02	158
	1980-81	907.56	1446.08	159
	1981-82	944.33	1555.40	165
	1982-83	958.67	1725.08	180

Notes:
(a)   the season is different for different products;
(b)   EEC import prices minus levies and duties, i.e. c.if. at EEC ports;
(c)   threshold prices (cereals, sugar and butter); guide price (beef).

Sources: EEC statistics and IMF.

Figure 30.5 Prices of certain agricultural commodities in the EEC and on world markets: 1979-83 (ECUs per tonne)

WORLD MARKETS FOR FOOD COMMODITIES

Many food commodities and their downstream derivatives fall outside the direct influence of the CAP, particularly tropical and semi-tropical products such as edible vegetable oils, cocoa beans, coffee, tea and pulses, for example.

Within a free market framework prices of agricultural commodities fluctuate wildly, principally influenced by the weather. The most dramatically sensitive is coffee where rumours of frost in Brazil are enough to send prices rocketing. In 1979 the futures price of coffee in London rose to £600 a tonne (up by 40 per cent) within a month only to fall all the way back the following month. In 1977 severe frost damage pushed coffee prices up by nearly 100 per cent in just five months – such is the life of the coffee buyer!

Source: Public Ledger.

Figure 30.6 Market reaction to drought: soyabean oil

Figures 30.6 and 30.7 show how the markets for soyabean oil and groundnut oil reacted violently to the severe drought in the US midwest during the 1983 season. As rumours of drought damage to the soyabean crops of Iowa and Illinois turned to reality the price of soyabean oil soared by 60 per cent in just 20 days. Soyabeans comprise nearly 50 per cent of the world production of the major exportable oilseeds. Soyameal represents three-quarters of all world exports of protein meal and soyabean oil one-quarter of all vegetable and animal oil exports. With the USA traditionally

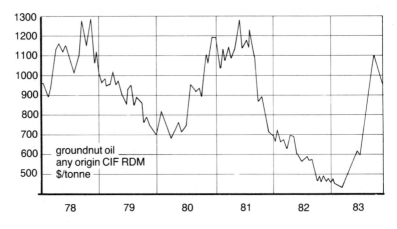

Source: Public Ledger.

Figure 30.7 Market reaction to drought: groundnut oil

supplying two-thirds of the world's soyabeans, the impact of the midwest drought is hardly surprising. It is estimated that 30 per cent of all UK food manufacturers use oils and fats in some form or other and so the US drought of 1983 will have special significance for most raw material buyers.

A close study of the dynamics of the market for edible oils and fats during 1983/4 will reward those buyers seeking a deeper knowledge of the curious and fickle nature of agricultural commodity markets. Examples of most of the independent variables making up the complex market model will be found; some of the most significant being:

- The surge in demand from speculators on the Chicago grain market as Wall Street journalists 'napped' soyabean futures.
- The sudden swing from abundant 1982 crop carryover stocks to a predicted 1983 crop shortfall and consequent supply lag until 1984 crops.
- The substitute switching from soyabean oil to other edible oils as buyers seek to temper costs, thus affecting the markets for other edible oils (see Figure 30.7: the market price of groundnut oil reacted in sympathy even though the groundnut crop was not damaged by drought).
- Rumours of political intervention by southern hemisphere

producer countries in 'cancelling' undelivered low price contracts.

- The inability of crop experts to predict with accuracy crop yields before harvest.
- The marginal improvement in supply as the droughted soyabeans produced unexpected above average oil yields.
- The psychological effect of user buyers not reacting positively to bullish facts as they emerged from several years of supply security and falling prices.
- The likelihood of 'demand rationing' when market prices escalate to totally uneconomic levels. This can be brought about by individual buyers withdrawing from the market and ceasing using the commodity temporarily or by poorer countries simply not being able to afford them.

DETERMINING AGRICULTURAL COMMODITY PRICES

The theory of competitive markets tells us that there will be an equilibrium price at which a particular commodity will trade in a particular time period. Variations in supply conditions will change this price, as will fluctuations in demand. One would expect, therefore, to be able to predict the impacts of short-run changes in supply and demand on price and its movements over time as costs and demand conditions change. But in the real world of agricultural commodities this equilibrium price is surprisingly elusive. The determinants of prices in world commodity markets are much more complex than would be suggested by the competitive model of the microeconomist.

Consequently price forecasting techniques have been aimed at predicting price 'bands' within which prices may fluctuate rather than specific unit prices which will prevail at a particular point in time. Kingsman,[1] recognising this, points out that prices do not increase or decrease at a smooth rate but tend to meander up or down about some overall trend with upper and lower limits which he terms the 'forecast envelope' (see Figure 30.8).

Commodity traders and buyers synonymously talk of 'upside' and 'downside' risk. Having determined the general price direction, their principal day-to-day concern is with fluctuations around the

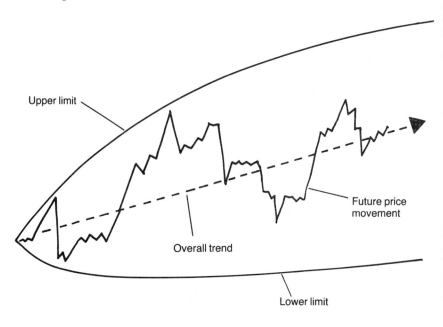

Upper limit

Future price movement

Overall trend

Lower limit

Figure 30.8 Forecast envelope

trend. Some multinational food manufacturers have commodity analysis departments for the sole purpose of guiding their buyers and sellers in making sound and profitable market price decisions.

The buyer of agricultural commodities ought to feel quite comfortable, surrounded as he is by a proliferation of published price forecasting techniques, an army of consultants all keen to advise him when to buy, in exchange for a vast fee and no guarantee of success, and the marvels of modern communications which enable him to be bombarded hourly with market intelligence. In practice he needs to be cautious and unruffled, yet not unresponsive to all the information available to him. He will sift and analyse in his search for the most significant price determinants, call on his or the experience of others, but the ultimate buying decision is likely to be his alone – as price volatile commodity markets do not wait for committee decisions. Neither do they close when the buyer leaves his desk in the evening or takes his annual leave. Total immersion of the buyer in his key markets is the only safe philosophy. There is no compromise.

Greig[2] makes two pertinent observations with respect to food commodity buying:

> Know your commodity. There is a great tendency to substitute statistical complexity for knowledge of the commodity. The results are usually disastrous.
> For most major food commodities, the supply of the commodity has a much greater impact on price than does the demand.

A degree of purchasing specialisation is clearly called for, particularly as many primary commodities and their downstream derivatives are influenced by the same market forces. The purchase of whole cereals, flours, and cereal-based thickeners, for example, fall into this category. Kraljic[3] recognised this need in his discussion on the development and implementation of specific purchasing strategies and action plans suggesting that the structure of the purchasing function is best oriented towards sympathetic commodity areas or 'skill centres', rather than towards internal company organisational centres.

LIMITING THE RISK

The foolish activities of certain UK cocoa buyers in 1973 incurred buying losses for their companies to the tune of £20 million. This speculative misuse of the cocoa futures market did more to set back the effective use of the food commodity futures markets by food manufacturers than any other single event. In consequence some buyers were directed not to use futures markets to hedge their risks, particularly in companies where there was a distinct misunderstanding of the operation of futures markets.

For commodities where a formal futures market exists, for example, the recently introduced UK potatoes and soyabean oil futures terminals, most of the forward price volatility can be ironed out by judicious use of various hedging techniques. Such techniques are far from speculative when used in a restrained way; indeed it can be argued that to ignore the hedging facility when it exists is speculation. Almost all of the formal organisations which administer the various futures markets publish simple guides with examples as to how the manufacturer can use the market to protect himself against unforeseen price fluctuations for his key raw materials.

Notwithstanding the very obvious advantages to be gained, prudent businesses should lay down clear and unambiguous operating guide lines if the 1973 cocoa débâcle is not to be repeated. There should also be written instructions to the company's commodity brokers setting out the conditions on which they are to deal with the authorised buyer. As well as stating by name who is authorised to deal, there should be limitations on the extent of their trading and the markets in which they may trade.

For example, a food manufacturer might specify the limits of authority as follows:

> Mr X is authorised to trade in soyabean oil futures on behalf of *XYZ* plc. Dealings are limited to the London soyabean oil market and will only be done through broker A and broker B. A total long position will not exceed 1,000 tonnes or £500,000 whichever is the greater with any one broker. A short position will not exceed 200 tonnes or £100,000 whichever is the greater with any one broker. Any price movement which takes the company's position above these limits will be reported to the managing director within 24 hours of occurrence.

HIGH RISK COMMODITIES

Certain commodities are not suitable for futures trading. This is primarily due to their lack of continuous availability or because they are not capable of standardisation so as to form a reliable basis for contract. It may be simply because the world volume of trade is inadequate to support a futures market.

Spices, edible nuts and pulses such as dry beans for baked beans and dried peas fall into this category. The buyer does not have the facilities of a futures market in which to hedge his risk, therefore his company is totally exposed in markets which are historically the most price volatile. It is in this area that the food raw materials buyer can be said to hold the company profits in the palm of his hand, particularly when the commodity in question happens to be strategically important to the business. A correct buying decision can give his company such a competitive edge that windfall profits ensue, especially if supplies become virtually unobtainable due to crop failure. Such markets demand continuous and expert attention, as prices can move for the most trivial and ephemeral reasons. As a result it is not surprising that professional speculators are attracted to these markets seeing them as sources of quick trading profits.

The buyer must, therefore, seek and identify genuine price trends, and try to leave the day-to-day fluctuations to the speculative traders. Most of all he must stick to the trading principles that have served him well in the past when his market takes on one of its all-too-frequent volatile postures. Time and experience will teach him to judge the quality of information from his many sources; which market contacts he can rely upon and which invariably proliferate or originate rumours!

Over time the buyer can devise his own rules and techniques which specifically apply to the commodities he buys. These may or may not involve the use of futures markets, inventory building, hand-to-mouth buying and long-term price agreements. The challenge for improvement is constant.

REFERENCES

(1) B. G. Kingsman, 'Forecasting and Research for Supply Markets', in Farmer and Taylor (eds), *Corporate Planning and Procurement* Heinemann, reprinted 1982.
(2) Dr W. Smith Greig, *The Economics of Food Processing,* The Avi Publishing Co. Inc., 1971.
(3) Dr Peter Kraljic, 'Practical Aspects and Implementation of Purchasing Strategy in Enterprises' in *IFDMM Journal,* no. 1, October 1981.

FURTHER READING

R. G. Lipsey, *An Introduction to Positive Economics,* Weidenfeld and Nicholson, 6th edition, 1983.
C. W. J. Granger, 'Trading in Commodities', An *Investors' Chronicle* Guide, Woodhead-Faulkner, 4th edition, 1983.
Allan N. Rae, *Crop Management Economics,* Crosly, Lockwood & Staples, 1982.

31

Purchasing for the pharmaceutical industry

Clive Butler

PROFILE OF THE INDUSTRY

As an introduction to this chapter it is intended to identify some of
the important facts relating to the pharmaceutical industry, the
companies operating in it, and some of the major products and
materials in use. This background, though brief, will assist in a
better understanding of the industry itself and it is suggested that
such knowledge is essential to successful purchasing of the material
needs of the industry.

The industry itself, though small, is an international one; only
about 25 per cent of approximately 120 companies in the field are
British owned, the rest having parents who are mainly American,
though there has been some growth in European-owned companies
in recent years. However amongst the 25 per cent British companies
are some very well known large corporations, e.g. Boots, Glaxo,
Beechams and Fisons.

By many standards the industry may be regarded as small; it
employs about 70,000 which is less than 0.5 per cent of the working
population, yet it manages a remarkable performance in exporting
£1bn in 1982 with a trade surplus of £600m.

Some of the problems facing the industry are worth noting for
they can have an influence on the purchase of materials; though the
following is not meant to be a complete list it does identify some of
the major difficulties:

- extensive and expensive legally enforced manufacturing practices
- restriction of selling prices of ethical (or prescription only) drugs
- long and expensive periods of time to develop safe drugs
- short product life
- patent infringements especially from overseas manufacturers
- control in advertising its products.

Products of the industry can broadly be divided into two categories:

- those sold over the counter mainly in chemist shops, but also some products in grocery outlets – these are generally called OTC products, and
- those which are available only against prescription from a doctor or dentist (mainly called ethicals).

OTC products need little description for we are all buyers in this area at one time or another; in the main these are simple remedies suitable for home medication with analgesics, cough preparations and medicated confectionery being the most important groups.

Ethical drugs, available only if prescribed by a qualified medical practitioner, are the results of millions of pounds spent on research and the most important ones are antibiotics, antidepressants and those concerned with the treatment of heart disease.

The industry is different from most others in that its major customer for ethicals is the government; for example, the British National Health Service in 1982-3 paid about £1.5bn for its drugs and national governments throughout the world are generally the industry's largest customer. In Britain, prices the industry can charge for its drugs are controlled through a Pharmaceutical Price Regulation Scheme which regulates the prices for drugs sold to the NHS by monitoring the levels of profits, and controls matters of expenditure on, for example, promotional spending.

QUALITY CONSIDERATIONS

Inevitably the pharmaceutical industry is greatly concerned with the quality standards necessary for it to produce safe and effective products; this chapter will study in some detail these considerations for they effect sourcing decisions to considerable extent.

Background

Legislation introduced to protect the consumer against malpractices of traders, goes back to the sixteenth century – the earliest recorded Act (in 1540) empowered physicians in London to appoint four inspectors of medicine. During the nineteenth century the Pharmaceutical Society of Great Britain was established, and legislation was introduced to control the retail supply of poisons and to establish a register of pharmacists. In 1858 the necessary statutory provision was made for the publication of the British Pharmacopeia and in 1925 the first Therapeutic Substances Act provided for control over biological products. Later, mainly with the 1933 Pharmacy Act, antibiotics and certain other products were placed on a prescription only basis.

However, except for biological substances and dangerous drugs like narcotics, no limitations were placed on the freedom of a manufacturer to put a new drug on the market. Clearly most reputable companies carried out thorough testing procedures but they had no legal obligation to do so. The need for further legislation was being considered when, in late 1961, the thalidomide tragedy occurred; by 1964 an expert committee (The Committee on Safety of Drugs) had been set up under the chairmanship of Sir Derrick Dunlop to review evidence available for new drugs and to offer advice on their toxicity. The pharmaceutical industry voluntarily agreed to submit data on new products to this committee and to accept its decisions. It was clear though that such circumstances could only be temporary and after a period of consultation it was decided to introduce new legislation giving statutory backing to the committee's advice, and also to overhaul all other legislation relating to medicines. Thus came about the most important and all embracing piece of legislation known as The Medicines Act 1968.

The Medicines Act 1968

The Act is a comprehensive measure replacing almost all of the earlier legislation on the control of medicines for human and veterinary use. Under the Act:

1 A body called the Medicines Commission was established to give advice and make recommendations to the Minister.
2 A licensing system was established to regulate marketing, importation, manufacture and distribution.
3 A revised code of law as to the retail sale and supply of products was introduced.
4 Ministers were empowered to make regulations relating to labelling containers and selling presentations.
5 Ministers could establish committees with specific advisory functions.

It is not necessary for present purposes to go into much detail on these main provisions, except over that relating to licensing, for this also has a significant impact on purchasing decisions.

The licensing procedures require the Medicines Inspectorate to consider the suitability of premises of manufacture, the equipment, the procedures in use and the competence of the personnel for the purpose of the operation. Thus the Medicines Inspectorate will visit establishments in order to assess and review these matters in considerable detail.

Impact on sourcing decision

The concern in legislation that the premises and good manufacturing procedures at manufacturers and wholesalers measure up to the highest standards affects suppliers, for a knowledge of supplying companies and its procedures are required in much more detail than hitherto.

Data accompanying an application for a product licence must include a considerable amount of information relating to starting materials (see Appendix 1). It will be seen that supplying companies are required to provide information on the starting material which they may be reluctant to do for a number of reasons; batch production is not really an appropriate description ccovering the production of some natural materials like sugar for example. In other cases where batch production is the normal method, as in production of chemicals, manufacturers may be reluctant to go to the trouble of providing special data to an industry which is often only a small buyer of its materials. Thus in the raw material area much work has to be done in acquainting suppliers with the industry's special needs, and persuading companies to take action, such as selecting particular batches, in order to provide materials of the required quality. In other instances it may be preferable to encourage suppliers to set up a specialised manufacturing unit, making low volume, high purity raw materials.

Packaging suppliers too have to concern themselves with specifications of their starting materials, e.g. PVC for making plastic bottles should be bought from manufacturers of repute who are able to guarantee purity and consistency from batch to batch. In all forms of packaging, from immediate containers (like bottles) or outer packaging, standards of operating and their quality assurance is important. Supplying companies to pharmaceutical manufacturers have to recognise the special needs of the industry, and if necessary adapt in order to provide the industry with its material requirements.

SUPPLY MARKETS

The industry purchases a wide range of raw materials, both synthetically produced and those of natural origin; its usage of packaging components is relatively small.

Synthetic materials

Most synthetics are derivatives of petrochemicals and the large international chemical companies in Europe have sold pharmaceutical chemicals in the UK for many years even when faced with tariff barriers. Today, in general, there is free movement of materials and most supplies come from within the EEC, where Britain, Germany, France and the Netherlands are the most important source countries. Others worth mentioning include Japan, who can be highly competitive despite duty barriers, though there is some doubt about their long-term interest in selling to the UK when they can obtain better prices in markets such as the USA. America traditionally sells only specialised intermediates in the UK, but increasingly is being seen as a cheap source for more materials (mainly because of low energy costs) again despite tariff barriers. Other countries present an interesting situation, particularly third world countries where costs of production can be very low and as they have preferential tariff barriers (or none at all) then it is possible for them to sell throughout Europe at very cheap prices – Korea and Indonesia would be good examples here. Elsewhere, primarily in the Middle-East, considerable investment is being made both in petrochemicals and downstream chemicals and from the mid-1980s these countries may well emerge as important sources to the industry.

As has been noted, most synthetic materials are derived from petrochemicals, thus a detailed knowledge of the petrochemical industry and the supply influences is essential to successful purchasing of pharmaceutical chemicals. The reporting of price movements and availability of crude oil has been extensive since 1974 when the producers increased their prices dramatically overnight, and caused in the following few years widespread economic problems. The more relevant results to this chapter concern the subsequent, and the continuing, rationalisation in the chemical industry with widespread refinery and downstream closures, and further amalgamation by producers. The general drift to a smaller number of producers is likely to continue as most petrochemical operators are still showing significant losses.

In the medium term such moves in the supply market will mean less competition, resulting in higher prices. This does not seem to have happened in all product areas in the last year or so, mainly due to a glut of crude oil, its price stability and continued weak demand; but also fierce competition amongst petrochemical producers existed for much of the time as producers resisted unpalatable decisions relating to refinery closures.

If the crude oil scene looks reasonably comfortable some attention has to be given to the main 'building blocks' of the industry like ethylene, benzene, toluene and phenol. Out of these ethylene has increased markedly in the last twelve months with a determination amongst producers to obtain a satisfactory pricing level, whereas the others have seen much lower increases.

In addition to these base costs, petrochemical producers are large users of energy which has also increased substantially in price,

575

though much successful work has been carried out by all manufacturers to conserve energy. In the UK chemical companies have argued that industrial energy costs are much higher than continental competitors, so making them less competitive, but there does not seem to be any move on the government's part to change these costs significantly.

As a result, manufacturers of pharmaceutical intermediates have been faced with these changes in their feedstock and have, of course, tried to pass some of it on to their customers, the pharmaceutical manufacturers. At the same time the pharmaceutical manufacturer is undergoing his own 'squeeze' with the various National Health Services looking for price reductions – stability is not good enough.

This is a time for manufacturer and customer to get closer together; the tradition of overseas suppliers selling chemicals through UK agents must surely change, for the complexity of business negotiations today requires principal and customer to have a much closer relationship, and to offer the same level of direct communication as British chemical companies. If agents are to survive in the future it is clear they must (and some have already) adapt their business to offer facilities required by pharmaceutical manufacturers, relating to areas such as quality control and warehousing which in the past have been non-existent or minimal.

Natural materials

Many different natural materials are used in the industry. Some are easily defined, e.g. sugar, but others may be more of a complex nature, e.g. colours, and used in small quantities, though vital to the formulation. As a result many of these materials are soft commodities, the markets often fluctuating violently and being influenced by crop time/size, weather conditions and speculation as well as by normal supply and demand considerations.

A number of significant materials, like sugar, milk and cereals, have their prices influenced to a great extent by the Common Agricultural Policy of the EEC. To set prices for CAP materials, the EEC Commission tables proposals for new price levels in January of each year. The proposals take into account levels of EEC inflation, incomes of farmers and the relative strengths of member country currencies and thus the levels of the monetary compensation amounts (MCA) which is a device used to equalise prices paid for CAP materials within the community. The proposals must be ratified by the EEC Council of Ministers so that inevitably political pressures influence the final price agreement.

The level of the green pound further influences the cost of CAP materials; a reduction in value of the green pound would increase prices in the UK and UK farmers' incomes, and a revaluation would reduce prices and decrease the farmers' income – so here again political pressures influence the level of the green pound.

Implementation dates for different products can vary and certainly the amount is different, though we have consistently seen increases in the range of 5-9 per cent each year so that forward purchasing can often produce substantial savings.

In some cases, such as sugar, markets are somewhat restricted, though there are some special arrangements for countries (like the Caribbean area on sugar) which the UK negotiated as part of its entry into the EEC.

Natural products have traditionally been sold through merchants who still transact a large amount of business, working for a small commission of around 3 per cent. Their effect on the price paid is small but they can provide information and advice (particularly important on soft commodities), shipping and payment facilities.

However, increasingly it has become the practice of the larger users to deal directly with producers, perhaps utilising the merchant for essential spot purchasing arrangements where the buyer has an immediate need. Of course in some cases, and this is particularly true where little or no quality control exists at origin, it may well be worth paying the merchant's small commission. In the event of default on the part of the overseas supplier the buyer will not be involved in the lengthy and expensive business of obtaining redress, so that the buyer is often happier to place his order with a merchant house and to pay a small premium.

Packaging materials

The industry is a small, but important user of most packaging components, with glass and plastic amongst the most important where they are used for immediate containers. Aluminium, whilst still extensively used for tubes, is fast declining.

The UK glass industry has seen a very substantial fall in demand during the last five years; indeed the number of people employed in the industry has fallen by half since 1979 and even taking into account some major furnace closures in the last twelve months there is still overcapacity in the industry and it is probable that further closures will take place. The glass industry is a larger user of energy as temperatures in furnaces reach 400°C and reference has been made earlier in this chapter to UK energy costs versus continental companies. Some work has been undertaken recently by British Gas on the development of a ceramic burner and this promises to increase furnace efficiency by 20-30 per cent. In 1983 imports of glass containers accounted for about 11 per cent of the demand for glass containers and these were mainly for specialised or decorative containers in volumes which the large UK manufacturers like United Glass, Rockware or Beatson Clark have not been able to produce; certainly the sheer logistics of moving large and certainly breakable containers, will continue to keep imports into the UK at a relatively low level.

Plastic containers for use with pharmaceuticals have expanded just as fast as in other product areas, and even in some traditional areas (like tablet bottles) it is still gaining ground and contributing to the continuing decline of glass containers referred to earlier. As might be expected there are a number of reasons for this gradual but continuing change. Plastics have a modern image and low breakages which marketing departments can exploit; prices have been very low, artificially so, for some time and particularly when compared with glass containers; supplies can be moved within the UK and imported into the UK cheaply, due to lightness, and safety.

The low investment cost to set up manufacturing plants for packaging components has meant the establishment of a large number of small producers. Clearly many of these companies offer a restricted range of components and/or materials, e.g. tablet bottles in stock sizes from polypropylene, but the larger organisations like United Closures and Plastics or BXL offer not only stock and custom-made containers, but closures as well.

We have discussed earlier in this chapter the desire for petro-chemical price increases, and the action being taken by the large international petrochemical companies in (strategically) closing plants in an effort to reduce capacity for producing the major plastic materials – polypropylene, polyethylene, polystyrene and PVC and their action appears to have 'paid off'. The rise in demand for packaging plastics has gained sufficient movement during the last year to persuade producers to increase polymer prices, with the consequence of this being transferred into increases in component prices. Though major polymer producers like BP and ICI have made losses in these areas, the stable price of oil and the coming on-stream in the next few years of new petrochemical complexes in, for example, Saudi Arabia, makes it unlikely that present prices will be maintained and it is possible that current prices will fall in the medium term.

The overall future for plastics looks bright; not only will its prices be held in check but it is believed that demand will continue to increase as technology produces more materials like polyethylene terephthalate (PET), which will give price, weight and appearance benefits over traditional materials.

Energy costs

Reference has already been made to energy costs, including those which suppliers to the industry carry and also which pharmaceutical manufacturers are faced with. Here, depending on the products being manufactured, the industry can be large users, e.g. antibiotics require a great deal of energy.

An understanding of energy costs is therefore required and Appendix 3 provides much detail of competitive costs in Europe, because UK companies have argued for some time that their industrial prices are far too high when compared with continental competitors, and that this is a major factor in their difficulty in competing with EEC sources. It would also be worth making observations on the UK source as a general overview on the main fuels as follows:

> *Oil* is crucial to UK fuel pricing in general and it is felt at the time of writing that the marker (Saudi Arabian Light) will remain stable in US$ terms of $29 barrel for the next 2/3 years. Clearly some changes such as a build up of the conflict between Iran and Iraq could cause a short-term uplift in price. Oil will

eventually run out unless new fields are discovered.

Coal could be the boiler fuel of the future. Much surplus capacity has to be closed with a further sharpening of the cost difference between coal and oil (even now the price of coal per therm is almost half that of heavy fuel oil) and the National Coal Board has been successful in persuading some large industrial users to switch to coal-fired equipment. Resources are sufficient for a long time and coal might also be used as a chemical feedstock, replacing oil.

Gas is the uncertain industrial fuel, with the future supply/ demand balance being unclear. In the meantime the Gas Board has promoted its product very successfully to the consumer.

Electricity prices are such that its use as an industrial fuel cannot be contemplated on a large scale and already UK costs are substantially higher than the other EEC countries especially as loading increases.

PROBLEMS AND OPPORTUNITIES FOR SUCCESSFUL PURCHASING

Future developments in synthetics production

We have seen earlier in this chapter the importance of oil and petrochemical feedstocks to synthetic materials used in the pharmaceutical industry. Clearly the industry itself is not going to influence at all the price of oil or the petrochemical building blocks, but it is important for astute buyers to be aware of changes in the petrochemical industry which have been referred to in an earlier chapter. It is also important to look further ahead for over the next five to ten years new petrochemical complexes will come on stream in countries like Saudi Arabia and consideration must be given to the opportunities presented to the buyer as a result of these moves. Whilst there is still some doubt on the precise range of products which will be produced, certainly the major building blocks will be produced and it is fascinating to consider not only the impact on feedstock markets but how far downstream production will eventually be taken.

Obviously countries like Saudi Arabia do not, and will not in the foreseeable future, have a large internal demand for feedstocks/ finished products. The impact of large quantities of feedstock on world markets will inevitably mean a glut, and notwithstanding earlier comments on European refinery closures, we can expect to see feedstock prices drop, which the professional buyer must take to his advantage when negotiating prices for pharmaceutical chemicals or plastic packaging components. The possibilities go further than this, for it may be that the Arab countries will go much further downstream and produce pharmaceutical and other fine chemicals and perhaps even, though this is more unlikely, plastic packaging components. The possibilities of these countries opening up as new source countries for a wide range of materials in the next decade presents a challenge to purchasing people. Further it is necessary to take positive action *now* to develop a supplier development policy, for as we have seen, the pharmaceutical industry has special quality requirements which its suppliers must understand and to which they have to conform.

Natural material markets

In the natural products area, successful purchasing of soft commodities demands an attitude of mind which can weigh up a whole series of considerations at the same time. In these markets so much influences the price and availability – some of it true, but some put about by speculation or producers anxious to 'talk the market up'. Also as a number of materials are sometimes interchangeable, it is necessary not just to study the market for that particular material, but for others which could replace it. With almost all purchases coming into the UK from overseas the values of the pound sterling, French franc, Italian lire etc. can have a considerable effect on the final delivered cost to the buyer, though outside the control of the sellers. Buyers in this area, and to a certain extent too in synthetic materials, need to be closely aware of currency levels and to give careful consideration to this aspect in their negotiations. Buyers should also take the lead in encouraging suppliers at a practical level; they should be prepared to devote time and money in encouraging producers, particularly in developing countries, to examine matters such as plant culture and to increase the yields of plantations. Processors at source should be encouraged to give top priority to quality control and it could be that members of the industry should examine the possibility of entering into joint ventures with the processors in countries of origin where financial help is needed in order to introduce better methods.

Commodities controlled by the EEC present a different problem; essentially these are controlled markets under the CAP scheme which has meant higher prices in recent years. In company with other industries, the pharmaceutical industry must continue to exert every possible pressure at the political level to ensure that commercial manufacturing organisations have a better deal. Opportunities to purchase some items outside the EEC exist, but such countries often have to be encouraged to deal with the UK and usually their standards are not as high.

Packaging materials – the future

Most packaging materials tend to be bought nationally rather than imported, and this trend can be expected to continue where fragile large containers, such as glass are involved. In other areas, particularly plastic containers, it is felt that there will be a concentration of business in countries where feedstocks/energy and conversion costs are low. This may well result in increased purchases from countries not currently regarded as important source areas. Also innovative suppliers are going to be in a strong position – more R & D expenditure in the packaging industry is needed.

Suppliers – a profile

Companies supplying the pharmaceutical industry have to accept its requirements for the highest quality standards, even if this means setting up special procedures.

The trend towards buyer and manufacturer dealing directly with one another will continue, with the probable demise of trading or merchanting organisations. Those that remain will have to provide higher facilities to offer a totally satisfactory supplies service.

New companies will be examined outside the traditional market-place of the EEC; the search for these sources will be concentrated in the low-cost production countries of the world. This will be further promoted by the continuing push on pharmaceutical selling prices and the willingness of government purchasing bodies to buy cheaper drugs from countries who are often breaking international patents.

So the future of the industry will continue to depend to a large extent upon its relationship with its suppliers: the needs of the industry must be clearly defined, but its purchasing staff will need a blend of product and supply market knowledge, financial awareness and interest in the international development of new supply markets. It is and will be an exacting task.

APPENDIX 1

Extract from HMSO publication *Guide to Good Manufacturing Practices,* "Starting material specifications":

5.7   There should be a starting material specification, approved by quality control for every starting material.

5.8   The specification should be dated and include:

(*a*)   a designated name with reference to monograph specifications where appropriate and preferably a code reference unique to the material;

(*b*)   a reference to any alternative proprietary designation of the material;

(*c*)   a description of the physical form of the material;

(*d*)   sampling instructions;

(*e*)   tests and limits for identity, purity and assay;

(*f*)   details of, or reference to, the analytical methods to be used to assess identity and purity, and to perform the assay;

(*g*)   approved supplier(s) of the material;

(*h*)   safety precautions to be observed;

(*i*)   storage conditions;

(*j*)   frequency of retesting of stored materials.

APPENDIX 2

Records on starting materials

5.21 The receipt of each delivery should be recorded and this record should include:

    (*a*)   date of receipt;

    (*b*)   name of material, and name on delivery notes and containers if different;

    (*c*)   supplier's name;

    (*d*)   supplier's batch or reference number;

    (*e*)   total quantity and number of containers received;

    (*f*)   the batch identifying number awarded on or after receipt.

5.22 The testing of each starting material should be recorded and this record should include:

    (*a*)   date of testing;

    (*b*)   name of material and the batch identifying number;

    (*c*)   results of all tests;

    (*d*)   names of personnel who performed the tests;

    (*e*)   a cross reference to any relevant certificate of analysis;

    (*f*)   the signed release on rejection of the material by quality control.

APPENDIX 3

Comparison of energy costs within EEC countries

Heavy fuel oil	*£/tonne*
UK	126.59
France	117.59
Italy	117.42
Germany	112.87

Gas	*p/therm*
UK	30.3
Italy	31.7
Germany	31.6
France	27.8

Electricity		*p/kw/h*	
40% loading		*80% loading*	
Italy	3.91	UK	3.03
Germany	3.70	Germany	2.68
UK	3.30	France	2.12
France	2.49	Italy	2.07

Note: Prices and exchange rates as at May 1983.

32

Purchasing for the motor industry

Tony Skidmore

The relationship between the motor vehicle manufacturers and their suppliers has historically varied from one of 'arm's length' ordering of parts to a drawing specification with an almost patronising attitude to the supplier, to occasional bursts of 'our' problems and 'we are all in this business together'. At best an uneasy mutual caution, at worst hostility and suspicion.

Purchasing as a function inside motor companies seems to have emerged out of the 'stores department', with clerks requisitioning parts from 'outside' companies to complement the in-house manufacture and assembly of those early vehicles. Many of the outside sources were trades carried over from horse-drawn carriage making – notably bodies, seat trims, oil lamps etc.

Companies such as Joseph Lucas can trace their own early days to involvement with the emerging UK motor industry, supplying the first petrol-burning lamp in 1902 and in 1911 an electric lighting set called 'King of the Road' sold for £24 in brass and £25 plated. At that time UK car production was 72,000 a year.

Buying continued to retain a stores department image for many years with a less than prestigious position in most companies. Buyers were perceived as a dubious link with outside suppliers living in a world of supplier lunches, defending the supplier's position and seen by other people in the company as having at best divided loyalties. Clearly this was not the best atmosphere in which to develop and build a trusting partnership between a supplier and a motor manufacturer.

THE 1950s AND 1960s

UK vehicle production in 1953 was 800,000 and by 1963 had reached 2 million units, 9.7 per cent of the world total production of 20 million.

The basics of buying in the early 1950s were the same fundamentals that apply today – price, delivery and quality, but at that time the emphasis was biased towards pricing with cost reduction achieved by dual and multiple sourcing, and suppliers competing keenly for volume business. Profits were good in a captive automotive home market and a virtually captive export market, at least as far as Commonwealth and EFTA countries were concerned.

Delivery and quality performance were not always taken into consideration as part of the whole purchasing arrangement and it is probable that costing systems were not sufficiently detailed to identify on-costs associated with poor delivery performance and unsatisfactory quality. These were exciting growth times with many basic commodities, including steel, only recently off allocation and much of the supplier industry operating with out-of-date plant and shortage of labour.

As the industry grew, the supply base, of necessity, expanded in line. Not all the supply chain was of UK origin; many American companies came to Britain encouraged by the overseas expansion moves of Ford and General Motors (Vauxhall in the UK). Such names as Firestone, A. C. Delco, Bendix, Kelsey Hayes and Briggs Motor Bodies were in the van of this transatlantic component support expansion. It is interesting to note here that some 40 years later a reverse trend has taken place with UK and continental specialised small car know-how such as constant velocity joints for front-wheel drive cars, carburettors, cylinder heads and gaskets flowing the other way. This development has included the building of plants in America to support production of the US sub-compact J Car, Escort and other car lines.

MAKE/BUY STRATEGY

The major motor companies had, and still have, different styles and fashions as regards the parts to be made in-house (captive) and those to be bought from outside suppliers. The view at times is that car companies should stick to their basic skills of designing, assembling and selling vehicles, making only the basic parts such as bodies, engines, gearboxes and axles, and buying everything else. Others would argue that with some 60 per cent of the manufactured cost in bought-out components, a major profit opportunity was available with appropriate in-house investment.

It is the opinion of the writer that such apparent profit opportunities can be expensively short-sighted, as the car companies may integrate a part profitably for two to three years. Without the appropriate in-house research and development capability to keep that specialised part up to date with new technology the design becomes obsolete. Worse still, the previous outside source may not exist any more when the buying company needs to reconsider or indeed reverse the decision to make the part inside in favour of alternative uses of funds or space for new product development in the car company.

Integration is a tricky subject and never more so than when there is a downturn in the economy. When a car company has spare capacity in a press shop, a foundry or a machine shop, plant managers and controllers are eager for volume to contribute to fixed-cost recovery. In purchasing it is sometimes difficult to argue against this logic in the short term, but such action may have an irretrievable effect on outside supplier capacity and could indeed trigger plant closures where a supplier loses major volume as a result of integration actions by its customers.

Uncertainty in the industry is perhaps even worse where the make/buy strategy is not clear and may become involved with the investment policies of a nationalised group such as BL. Such uncertainty has caused concern in the foundry and forging industries and, to some extent, the rationalisation of steel-finishing activities.

With steady growth business planning is usually more orderly and purchasing can negotiate long-term contracts which will in turn encourage supplier investment in specialised areas. The steady growth of the Japanese motor car industry has enabled both the suppliers and the producers to develop a business strategy and to achieve a more orderly make/buy production pattern. This is just one part of the whole success story of the Japanese car industry. The supplier relationship is a key factor in Japanese manufacturing efficiency, with their suppliers operating in a loose confederation with the major customer car companies.

Purchasing for the motor industry is now a more visible and increasingly important strategic element in the automotive business and is no longer a simple job of switching sources for short-term gain. Competitive pressures still play the same vital part in the buyer's job; even more so, when the fact that the finished car or truck will be competing in markets against overseas makers whose supplier base is probably more cost and quality effective than for a UK-sourced part is taken into account.

WORLD PRODUCTION AND UK IMPORTS

The motor industry in the UK has changed from a net exporter to a situation where imports are currently running at 57 per cent of registrations. (In 1953 and 1963 imports were 0.6 and 4.5 per cent respectively). This import competition is primarily from Germany, France, Italy, Spain and significantly Japan.

Figures 32.1 and 32.2 illustrate world vehicle production from 1953 to 1982.

	1953		1963		1973		1982	
	'000s	%	'000s	%	'000s	%	'000s	%
UK	834.9	8.4	2,011.7	9.7	2,163.9	5.7	1,156.5	3.3
Europe	2,035.1	20.4	7,905.7	38.2	13,004.7	34.0	11,347.7	32.1
USA	7,323.2	73.5	9,100.4	44.0	12,681.7	33.1	6,975.7	19.8
Japan	46.6	0.5	1,283.5	6.2	7,082.8	18.5	10,731.8	30.4
Others	558.5	5.6	2,386.9	11.6	5,515.8	14.4	6,251.1	17.7
World total	9,963.4	100.0	20,676.5	100.0	38,285.0	100.0	35,306.3	100.0

Figure 32.1 World vehicle production (cars and commercials) 1953-1982

Figure 32.1 shows:
- UK declining share of world production from 8.4 per cent in 1953 to 3.3 per cent in 1982, and volume halved from 2.1M vehicles in 1973 to 1.1M in 1982.

- Total Europe with some slippage in percentage of world production, but holding volume at 11 to 13M vehicles.
- The major losers in world production volume terms have been the USA, whose domestic production has been halved from 12.6M in 1973 to 6.9M in 1982. In percentage terms this represents a reduction from 33 to 19 per cent of world production.
- The dramatic winners have been the Japanese who produced 46,000 vehicles in 1953, less than 1 per cent of world production, and in 1982 10.7M, 30 per cent of world production.

Figure 32.2 shows UK vehicle registrations and imports from 1953 to 1982 with imports rising from 0.6 per cent in 1953 to 54.2 per cent in 1982.

	1953		1963		1973		1982	
	'000s	%	'000s	%	'000s	%	'000s	%
UK produced	398.8	99.4	1,190.8	95.8	1,466.8	74.7	816.3	45.8
Imports from								
Rest of Europe	1.9	0.5	50.4	4.1	361.6	18.4	731.7	41.0
Japan	NIL	NIL	NEG	NIL	96.3	4.9	192.2	10.8
Other	0.2	0.1	1.1	0.1	39.3	2.0	42.1	2.4
Total	400.9	100.0	1,242.3	100.0	1,964.0	100.0	1,782.3	100.0

Figure 32.2 UK vehicle registrations 1953-1982

A RESTATEMENT OF BUYING OBJECTIVES

This competitive pressure is now felt in motor company purchasing departments, with buyers involved in more radical thinking than the basics of price, delivery and quality. What is happening is a realisation that the suppliers, particularly of proprietary systems, have a whole wealth of research and development expertise and there is really no point in the car companies continuing treatment of a supplier as someone called in to bid for business at the eleventh hour in a new programme. This attitude survives perhaps from the days when car designers felt that they had to design the whole vehicle, as they were responsible for the final 'sign off'.

Cars and trucks are now a high-technology, high-quality business and suppliers to the car assembly companies are an integral part of this concept. This necessitates supplier involvement earlier in the design stage, preselection of single-source suppliers, and longer-term contracts of, say, three to five years' duration with real incentives for suppliers to boost quality and productivity. The industry still buys some 60 per cent of the manufacturing costs of a vehicle and its involvement with its suppliers must be total if the partners are to be mutually cost effective.

A restatement of the basics of purchasing for the motor industry is appropriate with an expansion of the relationships relevant to today's way of conducting this business:

1 Working with suppliers at the design stage means taking them into your confidence, using their know how in specialised areas such as braking, lighting, suspension, carburettors and new and complex electronic control systems for emission and fuel economy, etc.

2 Reducing the number of suppliers, particularly of high-volume parts and encouraging suppliers to make the appropriate specialised investment rather than 'shopping around' for dual and multi-sourcing. This same rationale has a spin-off in other areas, such as quality and supplier cost reduction.

3 Long-term contracts: part of this trusting means that the motor companies must put their business on a long-term basis, leaving the supplier free from integration threats for a reasonable period. He can then make the appropriate investment knowing where a major part of his output is going.

4 Quality is paramount in all of this and can only come fundamentally from a good product design, tooling that is not rushed into production at the last minute and is properly constructed; and the recognition that quality is designed into the product rather than 'inspected-in' afterwards. This again relates to the volume of business given to a supplier and the fact that the supplier knows that he will have 100 per cent of the business and can invest accordingly. Process quality is an

essential element in the relationship with ongoing statistical process control to monitor the making of a consistent quality product in volume production. The fear that some suppliers have had that this drive for quality will cost money, is largely unfounded. Certainly to train people and instal the disciplines may involve some expense, but the reduction in cost pay-back is considerable through, for example, the elimination of scrap, the need to inspect afterwards, and avoidance of the risk of returned shipments from customers.

5 Just-in-time supply: it is not cost effective to tie up money in inventory. It is recognised that many motor industry buyers have had problems with strikes and poor supply records and, as a consequence, have dual or multi-sourced parts to protect supply lines. The approach now is to select a source, preferably a domestic one, which is competent to supply a quality product on a continuous basis with minimum inventory through the whole supply chain. (Maybe the long-term contract with the supplier includes a union no strike agreement?)

6 Cost reduction, which, frequently involves increased productivity and arises from installing the right facilities, having the volume to produce, getting the quality right and eliminating scrap and the need to rework parts.

7 Organisation: in many motor companies there has been much rethinking about the supply organisation, how purchasing should be organised, whether it should be centralised or decentralised into the various divisions of a car company; whether buying should be undertaken for the different car or product lines or whether it should be organised centrally on a commodity basis. And whether the supply organisation should include such functions as quality control, liaison engineering, material handling engineering and purchase cost analysis.

THE UK COMPONENT SUPPLIERS

While the car companies as discussed earlier were being buffeted by import competition and a 50 per cent plus loss of UK produced volume, what of the component supply base which has seen half of its business disappearing?

The Economist Intelligence Unit (EIU) Special report No. 91 in January 1981 summarised the situation thus:

The years of 1979 and 1980 were without doubt the watershed years for the UK components sector. With remarkable uniformity most companies had been able to report five, ten or even more years of uninterrupted increases in sales, in pretax profits, and in general expansion. But then, with few exceptions, the accounts for the year ending in 1980 presented a changed picture. While sales figures might still be ahead of the effects of inflation, pretax profits had tumbled, in some cases very severely, and the outlook was bleak indeed.

The ability to have foreseen all this varied widely from company to company. However, two simple facts had been evident for a number of years: first, that at some future stage in this continuing period of profitability a reversal must inevitably come; and, secondly, that provisions for safeguarding cashflow through the ensuing recession were of paramount importance.

It appears that virtually all of the leading component manufacturers were in a fit condition to withstand this reversal of fortunes, in all respects but one. In the UK most were suffering seriously from overmanning, and, although some initial movement had begun in the direction of realism, effective action was frequently thwarted by political and trade union opposition.

Steps taken by leading UK component manufacturers in an effort to match up to these problems have included strategic moves to become more multinational in order to survive the decline in vehicle manufacturing output at home. Among such moves there has been an early realisation of the need for new worldwide production facilities. Emphasis has been upon the provision of support facilities in close proximity to the expanding vehicle production plants, many in the third world and in the new foreign vehicle population centres such as Spain.

It is not surprising that there has been a contraflow in this strategic field. Systematic progress has been made by component manufacturers from the USA in getting first a foothold, and then fairly rapidly establishing a complete base in the UK, from whence to develop their business in Western Europe, and further afield.

This has been a notable feature of the industrial scene during the last few years. Despite the well-publicised hardships endured by British industry generally, and anything to do with vehicle production in particular, the US companies seem confident enough as to the long term, and moreover usually have the advantage of not being overmanned to start with. Among the advantages associated with choosing the UK on this side of the Atlantic is the common language, closely followed by the strength of the indigenous workforce already knowledgeable in the components industry. Of the top sixty outside companies supplying the motor industry today, thirteen are of US parentage, and two are Canadian.

The Americans are not alone in increasing their participation in this 'Top 60' sector of British industry. France and West Germany have each increased from one company to two, while the remaining foreign owned large company is of Swedish parentage. Thus, the leading sixty automotive component manufacturers are now in the proportion of one foreign owned to every two British owned.

The indications are that of foreign vehicle manufacturers enjoying growing sales in the UK, Volvo leads the way in reciprocating – placing contracts with British suppliers to the value of more than £100m annually. A recent survey showed that, after Volvo, next in order of importance was Renault, apparently spending some £60m, followed by Opel and Fiat at about £45m each. Scania and VW/Audi are thought to spend about £25m each.

These basics are still very much the challenge to component suppliers. In the two years since the EIU report was written much impressive progress has been made by suppliers in becoming leaner and fitter, winning export business, and working with the UK-based vehicle producers to ensure that both parties stay in business in terms of producing a competitive quality product.

TODAY'S BUYER

What of the buyer in this industry who started life arranging the supply of parts from a local supplier in an expanding domestic market? He (or she) is now required to be a multi-disciplined linguist to handle the job which is more than ever an international function.

Purchasing in the motor industry is a key function in the company, but in terms of recognition, engineering, finance and manufacturing are probably pre-eminent in status, salary, and board representation. Nevertheless the job satisfaction of handling 60 per cent of a company's manufacturing costs is still a challenge that in the writer's company continues to attract an increasing number of its graduate intake as buyers each year.

33

Purchasing for the airline industry

James McConville

The challenge of purchasing for an international airline is expressed in the size, complexity and diversity of requirements and the need to operate in the worldwide marketplace. Approximately two-thirds of an airline's operating expenditure is accounted for by purchases of goods and services from third parties. A large airline may spend well over £1,000 million per annum on such purchases and perhaps a further £200 million on capital equipment. Clearly the performance of the purchasing function has a crucial bearing on profitability.

Complexity and the importance of maintaining supply lines can be illustrated by the purchasing involvement in a typical 747 'jumbo jet' departure from London. On board are 350 passengers and 20 tons of baggage and cargo as well as 25,000 separate items of food, drink and other inflight amenities to sustain the passengers on their journey. The total weight of the aircraft on take-off is nearly 350 tons, including 100 tons of fuel. Many of the passengers have started their journeys in London, some are completing return journeys, others are continuing journeys which started in another continent. All passengers have been booked onto the flight through real-time worldwide reservation systems. On board the flight crew use computers, radio, radar and inertial navigation systems to fly the aircraft to its destination. The cost of the aircraft as delivered from the Boeing plant at Seattle is around $55 million and the engines cost a further $25 million. Support is provided through a complex array of engineering spares and equipment which amount to more than 500,000 items for the British Airways fleet. In a monopoly market situation the availability and price of the spares required to service an aircraft throughout its lifespan of perhaps fifteen years may depend entirely on contract negotiations undertaken at the time of initial purchase of the aircraft type. Availability of engineering and other spares and supplies at perhaps 100 airports around the world is critically important to an airline operation. A 747 jet may average nearly twelve hours in the air each day of the year, even after allowing for loading, off-loading, cleaning, servicing and major overhaul. Delay is unacceptable in a business where the product is a highly perishable commodity and a cancelled flight, through lack of spares or supplies, means that revenue is lost irretrievably, even though most of the cost of the service must still be absorbed.

DIVERSITY OF PURCHASING ACTIVITY

The diversity of purchasing activity is illustrated in Figure 33.1, which shows the range of goods and services required by an international airline with an annual operating expenditure on purchases of £1,000 million. At one end of the spectrum technological and financing expertise is involved in the procurement of aircraft and engines together with the essential support equipment of flight simulators and avionics. At the other extreme, an airline is involved in the bulk purchase of common household items such as food, wines, tobacco, cutlery, china, glass and toiletries. Flight planning and passenger reservations are dependent on worldwide tele-communication and computer systems which must operate on a twenty-four hour basis without failure. Fuel and services for aircraft handling, baggage, catering and engineering must be provided at every airport. These goods and services are bought on a worldwide basis and paid for in more than fifty currencies.

Although the sheer logistics are breathtaking, high inventories are not the answer in an industry which has been forced to become extremely cost conscious. This is reflected in the changes in the role and significance of the purchasing function in the airline industry which have taken place in recent years. After the Second World War, airlines enjoyed a period of rapid expansion and 5 or 10 per

Purchasing group	Type of activity	Expenditure £m
Capital expenditure	Aircraft, engines, flight simulators and training equipment, computer and telecommunications equipment, cargo and baggage handling equipment	200
Operating expenditure		
Fuel	Aviation fuel and oil, motor transport fuel and oil, airport fuel systems	500
Engineering	Airframe spares, mechanical systems and propulsion spares, instruments, radio and electrical spares, tools and equipment	100
Service contracts	Catering services, passenger, engineering and cargo handling, marketing contracts, hotel accommodation, navigation charges, landing fees	300
Operations support	Uniforms, protective clothing, catering equipment, food, drink and tobacco, inflight entertainment, motor transport and ground equipment spares, building and plant spares, office equipment, security and fire equipment, stationery and printing, medical, paper products	100
Total operating purchases		1,000

Figure 33.1 Purchasing activities in an international airline

cent growth per annum was not unusual. In this environment the drive to maintain and increase market share was the dominant influence with the assumption that any cost increase could always be absorbed by the next year's increase in revenues. The period of sustained growth was halted by the fuel crises of 1973 and 1979 and the consequent economic recessions which raised costs dramatically and simultaneously arrested the growth of traffic volumes. Over-capacity resulted in severe price competition and, virtually over-night, control of costs became essential for survival. Hitherto, purchasing performance had been measured primarily by the ability to maintain the logistics pipeline necessary to keep aircraft flying on schedule. The cost of goods and services purchased and the cost and funding of inventories have now become of fundamental import-ance. In turn this has given new dimensions to the role of the purchasing function.

CREATING AN EFFECTIVE PURCHASING STRUCTURE

The task of the airline purchasing function is to ensure that the best value for money is obtained on an internationally competitive basis as well as safeguarding the logistical pipelines. However, creating an effective structure to achieve this is not a simple matter because there are few areas of purchasing activity which stand alone without overlapping elsewhere. The interactions in the commitment process require that an effective airline purchasing organisation should work as a whole rather than as a series of self-sufficient units, each relating to a specific resource department.

A typical airline organisation will include sales and marketing, engineering, flight operations and ground operations among the main resource departments as measured in terms of manpower and demand for the procurement of goods and services. These departments may also have responsibility for other activities so that, for example, the catering service may be part of flight operations or ground operations or, indeed, may report as a separate entity. Although the main departments employ different skills and technologies, they all share, to a greater or lesser extent, common interests in the equipment and services which are purchased and thus can properly lay claim to active involvement in the procurement process. This is illustrated in the purchase of the single most important item of capital equipment, namely an aircraft. Clearly, engineering must have a major voice in the determination of technical specifications, but sales and marketing will wish to influence cabin interior design; catering services will be interested in galley layout; flight operations are concerned with flight deck equipment; ground operations will be involved in standards for passenger boarding and baggage and cargo handling facilities. If each of these departments were to be given a free hand then, very probably, the aircraft finally specified would be late in delivery, very expensive and so loaded with equipment that it might have difficulty in becoming airborne!

The mutual interest shared by different functions of an airline extends to many of the other goods and services which are purchased. Fuel is the largest single item of operating expenditure and both flight operations and engineering have a direct interest in fuel costs together with the planning and finance functions. Another example is the purchase of hotel accommodation where sales and marketing and flight operations are concerned with the respective requirements of passengers and flight crews. For maximum effectiveness the purchasing function must be structured in a way which recognises the complexity of the airline organisation and the interdependence of the many technical functions.

A basic principle of effective purchasing is that supplier contact should be managed through a single focal point which brings together the varied and, perhaps, conflicting requirements of different parts of an organisation so that there is no erosion of potential purchasing power in the marketplace. Adoption of this principle suggests that the purchasing structure must be capable of spanning the airline organisation wherever the final specification represents the combined requirements of different areas.

The principles involved in the management of supplier contact apply not only to the procurement of common goods and services, but wherever a range of goods and services are provided by a common supplier, a situation which is likely to be found at every airport served away from the home base. By means of separately negotiated contracted services, passengers are directed to and from aircraft; baggage and cargo is loaded and off-loaded; aircraft are refuelled and serviced; meal trays and drinks are loaded in pre-packed containers; and navigation, landing and aircraft parking facilities are provided. Frequently the suppliers concerned provide a number of services at one airport or, alternatively, the same service at several airports. These suppliers will include other airlines operating at their home base and receiving a reciprocal service at the opposite end of the route. In these cases it is sensible to combine the management for both the purchase and the sale of reciprocal services.

Finally, in considering the purchasing structure required in an international environment, foreign exchange risk must always be a leading consideration. British Airways, for example, trades in over a hundred different currencies and, in order to minimise risk, there must be complete awareness of the significance, not only of currency of payment, but the underlying currency of contract. Fuel purchases, for example, may be paid in a variety of currencies but the basic price is established in US dollar terms and the foreign exchange risk relates to this currency. Many opportunities arise to reduce risk by varying the source of overseas purchases and cash flow can be improved by selective local buying in soft currencies where there are delays in the release of hard-won revenue. This underlines the need for the total involvement and awareness of the purchasing function in all aspects of cash management.

Given the complexities which have been described above, it is not surprising that there is no common organisational pattern in airline purchasing. Many airlines have traditionally located purchasing in the engineering area which is the most demanding in terms of logistical management. Others continue to operate with a series of independent purchasing units which are loosely co-ordinated through joint committees and working groups set up to consider areas of mutual involvement. Few airlines have extended the formal involvement of purchasing to all procurement activity including contracts at airports away from the home base. Whatever internal organisational benefits may be derived from these variations, optimum purchasing performance depends on the efficiency of the whole rather than the sum of its constituent parts. This principle has been fully recognised in the unified purchasing organisation at British Airways which is responsible for all procurement activity together with sales of related goods and services.

PURCHASING FOR BRITISH AIRWAYS

Purchasing at British Airways is founded on a short and succinct statement of policy. In essence this requires that purchasing shall meet the agreed requirements for goods and services at the lowest cost as measured on an internationally competitive basis, taking into account price, specification, quality, timing, inventory, payment and other commercial terms. Emphasis is placed on the mainten-ance of high professional and ethical standards and on supplier relationships based on mutual confidence.

Purchasing has a unified organisational structure which tran-scends internal departmental boundaries while clearly identifying responsibilities for particular commodity groups. In designing these interrelationships it is accepted that, to achieve the maximum contribution, purchasing must have active involvement at every stage of the procurement process, starting from initial planning conception through to eventual delivery and payment. Performance is measured by the ultimate effect of every purchasing action on airline profitability.

The purchasing organisation is divided into six main groups: engineering, operations support, service contracts, fuel, capital expenditure and control.

The engineering group has responsibility for the purchasing and supply of spares and equipment for aircraft and engines. More than 500,000 separate items are controlled using real-time computer systems which extend throughout the workshop and stores facilities and to selected locations elsewhere. The operations support group is similarly responsible for the multitude of items which are required for many other areas of the airline, such as uniforms, transport workshops, medical, stationery and printing. The service contracts group also spans several line functions with responsibility for catering equipment and foodstuffs and for contracts at more than 100 airports, involving the purchase and sale of catering services and passenger, engineering and cargo facilities.

The fuel group controls the purchase and supply of all fuel products, including aviation fuel, motor transport fuel and oil on a worldwide basis. The group must respond rapidly not only to changes in the marketplace, but to frequent variations in demand arising from changes in flight schedules, route structures, aircraft types and engine technology. The capital group has responsibility for the direction, management and control of contracts covering the purchase, lease and sale of all capital equipment. Control is exercised by full participation in the strategic planning processes with all capital proposals being passed through the group. Finally, the control group is required to ensure that agreed policies, procedures and controls are implemented and to provide a comprehensive overview of all purchasing activity at every stage in the commitment process. The group also has responsibility for performance reporting, systems and economic and cost analysis.

Many different approaches have been made to purchasing for an international airline and the unified structure adopted by British Airways represents only one solution. There is probably no single correct answer to the organisational question, but this serves only to add spice to the challenge of purchasing for an international airline.

PURCHASING AVIATION FUEL

A description of purchasing for an international airline would not be complete without special reference to the procurement of aviation fuel which accounts for around half an airline's purchasing expenditure. Successful trading in any commodity demands a full appreciation of the industry infrastructure and the underlying economic pressures which determine supply and demand. In this respect aviation fuel is no exception and provides an interesting case study.

The postwar years were a period of rapid growth for the airline industry which benefited from cheap and plentiful supplies of aviation fuel, priced at around 10 cents per gallon. One of the major assumptions in the development of early turbine engines was that there would be no change in the availability and price of fuel. At the same time, fuel distribution facilities were provided at the major airports to accommodate the increasing demands of airlines. These facilities required considerable investment, and the airline industry, being primarily concerned with the financing of aircraft, was reluctant to divert capital to the provision of airport fuel distribution systems. Naturally, large aviation fuel suppliers were willing to provide the necessary investment, thereby obtaining ownership and control of fuel systems. As a result aviation fuel became a 'value added' commodity with a few suppliers enjoying a virtual monopoly of the business. Both airlines and fuel companies enjoyed the benefits of growth until the first oil crisis of 1973, when oil was suddenly in short supply and prices quadrupled. With the oil embargo came a battery of controls on crude oil petroleum which dictated buyer/seller relationships and determined prices.

Aviation fuel and kerosene are both petroleum distillates derived from the same part of the petroleum barrel as diesel fuel and heating oil. Refiners, therefore, have the option of increasing aviation fuel production at the expense of diesel fuel and heating oil or vice versa. Thus consumers of aviation fuel and consumers of other distillates compete with each other for supplies of energy. After 1973, with the simultaneous economic recovery and the deregulation of the domestic airline business in the USA, aviation fuel consumers were placed at a competitive disadvantage, needing more fuel but unable to compete effectively with other distillate consumers because of regulatory controls. In 1979 these controls were eased, new suppliers entered the business and airlines began to purchase in a new free market for aviation fuel. Almost immediately, however, the Iranian revolution created a further oil shortage and, although prices rose, the airline industry was then better placed to cope with the problem. However, the longstanding control of airport facilities by major suppliers continued to prevent airlines obtaining the fuel which was then available from new suppliers. This problem was clearly recognised by the airline industry which is now beginning to provide access at all major airports to any source of fuel that can be acquired, enabling fuel supplies to be supplemented during periods of shortage and maximising competitive advantage when supplies are in surplus.

Longer-term purchasing strategy has, thus, evolved slowly as constraints within the free market supply system have been recognised and addressed. In the medium term, economic and political factors continue to determine the supply and demand equation with a degree of fluctuation and unpredictability which is common to most commodity markets. In the very short term the volume of aviation fuel purchases is determined by complex planning systems which not only determine the cheapest points to pick up fuel, but the most economic way of flying the aircraft to minimise fuel burn. With a fully loaded aircraft much of the cost of fuel burn is accounted for simply by the cost of carrying fuel for later stages of flight. Given that a 1 per cent saving in fuel consumption or in fuel price may be reckoned in terms of millions of pounds, then the scope for further refinement in both the strategy and tactics of aviation fuel purchasing is considerable.

This brief description of the evolution of purchasing strategy for aviation fuel is only one example of the many specialised areas of procurement activity to be found within an international airline. The purchasing techniques and skills required range from the control of high-volume flow materials to the multi-million pound negotiation of intricate international contracts for the procurement of high-technology equipment. The challenge is immense and the ultimate measure of success is the contribution made to profitability in a highly competitive international environment.

34

Purchasing for the defence industry

Brian Kenny

This chapter concentrates upon military procurement which involves contracting for a highly engineered package to design, develop and produce a product to specific government requirements and for which there are no established private markets. Whilst other types of purchase are made by defence procurement staff, it is this kind of activity which differentiates defence procurement from most others.

The UK defence establishment employs an elaborate mechanism for conceptualisation, source solicitation, source selection, price negotiation and development monitoring and control. Frequently, price is not the main consideration in contractor selection, since the buyer is concerned with securing a product of superior quality and, since some competition may exist before the final product is completely specified, estimates of both final performance and costs often remain tentative. As a result, a potential contractor's technical capability may be given more weight than his comparative price positioning among the bidders.

In general, the government is not a buyer of products in the accepted sense since the product is rarely beyond the concept stage prior to industry involvement. Thus, at this stage the authority seek to procure research and development capability and ultimate conversion of results, e.g. a finished weapon system. Other criteria for choosing a particular supplier may include the attractiveness of the concepts and designs put forward and the buyer's knowledge of the technical, physical and managerial resources which the contractor has at his disposal.

HISTORICAL PERSPECTIVE

The need to rationalise supply management for the British armed forces was identified as early as 1926:

> (The term supply is to describe all the processes involved in) obtaining or producing the material needs of the Fighting Services from the requisitioning stage to the delivery of those needs to the Service Store Depots or distribution authority. (Cmnd 2649, 1926)

At the beginning of the First World War the supply of general stores was the responsibility of the individual service departments. The Ministry of Munitions was created in June 1915 and took over from the War Office the job of supplying war-like stores. The Admiralty remained responsible for almost the whole of its needs apart from steel, explosive and propellant and later aircraft, which were obtained through the Ministry of Munitions. In December 1946 a Minister of Defence was appointed with the power to take charge of the formulation and general application of a unified policy relating to the armed forces of the Crown as a whole and their requirements. The ministry's responsibility was further extended in 1957 when Mr Duncan Sandys was made responsible for reshaping and reorganising the armed forces in accordance with current strategic needs and in light of the economic capacity of the country. The culmination of this was the merging of the Admiralty, War Office and Air Ministry into the single identity of the Ministry of Defence, in 1964.

In 1970 the government announced their intention to rationalise the whole function of defence procurement and the overlapping aerospace responsibilities on a lasting basis.

Dereck Rayner (now Sir Dereck) headed a project team whose terms of reference included recommendations for reorganisation and integration of procurement policy and procedures (Cmnd 4641, 1971). Reorganisation was a question of a complete restructuring of the procurement organisation through a thorough analysis of the existing problem areas whilst maintaining political, military and industrial acceptance. Some of the problems appeared largely or wholly insoluble. For example, the fact that the procurement organisation could not operate on fully commercial lines and that it existed only to meet the needs of its users and therefore was not its own master. Likewise, it could not escape from policy changes implemented by the government which affected the armed forces and their tasks within the long-term acquisition process or from changes in strategic thinking.

THE MOD PROCUREMENT EXECUTIVE

The implementation of the Rayner Report recommendations gave rise to the formation of the Procurement Executive which also encompassed responsibility for civil aerospace supplies. In its present form the executive is responsible to the Secretary of State for Defence for the Royal Ordnance factories and the Defence Research Establishments in addition to the requisition of supplies from industry.

The Procurement Executive is headed by the Chief of Defence Procurement under political direction of ministers (see Figure 34.1). The central divisions are responsible for procurement policy which encompasses purchasing, quality assurance arrangements, contracts policy and international aspects. Three systems controllerates are responsible for procurement of land, sea and air systems/equipment respectively, each acting for all three services. The Controllerate of Research and Development/Nuclear provides support to the systems controllerates in addition to its prime responsibility for work of the defence R & D establishments.

The head of defence sales is responsible for the sale of UK-manufactured defence equipment abroad, whilst acting as an advisory body to industry.

The procurement process

The Procurement Executive plays a key role in the early phases of the procurement cycle which, of course, varies in time span according to the complexity of the task in hand. Constant collaboration with the respective military staff and ministry officials

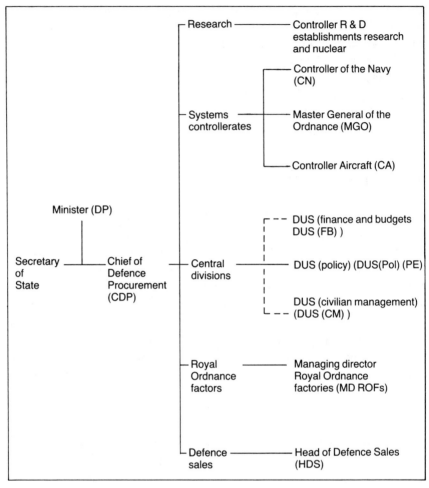

NOTE: DUS (FB) and DUS (CM) are responsible to PUS. HDS is also responsible to PUS.

Source: MOD/PE, 1983.

Figure 34.1 Procurement Executive organisation

forms an essential part of the process which, in addition, requires formal endorsement at various stages of the procurement cycle. Once service needs have been established and the target endorsed, the Procurement Executive takes on the role of prime co-ordinator from feasibility to acceptance (see Figure 34.2).

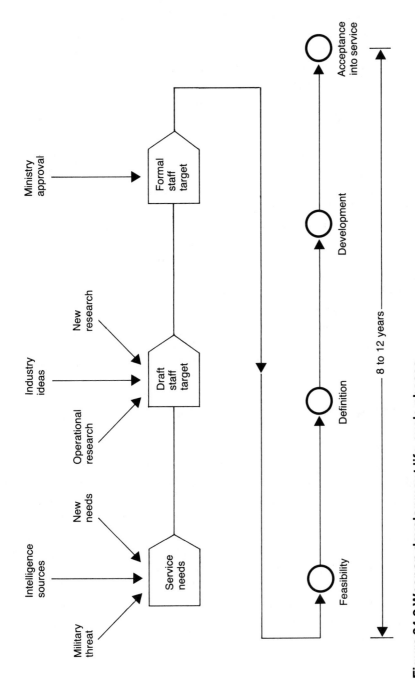

Figure 34.2 Weapon development life-cycle phases

This co-ordinating role is an important link between the supplier, the central staffs and the ultimate service user. Firstly, the Procurement Executive is able to apply multidisciplinary expertise to the evaluation and control of contracts, such as financial, technical and legal matters. Secondly, central co-ordination ensures that developments are not unnecessarily duplicated or overlapped, which was a shortcoming of the earlier, decentralised systems (see Figure 34.3).

The need of 'staff target' is a broad statement of the function and performance requirement of equipment or system concerned. However, the final specification will depend upon a variety of factors, not least of these being the size of the defence budget allocation – published annually in the Public Expenditure White Paper – and the share of this budget that the requirement can reasonably command. Given that negotiations subsequently prove the feasibility of the project, the go-ahead to proceed will be a matter of economic and military priorities existing at the time. However, commencement of the project itself is no guarantee of successful completion as political, economic or technological change may cause project deferment or even cancellation, and the relative long-term nature of projects, of course, exacerbates this situation.

ORGANISATION AND MANAGEMENT OF DEFENCE R & D

UK Government investment in defence research and development, estimated at some £1,800m in 1982/83[1], currently represents over half of the total national R & D budget. More than three-quarters of defence R & D expenditure is accounted for through industry contracts, the remainder funding 'in-house' projects within the defence research establishments. The procedures for research management are highly formalised and closely integrated with the weapons development and procurement cycle.

The Controller Research and Development Establishments (CER) is responsible for the defence research programme and management of some twenty R & D establishments, located in various parts of the UK. All of the establishments, including the

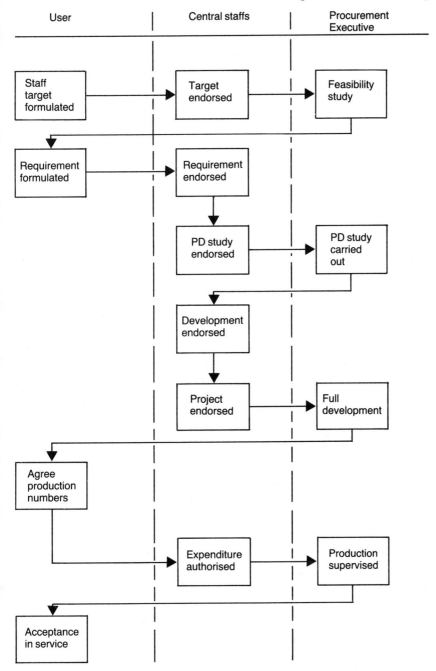

Figure 34.3 Flowpath for introduction of a new weapon project

Atomic Energy Authority's Atomic Weapons Research Establishment, come under the responsibility of the Procurement Executive, thus providing centralised management and control for the research activities of the three services including Civil Aerospace. The technology establishments are primarily concerned with technological research and related subsystems development, rather than with specific environmental weapon systems R & D.

INDUSTRY R & D INVOLVEMENT

The evolution and structure of the military-industrial complex has been shaped by procurement practices over the decades, and in particular by attitudes toward sensitive research and development programmes. The pressure to safeguard national security has traditionally focused 'basic' research in the Defence Research Establishments and allocated complex targeted research (and subsequent development and production) to a select part of the total industrial base. A significant proportion of this applied research is carried out by a small number of established suppliers who possess approved research, development, design and production facilities ('05-21' standard of defence quality assurance approved). Since the Second World War a close working relationship has evolved between the procuring authorities and these established organisations where 'long lead times, high capital expenditure, the perceived need to maintain national capacity to produce strategic goods and the uncertainties of the technology itself, have been among the factors educating this interdependence'.[2]

The intellectual property rights (IPR), which derive from defence contracts with industry, are vested in the contractor concerned with the reservation to the MOD, of the minimum rights required for its procurement purposes.[3] These rights are generally exercised in favour of the contractor concerned as a means of providing an incentive to undertake complex research and development, e.g. the contractor will obviously have a distinct advantage when selection for production contracts is considered and he will have the opportunity to benefit from exports 'spin-off'.

SOURCE SELECTION

Buyer preferences in weapons programmes reflect three essential components making up source-selection decision criteria:[4]

1 State of the art – technological capability and its application to performance enhancement.
2 Development time.
3 Development cost.

A problem faced by the Procurement Executive is that for the bulk of their work they cannot rely on 'competition' to promote supply efficiency. As C. B. Dodds puts it: 'For more than three-quarters of the Procurement Executives' business it is impracticable to rely on competitive tendering as a means of securing the best value for money'.[5]

The limited number of potential bidders and the difficulty of defining exact equipment specification make the task of cost estimating problematic and for complex long-term projects it is often not possible to demand firm, fixed prices.

For such contracts it is often the practice to deal with a number of specialist subsystem contractors with one of the latter having responsibility for prime contractorship. The prime contractor is responsible for ultimate delivery of the requirement, including design co-ordination, systems engineering, overall planning, programming and progressing of work and overall financial management.[6] Obviously, the ultimate selection of the prime contractor will depend upon satisfying the selection criteria previously identified, given the problems of development cost uncertainties which are likely to be common to any potential supplier. The nature of the UK defence industry is such that major sources of weapons supply are the nationalised industries of aerospace and ship building and the Royal Ordnance factories. The process of source solicitation and selection in this environment is not subject to the usual forces of competitive bidding associated with other sectors of the industry, although a competitive element may exist in the form of alternative import considerations, e.g. the Nimrod Early Warning System versus the US Boeing AWACS. Additionally, there may be contracts of an engineering nature for which the Royal Ordnance factories may compete against private industry. (At the time of writing there is discussion on the privatisation of these factories, which of course may remove this distinction.)

Quality assurance

Contracts are normally placed only with firms whose arrangements for quality and product reliability reduce MOD direct inspection to a minimum level or indeed, totally eliminate the need. It is policy to restrict direct contract opportunity, where possible, to firms possessing formally approved quality assurance facilities. Confidence in a direct contractor's quality control arrangements is based on compliance with one of the various quality assurance standards (Def. Stan.) which cover for levels of quality control and inspection demands appropriate to the contract requirements.

These standards specify those elements for a quality control management system which the contractor must possess if the MOD is to be confident that it will ultimately obtain products of the required quality.[7]

CONTRACT SYSTEMS

Project Definition Study (PDS)

The initiation of a 'staff target' and 'operational requirement' have been referred to previously in evaluating R & D management and procedures. For the Project Definition Study contract the Procurement Executive may invite a selection of capable suppliers to tender proposals detailing the proposed study, ultimate weapon specification, time-scales, project management, contractual commitments and quality assurance statement.

The bidder is generally required to submit budgetary prices for the development and production phases although, depending on the scale of the operation, a fixed price may be called for. Two contractors may be selected to carry out the PDS in order to maintain a competitive element at the study phase and to provide for some level of comparative specification and pricing appraisal.

Design and development contract

A detailed user requirement is issued to selected capable contractors outlining the operational requirements, delivery schedule, contractual demands, quality requirements and usually calling for a fixed price, if not negotiable. Selection is generally based on the overall excellence of the proposed system, expected cost/performance effectiveness, conformity to delivery schedules and the judgement of the potential contractor's capability based on past performance.

Invitation cycle

Where the contract is for design and development of a complex weapon system there are obviously inherent risks for the contractor. The inclusion of penalty clauses may reduce the bid response to one or two main suppliers who, whilst having the necessary capability and reputation in defence work, would regard themselves as having a powerful negotiating position. Often the user will know what he wants but have little idea of how it can be done, and thus the contract, in a sense, can be regarded as an invitation to participate at an early stage in the weapon's life cycle.

The later in the development cycle the procurement authority waits before soliciting bids, the better it will be able to identify the most suitable bidder; but more of its own resources are used up and less risk is transferred to the contractor. Theoretically, the more firms that are invited to bid the more chance there is of being offered a clearly superior product, but too many bidders may delay the selection unnecessarily and add to the cost of selection.

For repeat contracts in which the original equipment or system has been produced and is in operational use, source selection may be narrowed down to the original contractor, in the interests of both the buyer and supplier.

CONTRACT PRICING AND NEGOTIATION

For many of the complex systems procured by the authorities, it is difficult to estimate costs with any degree of accuracy and thus the agreement of a 'fixed price' before aceptance of a proposal may be waived. In order that a 'fair and reasonable' price may subsequently be agreed, the Procurement Executive requires complete and continuing information on the contractor's production plans, costs and estimating techniques, together with access to his records and manufacturing facilities. In turn, the contractor needs to be fully acquainted with the system requirements in order to translate these into meaningful costs, although certain operational details may be withheld for security reasons.

This principle of 'equality of information' is necessary in view of the high ratio of non-competitive contracts – in the region of 80 per cent – handled by the Procurement Executive. The post-costing approach enables the Procurement Executive to refine estimating techniques through 'experience' and to calculate more effectively the pricing of follow-on contracts (Standard Condition 48, 1968).

The basic of a 'fair and reasonable price' takes into consideration the contractor's profit which is calculated from the capital employed on the particular project.

This negotiative approach is part of the Procurement Executive's deliberate attempt to sustain a 'dialogue' between itself and industry to ensure that thinking is on converging lines in order to ensure value for money for the user and a reasonable profit for the contractor.

The factor of price is thus an element of the total negotiation strategy and is not determined purely on economic grounds. Pricing may be regarded as an extension of the close relationship between the Procurement Executive and the contractor, where negotiation will ultimately lead to mutual agreement. It remains for the contractor to justify the cost targets he has set and for the procuring authority to facilitate negotiations for any additional costs to cover for modifications and/or changes to the original requirements, other than those arising from contractor default.

In the case of large weapon systems, price is only one of several factors considered by the customer. The major products purchased in the defence market epitomise perfect examples of product differentiation at the extreme.

INCENTIVE CONTRACTS

Incentive contracts are used in those cases where neither the supplier nor the customer can estimate the cost of the work covered by the contract with sufficient confidence to enable a fixed price to be agreed before starting, or in the early stages of the work, but where both parties can reasonably forecast the area in which the actual costs of performing the work will fall and agree a most likely, or target, cost. A fee is also agreed for the profit which would be payable if the cost of the work comes out on target, together with a ratio in which any under-runs or over-runs from target cost will be shared between the supplier and the customer. The supplier has a positive incentive to keep his costs down, because by so doing he can increase his profit or avoid contributing towards an over-run on costs. The incentive thus provided motivates the supplier to act in the customer's best interests (see Figure 34.4).

Target cost	£500,000.00
Profit (at target)	£40,000.00
Share ratio for	
over and under-runs, 75% customer, 25% supplier	
Outcome (i.e. actual cost) = £487.495	
Fee for profit payable: Target profit	£40,000.00
Supplier's share of under-run	
(500,000 − 487,495) × 25%	£3,126.25

Total £43,126.25

Thus:	Expected price				Actual price	
Target cost	500,000		Cost		487,495.00	
Target profit	40,000	= 8%	Fee		40,000.00	= 8.85%
			Share of under-run		3,126.25	

Total 540,000   Total 530,621.25

Customer saved £9,378.75   Supplier earned £3,126.25 bonus

Figure 34.4 Example of incentive contract

PROJECT MANAGEMENT

Project management involves development cost estimating, programming and cost and achievement comparison.

Development cost estimating is a highly specialised activity, the major purposes of which are:

- to assess the total R & D cost and decide if development should proceed
- to forecast annual funding
- to set budgets for control of costs
- to evaluate the cost of changes.

Parametric estimates using data taken from past similar contracts, may be used for cost estimating or, if the contract poses many new problems, comparative methods may be applied where a simple ratio may be found to exist between the efforts, or costs, for different sections of the same project.

A 'work package' system is used for expressing estimates, budgets and for cost collection. This is regarded as the smallest, composite unit of activities for which efficient cost-collection can be achieved.

Development programming

The task of programming the project provides for estimating time and costs, establishing a framework for co-ordinating all project activities and for creating a standard against which to control technical, time and eventually cost progress.

Essential inputs to the programme comprise:

(*a*) the in-service Date, which becomes the target milestone to which all other milestones are related and which determines the initial duration of the programme;

(*b*) the staff target, becoming the staff requirement incorporating engineering performance, trials and acceptance specification which set the preliminary detail of the programme.

Outputs of the programme should be capable of expressing the major and intermediate tasks, the logical task sequences, the responsibilities for tasks and the estimates of time, resources and the notification of the end date.

Cost and achievement comparison

The measurement of project progress or achievement against a plan is made more effective by attention to formal planning and frequent monitoring of progress. This necessitates regular contact with the contractor's team by the PE staff involved. The monitoring task requires an examination of the planned work to date, how much has been done, the planned cost of the work and the actual cost incurred.

Collaborative projects

The management of international collaborative projects poses a number of problems for the Procurement Executive, although the considerations at the higher level of decision making involve both specific benefits and disadvantages:[8]

(*a*) standardisation – procurement on a collaborative basis ensures inter-operability of equipment with that of allies concerned, and hence greater cost-effectiveness against an enemy with the problems of standardisation;

(*b*) political – collaboration is a means of expressing, and cementing, NATO and/or European solidarity.

In the complex field of aerospace it is considered that the necessary degree of co-operation can only be achieved by the commercial integration of the co-operating firms. A system of prime contractor in one country and subcontractor in another may be adopted as occurred in the Anglo-French helicopter project. The management arrangements were such that the Procurement Executive acted as executive agent and let the LYNX contracts on the prime contractor who in turn subcontracted out an agreed proportion. A joint administrative subcommittee dealt with the financial, legal and contractual aspect of the project.

SOME PROBLEM AREAS

Increasing weapon sophistication has given rise to increased uncertainties in cost projections, greater R & D funding and higher costs of weapon ownership and deployment. The defence industries have tended to take on an increasing proportion of skilled engineers and scientists in relation to a given output, whilst the increased specialisation of tooling and plant needed for weapons development has called for more government investment.

Economies of scale through longer production runs have been sought from arms exports, but Britain's achievements have not been sufficient to offset the pressures of rising costs. Over the past years there has been a general levelling off in the contribution to defence expenditure from arms exports.[9]

Attempts to lower costs through co-operative ventures in the form of a 'European approach' have only had a limited success.

Co-production of the Jaguar and MRCA aircraft led to the incursion of 'costs of co-operation' through larger overheads on research and development and production, difficulties in co-ordinating the work of remote sites and reconciling working methods and standards. 'The complexity of these problems and the time and effort necessary to reconcile them increase overheads'.[10] Many of these problems are being solved as collaborative ventures move along the learning curve, but the propensity for individual countries to maintain sovereignty over particular defence equipment development has inhibited the move towards larger-scale standardisation.[11]

DISTINGUISHING CHARACTERISTICS

In comparing the defence sector with that of its commercial counterpart a number of distinguishing characteristics can be identified.[12] These can be summarised as follows:

1 The market consists essentially of a single buyer (monopsonistic).
2 Demand is a function of the potential threat imposed by perceived military advantage of the enemy or the possible gains

from exploiting technological development.

3 The market is highly personalised and dependent upon close dialogue between buyer and seller – the former having access to inspect the supplier's resources, accounting and control procedures.

4 Price is determined by an evaluation of anticipated and actual costs, plus a percentage *assessed by the buyer.*

5 Protracted development times often lead to technological obsolescence before the product is completed.

6 The buyer is willing to invest in product research and development and provide equipment and facilities.

7 Price is rarely the dominant factor; quality, performance and timely delivery being amongst the key considerations.

8 Although the buyer may have a number of research, development and production sources to choose from, relatively few products are ultimately produced simultaneously, for the same end use.

These characteristics may be contrasted with conditions prevailing in the commercial market where:

1 The market consists of several buyers.

2 Demand is based on disposable income.

3 A generally impersonal relationship exists between buyer and seller.

4 There is a relative dominance of price.

5 There is a relatively wide choice of products.

6 The producer must finance own R & D and provide for investment, i.e. the buyer is not willing to invest.

7 Design changes remain relatively slow and technological exploitation is mainly supplier controlled.

8 The industrial base is largely allowed to 'float' although social pressures may initiate government investment in a time of recession.

Thus the procurement system has helped to shape a relatively unique environment in which the military-industrial supplier has almost become an arm of its buyer, the government. It is hardly surprising that, given the additional burden of complex and protracted product development, defence procurement should have its own peculiar problem areas.

621

RECENT PERSPECTIVES ON DEFENCE PROCUREMENT

The escalation in the cost of defence equipment has led to major reviews of policy following the defence review in 1981. The MOD is introducing a series of measures designed to increase the role of private industry involvement in decisions affecting British defence business and to cut costs and boost efficiency.

The government had decided as early as 1981 to move towards a more positive partnership with the defence industries which would involve companies at a much earlier stage in the definition and refinement of equipment needs. Alongside of this, attempts to increase the level of collaborative ventures and to stimulate greater competition for weapons contracts are seen as being essential to combating the increasing burden on defence spending, while maintaining existing high standards of weapons performance and superiority. The services are being persuaded to simplify staff requirements in terms of what they wish the weapon or equipment to do, leaving industry to come up with a precise solution.

Over the past few years the number of defence research establishments has been reduced in an attempt to rationalise the high R & D costs incurred annually and to phase in industry's involvement at the early phases of the development cycle. A more 'commercial' approach at this stage will, it is hoped, allow export potential to be evaluated and acted upon accordingly.

In return suppliers will be required to take on more responsibility in the way of prime contractorship and subcontractor management, and such changes will be likely to lead to greater pressures for firm, fixed contract prices.

The shift of responsibility brought about by these changes should prove mutually beneficial. The bringing in of competitive entrepreneurial skills from industry and the subsequent reduced pressures on a presently stretched Procurement Executive should eventually lead to more efficient co-ordination of activities and a reduction in the level of uncertainty in the design, planning and execution of contracts.

REFERENCES

(1) 'Supply Estimates', 1982/83, HMSO.

(2) Philip Gummett, 'The Contract Mechanism and the Promotion of British Technology' in *Directing Technology,* Ron Johnston and Philip Gummett (eds), Croom Helm, London, 1979.

(3) Sir Ieuan Maddock, *Civil Exploitation of Defence Technology,* NEDC, London, 1983.

(4) B. Kenny, 'The Defence Industry Environment and its Impact on the Military-Industrial Firm', PhD Thesis, University of Salford, 1982.

(5) C. B. Dodds, 'Corporate Planning for Procurement – Government' in *Corporate Planning and Procurement,* D. H. Farmer and B. Taylor (eds), Heinemann, London, 1975.

(6) A. H. Blyth, Head, Contracts Policy MOD/PE, 'Recent Trends in MOD Contract Practice', Symposium RAS, 22 January 1975.

(7) 'Selling to the MoD', MoD CS (PS), London, 1983.

(8) 'Proceedings of MOD/PE Seminar', University of Bradford, November 1974.

(9) B. Kenny, op. cit.

(10) John Stanley and Maurice Pearton, *International Trade in Arms,* Chatto and Windus, London, 1972.

(11) Lynton McLain, 'Joint ventures run into problems', *Financial Times* 10 October 1983.

(12) B. Kenny, op. cit.

35

Purchasing for the paint industry

Bernard Hammond

Whilst the casual observer of the paint industry could be forgiven for believing that it is a relatively simple environment within which to manage, the converse is true. As far as procurement is concerned, the industry provides management with many challenges which have a considerable impact upon a company's success in its end markets. Apart from any other factor, expressed as a proportion of ex-works prices, procurement expenditure can be as much as 65 per cent of company income. Effective procurement performance, therefore, is a prerequisite of profitable company trading in what is an extremely competitive end market.

In this chapter, some of the key aspects of purchasing in this environment are examined so as to highlight the important relationships between the supply and sales markets.

In order that the reader might consider the procurement task in context, the discussion is related initially to the product itself. Thereafter some important materials are considered prior to examining some of the major constraints which impinge upon the task of purchasing for the paint industry.

CONCEPT OF PURCHASING

The purchasing functions in any industry must be aware of two important interfaces: the external and the internal. In other words, it needs to understand the environment from which it is buying and for what purpose. The policies and strategies adopted and the organisation selected, should reflect the supply market from which purchases are made and the end market in which the company is trading. It is vital, particularly in the current economic climate, that the purchasing function should be aware of the key factors in each of these environments when organising the purchasing of goods and services. This is as true of the paint industry as it is of any other.

Given the changing nature of the paint market, the purchasing function should be applying policies and strategies which not only allow for short-term fluctuations, but which take into account the long-term aims of the company, as well as the long, medium and short-term factors which impinge upon the supplying companies. All purchasing policies must take account of these factors and perhaps the easiest way to organise this 'thought process' is to think in terms of a company's selling functions.

Marketing departments are responsible for key input to strategic plans, which includes consideration of the number of suppliers to customers in the market, its capacity and the means by which the company concerned might position itself most effectively in the market. As far as purchasing is concerned, this aspect of the task has been more neglected than any other. In marketing, while someone has to develop the strategy, it is also necessary for it to be implemented through tactical and operational activities in order to sell goods. The same is true of purchasing, in that it is necessary for some to actually buy products and services and implement the strategies which have been developed and hence relate to the medium and short term. Finally, the goods have to be delivered and, in this context, both the purchasing and selling functions have comparable logistics and warehousing problems. Under normal circumstances, the strategic element of the overall task is the aspect which is often overlooked or given less than adequate attention. In the paint industry there has to be a fast response to consumer demands and, thus, individuals in the purchasing team have to be extremely flexible in order to be able to recognise the strategic and tactical aspect of their role and to implement accordingly.

BACKGROUND TO THE PRODUCT

Paint has been described as a 'miracle in a can'. It remains a stable liquid whilst in the pack, sometimes for many years, but when opened it can be spread easily to a thin film which within hours can dry to a hard decorative, protective coating, of only one-thousandth of an inch thickness which can last for years – and at a present day cost of 10-50p per square metre. The protective properties of paint are taken for granted, e.g. if a 1 thou. skin of stainless steel were put out to weather, it would be expected to corrode unless protected by paint.

There are three main ingredients of paint: firstly pigment, which may be white, coloured or colourless and which has several functions, i.e. providing colours, obliteration and controlling flatness of the finish; secondly resins, solvent or water thinned, which bind the pigment particles into a continuous film and bind the paint to the surface as well as providing durability; and thirdly, solvents, which adjust viscosity and help ensure ease of application.

The ultimate performance of a paint depends upon the correct choice and proportions of the various ingredients, whilst the overall composition can range from the very simple to the very complex, depending upon the types of product. When these factors are taken into account and the packaging and marketing aspects and production constraints of the paint business are considered, it will be seen that there will be a wide variety of purchases required and that the task can be complex and demanding.

SCOPE OF PURCHASES

In order to provide a broad picture of products and materials typically purchased, it would be helpful to review certain examples. The list which follows gives some indication of the variety of purchase, the spread and depth of knowledge necessary to deal with them and the factors which affect the cost base of a paint company.

The following items are major purchases of the paint industry:

- titanium dioxide
- paint containers
- resins
- extenders
- colour pigments
- marketing aids.

Titanium dioxide

This product begins life as dark grey-to-black rock or sand and ends up as the white basis of paint. Vast amounts of energy are used in processing it and as a result the commensurate expenditure, together with transport, accounts for a high percentage of costs. There are only a small number of manufacturers of titanium dioxide in the world, who may each have one or more plants. This product, in terms of a purchasing approach, is not too complicated, but since it accounts for between 10 and 20 per cent of raw material costs, it has an important part to play in the profitability of the company.

It is still possible, even with four or more potential suppliers in the UK market, to be faced with a monopoly supply position because of technical or physical differences in the product. A purchasing function must therefore ensure that a close relationship is established with technical and production colleagues, in order that maximum purchasing flexibility is maintained.

Given the limited number of manufacturers and the relatively high price of titanium dioxide, it is important to be aware of all the manufacturers worldwide and to monitor new developments, plant closures and changes in process and technology, because over the space of even a few months, the marketplace in the UK can change drastically. This could be caused by happenings a continent away, let alone a country away, and whilst it might not affect UK purchases directly in the short term, in time, the world market will be affected and, in turn, the local market.

Paint containers

When the paint industry purchases cans, it is dealing with an engineering-based supplier. The can industry has high cost of entry for newcomers and is capital intensive; consequently, in the short to medium term, it has a relatively fixed capacity. The vast majority of containers are made from tinplate, most of which is supplied in the UK by British Steel, in effect, a monopoly supplier. As a result price competition up to the present has been virtually non-existent. When it is realised that in the shipping of cans, the vast majority of the load is air, then location of production is important and as a consequence the can market is not normally subject to the vagaries of imported products. The only effective foreign competition can come in the purchase of imported tinplate but, because of quota arrangements, this cannot change the position dramatically.

There are problems, too, with regards to the shape of the can itself, not least of which relate to stockholding. The majority of such stock is kept in the form of flat-printed plate at the supplier's plant prior to being formed into cans. The management of this stock of printed tinplate held at the suppliers is a major challenge faced by purchasing. It would be easy to acquiesce and allow suppliers to take total responsibility for this inventory. However, there is the danger that this would result in either surplus stock of specifically printed plate (and the commensurate cost of washing off the print if design is changed), the finance of stock when changes occur, or shortages which could result in the stoppage of production and the commensurate cost of lost orders.

A key problem for purchasing with cans is a design change. The time from conception to sale of a paint formulation can seem an infinity; however from finalisation of design idea to can delivery may take as little as six to eight weeks. Whilst the planning of these changes may be conceived when there is adequate time, it is not unusual for last-minute changes, to be made or for marketing to adopt a different tactical approach. As a result the buyer rarely has sufficient time to source properly. This necessitates the changing of stock levels, design, artwork, bromides and plates, all of which have to be managed at a tactical level. Quite often these changes can be detrimental to the purchased price, since all the hard work carried out in the formative days can be negated in the desire to bring in cans for immediate use. This is particularly true when promotions are involved.

The technology of paint containers is changing, and the fact that lengthy trials with paint in the pack are needed before approval of these changes can be given, causes a further problem in purchasing. Given that alterations in can design will cause problems, it can be appreciated that any change in can technology which affects design, and hence needs testing, causes further difficulties. Changes can occur in welding, riveting, types of lids, tin or plastic, types of paint within containers, and finally, the biggest choice facing the purchaser in the paint industry, that of the tinplate, or the plastic container. The implications of such a change include the need to consider the number of viable suppliers and the shape of the packing industry.

Given the likelihood of design change, the progress of technology, and fashion developments, there is always the danger of making poor decisions, for example, as a result of not examining unit costs closely, or applying strategies which are too general, or by concentrating upon the short term at the expense of the long term or vice versa. The skilled purchasing manager will need to ensure that all pertinent issues are taken account of in making his sourcing decisions.

Resins

Most paint manufacturers either have their own resin plants or are associated closely with a manufacturer who has one. The process of manufacture is relatively simple and the profit is to be found in raw material purchase, throughput and technical advance. Basically, resin is obtained from three types of raw materials: vegetable oil, white spirit and commodity petrochemicals.

The vegetable oil most commonly used in the manufacture of resins is derived from the soya bean. This product is sold on world commodity markets which are open and thus freely reported. As a result the product price behaves in the same way as any other commodity and has, therefore, an underlying potential for speculation. As a result this brings an added dimension to its purchase for use as a raw material. Whilst, as yet, the material has not been affected, as has silver for example, there have been some fairly drastic changes in price. In July 1983 the price of soya was between £307 and £309 per tonne, but by November it was hovering around £600. The potential for speculative gain in the purchasing field is clear. If company A had purchased one year's supply of oil at £318 per tonne, whilst company B had purchased at £600 per tonne, their paint costs could differ by as much as 10 per cent, and hence fundamentally affect the profitability of the company (even when stockholding costs were taken into account). Nevertheless, whether a purchasing function should involve itself in speculation is a matter for very careful consideration and firm policy. The purchasing of commodities has been dealt with elsewhere in this handbook, but apart from knowledge of techniques like hedging, buying long or short, taking forward positions and buying spot, other factors which can affect the product itself must be considered. Among these are:

(a) weather, in USA or South America;
(b) political situations;
(c) values of alternative oils;
(d) the market for other uses of the relevant oils.

It is through effective decision making after taking all these factors into account, that purchasing can make a large contribution to company profitability.

White spirit is a petrochemical whose feedstocks can be used for a number of products, not least of which is jet aircraft fuel. The price of white spirit is subject to constant fluctuations, due not only to alternative values resulting from competition for feedstock, but also to the fact that it is produced in large quantities over short periods, and that there are a large number of suppliers, be they manufacturers, merchants, agents or distributors. Prices can change drastically overnight and therefore the purchase price for the professional can differ from that of the uninformed by as much as 10 per cent.

Commodity petrochemicals, which include phthalic anhydride, styrene monomer, maleic anhydride and adipic acid, are also subject to fluctuations. They all have numerous suppliers and buyers and react fairly quickly to changes in volume, the economy, currency, feedstocks and alternative uses. All of these factors are important in covering the cost and price of this type of petrochemical.

The foregoing brief discussion, refers only to the basic air-drying resins. Since more complicated resins are manufactured to meet specific needs, it is necessary for the buyer to be aware of the raw materials involved, process times and, as relevant, to be technically aware of the number of alternative resins which may be used in the more sophisticated paint formulations, such as those for the car industry, protective coatings and marine applications. The number of feedstocks for resins, the complexity of factors affecting predictions, the variety of product available and the techniques of purchasing needed, make the purchasing of resins and their feedstock a fascinating and complicated area for any paint company.

Colour pigments

In purchasing colour pigments, it is essential that the purchasing and the technical/chemical function should act together. Since no two pigments are the same, even simple decorative formulation pigments are technically specified. Thus, if only one formulation is specified, this leads to a monopoly supply position, which the buyer wishes to avoid; while it is the seller's objective to ensure that he is in that position. Consequently, the skill in purchasing pigments is to evolve a commercial strategy which is accepted by all relevant people in the paint company. Research chemists, who are required to formulate products which may not be launched onto the market for many years, have to be aware of this policy and of the potential for change as markets fluctuate. In addition to the chemical formula which they are evolving, they have to consider both long-term commercial strategy and short-term tactical needs of the business. A key task for the buyer in this respect is to assist his colleagues to understand the many commercial factors which stem from their technical decisions. For his part, the buyer needs an understanding of the technical problems which the chemists face.

Marketing/sales aids

Paint, at least, decorative paint, is a fashion product which most people buy at some time or other. There is a wide variety of consumer, each having different needs. Consequently expenditure by paint companies in the area of sales support is vast, especially in the decorative market. Items which need to be purchased to support promotional activity can range from video machines for in-store promotions, to colour cards, from labels to point-of-sale promotional items and from conference facilities to colour buttons. In competing in such a market the marketing man has to be extremely creative in order to maintain or improve marketshare. He may not welcome what he sees as cost and time constraints as purchasing people attempt to do their job. As a result, it is essential that the purchasing function involves itself at an early stage. When purchasing and marketing work together effectively the creative needs of the marketing man can still be met, but at a far lower cost and often more efficiently than might otherwise be the case.

The first step in this liaison must be to ensure that the objectives of the programme are clearly defined, not only in terms of items to be purchased, but also in terms of budget, availability and lead times. Trusted potential suppliers must be involved as soon as possible, since their expertise can be of considerable value. This is true not only as regards cost, but also in the artistic sense. A creative person is prone to change and, of course, should be encouraged to bring all his available flair to the job. However, he should be made aware of the consequences which changes bring, not least of which may be in regard to lead time.

In setting out to solve these problems, effective collaborative planning between marketing and purchasing professionals can, frequently, prove to be a most worthwhile investment. This is especially true in areas that are subject to frequent changes. If it is possible to involve the purchasing department prior to any annual budgets, then the return in the form of deliveries on time, and the achievement of 'cost targets' can be considerable.

OTHER FACTORS WHICH INFLUENCE PURCHASING

The volume output of each type of paint can vary from a continuous process, to small batch production; paints can be standard, which in the case of whites for the decorative market may be a continuous process, or they can be special, as for example in the case of some vehicle refinish or marine applications.

The changing nature of the paint industry has led to manufacturers seeking more continuous production for whites in order to take advantage of the considerable potential for savings which results from the move to bulk powders and liquids. In some cases this has resulted in companies only slightly amending the continuous white process to produce fashion colours by tinting. These changes have led to evaluation of bulk versus bags versus drums, to the different types of storage and methods of receipt, all of which, have a vital impact on purchasing performance. When dealing with special small-lot paints, the problems are those of slow-moving stocks, of relatively high costs of production and proportionally high cost of small quantities of special raw materials.

The scope of raw materials purchases in the paint industry can vary from large-volume multimillion pounds per annum products to vital small ingredients which may cost only a few hundred pounds per year. One problem for paint producers is that there is an extraordinary number of small items on which the company may spend less than £1,000 per annum. The difficulty with most items in this vast array of small-value products, is that there is very rarely an alternative, since the costs in time alone of testing and approving is prohibitive. Consequently, the purchasing department has to adopt some simple expedients such as:

1 Always endeavour to establish what a proprietory brand constitutes, since more often than not, the same material can be bought at lower costs as a generic product.
2 Locate and develop a supplier who sells or manufactures a number of these products and then emphasise turnover in negotiation rather than individual product cost.
3 Attempt to locate a middleman, with low overheads, who can aggregate the needs of a number of companies and provide a lower-cost service as a result of the combined power of his purchases. Whilst this approach will not be feasible with all products, it could be successful with many. In addition, the expertise of these types of supplier can be valuable because they will be able to afford the time to evaluate alternatives and negotiate with their suppliers from a position of greater strength.

CONCLUSION

As can be seen from this discussion the aim of a purchasing department in the paint industry is easy to understand, but achieving the desired ends can be extremely difficult. It is important that a buyer should have knowledge of different types of markets in which he works, together with an awareness of the types of products produced and that he has cognisance of the constraints inherent in the environment within which his suppliers operate. His operational and tactical actions must be closely related to the strategic approaches which he wishes to follow. It is also vital that the purchasing function is seen by its marketing colleagues as a key resource in competing in the collective markets in which the paint industry is involved.

36

Purchasing for the petrochemical industry

Richard Brasher

Procurement in the petrochemical industry is the activity which includes purchasing, expediting, inspection, transport and documentation. Each of these activities is related to the others; the failure of one can negate the success of the others and be severely detrimental to the execution of a project.

The approach to procurement for a major project described here has been used successfully for many years. Although there are probably other ways to approach specific aspects of the task, the key elements are included in this chapter. The handling of construction subcontracts has been omitted because this subject merits a separate chapter.

Procurement for a large project such as the building of a multi-million pound petrochemical complex, should start before the final decision to proceed is made. The purchasing section of a procurement department should assist the project team by obtaining estimated prices for high-value, or unusual, pieces of equipment and also in enquiring about anticipated deliveries. Examples of the type of equipment and facilities required are shown in the Appendix to this chapter. Failure to undertake these checks properly can lead to under- or over-estimating the total cost, or to faulty planning – which can play havoc with construction and completion dates.

In the proposal stages of a project, purchasing should not act in isolation from the other procurement sections. There must be continuing dialogues with expediting and inspection to check on supplier performance, capabilities and capacities – all of which can change – and to confirm that deliveries quoted are feasible. There must also be discussions with transport and documentation sections to ensure that client requirements in these disciplines are achievable.

Procurement may still be a Cinderella activity in many businesses, but any company which treats it as such in the petrochemical industry is taking a very grave risk. Failure to involve procurement at the planning stage can lead to many different problems, e.g. a multi-million pound investment standing idle beause of a delivery failure on one piece of equipment! This failure could be caused by poor supplier selection, a certification problem, a transport problem, or various other reasons.

PROCUREMENT FOR A PROJECT

After the decision to proceed, a project task force has to be selected of which the procurement section will be an important part. This team will be headed by the project procurement manager (PPM) who will be supported by a senior buyer, senior expeditor, inspection co-ordinator, traffic co-ordinator and documentation supervisor. Each of these leaders will have several people, from the discipline concerned, reporting to him. The number of staff, and the dates on which they join the project team, will depend on the size and complexity of the project, and the timing of its various phases. The PPM should report to both the head of procurement and the project director. Similarly, the leaders from the procurement disciplines should report to the project procurement manager and the heads of their departments, who also report to the head of procurement. This reporting system should enable performance to be properly controlled and monitored which in turn should enable problems to be identified and attended to before they become too serious.

Procurement procedures and reports

The PPM will be responsible for preparing procurement procedures for the project taking into account client and company procedures and specific requirements of the project. He will also be responsible for obtaining approval of these procedures from the heads of departments in procurement, the project director and, if appropriate, the client. The PPM must also enure that the procedures are complied with by all concerned. Project procedures will be considerably affected by the type of project, both technically and commercially, and by type of client and the country in which the plant is to be built. For example, project procedures for building a plant in the UK for a sophisticated client who is paying cash will be far simpler than those for a client located in a third world country which has borrowed money from a consortium of banks in the UK backed by ECGD – and also perhaps from sources in other countries. If the project is to be financed by a project line of credit, or another type of loan, certain very complex procedures have to be followed, necessitating the preparation and, in due course, completion of several different types of form. In addition it may be mandatory to have selected quotations and orders approved before final commitment.

Included in the project procedures will be a section on reports and meetings – their frequency, distribution and attendance. In most cases detailed reports on each activity are submitted monthly. However it is recommended that a skeleton report, in a set format, is submitted weekly so that remedial action, if necessary, can be taken as quickly as possible. Reporting on a monthly basis only can result in a serious problem being left unattended for too long with consequential knock-on effects. For example, a delay by a contractor's or client's engineering staff of one month may well cause a much longer delay in fabrication and an even greater delay in construction of the total plant.

Location of procurement team

Before the purchasing activity commences with issuing of enquiry packages, a decision has to be made on where to locate the project procurement section. For a large project it is advisable to locate it with the rest of the project team in a task force area. This has many obvious advantages and is much favoured by clients and project directors. However, it also has certain drawbacks, such as failure to confirm verbal communications in writing which can lead to important matters being misunderstood or forgotten and not acted upon. It is essential to maintain very strict operating disciplines and adherence to project procedures.

Suppliers' lists and enquiries

The PPM also has to prepare a suppliers' list, for the project, probably using his company's standard list and perhaps that of the client. If the project is for an overseas country, very careful research must be done into import restrictions and regulations to determine whether use of indigenous fabricators or agents, or both, is mandatory. Obviously, this will have a bearing on preparation of the suppliers' list and organisations that have not been used before should be surveyed to evaluate their viability and capability.

When enquiries are placed they should be as complete and intelligible as possible and the proposed terms of contract should also be included. Omissions should be highlighted so that a supplier does not have to guess or make assumptions. In particular, technical documentation included with enquiry packages should avoid conflicting specifications and if more than one standard or code is to apply, the one which takes precedence should be indicated.

Selecting suppliers and pre-award meetings

Selection of potential suppliers should be very carefully made so that only those which have an equal chance of obtaining the order are included. This not only avoids putting suppliers to unnecessary expense, but also saves the contractor, and perhaps client, time spent in evaluating bids. The number of enquiries issued will vary, depending on the item and circumstances, but it is seldom less than three or more than eight and it is desirable to obtain at least three competitive tenders. Obviously, the date by which bids must be received should be clearly stated and adhered to. In the writer's opinion if one supplier asks for an extension, which is granted, then the others should also be given the same concession. Similarly, if a supplier offers a rebid after the due date then other suppliers, which have quoted competitively, should be given an opportunity to revise their quotations. It is extremely important that the highest possible standards of business ethics are observed and that information provided by one supplier is not passed inadvertently to others.

Bid evaluation is normally done by at least one commercial and one technical person. Many different aspects have to be considered, but the main points are probably technical, price and delivery. Allowance should also be made for currency exchange rates, if more than one currency is involved, and the cost of transport, spares and other items. Past performance on quality and completion and current capacity should also be considered. It is beneficial to have bid comparison sheets for high value or important orders approved by the heads of purchasing, expediting and inspection – besides the project director and, if required, the client's representative – because they are likely to know if there has been any change in the selected supplier's circumstances.

At the time of writing, there is a tendency to place orders with the lowest bidder, regardless of other considerations and even if the price is much lower than others quoted. This practice has developed because the recession has eroded the profitability of most client companies and, while understandable, is ill advised except in special circumstances.

There is a right price for almost anything and buying from a company which is selling at a genuine loss is tantamount to buying trouble. A supplier that has quoted too low a price may try to save on material, quality, or labour and may also submit very high charges for changes. Besides this, quality companies which quote reasonable prices are likely to be forced out of business, through lack of work, or compelled to adopt some of the practices of the subnormally low bidders. Ultimately the buying company and the industry at large will suffer and purchasing professionals should seek to avoid this occurrence.

Before the award of an order, for equipment and materials, of any value or importance, it is customary to have a pre-award meeting to clarify outstanding technical matters and to negotiate commercial terms and prices. These meetings can be extremely valuable to both parties if properly managed and attended by the right people. Ideally, there should be an agenda circulated in advance, with a copy to the supplier. The specifications, standards and codes that apply should be discussed to ensure that the supplier understands completely the requirements. Therefore, it may be appropriate to ask representatives from several different disciplines to attend these meetings on a part-time basis, or at least to ensure that one of their colleagues covers their points for them.

After the award of an order or contract, a complete copy of the commercial conditions and technical package should be sent to the supplier as quickly as possible. Copies must also be distributed internally to other departments involved and the other sections of procurement. At this stage, purchasing will normally hand over the order to expediting and inspection, in order that they might monitor progress and quality of fabrication. However, besides being involved in invoice approval, purchasing should maintain an interest and should handle any amendments, claims or backcharges.

It is not proposed to discuss negotiations because this subject is dealt with elsewhere in the handbook. However, it should be emphasised that commercial terms and conditions should be comprehensive, but drafted in simple English, and any onerous clauses should be highlighted and their impact discussed. Terms of payment should be related to activities, not just to dates, and an escalation formula, if applicable, should be workable with separate formulae for labour and material costs. Payments made in advance of delivery should be secured against a performance bond, or bank guarantee, and clauses covering insurance, passing of risk and property, guarantees and many others should also be included.

EXPEDITING

On receipt of a purchase order, expediting should immediately enter the relevant details such as the item number, description, quantity and promised delivery date on the material status report. The expeditor should pass a complete copy of the order to the inspection co-ordinator for allocation to an outside inspector who will be responsible for the quality of fabrication. Thereafter, the expeditor should check with the supplier to determine when fabrication programmes, copies of sub-orders and drawings are to be delivered and to establish works order numbers.

After organising the initial expediting activity for an order, the expeditor has to make regular telephone and telex contact to monitor fabrication progress. The frequency of checking, whether monthly, weekly or daily, will depend on how the work is proceeding and criticality to the schedule of the item concerned. The expeditor must also ensure that queries to and from a supplier are answered as quickly as possible and that drawings are commented on, approved or otherwise, and returned promptly. In this latter activity the expeditor will be assisted by a drawings control clerk.

Most of the information that an expeditor receives on progress will be from personnel within a supplier's organisation. How much reliance an expeditor places on information received should depend on his knowledge of the person concerned, their level of seniority, and previous performance of their company. In addition, the expeditor can gain significant information by asking pertinent questions and by checking with the supplier's sub-suppliers. However, the most dependable source of information should be the contractor's inspector who will be making visits. If inspection has been waived, or there is to be only final inspection or if there is uncertainty about satisfactory performance, the expeditor himself should either make a visit, or arrange for an inspector to do so.

Expediting should be informed about any activity which may adversely affect the delivery of an order and should remain involved until arrival of the equipment concerned has been confirmed by site warehouse staff. There is a tendency to allow expediting to delegate its responsibility to the transport or shipping department after completion of final inspection. However, it is prudent for expediting to remain involved until written confirmation of safe receipt, in order to avoid the possibility of an item being left behind in a supplier's works while all concerned believe that it has been shipped! Expediting should be involved in approval of invoices for payment, particularly those in respect of progress and final payments.

In many organisations, expediting is considered to be of less consequence than purchasing because the latter is involved in committing substantial sums of money most effectively. This philosophy is mistaken because, although the two activities are closely interrelated, the failure to achieve required deliveries can far outweigh any savings made by purchasing.

INSPECTION

Inspection and reporting of progress during fabrication is of paramount importance in the petrochemical industry. On receipt of a copy of the purchase order the inspection co-ordinator should check that it is complete in all respects, i.e. that the correct specification, drawings, applicable codes and test requirements are included. The next task is to grade the order to indicate the amount of inspection required. Gradings might be as follows:

Grade A – critical item requiring careful inspection and record-
ing at all stages of manufacture.
Grade B – less critical item but one that still requires regular
inspection at various stages of manufacture.
Grade C – check of test certification only in the home office.
Grade D – no inspection or outside expediting required.
Grade E – outside expediting only.
Grade F – final inspection only.

Having graded an order, the inspection co-ordinator then has to assign it to an inspector. Allocation will depend on the location of the supplier's works and the inspector's home, current workload and, most essential, experience in inspecting similar items.

The inspector responsible for a purchase order should visit the selected supplier shortly after the purchase order has been placed, to ensure that production personnel fully understand all requirements and have no queries. Thereafter, the inspector should make visits, as required, to confirm quality of materials and fabrication, dimensions, weld procedures, welders' qualifications (where necessary), witness tests and to check on certification and documentation. In addition, he may have to examine painting, marking for transportation, packing and loading on to transport.

Failure by an inspector to carry out his duties in the most meticulous manner could, at worst, be catastrophic if a defective item is put into service before the fault is discovered and rectified. If an item has to be corrected on site, or if the certification and documentation is incorrect, the delay caused by taking remedial action might be extremely expensive because of disruption to construction and ultimate completion.

Quality requirements are becoming more stringent, both onshore and offshore, and it is totally incorrect to assume that standards that applied previously will be acceptable today. The importance of emphasising this point to both inspectors and suppliers cannot be overstressed. In addition, quality and certification regulations vary considerably depending on the country and the client. These requirements, which in certain cases can be extremely exacting, must be fully researched and understood by all concerned.

TRANSPORT

The transport section should be involved in a project at an early stage, particularly for overseas construction sites. This section is involved in investigating transport requirements, preparation of transport enquiry documents, bid evaluation and assisting in negotiation with the selected forwarding agent or shipping company. Thereafter transport must ensure that marking and shipping instructions are included in purchase orders and that regular contact is maintained with expediting on progress of manufacture of equipment. It is transport's responsibility to inform forwarding agents when equipment is likely to be ready for collection and to monitor their performance. Transport is also involved in customs procedures, and in handling the documentation for export and import and duties payable. Data concerning ports near the job site, facilities and regulations at these ports, and shipping lines serving the relevant country has to be assembled and disseminated to those concerned. It is essential to ensure that selected ports can handle the size of vessel to be used and that there is satisfactory craneage and other equipment for unloading.

Movement of large items

For unusual and large pieces of equipment the methods of loading and unloading and the facilities available for lifting should be studied. In addition the route to be taken should be surveyed in advance and the following points should be investigated: movement through gates, around corners, over and under bridges, under power cables, across level crossings and culverts, up and down steep gradients, and local authority and police regulations concerning movements of large and/or heavy items. These points should be considered either when moving a large load from a supplier's works to the port of shipment or from the port of destination to the site, or both. On certain occasions it may be necessary physically to follow actual movement.

Loads may move from a supplier's works to the port of embarkation by barge down a canal or by river or both. In these cases lifting or driving on to the barge or ship have to be taken into acount and may be affected by tides or level of water. Prolonged droughts can affect water level and extreme cold can freeze the water in a canal. Delays in moving a big load to a port can result in a demurrage charge from shipowners – or in missing the ship, leading to storage charges for the item concerned.

Marshalling yards

For certain projects involving job sites in more remote parts of the world, it may be necessary to use chartered or dedicated ships. This in turn will almost certainly lead to the requirement for one or more marshalling yards where equipment and material can be delivered and stored while awaiting a chartered vessel. It is essential that a marshalling yard is properly staffed to record, inspect, and off-load goods on arrival. Areas must be prepared to hold large and heavy equipment and certain items, such as control panels and electronic equipment, may require not only weather-proof storage but storage at a certain temperature.

As a minimum, a marshalling yard will require adequate secure storage facilities, lifting equipment, easy access by road and sea, and close proximity to an airport and rail head. If equipment has to be stored or subjected to a long journey it should be properly packed, or protected, to prevent rust or damage in transit.

Use of shipping and forwarding agents

There is frequent debate as to whether or not a company should handle its own transport requirements or use the services of a shipping and forwarding agent, or subcontract this activity to suppliers. To handle transport in-house entails maintaining a large and highly-skilled staff, which can be justified only if there is a heavy and continuous workload. On the other hand, subcontracting this activity to suppliers is likely to lead to significant extra costs. Therefore, it is probably best to have a small but experienced in-house transport section and to appoint a shipping and forwarding agent to actually arrange movements of the goods. This method has many advantages, one of which is that agents normally have offices, or local agents, in the country into which the equipment is being imported, who are familiar with local requirements.

DOCUMENTATION

Documentation requirements for a project vary according to whether the project is a cash contract or paid for out of a bank loan or loans. In addition, there will be a considerable amount of other commercial and technical documentation required. If possible, the extact requirements should be identified before the bid is made and certainly as soon as possible thereafter. When dealing with a new client or a new territory, or both, discussions with banks, lawyers, accountants and technical authorities familiar with that country are recommended. Documentation requirements are becoming more demanding and complex, but it is not necessary to re-invent the wheel.

OFFSHORE

Procurement for the topsides of an offshore production platform is similar to procurement for an onshore project. However, although many of the items are the same, there may be differences in the materials of construction and the paint finish because of safety requirements and the highly corrosive environment. Another important factor is that size of equipment and weight can affect selection of a supplier. Due to difficulties of access to a platform, for replacement or repair, offshore specifications tend to be more demanding with greater quality assurance and quality control involvement. Delivery requirements for offshore projects are even more important than for onshore. The cost of missing a weather window or having the work completed on a platform, instead of in the construction yard, can be horrific. In addition even greater emphasis is put on material certification and many items require design approval and tests witnessed by a certifying authority.

PERSONNEL

There is a continuing debate as to whether or not procurement personnel should have an engineering qualification, which in certain companies is mandatory. However, with the exception of inspection, it is the author's opinion that personal qualities and intellectual ability is of greater importance than a technical qualification. While the latter is advantageous it should be emphasised that procurement, apart from inspection, should be more concerned with the commercial side of a project leaving technical matters to be handled by the engineers. However procurement personnel must be familiar with the items being purchased and be prepared when necessary to offer their engineering colleagues alternative sources of supply and possibly to suggest alternative equipment or materials. Procurement in the petrochemical industry probably involves a wider range of equipment, materials and facilities than in most other industries. In addition the sums of money involved, stringency of quality requirement, complexity of documentation and varied sources of supply make it essential to employ, train and develop high quality and dedicated staff. These people have to be hardworking, conscientious, intelligent and flexible if they are to satisfy the demands of an industry in which the pressures are probably greater than most.

APPENDIX: EQUIPMENT LIST FOR A TYPICAL PETROCHEMICAL COMPLEX

Onsite equipment

Distillation towers
Reactors
Drums and onsite tanks
Pumps (including spares)

Compressors
Vacuum sets
Exchangers
Fired heaters
Miscellaneous equipment

Utility generation equipment

Boiler facility
Power generation
Water treatment
Inert gas generation
Cooling water system
Fuel oil/fuel gas system

Offsite equipment

Storage tanks – feed, intermediate product
Product loading – marine and road
Flare system
Drainage systems
Hydrocarbon slop system
Effluent treatment

Buildings

Control room
Laboratories
Switchroom
Boiler house
Power house
Analyser houses
Workshop
Warehouse
Canteen and mess facilities
Administration offices
Gate house
Fire station

37

Purchasing for maintenance, repair and operating

John Stevens

When any part of the purchasing activity is decentralised, and users do the buying, it is quite conceivable that the impact of those purchases on corporate profitability is entirely overlooked. In the case of MRO items – maintenance, repair and operating supplies – items which are consumed but do not go into the product – this is often the case. Some individual departments may do their own buying, despite the fact that purchasing handles all raw materials and other bought out production materials and components. As a result of this, the global expenditure on MRO items may not be clearly established, and this is usually a substantial outgoing. A typical breakdown of the spend in a manufacturing company producing automotive parts is shown in Figure 37.1.

A relationship of £21.2 to £5.35 between direct materials to MRO purchases is not untypical. It indicates that for approximately every pound sterling spent on inputs which are incorporated into the product, 25p is spent on materials which are used to aid the manufacturing facilities and other aspects of the business. It must be stressed that the MRO budget would not generally include items on the capital account, but those such as motors, pumps, piping, bearings, valves, fasteners, fittings, paints, lubricants, tools, uniforms, stationery and print services, and many others too numerous to mention, might well come within this blanket heading. The magnitude of this expenditure is sometimes immense, even in a manufacturing concern as opposed to a utility (where almost all

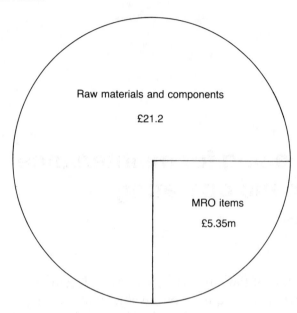

Figure 37.1 MRO purchases as a proportion of total revenue expense

expenditure is MRO by circumstance). One UK car manufacturer reckoned its global expenditure in 1982 on consumables to be around £90m, in other words something in excess of the total revenue spend of, say, The Dunlop Tyre group and Girling Limited, who both supply the company, put together!

Wearing a consultant's hat concentrates one's attention on seeking weak spots in any organisation's operations. A checklist of questions asked of any client company may quickly point to uncontrolled situations, under-investment in purchasing know-how and techniques, and sometimes blind spots as regards where there may still be potential pockets of lost profit within the materials administration sector. Readers might like to check their own department's control over MRO buying by answering the following questions themselves. Those who work in a professional environment should be able to give a reasonable answer to every question immediately, and a precise answer in a matter of hours after having consulted the departmental information system.

AN AUDIT OF THE MRO PURCHASING OPERATION

1 What is the approximate size of your annual spend on MRO items?

2 What is the average value of your inventory of MRO items?

3 What is the total number of MRO items held as stock-in-stores?

4 What is the percentage of your total MRO stock which you consider to be 'strategic spares'? These are sometimes called 'critical spares'. They are replacement parts for which the probability of being needed as a replacement in a piece of plant or machinery is either unknown, or very slight. They are thus stocked as an 'insurance' against breakdown.

5 What is the percentage of your total MRO stock which you consider to be 'wear spares'? These are spares which are stocked to replace those items which are subject to wear or deterioration, and which require replacement at intervals. The rate of wear if often a function of plant running time, and the replacement factor can be predicted with considerable accuracy. They tend to be relatively high in value, with larger than average lead times.

6 What is the percentage of your total MRO stock which you consider to be consumable items? These are often common usage items, normally having a demand of some volume which is predictable. They can frequently be obtained from a large number of suppliers, have reasonably short lead times, and are normally in the low-value range.

7 Which of the following do you employ for inventory control of consumable items:

(a) two-bin systems

(b) max/min re-order system

(c) EOQ formula

(d) time interval re-ordering

(e) visual systems – varieties of (a)?

8 Which of the following do you employ for inventory control of wear spares:

(a) two-bin systems

(b) max/min re-order system

(c) EOQ formula

  (*d*) time interval re-ordering
  (*e*) visual systems – varieties of (*a*)
  (*f*) re-order when a spare is used from stock?
9 Is a coding system employed for MRO items?
  (*a*) All?   (*b*) Some?
10 Is a computer used to control the stock of MRO items?
11 What is the target and actual 'level of service' that is required, and provided, to user departments who utilise MRO items? (A 99 per cent service level would mean that for every 100 occasions when the user department wanted the items, the user would be satisfied from stock 99 times.)
12 What is the average level of obsolescence of your MRO items per annum, expressed as a percentage of the total number of MRO items held in stock?
13 Is the purchase of MRO items carried out by:
  (*a*) purchasing manager
  (*b*) senior buyer
  (*c*) buyer
  (*d*) assistant buyer/clerk
  (*e*) personnel outside purchasing?
14 If (*e*) above, who?
15 After the purchase of a piece of plant and machinery, is the decision to stock a range of spare parts determined by:
  (*a*) purchasing using historical data on similar items of plant/machinery?
  (*b*) purchasing using manufacturer's recommended list of spares?
  (*c*) engineers providing their own list of spares?
  (*d*) purchasing in consultation with user departments?
16 Is there a planned maintenance programme in operation in your company?
17 If there is a planned maintenance programme, does purchasing have a programmed supply related to the planned maintenance programme? This may sometimes be referred to as 'provisioning for planned usage'.
18 Does the MRO buyer have access to a detailed list of all plant and machinery within the company, together with their maintenance histories, i.e. date of purchase, number of

breakdowns, number of overhauls, parts and major items replaced etc?

19 How often is the MRO buyer in contact with personnel from the maintenance engineering department?

20 What percentage of the total MRO items is supplied by distributors/stockists?

21 Are outside contractors used to carry out maintenance?

22 Does purchasing select maintenance contractors?

23 Do maintenance contractors supply their own materials and spare parts?

24 Do you have any arrangements with suppliers whereby the inventory responsibility of some MRO items has been transferred to the supplier?

25 Do suppliers maintain a stock of items supplied by them on your site on a 'pay-as-used' basis?

26 Do you carry out any joint purchasing with other companies for common items?

27 Do you use 'buyback' clauses in contracts for maintenance or repair parts? (A buyback clause is an agreement with a source who agrees to buy back supplied items after a certain period of no consumption by the customer, provided the items are not obsolete.)

28 Do you use any means in order to measure specifically the performance of the MRO buyer or staff?

29 Does the individual in charge of purchasing MRO items have specific training or experience applicable to the job?

30 Is MRO buying used as a training ground for buyers moving later to the purchase of materials used and incorporated in the final product?

It is hoped that these questions might serve as a useful checklist in the examination of the supply activity in carrying out the MRO provisioning task. They were originally included in a research exercise carried out at Coventry (Lanchester) Polytechnic. One hundred companies were mailed and thirty-two usable replies were returned. Of the returned group, a purchasing manager of a well-known compressor manufacturer expressed the view that the list of questions had made him aware of possible improvements in the purchase of non-production materials for his company, and that he had already implemented some procedural changes which would give him better control over MRO purchases.

The feedback from the returned questionnaires disclosed the following 'present state of the art' in MRO buying which, despite the limited sample size, is informative and may serve as a guideline. These results refer to the relevant question as numbered in the audit.

7   The max/min method appears to be the most commonly employed technique to control consumable items; the EOQ method ranked only third, despite its applicability.

8   The max/min method was also commonly employed to control wear spares. It is not the ideal method for this group.

9   The MRO stores vocabulary had not been coded by all respondents.

10   Computers were not used universally for the MRO stock file.

11   Service level targets varied from <75 to 99 per cent.

12   One-quarter of the respondents indicated that obsolescence on MRO items exceeded 5 per cent per annum.

15   The range of spare parts to support capital items were determined by the purchasing manager's engineering department.

16   Planned maintenance is very commonly employed.

17   Programmed supply, to tie in with planned maintenance, was a sadly neglected technique.

18   MRO buyers had neither sufficient information on installed plant and equipment nor maintenance histories.

20   Distributors played an important role in supplying MRO items; over one-quarter of the respondents sourced more than 60 per cent of their MRO needs from stockists. Quick delivery and aid to continuity of supply were considered the main advantages in being stockists; lower inventory costs came third.

21   Outside contractors were universally employed to carry out maintenance.

23   The contractors supplied their own materials and spare parts.

22   Maintenance contractors were selected by non-purchasing personnel.

24   Only half the respondents had transferred responsibilities of

25 MRO inventories to suppliers, and far fewer had employed consignment stocking systems.
26 Joint contracting was a rarity.
27 Buyback arrangements were rarely explored.
28 Specific measuring methods for MRO items were uncommon.
29 MRO buyers were experienced but not trained.
30 MRO buying is commonly a starting job for the new recruit.

A brief analysis of this snapshot of the MRO scene suggests that there is scope for more attention to be paid to this buy. It is hoped that the research into what goes on in a representative sample of companies can be of value to others doing similar jobs by providing a useful set of reference points.

Appendix: national purchasing organisations*

Argentine
Asociación Argentina de Compradores
Adolfo M. Salas, Secretary
Tucuman 141-6° Piso,
(1049) Buenos Aires – Tel. 32-2178,
31-8421

Australia
Australian Institute of Purchasing and
Supply Management
A. G. Greig, National Secretary
Treasurer
12 Rowena Street
Kenmore, Queensland 4069
Tel. 617-378 68 39
Telex: Davignon AR 40 443

Austria
Arbeitsgemeinschaft Einkauf
H. Pechek, Secretary General
Postfach 131
Hohenstaufengasse 3, A - 1014 Wien
Tel. 63 86 36, Telex 7-5718

Belgium
Association Belge des Chefs
d'Approvisionnement – ABCA
J. P. Trum, Secretary-General
Chemin de Gros-Tienne 36
1328 Ohain – Tel. 02/653 8094

Vereniging voor Inkoop en
Bevoorrading – VIB
Mr. Maurits Henne, Secretary-General
c/o VEV Brouwersvliet 15 (Bus 7)
B-2000 Antwerpen

Brazil
Associacão Brasileira de Administracão
de Material – ABAM
Vander Faria, Secretary
Avenida Beira Mar 406, Groupo 207
Rio de Janeiro – (RJ) CEP 20.021
Tel. (021) 220 8141/256 38 68

---

* Reproduced with permission of the IFPMM.

Canada
Purchasing Management Association of
Canada
David Tyler, Executive Vice-President
PMAC
2 Carlton Street, Suite 917
Toronto, Ontario M5B 1J3
Tel. (416) 977-7111
Telex: 06 218249

Denmark
Danske Indkøbschefers Landsforening
– DILF
Ms. G. Olsbro, Secretary-General
Charlottenlundvej 26
DK - 2900 Hellerup – Tel. (1) 622401

Finland
Suomen Materiaalitaloudellinen
Yhdistys R. Y. – SMTY
Ms. Marjatta Kauppinen, Secretary
Vuorimiehenpuistikko 4 D 50
SF-00140 Helsinki 14 – Tel. 90-174469

France
Compagnie des Dirigeants
d'Approvisionnement et Acheteurs
de France
Ph. Colaneri, Secretary-General
8, rue du Conservatoire
75009 Paris – Tel. 7704335

Germany
Bundesverband Materialwirtschaft und
Einkauf e.V.
U. Jekewitz, Hauptgeschäftsführer
Waidmannstrasse 25
6000 Frankfurt am Main 70
Tel. (0611) 633041/42

Greece
Hellenic Purchasing Institute
C. Cambas, Secretary-General
15 Omirou Street
Athens 135
Tel. 3621 745

Great Britain
Institute of Purchasing and Supply
I. G. S. Groundwater, Director-
General
Easton House, Easton on the Hill
Stamford, Lincolnshire, PE9 3NZ
Tel. 0780-56777

Hong Kong
Institute of Purchasing and Supply
(Hong Kong)
Tony Mak, Hon. Secretary
P.O. Box 72241
Kowloon Central Post Office
Kowloon/Hong Kong

India
Indian Association of Materials
Management
Ms. Dhun S. Dastoor, Executive
Secretary
406, Vyapar Bhavan, 4th Floor
P. D'Mello Road, Carnac Bunder
Bombay 400009 – Tel. 346081
Telex 11-5944

Ireland
Irish Institute of Purchasing and
Materials Management
D. Donnelly, Hon. Secretary
16 Hume Street
Dublin 2 – Tel. 01-605608/681601

Israel
Irgoun Israeli Le'Menahalei Rechesh
Ve'Haspaka
Israeli Purchasing Managers Ass.
Kalman Magen Street 11
P.O. Box 7128
Tel Aviv 61071 – Tel. 256705

Netherlands
Nederlandse Vereniging voor Inkoop
Efficiency – NEVIE
F. J. de Kraker, Director
Van Alkemadelaan 700
2597 AW Den Haag – Tel. 070-264341
Telex 32626

Italy
Associazione degli Approvvigionatori e
Compratori Italiani – ADACI
Dr. D. Giuliani, Secretary-General
Via Ranzoni 17
20149 Milan – Tel. 4082474

New Zealand
New Zealand Institute of Purchasing
and Supply
Ross D. Douglas, National Secretary
P.O. Box 3590
Wellington – Tel. 845475

Japan
Japan Materials Management
Association
Dr. Toshio Minamikawa, Vice-
President
Kyodo Building
1 Nihonbashi-Honcho 1-Chome
Chuo-Ku, Tokyo 103

Nigeria
Nigerian Institute of Purchasing and
Materials Management
A. O. Odusote, Secretary
6, Barikisu-Iyede Street
Onitiri
Yaba-Lagos

Kenya
The Kenya Institute of Supplies
Management
J. S. M. Mativo, Secretary-General
P.O. Box 30400
Nairobi
Tel. 338 111/426

Norway
Norsk Innkjøps og
Materialadministrasjonsforbund –
NIMA
Trondheimsveien 80
Oslo 5 – Tel. 379710/378679

Mexico
Federación Mexicana de Asociaciones
de Compras, Abastecimiento y
Materiales – FEMACAM
Ap. Postal No. 20-623, Delegación
Alvaro Obregon, 01000 Mexico
Tel. 5-478757

Philippines
Purchasing Association of the
Philippines, Inc.
I. B. Handinero, Jr., Executive
Secretary
P.O. Box 1876, MCC
Makati, Rizal – Tel. 864711/878822

Portugal
Associacão Portuguesa de Compras e
Aprovisionamento
C. Silva Marques, Secretary-General
Alameda das Linhas de Torres
201-3° – Dto, 1700 Lisboa
Tel. 795348

Singapore
Singapore Institute of Purchasing and
Supply
Tan Soo Tuan, Hon. Secretary
Rm. 602, 6th Floor
Maxwell Road, P.O. Box 3429
Tel. 2208451

South Africa
Institute of Purchasing South Africa
P.O. Box 35495
Northcliff 2115, Transvaal
Tel. (011) 6787081

Spain
Asociación Española de Responsables
de Compras y de Existencias (AERCE)
Dr. Simón Pallarés Mellado
Secretary-General
Maria de Molina, 44
Madrid 6 – Tel. 91-261 82 63

Sri Lanka
Institute of Supply and Materials
Management
C. S. Chinniah, Secretary
148/3 Kynsey Road, Colombo 8
Tel. 95908

Sweden
Sveriges Inköpsledares Förbund – SILF
Ms. E. Schönström, Secretary-General
Box 70, 16126 Bromma
Tel. (46) 880 20 75

Switzerland
Schweizerischer Verband für
Materialwirtschaft und Einkauf
(SVME)
A. J. Röösli, Secretary-General
Postfach 87
Laurenzenvorstadt 90, CH-5001 Aarau
Tel. (064) 247131

Uganda
Uganda Association of Purchasing and
Supply Management
Joseph R. Owor, Secretary-General
P.O. Box 2017
Kampala
Tel. 6 10 11/4

USA
NAPM
National Association of Purchasing
Management Inc.
R. J. Baker, Executive Vice-President
496 Kinderkamack Road, P.O. Box 418
Oradell, N.J. 07649
Tel. (201) 967-8585

NIGP
National Institute of Governmental
Purchasing Inc.
Lewis Spangler, Executive Vice-
President
Suite 101, Crystal Square Bldg. 3
1735 Jefferson Davis Highway
Arlington, Virginia 22202
Tel. (703) 920-4020

Venezuela
Asociación Venezolana de
Compradores – AVEC
Ed. Fedecamaras, Secretary
2° Piso, Oficina «G»
Urb. El Bosque, Caracus 1050-A
Tel. 72 27 64

Further reading

Geoffrey W. Aljian (ed.) *Purchasing Handbook,* 3rd ed., McGraw-Hill, New York, 1973.

Dean S. Ammer, *Materials Management and Purchasing,* 4th ed., Richard D. Irwin, Homewood, 1980.

Peter J. H. Baily and D. H. Farmer, *Purchasing Principles and Management,* 4th ed., Pitman, London, 1981.

Peter J. H. Baily and David Farmer, *Materials Management Handbook,* Gower, 1982.

Peter J. H. Baily, *Purchasing and Supply Management,* 3rd ed. Chapman & Hall, London, 1973.

D. E. Barker and Brian Farrington, *The Basic Arts of Buying,* Business Books Ltd, London, 1976.

C. Wayne Barlow, *Purchasing for the Newly Appointed Buyer,* AMA, New York, 1970.

G. K. Beekman-Love and L. Niger, *Materials Management,* Martinus Nijhoff, Leiden, 1978.

P. H. Combs, *Handbook of International Purchasing,* 2nd ed., Cahners, Boston, 1976.

E. Raymond Corey, *Procurement Management,* CBI, Boston, 1978.

Richard David and David H. Farmer, *Purchasing in the Construction Industry*, Gower, 1970.

J. Dramond and G. Purtel, *Retail Buying*, Prentice-Hall, Englewood Cliffs, 1976.

Somerby Dowst, *Basics for Buyers*, Cahners, Boston, 1971.

W. B. England, *The Purchasing System*, Richard D. Irwin, Homewood, 1967.

Dag Ericsson, *Materials Administration*, McGraw-Hill, London, 1974.

David H. Farmer, *Insights in Procurement*, MCB, Bradford, 1981.

David H. Farmer and B. Taylor, *Corporate Planning and Procurement*, Heinemann, London, 1975 and 1983.

P. V. Farrel, *Aljians Purchasing Handbook*, 4th ed., McGraw-Hill, New York, 1982.

Brian Farrington, *Industrial Purchase Price Management*, Gower, 1980.

Harold E. Fearon, *Purchasing Economics*, AMA, New York, 1968.

H. E. Fearon and K. Hamilton (eds) *Purchasing in South Africa*, McGraw-Hill, Johannesburg, 1980.

V. P. Gravereau and L. J. Konopa (eds) *Purchasing Management*, Grid. Inc., Columbus, 1973.

F. A. Hayes and G. A. Renard, *Evaluating Purchasing Performance*, AMA, New York, 1964.

Floyd Hendrick, *Purchasing Management in the Smaller Company*, AMA, New York, 1971.

S. F. Heinritz and P. V. Farrell, *Purchasing, Principles and Applications*, 6th ed., Prentice-Hall, Englewood Cliffs, 1981.

Lamar Lee and Donald Dobler, *Purchasing and Materials Management*, 3rd ed., McGraw-Hill, New York, 1977.

M. R. Leenders, H. Fearon and W. England, *Purchasing and Materials Management*, 7th ed., Richard D. Irwin, Homewood, 1980.

M. Manente, *The Functions of the Purchasing Manager,* AMA, New York, 1969.

R. M. Monczka and P. L. Carter, *Purchasing Performance, Measurement and Control,* MSU, East Lansing, 1973.

W. J. Parsons, *Improving Purchasing Performance,* Gower, 1982.

V. H. Pooler, *The Purchasing Man and His Job,* Houghton Mifflin, Boston, 1969.

W. R. Stelzer, *Materials Management,* Prentice-Hall, Englewood Cliffs, 1970.

John Stevens, *Measuring Purchasing Performance,* Business Books, London, 1978.

J. H. Westing, I. V. Fine and G. J. Zenz, *Purchasing Management,* 4th ed., John Wiley, New York, 1976.

J. W. Wingate and J. S. Friedlander, *The Management of Retail Buying,* Prentice-Hall, Englewood Cliffs, 1963.

G. J. Zenz, *Purchasing and the Management of Materials,* 5th ed., John Wiley, New York, 1981.

Index

compiled by Richard Raper

Note
As well as listing all cited authors, the index under 'references' lists their bibliographical location at the ends of chapters.

Index